Pricing and Hedging of Derivative Securities

Pricing and Hedging of Derivative Securities

LARS TYGE NIELSEN

OXFORD
UNIVERSITY PRESS

OXFORD
UNIVERSITY PRESS

Great Clarendon Street, Oxford OX2 6DP

Oxford University Press is a department of the University of Oxford.
It furthers the University's objective of excellence in research, scholarship,
and education by publishing worldwide in

Oxford New York

Athens Auckland Bangkok Bogotá Beunos Aires Calcutta
Cape Town Chennai Dar es Salaam Delhi Florence Hong Kong Istanbul
Karachi Kuala Lumpur Madrid Melbourne Mexico City Mumbai
Nairobi Paris São Paulo Singapore Taipei Tokyo Toronto Warsaw
with associated companies in Berlin Ibadan

Oxford is a registered trade mark of Oxford University Press
in the UK and certain other countries

Published in the United States
by Oxford University Press Inc., New York

British Library Cataloguing in Publication Data
Data available

Library of Congress Cataloging in Publication Data
Data available

ISBN 0–19–877619–5

3 5 7 9 10 8 6 4 2

Typeset by the author
Printed in Great Britain on acid-free paper by
Biddles Ltd, www.biddles.co.uk

To Karen, Vilhelm, Maria, and Philip

PREFACE

This book is an introduction to pricing and hedging of derivative securities for academics and practitioners. It has grown out of my doctoral course in continuous-time finance theory at INSEAD. It can be used as a text in graduate programs in finance, mathematical finance, economics, mathematical economics, financial engineering, or pure or applied mathematics. It can also be used as a reference, or for self-study. I have used various versions of the manuscript in lecture series at Tilburg University and at New York University's Stern School of Business, as well as in public and private executive courses in the mathematics of derivative securities.

The theory of pricing and hedging of derivative securities is mathematically sophisticated and requires the use of advanced probability theory. My aim has been to make the mathematics available in a precise and rigorous manner, even though the focus of the book is on financial economics. Exposure to the mathematics is necessary in order to give the reader the background to read the journal literature with confidence, apply the methods to new problems, or to do original research in the field.

An area of probability theory which is particularly important is the theory of continuous-time stochastic processes. It is an essential prerequisite for continuous-time finance, it is not easily accessible, and it has for a long time formed a barrier of entry into the field. One of my purposes in writing this book has been to help break down that barrier and make it possible for the reader actually to learn this material.

The book begins with three chapters on stochastic processes, stochastic integration with respect to Wiener processes, Itô processes and Itô's lemma, Girsanov's theorem, the martingale representation theorem, and Gaussian processes. I have put quite a lot of effort into deciding what to include and what not to include in these chapters. The guiding principle has been that all the stochastic process theory needed later on in the book should be explained here, while on the other hand very little material should be covered that is not useful in finance.

The theory of stochastic processes uses measure and integration theory, the relevant parts of which are covered in two appendices. Depending on his or her interests and background, the reader may begin by reading those appendices or may alternatively just use them as a reference. For most people, I would recommend the latter option. Go easy on the measure theory to begin with unless you already know it well. After having read the main body of the book, you may be motivated to look deeper into measure and integration, and you should in fact do so if you are seriously interested in continuous-time finance. In that case, I hope you will find the appendices to be an efficient introduction to the subject.

Building on the foundations laid in the three chapters on stochastic processes, the following two chapters cover the general theory of trading, pricing, and hedging in continuous time, using the martingale approach. The exposition emphasizes the concepts of prices of risk, state price processes, and risk-adjusted probabilities.

The last two chapters are devoted to applications. Rather than cover a large number of applications in survey form, I have chosen to include only a small number but develop them in detail. The applications that I have selected are the Black–Scholes model and the Gaussian one-factor models of the term structure of interest rates. I believe it is more important for the reader to see a few topics developed in depth than to get a broad but less detailed overview. In any case, most instructors will want to choose their own applications from the journal literature.

In order to keep the length of the book finite, it has been necessary not only to limit the number of applications but also to omit some topics from the fundamental theory. Most notably, I have not covered stochastic differential equations and the associated partial differential equations beyond the heat equation and the Black–Scholes PDE. Stochastic differential equations are an extremely useful tool in financial economics, but their theory is more subtle than most finance books would lead you to suspect, and it requires a fairly lengthy mathematical presentation. There was no way these equations could be included and be given a satisfactory treatment in this book.

My vision is that the reader will appreciate learning some mathematics without being overburdened with it, will get a certain sense of satisfaction from the general theory and the applications, and in the end will be hungry for more.

I would like to thank a number of people who have influenced this book.

I initially learned continuous-time finance from Chi-fu Huang after having tried but failed to learn it from other sources. His lecture notes have had a significant influence on the way this book is structured.

The students who took my course at INSEAD gave me feedback and comments which have been incorporated in successive revisions of the manuscript. They include João Amaro de Matos (New University of Lisbon), Benoit Leleux (Babson College), Saugata Banerjee (Koç University), Fatma Lajeri (Koç University), Jesús Saá-Requejo, Finn Erling Bendixen, P. Raghavendra Rau (Purdue University), Pedro Santa-Clara Gomes (University of California, Los Angeles), Salvatore Cantale (Tulane University), Yrjö Koskinen (Stockholm School of Economics), Aris Stouraitis, Georges Hübner (University of Liège and Limburg University), Stephen Sapp, Arturo Bris (Yale University), Aine NiShuilleabhain, Dmitry Lukin (University of California, Irvine), Jos van Bommel (Babson College), Swookeun Jeon, Dima Leshchinskii, Neil Brisley, Arzu Ozoguz, Merih Sevilir, and Andrei Simonov.

Georges Constantinides read a version of the manuscript and gave me written comments. So did David Nachman and Steven Raymar, who used the manuscript in their courses, and Alexander Reisz, who followed my lecture series at New York University. Maria Vassalou used the manuscript in a doctoral course at Columbia University and gave me detailed feedback on the substance as well as on how to restructure some of the material to make it more teachable.

Finally, a practical remark on the organization of the material. Certain sections, subsections, theorems, propositions, proofs, etc., are marked with an asterisk "(*)." This means that they can be skipped on a first reading. If a theorem or proposition or the like is marked by (*), then the proof can be skipped too.

CONTENTS

INTRODUCTION

The principle behind the modern theory of pricing and hedging of derivatives or contingent claims is as follows. The future payoff to a claim, such as an option on a stock, will in general depend on the price paths of one or more basic securities. Using those basic securities, one can try to construct a trading strategy which replicates the payoff in the sense that in every possible future scenario, its value at the time of maturity of the claim will equal the payoff to the claim. The trading strategy should be self-financing and satisfy an admissibility condition which is imposed in order to rule out the possibility of arbitrage. If such a replicating trading strategy can be found, then the current price of the claim will be equal to the initial amount of money needed to start off the trading strategy.

It turns out that if the claim can be replicated like this, then its discounted value is a martingale under the so-called risk-adjusted probabilities. Hence, its present value can be calculated as the conditional expectation of the future payoff discounted back to the present. This valuation procedure is called the martingale method or the martingale valuation principle. In many cases, the conditional expectation can be calculated fairly explicitly, because we know the probability distributions that are involved. For example, the payoff is often a function of a random variable which is known to be normally distributed under the risk-adjusted probabilities.

A variant of the martingale method uses the so-called state prices or pricing kernel. If the claim can be replicated, then its value multiplied by the state prices is a martingale, not under the risk-adjusted but under the original probabilities. Again, the claim can be valued by calculating a conditional expectation.

The surprising and powerful complete markets theorem says that in a wide range of situations, every contingent claim can be replicated by a trading strategy, and therefore it can be priced by the martingale method.

Once the value of the claim has been calculated by the martingale method, it remains to find the replicating trading strategy. Usually, the value will be expressed as a function of the current prices of the basic securities. If so, then this function carries the information necessary to construct the replicating trading strategy. The derivatives of the function with respect to the basic securities prices are called the deltas of the claim, and they tell us how many shares of each security to hold in the replicating trading strategy.

To flesh out this story, we need to model the securities prices as Itô processes, define what it means for a trading strategy to be self-financing, and introduce the concepts of state price processes and risk-adjusted probabilities. All of this requires stochastic processes and Itô calculus, and that is where we shall begin.

1

STOCHASTIC PROCESSES

Stochastic processes are a fundamental concept in finance theory. They describe random phenomena that evolve over time, such as securities prices, interest rates, trading strategies, the value of an investor's portfolio, etc. Most processes used in finance belong to a particularly important class called Itô processes, which are the subject of the following chapter. In this chapter, we introduce some more elementary notions which are needed before we can understand Itô processes.

1.1 Basic Notions

Let $(\Omega, \mathcal{F}, P)$ be a probability space, and let $\mathcal{T}$ be an interval on the real line, interpreted as a time interval. Specifically, assume that $\mathcal{T} = [0, \infty)$ or $\mathcal{T} = [0, T]$ for some T.

In financial models, securities prices, exchange rates, price levels, and trading strategies will usually be modeled as stochastic processes.

A K-dimensional *stochastic process* (or process, for short) is a mapping $X : \Omega \times \mathcal{T} \to I\!\!R^K$ such that for each fixed $t \in \mathcal{T}$, the mapping

$$X_t : \omega \mapsto X(\omega, t) = X_t(\omega) : \Omega \to I\!\!R^K$$

is measurable (thus, a random vector or random variable). We will also write this random vector or variable as $X(t) = X_t$. Thus,

$$X_t(\omega) = X(t)(\omega) = X(\omega, t)$$

If X is a stochastic process, then for each fixed $\omega \in \Omega$, the function $t \mapsto X(\omega, t) : \mathcal{T} \to I\!\!R^K$ is called a *sample path* of the process.

Figure 1.1 illustrates a process X as a function of (ω, t). If you restrict it to a fixed state of the world ω (a horizontal line), you get a path of the process. If you restrict it to a fixed point in time t (a vertical line), you get a random variable.

A process is said to be *continuous* (*right-continuous*, *left-continuous*) if every sample path is continuous (right-continuous, left-continuous).

Two random variables are usually considered to be equivalent or to be the same if they are identical with probability one. In a similar manner, we shall often identify processes that are in some sense "almost the same." But there are several possible concepts of what it means for two processes to be almost the same: they may be indistinguishable, they may be stochastically equivalent (versions or modifications of each other), or they may be almost everywhere

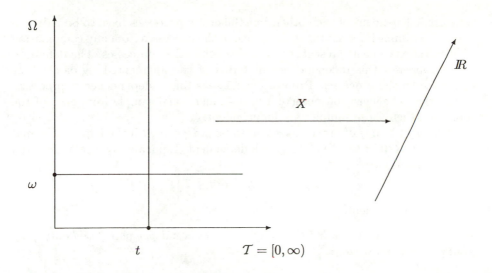

FIG. 1.1. A process X as a function of (ω, t)

identical. Indeed, the stochastic integral with respect to a Wiener process will
be defined initially only up to stochastic equivalence, but when we subsequently
require the paths to be continuous with probability one, the integral is defined
up to indistinguishability. The coefficient or integrand processes will be identified
if they are almost everywhere identical.

Two processes X and Y are *indistinguishable* if their paths are identical with
probability one: there exists a set $N \in \mathcal{F}$ such that $P(N) = 0$ and

$$X(\omega, t) = Y(\omega, t) \text{ for all } \omega \in \Omega \setminus N \text{ and all } t \in \mathcal{T}$$

Two stochastic processes X and Y are *stochastically equivalent*, and they are
said to be *modifications* or *versions* of each other, if for all $t \in \mathcal{T}$, $X(t) = Y(t)$
with probability one.

Two processes X and Y are *almost everywhere identical* (with respect to the
measure $P \otimes \lambda$ on $(\Omega \times \mathcal{T}, \mathcal{F} \otimes \mathcal{B}(\mathcal{T}))$ if there exists a set $M \in \mathcal{F} \otimes \mathcal{B}(\mathcal{T})$ such
that $(P \otimes \lambda)(M) = 0$ and

$$X(\omega, t) = Y(\omega, t) \text{ for all } (\omega, t) \in (\Omega \times \mathcal{T}) \setminus M$$

See Section 1.7 for a detailed discussion of these concepts.

We need to know what it means that several processes are independent of
each other. For example, in the next section we shall study multi-dimensional
Brownian motions. A K-dimensional standard Brownian motion consists of K
independent one-dimensional standard Brownian motions. What does independence mean? It means not only that the realizations of the processes at any one

time are independent of each other, but the entire processes have to be independent. You cannot infer anything about one of the processes from any combination of observations—past, present, or future—of the other processes. The definition below expresses this independence in terms of the augmented sigma-algebras generated by the processes. Proposition 1.1 says that independence of processes means that whenever you observe a finite-dimensional sample from each of the processes, then those samples are independent.

A family $(X^i)_{i \in I}$ of processes is said to be *independent* if the family of sigma-algebras $\sigma(\{X^i(t) : t \in T\})$, $i \in I$, is independent. Equivalently, the augmented sigma-algebras

$$\mathcal{F}^{X^i}_\infty = \tilde{\sigma}(\{X^i(t) : t \in T\})$$

$i \in I$, are independent.

Proposition 1.1 *A family $(X^i)_{i \in I}$ of processes is independent if and only if the family of random vectors*

$$\left[(X^i(t_1), \ldots, X^i(t_n)) \right]_{i \in I}$$

is independent whenever $n \in I\!N$ and $t_1 < \cdots < t_n$.

Proof (*)   First, suppose the processes are independent, and let $t_j \in [0, T]$ for $j = 1, \ldots, n$. Since

$$\sigma(\{X^i_{t_1}, \ldots, X^i_{t_n}\}) \subset \sigma(\{X^i_t : 0 \le t \le T\})$$

for $i \in I$, and since the sigma-algebras $\sigma(\{X^i_t : 0 \le t \le T\})$ are independent, the sigma-algebras $\sigma(\{X^i_{t_1}, \ldots, X^i_{t_n}\})$, $i \in I$, are also independent. So, the corresponding random vectors

$$\left[(X^i(t_1), \ldots, X^i(t_n)) \right]_{i \in I}$$

are independent.

Conversely, suppose that the random vectors $(X^i_{t_1}, \ldots, X^i_{t_n})$, $i \in I$, are independent whenever $n \in I\!N$ and $t_j \in [0, T]$ for $j = 1, \ldots, n$.

The critical step will be an application of Proposition A.40. Consider the following classes of events:

$$\mathcal{A}^i = \bigcup_{n; t_1, \ldots, t_n} \sigma(\{X^i_{t_1}, \ldots, X^i_{t_n}\})$$

The classes $\mathcal{A}^i$, $i \in I$, are independent. Each $\mathcal{A}^i$ is stable under the formation of finite intersections. Therefore, it follows from Proposition A.40 that the sigma-algebras $\sigma(\mathcal{A}^i)$ are independent.

It is easily seen that $\sigma(\mathcal{A}^i) = \sigma(\{X^i_t : 0 \le t \le T\})$ for each i. Hence, the processes are independent.   □

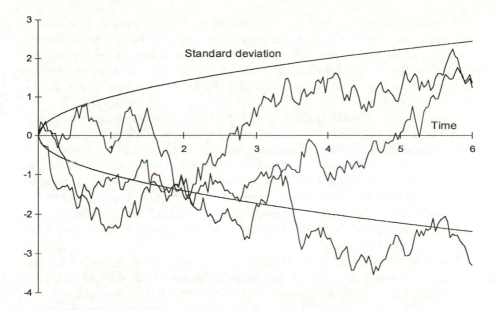

FIG. 1.2. Three sample paths of a standard Brownian motion

1.2   Brownian Motions

The basic building block of 98 percent of all finance theory in continuous time is a Brownian motion (or a Wiener process).

A K-dimensional *standard Brownian motion* is a K-dimensional process B such that

1. $B(0) = 0$ with probability one.

2. B is continuous.

3. If $0 \leq t_0 < \cdots < t_n$, then the increments $B(t_1) - B(t_0), \ldots, B(t_n) - B(t_{n-1})$ are independent.

4. If $0 \leq s \leq t$, then the increment $B(t) - B(s)$ is normally distributed with mean zero and covariance matrix $(t - s)I$, where I is the $K \times K$ identity matrix.

In particular, if B is a one-dimensional standard Brownian motion, and if $0 \leq s \leq t$, then the increment $B(t) - B(s)$ is normally distributed with mean zero and variance $t - s$.

Figure 1.2 shows three sample paths of a one-dimensional standard Brownian motion, together with the standard deviation curves $\pm\sqrt{t}$. Time, t, is on the horizontal axis, and the value of the Brownian motion is measured along the vertical axis. The unconditional mean of the value of the process at each point in time, given information at time zero, is zero. The standard deviation curves delineate a range of plus or minus one standard deviation around the mean.

The unconditional probability that the process at a given point in time takes a value within those curves is approximately 66 percent. Of course, the conditional probability given information at a time where you have observed the beginning of the path is different. In particular, once the path is outside the range between the two standard deviation curves, there is probability one that it will stay outside at least for a little while.

It is not really possible to draw sample paths of a Brownian motion exactly. The picture has to be an approximation. The sample paths in Fig. 1.2 have been generated in the following manner. For each of them, I first generated 180 independent, standard normally distributed numbers, using a random number generator. Then I multiplied them by $\sqrt{1/30}$ in order to change their variance to 1/30. Each number is now the increment of the Brownian motion over a time interval of length 1/30. Adding them up gives the levels of the Brownian motion, sampled at discrete points in time that are 1/30 apart. Successive sampled levels were finally joined by straight lines.

The term "Wiener process" is often used interchangeably with the term "standard Brownian motion," cf. the notes in Section 1.12. As I shall explain in Section 1.5, I use the two terms to evoke slightly different concepts.

The increments $B(t_1) - B(t_0), \ldots, B(t_n) - B(t_{n-1})$ are the continuous-time analog of a sequence of independent normally distributed errors or shocks in a discrete-time framework. The process B itself corresponds to the sum of the errors or shocks.

In discrete-time modeling, it is necessary to pick the minimum time intervals once and for all and to assign an error or shock variable to each of them. In continuous time, there are no minimum time intervals, except if we consider them to be instants. To avoid having to model instantaneous errors or shocks, we model the cumulative process B instead.

Theorem 1.2 *There exists a probability space $(\Omega, \mathcal{F}, P)$ and a K-dimensional standard Brownian motion on $\mathcal{T} = [0, \infty)$.*

Proof (*) See for example the construction in Billingsley [8, 1986, Section 37] of a probability space $(\Omega, \mathcal{F}, P)$ with a one-dimensional standard Brownian motion on $\mathcal{T} = [0, \infty)$. To construct a K-dimensional standard Brownian motion, take the product of K (independent) replicas of the probability space with a Brownian motion B^k defined on each.   □

Exercise 1.1 *Suppose B is a one-dimensional standard Brownian motion. Let $\sigma > 0$. Calculate a constant number $c > 0$ such that the process*

$$X(t) = cB\left(t/\sigma^2\right)$$

is a standard Brownian motion.

Proposition 1.3 *A K-dimensional process B is a standard Brownian motion if and only if the component processes B^k are independent standard Brownian motions.*

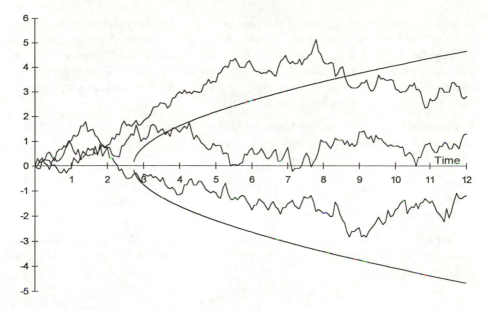

FIG. 1.3. The law of the iterated logarithm

Exercise 1.2 *Prove Proposition 1.3.*

Proposition 1.4 The law of the iterated logarithm. *If B is a standard Brownian motion, then*

$$\limsup_{t \to \infty} \frac{B(t)}{\sqrt{2t \ln \ln t}} = 1$$

with probability one.

Proof (*) See Karatzas and Shreve [64, 1988, Theorem 2.9.23]. □

The law of the iterated logarithm (Proposition 1.4) means the following. If $0 \le a < 1 < b$, then with probability one,

$$B(t) < b\sqrt{2t \ln \ln t}$$

for all sufficiently large t, whereas for all $s \ge 0$, no matter how large, there exist even larger $t > s$ such that

$$B(t) > a\sqrt{2t \ln \ln t}$$

Figure 1.3 illustrates the law of the iterated logarithm. It shows three sample paths of a one-dimensional standard Brownian motion, together with the iterated logarithmic curves $\pm\sqrt{2t \ln \ln t}$. Time, t, is on the horizontal axis, and the value of the Brownian motion is measured along the vertical axis. Note that the iterated logarithmic curves start at $t = e \sim 2.718$, because $\ln \ln t$ has to be non-negative.

In terms of the figure, the law of the iterated logarithm says the following. If we scale up the iterated logarithmic curves vertically, and even if we do it ever so slightly (by a factor $b > 1$ close to 1), then every path of the Brownian motion will, as time goes by, eventually stay between these curves. Conversely, if we contract the curves slightly, then every path of the Brownian motion will, as time goes by, continue to cross both of them.

Proposition 1.5 The law of large numbers for Brownian motion. *If B is a standard Brownian motion, then*

$$\frac{B(t)}{t} \to 0$$

with probability one, as $t \to \infty$.

Proof (*) See Karatzas and Shreve [64, 1988], Problem 2.9.3 and its solution. Alternatively, the result follows from the law of the iterated logarithm (Proposition 1.4). Since

$$\frac{\sqrt{2t \ln \ln t}}{t} \to 0$$

as $t \to \infty$, the law of the iterated logarithm implies that

$$\limsup_{t \to \infty} \frac{B(t)}{t} = \limsup_{t \to \infty} \frac{B(t)}{\sqrt{2t \ln \ln t}} \frac{\sqrt{2t \ln \ln t}}{t} = 0$$

Moreover, since $-B$ is also a standard Brownian motion,

$$\liminf_{t \to \infty} \frac{B(t)}{t} = -\limsup_{t \to \infty} \frac{-B(t)}{t} = 0$$

$\square$

Proposition 1.6 (*) *If B is a standard Brownian motion, then the process $\hat{B}$ defined by*

$$\hat{B}(t) = \begin{cases} tB(1/t) & \text{if } t > 0 \\ 0 & \text{if } t = 0 \end{cases}$$

is also a standard Brownian motion.

Proof By definition, $\hat{B}(0) = 0$.
It is clear that $\hat{B}$ is continuous at $t > 0$. By the law of large numbers for Brownian motion (Proposition 1.5),

$$\hat{B}(t) = \frac{B(1/t)}{1/t} \to 0 = \hat{B}(0)$$

with probability one, as $t \to 0$. Hence, $\hat{B}$ is continuous also at $t = 0$.

If $0 < s < t$, then the increment $\hat{B}(t) - \hat{B}(s)$ is normally distributed with mean zero and variance $t - s$:

$$\hat{B}(t) - \hat{B}(s) = tB(1/t) - sB(1/s) = -s(B(1/s) - B(1/t)) + (t - s)B(1/t)$$

which follows a normal distribution with mean zero and variance

$$(-s)^2(1/s - 1/t) + (t - s)^2(1/t) = s - s^2/t + (t^2 - 2ts + s^2)/t = t - s$$

The same is true if $s = 0$, since $\hat{B}(t)$ is normally distributed with mean zero and variance $t^2(1/t) = t$.

It now follows that any two consecutive increments are uncorrelated. If $0 \leq s \leq t \leq u$, then

$$\begin{aligned}
u - s &= \text{var}(\hat{B}(u) - \hat{B}(s)) \\
&= \text{var}(\hat{B}(u) - \hat{B}(t)) + \text{var}(\hat{B}(t) - \hat{B}(s)) \\
&\quad + 2\text{cov}(\hat{B}(u) - \hat{B}(t), \hat{B}(t) - \hat{B}(s)) \\
&= u - t + t - s + 2\text{cov}(\hat{B}(u) - \hat{B}(t), \hat{B}(t) - \hat{B}(s)) \\
&= u - s + 2\text{cov}(\hat{B}(u) - \hat{B}(t), \hat{B}(t) - \hat{B}(s))
\end{aligned}$$

which implies that

$$\text{cov}(\hat{B}(u) - \hat{B}(t), \hat{B}(t) - \hat{B}(s)) = 0$$

Any two increments over non-overlapping but possibly not consecutive time intervals will also be uncorrelated. If $0 \leq s \leq t \leq u \leq v$, then

$$\begin{aligned}
v - s &= \text{var}(\hat{B}(v) - \hat{B}(s)) \\
&= \text{var}(\hat{B}(v) - \hat{B}(u)) + \text{var}(\hat{B}(u) - \hat{B}(t)) + \text{var}(\hat{B}(t) - \hat{B}(s)) \\
&\quad + 2\text{cov}(\hat{B}(v) - \hat{B}(u), \hat{B}(u) - \hat{B}(t)) \\
&\quad + 2\text{cov}(\hat{B}(u) - \hat{B}(t), \hat{B}(t) - \hat{B}(s)) \\
&\quad + 2\text{cov}(\hat{B}(v) - \hat{B}(u), \hat{B}(t) - \hat{B}(s)) \\
&= v - u + u - t + t - s + 2\text{cov}(\hat{B}(v) - \hat{B}(u), \hat{B}(t) - \hat{B}(s)) \\
&= v - s - 2\text{cov}(\hat{B}(v) - \hat{B}(u), \hat{B}(t) - \hat{B}(s))
\end{aligned}$$

Hence,

$$\text{cov}(\hat{B}(v) - \hat{B}(u), \hat{B}(t) - \hat{B}(s)) = 0$$

Since all the increments are mutually uncorrelated, it follows that any finite sequence of consecutive increments is independent.

This proves that $\hat{B}$ is a standard Brownian motion. □

1.3   Generalized Brownian Motions

While the standard Brownian motion is an indispensable building block of financial models, it cannot by itself represent all the varied phenomena we encounter. The prices of securities such as stocks, for example, are not well described by standard Brownian motions. They do not start at zero. Their increments have positive means, or so we like to believe, and they have variances that are not necessarily one per unit of time. If we consider the prices of several stocks simultaneously, their increments will typically be correlated with each other.

We introduce the notion of a generalized Brownian motion as a first step in constructing more complicated processes. A generalized Brownian motion may start at a value different from zero, and it has increments which may have means different from zero, variances different from one per unit of time, and covariances different from zero.

The means, variances, and covariances continue to be constant like those of a standard Brownian motion. Later on, we shall introduce the stochastic integral, which is essentially a way of building processes with time-varying and stochastic variances and covariances, and the time integral, which will allow us also to add a time-varying and stochastic mean.

The generalized Brownian motion is more flexible than the standard Brownian motion, but it is still not good enough as a model of stock prices. Its values are normally distributed, which means that they have positive probability of being negative. This is not a realistic property of stock prices. Moreover, the increments of a Brownian motion are, in a sense, additive, while the increments of stock prices ought to be multiplicative. The fact that the increments of the Brownian motion have constant expectation implies that the percentage increment in the stock price, or percentage rate of return to the stock, would be declining as the stock price increases.

To correct these shortcomings of the generalized Brownian motion as a model of stock prices, we shall introduce the notion of a "geometric Brownian motion." It comes about by an exponential transformation of a generalized Brownian motion. The exponential transformation maps additive increments into multiplicative increments. The percentage increments of a geometric Brownian motion have constant mean.

A K-dimensional process Z is a K-dimensional *generalized Brownian motion* (or a K-dimensional *arithmetic Brownian motion* or simply a K-dimensional *Brownian motion*) if

1. $Z(0)$ is deterministic.

2. Z is continuous.

3. If $0 \leq t_0 < \cdots < t_n$, then the increments $Z(t_1) - Z(t_0), \ldots, Z(t_n) - Z(t_{n-1})$ are independent.

4. There exist a K-dimensional vector μ and a $(K \times K)$-dimensional square matrix Σ such that whenever $0 \leq s < t$, the increment $Z(t) - Z(s)$ is normally distributed with mean $(t - s)\mu$ and covariance matrix $(t - s)\Sigma$.

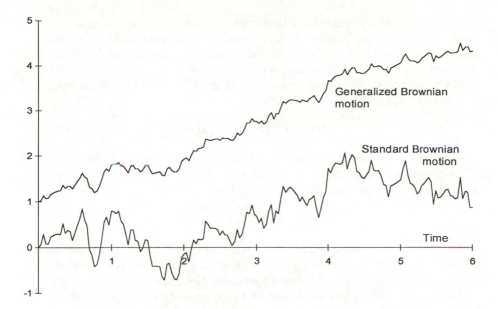

FIG. 1.4. A standard and a generalized Brownian motion

The vector μ and the matrix Σ are uniquely determined and will be called the *increment mean vector* and the *increment covariance matrix*, respectively.

Figure 1.4 shows a path of a standard Brownian motion and the corresponding path of a generalized Brownian motion with initial value one, increment mean 0.5, increment standard deviation 0.4, and increment variance 0.16 per unit of time.

If Z is a K-dimensional generalized Brownian motion, then each of the components Z_k, $k = 1, \ldots, K$, is a generalized Brownian motion

A standard Brownian motion is of course a special case of a generalized Brownian motion. Specifically, a K-dimensional standard Brownian motion is a K-dimensional generalized Brownian motion with initial value zero, increment mean vector zero, and increment covariance matrix I.

If we start from a standard Brownian motion and rescale it by a constant matrix and add an initial value and a linear increment, then the result is a generalized Brownian motion. Specifically, if B is a K-dimensional standard Brownian motion, and if σ is a constant $(N \times K)$-dimensional matrix, Z_0 is any N-dimensional vector, and μ is a constant N-dimensional vector, then the process

$$Z(t) = Z_0 + t\mu + \sigma B(t)$$

is an N-dimensional generalized Brownian motion, with initial value $Z(0) = Z_0$, increment mean vector μ, and increment covariance matrix $\Sigma = \sigma\sigma^{\mathsf{T}}$.

Conversely, every generalized Brownian motion with positive definite increment covariance matrix arises from a standard Brownian motion by rescaling and adding an initial value and a linear increment. Specifically, let Z be a K-dimensional generalized Brownian motion with positive definite increment covariance matrix Σ. There exists an invertible $(K \times K)$-dimensional matrix A such that $\Sigma = AA^\mathsf{T}$. Now the process

$$B(t) = A^{-1}[Z(t) - Z(0) - \mu t]$$

is a K-dimensional standard Brownian motion. The process Z arises from B by a linear transformation by A combined with adding the initial value $Z(0)$ and the deterministic function μt:

$$Z(t) = Z(0) + \mu t + AB(t)$$

Of course, it is also true that if we start from a generalized Brownian motion and rescale it by a constant matrix and add an initial value and a linear increment, then the result is a new generalized Brownian motion.

Most of the time, our models will be based on a standard Brownian motion. Sometimes, however, it will be convenient to base them on a special kind of generalized Brownian motion which we will call a "correlated Brownian motion." A correlated Brownian motion starts at zero and its components have variance one per unit of time but may be correlated. Formally, a K-dimensional *correlated Brownian motion* is a K-dimensional generalized Brownian motion with zero initial value and zero increment mean, such that the increment covariance matrix is invertible and has diagonal elements that are equal to one. The off-diagonal elements may be interpreted as *increment correlation coefficients*.

A process is a correlated Brownian motion with positive definite increment covariance matrix if and only if it arises from a standard Brownian motion by a rescaling of a particular form. Specifically, a K-dimensional process Z is a K-dimensional correlated Brownian motion with positive definite increment covariance matrix if and only if there exists a K-dimensional standard Brownian motion B and a K-dimensional invertible square matrix A such that $Z = AB$ and the matrix AA^T has diagonal elements that are equal to one. The matrix AA^T will be the increment covariance matrix.

If Z is a K-dimensional correlated Brownian motion, then each of the components Z_k, $k = 1, \ldots, K$, is a standard Brownian motion (but because of their possible correlation they do not necessarily form a K-dimensional standard Brownian motion).

A one-dimensional process is a *geometric Brownian motion* if it has the form e^Z, where Z is a one-dimensional generalized Brownian motion with deterministic initial value $Z(0)$.

A reason why a generalized Brownian motion is sometimes called an "arithmetic Brownian motion" is that the term brings out the contrast to a geometric Brownian motion.

Example 1.7 In the Black–Scholes option pricing model, there are two securities, a stock and a money market account. Let $K = 1$, and let B be a one-dimensional standard Brownian motion.

The stock price is described by a process of the form

$$S(t) = S(0) \exp\left[\left(\mu - \frac{1}{2}\sigma^2\right)t + \sigma B(t)\right]$$

where $S(0) > 0$, μ and $\sigma > 0$ are constants. This process is a geometric Brownian motion. It is also often used to describe a stock index or an exchange rate.

Observe that

$$\ln S(t) = \ln S(0) + \left(\mu - \frac{1}{2}\sigma^2\right)t + \sigma B(t)$$

is a generalized Brownian motion. The distribution of $\ln S(t)$ is normal with mean

$$\ln S(0) + \left(\mu - \frac{1}{2}\sigma^2\right)t$$

and variance $\sigma^2 t$. $\qquad E[\sigma^2 B^2(t)] = \sigma^2 t$

The continuously compounded rate of return to the stock, per unit of time, over a time interval $[t, t+\tau]$, is

$$\frac{1}{\tau}\ln\left(\frac{S(t+\tau)}{S(t)}\right) = \mu - \frac{1}{2}\sigma^2 + \frac{1}{\tau}\sigma(B(t+\tau) - B(t))$$

It is normally distributed with mean $\mu - \frac{1}{2}\sigma^2$, variance σ^2/τ, and standard deviation $\sigma/\sqrt{\tau}$. Note that the variance goes to zero as $\tau \to \infty$.

In fact, the rate of return converges to the mean $\mu - \frac{1}{2}\sigma^2$ with probability one as $\tau \to \infty$. This follows from the law of large numbers for Brownian motion (Proposition 1.5) combined with the observation that for given t, the process $\tau \mapsto B(t+\tau) - B(t)$ is a standard Brownian motion.

Besides the stock, there is also a money market account in the Black–Scholes model. The money market account is a security which earns a constant continuously compounded interest rate r and accumulates the interest instead of paying it out. The price process of a unit of the money market account is

$$M(t) = M(0)e^{rt}$$

where $M(0) > 0$ is a constant. This process is a (degenerate, deterministic) geometric Brownian motion. The deterministic process

$$\ln M(t) = \ln M(0) + rt$$

is a generalized Brownian motion with increment mean r and increment variance zero.

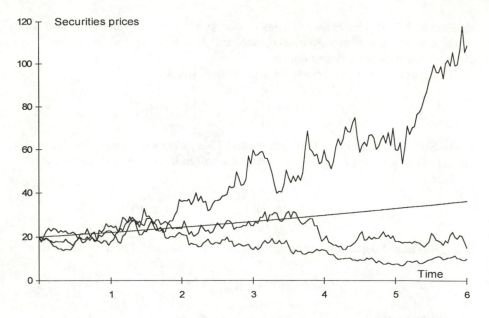

FIG. 1.5. Securities price processes in the Black–Scholes model

Figure 1.5 shows three paths of the stock price and one path of the value of the money market account in the Black–Scholes model. Both the stock and the money market account start at an initial value of 20. The interest rate is $r = 0.1$, the instantaneous expected rate of return to the stock is $\mu = 0.2$, and the volatility of the stock is $\sigma = 0.4$.   □

1.4   Information Structures

Very often when dealing with stochastic processes, it is useful or even necessary to specify what information is available to the observer at each point in time. For example, if we want to calculate the conditional expectation of future values of a process, then we need to specify the current information that goes into the calculation. In financial models, we will usually require that current and past securities prices are known to the investors, and that the investors can make use only of current information, not future information, when trading. This is formalized by means of the concept of a filtration.

A *filtration* is a family $F = (\mathcal{F}_t)_{t \in \mathcal{T}}$ of sigma-algebras $\mathcal{F}_t \subset \mathcal{F}$ which is increasing in the sense that $\mathcal{F}_s \subset \mathcal{F}_t$ whenever $s, t \in \mathcal{T}$, $s \le t$.

A filtration may be thought of as a dynamic information structure. The interpretation is that $\mathcal{F}_t$ represents the information available at time t. The fact that the filtration is increasing means that more and more is known as time goes forward: past information is not forgotten.

A filtration $F = (\mathcal{F}_t)$ is said to be *augmented* if $\mathcal{F}_t$ is augmented for each t. This requires only that $\mathcal{F}_0$ be augmented.

A stochastic process X is said to be *adapted* to the filtration F if for each fixed $t \in \mathcal{T}$, the random vector or random variable

$$X_t : \omega \mapsto X(\omega, t) = X_t(\omega) = X(t)(\omega) : \Omega \to \mathbb{R}^K$$

is measurable with respect to $\mathcal{F}_t$. This means that the value $X(t)$ of X at t depends only on information available at time t; or that an individual with information structure F is able to observe or infer the value of X at each point in time.

Adaptedness is a very important concept. Most of the processes that we shall encounter will be adapted.

If X is a process and $t \in \mathcal{T}$, let $\mathcal{F}_t^X$ be the augmented sigma-algebra generated by the values of the process up to time t:

$$\mathcal{F}_t^X = \sigma\left(\sigma\left(\{X_s : s \in \mathcal{T},\, s \le t\}\right) \bigcup \mathcal{N}\right)$$

where $\mathcal{N}$ is the set of null sets in $\mathcal{F}$, that is the events that have probability zero. The *augmented filtration generated by* X is the filtration $F^X = (\mathcal{F}_t^X)_{t \in \mathcal{T}}$.

Any stochastic process X is adapted to the augmented filtration F^X that it generates.

A stochastic process X is *measurable* if it is measurable as a mapping

$$X : (\Omega \times \mathcal{T}, \mathcal{F} \otimes \mathcal{B}(\mathcal{T})) \to (\mathbb{R}^K, \mathcal{B}(\mathbb{R}^K))$$

Most of the processes that we shall encounter will be measurable. Measurability of a process is a purely technical concept which does not have any interpretation in terms of economics or decision theory.

Proposition 1.8 *Every adapted right-continuous or left-continuous process is measurable.*

Proof (*) Let X be a right-continuous process. Define a sequence of processes X_n as follows. Set

$$X_n(\omega, 0) = X(\omega, 0)$$

For $t \in \mathcal{T}$, $t > 0$, let $k_{n,t}$ be the positive integer such that $(k_{n,t} - 1)/n < t \le k_{n,t}/n$. Set

$$s_{t,n} = \begin{cases} \min\{T, k_{n,t}/n\} & \text{if } \mathcal{T} = [0, T] \\ k_{n,t}/n & \text{if } \mathcal{T} = [0, \infty) \end{cases}$$

and

$$X_n(\omega, t) = X(\omega, s_{n,t})$$

Then X_n is a measurable process. Since $s_{n,t} \ge t$ and $s_{n,t} \to t$ as $n \to \infty$, and X is right-continuous, $X_n(\omega, t) \to X(\omega, t)$ for all $(\omega, t) \in \Omega \times \mathcal{T}$. Hence, X is measurable.

The proof for the case where X is a left-continuous process is similar. $\square$

A process X is said to be *integrable* if $X(t)$ is an integrable random vector for each $t \in \mathcal{T}$.

Let $F = (\mathcal{F}_t)$ be a filtration. A process X is a *martingale* if it is integrable and adapted and

$$E[X(t) \mid \mathcal{F}_s] = X(s)$$

whenever $s, t \in \mathcal{T}$, $0 \le s \le t$.

It is clear that a K-dimensional process X is continuous (right-continuous, left-continuous, adapted, measurable, integrable, a martingale) if and only if each of its one-dimensional component processes X_k, $k = 1, \ldots, K$, has that same property.

Proposition 1.9 *Let Q be a probability measure with density $dQ/dP = \xi$ with respect to P, and set*

$$\eta(t) = E\left[\xi \mid \mathcal{F}_t\right]$$

A process X is Q-integrable if and only if ηX is P-integrable. If so, then

$$E[\eta(t)X(t) \mid \mathcal{F}_s] = \eta(s)E_Q[X(t) \mid \mathcal{F}_s]$$

whenever $s \le t$. In particular, ηX is a martingale with respect to P if and only if X is a martingale with respect to Q.

Exercise 1.3 *Prove Proposition 1.9.*

We close this section with a result about independence which will be used later on in the proof of Theorem 4.1. It says that if all increments of a process starting at a particular time s are independent of the information available at time s, then any event that can be defined on the basis of all those increments is also independent of the information avaliable at time s.

Proposition 1.10 *Suppose X is a process such that whenever $0 \le s \le t$, the increment $X(t) - X(s)$ is independent of $\mathcal{F}_s$. Then the sigma-algebra*

$$\sigma\left(X(t) - X(s) : s \le t\right)$$

is independent of $\mathcal{F}_s$, for all $s \ge 0$.

Proof (*) Suppose $t_0, t_1, \ldots, t_N$ is a sequence of times such that

$$0 \le t_0 \le t_1 \le \cdots \le t_N$$

Then the random vector

$$(X(t_1) - X(t_0), X(t_2) - X(t_0), \ldots, X(t_N) - X(t_0))$$

is independent of $\mathcal{F}_{t_0}$. To see this, set $\mathcal{G}^0 = \mathcal{F}_{t_0}$ and

$$\mathcal{G}^i = \sigma(X(t_i) - X(t_{i-1}))$$

for $i = 1, \ldots, N$. For each $n = 0, \ldots, N-1$,

$$\sigma\left(\mathcal{G}^0 \bigcup \cdots \bigcup \mathcal{G}^n\right) \subset \mathcal{F}_{t_n}$$

and so the sigma-algebra $\mathcal{G}^{n+1}$ is independent of the sigma-algebra

$$\sigma\left(\mathcal{G}^0 \bigcup \cdots \bigcup \mathcal{G}^n\right)$$

It follows from Proposition A.42 that the sigma-algebras $\mathcal{G}^0, \ldots, \mathcal{G}^N$ are independent, and hence the random vectors

$$(X(t_1) - X(t_0), X(t_2) - X(t_1), \ldots, X(t_N) - X(t_{N-1}))$$

and

$$(X(t_1) - X(t_0), X(t_2) - X(t_0), \ldots, X(t_N) - X(t_0))$$

are independent of $\mathcal{F}_{t_0}$.

Let $\mathcal{A}$ be the class of events

$$\mathcal{A} = \bigcup_{N; t_0, \ldots, t_N} \sigma\left(X(t_1) - X(t_0), \ldots, X(t_N) - X(t_0)\right)$$

where the union is over finite sequences $t_0, t_1, \ldots, t_N$ such that

$$0 \le s = t_0 \le t_1 \le \cdots \le t_N$$

By what has already been shown, $\mathcal{A}$ is independent of $\mathcal{F}_s$. Since $\mathcal{A}$ is stable under finite intersections and generates

$$\sigma(\mathcal{A}) = \sigma\left(X(t) - X(s) : s \le t\right)$$

it follows from Proposition A.40 that the latter is independent of $\mathcal{F}_s$. □

1.5 Wiener Processes

Let $F = (\mathcal{F}_t)$ be a filtration. A K-dimensional process W on $\mathcal{T} = [0, \infty)$ is a K-dimensional *Wiener process relative to F* if

1. $W(0) = 0$ with probability one.
2. W is continuous.
3. W is adapted to the filtration F.
4. If $0 \le s \le t$, then the increment $W(t) - W(s)$ is independent of $\mathcal{F}_s$ and normally distributed with mean zero and covariance matrix $(t-s)I$, where I is the $K \times K$ identity matrix.

The formal difference between the concept of a Wiener process and the concept of a standard Brownian motion (according to my use of the terminology) is that the definition of a Wiener process refers to a particular information structure, whereas the definition of a Brownian motion does not. A process may be a Wiener process relative to one filtration but not relative to another, while a Brownian motion will be a Brownian motion no matter which filtration we have in mind. The substantial difference is in the independence requirement for the increments. Future increments of a Brownian motion are assumed to be independent of past increments, whereas future increments of a Wiener process are assumed to be independent of all currently available information, including but not limited to information about past increments.

If W is a K-dimensional Wiener process relative to a filtration $F = (\mathcal{F}_t)$, and if $G = (\mathcal{G}_t)$ is a filtration such that $\mathcal{F}_t \subset \mathcal{G}_t$ for all t and such that if $0 \leq s \leq t$, then the increment $W(t) - W(s)$ is independent of $\mathcal{G}_s$, then W is also a K-dimensional Wiener process relative to G.

According to Proposition 1.11 below, every Wiener process is a standard Brownian motion. Conversely, Proposition 1.12 says that every standard Brownian motion is a Wiener process relative to the augmented filtration that it generates (the information structure consisting in observing the path of the standard Brownian motion). For a standard Brownian motion to be a Wiener process relative to some other information structure requires, according to Proposition 1.11, that it be adapted and that its increment over any time interval be independent of the information available at the beginning of that time interval.

Proposition 1.11 *A process W is a K-dimensional Wiener process relative to F if and only if*

1. *W is a K-dimensional standard Brownian motion.*
2. *W is adapted to the filtration F.*
3. *$W(t) - W(s)$ is independent of $\mathcal{F}_s$ whenever $0 \leq s \leq t$.*

Proof Suppose W is a K-dimensional Wiener process relative to F. It has to be shown that W is a K-dimensional standard Brownian motion. The only part which requires some thought is to show that if $0 \leq t_0 < \cdots < t_n$, then the increments $W(t_1) - W(t_0), \ldots, W(t_n) - W(t_{n-1})$ are independent. Since they are jointly normally distributed, it is enough to show that they are pairwise independent. But if $0 \leq i < j < n$, then the increment $W(t_{j+1}) - W(t_j)$ is independent of $\mathcal{F}_{t_j}$ and hence independent of the increment $W(t_{i+1}) - W(t_i)$.

Conversely, it is clear from the definitions that if W satisfies 1–3 above, then W is a Wiener process relative to F.   □

Proposition 1.12 *If B is a K-dimensional standard Brownian motion, then B is a K-dimensional Wiener process relative to the augmented filtration $F^B = (\mathcal{F}_t^B)$ that it generates.*

Proof (*) According to Proposition 1.11, all that needs to be shown is that the increment $B(t) - B(s)$ is independent of $\mathcal{F}_s^B$ whenever $0 \leq s \leq t$.

For each positive integer n and each finite series of times $t_1, t_2, \ldots, t_n$ with $0 \leq t_1 < \cdots < t_n \leq s$, the random variables

$$B(t_1), B(t_2) - B(t_1), \ldots, B(t_n) - B(t_{n-1}) \text{ and } B(t) - B(s)$$

are independent. Hence, the sigma-algebra

$$\sigma(B(t_1), B(t_2), \ldots, B(t_n)) = \sigma(B(t_1), B(t_2) - B(t_1), \ldots, B(t_n) - B(t_{n-1}))$$

is independent of $B(t) - B(s)$.

Consider the following class of events:

$$\mathcal{A} = \bigcup_{n; 0 \le t_1 < \cdots < t_n \le s} \sigma(B(t_1), \ldots, B(t_n))$$

It is closed under the formation of finite intersections, and it is independent of $B(t) - B(s)$. Hence, it follows from Proposition A.40 that the sigma-algebra

$$\sigma(\mathcal{A}) = \mathcal{F}_s^B$$

is also independent of $B(t) - B(s)$. □

Observe that if W is a K-dimensional Wiener process relative to F then its components are independent one-dimensional Wiener processes relative to F.

Example 1.13 A Brownian motion may well be a Wiener process with respect to a filtration generated by a process which is not a Brownian motion. The filtration might be generated by the Brownian motion itself plus some other processes that are independent of it but are not Brownian motions.

Let W be a one-dimensional standard Brownian motion, and let a and b be two processes such that (a, b) and W are independent of each other (we take two processes a and b rather than just one because we shall need both in Exercise 1.12 later on). Then W is a Wiener process with respect to the augmented filtration generated by a, b, and W.

For concreteness, let us construct two such processes. Suppose a one-dimensional standard Brownian motion B is defined on a complete probability space $(\Omega^1, \mathcal{F}^1, P^1)$. We shall enlarge the probability space in order to make sure it has sufficiently many events that are independent of B. This is accomplished by constructing a product space. Let

$$\Omega^2 = \{0, 1\} \times \{0, 1\} = \{(0, 0), (0, 1), (1, 0), (1, 1)\}$$

let $\mathcal{F}^2$ be the sigma-algebra on Ω^2 consisting of all subsets of Ω^2, and let P^2 be the probability measure on $(\Omega^2, \mathcal{F}^2)$ which assigns probability $1/4$ to all elements of Ω^2:

$$P^2(\{(0, 0)\}) = P^2(\{(0, 1)\}) = P^2(\{(1, 0)\}) = P^2(\{(1, 1)\})$$

Let $(\Omega, \mathcal{F}, P)$ be the product space:

$$(\Omega, \mathcal{F}, P) = (\Omega^1 \times \Omega^2, \mathcal{F}^1 \otimes \mathcal{F}^2, P^1 \otimes P^2)$$

It is a complete probability space. Let $F^B = (\mathcal{F}_t^B)$ be the augmented filtration of $(\Omega^1, \mathcal{F}^1, P^1)$ generated by B. Let $F^2 = (\mathcal{F}_t^2)$ be the filtration of $(\Omega^2, \mathcal{F}^2, P^2)$ defined by

$$\mathcal{F}_t^2 = \begin{cases} \{\emptyset, \Omega^2\} & \text{for } t < 2 \\ \mathcal{F}^2 & \text{for } 2 \leq t \end{cases}$$

This means that before time 2, there is no information, but at time 2 the true state in Ω^2 is revealed. Finally, let $F = (\mathcal{F}_t)$ be the filtration of $(\Omega, \mathcal{F}, P)$ given by $F = F^B \otimes F^2$, which is supposed to mean

$$\mathcal{F}_t = \mathcal{F}_t^B \otimes \mathcal{F}_t^2$$

for all $t \geq 0$. Define a process W on $(\Omega, \mathcal{F}, P)$ by

$$W(\omega^1, i, j, t) = B(\omega^1, t)$$

for

$$(\omega^1, i, j) \in \Omega^1 \times \{0, 1\} \times \{0, 1\} = \Omega^1 \times \Omega^2 = \Omega$$

and $t \geq 0$. Then W is a standard Wiener process relative to F. Define a and b on Ω by

$$a(t) = b(t) = 1$$

for $0 \leq t < 2$, and

$$a(\omega^1, 0, 0, t) = a(\omega^1, 0, 1, t) = 2$$

$$a(\omega^1, 1, 0, t) = a(\omega^1, 1, 1, t) = 1$$

$$b(\omega^1, 0, 0, t) = b(\omega^1, 1, 0, t) = 3$$

$$b(\omega^1, 0, 1, t) = b(\omega^1, 1, 1, t) = 1$$

for $2 < t$. Both processes are constant equal to one up to time 2. At time 2, each of them can jump with probability one-half. The process a may jump up to two or stay at one, and the process b may jump up to three or stay at one. They jump independently of each other and independently of W.

Now $F = F^B \otimes F^2$ is the augmented filtration generated by (a, b, W), and W is a Wiener process relative to F. $\qquad\square$

If W is a Wiener process relative to F, then W is a martingale: if $0 \leq s \leq t$, then

$$E[W(t) \mid \mathcal{F}_s] = W(s) + E[W(t) - W(s) \mid \mathcal{F}_s] = W(s)$$

because $W(t) - W(s)$ is independent of $\mathcal{F}_s$ and has mean zero.

An N-dimensional process X is *square integrable* if $EX_i(t)^2 < \infty$ for each $t \in \mathcal{T}$ and each $i = 1, \ldots, N$.

The following theorem characterizes Wiener processes in terms of four properties which are quite similar to those that make up the definition of a Wiener process. What is remarkable about it is that those four properties do not include a requirement that increments should be normally distributed. Yet, they imply that the process is a Wiener process, and, hence, that the increments are normally distributed.

Theorem 1.14 *Let W be a K-dimensional process and $F = (\mathcal{F}_t)$ a filtration. Then W is a K-dimensional Wiener process relative to F if and only if it has the following properties:*

1. *$W(0) = 0$ with probability one.*
2. *W is continuous.*
3. *W is a square integrable martingale with respect to F.*
4. *For $0 \le s \le t$,*

$$E\left[(W(t) - W(s))(W(t) - W(s))^\top \mid \mathcal{F}_s\right] = (t - s)I$$

where I is the $K \times K$ identity matrix.

Proof (*) Karatzas and Shreve [64, 1988, Theorem 3.16], Liptser and Shiryayev [65, 1977, Theorem 4.2]. □

1.6   Generalized Wiener Processes

A K-dimensional process Z is a K-dimensional *generalized Wiener process* relative to F if

1. $Z(0)$ is deterministic.
2. Z is continuous.
3. Z is adapted to the filtration F.
4. There exist a K-dimensional vector μ and a K-dimensional square matrix Σ such that whenever $0 \le s < t$, the increment $Z(t) - Z(s)$ is independent of $\mathcal{F}_s$ and normally distributed with mean $(t - s)\mu$ and covariance matrix $(t - s)\Sigma$.

A K-dimensional generalized Wiener process relative to F is, in particular, a K-dimensional generalized Brownian motion. As in the case of a generalized Brownian motion, the vector μ and the matrix Σ are uniquely determined and will be called the *increment mean vector* and the *increment covariance matrix*, respectively.

A K-dimensional Wiener process relative to F will sometimes be called a K-dimensional *standard Wiener process* relative to F in order to distinguish it from a generalized Wiener process. So, a K-dimensional standard Wiener process relative to F is a K-dimensional generalized Wiener process relative to F with initial value zero, increment mean vector zero, and increment covariance matrix I.

If Z_0 is a deterministic N-dimensional vector, if W is a K-dimensional Wiener process relative to F (and, hence, a K-dimensional standard Brownian motion), and if μ is a constant N-dimensional vector and σ is a constant $(N \times K)$-dimensional matrix, then we have observed that the process

$$Z(t) = Z_0 + t\mu + \sigma W(t)$$

is an N-dimensional generalized Brownian motion with increment mean vector μ and increment covariance matrix $\Sigma = \sigma\sigma^\top$. In fact, Z is an N-dimensional generalized Wiener process relative to F.

Every K-dimensional generalized Wiener process Z relative to F with positive definite increment covariance matrix arises from a K-dimensional standard Wiener process relative to F by a linear transformation combined with adding an initial value and a linear deterministic function of time. Specifically, if the increment covariance matrix Σ of Z is positive definite, then there exists an invertible $(K \times K)$-dimensional matrix A such that $\Sigma = AA^\top$. We have observed that the process

$$W(t) = A^{-1}[Z(t) - Z(0) - \mu t]$$

is a K-dimensional standard Brownian motion, and that the process Z arises from W by a linear transformation by A combined with adding the initial value $Z(0)$ and the deterministic function μt:

$$Z(t) = Z(0) + \mu t + AW(t)$$

In fact, W is a K-dimensional standard Wiener process relative to F.

A K-dimensional *correlated Wiener process* relative to F is a K-dimensional generalized Wiener process which is a correlated Brownian motion. In other words, it has zero initial value and zero increment mean, and the increment covariance matrix is invertible and has diagonal elements that are equal to one.

A K-dimensional process Z is a K-dimensional correlated Wiener process relative to F with positive definite increment covariance matrix if and only if there exists a K-dimensional standard Wiener process W and a K-dimensional invertible square matrix A such that $Z = AW$ and the matrix $AA^\top$ has diagonal elements that are equal to one. The matrix $AA^\top$ will be the increment covariance matrix.

If Z is a K-dimensional correlated Wiener process relative to F, then each of the components Z_k, $k = 1, \dots, K$, is a standard Wiener process relative to F (but because of their possible correlation they do not necessarily form a K-dimensional standard Wiener process).

Example 1.15 *Continuation of Example 1.7.* Suppose W is a one-dimensional standard Wiener process relative to F. Consider the Black–Scholes stock price process:

$$S(t) = S(0) \exp\left[\left(\mu - \frac{1}{2}\sigma^2\right)t + \sigma W(t)\right]$$

Let us calculate the expectation at time t of the stock price at time $t + \tau$, $\tau \geq 0$. Observe that

$$S(t + \tau) = S(t) \exp\left[\left(\mu - \frac{1}{2}\sigma^2\right)\tau + \sigma(W(t + \tau) - W(t))\right]$$

Since the increment $W(t+\tau) - W(t)$ is independent of $\mathcal{F}_t$ and $S(t)$ is measurable with respect to $\mathcal{F}_t$,

$$E\left[S(t + \tau) \mid \mathcal{F}_t\right]$$

$$= E\left\{S(t)\exp\left[\left(\mu - \frac{1}{2}\sigma^2\right)\tau + \sigma(W(t+\tau) - W(t))\right]\,\Big|\,\mathcal{F}_t\right\}$$

$$= S(t)E\exp\left[\left(\mu - \frac{1}{2}\sigma^2\right)\tau + \sigma(W(t+\tau) - W(t))\right]$$

Use the formula for the mean of a lognormally distributed random variable (see Proposition 2.29):

$$E\exp\left[\left(\mu - \frac{1}{2}\sigma^2\right)\tau + \sigma(W(t+\tau) - W(t))\right]$$

$$= \exp\left[\left(\mu - \frac{1}{2}\sigma^2\right)\tau + \frac{1}{2}\sigma^2\tau\right]$$

$$= e^{\mu\tau}$$

Hence,

$$E\left[S(t+\tau)\mid\mathcal{F}_t\right] = S(t)e^{\mu\tau}$$

The expected future stock price, given today's information, depends on today's stock price, but the expected relative increment,

$$E\left[\frac{S(t+\tau)}{S(t)}\,\Big|\,\mathcal{F}_t\right] = e^{\mu\tau}$$

is unaffected by today's information. In particular, it is independent of information about past relative increments.

The expected future stock price, given today's information, grows exponentially at the rate μ as we look further and further into the future.

This calculation provides the first explanation of why we include the curious term $-\frac{1}{2}\sigma^2$ in the parameterization of the Black–Scholes stock price. This term gets offset by the $+\frac{1}{2}\sigma^2$ that comes from the formula for the expectation of a lognormally distributed variable.

The second, and related, explanation has to do with Jensen's inequality and the convexity of the exponential function. The future stock price is the current stock price times the exponential of a normally distributed random variable. The variance of this normally distributed random variable is $\sigma^2\tau$ and the expectation is

$$E\left[\left(\mu - \frac{1}{2}\sigma^2\right)\tau + \sigma(W(t+\tau) - W(t))\right] = \left(\mu - \frac{1}{2}\sigma^2\right)\tau$$

Because of the strict convexity of the exponential function, we cannot compute the expectation of the future stock price simply by applying the exponential function to this expression:

$$E\left[S(t+\tau)\mid\mathcal{F}_t\right] \neq S(t)\exp\left[\left(\mu - \frac{1}{2}\sigma^2\right)\tau\right]$$

The expectation of the future stock price will be higher than that, and more so the higher the variance $\sigma^2\tau$. The convexity effect will exactly make the $-\frac{1}{2}\sigma^2$ term disappear, and we get the formula above:

$$E\left[S(t+\tau) \mid \mathcal{F}_t\right] = S(t)e^{\mu\tau}$$

In Chapter 2, Example 2.3, we shall encounter yet another explanation of the $-\frac{1}{2}\sigma^2$ term based on Itô's formula.

It follows from the above formula for the expectation that given $\sigma > 0$, the stock price is a martingale relative to F if and only if $\mu = 0$. □

Example 1.16 *Two correlated one-dimensional Wiener processes.* Let W be a two-dimensional standard Wiener process relative to a filtration F, and let

$$Z(t) = AW(t)$$

where

$$A = \begin{pmatrix} \sqrt{\frac{1+\rho}{2}} & \sqrt{\frac{1-\rho}{2}} \\ \sqrt{\frac{1+\rho}{2}} & -\sqrt{\frac{1-\rho}{2}} \end{pmatrix}$$

and ρ is a constant with $-1 \le \rho \le 1$. Then

$$Z(t) = \begin{pmatrix} Z_1(t) \\ Z_2(t) \end{pmatrix} = \begin{pmatrix} \sqrt{\frac{1+\rho}{2}}W_1(t) + \sqrt{\frac{1-\rho}{2}}W_2(t) \\ \sqrt{\frac{1+\rho}{2}}W_1(t) - \sqrt{\frac{1-\rho}{2}}W_2(t) \end{pmatrix}$$

is a two-dimensional correlated Wiener process relative to F with increment mean vector zero and increment covariance matrix

$$AA^{\mathsf{T}} = \begin{pmatrix} \sqrt{\frac{1+\rho}{2}} & \sqrt{\frac{1-\rho}{2}} \\ \sqrt{\frac{1+\rho}{2}} & -\sqrt{\frac{1-\rho}{2}} \end{pmatrix} \begin{pmatrix} \sqrt{\frac{1+\rho}{2}} & \sqrt{\frac{1+\rho}{2}} \\ \sqrt{\frac{1-\rho}{2}} & -\sqrt{\frac{1-\rho}{2}} \end{pmatrix}$$

$$= \begin{pmatrix} 1 & \rho \\ \rho & 1 \end{pmatrix}$$

Each of the processes Z_1 and Z_2 is a Wiener process relative to F (with increment mean zero and increment variance one), but their increments are correlated. If $0 < s \le t$, then $Z_1(t) - Z_1(s)$ and $Z_2(t) - Z_2(s)$ have variance $t - s$, covariance $(t-s)\rho$, and correlation coefficient ρ. So ρ is the increment correlation coefficient.

Conversely, if Z is a two-dimensional correlated Wiener process relative to F with increment correlation coefficient ρ, then the process $W = A^{-1}Z$ is a two-dimensional standard Wiener process relative to F, and $Z = AW$. The inverse of A is

$$A^{-1} = \frac{1}{\sqrt{1-\rho^2}} \begin{pmatrix} \sqrt{\frac{1-\rho}{2}} & \sqrt{\frac{1-\rho}{2}} \\ \sqrt{\frac{1+\rho}{2}} & -\sqrt{\frac{1+\rho}{2}} \end{pmatrix}$$

□

Exercise 1.4 *As in Example 1.16, let Z be a correlated two-dimensional Wiener process relative to F with increment correlation coefficient ρ, where $-1 < \rho < 1$. Let $\sigma_1 > 0$ and $\sigma_2 > 0$. Then $\sigma_1 Z_1$ and $\sigma_2 Z_2$ are correlated generalized Wiener processes with variance rates σ_1^2 and σ_2^2, respectively. Calculate a constant number c such that*

$$\tilde{W} = c\,(-\sigma_1 Z_1 + \sigma_2 Z_2)$$

is a standard Wiener process relative to F.

Example 1.17 *Two risky securities whose price processes are correlated geometric Brownian motions.* Let

$$Z(t) = \begin{pmatrix} Z_1(t) \\ Z_2(t) \end{pmatrix}$$

be a two-dimensional correlated Wiener process with initial value zero and increment correlation ρ, as in Example 1.16. Consider the following two financial price processes:

$$S_1(t) = S_1(0) \exp\left[\left(\mu_1 - \frac{1}{2}\sigma_1^2 \right) t + \sigma_1 Z_1(t) \right]$$

$$S_2(t) = S_2(0) \exp\left[\left(\mu_2 - \frac{1}{2}\sigma_2^2 \right) t + \sigma_2 Z_2(t) \right]$$

where $S_1(0) > 0$, $S_2(0) > 0$, μ_1, μ_2, $\sigma_1 > 0$, and $\sigma_2 > 0$ are constants. These processes may represent the prices of two stocks, or stock indexes, or an exchange rate and a stock index. They are geometric Brownian motions, and they are correlated.

The processes $\ln S_1$ and $\ln S_2$ form a two-dimensional generalized Wiener process:

$$\ln S_1(t) = \ln S_1(0) + \left(\mu_1 - \frac{1}{2}\sigma_1^2 \right) t + \sigma_1 Z_1(t)$$

$$\ln S_2(t) = \ln S_2(0) + \left(\mu_2 - \frac{1}{2}\sigma_2^2 \right) t + \sigma_2 Z_2(t)$$

The increment covariance matrix is

$$\begin{pmatrix} \sigma_1^2 & \rho\sigma_1\sigma_2 \\ \rho\sigma_1\sigma_2 & \sigma_2^2 \end{pmatrix}$$

The continuously compounded rates of change in the prices, over a time interval $[t, t+\tau]$, are

$$\frac{1}{\tau} \ln \left(\frac{S_1(t+\tau)}{S_1(t)} \right) = \mu_1 - \frac{1}{2}\sigma_1^2 + \frac{1}{\tau}\sigma_1(Z_1(t+\tau) - Z_1(t))$$

and

$$\frac{1}{\tau} \ln \left(\frac{S_2(t+\tau)}{S_2(t)} \right) = \mu_2 - \frac{1}{2}\sigma_2^2 + \frac{1}{\tau}\sigma_2(Z_2(t+\tau) - Z_2(t))$$

They are jointly normally distributed with means $\mu_1 - \frac{1}{2}\sigma_1^2$ and $\mu_2 - \frac{1}{2}\sigma_2^2$, standard deviations $\sigma_1/\sqrt{\tau}$ and $\sigma_2/\sqrt{\tau}$, and correlation ρ. □

1.7　(*) Identification of Processes

In this section, we elaborate on the various concepts of processes being almost the same.

Recall that two processes X and Y are *indistinguishable* if their paths are identical with probability one: there exists a set $N \in \mathcal{F}$ such that $P(N) = 0$ and

$$X(\omega, t) = Y(\omega, t) \text{ for all } \omega \in \Omega \setminus N \text{ and all } t \in T$$

Note that we have to be a bit careful in this definition. The set

$$\{\omega \in \Omega : X(\omega, t) = Y(\omega, t) \text{ for all } t \in T\}$$

is not necessarily measurable. Hence, we cannot require it to have probability one. Instead, we require its complement to be contained in a null set N. But if the underlying probability space is complete, then this requirement is equivalent to the assumption that the set be measurable and have probability one.

Recall that two stochastic processes X and Y are *stochastically equivalent*, and they are said to be *modifications* or *versions* of each other, if for all $t \in T$, $X(t) = Y(t)$ with probability one.

Finally, recall that two processes X and Y are *almost everywhere identical* (with respect to the measure $P \otimes \lambda$ on $(\Omega \times T, \mathcal{F} \otimes \mathcal{B}(T))$) if there exists a set $M \in \mathcal{F} \otimes \mathcal{B}(T)$ such that $(P \otimes \lambda)(M) = 0$ and

$$X(\omega, t) = Y(\omega, t) \text{ for all } (\omega, t) \in (\Omega \times T) \setminus M$$

Again, we have been careful in formulating this definition, because the set

$$\{(\omega, t) \in \Omega \times T : X(\omega, t) \neq Y(\omega, t)\}$$

is not necessarily measurable (unless we assume the processes X and Y to be measurable). If we do not assume the set to be measurable, then we cannot require it to have measure zero. Instead, we require it to be contained in a null set M. But if the underlying probability space is complete, then this requirement is equivalent to the assumption that the set is measurable and has measure zero.

If the processes X and Y are measurable, then the set

$$\{(\omega, t) \in \Omega \times T : X(\omega, t) \neq Y(\omega, t)\}$$

is measurable, and X and Y are almost everywhere identical if and only if the set has measure zero (whether or not the probability space is complete).

It is clear that two K-dimensional processes X and Y are indistinguishable (stochastically equivalent, almost everywhere identical) if and only if for each $k = 1, \ldots, K$, the corresponding one-dimensional component processes X_k and Y_k are indistinguishable (stochastically equivalent, almost everywhere identical).

Proposition 1.18 *If two processes are indistinguishable, then they are stochastically equivalent and almost everywhere identical.*

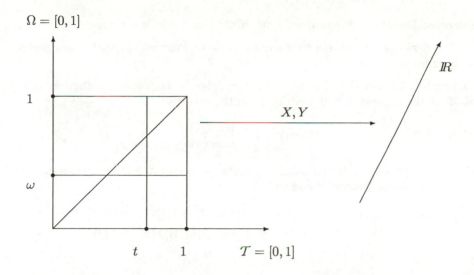

$\Omega = [0,1]$

$\mathbb{R}$

X, Y

ω

$t \qquad 1 \qquad \mathcal{T} = [0,1]$

FIG. 1.6. The processes X, Y in Example 1.19

Exercise 1.5 *Prove Proposition 1.18.*

The converse of Proposition 1.18 is not necessarily true, as illustrated in the following example.

Example 1.19 Let $\Omega = \mathcal{T} = [0,1]$, let $P = \lambda$ be the Lebesgue measure on $[0,1]$, let X be the process $X = 0$, and let the process Y be the indicator function along the diagonal in $[0,1] \times [0,1]$:

$$Y(\omega, t) = \begin{cases} 1 & \text{if } \omega = t \\ 0 & \text{if } \omega \neq t \end{cases}$$

These processes X and Y are stochastically equivalent and almost everywhere identical, but they are not indistinguishable.

The processes X and Y are illustrated in Fig. 1.6. The process X is zero everywhere, whereas Y is one on the diagonal and zero off the diagonal. They are almost everywhere identical, because they differ only on the diagonal, which has measure zero. They are stochastically equivalent, because for each fixed time t (corresponding to a vertical line), they differ only at one state ω (the point where the vertical line crosses the diagonal), which again has measure (probability) zero. The processes X and Y are not indistinguishable, because for each fixed state ω (corresponding to a horizontal line), their paths differ, because they differ where the horizontal line crosses the diagonal.   □

Proposition 1.20 *If two measurable processes are stochastically equivalent, then they are almost everywhere identical.*

Exercise 1.6 *Prove Proposition 1.20. Hint: Use Fubini's theorem.*

The next example shows that the converse of Proposition 1.20 is not necessarily true.

Example 1.21 Let $\Omega = T = [0, 1]$, let $P = \lambda$ be the Lebesgue measure on $[0, 1]$, let X be the process $X = 0$, and let Y be the process

$$Y(\omega, t) = \begin{cases} 1 & \text{if } t \in Q \\ 0 & \text{otherwise} \end{cases}$$

where Q is the set of rational numbers. These processes X and Y are measurable and $P \otimes \lambda$ almost everywhere identical:

$$\begin{aligned}
(P \otimes \lambda)(\{(\omega, t) : X(\omega, t) \neq Y(\omega, t)\}) &= (P \otimes \lambda)([0, 1] \times ([0, 1] \cap Q) \\
&= P([0, 1]) \lambda([0, 1] \cap Q) \\
&= 0
\end{aligned}$$

But X and Y are not stochastically equivalent, because for all $t \in [0, 1] \times ([0, 1] \cap Q)$, $X(t) \neq Y(t)$ with probability one.   □

Proposition 1.22 *If the processes X and Y are stochastically equivalent, and if both are right-continuous or both are left-continuous, then they are indistinguishable.*

Proof Let T' be the set of rational numbers in T plus the right end-point if there is one:

$$T' = \begin{cases} Q \cap [0, \infty) & \text{if } T = [0, \infty) \\ (Q \cap [0, T]) \cup \{T\} & \text{if } T = [0, T] \end{cases}$$

where Q is the set of rational numbers. Since Q is countable, so is T'.

Set

$$N = \{\omega \in \Omega : X(\omega, t) \neq Y(\omega, t) \text{ for some } t \in T'\}$$

Since T' is countable, N is measurable and $P(N) = 0$.

Assume first that X is right-continuous. To show that X and Y are indistinguishable, it suffices to show that if $\omega \in \Omega \backslash N$, then the paths $X(\omega, \cdot)$ and $Y(\omega, \cdot)$ coincide not only at times $t \in T'$ but at all times $t \in T$. This is a consequence of the fact that they are both right-continuous.

To see this, let $t \in T$. Pick a sequence (q_n) of numbers $q_n \in T'$ such that $q_n \geq t$ and $q_n \to t$. Since the paths $X(\omega, \cdot)$ and $Y(\omega, \cdot)$ are right-continuous, $X(\omega, q_n) \to X(\omega, t)$ and $Y(\omega, q_n) \to Y(\omega, t)$; but since $X(\omega, q_n) = Y(\omega, q_n)$ it follows that $X(\omega, t) = Y(\omega, t)$.

The proof for the case where X and Y are left-continuous is similar.   □

Example 1.23 We have shown that every K-dimensional generalized Wiener process Z relative to F with positive definite increment covariance matrix arises from a K-dimensional standard Wiener process relative to F by a linear transformation combined with adding an initial value and a linear deterministic function of time. We can now use Proposition 1.22 to show that if the increment covariance matrix is positive semi-definite with rank $N \leq K$, then Z arises in a similar way from an N-dimensional standard Wiener process relative to F.

Specifically, if the increment covariance matrix Σ of Z has rank N, then there exists a $(K \times N)$-dimensional matrix A with rank N such that $\Sigma = AA^{\mathsf{T}}$. Set $C = (A^{\mathsf{T}}A)^{-1}A^{\mathsf{T}}$. Then $C\Sigma C^{\mathsf{T}} = I$, the N-dimensional identity matrix. Now the process
$$W(t) = C[Z(t) - Z(0) - \mu t]$$
is an N-dimensional Wiener process relative to F. The process Z arises from W by a linear transformation by A combined with adding the initial value $Z(0)$ and the deterministic function μt:

$$Z(t) = Z(0) + \mu t + AW(t)$$

in the sense that the right hand and left hand sides of this equation are indistinguishable processes. To see this, observe that they are continuous and stochastically equivalent. The fact that they are stochastically equivalent means that for each t, the random vector

$$Z(t) - Z(0) - \mu t - AW(t)$$

is equal to zero with probability one. This follows from the observation that it is normally distributed with mean zero and covariance matrix

$$(I - AC)\Sigma(I - AC)^{\mathsf{T}} = (I - AC)AA^{\mathsf{T}}(I - AC)^{\mathsf{T}}$$

which equals zero because
$$(I - AC)A = 0$$

$\square$

Exercise 1.7 *Suppose the processes X and Y are almost everywhere identical. Assume that either*

1. *both X and Y are right-continuous, and if $T = [0, T]$ then $X(T) = Y(T)$ with probability one, or*
2. *both X and Y are left-continuous, and $X(0) = Y(0)$ with probability one.*

Show that X and Y are indistinguishable.

Note that Proposition 1.22 follows from Propositions 1.8 and 1.20 and Exercise 1.7.

Any version of an integrable process is integrable.

If $F = (\mathcal{F}_t)$ is an augmented filtration, then any version of an adapted process is adapted, and any version of a martingale is a martingale.

If $(X^i)_{i \in I}$ and $(Y^i)_{i \in I}$ are families of processes such that for each $i \in I$, X^i and Y^i are stochastically equivalent, and if the family $(X^i)_{i \in I}$ is independent, then the family $(Y^i)_{i \in I}$ is also independent.

1.8   Time Integrals

An important way of creating or defining a new process is to integrate a process
either with respect to time or with respect to a Wiener process. Stochastic integrals, which are integrals with respect to a Wiener process, will be introduced
in the next section. In this section, we briefly consider time integrals.

The purpose of integrating a process with respect to time is to create a new
process with a possibly random and time-varying increment mean.

Standard Wiener processes have increments with zero mean, zero covariances,
and variance one per unit of time. We can subject a standard Wiener process
to a linear transformation and add a linear deterministic drift. This results in
a generalized Wiener process, whose increments may have means different from
zero, contemporaneous covariances different from zero, and variances which are
larger or smaller than one per unit of time. Still, these increments have means,
variances, and covariances that are deterministic and constant per unit of time.

A process with randomly time-varying increment mean can be constructed
by integrating another process up against time. The integrand process essentially represents the instantaneous increment mean, which may be randomly
time varying.

From now on, assume that the underlying probability space $(\Omega, \mathcal{F}, P)$ is complete and that there is given an augmented filtration $F = (\mathcal{F}_t)$. These assumptions are convenient and harmless. The assumption that the filtration is augmented has the desirable consequence that every version of an adapted process
is adapted.

We need to impose some minimal conditions on integrand processes before
they can be meaningfully integrated.

Let $\mathcal{L}^1$ denote the set of adapted measurable processes a (whose values may
be scalars or column vectors) such that for every $t \in \mathcal{T}$,

$$\int_0^t \|a\| \, dt < \infty \qquad P \text{ almost surely}$$

The processes in $\mathcal{L}^1$ are those that can be integrated with respect to time.

If a is N-dimensional, then $\|a\|$ is the Euclidean length of a:

$$\|a\| = \sqrt{a_1^2 + \cdots + a_N^2}$$

If a is one dimensional, then $\|a\|$ is the absolute value of a, $\|a\| = |a|$.

If a is N-dimensional, then for each $i = 1, \ldots, N$,

$$|a_i(\omega, t)| \leq \|a(\omega, t)\| \leq |a_1(\omega, t)| + \cdots + |a_N(\omega, t)|$$

for all (ω, t). Hence, a is in $\mathcal{L}^1$ if and only if each of the component processes a_i
is in $\mathcal{L}^1$.

It is clear that $\mathcal{L}^1$ is a linear space: if $a, \alpha \in \mathcal{L}^1$, then $a + \alpha \in \mathcal{L}^1$, and if
$a \in \mathcal{L}^1$ and c is a number, then $ca \in \mathcal{L}^1$.

Proposition 1.24 *If $a \in \mathcal{L}^1$ is $N \times 1$ dimensional and ϕ is a continuous adapted $(N \times 1)$-dimensional process, then $\phi^\top a \in \mathcal{L}^1$.*

Exercise 1.8 *Prove Proposition 1.24.*

If $a \in \mathcal{L}^1$, we define the corresponding *time integral process* by the pathwise time integral

$$(\omega, t) \mapsto \int_0^t a \, ds = \int_0^t a(s) \, ds = \int_0^t a(\omega, s) \, ds$$

If a is K-dimensional, then so is the time integral process. The integrand will often be written as a instead of $a(s)$ even if it does depend on time and is being integrated with respect to time.

It is important to notice that the integrand process a does not have to be continuous. It may well exhibit jumps or indeed any kind of discontinuities, so long as it is measurable and adapted. The integral process will be continuous in any case.

Proposition 1.25 *If $a \in \mathcal{L}^1$, then the process*

$$X(t) = \int_0^t a \, ds$$

is continuous and adapted.

Proof (*) See Liptser and Shiryayev [65, 1977, p. 95], Chung and Williams [17, 1983, Lemma 3.8]. □

Proposition 1.25, combined with Proposition 1.8, implies that the time integral process is measurable.

Proposition 1.26 *If $a \in \mathcal{L}^1$, then a is almost everywhere identical to zero if and only if the integral process $\int_0^t a(s) \, ds$ is indistinguishable from zero.*

Proof (*) It is clear from Fubini's theorem that if $a = 0$ almost everywhere with respect to $P \otimes \lambda$, then for all $t \in \mathcal{T}$, $\int_0^t a(s) \, ds = 0$ with probability one. Therefore, the integral process is stochastically equivalent to zero. Since it is continuous, it follows from Proposition 1.22 that it is indistinguishable from zero.

Conversely, suppose the integral process is indistinguishable from zero. Let $\mathcal{A}$ be the subset of $\mathcal{F} \otimes \mathcal{B}(\mathcal{T})$ consisting of sets of the form $C \times (b, c]$, where $C \in \mathcal{F}$ and $b, c \in \mathcal{T}$, $b < c$. Then $\mathcal{A}$ is stable under the formation of finite intersections, $\mathcal{A}$ generates the product sigma-algebra $\mathcal{F} \otimes \mathcal{B}(\mathcal{T})$, $\Omega \times \mathcal{T}$ is a finite or countable union of sets in $\mathcal{A}$, and by Fubini's theorem,

$$\int_{C \times (b,c]} a \, d(P \otimes \lambda) = \int_C \left[\int_0^c a(t) \, dt - \int_0^b a(t) \, dt \right] dP = 0$$

for each $C \times (b, c] \in \mathcal{A}$. By Proposition B.15, $a = 0$ almost everywhere with respect to $P \otimes \lambda$. □

It follows from Proposition 1.26 that two processes in $\mathcal{L}^1$ have indistinguishable time integrals if and only if they are almost everywhere identical. Hence, we do not need to distinguish integrand processes that are almost everywhere identical.

1.9   Stochastic Integrals

In this section, we define and study the stochastic integral with respect to a Wiener process.

The purpose of integrating a process with respect to a Wiener process is to create a new process with a possibly random and time-varying increment variance (and random and time-varying contemporaneous increment covariances in the case of multi-dimensional processes). The square of the integrand process essentially represents the variance (or the covariance matrix, in the multi-dimensional case) of the instantaneous increment.

The stochastic integral with respect to a Wiener process will be defined for integrands which are adapted and measurable and satisfy an appropriate integrability condition. Two integrands will be identified if they are almost everywhere identical.

We shall first define the stochastic integral of a one-dimensional process over a fixed bounded time interval $[0, t]$. This integral will be a random variable. By considering it as a function of the upper integration limit, we shall turn it into a stochastic process. Based on the one-dimensional case, a K-dimensional row vector process can be integrated with respect to a K-dimensional Wiener process by integrating each component with respect to the corresponding component of the Wiener process and adding them up. Finally, an $(N \times K)$-dimensional matrix valued process can be integrated with respect to a K-dimensional Wiener process by integrating each row in the matrix and stacking the resulting integrals on top of each other to form an N-dimensional process.

Recall that the probability space is assumed to be complete and that the filtration F is assumed to be augmented. Let W be a one-dimensional Wiener process relative to F.

A one-dimensional process b on $[0, t]$ is a *simple process* if there exists a subdivision $0 = t_0 < t_1 < \cdots < t_n = t$ of $[0, t]$ and random variables $\beta, \beta_0, \beta_1, \ldots, \beta_{n-1}$ with $\beta \in \mathcal{F}_0$ and $\beta_i \in \mathcal{F}_{t_i}$ for each $i = 0, \ldots, n - 1$, such that b has the form

$$b = \beta 1_{\{0\}} + \sum_{i=0}^{n-1} \beta_i 1_{(t_i, t_{i+1}]}$$

This means that $b(0) = \beta$ and $b(t) = \beta_i$ when $t \in (t_i, t_{i+1}]$. In other words, each path of the process is constant on each subinterval, and the random value of the process on the subinterval $(t_i, t_{i+1}]$ is measurable with respect to $\mathcal{F}_{t_i}$.

Figure 1.7 shows a sample path of a simple process. Our convention is that the subintervals where it is constant are open on the left and closed on the right. This is actually of minor importance. What is important is that the random

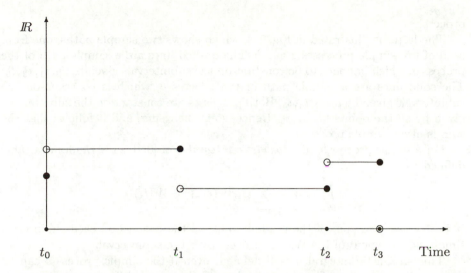

FIG. 1.7. A sample path of a simple process

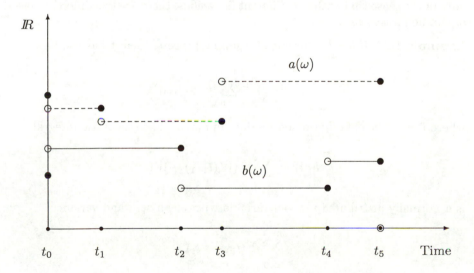

FIG. 1.8. Sample paths of two simple processes

value of the process on each subinterval is known at the left end-point of that
subinterval, whether the left end-point is contained in the subinterval or not.

It is clear that if b is a simple process, then cb is a simple process for every
constant c; and if a and b are simple processes, then the sum $a + b$ is a simple

process.

The latter is illustrated in Fig. 1.8, which shows two sample paths, one from each of two simple processes a and b. The dashed lines are a sample path of the process a, which happens to be constant on the subintervals given by t_0, t_1, t_3, t_5. The solid lines are a sample path of the process b, which is constant on the subintervals given by t_0, t_2, t_4, t_5. Both processes are constant on the subintervals given by all the points $t_0, \ldots, t_5$. Hence, so is their sum, and it follows that the sum is also a simple process.

For a simple process b, the *stochastic integral* over $[0, t]$ is the random variable defined by

$$\int_0^t b\, dW = \sum_{i=0}^{n-1} \beta_i(W(t_{i+1}) - W(t_i))$$

It is the weighted sum of the random value of the process on each subinterval times the increment of the Wiener process over the subinterval.

This stochastic integral is well defined: even if the simple process b can be expressed in the above form in several ways (based on different subdivisions), the corresponding integrals are identical.

The stochastic integral of simple processes over $[0, t]$ depends on the filtration only in the sense that with two different filtrations, there are two different classes of simple processes.

Example 1.27 If b is a deterministic simple process, then it has the form

$$b = \beta 1_{\{0\}} + \sum_{i=0}^{n-1} \beta_i 1_{(t_i, t_{i+1}]}$$

where the coefficients β_i are non-random numbers. The stochastic integral

$$\int_0^t b\, dW = \sum_{i=0}^{n-1} \beta_i(W(t_{i+1}) - W(t_i))$$

is a normally distributed random variable with mean zero and variance

$$\sum_{i=0}^{n-1} \beta_i^2(t_{i+1} - t_i)$$

□

Exercise 1.9 *Show the following directly on the basis of the definition of the stochastic integral of simple processes.*

1. *If a and b are simple processes, and γ and δ are numbers, then*

$$\gamma \int_0^t a\, dW + \delta \int_0^t b\, dW = \int_0^t (\gamma a + \delta b)\, dW$$

2. *If a and b are bounded simple processes, then*

$$E\left[\left(\int_0^t a\, dW\right)\left(\int_0^t b\, dW\right)\right] = E\left[\int_0^t ab\, ds\right]$$

3. *If b is a bounded simple process, then the stochastic integral process $t \mapsto \int_0^t b\, dW$ is a continuous martingale.*

Before we can meaningfully integrate non-simple processes with respect to a Wiener process, we need to impose some minimal conditions on them.

Let $\mathcal{L}^2$ denote the set of adapted measurable processes b (whose elements may be matrices, vectors, or scalars) such that for every $t \in \mathcal{T}$,

$$\int_0^t \|b\|^2\, ds < \infty \qquad P \text{ almost surely}$$

The processes in $\mathcal{L}^2$ turn out to be those that can be integrated with respect to a Wiener process.

If b is a vector- or matrix-valued process, then $\|b\|^2$ equals the sum of squares of its elements:

$$\|b\|^2 = \sum_{i,j} b_{ij}^2$$

Hence, b is in $\mathcal{L}^2$ if and only if each of its component processes is in $\mathcal{L}^2$.

It is clear that $\mathcal{L}^2$ is a linear space: if $b, \beta \in \mathcal{L}^2$, then $b + \beta \in \mathcal{L}^2$, and if $b \in \mathcal{L}^2$ and c is a number, then $cb \in \mathcal{L}^2$.

If b is a matrix-valued process, then

$$\|b\|^2 = \mathrm{tr}(bb^\top)$$

Here, $\mathrm{tr}(bb^\top)$ denotes the trace of the matrix $bb^\top$, which is defined as the sum of its diagonal elements.

Recall the following two manipulation rules for traces of matrices. If A is a square matrix, then

$$\mathrm{tr}(A) = \mathrm{tr}(A^\top)$$

and if A and B are matrices of dimension $N \times K$ and $K \times N$, respectively, then

$$\mathrm{tr}(AB) = \mathrm{tr}(BA)$$

Proposition 1.28 *Let b be an adapted, measurable $(N \times K)$-dimensional matrix-valued process. Then $b \in \mathcal{L}^2$ if and only if $bb^\top \in \mathcal{L}^1$.*

Exercise 1.10 *Prove Proposition 1.28.*

Proposition 1.29 *If $b \in \mathcal{L}^2$ is $N \times K$ dimensional, and if ϕ is a continuous adapted $(N \times N)$-dimensional process, then $b^\top \phi b \in \mathcal{L}^1$.*

Exercise 1.11 *Prove Proposition 1.29.*

To define the stochastic integral of a non-simple scalar-valued process in $\mathcal{L}^2$, we approximate it by a sequence of simple processes, as follows.

Proposition 1.30 *Let $K = N = 1$. Let $b \in \mathcal{L}^2$ and $t \in \mathcal{T}$.*

1. *There exists a sequence (b_n) of simple processes in $\mathcal{L}^2$ such that*

$$\int_0^t |b - b_n|^2 \, ds \to 0$$

   in probability.
2. *For every sequence (b_n) as in 1, the sequence $\int_0^t b_n \, dW$ converges in probability.*
3. *The limit in 2 is unique with probability one, and it does not depend on the choice of the sequence (b_n).*

Proof (*)   Statement 1 follows from Liptser and Shiryayev [65, 1977, Lemma 4.5] or Arnold [1, 1974, Lemma 4.4.5]. For 2 and 3, see Arnold [1, 1974, Lemma 4.4.9]. □

If $b \in \mathcal{L}^2$, define the *stochastic integral* $\int_0^t b \, dW$ as the probability limit of the integrals $\int_0^t b_n \, dW$ of the simple approximating processes from Proposition 1.30.

If b happens to be a simple process, then the integral of b according to this definition coincides with the integral of b as a simple process.

The index n going to infinity in Proposition 1.30 should not be interpreted as time going forward. It means that the process b_n approximates b better and better.

Suppose $F = (\mathcal{F}_s)_{s \in \mathcal{F}}$ and $\hat{F} = (\hat{\mathcal{F}}_s)_{s \in \mathcal{F}}$ are two augmented filtrations such that W is a Wiener process relative to each. Then the integrals based on F and $\hat{F}$ differ only in the sense that the sets $\mathcal{L}^2$ of processes that can be integrated differ. Define the intersection $F \cap \hat{F}$ of the filtrations as the filtration $(\mathcal{F}_s \cap \hat{\mathcal{F}}_s)$. If b is in $\mathcal{L}^2$ based on both F and $\hat{F}$, then it is in $\mathcal{L}^2$ based on $F \cap \hat{F}$, and so it can be approximated by a sequence of processes that are simple processes with respect to $F \cap \hat{F}$. These processes are also simple processes with respect to both F and $\hat{F}$. Hence, the integral of b based on each of the three filtrations is the same.

Now let W be a K-dimensional Wiener process relative to F. Let b be an $(N \times K)$-dimensional matrix-valued process:

$$b = \begin{pmatrix} b_{11} & \ldots & b_{1K} \\ \vdots & & \vdots \\ b_{N1} & \ldots & b_{NK} \end{pmatrix}$$

Recall that b is in $\mathcal{L}^2$ if and only if each of the component process b_{nk} is in $\mathcal{L}^2$. If so, define the stochastic integral of b as

$$\int_0^t b \, dW = \begin{pmatrix} \sum_{k=1}^K \int_0^t b_{1k} \, dW_k \\ \vdots \\ \sum_{k=1}^K \int_0^t b_{Nk} \, dW_k \end{pmatrix}$$

Proposition 1.31 Properties of the stochastic integral. *Let $a, b \in \mathcal{L}^2$ and $t \in \mathcal{T}$.*

1. *Linearity: if γ and δ are numbers, then*

$$\gamma \int_0^t a \, dW + \delta \int_0^t b \, dW = \int_0^t (\gamma a + \delta b) \, dW$$

2. *Time consistency: if $0 \le s \le t$, then*

$$\int_0^s b \, dW = \int_0^t 1_{\Omega \times [0,s]} b \, dW$$

Proof (*) It suffices to prove this for the case $N = K = 1$, since the multidimensional case follows immediately from the one-dimensional case.

1: See Liptser and Shiryayev [65, 1977, pp. 96–97 and 105] or Arnold [1, 1974, Theorem 4.4.14].

2: If b is a simple process, then so is $1_{\Omega \times [0,s]} b$, and it is clear that the equation holds. If b is not necessarily simple, choose a sequence of simple processes $b_n \in \mathcal{L}^2$ such that

$$\int_0^t |b_n - b|^2 \, ds \to 0$$

in probability. Then $(1_{\Omega \times [0,s]} b_n)$ is a sequence of simple processes in $\mathcal{L}^2$, and since

$$\int_0^t |b_n 1_{\Omega \times [0,s]} - b 1_{\Omega \times [0,s]}|^2 \, du \le \int_0^t |b_n - b|^2 \, du$$

it follows that

$$\int_0^t |b_n 1_{\Omega \times [0,s]} - b 1_{\Omega \times [0,s]}|^2 \, du \to 0$$

in probability. Hence,

$$\int_0^s b_n \, dW = \int_0^t b_n 1_{\Omega \times [0,s]} \, dW \to \int_0^t b 1_{\Omega \times [0,s]} \, dW$$

But since

$$\int_0^s b_n \, dW \to \int_0^s b \, dW$$

it follows that

$$\int_0^s b \, dW = \int_0^t b 1_{\Omega \times [0,s]} \, dW$$

$\square$

For each fixed $t \in \mathcal{T}$, the stochastic integral $\int_0^t b\, dW$ is a random variable. We shall now consider the stochastic integral as a stochastic process by allowing t to vary.

Proposition 1.32 *For every $b \in \mathcal{L}^2$, the stochastic integral process $\int_0^t b\, dW$ is adapted.*

Proof For each t, the random variable $\int_0^t b\, dW$ is measurable with respect to $\mathcal{F}_t$ because it is the probability limit of a sequence of variables that are measurable with respect to $\mathcal{F}_t$. □

Note that for each t, the integral is only defined with probability one, so the integral process is only defined up to stochastic equivalence. According to the following proposition, it has a continuous version.

Proposition 1.33 *If $b \in \mathcal{L}^2$, then the stochastic integral process $\int_0^t b\, dW$ has a continuous version.*

Proof (*) It suffices to consider the case $N = K = 1$. See Liptser and Shiryayev [65, 1977, pp. 96–97 and 105] or Arnold [1, 1974, Theorem 5.1.1]. □

From now on, we shall always assume that we select a continuous version of the stochastic integral process. Under this assumption, the process is defined up to indistinguishability.

Since we assume the filtration to be augmented, any version of an adapted process is adapted. Hence, choosing a continuous version of the stochastic integral process does not affect the fact, stated in Proposition 1.32, that it is adapted.

Proposition 1.34 *If $a, b \in \mathcal{L}^2$ are almost everywhere identical, then*

$$\int_0^t a\, dW = \int_0^t b\, dW$$

in the sense of indistinguishability.

Proof It suffices to show that if b is almost everywhere identical to zero, then $\int_0^t b\, dW = 0$ in the sense of indistinguishability. For each fixed t, consider the sequence of simple processes $b_n = 0$. Each of these processes has integral $\int_0^t b_n\, dW = 0$, and the sequence approximates b since $\int_0^t |b_n - b|^2\, ds = 0$ for all n. Hence, the integral process $\int_0^t b\, dW$ is stochastically equivalent to zero. By Proposition 1.33 and by convention, it is a continuous process. Hence, by Proposition 1.22, it is indistinguishable from zero. □

The converse of the statement in Proposition 1.34 is also true: if the two integral processes are indistinguishable, then the two integrand processes are almost everywhere identical. This will follow from Proposition 2.6, which in turn is a consequence of Itô's lemma.

We defined simple processes so as to be constant on time subintervals that are open on the left and closed on the right. This is not important. We might just as well have used intervals that are open on the right and closed on the left. Indeed, suppose

$$0 = t_0 < t_1 < \cdots < t_n = t$$

is a subdivision of $[0, t]$ and $\beta, \beta_0, \beta_1, \ldots, \beta_{n-1}, \beta_n$ are random variables with $\beta \in \mathcal{F}_0$ and $\beta_i \in \mathcal{F}_{t_i}$ for each $i = 0, \ldots, n$. Let b be the simple process

$$b = \beta 1_{\{0\}} + \sum_{i=0}^{n-1} \beta_i 1_{(t_i, t_{i+1}]}$$

and let $\tilde{b}$ be the process

$$\tilde{b} = \sum_{i=0}^{n-1} \beta_i 1_{[t_i, t_{i+1})} + \beta_n 1_{\{t\}}$$

Then

$$\int_0^t \tilde{b}\, dW = \int_0^t b\, dW = \sum_{i=0}^{n-1} \beta_i (W(t_{i+1}) - W(t_i))$$

This follows from Proposition 1.34 combined with the fact that $b = \tilde{b}$ almost everywhere.

What is important, however, is that simple processes should be defined in such a way that they are adapted.

If $b \in \mathcal{L}^2$ and $0 \le s \le t$, define

$$\int_s^t b\, dW = \int_0^t b\, dW - \int_0^s b\, dW$$

It follows from property 2 of Proposition 1.31 that

$$\int_s^t b\, dW = \int_0^t 1_{\Omega \times (s, t]} b\, dW$$

Proposition 1.35 *If $b \in \mathcal{L}^2$, $0 \le s \le t$, and Y is a random variable measurable with respect to $\mathcal{F}_s$, then*

$$\int_s^t Y b\, dW = Y \int_s^t b\, dW$$

Proof (*) It suffices to prove this for the case $N = K = 1$, since the multi-dimensional case follows immediately from the one-dimensional case.

First, suppose b is a simple process: there exists a subdivision

$$0 = t_0 < t_1 < \cdots < t_n = t$$

of $[0, t]$ and random variables $\beta, \beta_0, \beta_1, \ldots, \beta_{n-1}$ with $\beta \in \mathcal{F}_0$ and $\beta_i \in \mathcal{F}_{t_i}$ for each $i = 0, \ldots, n-1$, such that

$$b = \beta 1_{\{0\}} + \sum_{i=0}^{n-1} \beta_i 1_{(t_i, t_{i+1}]}$$

We may assume without loss of generality that there exists $m \in \{0, \ldots, n-1\}$ such that $t_m = s$. Now,

$$Y b 1_{(s,t]} = \sum_{i=m}^{n-1} Y \beta_i 1_{(t_i, t_{i+1}]}$$

which is a simple process. So

$$\int_0^t Y b 1_{(s,t]} \, dW = \sum_{i=m}^{n-1} Y \beta_i \left(W_{t_{i+1}} - W_{t_i} \right)$$

$$= Y \sum_{i=m}^{n-1} \beta_i \left(W_{t_{i+1}} - W_{t_i} \right)$$

$$= Y \int_0^t b 1_{(s,t]} \, dW$$

In the general case, pick a sequence of simple processes (b_n) such that

$$\int_0^t |b_n - b| \, du \to 0$$

in probability. This can be done by Proposition 1.30. Then

$$|b_n 1_{(s,t]} - b 1_{(s,t]}| \leq |b_n - b|$$

and

$$|Y b_n 1_{(s,t]} - Y b 1_{(s,t]}| = |Y 1_{(s,t]}||b_n - b| \leq |Y||b_n - b|$$

So,

$$\int_0^t |b_n 1_{(s,t]} - b 1_{(s,t]}| \, du \leq \int_0^t |b_n - b| \, du \to 0$$

and

$$\int_0^t |Y b_n 1_{(s,t]} - Y b 1_{(s,t]}| \, du \leq |Y| \int_0^t |b_n - b| \, du \to 0$$

in probability. Hence,

$$\int_0^t b_n 1_{(s,t]} \, dW \to \int_0^t b 1_{(s,t]} \, dW$$

and

$$\int_0^t Y b_n 1_{(s,t]} \, dW \to \int_0^t Y b 1_{(s,t]} \, dW$$

in probability. But since $Y b_n 1_{(s,t]}$ is a simple process,

$$\int_0^t Y b_n 1_{(s,t]} \, dW = Y \int_0^t b_n 1_{(s,t]} \, dW$$

$$\to Y \int_0^t b 1_{(s,t]} \, dW$$

Hence,

$$\int_s^t Y b \, dW = \int_0^t Y b 1_{(s,t]} \, dW = Y \int_0^t b 1_{(s,t]} \, dW = Y \int_s^t b \, dW$$

$\square$

The integral on the right hand side in the formula in Proposition 1.35 is interpreted as

$$\int_s^t Y b \, dW = \int_0^t 1_{(s,t]} Y b \, dW$$

The requirement that Y be measurable with respect to $\mathcal{F}_s$ ensures that the integrand $1_{(s,t]} Y b$ is an adapted process.

An analogous formula is also true for time integrals. If $a \in \mathcal{L}^1$, $0 \le s \le t$, and Y is a random variable measurable with respect to $\mathcal{F}_s$, then

$$\int_s^t Y a \, du = Y \int_s^t a \, du$$

This follows trivially from the fact that the time integral is defined pathwise:

$$\int_s^t Y(\omega) a(\omega, u) \, du = Y(\omega) \int_s^t a(\omega, u) \, du$$

for each $\omega \in \Omega$. By contrast, the formula for the stochastic integral in Proposition 1.35 requires a more involved proof because the stochastic integral is not defined path by path.

Let $\mathcal{H}^2$ denote the set of adapted measurable processes b such that

$$E \int_0^t \|b\|^2 \, du < \infty$$

for all $t \in \mathcal{T}$. Note that $\mathcal{H}^2 \subset \mathcal{L}^2$. In fact, $\mathcal{H}^2$ is strictly smaller than $\mathcal{L}^2$, because the random time integral may take finite values with probability one and yet have infinite expectation.

If b is a vector or matrix valued process, then b is in $\mathcal{H}^2$ if and only if each of its components is in $\mathcal{H}^2$.

The following proposition says that if the integrand process is in $\mathcal{H}^2$, then the integral can be defined by approximation in L^2 instead of approximation in probability.

Proposition 1.36 Convergence of the stochastic integral. *Let* $b \in \mathcal{H}^2$. *Assume that* $N = K = 1$.

1. *There exists a sequence* (b_n) *of simple processes in* $\mathcal{H}^2$ *such that for all* $t \in T$,

$$E \int_0^t |b(s) - b_n(s)|^2 \, ds \to 0$$

as $n \to \infty$.

2. *If* b *is deterministic, then the simple processes* b_n *in (1) can be chosen such as to be deterministic.*

3. *If* $t \in T$ *and if* (b_n) *is a sequence of simple processes in* $\mathcal{H}^2$ *such that*

$$E \int_0^t |b(s) - b_n(s)|^2 \, ds \to 0,$$

then

$$E \left(\int_0^t b_n \, dW - \int_0^t b \, dW \right)^2 \to 0$$

as $n \to \infty$.

Proof (*)

1: See Liptser and Shiryayev [65, 1977, Lemma 4.4] or Arnold [1, 1974, Lemma 4.4.12].

2: Arnold [1, 1974, Lemma 4.4.5].

3: First, the sequence $(\int_0^t b_n \, dW)$ converges in $L^2(\Omega, \mathcal{F}, P)$. This is shown as in Liptser and Shiryayev [65, 1977, p. 96]. But then it converges to the same limit in probability, and by Proposition 1.30, the limit is $\int_0^t b \, dW$. □

In general, a stochastic integral is not necessarily a martingale. The next proposition says that if the integrand process is in $\mathcal{H}^2$, then the stochastic integral is a martingale. Furthermore, it has finite second moments, and there is a formula for calculating the variances and covariances of its components.

Proposition 1.37 Conditional mean and covariance of the increments of the stochastic integral.

1. *If* b *is a* K-*dimensional row-vector-valued process in* $\mathcal{H}^2$, *then the process* $\int_0^t b \, dW$ *is a martingale.*

2. *If b and β are K-dimensional row-vector-valued processes in $\mathcal{H}^2$, then the process*

$$\left(\int_0^t b\,dW \right) \left(\int_0^t \beta\,dW \right)$$

is integrable, and

$$E\left[\left(\int_s^t b\,dW \right) \left(\int_s^t \beta\,dW \right) \Big| \mathcal{F}_s \right] = E\left[\int_s^t b\beta^\top\,du \,\Big|\, \mathcal{F}_s \right]$$

$$= \int_s^t E\left[b(u)\beta(u)^\top \mid \mathcal{F}_s \right]\,du$$

for $0 \le s \le t$.

Proof (*) It suffices to prove this in the case $N = K = 1$.

1: See Liptser and Shiryayev [65, 1977, pp. 97 and 99], or Arnold [1, 1974, Theorem 5.1.1].

2: See Liptser and Shiryayev [65, 1977, p. 97]. The last equation follows from Theorem B.28 (the conditional Fubini theorem). $\qquad\square$

Exercise 1.12 *Consider the processes a, b, and W and the filtration F from Example 1.13. Calculate*

$$\mathrm{var}\left(\int_0^3 a\,dW \right)$$

$$\mathrm{var}\left(\int_1^3 a\,dW \,\Big|\, \mathcal{F}_1 \right)$$

$$\mathrm{cov}\left(\int_0^3 a\,dW, \int_0^3 b\,dW \right)$$

and

$$\mathrm{cov}\left(\int_1^3 a\,dW, \int_1^3 b\,dW \,\Big|\, \mathcal{F}_1 \right)$$

It follows from Proposition 1.37 that if $b \in \mathcal{H}^2$ is an $(N \times K)$-dimensional matrix-valued process, then the stochastic integral process is square integrable with conditional covariance matrix

$$E\left[\left(\int_s^t b\,dW \right) \left(\int_s^t b\,dW \right)^\top \Big| \mathcal{F}_s \right] = E\left[\int_s^t bb^\top\,du \,\Big|\, \mathcal{F}_s \right]$$

$$= \int_s^t E\left[b(u)b(u)^\top \mid \mathcal{F}_s \right]\,du$$

Therefore, we call the process $bb^\top$ the *instantaneous covariance matrix* of the stochastic integral.

Corollary 1.38 Uncorrelated increments of the stochastic integral. *Let $b, \beta \in \mathcal{H}^2$ be K-dimensional row-vector-valued processes. If $0 \leq s \leq t \leq u$, then*

$$E\left[\left(\int_s^t b\,dW\right)\left(\int_t^u \beta\,dW\right)\,\bigg|\,\mathcal{F}_s\right] = 0$$

Warning: The fact that the increments of the stochastic integrals have zero covariance does not necessarily imply that they are stochastically independent. They will be stochastically independent if they are jointly normally distributed. That will be the case if the integrand processes b and β are deterministic, as we shall see later, in Theorem 3.1.

The following theorem, called the martingale representation theorem, will be the key ingredient in the proof of the complete markets theorem (Theorem 5.6), which says that under appropriate assumptions, financial markets are dynamically complete.

Theorem 1.39 The martingale representation theorem. *Let W be a standard Brownian motion of dimension K. If X is a martingale with respect to the filtration F^W, then there exists a process $b \in \mathcal{L}^2$ such that*

$$X(t) - X(0) = \int_0^t b\,dW$$

(in the sense that the two processes are indistinguishable).

Proof (*) Rogers and Williams [79, 1987, Theorem 36.5], Karatzas and Shreve [64, 1988, Problem 4.16]. □

1.10 (*) Predictable Processes

We have assumed that the integrand processes that are integrated up against the Wiener process to form stochastic integrals are adapted and measurable. The mathematical literature often imposes the slightly stronger assumption that the integrand processes are "predictable" or "previsible." This is, in particular, true of expositions of the stochastic integral that allow for integrators which are more general than Wiener processes. It is possible to define a stochastic integral with respect to integrators that are so-called "semi-martingales," at the cost of assuming that the integrands are predictable.

When we consider only stochastic integrals with respect to Wiener processes, as is most often the case in finance, it is not necessary to assume that the integrands are predictable. Even so, the concept of predictable processes and the related concepts of "optional" and "progressive" processes do occasionally appear in the finance literature. For this reason we briefly define them and investigate their interrelations in this section, although we are not really going to need them. As we shall argue, these classes of processes essentially coincide with the class of adapted measurable processes. More precisely, every predictable (or optional or progressive) process is adapted and measurable, and every adapted and measurable process is almost everywhere identical to a process which is predictable (and optional and progressive).

Let $(\Omega, \mathcal{F}, P)$ be a complete probability space with an augmented filtration $F = (\mathcal{F}_t)_{t \in \mathcal{T}}$. Assume that the filtration is *right-continuous*, which means that

$$\mathcal{F}_s = \bigcap_{s < t} \mathcal{F}_t$$

for all $s \in \mathcal{T}$ (except if s is a right end-point of $\mathcal{T}$).

Proposition 1.40 *Let $(\Omega, \mathcal{F}, P)$ be a complete probability space, and B a K-dimensional standard Brownian motion. Then the augmented filtration F^B generated by B is right-continuous.*

Proof Liptser and Shiryayev [65, 1977, Theorem 4.3]. □

Let $\mathcal{P}$ denote the sigma-algebra on $\Omega \times \mathcal{T}$ generated by the adapted left-continuous processes. It is called the *predictable* sigma-algebra. A process is said to be *predictable* if it is measurable with respect to $\mathcal{P}$.

Note that this concept of a predictable process is of a technical mathematical nature and is quite different from the concept found in the empirically oriented finance literature. There, it is usually not precisely defined, but it typically means a process with independent increments.

Let $\mathcal{O}$ denote the sigma-algebra on $\Omega \times \mathcal{T}$ generated by the adapted right-continuous processes. It is called the *optional* sigma-algebra. A process is said to be *optional* if it is measurable with respect to $\mathcal{O}$.

A process X is said to be *progressively measurable* or simply *progressive* if, for every $t \in \mathcal{T}$, the restriction of X to $\Omega \times [0, t]$ is measurable with respect to $\mathcal{F}_t \otimes \mathcal{B}([0, t])$. Any progressive process is measurable and adapted.

Let $\mathcal{M}$ denote the sigma-algebra on $\Omega \times \mathcal{T}$ generated by the progressive processes. It is called the *progressive* sigma-algebra.

Proposition 1.41 *A process is progressive if and only if it is measurable with respect to $\mathcal{M}$.*

Proof It follows directly from the definition of $\mathcal{M}$ that every progressive process is measurable with respect to $\mathcal{M}$. Conversely, to show that every process which is measurable with respect to $\mathcal{M}$ is progressive, let B be the set of bounded progressive processes. Then $\sigma(B) \subset \mathcal{M}$. Every progressive process is a pointwise limit of processes from B, and hence it is measurable with respect to $\sigma(B)$. This shows that $\mathcal{M} = \sigma(B)$. It follows from Theorem A.36 (with $H = B$) that B contains all bounded processes measurable with respect to $\sigma(B)$. Therefore, all such processes are progressive. Every process which is measurable with respect to $\mathcal{M} = \sigma(B)$ is a pointwise limit of bounded processes measurable with respect to $\sigma(B)$. Hence, it is progressive. □

Proposition 1.42 $\mathcal{P} \subset \mathcal{O} \subset \mathcal{M} \subset \mathcal{F} \otimes \mathcal{B}(\mathcal{T})$.

Proof See Chung and Williams [18, 1990, p. 63]. ☐

Observe that Proposition 1.8 above follows from Proposition 1.42.

Since all progressive processes are adapted, it follows from Propositions 1.41 and 1.42 that all optional processes are adapted and all predictable processes are adapted.

Finally, let $\mathcal{P}^*$ denote the augmentation of $\mathcal{P}$ by null sets (sets of measure zero) from $(\Omega \times \mathcal{T}, \mathcal{F} \otimes \mathcal{B}(\mathcal{T}), P \otimes \lambda)$ where λ is the Lebesgue measure on $\mathcal{T}$.

Proposition 1.43 *Any measurable adapted process is $\mathcal{P}^*$-measurable.*

Proof Chung and Williams [18, 1990, Theorem 3.7]. ☐

Proposition 1.44 *Let b be a measurable process. Then b is $\mathcal{P}^*$-measurable if and only if there exists a predictable process β such that b and β are almost everywhere identical.*

Proof Chung and Williams [18, 1990, Lemma 3.5 (ii)]. ☐

It follows from these propositions that so long as we identify processes that are almost everywhere identical, there is no difference between adapted measurable processes, predictable processes, optional processes, and progressively measurable processes.

1.11 Summary

This chapter has introduced the fundamental concept of stochastic processes and the most important related ideas. We can think of a stochastic process as the dynamic generalization of a random variable. Formally, a stochastic process is a family of random variables indexed by time.

An important example of a stochastic process is Brownian motion. It is the basic building block from which we build almost all of our other stochastic processes. A Brownian motion has initial value zero, and it is continuous, which means that it does not jump. Successive increments of a Brownian motion are independent of each other, which means that information about past increments cannot be used to predict future increments. The increments are normally distributed with mean zero and with variance equal to the length of the time interval. In this sense, Brownian motion is the dynamic, continuous-time counterpart of a normal distribution.

We can stack a number of independent one-dimensional Brownian motions on top of each other to get a multi-dimensional Brownian motion. That is useful in models where we want several sources of uncertainty. We can then add initial values and linear deterministic drifts to the component processes. The drift terms will make the increment means proportional to time. Finally, we can replace the original Brownian motions with linear combinations which are correlated and scaled in such a way that they no longer have unit variance. The result will be what we call a generalized Brownian motion.

A one-dimensional generalized Brownian motion is still not a good model of a securities price, although it does have some desirable properties. It may start at a value different from zero, and its increments do not necessarily have mean zero and variance one per unit of time. Like securities prices, the components of a multi-dimensional generalized Brownian motion may be correlated with each other. However, a generalized Brownian motion has positive probability of taking negative values, and it tends to change by the same absolute amount regardless of whether its level is high or low. The percentage increment will tend to decline as the level increases.

To correct this, we introduced the notion of a geometric Brownian motion, which is the exponential of a generalized Brownian motion. The percentage increments of a geometric Brownian motion have constant mean and variance per unit of time. The stock price in the Black–Scholes model follows a geometric Brownian motion.

However, we want to go beyond generalized and geometric Brownian motions and construct processes whose increment means, variances, and covariances can vary over time in a random manner. The so-called Itô processes have this property. They are the processes most often used to describe the prices of securities and the values of trading strategies, and we shall study them in detail in the next chapter. For now, we note that an Itô process is the sum of an initial value, a time integral, and a stochastic integral.

Time integration is a way of creating a process with an expected increment mean that varies randomly over time. A time integral can be thought of as the sum over time of the values of an integrand process. It is random because it depends on the path of the integrand process. It will also depend on time, because it depends on the integration limit. Hence, the time integral is a stochastic process. We can think of the instantaneous increment of the time integral at a point in time as having expectation equal to the value of the integrand process, given the information available at that point in time.

Stochastic integration is a way of creating a process with an increment variance that varies over time. It is conceptually a little bit more complicated than time integration. A stochastic integral is an integral not simply with respect to time but with respect to a Brownian motion. It can be thought of as a sum over time of the value of an integrand process times the instantaneous increment of the underlying Brownian motion. If we think of the instantaneous increment of the Brownian motion as having mean zero and variance one, then the instantaneous increment of the stochastic integral at a point in time has mean zero and variance equal to the square of the value of the integrand process.

It is necessary to impose a restriction on the integrands of the time integrals and stochastic integrals which says that although they can vary randomly, they can do so only by depending at each point in time on information that is available at that time. Indeed, virtually all of our processes, including price processes, interest rate processes, and trading strategies, have to satisfy this restriction. So it is necessary to model the information available in the economy at each point in time. We did this by the concept of an information structure, or formally, a filtration. An information structure or filtration is a mathematical representation of how information evolves over time. A stochastic process which is consistent with the filtration in the sense that its value at each point in time is random only through dependence on the information available at that time, is said to be adapted. Virtually all of the processes that we use will have to be adapted.

The Brownian motions driving the stochastic integrals also have to interact properly with the information structure. They have to be adapted, and their increments over a time interval have to be independent not only of past increments but of all information available at the beginning of the time interval. A Brownian motion with these informational properties is called a Wiener process relative to the filtration. As documented in the notes in the following section, there is some ambiguity in the literature about the use of the terms "Brownian motion" and "Wiener process," but this is how we use them here.

Given that the integrand processes are adapted, both the time integral and the stochastic integral will also be adapted. That is, the integral up to a particular point in time will depend on information available at that time, but it will not anticipate the future.

How do we construct the stochastic integral? In the case where the integrand process is a so-called simple process, this is not difficult. A simple process is one whose value can change only at a finite number of prespecified points in time. Between those changes, the paths of the process are constant. We calculate the stochastic integral of a simple process by summing up the value of the process times the increment of the Wiener process over each of the subintervals. It turns out that this integral is normally distributed with zero mean and with a variance that can easily be calculated.

To define the stochastic integral over a fixed time interval for more complicated integrand processes, we approximate the integrand process in a certain sense by a sequence of simple processes. As the simple processes get closer and closer to the complicated integrand processes that we want to integrate, their integrals converge to some random variable. That random variable will be the integral of the complicated process over the given time interval. This approximation is not to be interpreted as something that happens over time, although we often use a time metaphor for an approximating process. The stochastic integral becomes a stochastic process when we vary the upper limit of the time interval over which we integrate.

The stochastic integral is a continuous process, it is consistent with the information structure, and it is linear in the sense that the integral of a sum of processes is the sum of the integrals, and the integral of a constant times a process is the constant times the integral of the process.

Additional properties of the integral require a square integrability condition on the integrand process which ensures that the integral has finite variance. When this condition is satisfied, the integral is a martingale, and there are formulas for calculating its variance as well as the covariance between two stochastic integrals.

A martingale is a process whose conditional expected future value, given current information, equals its current value. The square integrability condition is sufficient for the stochastic integral to be a martingale, but it is not necessary. The integral may well be a martingale even if it does not have finite variance.

To calculate the variance of a stochastic integral, square the integrand process, take the expectation, and integrate it over time. The expectation of the squared integrand measures the variance of the increment of the integral over each instant. By integrating over time, we get the variance of the integral itself. To calculate the covariance between two stochastic integrals, multiply the integrand processes with each other, take the expectation, and integrate over time. The expectation of the product of the integrand processes measures the covariance of the increments of the integrals. By integrating over time, we get the covariance of the integrals themselves.

The martingale representation theorem says the following. Suppose a multi-dimensional Wiener process is given, and suppose the information available at each point in time consists in knowing the entire path of the Wiener process up to that time. Then any martingale is equal to a constant plus a stochastic integral with respect to the Wiener process.

The martingale representation theorem will be the key ingredient in proving the complete markets theorem in Chapter 4.

In some of the literature on continuous-time finance, the integrand processes are assumed to be predictable rather than simply adapted and measurable. In some cases, this is necessary because the integrator processes are not just Wiener processes but so-called semi-martingales. In other cases, the authors use the concept of predictable processes without really needing it. When the integrator is a Wiener process, there is no need to distinguish between integrand processes that are predictable and integrand processes that are adapted and measurable. Every predictable process is adapted and measurable, and every adapted and measurable process is almost everywhere identical to a predictable process.

1.12   (*) Notes

I have obviously relied quite a bit on Arnold [1, 1974], Liptser and Shiryayev [65, 1977], and Karatzas and Shreve [64, 1988] in writing this chapter. The book by Arnold is short but contains many of the most important concepts and results. Karatzas and Shreve [64, 1988] is an indispensable handbook.

We have defined two processes to be versions of each other if at each point in time they are equal with probability one. This terminology is consistent with Arnold [1, 1974], Friedman [38, 1975], and Chung and Williams [17, 1983]. Ethier and Kurtz [36, 1986] use a different terminology: they call two processes "versions" of each other if they have the same finite-dimensional distributions, and even if they are defined on different probability spaces.

The definition of an augmented filtration in Karatzas and Shreve [64, 1988] is slightly different from the one adopted here.

In 1827 or 1828 the Scottish botanist Robert Brown observed that pollen suspended in liquid moves about in an irregular fashion. This movement arises because molecules of the liquid randomly bump into the pollen particles. Brownian motion gets its name from this phenomenon.

The mathematics of Brownian motion was first studied by Bachelier [4, 1900], in a thesis about option pricing, and by Albert Einstein. Norbert Wiener proved that Brownian motion exists and that its paths are nowhere differentiable.

There seems to be no consensus in the literature about the precise meaning of the terms Brownian motion and Wiener process.

The distinction we have made between a standard Brownian motion and a Wiener process relative to a filtration is consistent with the terminology of Liptser and Shiryayev [65, 1977]. In dimension one, they define a Brownian motion the way we have defined a standard Brownian motion. They use higher-dimensional Brownian motions without an explicit definition, but presumably the appropriate definition would be the same as our definition of a higher-dimensional standard Brownian motion. They define a Wiener process relative to a filtration F (explicitly in dimension one, implicitly in higher dimensions) by the properties in Theorem 1.14, which is equivalent to our definition.

Gihman and Skorohod [39, 1972] define a Wiener process the way we have defined a standard Brownian motion and use the term "Brownian motion" only to refer to physical phenomena of motion.

Arnold [1, 1974] defines a Wiener process in a way which is equivalent to our definition of a standard Brownian motion. He uses the term "Brownian motion" to refer to various physical phenomena of motion rather than a class of stochastic processes.

Friedman [38, 1975] defines a Brownian motion the way we have defined a generalized Brownian motion and uses the terms Brownian motion and Wiener process interchangeably.

Harrison [42, 1985] defines a Brownian motion as we have done here and mentions the term Wiener process as a synonym. What he calls a Brownian motion with respect to a filtration is the same as what we call a Wiener process relative to a filtration.

Billingsley [8, 1986] and Chung and Williams [18, 1990] define Brownian motion as we have done here. Chung and Williams do not use the term Wiener process. Billingsley mentions it as a synonym of Brownian motion.

What we call a Wiener process here is what Karatzas and Shreve [64, 1988] call a standard Brownian motion.

The geometric Brownian motion for stock prices and the exponential money market account, which we refer to as the "Black–Scholes model," may have been introduced by Samuelson [82, 1965].

Paley, Wiener, and Zygmund [75, 1933] defined the stochastic integral for continuousy differentiable deterministic integrands by integration by parts, and extended it to deterministic integrands in $\mathcal{H}^2$ by approximation. Itô [55, 1944] extended the integral to "non-anticipating" functionals of the Brownian path.

Non-anticipating functionals correspond to adapted processes.

McKean [66, 1969] and Arnold [1, 1974] also use the term "non-anticipating" instead of "adapted."

Note that Karatzas and Shreve [64, 1988] and Chung and Williams [18, 1990] assume that the filtration is right-continuous.

Proposition 1.35 is related to Karatzas and Shreve [64, 1988, Exercise 3.2.30].

2

ITÔ CALCULUS

Most processes used in continuous-time finance to represent prices or portfolio values are Itô processes, essentially for three reasons. First, the class Itô processes is sufficiently rich to describe a large number of interesting and important phenomena. Secondly, a smooth transformation of an Itô process is again an Itô process, according to Itô's lemma. Thirdly, when securities prices follow Itô processes, markets will often be dynamically complete, which implies that virtually every derivative security can be priced by replication.

This chapter defines Itô processes and integration with respect to Itô processes, explains Itô's lemma, and develops the associated Itô calculus. We work in detail through a number of examples of how to use Itô's formula, such as Example 2.3, where we calculate the dynamics of the Black–Scholes stock price. Section 2.4 studies positive Itô processes, or stochastic exponentials. These are particularly important because many processes in finance, such as exchange rate processes and most securities price processes, have to be positive. Finally, Section 2.5 discusses Girsanov's theorem, which will be fundamental in applications of the so-called risk-adjusted probabilities.

We continue to assume that the underlying probability space $(\Omega, \mathcal{F}, P)$ is complete, and that the filtration $F = (\mathcal{F}_t)$ is augmented.

Let W be a K-dimensional Wiener process relative to a filtration F.

2.1 Itô Processes and Itô's Lemma

An N-dimensional *Itô process* is an N-dimensional process X of the form

$$X(t) = X_0 + \int_0^t a \, ds + \int_0^t b \, dW$$

where X_0 is a random N-vector which is measurable with respect to $\mathcal{F}_0$, $a \in \mathcal{L}^1$, and $b \in \mathcal{L}^2$.

An Itô process is continuous and adapted.

There is a useful differential notation associated with Itô processes. For the stochastic integral equation above, defining the Itô process X, we write in differential form,

$$dX(t) = a(t) \, dt + b(t) \, dW(t)$$

or, notationally suppressing t as an argument in the processes,

$$dX = a \, dt + b \, dW$$

We do not attribute any rigorous mathematical meaning to this equation. From the mathematical point of view, it is simply shorthand for the integral equation.

We treat dW as a K-dimensional and dX as an N-dimensional column-vector-valued object.

The equation in differential form can be interpreted heuristically as expressing the increment dX in X during an instant of time dt. The expected increment is a. The increment also has a random component which is b times the increment dW in the Wiener process during dt. If we think of dW as a normally distributed K-vector with mean zero and unit covariance matrix (per unit of time), then $b\,dW$ is normally distributed with mean zero and covariance matrix bb^T. In particular, if $N = K = 1$ and $b \geq 0$, then b is the standard deviation of the increment in X over the instant dt.

We refer to a as the *drift* of X and to b as the *dispersion* of X. We shall see in Proposition 2.6 below that these processes are uniquely determined (up to equality almost everywhere) given the process X. The process bb^T will be interpreted as the *instantaneous covariance matrix* of X.

Example 2.1 If Z_0 is any N-dimensional random vector measurable with respect to $\mathcal{F}_0$, if μ is a constant N-dimensional vector, and if σ is a constant $(N \times K)$-dimensional matrix, then the generalized Wiener process

$$Z(t) = Z_0 + t\mu + \sigma W(t)$$

is an Itô process with drift μ and dispersion σ, since

$$Z(t) = Z_0 + \int_0^t \mu\,ds + \int_0^t \sigma\,dW$$

In differential notation,

$$dZ = \mu\,dt + \sigma\,dW$$

In particular, the Wiener process itself is a K-dimensional Itô process:

$$W(t) = \int_0^t 1\,dW$$

and time is a one-dimensional Itô process:

$$t = \int_0^t 1\,ds$$

□

The set of Itô processes is a linear space. If X and Y are Itô processes, then so is $X + Y$, and if X is an Itô process and c is a number, then cX is an Itô process. This follows from the fact that $\mathcal{L}^1$ and $\mathcal{L}^2$ are linear spaces.

If $f : x \mapsto f(x)$ is a twice continuously differentiable function defined on an open set in $\mathbb{R}^N$, let f_x denote the gradient, construed as a row vector:

$$f_x(x) = \left(\frac{\partial f}{\partial x_1} \cdots \frac{\partial f}{\partial x_N} \right)$$

and let f_{xx} denote the Hessian (the matrix of second derivatives)

$$f_{xx}(x) = \left(\frac{\partial^2 f(x)}{\partial x_i \partial x_j} \right)_{i,j=1}^N$$

Theorem 2.2 Itô's lemma. *Let $D \subset \mathbb{R}^N$ be an open set, let X be an N-dimensional Itô process*

$$X(t) = X_0 + \int_0^t a\, ds + \int_0^t b\, dW$$

such that, with probability one, $X(t) \in D$ for all t, and let $f : D \to \mathbb{R}$ be a function which is twice continuously differentiable in D. Then the process $f(X)$ is an Itô process. Specifically,

$$f(X(t)) = f(X_0) + \int_0^t \left[f_x(X)a + \frac{1}{2}\mathrm{tr}(b^\top f_{xx}(X)b) \right] ds$$
$$+ \int_0^t f_x(X)b\, dW$$

If $1 \leq m < N$ and the last $N - m$ components of X are pure time integrals, that is $b_{nk} = 0$ for all k when $m < n \leq N$, then it is not required that the second derivatives involving the last $N - m$ variables exist (there will be no ambiguity in computing the expressions above since these derivatives will be multiplied by zero).

Proof (*) See Chung and Williams [18, 1990, Theorem 5.10]. The fact that they assume a right-continuous filtration does not matter.   □

Various versions of the formula in Theorem 2.2 will be referred to as Itô's formula.

In differential form, Itô's formula says

$$df(X) = \left[f_x(X)a + \frac{1}{2}\mathrm{tr}(b^\top f_{xx}(X)b) \right] dt + f_x(X)b\, dW$$

The expression $\mathrm{tr}(b^\top f_{xx}(X)b)$ in Itô's formula means the trace of the $(K \times K)$-dimensional random time-dependent matrix $b^\top f_{xx}(X)b$, which is defined as the sum of the diagonal elements.

The expression $\mathrm{tr}(b^\top f_{xx}(X)b)$ can also be computed as follows:

$$\mathrm{tr}(b^\top f_{xx}(X)b) = \mathrm{tr}(bb^\top f_{xx}(X))$$

$$= \sum_{i,j=1}^{N} \frac{\partial^2 f}{\partial x_i \partial x_j}(X)\left(bb^\top\right)_{ij}$$

$$= \sum_{i,j=1}^{N} \sum_{k=1}^{K} \frac{\partial^2 f}{\partial x_i \partial x_j}(X) b_{ik}b_{jk}$$

These expressions can be used in combination with several of the various versions of Itô's formula that we shall present below.

Since X has continuous paths and the derivatives of f are continuous, the processes $f_x(X(t))$ and $f_{xx}(X(t))$ are continuous. Hence, it follows from Propositions 1.24, 1.28, and 1.29 that the coefficient processes in Itô's formula are in the spaces $\mathcal{L}^1$ and $\mathcal{L}^2$ where they are supposed to be.

The role of the set D in Theorem 2.2 is this: it may be that the function f is defined only on a subset of $I\!R^N$ and cannot be extended to a continuous and sufficiently smooth function on all of $I\!R^N$. For example, $N = 1$, $D = (0, \infty)$, and $f = \ln$.

When $N = 1$, Itô's formula can be written like this:

$$df(X) = \left[f'(X)a + \frac{1}{2}f''(X)bb^\top\right]dt + f'(X)b\,dW$$

and when $N = K = 1$,

$$df(X) = \left[f'(X)a + \frac{1}{2}f''(X)b^2\right]dt + f'(X)b\,dW$$

Example 2.3 *Continuation of Examples 1.7 and 1.15. The price processes in the Black–Scholes model expressed as Itô processes.* Let $K = 1$, and let W be a one-dimensional Wiener process relative to a filtration F. The stock price process has the form

$$S(t) = S(0)\exp\left[\left(\mu - \frac{1}{2}\sigma^2\right)t + \sigma W(t)\right]$$

where $S(0) > 0$, μ and $\sigma > 0$ are constants. Let X be the generalized Wiener process

$$X(t) = \ln S(t)$$

$$= \ln S(0) + \left(\mu - \frac{1}{2}\sigma^2\right)t + \sigma W(t)$$

$$= \ln S(0) + \int_0^t \left(\mu - \frac{1}{2}\sigma^2\right)ds + \int_0^t \sigma\,dW(s)$$

Then X is an Itô process with

$$dX = \left(\mu - \frac{1}{2}\sigma^2\right) dt + \sigma \, dW$$

and

$$S(t) = \exp(X(t))$$

According to Itô's lemma, applied to X and to the function $f = \exp$, S is an Itô process with

$$
\begin{aligned}
dS &= df(X) \\
&= \left[f'(X) \left(\mu - \frac{1}{2}\sigma^2 \right) + \frac{1}{2}\sigma^2 f''(X) \right] dt + f'(X)\sigma \, dW \\
&= \left[\exp(X) \left(\mu - \frac{1}{2}\sigma^2 \right) + \frac{1}{2}\sigma^2 \exp(X) \right] dt + \exp(X)\sigma \, dW \\
&= \exp(X)\mu \, dt + \exp(X)\sigma \, dW \\
&= S\mu \, dt + S\sigma \, dW
\end{aligned}
$$

or, equivalently,

$$\frac{dS}{S} = \mu \, dt + \sigma \, dW$$

This equation can be interpreted heuristically as expressing the relative or percentage increment dS/S in S during an instant of time dt. Assuming that the stock does not pay any dividends, all the return to an investment in the stock comes in the form of stock price appreciation (or depreciation), and so the relative increment dS/S can also be interpreted as the instantaneous rate of return on the stock. The expected instantaneous rate of return is μ, and the standard deviation of the instantaneous rate of return is σ (assuming that σ is positive). We also call σ the *volatility* of S.

In the calculations above, the $-\frac{1}{2}\sigma^2$ term in the Black–Scholes stock price process gets eaten up by the second-order term from Itô's lemma. This is a third way of looking at why the term is there in the parameterization of the stock price. The other two explanations were given in Chapter 1, Example 1.7.

The money market account has a price process of the form

$$M(t) = M(0)e^{rt}$$

where $M(0) > 0$ and r are constants. Let $Y(t)$ be the (degenerate, deterministic) generalized Wiener process

$$Y(t) = \ln M(t) = \ln M(0) + rt = \ln M(0) + \int_0^t r \, ds$$

Then Y is an Itô process with

$$dY = r \, dt$$

and

$$M(t) = \exp(Y(t))$$

According to Itô's lemma (or, in this case, the ordinary chain rule of calculus), applied to Y and to the function $f = \exp$, M is an Itô process with

$$dM = df(Y) = f'(Y)r\,dt = \exp(Y)r\,dt = Mr\,dt$$

or, equivalently,

$$\frac{dM}{M} = r\,dt$$

The instantaneous rate of return to the money market account is r. □

Example 2.4 *Itô's formula for a logarithmic transformation of an Itô process.* If Y is a positive one-dimensional Itô process, then its differential can be written in the form

$$dY = Y(\alpha\,dt + \beta\,dW)$$

where $\alpha \in \mathcal{L}^1$ is a one-dimensional process and $\beta \in \mathcal{L}^2$ is a $(1 \times K)$-dimensional process.

The differential of $\ln Y$ is

$$d\ln Y = \left(\alpha - \frac{1}{2}\beta\beta^{\mathsf{T}}\right)dt + \beta\,dW$$

To see this, consider the function $f(y) = \ln y$. It is defined on $D = (0, \infty)$ and (at least) twice continuously differentiable, with

$$f'(y) = \frac{1}{y}$$

and

$$f''(y) = -\frac{1}{y^2}$$

According to Itô's lemma, $f(Y) = \ln Y$ is an Itô process with

$$d\ln Y = \left[f'(Y)Y\alpha + \frac{1}{2}f''(Y)Y^2\beta\beta^{\mathsf{T}}\right]dt + f'(Y)Y\beta\,dW$$

$$= \left(\alpha - \frac{1}{2}\beta\beta^{\mathsf{T}}\right)dt + \beta\,dW$$

In the special case where $Y = S$ is the Black–Scholes stock price, we already know from Example 2.3 that

$$\frac{dY}{Y} = \frac{dS}{S} = \mu\,dt + \sigma\,dW$$

and that

$$\ln Y(t) = \ln S(t) = \ln S(0) + \left(\mu - \frac{1}{2}\sigma^2\right)t + \sigma W(t)$$

and

$$d \ln Y = \left(\mu - \frac{1}{2}\sigma^2 \right) dt + \sigma \, dW(t)$$

If $Y = M$ is the Black–Scholes money market account value, then

$$\frac{dY}{Y} = \frac{dM}{M} = r \, dt$$

and

$$\ln Y(t) = \ln M(t) = \ln M(0) + rt$$

and

$$d \ln Y = r \, dt$$

$\square$

Most of the time when Itô's formula is used in this book, the function f is an exponential or logarithmic function, or it is a function which maps a two-dimensional Itô process into the product or the ratio of its components. Exponential and logarithmic transformations were exemplified in Examples 2.3 and 2.4 above. Exponentials will be dealt with more systematically below under the heading of stochastic exponentials. Examples 2.12, 2.13, and 2.14 below will discuss Itô's formula for products and ratios.

Itô's lemma is a powerful tool for computing stochastic integrals. It is rarely possible or efficient to compute them directly from the definition. The situation is the same as for ordinary Lebesgue integrals. They are most often computed by means of the fundamental theorem of calculus and the chain rule.

Example 2.5 Let $K = 1$. We shall use Itô's lemma to show that the integral

$$\int_0^t W \, dW$$

is a function of $W(t)$ and t and to compute that function.

The Wiener process W itself is an Itô process:

$$W(t) = 0 + \int_0^t 0 \, ds + \int_0^t 1 \, dW$$

Consider the function f defined on the real line by $f(x) = x^2$. It is (at least) twice continuously differentiable. By Itô's lemma, the process $f(W(t)) = W(t)^2$ is an Itô process with differential

$$dW(t)^2 = \left[f'(W) \times 0 + \frac{1}{2}f''(W) \times 1 \right] dt + [f'(W) \times 1] \, dW$$

$$= 1\,dt + 2W\,dW$$

Hence,

$$W(t)^2 = \int_0^t 1\,ds + \int_0^t 2W\,dW$$

and so

$$\int_0^t W\,dW = \frac{1}{2}(W(t)^2 - t)$$

$\square$

Since the time process t is an Itô process, so is the process $(X(t), t)$. This leads to the following time-dependent version of Itô's formula:

$$df(X(t), t)$$
$$= \left[f_x(X(t), t)a(t) + f_t(X(t), t) + \frac{1}{2}\mathrm{tr}(b(t)^\top f_{xx}(X(t), t)b(t))\right] dt$$
$$+ f_x(X(t), t)b(t)\,dW_t$$
$$= f_x(X(t), t)\,dX_t + \left[f_t(X(t), t) + \frac{1}{2}\mathrm{tr}(b(t)^\top f_{xx}(X(t), t)b(t))\right] dt$$

Here, only f_t, f_x, and f_{xx} need to exist and to be continuous. These symbols mean, respectively, the partial derivative with respect to time, the vector of partial derivatives with respect to X, and the matrix of second derivatives with respect to X.

In compact notation,

$$df = \left[f_x a + f_t + \frac{1}{2}\mathrm{tr}(b^\top f_{xx}b)\right] dt + f_x b\,dW$$
$$= f_x\,dX + \left[f_t + \frac{1}{2}\mathrm{tr}(b^\top f_{xx}b)\right] dt$$

Exercise 2.1 *Use Itô's lemma to show that*

$$\int_0^t (t - s)\,dW(s) = \int_0^t W\,ds$$

Exercise 2.2 *Assume that $K = 1$. Show that*

$$\int_0^t W^2\,dW$$

is a function of t, $W(t)$, and $\int_0^t s\,dW(s)$, and compute that function.

Proposition 2.6 Uniqueness of the coefficients in an Itô process. *Let $a, \alpha \in \mathcal{L}^1$ be N-dimensional vector processes, let $b, \beta \in \mathcal{L}^2$ be $(N \times K)$-dimensional matrix-valued processes, and let X_0 and Y_0 be constants. If the processes*

$$X(t) = X_0 + \int_0^t a \, ds + \int_0^t b \, dW$$

and

$$Y(t) = Y_0 + \int_0^t \alpha \, ds + \int_0^t \beta \, dW$$

are indistinguishable, then $X_0 = Y_0$, a and α are almost everywhere identical, and b and β are almost everywhere identical.

Proof It suffices to show that if X is indistinguishable from the zero process, then $X_0 = 0$, a equals zero almost everywhere, and b equals zero almost everywhere. It suffices to consider the case where $N = 1$. Apply Itô's lemma to the function $f = \exp$. This yields, for all t,

$$
\begin{aligned}
0 &= \exp(X(t)) - \exp(X(0)) \\
&= \int_0^t \left[\exp(0)a + \frac{1}{2}\exp(0)bb^\top \right] ds + \int_0^t \exp(0)b \, dW \\
&= \int_0^t \left[a + \frac{1}{2}bb^\top \right] ds + \int_0^t b \, dW \\
&= \frac{1}{2} \int_0^t bb^\top \, ds
\end{aligned}
$$

Hence, $b(\omega, t) = 0$ for almost all (ω, t). That implies $\int_0^t b \, dW = 0$, and so $\int_0^t a \, ds = 0$ for all t. By Proposition 1.26, $a(t, \omega) = 0$ for almost all (ω, t). $\qquad\square$

Proposition 2.7 *An Itô martingale has zero drift. If the Itô process*

$$X(t) = X(0) + \int_0^t a \, ds + \int_0^t b \, dW$$

is a martingale with respect to F^W, then $a = 0$ almost everywhere.

Proof Use the martingale representation theorem. Since X is a martingale, there exists $\gamma \in \mathcal{L}^2$ such that

$$X(t) = X(0) + \int_0^t \gamma \, dW = X(0) + \int_0^t 0 \, ds + \int_0^t \gamma \, dW$$

Since the coefficients in an Itô process are unique by Proposition 2.6, $a = 0$ almost everywhere. $\qquad\square$

Warning: It is not true, conversely, that an Itô process with zero drift is necessarily a martingale. It is true if, additionally, the dispersion coefficient is in $\mathcal{H}^2$. We shall encounter other sufficient conditions below in the section on stochastic exponentials.

2.2 Integrals with Respect to Itô Processes

We shall now define the stochastic integral of a process with respect to an Itô process.

Let X be an N-dimensional Itô process

$$X(t) = X_0 + \int_0^t a \, ds + \int_0^t b \, dW$$

where it is understood that X_0 is a random N-vector which is measurable with respect to $\mathcal{F}_0$, and that $a \in \mathcal{L}^1$ and $b \in \mathcal{L}^2$.

Let $\mathcal{L}(X)$ denote the set of adapted, measurable $(M \times N)$-dimensional matrix-valued processes γ such that $\gamma a \in \mathcal{L}^1$ and $\gamma b \in \mathcal{L}^2$. These are the processes that can be integrated with respect to X. The definition makes sense because by Proposition 2.6, the processes a and b are determined given X, up to equality almost everywhere.

The set $\mathcal{L}(X)$ is a linear space. If $\gamma, \delta \in \mathcal{L}(X)$, then $\gamma + \delta \in \mathcal{L}(X)$, and if $\gamma \in \mathcal{L}(X)$ and c is a constant number (or row vector, for that matter), then $c\gamma \in \mathcal{L}(X)$.

If $\gamma \in \mathcal{L}(X)$, define the *stochastic integral* of γ with respect to X by

$$\int_0^t \gamma \, dX = \int_0^t \gamma a \, dt + \int_0^t \gamma b \, dW$$

In differential notation,

$$\gamma(t) \, dX(t) = \gamma(t) a(t) \, dt + \gamma(t) b(t) \, dW(t)$$

or, more compactly,

$$\gamma \, dX = \gamma a \, dt + \gamma b \, dW$$

It is clear that the stochastic integral with respect to X is an Itô process. In particular, it is adapted and continuous.

Recall that an N-dimensional vector-valued process a is in $\mathcal{L}^1$ if and only if its components a_i are in $\mathcal{L}^1$, and that an $(N \times K)$-dimensional matrix-valued process b is in $\mathcal{L}^2$ if and only if the entries b_{ik} are in $\mathcal{L}^2$. Be careful about generalizing this to the integrands in $\mathcal{L}(X)$. If γ is an $(M \times N)$-dimensional matrix-valued process, let $\gamma_{|i}$, $i = 1, \ldots, N$, denote the ith column. If $\gamma_{|i} \in \mathcal{L}(X_i)$ for all i, then $\gamma \in \mathcal{L}(X)$. But the converse may not be true, as illustrated by the following example.

Example 2.8 *A variation of Müller [73, 1989] and Jarrow and Madan [60, 1991].* Let $K = N = 2$, $M = 1$, let $a = 0$, and let b be the two-dimensional deterministic process given by

$$b(t) = \begin{pmatrix} b_{1-}(t) \\ b_{2-}(t) \end{pmatrix} = \begin{pmatrix} b_{|1}(t) & b_{|2}(t) \end{pmatrix} = \begin{pmatrix} 1 & 0 \\ 1-t & t \end{pmatrix}$$

for $t \geq 0$, where b_{1-} and b_{2-} denote the two rows of b and $b_{|1}$ and $b_{|2}$ denote the two columns of b. Let X be the two-dimensional Itô process given by

$$X(t) = \int_0^t b \, dW$$

In differential form,

$$dX = \begin{pmatrix} dX_1 \\ dX_2 \end{pmatrix} = b \, dW = \begin{pmatrix} b_{1-} \, dW \\ b_{2-} \, dW \end{pmatrix} = b_{|1} \, dW_1 + b_{|2} \, dW_2$$

Let γ be the deterministic process given by

$$\gamma(t) = \left(\frac{t-1}{t}, \frac{1}{t} \right)$$

for $t > 0$, and, arbitrarily, $\gamma(0) = (0,0)$. Then

$$\gamma(t)b(t) = \begin{cases} (0,1) & \text{for } t > 0 \\ (0,0) & \text{for } t = 0 \end{cases}$$

Clearly, $\gamma b \in \mathcal{L}^2$. Hence $\gamma \in \mathcal{L}(X)$, and the stochastic integral

$$\int_0^t \gamma \, dX = \int_0^t \gamma b \, dW = \int_0^t \gamma_1 b_{|1} \, dW_1 + \int_0^t \gamma_2 b_{|2} \, dW_2$$

and the stochastic differential

$$\gamma \, dX = \gamma b \, dW = \gamma_1 b_{|1} \, dW_1 + \gamma_2 b_{|2} \, dW_2$$

are well defined.

It is also tempting to write

$$\gamma \, dX = \gamma_1 \, dX_1 + \gamma_2 \, dX_2 = \gamma_1 b_{1-} \, dW + \gamma_2 b_{2-} \, dW$$

or

$$\int_0^t \gamma \, dX = \int_0^t \gamma_1 \, dX_1 + \int_0^t \gamma_2 \, dX_2 = \int_0^t \gamma_1 b_{1-} \, dW + \int_0^t \gamma_2 b_{2-} \, dW$$

However, this is not correct, because γ_1 does not belong to $\mathcal{L}(X_1)$ and γ_2 does not belong to $\mathcal{L}(X_2)$. Equivalently, $\gamma_1 b_{1-}$ and $\gamma_2 b_{2-}$ do not belong to $\mathcal{L}^2$. To see this, first observe that

$$\gamma_1(t)b_{1-}(t) = \begin{cases} (1 - \frac{1}{t}, 0) & \text{for } t > 0 \\ (0,0) & \text{for } t = 0 \end{cases}$$

and

$$\gamma_2(t)b_{2-}(t) = \begin{cases} (\frac{1}{t} - 1, 1) & \text{for } t > 0 \\ (0,0) & \text{for } t = 0 \end{cases}$$

Now for $0 < c \leq 1$,

$$\int_c^1 \left| \frac{1}{s} - 1 \right| ds = \int_c^1 \left(\frac{1}{s} - 1 \right) ds$$

$$= \ln 1 - \ln c - (1 - c)$$
$$\rightarrow +\infty$$

as $c \rightarrow 0$. Hence,

$$\int_0^1 \left| \frac{1}{s} - 1 \right| ds = \infty$$

which implies that

$$\int_0^1 \left| \frac{1}{s} - 1 \right|^2 ds = \infty$$

This implies that $\gamma_1 b_{1-}$ and $\gamma_2 b_{2-}$ do not belong to $\mathcal{L}^2$. □

The stochastic integral is linear in the integrator X. If X and Y are Itô processes, and if $\gamma \in \mathcal{L}(X)$ and $\gamma \in \mathcal{L}(Y)$, then $\gamma \in \mathcal{L}(X + Y)$, and

$$\int_0^t \gamma \, d(X + Y) = \int_0^t \gamma \, dX + \int_0^t \gamma \, dY$$

If X is an Itô process, and if $\gamma \in \mathcal{L}(X)$ and c is a constant (number or row vector), then $\gamma \in \mathcal{L}(cX)$ and

$$\int_0^t \gamma \, d(cX) = c \int_0^t \gamma \, dX$$

In differential notation,

$$\gamma \, d(X + Y) = \gamma \, dX + \gamma \, dY$$

and

$$\gamma \, d(cX) = c(\gamma \, dX)$$

The stochastic integral is linear in the integrand γ. If $\gamma, \delta \in \mathcal{L}(X)$, then

$$\int_0^t (\gamma + \delta) \, dX = \int_0^t \gamma \, dX + \int_0^t \delta \, dX$$

and if $\gamma \in \mathcal{L}(X)$ and c is a constant (number or row vector), then

$$\int_0^t c\gamma \, dX = c \int_0^t \gamma \, dX$$

In differential notation,

$$(\gamma + \delta) \, dX = \gamma \, dX + \delta \, dX$$

and

$$(c\gamma) \, dX = c(\gamma \, dX)$$

If X is an N-dimensional Itô process, if $\gamma \in \mathcal{L}(X)$ has dimension $M \times N$, and if

$$Y(t) = Y(0) + \int_0^t \gamma\, dX$$

then an adapted measurable M-dimensional row vector process δ is in $\mathcal{L}(Y)$ if and only if $\delta\gamma \in \mathcal{L}(X)$, in which case

$$\int_0^t \delta\, dY = \int_0^t \delta\gamma\, dX$$

In differential notation,

$$\delta\, dY = \delta(\gamma\, dX) = (\delta\gamma)\, dX$$

The stochastic integral with respect to an Itô process X has the same time consistency property as the stochastic integral with respect to the underlying Wiener process, cf. Proposition 1.31. If $\gamma \in \mathcal{L}(X)$ and if $0 \le t \le T$, then

$$\int_0^t \gamma\, dX = \int_0^T 1_{\Omega \times [0,t]} \gamma\, dX$$

As for the integral with respect to the Wiener process, define

$$\int_t^T \gamma\, dX = \int_0^T \gamma\, dX - \int_0^t \gamma\, dX = \int_0^T 1_{\Omega \times (t,T]} \gamma\, dX$$

Corollary 2.9 *Let X be an Itô process. If $0 \le t \le T$ and Y is a random variable measurable with respect to $\mathcal{F}_t$, then*

$$\int_t^T Y\, dX = Y \int_t^T dX = Y(X(T) - X(t))$$

Proof Follows from Proposition 1.35. Suppose $dX = a\, dt + b\, dW$. Then

$$\int_t^T Y\, dX = \int_t^T Y a\, dt + \int_t^T Y b\, dW$$

$$= Y \int_t^T a\, dt + Y \int_t^T b\, dW$$

$$= Y \int_t^T dX = Y(X(T) - X(t))$$

$$\square$$

It follows from Corollary 2.9 that simple processes are integrated with respect to an Itô process in much the same way as they are integrated with respect to the Wiener process. This will be true whether the simple processes are defined to be constant on time subintervals that are open to the left or open to the right.

If f is a twice continuously differentiable function of X (as in Itô's lemma), then any process γ which can be integrated with respect to X can also be integrated with respect to $f(X)$. That is the content of the following proposition.

Proposition 2.10 *Under the assumptions of Itô's lemma (Theorem 2.2), assuming that $N = 1$,*

$$\mathcal{L}(X) \subset \mathcal{L}(f(X))$$

Proof According to Itô's formula,

$$df(X) = \left[f'(X)a + \frac{1}{2}f''(X)bb^\top \right] dt + f'(X)b\, dW$$

If $\gamma \in \mathcal{L}(X)$ (γ is a one-dimensional process), then $\gamma a \in \mathcal{L}^1$ and $\gamma b \in \mathcal{L}^2$. Since also $b \in \mathcal{L}^2$, the latter implies that $\gamma bb^\top \in \mathcal{L}^1$. Since the processes $f'(X_t)$ and $f''(X_t)$ are continuous, they are pathwise bounded on bounded time intervals. Hence,

$$\gamma[f'(X)a] = f'(X)\gamma a \in \mathcal{L}^1$$
$$\gamma[f'(X)b] = f'(X)\gamma b \in \mathcal{L}^2$$

and

$$\gamma[f''(X)bb^\top] = f''(X)\gamma bb^\top \in \mathcal{L}^1$$

Hence, $\gamma \in \mathcal{L}(f(X))$. $\qquad\square$

In Proposition 2.10, if f is invertible in the sense that there exists a twice continuously differentiable function g such that $g(f(X)) = X$, then of course

$$\mathcal{L}(X) = \mathcal{L}(f(X))$$

2.3 Further Manipulations of Itô's Formula

Using stochastic integration with respect to an Itô process, we can now rewrite Itô's formula like this:

$$f(X(t)) = f(X_0) + \int_0^t f_x(X)\, dX + \frac{1}{2}\int_0^t \operatorname{tr}(b^\top f_{xx}(X)b)\, ds$$

In differential notation,

$$df(X) = f_x(X)\, dX + \frac{1}{2}\operatorname{tr}(b^\top f_{xx}(X)b)\, dt$$

When $N = 1$, this specializes to

$$df(X) = f'(X)\, dX + \frac{1}{2}f''(X)bb^\top dt$$

and when $N = K = 1$,

$$df(X) = f'(X)\, dX + \frac{1}{2}f''(X)b^2\, dt$$

Itô's formula can be stated and manipulated heuristically using the following formal multiplication rules:

$$(dt)^2 = 0$$

$$dt\, dW_k = dW_k\, dt = 0$$

for all $k = 1, \ldots, K$, and

$$dW_k\, dW_l = \begin{cases} 0 & \text{if } k \neq l \\ dt & \text{if } k = l \end{cases}$$

for all $k, l = 1, \ldots, K$. In vector notation,

$$dt\, dW = dW\, dt = 0$$

and

$$dW\,(dW)^\top = I\, dt$$

where I is the $(K \times K)$-dimensional identity matrix. It follows by formal manipulation of these rules that

$$\begin{aligned}
dX\,(dX)^\top &= (a\, dt + b\, dW)(a\, dt + b\, dW)^\top \\
&= b\, dW\,(dW)^\top b^\top \\
&= bb^\top dt
\end{aligned}$$

This further illustrates why we think of $bb^\top$ as the instantaneous increment covariance matrix. Equivalently,

$$dX_i\, dX_j = \left(dX\,(dX)^\top\right)_{ij} = (bb^\top)_{ij}\, dt = \sum_{k=1}^{K} b_{ik} b_{jk}\, dt$$

for $i, j = 1, \ldots, N$.

Since the matrix $bb^\top$ is symmetric, of course

$$dX_i\, dX_j = dX_j\, dX_i$$

We can now write Itô's formula in the form

$$\begin{aligned}
df(X) &= f_x(X)\, dX + \frac{1}{2} \operatorname{tr}(bb^\top f_{xx}(X))\, dt \\
&= f_x(X)\, dX + \frac{1}{2} \sum_{i,j=1}^{N} \frac{\partial^2 f}{\partial x_i \partial x_j}(X)\left(dX\,(dX)^\top\right)_{ij} \\
&= f_x(X)\, dX + \frac{1}{2} \sum_{i,j=1}^{N} \frac{\partial^2 f}{\partial x_i \partial x_j}(X)\, dX_i\, dX_j \\
&= f_x(X)\, dX + \frac{1}{2}(dX)^\top f_{xx}(X)\, dX
\end{aligned}$$

Observe that the version of Itô's formula above is expressed in terms of dX and does not directly involve the differential dW of the underlying Wiener process.

Itô's formula can be interpreted in terms of a second-order Taylor expansion:

$$df(X) = f(X + dX) - f(X)$$
$$\sim f_x(X)\, dX + \frac{1}{2}(dX)^\top f_{xx}(X)\, dX$$

Example 2.11 *Correlated Wiener process.* Suppose A is a K-dimensional invertible square matrix such that the matrix $AA^\top$ has diagonal elements that are equal to one, and consider the process $Z = AW$, which is a correlated K-dimensional Wiener process relative to F. Denote the elements of $AA^\top$ by ρ_{kl}, $k, l = 1, \ldots, K$.

We find the following formal multiplication rules. In vector notation,

$$dZ = A\, dW$$

$$dt\, dZ = dt\, A\, dW = A\, dt\, dW = 0$$

$$dZ dt = A\, dW\, dt = 0$$

and

$$dZ\, (dZ)^\top = A\, dW\, (dW)^\top A^\top = AI\, dt\, A^\top = AA^\top\, dt$$

This implies that

$$dt\, dZ_k = dZ_k\, dt = 0$$

for all $k = 1, \ldots, K$, and

$$dZ_k\, dZ_l = \rho_{kl}\, dt$$

for all $k, l = 1, \ldots, K$. $\qquad\qquad\square$

Example 2.12 *Itô's formula for a product of Itô processes.* Let X and Y be Itô processes with these differentials:

$$dX = a\, dt + b\, dW$$

$$dY = \alpha\, dt + \beta\, dW$$

Assume that X has dimension N and Y has dimension one, which implies that b has dimension $N \times K$ and β has dimension $1 \times K$. Then XY is an N-dimensional Itô process with differential

$$d(XY) = X\, dY + Y\, dX + dX\, dY$$
$$= (X\alpha + Ya + b\beta^\top)\, dt + (X\beta + Yb)\, dW$$

To see this, consider each of the coordinates of X separately, or, in other words, assume that $N = 1$. Now the values of a and α are numbers, while the values of b and β are K-dimensional row vectors.

The processes X and Y jointly form a vector process

$$d\begin{pmatrix} X \\ Y \end{pmatrix} = \begin{pmatrix} a \\ \alpha \end{pmatrix} dt + \begin{pmatrix} b \\ \beta \end{pmatrix} dW$$

The coefficients are a two-dimensional column-vector-valued process and a $(2 \times K)$-dimensional matrix-valued process, respectively.

Define the function f by

$$f : \begin{pmatrix} x \\ y \end{pmatrix} \mapsto xy : I\!R^2 \to I\!R$$

It is (at least) twice continuously differentiable, with first derivatives

$$f_x = y$$
$$f_y = x$$

and second derivatives

$$f_{xy} = f_{yx} = 1$$

and

$$f_{xx} = f_{yy} = 0$$

Now

$$d(XY) = \begin{pmatrix} f_x & f_y \end{pmatrix} d\begin{pmatrix} X \\ Y \end{pmatrix}$$

$$+ \frac{1}{2} d\begin{pmatrix} X \\ Y \end{pmatrix}^{\mathsf{T}} \begin{pmatrix} f_{xx} & f_{yx} \\ f_{xy} & f_{yy} \end{pmatrix} \begin{pmatrix} X \\ Y \end{pmatrix} d\begin{pmatrix} X \\ Y \end{pmatrix}$$

$$= \begin{pmatrix} Y \\ X \end{pmatrix}^{\mathsf{T}} d\begin{pmatrix} X \\ Y \end{pmatrix} + \frac{1}{2} d\begin{pmatrix} X \\ Y \end{pmatrix}^{\mathsf{T}} \begin{pmatrix} 0 & 1 \\ 1 & 0 \end{pmatrix} d\begin{pmatrix} X \\ Y \end{pmatrix}$$

$$= Y\,dX + X\,dY + \frac{1}{2}(dX\,dY + dY\,dX)$$

$$= Y\,dX + X\,dY + dX\,dY$$

It remains to calculate $dX\,dY$:

$$dX\,dY = \left[\begin{pmatrix} b \\ \beta \end{pmatrix}\begin{pmatrix} b \\ \beta \end{pmatrix}^{\mathsf{T}}\right]_{12} dt = \begin{pmatrix} bb^{\mathsf{T}} & b\beta^{\mathsf{T}} \\ \beta b^{\mathsf{T}} & \beta\beta^{\mathsf{T}} \end{pmatrix}_{12} dt = b\beta^{\mathsf{T}}\,dt$$

Hence,

$$d(XY) = Y\,dX + X\,dY + dX\,dY$$
$$= Y(a\,dt + b\,dW) + X(\alpha\,dt + \beta\,dW) + b\beta^{\mathsf{T}}\,dt$$
$$= (X\alpha + Ya + b\beta^{\mathsf{T}})\,dt + (X\beta + Yb)\,dW$$

We can also calculate the latter expression on the basis of the original version of Itô's formula from Theorem 2.2.

We first calculate the following matrix:

$$\begin{pmatrix} b \\ \beta \end{pmatrix}^{\mathsf{T}} \begin{pmatrix} f_{xx} & f_{yx} \\ f_{xy} & f_{yy} \end{pmatrix} \begin{pmatrix} b \\ \beta \end{pmatrix} = (b^{\mathsf{T}} \ \beta^{\mathsf{T}}) \begin{pmatrix} 0 & 1 \\ 1 & 0 \end{pmatrix} \begin{pmatrix} b \\ \beta \end{pmatrix}$$

$$= b^{\mathsf{T}}\beta + \beta^{\mathsf{T}}b$$

The trace of this matrix is

$$2\operatorname{tr}(\beta^{\mathsf{T}}b) = 2\operatorname{tr}(b\beta^{\mathsf{T}}) = 2b\beta^{\mathsf{T}}$$

Alternatively,

$$\begin{pmatrix} b \\ \beta \end{pmatrix}\begin{pmatrix} b \\ \beta \end{pmatrix}^{\mathsf{T}} \begin{pmatrix} f_{xx} & f_{yx} \\ f_{xy} & f_{yy} \end{pmatrix} = \begin{pmatrix} bb^{\mathsf{T}} & b\beta^{\mathsf{T}} \\ \beta b^{\mathsf{T}} & \beta\beta^{\mathsf{T}} \end{pmatrix}\begin{pmatrix} 0 & 1 \\ 1 & 0 \end{pmatrix}$$

$$= \begin{pmatrix} b\beta^{\mathsf{T}} & bb^{\mathsf{T}} \\ \beta\beta^{\mathsf{T}} & \beta b^{\mathsf{T}} \end{pmatrix}$$

The trace of this matrix, again, is $2b\beta^{\mathsf{T}}$.

So,

$$df(X) = \left\{ (f_x \ f_y)\begin{pmatrix} a \\ \alpha \end{pmatrix} + \frac{1}{2}\operatorname{tr}\left[\begin{pmatrix} b \\ \beta \end{pmatrix}^{\mathsf{T}}\begin{pmatrix} f_{xx} & f_{yx} \\ f_{xy} & f_{yy} \end{pmatrix}\begin{pmatrix} b \\ \beta \end{pmatrix}\right] \right\} dt$$

$$+ (f_x \ f_y)\begin{pmatrix} b \\ \beta \end{pmatrix} dW$$

$$= (Ya + X\alpha + b\beta^{\mathsf{T}})\,dt + (X\beta + Yb)\,dW$$

□

Example 2.13 *Itô's formula for a ratio of Itô processes.* Let X be an N-dimensional Itô process with differential

$$dX = a\,dt + b\,dW$$

Let Y be a positive one-dimensional Itô process. Its differential can be written in the form

$$dY = Y(\alpha\,dt + \beta\,dW) = Y\alpha\,dt + Y\beta\,dW$$

where $\alpha \in \mathcal{L}^1$ and $\beta \in \mathcal{L}^2$.

Then $1/Y$ is a one-dimensional Itô process with differential

$$d\left(\frac{1}{Y}\right) = \frac{1}{Y}\left[(-\alpha + \beta\beta^{\mathsf{T}})\,dt - \beta\,dW\right]$$

and X/Y is an N-dimensional Itô process with

$$d\left(X\frac{1}{Y}\right) = \frac{1}{Y}\left\{[a - X\alpha - (b - X\beta)\beta^{\mathsf{T}}]\,dt + (b - X\beta)\,dW\right\}$$

To see this, apply Itô's lemma to the function

$$f : y \mapsto 1/y : (0, \infty) \to I\!R$$

It is (at least) twice continuously differentiable with

$$f'(y) = -\frac{1}{y^2}$$

and

$$f''(y) = \frac{2}{y^3}$$

By Itô's lemma,

$$d\left(\frac{1}{Y}\right) = df(Y)$$

$$= \left[f'(Y)Y\alpha + \frac{1}{2}f''(Y)Y^2\beta\beta^{\top}\right] dt + f'(Y)Y\beta \, dW$$

$$= \frac{1}{Y}\left[(-\alpha + \beta\beta^{\top})\, dt - \beta \, dW\right]$$

The formula for the differential of X/Y now follows from the formula for the differential of $1/Y$ combined with Itô's formula for a product of processes, Example 2.12.   □

Example 2.14 *The discounted stock price in the Black–Scholes model. Continuation of Examples 1.7, 1.15, and 2.3.* Let S and M be the stock price and the money market account in the Black–Scholes model. Then

$$\frac{dS}{S} = \mu \, dt + \sigma \, dW$$

and

$$\frac{dM}{M} = r \, dt$$

The stock price, measured in units of the money market account, or discounted at the rolled-over instantaneous interest rate r, is S/M, which has differential

$$d\left(\frac{S}{M}\right) = \left(\frac{S}{M}\right)[(\mu - r)\, dt + \sigma \, dW]$$

□

Proposition 2.15 Integration by parts. *If X and Y are one-dimensional Itô processes with*

$$dX = a \, dt + b \, dW$$

and

$$dY = \alpha \, dt$$

then

$$\int_0^t X \, dY = \int_0^t X\alpha \, ds = X(t)Y(t) - X(0)Y(0) - \int_0^t Y \, dX$$

Proof By Itô's lemma for a product, XY is an Itô process with

$$d(XY) = X\,dY + Y\,dX = X\alpha\,dt + Y\,dX$$

Hence,

$$X(t)Y(t) - X(0)Y(0) = \int_0^t d(XY) = \int_0^t X\alpha\,ds + \int_0^t Y\,dX$$

□

Example 2.16 If $a = 0$ and $b = \alpha = 1$ in Proposition 2.15, we find that $X = W$ and $Y(t) = t$, so

$$\int_0^t W\,ds = \int_0^t X\alpha\,ds$$

$$= X(t)Y(t) - X(0)Y(0) - \int_0^t Y\,dX$$

$$= W(t)t - 0 - \int_0^t s\,dW(s)$$

$$= \int_0^t (t - s)\,dW(s)$$

which was what was to be shown in Exercise 2.1. □

Proposition 2.17 Interchanging the order of integration. *Suppose $\alpha \in \mathcal{L}^1$ and $b \in \mathcal{L}^2$. Then*

$$\int_0^t \int_0^s \alpha(s)b(u)\,dW(u)\,ds = \int_0^t \int_u^t \alpha(s)b(u)\,ds\,dW(u)$$

Proof Define processes X and Y by

$$X(t) = \int_0^t b\,dW$$

and

$$Y(t) = \int_0^t \alpha(u)\,du$$

Apply Proposition 2.15:

$$\int_0^t \int_0^s \alpha(s)b(u)\,dW(u)\,ds = \int_0^t \alpha(s) \int_0^s b(u)\,dW(u)\,ds$$

$$= \int_0^t \alpha(s)X(s)\,ds$$

$$= X(t)Y(t) - \int_0^t Y(s)\,dX(s)$$

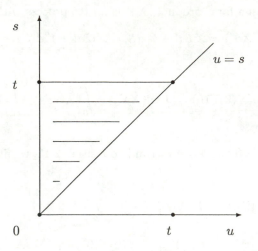

FIG. 2.1. The region $0 \le u \le s \le t$

$$= X(t) \int_0^t \alpha(s)\, ds - \int_0^t \int_0^s \alpha(u)\, du\, dX(s)$$

$$= \int_0^t \int_0^t \alpha(s)\, ds\, dX(u) - \int_0^t \int_0^s \alpha(u)\, du\, dX(s)$$

$$= \int_0^t \int_0^t \alpha(s)\, ds\, dX(u) - \int_0^t \int_0^u \alpha(s)\, ds\, dX(u)$$

$$= \int_0^t \int_u^t \alpha(s) b(u)\, ds\, dW(u)$$

$\square$

Figure 2.1 illustrates the interchange of the order of integration in Proposition 2.17. To calculate the left hand side of the equation, first fix s on the vertical axis and let u vary from zero to s. The point (u, s) moves across a horizontal line segment from the point $(0, s)$ on the vertical axis to the point (s, s) on the 45 degree line. Then allow s to vary from 0 to t. The horizontal line segment moves up and across the shaded region. To calculate the right hand side of the equation, first fix u on the horizontal axis and let s vary from u to t. The point (u, s) moves up along a vertical line segment from the point (u, u) on the 45 degree line to the point (u, t). Then allow u to vary from 0 to t. The vertical line segment moves over and across the shaded region. In both cases, we integrate over all points in the shaded region.

2.4   Stochastic Exponentials

If $\alpha \in \mathcal{L}^1$ and $\beta \in \mathcal{L}^2$ are processes of dimension 1×1 and $1 \times K$, respectively, define a one-dimensional process $\eta[\alpha, \beta]$ by

$$\eta[\alpha, \beta](t) = \exp\left[\int_0^t \left(\alpha - \frac{1}{2}\beta\beta^\top\right) ds + \int_0^t \beta \, dW\right]$$

A process of this form is called a *stochastic exponential*.

A stochastic exponential is obviously a positive process. It is an Itô process, by Itô's lemma. Conversely, every one-dimensional positive Itô process is a stochastic exponential (multiplied by a positive random initial value).

Proposition 2.18 Positive Itô processes. *If X is a one-dimensional positive Itô process, then there exist $\alpha \in \mathcal{L}^1$ and $\beta \in \mathcal{L}^2$ such that $X = X(0)\eta[\alpha, \beta]$.*

Proof   Since X is positive, $\ln X$ is a well-defined Itô process. Write its differential as

$$d \ln X = \gamma \, dt + \beta \, dW$$

Set

$$\alpha = \gamma + \frac{1}{2}\beta\beta^\top$$

Then

$$\ln X(t) = \ln X(0) + \int_0^t \left(\alpha - \frac{1}{2}\beta\beta^\top\right) dt + \int_0^t \beta \, dW$$

and, hence,

$$X = X(0)\eta[\alpha, \beta]$$

$\square$

An application of Itô's formula shows that

$$d\eta[\alpha, \beta] = \eta[\alpha, \beta]\,(\alpha \, dt + \beta \, dW)$$

or, alternatively,

$$\frac{d\eta[\alpha, \beta]}{\eta[\alpha, \beta]} = \alpha \, dt + \beta \, dW$$

This is the motivation for the particular parameterization we have chosen for stochastic exponentials.

Note the following manipulation rules:

$$\frac{1}{\eta[\alpha, \beta]} = \eta[-\alpha + \beta\beta^\top, -\beta]$$

if $\alpha \in \mathcal{L}^1$ and $\beta \in \mathcal{L}^2$, and

$$\eta[a, b]\eta[\alpha, \beta] = \eta[a + \alpha + b\beta^\top, b + \beta]$$

and

$$\frac{\eta[a,b]}{\eta[\alpha,\beta]} = \eta[a - \alpha - (b - \beta)\beta^\top, b - \beta]$$

if, in addition, $a \in \mathcal{L}^1$ and $b \in \mathcal{L}^2$. These rules can be derived by direct calculation.

Proposition 2.19 *If $\alpha \in \mathcal{L}^1$ and $\beta \in \mathcal{L}^2$, then $\eta = \eta[\alpha,\beta]$ is the unique one-dimensional Itô process such that*

$$d\eta = \eta\,[\alpha\,dt + \beta\,dW]$$

and $\eta(0) = 1$.

Proof It is clear that $\eta = \eta[\alpha,\beta]$ satisfies the boundary condition $\eta(0) = 1$. We have already observed that it solves the differential equation. Suppose $\tilde\eta$ is an Itô process, possibly different from η, which solves the differential equation. Using Itô's formula for a ratio of processes, Example 2.13,

$$d\left(\frac{\tilde\eta}{\eta}\right) = \frac{\tilde\eta}{\eta}\left\{[\alpha - \alpha + (\beta - \beta)\beta^\top]\,dt + [\beta - \beta]\,dW\right\} = 0$$

Consequently, $\tilde\eta/\eta$ is a constant. If $\tilde\eta(0) = \eta(0) = 1$, then the processes are identical. This shows the uniqueness of η.   □

We call the processes α, β, $\beta\beta^\top$, and $\sqrt{\beta\beta^\top}$ respectively the *relative drift* or *percentage drift*, the *relative dispersion* or *percentage dispersion*, the *squared volatility*, and the *volatility* or *relative standard deviation* or *percentage standard deviation* of $\eta[\alpha,\beta]$.

Given Proposition 2.19, we can interpret the manipulation rules for stochastic exponentials mentioned above as versions of Itô's formula for a ratio and for a product of positive Itô processes.

Example 2.20 *Securities prices in the Black–Scholes model. Continuation of Examples 1.7, 1.15, 2.3, and 2.14.* The stock price in the Black–Scholes model is

$$S = S(0)\eta[\mu, \sigma]$$

and the value of the money market account is

$$M = M(0)\eta[r, 0]$$

Their ratio, therefore, is

$$\frac{S}{M} = \frac{S(0)}{M(0)}\eta[\mu - r, \sigma]$$

□

Example 2.21 *Two risky securities whose prices are correlated geometric Brownian motions. Their ratio. Continuation of Example 1.17.* Let

$$Z(t) = \begin{pmatrix} Z_1(t) \\ Z_2(t) \end{pmatrix}$$

be a two-dimensional correlated Wiener process with increment correlation ρ, as in Example 1.16. It has the form $Z = AW$, where A is a $(2 \times K)$-dimensional matrix with

$$AA^\top = \begin{pmatrix} 1 & \rho \\ \rho & 1 \end{pmatrix}$$

Consider, as in Example 1.17, the following two financial price processes:

$$S_1(t) = S_1(0) \exp\left[\left(\mu_1 - \frac{1}{2}\sigma_1^2\right) t + \sigma_1 Z_1(t)\right]$$

$$S_2(t) = S_2(0) \exp\left[\left(\mu_2 - \frac{1}{2}\sigma_2^2\right) t + \sigma_2 Z_2(t)\right]$$

where $S_1(0) > 0$, $S_2(0) > 0$, μ_1, μ_2, $\sigma_1 > 0$, and $\sigma_2 > 0$ are constants.
    Since

$$\sigma_1 Z_1 = (\sigma_1, 0)AW$$

$$\sigma_2 Z_2 = (0, \sigma_2)AW$$

$$\sigma_1^2 = (\sigma_1, 0)AA^\top(\sigma_1, 0)^\top$$

and

$$\sigma_2^2 = (0, \sigma_2)AA^\top(0, \sigma_2)^\top$$

we can write S_1 and S_2 as stochastic exponentials with respect to W, as follows:

$$S_1 = S_1(0)\eta[\mu_1, (\sigma_1, 0)A]$$

and

$$S_2 = S_2(0)\eta[\mu_2, (0, \sigma_2)A]$$

The ratio of S_2 to S_1 is also a stochastic exponential with respect to W:

$$\frac{S_2}{S_1} = \frac{S_2(0)}{S_1(0)}\eta[\mu_2 - \mu_1 - [(0, \sigma_2)A - (\sigma_1, 0)A][(\sigma_1, 0)A]^\top, (0, \sigma_2)A - (\sigma_1, 0)A]$$

$$= \frac{S_2(0)}{S_1(0)}\eta[\mu_2 - \mu_1 + (\sigma_1, -\sigma_2)AA^\top(\sigma_1, 0)^\top, (-\sigma_1, \sigma_2)A]$$

$$= \frac{S_2(0)}{S_1(0)} \eta[\mu_2 - \mu_1 + \sigma_1^2 - \rho\sigma_1\sigma_2, (-\sigma_1, \sigma_2)A]$$

In particular, the squared volatility of the ratio is

$$(-\sigma_1, \sigma_2)AA^\top(-\sigma_1, \sigma_2)^\top = \sigma_1^2 + \sigma_2^2 - 2\rho\sigma_1\sigma_2$$

Assume that the increment correlation ρ satisfies $-1 < \rho < 1$. Recall from Exercise 1.4 that the process

$$\tilde{W} = \frac{1}{\sqrt{\sigma_1^2 + \sigma_2^2 - 2\rho\sigma_1\sigma_2}}(-\sigma_1 Z_1 + \sigma_2 Z_2)$$

is a standard Wiener process relative to F. Now,

$$\begin{aligned}
d\left(\frac{S_2}{S_1}\right) &= \frac{S_2}{S_1}\left[\left(\mu_2 - \mu_1 + \sigma_1^2 - \rho\sigma_1\sigma_2\right)dt + (-\sigma_1, \sigma_2)A\,dW\right] \\
&= \frac{S_2}{S_1}\left[\left(\mu_2 - \mu_1 + \sigma_1^2 - \rho\sigma_1\sigma_2\right)dt - \sigma_1\,dZ_1 + \sigma_2\,dZ_2\right] \\
&= \frac{S_2}{S_1}\left[\left(\mu_2 - \mu_1 + \sigma_1^2 - \rho\sigma_1\sigma_2\right)dt + \sqrt{\sigma_1^2 + \sigma_2^2 - 2\rho\sigma_1\sigma_2}\,d\tilde{W}\right]
\end{aligned}$$

The last expression shows that S_2/S_1 solves a SDE as in Proposition 2.19. Hence, it is a constant times a stochastic exponential based on $\tilde{W}$. The coefficients are constants, so the process is a geometric Brownian motion. □

2.5   Girsanov's Theorem

If λ is a $(1 \times K)$-dimensional process in $\mathcal{L}^2$, consider the process

$$\eta[0, -\lambda](t) = \exp\left[-\frac{1}{2}\int_0^t \lambda\lambda^\top ds - \int_0^t \lambda\,dW\right]$$

Proposition 2.22 *The process $\eta = \eta[0, -\lambda]$ is the unique Itô process such that*

$$d\eta = -\eta\lambda\,dW$$

and $\eta(0) = 1$.

Proof   Follows from Proposition 2.19. □

So $\eta[0, -\lambda]$ is a positive Itô process with zero drift and with initial value $\eta[0, -\lambda](0) = 1$. Every positive Itô process X with zero drift has the form $X = X(0)\eta[0, -\lambda]$ for some $\lambda \in \mathcal{L}^2$.

A process X is a *supermartingale* if it is integrable and adapted and

$$E[X(t) \mid \mathcal{F}_s] \leq X(s)$$

whenever $0 \leq s \leq t$.

Proposition 2.23 *The process $\eta[0, -\lambda]$ is a supermartingale.*

Proof (*) Liptser and Shiryayev [65, 1977, Chapter 6, Lemma 6.1]. □

It follows from Proposition 2.23 that any positive Itô process with zero drift is a supermartingale.

The following proposition gives some conditions for $\eta[0, -\lambda]$ to be a martingale on a finite time interval $\mathcal{T} = [0, T]$.

Proposition 2.24 *The process $\eta[0, -\lambda]$ is a martingale on $\mathcal{T} = [0, T]$ if and only if $E\eta[0, -\lambda](T) = 1$. A sufficient condition for this is the so-called Novikov condition:*

$$E \exp\left[\frac{1}{2} \int_0^T \lambda\lambda^\mathsf{T} ds\right] < \infty$$

Proof (*) Liptser and Shiryayev [65, 1977, Theorem 6.1]. □

Example 2.25 Suppose λ is a constant K-dimensional row vector. Then

$$\int_0^T \lambda\lambda^\mathsf{T} ds = T\lambda\lambda^\mathsf{T} < \infty$$

The random variable

$$-\frac{1}{2} \int_0^T \lambda\lambda^\mathsf{T} ds - \int_0^T \lambda\, dW = -\frac{1}{2}T\lambda\lambda^\mathsf{T} - \lambda W(T)$$

is normally distributed with mean $-T\lambda\lambda^\mathsf{T}/2$ and variance $T\lambda\lambda^\mathsf{T}$. Hence, the random variable

$$\eta[0, -\lambda](T) = \exp\left[-\frac{1}{2}T\lambda\lambda^\mathsf{T} - \lambda W(T)\right]$$

is lognormally distributed. Using the formula for the mean of a lognormally distributed random variable (see Proposition 2.29),

$$E\eta[0, -\lambda](T) = \exp\left[-\frac{1}{2}T\lambda\lambda^\mathsf{T} + \frac{1}{2}T\lambda\lambda^\mathsf{T}\right] = e^0 = 1$$

It follows that the process $\eta[0, -\lambda]$ is a martingale on $[0, T]$.

Alternatively, since

$$E \exp\left[\frac{1}{2} \int_0^T \lambda\lambda^\mathsf{T} ds\right] = \exp\left[\frac{1}{2}T\lambda\lambda^\mathsf{T}\right] < \infty$$

the Novikov condition is satisfied, and it follows from Proposition 2.24 that $\eta[0, -\lambda]$ is a martingale. □

Let $\mathcal{T} = [0, T]$. If $E_P \eta[0, -\lambda](T) = 1$, or equivalently, if $\eta[0, -\lambda]$ is a martingale with respect to P, then we can consider the probability measure Q on $(\Omega, \mathcal{F})$ which has density (Radon–Nikodym derivative) $\eta[0, -\lambda](T)$ with respect to P. Recall that Q is defined by

$$Q(A) = E_P \left[\eta[0, -\lambda](T) 1_A \right]$$

whenever $A \in \mathcal{F}$.

Since $\eta[0, -\lambda](T)$ is a positive random variable, Q is equivalent to P, which means that Q and P have the same null sets. This implies, in particular, that the probability space $(\Omega, \mathcal{F}, Q)$ is complete if and only if $(\Omega, \mathcal{F}, P)$ is complete, and the filtration F is augmented with respect to Q if and only if it is augmented with respect to P. Equivalence of P and Q also implies that the spaces $\mathcal{L}^1$ and $\mathcal{L}^2$ do not depend on which of these two probability measures we are using. The space $\mathcal{H}^2$, however, does depend on the probability measure.

Define a K-dimensional process W^λ by

$$W^\lambda(t) = \int_0^t \lambda^\top ds + W(t)$$

This process is adapted to F. It is an Itô process with

$$dW^\lambda = \lambda^\top dt + dW$$

It turns out to be a Wiener process relative to F if the probability measure P is replaced by Q.

Theorem 2.26 Girsanov's theorem. *If $E_P \eta[0, -\lambda](T) = 1$, then the process W^λ is a Wiener process with respect to F and Q, where Q is the probability measure which has density $\eta[0, -\lambda](T)$ with respect to P.*

Proof (*) Karatzas and Shreve [64, 1988, Theorem 3.5.1]. □

Example 2.27 Suppose $K = 1$ and let λ be a positive constant. Then

$$\eta[0, -\lambda](T) = \exp\left[-\frac{1}{2} \int_0^T \lambda^2 ds - \int_0^T \lambda\, dW \right]$$

$$= \exp\left[-\frac{1}{2}\lambda^2 T - \lambda W(T) \right]$$

The only random part of this expression is $W(T)$, and $\eta[0, -\lambda](T)$ is a decreasing function of $W(T)$. This means that those paths of W that happen to drift up and reach a high value at time T will be assigned a low probability under Q, whereas those paths that reach a low (large negative) value at T will get high probability under Q. The process W^λ is given by

$$W^\lambda(t) = \int_0^t \lambda\, ds + W(t) = \lambda t + W(t)$$

When going from W to W^λ and from P to Q, each path of W is being shifted up (by the amount λt), but at the same time probability mass is being shifted downwards onto the lower paths. The net result is that W^λ has no tendency to drift up or down under Q: it is a standard Wiener process. This is illustrated in Figs. 2.2–2.5.

Figure 2.2 shows nine paths of a standard Wiener process W over the time interval $[0,6]$. These paths have not been completely randomly selected: they have been chosen so as to end up at equally spaced values

$$W(T) = -4, -3, -2, -1, 0, 1, 2, 3, 4$$

at time $T = 6$. Paths that end up close to zero have higher probability than paths that end up further away from zero, because $W(T)$ is normally distributed with mean zero. This has been indicated in the figure by drawing the three paths that end up at $-1, 0, 1$ fatter than the others.

In Fig. 2.3, the same nine paths have been shifted up by a drift of $\lambda = 0.5$ per unit of time, and they are shown together with a straight line representing this linear drift. Of course, under P, the process is no longer a standard Wiener process. But the remarkable result of Girsanov's theorem is that it is a standard Wiener process under Q.

When changing from the original probability measure P to the new probability measure Q, probability mass is shifted downwards to the lower paths. This is illustrated in Fig. 2.4. It shows the same nine paths as Fig. 2.3, but now the lowest three paths have been drawn fatter than the others. This indicates that paths like them are more likely under Q than paths further away from zero.

The process has zero drift under Q. This is illustrated in Fig. 2.5, which is identical to Fig. 2.4, except that the three highest paths are no longer shown and have been replaced by three new low paths. The paths are now fairly evenly distributed around the horizontal axis.   □

Note that the augmented filtrations F^W and F^{W^λ} generated by W and W^λ, respectively, need not be identical. They are both coarser than F, because W and W^λ are adapted to F. If λ is deterministic, then $F^W = F^{W^\lambda}$.

Girsanov's theorem is used frequently in financial economics to change the drift of a process and, in many cases, turn it into a martingale. This is illustrated in the following example.

Example 2.28 *Risk-adjusted probabilities in the Black–Scholes model. Continuation of Examples 1.7, 1.15, 2.3, 2.14, and 2.20.* The discounted stock price in the Black–Scholes model is

$$\frac{S}{M} = \frac{S(0)}{M(0)}\eta[\mu - r, \sigma]$$

Set

$$\lambda = \frac{\mu - r}{\sigma}$$

Since λ is a constant, $\eta[0, -\lambda]$ is a martingale. Define the process W^λ by

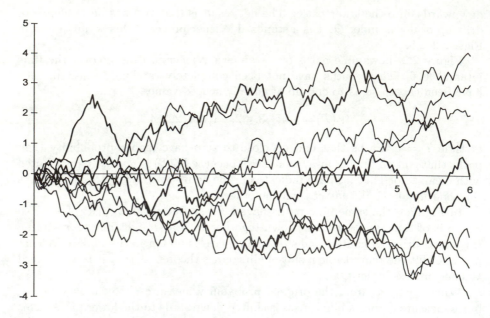

FIG. 2.2. Girsanov: nine paths of a Wiener process

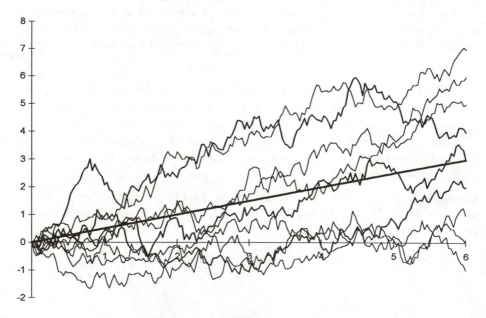

FIG. 2.3. Girsanov: drift added to the Wiener process

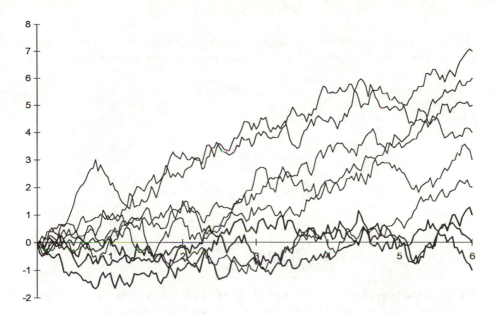

FIG. 2.4. Girsanov: probability mass shifted down

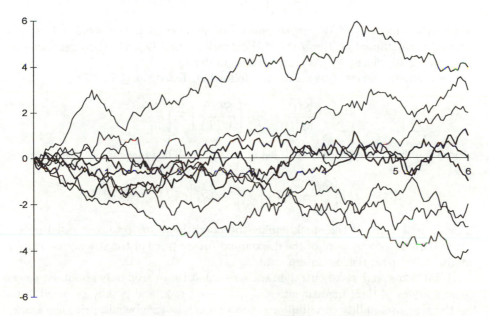

FIG. 2.5. Girsanov: three high paths replaced by three low paths

$$W^\lambda(t) = \lambda t + W(t)$$

and let Q be the probability measure with density $\eta[0, -\lambda](T)$ with respect to P. By Girsanov's theorem, W^λ is a Wiener process with respect to F and Q. Note that

$$dW^\lambda = \lambda\, dt + dW$$

Now,

$$
\begin{aligned}
d\left(\frac{S}{M}\right) &= \frac{S}{M}[(\mu - r)\, dt + \sigma\, dW] \\
&= \frac{S}{M}[(\mu - r)\, dt + \sigma\, dW^\lambda - \sigma\lambda\, dt] \\
&= \frac{S}{M}[(\mu - r)\, dt + \sigma\, dW^\lambda - (\mu - r)\, dt] \\
&= \frac{S}{M}\sigma\, dW^\lambda
\end{aligned}
$$

So, from the perspective of W^λ and Q, S/M is an Itô process with zero drift. In fact, S/M is a martingale under Q. To see this, note that

$$\frac{S}{M} = \frac{S(0)}{M(0)}\eta[0, \sigma; W^\lambda]$$

where the inclusion of W^λ in the notation signifies that the stochastic exponential is calculated on the basis of W^λ (rather than W). By the arguments of Example 2.25, $\eta[0, \sigma; W^\lambda]$ is a martingale under Q.

In economic terms, this means the following. Let $0 \le t \le T$. Then

$$\frac{S(t)}{M(t)} = E_Q\left[\frac{S(T)}{M(T)} \,\Big|\, \mathcal{F}_t\right]$$

where E_Q denotes expectation based on the probability measure Q. This implies that

$$S(t) = E_Q\left[\frac{M(t)}{M(T)}S(T) \,\Big|\, \mathcal{F}_t\right] = E_Q\left[e^{-r(T-t)}S(T) \,\Big|\, \mathcal{F}_t\right]$$

The current price of the stock equals the conditional expectation based on Q, given current information, of the discounted future price of the stock, discounted at the rolled-over riskless interest rate.

If investors were risk-neutral, in the sense that they cared only about expected future values of their investments and not about risk, and if they believed Q to be the true probability distribution, then this is how they would price the stock.

For this reason, Q will be called the "risk-adjusted" probability measure in this context.   □

Suppose $E\eta[0, -\lambda](T) = 1$. The process W^λ is a Wiener process based on Q, and at the same time it is an Itô process based on P. If $b \in \mathcal{L}^2$ then the integral

$$\int_0^t b \, dW^\lambda$$

can be interpreted in two potentially different ways. On the one hand, it can be seen as an integral with respect to a Wiener process W^λ based on Q. On the other hand, $b\lambda^\top \in \mathcal{L}^1$, so that the integral can also be seen as an integral with respect to the Itô process

$$W^\lambda(t) = \int_0^t \lambda^\top ds + W(t)$$

based on P:

$$\int_0^t b \, dW^\lambda = \int_0^t b\lambda^\top ds + \int_0^t b \, dW$$

These two integrals are indeed identical.

Proof (*)   To show this, assume first that b is a simple process; that is, there exists a subdivision $0 = t_0 < t_1 < \cdots < t_n = t$ of $[0, t]$ and random variables $\beta, \beta_0, \beta_1, \ldots, \beta_{n-1}$ with $\beta \in \mathcal{F}_0$ and $\beta_i \in \mathcal{F}_{t_i}$ for each $i = 0, \ldots, n-1$, such that b has the form

$$b(s) = \beta 1_{\{0\}}(s) + \sum_{i=0}^{n-1} \beta_i 1_{(t_i, t_{i+1}]}(s)$$

The stochastic integral based on Q is defined by

$$\int_0^t b \, dW^\lambda = \sum_{i=0}^{n-1} \beta_i (W^\lambda(t_{i+1}) - W^\lambda(t_i))$$

The stochastic integral with respect to the Itô process based on P is given by

$$\int_0^t b \, dW + \int_0^t b\lambda^\top ds = \sum_{i=0}^{n-1} \beta_i (W(t_{i+1}) - W(t_i)) + \sum_{i=0}^{n-1} \int_{t_i}^{t_{i+1}} b\lambda^\top ds$$

$$= \sum_{i=0}^{n-1} \beta_i (W(t_{i+1}) - W(t_i)) + \sum_{i=0}^{n-1} \beta_i \int_{t_i}^{t_{i+1}} \lambda^\top ds$$

$$= \sum_{i=0}^{n-1} \beta_i \left[\left(W(t_{i+1}) + \int_0^{t_{i+1}} \lambda^\top ds \right) \right.$$

$$\left. - \left(W(t_i) + \int_0^{t_i} \lambda^\top ds \right) \right]$$

$$= \sum_{i=0}^{n-1} \beta_i (W^\lambda(t_{i+1}) - W^\lambda(t_i))$$

If b is not simple, then there exists a sequence (b_n) of simple processes such that

$$\int_0^t |b - b_n|^2 \, ds \to 0$$

in probability. Note that convergence in P-probability and convergence in Q-probability are equivalent. The sequences $\int_0^t b_n \, dW^\lambda$ and $\int_0^t b_n \, dW$ converge in probability to $\int_0^t b \, dW^\lambda$ and $\int_0^t b \, dW$, respectively. Furthermore,

$$\left| \int_0^t b_n \lambda^\top ds - \int_0^t b \lambda^\top ds \right| = \left| \int_0^t (b_n - b) \lambda^\top ds \right|$$

$$\leq \left(\int_0^t |b_n - b|^2 \, ds \right)^{\frac{1}{2}} \times \left(\int_0^t \lambda \lambda^\top ds \right)^{\frac{1}{2}}$$

$$\to 0 \quad \text{in probability}$$

So, the sequence

$$\int_0^t b_n \, dW^\lambda = \int_0^t b_n \, dW + \int_0^t b_n \lambda^\top ds$$

converges in probability to

$$\int_0^t b \, dW + \int_0^t b \lambda^\top ds$$

Hence,

$$\int_0^t b \, dW^\lambda = \int_0^t b \, dW + \int_0^t b \lambda^\top ds$$

$\square$

The following proposition gives formulas for the means of a lognormal distribution and of a lognormal distribution which is truncated either above or below. The formula for the mean of a lognormal distribution has already been used in Examples 1.15 and 2.25. The formulas for the mean of a truncated lognormal distribution will be used at various points in calculations of option pricing formulas. The proof illustrates how Girsanov's theorem may sometimes be used to calculate expected values. Indeed, we give two alternative proofs. The first proceeds in a standard way by integrating with respect to the density function of a normal distribution. The second proof uses Girsanov's theorem.

Let N denote the standard normal cumulative distribution function.

Proposition 2.29 *If U is a normally distributed random variable with mean m and variance s^2, and if U_0 is a number, then*

$$E\left[e^U 1_{U \leq U_0}\right] = \exp\left(m + \frac{1}{2}s^2\right) N(d)$$

$$Ee^U = \exp\left(m + \frac{1}{2}s^2\right)$$

and

$$E\left[e^U 1_{U \geq U_0}\right] = \exp\left(m + \frac{1}{2}s^2\right) N(-d)$$

where

$$d = \frac{U_0 - m - s^2}{s}$$

Proof To prove the first equation in a standard way, set

$$V = \frac{U - m}{s}$$

Then V follows a standard normal distribution, $U = m + sV$, and $U \leq U_0$ if and only if

$$V \leq \frac{U_0 - m}{s} = d + s$$

Now,

$$E\left[e^U 1_{U \leq U_0}\right] = E\left[e^{m+sV} 1_{V \leq d+s}\right]$$

$$= \frac{1}{\sqrt{2\pi}} \int_{-\infty}^{d+s} e^{m+sv} \exp\left(-\frac{v^2}{2}\right) dv$$

$$= \exp\left(m + \frac{1}{2}s^2\right) \frac{1}{\sqrt{2\pi}} \int_{-\infty}^{d+s} \exp\left(-\frac{(v-s)^2}{2}\right) dv$$

$$= \exp\left(m + \frac{1}{2}s^2\right) \frac{1}{\sqrt{2\pi}} \int_{-\infty}^{d} \exp\left(-\frac{y^2}{2}\right) dy$$

$$= \exp\left(m + \frac{1}{2}s^2\right) N(d)$$

The alternative proof of the first equation goes as follows. Let B be a standard Brownian motion on a probability space $(\Omega, \mathcal{F}, P)$. Then U has the same distribution as $m + sB(1)$. Define a new process B^s by

$$B^s(t) = B(t) - st$$

Let Q be the probability measure with density $\eta[0, s](1)$ with respect to P. By Girsanov's theorem, B^s is a standard Brownian motion with respect to Q. Now,

$$\eta[0, s](1) = \exp\left(-\frac{1}{2}s^2 + sB(1)\right)$$

$$e^{m+sB(1)} = \exp\left(m + \frac{1}{2}s^2\right)\eta[0, s](1)$$

and

$$m + sB(1) = m + s(B^s(t) + s) = m + s^2 + sB^s(1)$$

Hence,

$$E\left[e^U 1_{U \leq U_0}\right] = E\left[e^{m+sB(1)} 1_{m+sB(1) \leq U_0}\right]$$

$$= \exp\left(m + \frac{1}{2}s^2\right) E[\eta[0, s](1) 1_{m+sB(1) \leq U_0}]$$

$$= \exp\left(m + \frac{1}{2}s^2\right) E_Q[1_{m+sB(1) \leq U_0}]$$

$$= \exp\left(m + \frac{1}{2}s^2\right) Q(m + sB(1) \leq U_0)$$

$$= \exp\left(m + \frac{1}{2}s^2\right) Q(m + s^2 + sB^s(1) \leq U_0)$$

$$= \exp\left(m + \frac{1}{2}s^2\right) N\left(\frac{U_0 - m - s^2}{s}\right)$$

$$= \exp\left(m + \frac{1}{2}s^2\right) N(d)$$

To prove the second and third equations, observe that $d \to \infty$ and $N(d) \to 1$ as $U_0 \to \infty$. Hence,

$$Ee^U = \lim_{U_0 \to \infty} E\left[e^U 1_{U \leq U_0}\right]$$

$$= \lim_{U_0 \to \infty} \exp\left(m + \frac{1}{2}s^2\right) N(d)$$

$$= \exp\left(m + \frac{1}{2}s^2\right)$$

and

$$E\left[e^U 1_{U \geq U_0}\right] = Ee^U - E\left[e^U 1_{U \leq U_0}\right]$$

$$= \exp\left(m + \frac{1}{2}s^2\right) - \exp\left(m + \frac{1}{2}s^2\right) N(d)$$

$$= \exp\left(m + \frac{1}{2}s^2\right) (1 - N(d))$$

$$= \exp\left(m + \frac{1}{2}s^2\right) N(-d)$$

$$\square$$

2.6 Summary

An Itô process is a sum of an initial value, a time integral, and a stochastic integral. The time integral has instantaneous increments whose means may vary stochastically over time, and the stochastic integral has instantaneous increments whose variances and covariances may vary stochastically over time. The integrand in the time integral, or the coefficient to time, is called the drift of the Itô process. The integrand in the stochastic integral, or the coefficient to the Wiener processes, is called the dispersion. Itô processes are continuous and adapted to the information structure.

Itô's lemma says that if you apply a twice continuously differentiable function to an Itô process, then the resulting process will also be an Itô process. In other words, it will be the sum of an initial value, a time integral, and a stochastic integral. Itô's formula identifies the drift and the dispersion. The dispersion is the first derivative of the function times the dispersion of the underlying Itô process. The drift is the first derivative times the drift of the underlying Itô process, plus a second-order adjustment term. The second-order adjustment term is a half times the second derivative of the function times the squared dispersion of the underlying Itô process. Apart from this term, Itô's formula is essentially the equivalent of the chain rule from ordinary calculus.

We illustrated Itô's lemma with a number of examples. Example 2.3 calculated the dynamics of the stock price in the Black–Scholes model and found that the parameters μ and σ can be interpreted as the mean and the standard deviation of the instantaneous rate of return to the stock. Example 2.4 calculated the dynamics of the logarithm of a positive Itô process. Example 2.5 and Exercises 2.1 and 2.2 showed how Itô's lemma can sometimes be used to calculate integrals that would otherwise be difficult to handle.

Two Itô processes are identical if and only if they have the same initial value, the same drift process, and the same dispersion process. Saying that two drift or dispersion processes are the same means that they are identical almost everywhere with respect to the product measure on states of the world and time. Saying that two Itô processes are identical means that the entire paths are identical with probability one.

If an Itô process is a martingale, then its drift is zero.

Given that we can integrate with respect to time and with respect to a Wiener process, it is an easy matter to go one step further and define a stochastic integral with respect to an Itô process. This integral is again an Itô process, and, in particular, it is a continuous and adapted process. The integral is linear both in the integrand and in the integrator.

The concept of a stochastic integral of a process with respect to an Itô process will be important in Chapter 4, where securities prices are modeled as Itô processes and the so-called cumulative gains process is defined as the integral of a trading strategy with respect to the securities price process. More immediately, the new integral allows us to rewrite Itô's formula in an alternative way that is easier to remember and to manipulate in certain situations.

Recall that Itô's lemma exhibits a function of an Itô process as the sum of an initial value, a time integral, and an integral with respect to the Wiener process, and that Itô's formula identifies the integrand processes in those integrals. Alternatively, it can be written as the sum of an initial value, an integral with respect to the Itô process itself, and a time integral. Now the coefficient to the Itô process is the first derivative of the function, and the coefficient to time is the second-order adjustment term.

We illustrated this alternative form of Itô's formula in Example 2.12, which calculates the dynamics of a product of Itô processes, and in Example 2.13, which calculates the dynamics of a ratio. The latter was specialized in Example 2.14 to the ratio between the stock price and the value of the money market account in the Black–Scholes model.

Stochastic integrals with respect to Itô processes obey a formula for integration by parts. As an application, we showed that when integrating a product both with respect to time and with respect to a Wiener process, it is possible to interchange the order of integration.

A stochastic exponential is simply the exponential of an Itô process. Every positive Itô process can be written as a stochastic exponential, and every stochastic exponential is a positive Itô process. We parameterize stochastic exponentials in much the same way as the Black–Scholes stock price, except that the percentage drift and dispersion are not constants but general processes.

Stochastic exponentials will be used frequently because many processes in finance can take only positive values. Stock prices, for example, and most securities prices in general, are positive. In the real world, interest rates take only positive values, although in some models they follow processes that can take negative values. Stochastic exponentials are convenient, because they obey some simple calculation rules which embody Itô's lemma for products and for ratios. These were illustrated in Example 2.21, which calculates the dynamics of the ratio of two correlated stock prices.

A positive Itô process which is a martingale must be a stochastic exponential with zero drift. Hence it is completely determined by its initial value and its relative dispersion coefficient. Conversely, an appropriate condition on the relative dispersion coefficient, such as the Novikov condition, will ensure that the corresponding zero-drift stochastic exponential is a martingale. For example, if the relative dispersion coefficient is constant, then the stochastic exponential is a martingale. We showed this in Example 2.25 by direct calculation and, alternatively, by using the Novikov condition.

Suppose we are working with a fixed finite time horizon, and suppose we are given a stochastic exponential which is a martingale. Define a new probability measure whose density with respect to the old measure is the final value of the stochastic exponential. Consider the process which arises from adding to the Wiener process a drift equal to the relative dispersion of the stochastic exponential. Girsanov's theorem says that this process is a Wiener process under the new probability measure.

As discussed in Example 2.27, adding a positive drift to the original Wiener process has the effect of shifting its paths upwards. Changing the probability measure moves probability mass downwards onto the lower paths, which neutralizes the drift. The net effect is that the process continues to be a Wiener process.

Girsanov's theorem is used frequently to change the drift of a process and turn it into a martingale. We illustrated this in Example 2.28, where we made the discounted stock price in the Black–Scholes model into a martingale. This implies that the current stock price equals the expected discounted future stock price. It will turn out that not only the stock but all derivative securities which are contingent on the stock have this property. They are priced as if investors were risk neutral. For that reason, the new probabilities will be called the risk-adjusted probabilities.

Another illustration of Girsanov's theorem was one of the two alternative proofs of the formula for the expectation of a truncated lognormally distributed variable, in Proposition 2.29.

2.7 (*) Notes

McKean [66, 1969] writes the following about "differential and integral calculus based upon the Brownian motion" in his preface:

> Roughly speaking, it is the same as the customary calculus of smooth functions, except that in taking the differential of a smooth function f of the one-dimensional Brownian path $t \mapsto b(t)$, it is necessary to keep two terms in the power series expansion and to replace $(db)^2$ by dt:

$$df(b) = f'(b)\,db + \frac{1}{2}f''(b)(db)^2 = f'(b)\,db + \frac{1}{2}f''(b)\,dt$$

or, what is the same,

$$\int_0^t f'(b)\,db = f(b)\Big|_0^t - \frac{1}{2}\int_0^t f''(b)\,ds$$

From Arnold's [1, 1974] preface, about stochastic differential equations:

> ...the existing detailed studies of the subject, as a rule, either are not written from a standpoint of applications or are inaccessible to the person intending to apply them. ...The shorter accounts ...are rather unsuited for the study and understanding of the subject.

It seems that Itô [56, 1951] is the original source of Itô's formula.

In this chapter, we have defined the stochastic integral for integrators that are multi-dimensional Itô processes. Some authors, such as for example Harrison and Pliska [44, 1981], [45, 1983], use integrals that are defined for more general integrators. To allow for more general integrators, it may be necessary to restrict the class of integrands.

When applied to the case where the integrator is an Itô process, a theory built on such a restriction yields a smaller class of integrands than the one we have employed here. If X is an N-dimensional Itô process and γ is an N-dimensional vector-valued candidate for an integrand process, then the requirement might be that $\gamma_i \in \mathcal{L}(X_i)$ for all $i = 1, \ldots, N$, rather than the weaker requirement $\gamma \in \mathcal{L}(X)$, cf. Example 2.8. See Jarrow and Madan [60, 1991]. See also the notes to Chapter 4.

Heath, Jarrow, and Morton [48, 1992] and Baxter [6, 1997] have results about interchanging the order of integration which are more fancy than our Proposition 2.17.

Girsanov's theorem is due to Girsanov [40, 1960]. The formula of Cameron and Martin [11, 1945], [12, 1949] is a precursor of Girsanov's theorem. It is based on the integral for non-random integrands, which was defined by Paley, Wiener, and Zygmund [75, 1933]. Girsanov's theorem is sometimes called the Cameron–Martin–Girsanov theorem.

3

GAUSSIAN PROCESSES

This chapter studies some examples of processes that are Gaussian or conditionally Gaussian.

3.1 Basic Notions

If X is a one-dimensional process, then a *sample vector* is a random vector of the form

$$(X(t_1), X(t_2), \ldots, X(t_n))$$

where

$$0 \leq t_1 \leq \cdots \leq t_n$$

is a finite number of times where the process is sampled.

Similarly, if X is an N-dimensional process, then a *sample matrix* is a random $(N \times n)$-dimensional matrix of the form

$$(X(t_1), X(t_2), \ldots, X(t_n))$$

where, again,

$$0 \leq t_1 \leq \cdots \leq t_n$$

is a finite number of times where the process is sampled.

An N-dimensional process X is said to be *Gaussian* if the distribution of every sample matrix is jointly normal: for every finite number of times

$$0 \leq t_1 \leq \cdots \leq t_n$$

the (unconditional) joint distribution of the elements of the $(N \times n)$-dimensional sample matrix

$$(X(t_1), X(t_2), \ldots, X(t_n))$$

is normal.

If X is Gaussian, then the distribution of every sample matrix can be found if we know only the *mean function* $EX_i(t)$, $0 \leq t$, $i = 1, \ldots, N$, and the *covariance function* $\operatorname{cov}(X_i(s), X_j(t))$, $0 \leq s \leq t$, $i, j = 1, \ldots, N$.

A generalized Brownian motion

$$Z(t) = Z(0) + \mu t + \sigma B(t)$$

is Gaussian with

$$EZ_i(t) = Z_i(0) + \mu_i t$$

and

$$\operatorname{cov}(Z_i(s), Z_j(t)) = \operatorname{cov}(Z_i(s), Z_j(s))$$

$$= s \left(\sigma \sigma^\top \right)_{ij}$$

$$= s \sum_{k=1}^{K} \sigma_{ik} \sigma_{jk}$$

for $0 \leq s \leq t$. Here, B is a K-dimensional standard Brownian motion, μ is an N-dimensional column vector, and σ is an $(N \times K)$-dimensional matrix.

An N-dimensional process X is said to be *conditionally Gaussian* (given the filtration F) if it is adapted to F and if the conditional distribution of every sample matrix is jointly normal: for every finite number of times

$$0 \leq s \leq t_1 \leq \cdots \leq t_n$$

the conditional joint distribution of the elements of the $(N \times n)$-dimensional sample matrix

$$(X(t_1), X(t_2), \ldots, X(t_n))$$

given $\mathcal{F}_s$ is normal.

If X is conditionally Gaussian, then the conditional distribution of every sample matrix can be found if we know only the *conditional mean functions* $E(X_i(t) \mid \mathcal{F}_s)$, $0 \leq s \leq t$, $i = 1, \ldots, N$, and the *conditional covariance functions* $\mathrm{cov}(X_i(t), X_j(u) \mid \mathcal{F}_s)$, $0 \leq s \leq t \leq u$, $i, j = 1, \ldots, N$.

If X is conditionally Gaussian and $X(0)$ is normally distributed, then X is Gaussian.

If the increment $X(t) - X(s)$ is normally distributed and independent of $\mathcal{F}_s$ whenever $0 \leq s \leq t$, then X is conditionally Gaussian.

A generalized Wiener process

$$Z(t) = Z(0) + \mu t + \sigma W(t)$$

is both Gaussian and conditionally Gaussian, with

$$E(Z_i(t) \mid \mathcal{F}_s) = Z_i(s) + \mu_i(t - s)$$

and

$$\mathrm{cov}(Z_i(t), Z_j(u) \mid \mathcal{F}_s) = \mathrm{cov}(Z_i(t), Z_j(t) \mid \mathcal{F}_s)$$

$$= (t - s) \left(\sigma \sigma^\top \right)_{ij}$$

$$= (t - s) \sum_{k=1}^{K} \sigma_{ik} \sigma_{jk}$$

for $0 \leq s \leq t \leq u$. Here, W is a K-dimensional standard Wiener process relative to F, μ is an N-dimensional column vector, and σ is an $(N \times K)$-dimensional matrix.

3.2   Deterministic Integrands

Theorem 3.1 *If $b \in \mathcal{L}^2$ is a deterministic $(N \times K)$-dimensional matrix-valued process and $0 \leq s \leq t$, then the N-dimensional random variable*

$$\int_s^t b\, dW$$

is independent of $\mathcal{F}_s$ and normally distributed with mean zero and covariance matrix

$$\int_s^t bb^\top\, du$$

Proof (*)   Arnold [1, 1974, Corollary 4.5.6] says that the integral is normally distributed with the indicated mean and covariance matrix. Denote the elements of the matrix b by b_{ik}, $i = 1, \ldots, N$, $k = 1, \ldots, K$. According to Proposition 1.36, for each (i, k) there exists a sequence $b_{ik;n}$ of simple deterministic processes in $\mathcal{L}^2$ (and hence in $\mathcal{H}^2$) such that

$$\int_0^t |b_{ik;n} - b_{ik}|^2\, du \to 0$$

and, hence,

$$\int_s^t |b_{ik;n} - b_{ik}|^2\, du = \int_0^t |1_{(s,t]}b_{ik;n} - 1_{(s,t]}b_{ik}|^2\, du \to 0$$

It follows, again using Proposition 1.36, that

$$\int_0^t 1_{(s,t]}b_{ik;n}\, dW_k \to \int_0^t 1_{(s,t]}b_{ik}\, dW_k$$

in probability. Since $1_{(s,t]}b_{ik;n}$ is a deterministic simple process, its integral $\int_s^t 1_{(s,t]}b_{ik;n}\, dW_k$ is a weighted sum of increments of W_k between s and t, and so it is measurable with respect to the augmented sigma-algebra

$$\mathcal{G}_s = \tilde{\sigma}(W(u) - W(s) : s \leq u)$$

It follows from Proposition 1.10 that $\mathcal{G}_s$ is independent of $\mathcal{F}_s$. Since the integrals of the simple processes converge in probability to

$$\int_s^t b_{ik}\, dW_k = \int_0^t 1_{(s,t]}b_{ik}\, dW_k$$

the latter is also measurable with respect to $\mathcal{G}_s$. But this implies that

$$\int_s^t b\, dW$$

is measurable with respect to $\mathcal{G}_s$ and hence independent of $\mathcal{F}_s$. $\square$

It follows from Theorem 3.1 that the stochastic integral process is both Gaussian and conditionally Gaussian. The unconditional distribution of a sample matrix equals the conditional distribution given $\mathcal{F}_0$. If $0 \leq s \leq t$, then the conditional mean of the integral between s and t, given $\mathcal{F}_s$, is zero. If $0 \leq s \leq t \leq u$, then the conditional covariance matrix of the integrals between s and t and between s and u, given $\mathcal{F}_s$, is

$$E\left[\left(\int_s^t b\,dW\right)\left(\int_s^u b\,dW\right)^{\mathsf{T}} \middle| \mathcal{F}_s\right] = E\left[\left(\int_s^t b\,dW\right)\left(\int_s^t b\,dW\right)^{\mathsf{T}} \middle| \mathcal{F}_s\right]$$

$$= \int_s^t b(v)b(v)^{\mathsf{T}}\,dv$$

The following two propositions assume that the integrand b is such that bb^{T} is deterministic, but they do not assume that b itself is deterministic.

Proposition 3.2 (*) *Let $b \in \mathcal{L}^2$ be a K-dimensional row-vector-valued process such that bb^{T} is deterministic and positive almost everywhere on $[0,T]$. Set*

$$A(t) = \int_0^t b\,dW$$

and

$$f(t) = \int_0^t \|b(s)\|^2\,ds$$

for $0 \leq t \leq T$, and set $T^* = f(T)$. Then the process B defined by

$$B(s) = A(f^{-1}(s))$$

for $0 \leq s \leq T^*$ is a Wiener process relative to the filtration

$$F_{f^{-1}} = \left(\mathcal{F}_{f^{-1}(s)}\right)_{0 \leq s \leq T^*}$$

and

$$A(t) = B(f(t))$$

for $0 \leq t \leq T^*$.

Proof Observe that the functions f and f^{-1} are strictly increasing and continuous. It follows directly that $B(0) = 0$ almost surely, B is continuous, and B is adapted to the filtration $F_{f^{-1}}$. It is square integrable because A is square integrable. It is a martingale. If $0 \leq s \leq t$, then

$$E\left[B(t) \mid \mathcal{F}_{f^{-1}(s)}\right] = E\left[A(f^{-1}(t)) \mid \mathcal{F}_{f^{-1}(s)}\right] = A(f^{-1}(s)) = B(s)$$

Finally,

$$E\left[(B(t) - B(s))^2 \mid \mathcal{F}_{f^{-1}(s)}\right] = E\left\{[A(f^{-1}(t)) - A(f^{-1})(s)]^2 \mid \mathcal{F}_{f^{-1}(s)}\right\}$$

$$= E\left[\left(\int_{f^{-1}(s)}^{f^{-1}(t)} b\,dW\right)^2 \middle| \mathcal{F}_{f^{-1}(s)}\right]$$

$$= E\left[\int_{f^{-1}(s)}^{f^{-1}(t)} \|b(s)\|^2\,ds \middle| \mathcal{F}_{f^{-1}(s)}\right]$$

$$= t - s$$

It now follows from Theorem 1.14 that B is a Wiener process relative to the filtration $F_{f^{-1}}$. Finally,

$$A(t) = A(f^{-1}(f(t))) = B(f(t))$$

$\square$

The functions f and f^{-1} in Proposition 3.2 can be interpreted as (deterministic) time changes. A process of the form A, which is a stochastic integral with deterministic instantaneous variance, can be transformed into a Wiener process (relative to a new filtration) by a deterministic change of the time scale. Alternatively, A can be seen as arising from a Wiener process (relative to a new filtration) by a time change.

It follows from Proposition 3.2 that the stochastic integral A is both Gaussian and conditionally Gaussian. The unconditional distribution of a sample vector equals the conditional distribution given $\mathcal{F}_0$. If $0 \le s \le t$, then the conditional mean of the integral between s and t, given $\mathcal{F}_s$, is zero, and the conditional variance is

$$f(t) - f(s) = \int_s^t \|b(u)\|^2\,du$$

Proposition 3.3 (*) *Let $b \in \mathcal{L}^2$ be a K-dimensional row-vector-valued process such that $bb^\top$ is deterministic and positive almost everywhere on $[0, T]$. Set*

$$B(t) = \int_0^t \frac{1}{\sqrt{bb^\top}} b\,dW$$

Then B is a Wiener process relative to the filtration F.

Proof This follows directly from either Proposition 3.2 or Theorem 1.14. $\square$

It follows from Proposition 3.3 that any one-dimensional stochastic integral with deterministic instantaneous variance can be written as a stochastic integral of a deterministic process with respect to a one-dimensional Wiener process. Specifically, if $b \in \mathcal{L}^2$ is a K-dimensional process such that $bb^\top$ is deterministic and positive almost everywhere on $[0, T]$, then

$$\int_0^t b\,dW = \int_0^t \sqrt{bb^\top}\,dB$$

where

$$B(t) = \int_0^t \frac{1}{\sqrt{bb^\top}} b\,dW$$

as in Proposition 3.3.

Exercise 3.1 *Let W be a one-dimensional Wiener process relative to F. Let $0 \leq s \leq t$ and let $a \neq 0$ be a constant number. Find the distribution of the random variable*

$$e^{-at} \int_s^t e^{au} \, dW(u) = \int_s^t e^{-a(t-u)} \, dW(u)$$

The random variable in Exercise 3.1 will show up later in connection with so-called Ornstein–Uhlenbeck processes in Section 3.5 and with the Vasicek model of the term structure of interest rates in Sections 7.2–7.5. It is an exponentially weighted sum of instantaneous increments of the Wiener process between s and t, giving most weight to increments that happen close to time t and less weight to increments that happen a long time before t.

3.3   (*) Brownian Bridge Processes

In this section, we shall construct a so-called Brownian bridge. It is a process defined on a finite time interval $[0, T]$. It starts at zero and ends at zero for sure. We shall show that it is an Itô process on $[0, T]$.

The analysis of the Brownian bridge illustrates the use of a time change in connection with Brownian motion, the law of large numbers for Brownian motion, the law of the iterated logarithm, and integration by parts, among other things.

The Brownian bridge was suggested by Ball and Torous [5, 1983] as an element in constructing a price process for a zero-coupon bond. It is useful for constructing various examples and counterexamples of properties of interest rate and bond price processes.

A *zero-coupon bond* with face value one and maturity T is a security which pays one (dollar) for sure at time T and nothing at all other times. The price process suggested by Ball and Torous was

$$S(t) = S(0)e^{Rt + \sigma Y(t)}$$

where $S(0) > 0$ is a deterministic initial value, $\sigma > 0$ is a constant, R is a constant related to $S(0)$ by

$$S(0)e^{RT} = 1$$

and Y is the Brownian bridge process. The price process S has the property that $S(T) = 1$, which is desirable since the value of the zero-coupon bond at maturity must be one. The parameter R can be interpreted as the continuously compounded yield on the bond at time zero:

$$R = \frac{1}{T} \ln \left(\frac{1}{S(0)} \right)$$

The Ball–Torous model will be analyzed further in Examples 4.7 and 4.9 below, as an illustration of the concepts of state prices, interest rates, and prices of risk.

Assume that W is a one-dimensional Wiener process relative to F, and let $0 < T$. Define a process α on $[0, T)$ by

$$\alpha(t) = \int_0^t \frac{1}{T - s}\, dW(s)$$

for $0 \leq t < T$.

By Theorem 3.1, if $0 \leq s \leq t < T$, then the increment $\alpha(t) - \alpha(s)$ is independent of $\mathcal{F}_s$ and normally distributed with mean zero and variance

$$\mathrm{var}(\alpha(t) - \alpha(s)) = \int_s^t \frac{1}{(T-u)^2}\, du = \frac{1}{T-t} - \frac{1}{T-s} = \frac{t-s}{(T-t)(T-s)}$$

Hence, α is Gaussian and conditionally Gaussian. The conditional mean of $\alpha(t)$ given $\mathcal{F}_s$ is

$$E(\alpha(t) \mid \mathcal{F}_s) = \alpha(s)$$

If $0 \leq s \leq t \leq u < T$, then the conditional covariance of $\alpha(t)$ and $\alpha(u)$ given $\mathcal{F}_s$ is

$$\mathrm{cov}(\alpha(t), \alpha(u) \mid \mathcal{F}_s) = \mathrm{var}(\alpha(t) \mid \mathcal{F}_s) = \frac{t-s}{(T-t)(T-s)}$$

Observe that

$$\mathrm{var}(\alpha(t)) = \int_0^t \frac{1}{(T-s)^2}\, ds = \frac{t}{(T-t)T} \to \infty$$

as $t \to T$. If we think of α as a weighted sum of increments dW in the Wiener process over $[0, t]$, then the weights assigned to increments close to t go to infinity as t approaches T, and hence the variance of $\alpha(t)$ goes to infinity.

Since

$$\int_0^T \frac{1}{(T-s)^2}\, ds = \lim_{t \to T} \mathrm{var}(\alpha(t)) = +\infty$$

α is not defined as a stochastic integral on $[0, T]$.

Define a process Y on $[0, T]$ by

$$Y(t) = \begin{cases} (T - t)\alpha(t) & \text{for } 0 \leq t < T \\ 0 & \text{for } t = T \end{cases}$$

Then Y is a *Brownian bridge*.

Since α is Gaussian and conditionally Gaussian, so is Y. For $0 \leq s \leq t < T$, the conditional mean of $Y(t)$ given $\mathcal{F}_s$ is

$$E(Y(t) \mid \mathcal{F}_s) = (T - t)E(\alpha(t) \mid \mathcal{F}_s) = (T - t)\alpha(s) = \frac{T-t}{T-s} Y(s)$$

This means that the value of Y is expected to go linearly to zero from its current value $Y(s)$ over the time interval $[s, T]$.

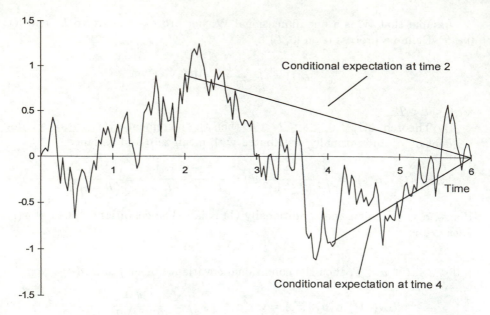

FIG. 3.1. Conditional expectation of a Brownian bridge

Figure 3.1 illustrates the conditional expectation of a Brownian bridge. It shows a path of a Brownian bridge which hits zero at time $T = 6$, together with two straight lines which represent conditional expectations. One of the lines connects the value of the Brownian path at time $t = 2$ with the zero value at time $T = 6$. It represents the conditional expectation, based on the information available at time $t = 2$, of the future values of the Brownian path at times in the interval $[2, 6]$. The other line connects the value of the Brownian path at time $t = 4$ with the zero value at time $T = 6$. It represents the conditional expectation, based on the information available at time $t = 4$, of the future values of the Brownian path at times in the interval $[4, 6]$.

If $0 \leq s \leq t \leq u < T$, then the conditional covariance of $Y(u)$ and $Y(t)$ given $\mathcal{F}_s$ is

$$
\begin{aligned}
\mathrm{cov}(Y(t), Y(u) \mid \mathcal{F}_s) &= \mathrm{cov}((T - t)\alpha(t), (T - u)\alpha(u) \mid \mathcal{F}_s) \\
&= (T - t)(T - u)\mathrm{cov}(\alpha(t), \alpha(u) \mid \mathcal{F}_s) \\
&= (T - t)(T - u)\frac{t - s}{(T - t)(T - s)} \\
&= (T - u)\frac{t - s}{T - s}
\end{aligned}
$$

Observe that

$$
\mathrm{var}(Y(t)) = \frac{(T - t)t}{T} \to 0 \text{ as } t \to T
$$

By Itô's lemma, Y is an Itô process on $[0, T)$. We shall show below that Y, unlike α, is in fact an Itô process on $[0, T]$.

On $[0, T)$, the differential of Y is

$$dY(t) = (T - t)\, d\alpha(t) - \alpha(t)\, dt = -\frac{Y(t)}{T - t}\, dt + dW(t) = -\alpha(t)\, dt + dW(t)$$

Hence,

$$Y(t) = -\int_0^t \alpha\, ds + W(t)$$

for $0 \le t < T$. The instantaneous standard deviation of the Brownian bridge is one, and the drift is $-\alpha$.

The variance of the drift $-\alpha$ of the Brownian bridge Y goes to infinity as time approaches T. Why? The instantaneous variance of Y is one, but Y converges to zero with probability one as time approaches T. This means that the drift has to pull Y very strongly towards zero when time is close to T. If the Wiener process pushes Y up above zero, then α has to become very large in order that $-\alpha$ can pull sufficiently toward zero, and if the Wiener process pushes Y down below zero, then, similarly, α has to become very negative. Given that the drift has to accomplish this in a shorter and shorter period of time while the standard deviation of Y stays constant, the variance of the drift has to go to infinity.

Proposition 3.4 Y *is continuous at* $t = T$. *With probability one,* $Y(t) \to 0$ *as* $t \to T$.

Proof Define a function $f : [0, T) \to [0, \infty)$ by

$$f(t) = \mathrm{var}(\alpha(t)) = \frac{1}{T - t} - \frac{1}{T} = \frac{t}{(T - t)T}$$

Since $f(t) \to \infty$ as $t \to T$, $f([0, T)) = [0, \infty)$. Let $g : [0, \infty) \to [0, T)$ be the inverse function:

$$g(s) = f^{-1}(s) = \frac{sT^2}{1 + sT}$$

Then by Proposition 3.2, the process B defined by

$$B(s) = \alpha(g(s))$$

for $0 \le s < T^*$ is a Wiener process relative to the filtration

$$F_g = \left(\mathcal{F}_{g(s)}\right)_{0 \le s \le T^*}$$

and

$$\alpha(t) = B(f(t)) = B\left(\frac{1}{T - t} - \frac{1}{T}\right) = B\left(\frac{t}{(T - t)T}\right)$$

for $0 \le t < T$.

Again since $f(t) \to \infty$ as $t \to T$, it follows from the law of large numbers for Brownian motion (Proposition 1.5) that

$$\frac{(T-t)T}{t}\alpha(t) = \frac{1}{f(t)}B(f(t)) \to 0 \text{ as } t \to T$$

Hence,

$$Y(t) = (T-t)\alpha(t) \to 0 \text{ as } t \to T$$

This shows that Y is continuous at $t = T$. □

The following proposition implies that if we define $\alpha(t)$ arbitrarily for $t = T$, for example by setting $\alpha(T) = 0$, then $\alpha \in \mathcal{L}^1([0,T])$. Hence, the integral

$$\int_0^T \alpha\, dW$$

is well defined, and by continuity, the equation

$$Y(t) = -\int_0^t \alpha\, ds + W(t)$$

holds also for $t = T$. So, Y is an Itô process on $[0,T]$.

Proposition 3.5

$$\int_0^T \frac{|Y(s)|}{T-s}\, ds = \int_0^T |\alpha(s)|\, ds < \infty$$

almost surely.

Proof Observe that

$$\int_0^t \alpha(s)\, ds = -Y(t) + W(t) \to W(T)$$

as $t \to T$, which is a finite limit. But this is not sufficient to show that α belongs to $\mathcal{L}^1([0,T])$.

Now,

$$\int_0^T |\alpha(s)|\, ds = \int_0^T |B(f(s))|\, ds = \int_0^\infty |B(u)||g'(u)|\, du = \int_0^\infty \frac{|B(u)|T^2}{(1+uT)^2}\, du$$

The law of the iterated logarithm applied to the standard Brownian motion B implies that

$$\frac{B(u)}{\sqrt{2u\ln\ln u}} < 2$$

for all sufficiently large u. Since the same is true of the standard Brownian motion $-B$, there exists, with probability one, a (path-dependent) number $U \geq 1$ such that

$$|B(u)| < 2\sqrt{2u \ln \ln u}$$

for all $u \in [U, \infty)$. Hence,

$$\frac{1}{T^2} \int_0^T |\alpha(s)| \, ds = \int_0^\infty \frac{|B(u)|}{(1 + uT)^2} \, du$$

$$\leq \int_0^U \frac{|B(u)|}{(1 + uT)^2} \, du + \int_U^\infty \frac{2\sqrt{2u \ln \ln u}}{(1 + uT)^2} \, du$$

The first term is finite because the integrand is continuous and hence bounded on $[0, U]$.

To show that the second term is finite, recall that we have chosen $U \geq 1$. This implies that for $u \geq U$,

$$2\sqrt{2u \ln \ln u} \leq 2\sqrt{2}\sqrt{u}\sqrt{u} = 2\sqrt{2}u^{3/4}$$

and

$$\frac{2\sqrt{2u \ln \ln u}}{(1 + uT)^2} \leq 2\sqrt{2}\frac{u^{3/4}}{(1 + uT)^2}$$

$$\leq \frac{2\sqrt{2}}{T^{3/4}} \frac{(uT)^{3/4}}{(1 + uT)^2}$$

$$\leq \frac{2\sqrt{2}}{T^{3/4}} \frac{(1 + uT)^{3/4}}{(1 + uT)^2}$$

$$\leq \frac{2\sqrt{2}}{T^{3/4}} (1 + uT)^{-5/4}$$

Hence,

$$\int_U^\infty \frac{2\sqrt{2u \ln \ln u}}{(1 + uT)^2} \, du \leq \frac{2\sqrt{2}}{T^{3/4}} \int_U^\infty (1 + uT)^{-5/4} \, du$$

$$= \frac{2\sqrt{2}}{T^{3/4}} \frac{4}{T} \lim_{s \to \infty} \left[(1 + UT)^{-1/4} - (1 + sT)^{-1/4} \right]$$

$$= \frac{2\sqrt{2}}{T^{3/4}} \frac{4}{T} (1 + UT)^{-1/4}$$

$$< \infty$$

This completes the proof that α belongs to $\mathcal{L}^1([0, T])$.   □

Proposition 3.6 α *does not belong to* $\mathcal{L}^2([0, T])$:

$$\int_0^T \frac{Y(s)^2}{(T - s)^2} \, ds = \int_0^T \alpha(s)^2 \, ds = \infty$$

Proof If it were the case that α did belong to $\mathcal{L}^2([0,T])$, then α^2 would belong to $\mathcal{L}^1([0,T])$, and

$$2\int_0^T \alpha \, dW - \int_0^T \alpha^2 \, ds$$

would be well defined and finite almost surely. However, we shall show that

$$2\int_0^t \alpha \, dW(s) - \int_0^t \alpha^2 \, ds \to -\infty$$

almost surely, as $t \to T$.

Integration by parts (Example 2.16) yields

$$\int_0^t \alpha(s)^2 \, ds = \int_0^t \frac{Y(s)^2}{(T-s)^2} \, ds$$

$$= \frac{Y(t)^2}{T-t} - \frac{Y(0)^2}{T-0} - \int_0^t \frac{1}{T-s} \, dY(s)^2$$

$$= \frac{Y(t)^2}{T-t} - \int_0^t \frac{1}{T-s} \, dY(s)^2$$

By Itô's lemma,

$$dY(t)^2 = dt + 2Y(t) \, dY(t) = dt - 2Y(t)\alpha(t) \, dt + 2Y(t) \, dW(t)$$

Hence,

$$\frac{1}{T-t} \, dY(t)^2 = \frac{1}{T-t} \, dt - 2\alpha(t)^2 \, dt + 2\alpha(t) \, dW(t)$$

and

$$\int_0^t \alpha(s)^2 \, ds = \frac{Y(t)^2}{T-t} - \int_0^t \frac{1}{T-s} \, dY(s)^2$$

$$= \frac{Y(t)^2}{T-t} - \int_0^t \frac{1}{T-s} \, ds + 2\int_0^t \alpha(s)^2 \, ds - 2\int_0^t \alpha(s) \, dW(s)$$

Rearranging terms,

$$2\int_0^t \alpha(s) \, dW(s) - \int_0^t \alpha(s)^2 \, ds = \frac{Y(t)^2}{T-t} - \int_0^t \frac{1}{T-s} \, ds$$

$$= (T-t)\alpha(t)^2 + \ln(T-t) - \ln T$$

It follows from the law of the iterated logarithm that when t is sufficiently large,

$$\alpha(t)^2 = B(f(t))^2 \le 8f(t) \ln \ln f(t) = 8\frac{t}{(T-t)T} \ln \ln f(t)$$

Hence,

$$(T-t)\alpha(t)^2 + \ln(T-t) \le \frac{8t}{T} \ln \ln f(t) - \ln \frac{t}{(T-t)T} + \ln \frac{t}{T}$$

$$= \frac{8t}{T} \left[\ln \ln f(t) - \frac{T}{8t} \ln f(t) \right] + \ln \frac{t}{T}$$

$$\to -\infty$$

as $t \to T$, and so

$$2 \int_0^t \alpha(s) \, dW(s) - \int_0^t \alpha(s)^2 \, ds \to -\infty$$

with probability one, as $t \to T$. $\qquad\square$

3.4 Conditionally Gaussian One-factor Processes

A *conditionally Gaussian one-factor processes* is an Itô process r whose stochastic differential has the form

$$dr = (\alpha - ar) \, dt + \sigma \, dW$$

where α, a, and σ are deterministic processes with $\sigma \in \mathcal{L}^2$ and $a, \alpha \in \mathcal{L}^1$. We shall show that such a process is indeed conditionally Gaussian.

Given the deterministic process $a \in \mathcal{L}^1$, let K denote its integral process

$$K(t) = \int_0^t a \, ds$$

(which is, of course, also deterministic).

Proposition 3.7 *Let* α, a, *and* σ *be deterministic processes with* $\sigma \in \mathcal{L}^2$, $a, \alpha \in \mathcal{L}^1$, *and let* r_0 *be a random variable, measurable with respect to* $\mathcal{F}_0$. *There exists a unique Itô process* r *such that*

$$dr = (\alpha - ar) \, dt + \sigma \, dW$$

and $r(0) = r_0$. *It is given by*

$$r(t) = e^{-K(t)} \left[r_0 + \int_0^t e^K \alpha \, ds + \int_0^t e^K \sigma \, dW \right]$$

Proof If r is a process which solves the stochastic differential equation, then

$$d\left(e^K r\right) = e^K \, dr + r e^K a \, dt$$
$$= e^K (\alpha - ar) \, dt + e^K \sigma \, dW + r e^K a \, dt$$
$$= e^K (\alpha \, dt + \sigma \, dW)$$

which implies

$$e^{K(t)} r(t) - r(0) = \int_0^t e^K \alpha \, ds + \int_0^t e^K \sigma \, dW$$

If, in addition, $r(0) = r_0$, then

$$r(t) = e^{-K(t)} \left[r_0 + \int_0^t e^K \alpha \, ds + \int_0^t e^K \sigma \, dW \right]$$

Conversely, this process has $r(0) = r_0$ and satisfies

$$e^K (\alpha \, dt + \sigma \, dW) = d(e^K r) = e^K \, dr + r e^K a \, dt$$

which implies

$$\alpha \, dt + \sigma \, dW = dr + r a \, dt$$

and

$$dr = (\alpha - ar) \, dt + \sigma \, dW$$

So, the process r solves the stochastic differential equation.   □

For $0 \le s \le t$, we can express $r(t)$ on the basis of $r(s)$ as follows. From

$$e^{K(t)} r(t) = r(0) + \int_0^t e^K \alpha \, du + \int_0^t e^K \sigma \, dW$$

we find

$$e^{K(t)} r(t) - e^{K(s)} r(s) = \int_s^t e^K \alpha \, du + \int_s^t e^K \sigma \, dW$$

and

$$r(t) = e^{-K(t)} \left[e^{K(s)} r(s) + \int_s^t e^K \alpha \, du + \int_s^t e^K \sigma \, dW \right]$$

This expression for $r(t)$ contains useful information about the conditional distribution of $r(t)$ given $\mathcal{F}_s$. By Theorem 3.1, the integral

$$\int_s^t e^K \sigma \, dW$$

is independent of $\mathcal{F}_s$ and is normally distributed with mean zero and variance

$$\int_s^t e^{2K} \sigma^2 \, du$$

So, given information at time s, $r(t)$ is normally distributed with conditional mean

$$E(r(t) \mid \mathcal{F}_s) = e^{-K(t)} \left[e^{K(s)} r(s) + \int_s^t e^K \alpha \, du \right]$$

and conditional variance

$$\mathrm{var}(r(t) \mid \mathcal{F}_s) = e^{-2K(t)} \int_s^t e^{2K} \sigma^2 \, du$$

Not only are individual future observations of r normally distributed given current information, but the same is true of finite-dimensional future samples. In other words, the process r is conditionally Gaussian. To see this, let

$$0 \leq s = t_0 < t_1 < \cdots < t_n$$

According to Theorem 3.1, the vector

$$\left(\int_s^{t_1} e^K \sigma \, dW, \ldots, \int_s^{t_n} e^K \sigma \, dW \right)$$

is normally distributed and independent of $\mathcal{F}_s$. This implies that the conditional distribution of the sample vector

$$(r(t_1), r(t_2), \ldots, r(t_n))$$

given $\mathcal{F}_s$ is an n-dimensional normal distribution. Hence, r is conditionally Gaussian.

To characterize the conditional distribution of the sample vector, it suffices to know the conditional mean function

$$E(r(t) \mid \mathcal{F}_s) = e^{-K(t)+K(s)} r(s) + e^{-K(t)} \int_s^t e^K \alpha \, du$$

which was calculated above, and the conditional covariance function

$$\text{cov}(r(t), r(u) \mid \mathcal{F}_s)$$

$0 \leq s \leq t \leq u$, which we shall calculate now.

Observe that if $0 \leq s \leq t \leq u$, then the level $r(t)$ and the integral

$$\int_t^u e^K \sigma \, dW$$

have zero conditional covariance given $\mathcal{F}_s$:

$$\text{cov}\left(r(t), \int_t^u e^K \sigma \, dW \;\Big|\; \mathcal{F}_s \right) = E\left[r(t) \int_t^u e^K \sigma \, dW \;\Big|\; \mathcal{F}_s \right]$$

$$= E\left\{ E\left[r(t) \int_t^u e^K \sigma \, dW \;\Big|\; \mathcal{F}_t \right] \;\Big|\; \mathcal{F}_s \right\}$$

$$= E\left\{ r(t) E\left[\int_t^u e^K \sigma \, dW \;\Big|\; \mathcal{F}_t \right] \;\Big|\; \mathcal{F}_s \right\}$$

$$= 0$$

Hence,

$$\text{cov}(r(t), r(u) \mid \mathcal{F}_s) = \text{cov}\left(r(t), e^{-K(u)+K(t)} r(t) \mid \mathcal{F}_s \right)$$

$$+ \operatorname{cov}\left(r(t), e^{-K(u)} \int_t^u e^K \sigma\, dW \mid \mathcal{F}_s\right)$$

$$= e^{-K(u)+K(t)} \operatorname{var}(r(t) \mid \mathcal{F}_s)$$

$$= e^{-K(u)+K(t)} e^{-2K(t)} \int_s^t e^{2K} \sigma^2\, dv$$

$$= e^{-K(u)-K(t)} \int_s^t e^{2K} \sigma^2\, dv$$

The process r is *Markovian*, which means that if

$$0 \le s = t_0 < t_1 < \cdots < t_n$$

then the conditional distribution of the sample vector

$$(r(t_1), r(t_2), \ldots, r(t_n))$$

given $\mathcal{F}_s$ is the same as the conditional distribution given $r(s)$. In other words, the conditional distribution is a "function" of $r(s)$. The conditional distribution is random in the sense that it depends on information at time s; but the only relevant part of that information is the level $r(s)$ of the process itself at time s.

Let $0 \le t$. If r_0 is integrable, then r is integrable, and the unconditional mean of $r(t)$ is

$$E(r(t)) = E[E(r(t) \mid \mathcal{F}_0)] = e^{-K(t)}\left[Er_0 + \int_0^t e^K \alpha\, du\right]$$

If r_0 is square integrable, then r is square integrable, and the unconditional variance of $r(t)$ is

$$\operatorname{var}(r(t)) = e^{-2K(t)}\left[\operatorname{var}(r_0) + \int_0^t e^{2K} \sigma^2\, du\right]$$

If $0 \le s \le t$, then the unconditional covariance between $r(s)$ and $r(t)$ is

$$\operatorname{cov}(r(s), r(t)) = \operatorname{cov}\left(r(s), e^{-K(t)+K(s)} r(s)\right)$$

$$+ \operatorname{cov}\left(r(s), e^{-K(t)} \int_s^t e^K \sigma\, dW\right)$$

$$= e^{-K(t)+K(s)} \operatorname{var}(r(s)))$$

$$= e^{-K(t)-K(s)}\left[\operatorname{var}(r_0) + \int_0^s e^{2K} \sigma^2\, du\right]$$

If r_0 is normally distributed, then the process is (unconditionally) *Gaussian*. The (unconditional) distribution of every sample can be computed on the basis of the (unconditional) mean function $Er(t)$ and the (unconditional) covariance function $\operatorname{cov}(r(s), r(t))$.

3.5 Ornstein–Uhlenbeck Processes

Assume that α, a, and σ are deterministic constants. Assume without loss of generality that W is a one-dimensional Wiener process relative to F.

If $a = 0$, then the equation

$$dr = (\alpha - ar)\, dt + \sigma\, dW$$

reduces to

$$dr = \alpha\, dt + \sigma\, dW$$

whose solution is the generalized Wiener process

$$r(t) = r_0 + \alpha t + \sigma W(t)$$

Assume for the remainder of this section that $a \neq 0$. We can reparameterize the equation by setting

$$b = \frac{\alpha}{a}$$

so that

$$\alpha - ar = a(b - r)$$

The function K and related expressions from the previous section can be calculated as follows:

$$K(s) = as$$

$$\alpha = ab$$

$$e^{-K(s)} r(0) = e^{-as} r(0)$$

$$e^{-K(s)} \int_0^s e^K \alpha\, du = e^{-as} \int_0^s e^{au} ab\, dW$$

$$= e^{-as} \left[e^{au} \right]_0^s b$$

$$= e^{-as} \left(e^{as} - 1 \right) b$$

$$= \left(1 - e^{-as} \right) b$$

and

$$e^{-K(s)} \int_0^s e^K \sigma\, dW = e^{-as} \int_0^s e^{au} \sigma\, dW$$

Proposition 3.8 *Let a, b, and σ be constants, and let r_0 be a random variable which is measurable with respect to $\mathcal{F}_0$. The process*

$$r(t) = e^{-at} r_0 + \left(1 - e^{-at} \right) b + \sigma e^{-at} \int_0^t e^{au}\, dW(u)$$

is the unique Itô process r such that

$$dr = a(b - r)\, dt + \sigma\, dW$$

and $r(0) = r_0$.

Proof Follows directly from Proposition 3.7.   □

Processes like the one in Proposition 3.8, with $a > 0$, are often used in finance to model the dynamics of interest rates (in the Vasicek model of the term structure of interest rates). We shall call them *Ornstein–Uhlenbeck processes*, although in part of the literature this term is reserved for the case where $b = 0$ and r_0 is deterministic.

Under the assumption that $a > 0$, the drift term $a(b-r)$ is positive whenever $b > r$ and negative when $b < r$, and more so if a is large. In this sense, the process has a tendency to drift toward b. The parameter b will be called the *mean reversion level*. The parameter a may be interpreted as a *speed of adjustment*.

For $0 \leq s \leq t$, we can express $r(t)$ in terms of $r(s)$ as follows:

$$r(t) = e^{-a(t-s)}r(s) + (1 - e^{-a(t-s)})b + \sigma e^{-at} \int_s^t e^{au}\, dW(u)$$

By Theorem 3.1,

$$\sigma e^{-at} \int_s^t e^{au}\, dW(u)$$

is independent of $\mathcal{F}_s$ and is normally distributed with mean zero and variance

$$\sigma^2 e^{-2at} \int_s^t e^{2au}\, du = e^{-2at}\frac{\sigma^2}{2a}(e^{2at} - e^{2as})$$

$$= \frac{\sigma^2}{2a}(1 - e^{-2a(t-s)})$$

So, given information at time s, $r(t)$ is normally distributed with conditional mean

$$E(r(t) \mid \mathcal{F}_s) = e^{-a(t-s)}r(s) + (1 - e^{-a(t-s)})b$$

and conditional variance

$$\text{var}(r(t) \mid \mathcal{F}_s) = \frac{\sigma^2}{2a}(1 - e^{-2a(t-s)})$$

If $0 \leq s \leq t$, then

$$E(r(t) \mid \mathcal{F}_s) = e^{-a(t-s)}r(s) + (1 - e^{-a(t-s)})b \to b$$

and

$$\text{var}(r(t) \mid \mathcal{F}_s) = \frac{\sigma^2}{2a}(1 - e^{-2a(t-s)}) \to \frac{\sigma^2}{2a}$$

as $t \to \infty$.

In the long run, the process forgets where it started at time s. It reverts toward the long-run mean b, with a finite long-run variance around it. The larger the speed-of-adjustment parameter a (and the smaller the dispersion coefficient σ), the less is the variance around b in the long run.

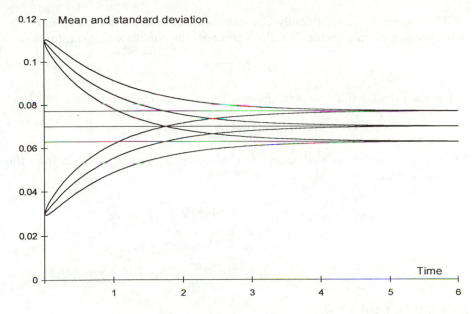

FIG. 3.2. Mean and standard deviation of forecast

Notice that the behavior of an Ornstein–Uhlenbeck process differs markedly from that of a generalized Wiener process. Today's conditional mean of the value at a future point in time of a generalized Wiener process with positive drift goes to infinity as that future time goes to infinity. The conditional variance also goes to infinity. The conditional mean of an Ornstein–Uhlenbeck process converges to b because of the mean reversion phenomenon. In the long run, the value of the Ornstein–Uhlenbeck process will not be too far away from b, also because of mean reversion. This is why the conditional variance converges to a finite long-run variance.

Figure 3.2 illustrates the means and standard deviations of the process r conditional on two different initial values, $r(0) = 0.03$ and $r(0) = 0.11$. Time, t, is on the horizontal axis, and the mean value of the process is measured along the vertical axis. The speed of adjustment is $a = 1$, the long-run mean is $b = 0.07$, and the volatility parameter is $\sigma = 0.01$. The three horizontal lines show the long-run mean and the long-run mean plus or minus one standard deviation. The three curves starting at $r(0) = 0.03$ show the expectation of $r(t)$ as a function of time t, as well as the expectation plus or minus one standard deviation. These expectations and standard deviations are calculated at time $t = 0$ and are conditional on the process being at $r(0) = 0.03$ at that time. Similarly, the three curves starting at $r(0) = 0.11$ show the expectation of r and the expectation plus or minus one standard deviation, conditional on the process being at $r(0) = 0.11$ at time $t = 0$.

The process r is conditionally Gaussian. To characterize the conditional distribution of a sample vector, it suffices to know the conditional mean function

$$E(r(t) \mid \mathcal{F}_s)$$

which was calculated above, and the conditional covariance function

$$\operatorname{cov}(r(t), r(u) \mid \mathcal{F}_s)$$

$0 \leq s \leq t \leq u$, which we shall calculate now, using the general formula from the previous section:

$$\begin{aligned}
\operatorname{cov}(r(t), r(u) \mid \mathcal{F}_s) &= e^{-K(u)-K(t)} \int_s^t e^{2K} \sigma^2 \, dv \\
&= e^{-a(u-t)} \operatorname{var}(r(t) \mid \mathcal{F}_s) \\
&= e^{-a(u-t)} \frac{\sigma^2}{2a} \left(1 - e^{-2a(t-s)}\right)
\end{aligned}$$

Note that for fixed $h \geq 0$,

$$\operatorname{cov}(r(t), r(t+h) \mid \mathcal{F}_s) = e^{-ah} \frac{\sigma^2}{2a} (1 - e^{-2a(t-s)}) \to e^{-ah} \frac{\sigma^2}{2a}$$

as $t \to \infty$. If you stand today at time s and calculate the conditional covariance of the values of r at two future dates that differ by a fixed length of time h, then this covariance converges to a finite number as the two dates are pushed into the distant future. The limit equals e^{-ah} times the long-run variance.

The process r is Markovian.

Let

$$0 \leq s = t_0 < t_1 < \cdots < t_N$$

For $n = 1, \ldots, N$, set

$$c_n = \left(1 - e^{-a(t_n - t_{n-1})}\right) b$$

$$\phi_n = e^{-a(t_n - t_{n-1})}$$

$$\epsilon_n = \sigma e^{-a t_n} \int_{t_{n-1}}^{t_n} e^{au} \, dW(u)$$

and

$$v_n = \frac{\sigma^2}{2a} \left(1 - e^{-2a(t_n - t_{n-1})}\right)$$

Then ϵ_n is a sequence of independent normally distributed random variables. Each variable ϵ_n is independent also of $\mathcal{F}_s$ for $s \leq t_{n-1}$ and it has mean zero and variance v_n. When sampled at the discrete times t_n, the process r has the following recursive structure:

$$r(t_n) = c_n + \phi_n r(t_{n-1}) + \epsilon_n$$

In particular, if the observations are equally spaced,

$$t_n - t_{n-1} = \tau$$

for all n, then c_n, ϕ_n, and v_n are independent of n:

$$c_n = c = (1 - e^{-a\tau})b$$

$$\phi_n = \phi = e^{-a\tau}$$

and

$$v_n = v = \frac{\sigma^2}{2a}(1 - e^{-2a\tau})$$

Now ϵ_n is a sequence of independent identically normally distributed random variables, independent also of $\mathcal{F}_s$, with mean zero and variance v, and

$$r(t_n) = c + \phi r(t_{n-1}) + \epsilon_n$$

This is an *autoregressive process of order one* or an AR(1) process.

We can use this autoregressive representation of the process r to plot some sample paths.

Figure 3.3 shows six sample paths of the process r. Time, t, is on the horizontal axis, and the values of the process are measured along the vertical axis. Three of the paths are conditional on the initial value $r(0) = 0.03$, and three are conditional on the initial value $r(0) = 0.11$. As in Fig. 3.2 the speed of adjustment is $a = 1$, the long-run mean is $b = 0.07$, and the volatility parameter is $\sigma = 0.01$. The three horizontal lines show the long-run mean and the long-run mean plus minus one standard deviation.

It is not really possible to draw sample paths of the process r exactly. The picture has to be an approximation. The sample paths in Fig. 3.3 have been generated in the following manner. For each of them, I first generated 180 independent standard normally distributed numbers, using a random number generator. Then I set $\tau = 1/30$ in order to simulate increments of the process over time intervals of length $1/30$. I then calculated the parameters c, ϕ, and v in the autoregressive representation, and multiplied my random numbers by the square root of v in order to generate the sequence ϵ_n. Finally, I calculated and plotted the sequence r_n.

If r_0 is integrable, then so is $r(t)$ for $0 \le t$, and the unconditional mean of $r(t)$ is

$$E(r(t)) = E[E(r(t) \mid \mathcal{F}_0)]$$

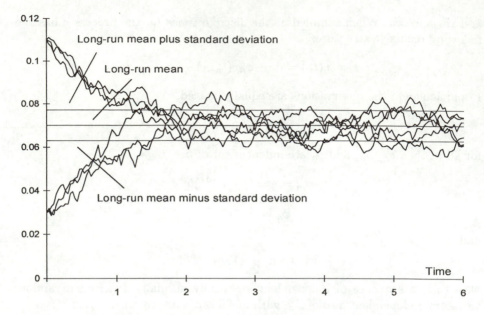

FIG. 3.3. Sample paths and long-run parameters

$$= E\left[e^{-at}Er_0 + \left(1 - e^{-at}\right)b\right]$$
$$= e^{-at}Er_0 + \left(1 - e^{-at}\right)b$$

If r_0 is square integrable, then so is $r(t)$ for $0 \le t$, and the unconditional variance is

$$\operatorname{var}(r(t)) = \operatorname{var}(e^{-at}r_0) + \operatorname{var}\left(\sigma e^{-at}\int_0^t e^{au}\, dW(u)\right)$$

$$= e^{-2at}\operatorname{var}(r_0) + \frac{\sigma^2}{2a}\left(1 - e^{-2at}\right)$$

If $0 \le s \le t$, then the unconditional covariance is

$$\operatorname{cov}(r(s), r(t)) = \operatorname{cov}\left(r(s), e^{-a(t-s)}r(s)\right)$$

$$+ \operatorname{cov}\left(r(s), \sigma e^{-at}\int_s^t e^{au}\, dW(u)\right)$$

$$= e^{-a(t-s)}\operatorname{var}(r(s))$$

$$= e^{-a(t-s)}\left(e^{-2as}\operatorname{var}(r_0) + \frac{\sigma^2}{2a}\left(1 - e^{-2as}\right)\right)$$

In particular, if $r(0)$ has mean

$$Er(0) = b$$

and variance

$$\mathrm{var}(r_0) = \frac{\sigma^2}{2a}$$

then

$$E(r(t)) = e^{-at}b + \left(1 - e^{-at}\right)b = b$$

$$\mathrm{var}(r(t)) = e^{-2at}\frac{\sigma^2}{2a} + \frac{\sigma^2}{2a}(1 - e^{-2at}) = \frac{\sigma^2}{2a}$$

and if $0 \le s \le t$, then

$$\mathrm{cov}(r(s), r(t)) = e^{-a(t-s)}\left(e^{-2as}\frac{\sigma^2}{2a} + \frac{\sigma^2}{2a}\left(1 - e^{-2as}\right)\right) = e^{-a(t-s)}\frac{\sigma^2}{2a}$$

If r_0 is normally distributed, then the process is unconditionally Gaussian. The unconditional distribution of every sample can be computed on the basis of the unconditional mean function $E(r(t))$ and the unconditional covariance function $\mathrm{cov}(r(t), r(u))$ which were calculated above. In particular, if r_0 is normally distributed with mean

$$Er_0 = b$$

and variance

$$\mathrm{var}(r_0) = \frac{\sigma^2}{2a}$$

then the process r is *stationary*. This means that if

$$0 = t_0 \le t_1 \le \cdots \le t_n$$

then the (unconditional) distribution of the sample vector

$$(r(t_1 + h), r(t_2 + h), \ldots, r(t_n + h))$$

is independent of $h \ge 0$. Indeed, it is an n-dimensional normal distribution whose elements all have mean b and variance $\sigma^2/2a$, and where the covariance between $r(t_i)$ and $r(t_j)$ is

$$\mathrm{cov}(r(t_i), r(t_j)) = \frac{\sigma^2}{2a}e^{-a(t_j - t_i)}$$

for $0 \le i \le j \le n$.

Let r be an Ornstein–Uhlenbeck process with initial value r_0 and differential

$$dr = a(b - r)\,dt + \sigma\,dW$$

If c is a constant, then $r + c$ is an Ornstein–Uhlenbeck process with initial value $r_0 + c$ and differential

$$d(r + c) = a[(b + c) - (r + c)]\,dt + \sigma\,dW$$

and cr is an Ornstein–Uhlenbeck process with initial value cr_0 and differential

$$d(cr) = a(cb - cr)\,dt + c\sigma\,dW$$

If $\tilde{r}$ is another Ornstein–Uhlenbeck process, driven by the same Wiener process W, with initial value $\tilde{r}_0$ and differential

$$d\tilde{r} = \tilde{a}(\tilde{b} - \tilde{r})\,dt + \tilde{\sigma}\,dW$$

and if $\tilde{a} = a$, then $r + \tilde{r}$ is an Ornstein–Uhlenbeck process with initial value $r_0 + \tilde{r}_0$ and differential

$$d(r + \tilde{r}) = a[(b + \tilde{b}) - (r + \tilde{r})]\,dt + (\sigma + \tilde{\sigma})\,dW$$

3.6   Summary

In this chapter, we have studied some examples of processes that are Gaussian or conditionally Gaussian. A process is said to be Gaussian if the distribution of every sample matrix is normal; and it is said to be conditionally Gaussian if the conditional distribution of every sample matrix is normal.

If the integrand process in a stochastic integral is a deterministic function of time, then the integral process is Gaussian and conditionally Gaussian. The integral over a time interval is independent of all information available at the beginning of the time interval. It has conditional mean zero, and we know how to calculate the conditional variance or the conditional covariance matrix. Hence, we know the conditional distribution of any sample matrix of the integral exactly.

If a stochastic integral is one dimensional, and if the instantaneous variance (but not necessarily the integrand process itself) is a deterministic function of time, then the integral is again Gaussian and conditionally Gaussian. Specifically, it can be seen as a Wiener process observed in time units different from the ordinary calendar time. As before, the integral over a time interval is independent of all information available at the beginning of the time interval, it has mean zero, and its variance is the integral of the instantaneous variance. This information suffices to characterize the distribution of any sample vector exactly.

Alternatively, a one-dimensional stochastic integral with deterministic instantaneous variance can be written as a stochastic integral of a deterministic process with respect to a one-dimensional Wiener process. This Wiener process is constructed by essentially normalizing the original stochastic integral so as to have instantaneous variance one.

Our first example of a Gaussian process was a so-called Brownian bridge. It is a one-dimensional Itô process defined on a finite time interval, it starts at zero, and it finishes at zero for sure. It is both Gaussian and conditionally Gaussian. The dispersion coefficient is the constant one. The drift is itself a Gaussian and conditionally Gaussian process, whose variance is finite on the interior of the time interval but goes to infinity as time approaches the right end-point. We showed that the drift process does not satisfy the integrability condition that is required in order to integrate it with respect to the Wiener process. The reason for this behavior of the drift is that it has to be highly variable close to the right end-point of the time interval in order to pull the Brownian bridge process back to zero with probability one.

Ball and Torous [5, 1983] suggested a price process for a zero-coupon bond which is constructed on the basis of a Brownian bridge. Over the life of the bond, its price increases by a factor which is the exponential of a linear function of time plus a constant times a Brownian bridge. This price process has the property that it equals the face value of the bond at maturity.

A conditionally Gaussian one-factor process is a one-dimensional Itô process whose dispersion is deterministic and whose drift is an affine function of the level of the process, with deterministic coefficients. Such a process will be used to describe the interest rate in the extended Vasicek or general Hull and White model of the term structure of interest rates.

A conditionally Gaussian one-factor process is Markovian. As the name suggests, it is also conditionally Gaussian. If the initial value of the process is normally distributed, then the process is (unconditionally) Gaussian. We calculated the conditional and unconditional mean functions and the conditional and unconditional covariance functions.

An Ornstein–Uhlenbeck process is a conditionally Gaussian one-factor process whose dispersion is constant and whose drift is a positive constant times the difference between a constant long-run mean and the current level of the process. Such a process is mean reverting in the sense that when the current level of the process is below the long-run mean, its drift will be positive, and when the current level is above the long-run mean, the drift will be negative. The strength of this effect is governed by the positive multiplicative constant in the drift term, which is interpreted as a speed of adjustment.

Ornstein–Uhlenbeck processes will be used to describe the interest rate in the Vasicek model of the term structure of interest rates.

Given current information, the conditional mean of the value of the process sometime in the near future will be close to the current value, whereas the conditional mean of the value of the process in the distant future approaches the long-run mean. The conditional covariance of the values of the process at two future dates is the same as the conditional variance of the value on the nearest of those dates. As that date recedes into the distant future, the conditional variance converges to a long-run variance which is proportional to the instantaneous variance and inversely proportional to the speed of adjustment.

If an Ornstein–Uhlenbeck process is sampled at a sequence of equidistant points in time, then it becomes an autoregressive process of order one.

If the initial value of an Ornstein–Uhlenbeck process is normally distributed, then the process is Gaussian. If, in addition, the mean and variance of the initial value equal the long-run mean and the long-run variance of the process, then the process is stationary.

3.7   (*) Notes

Cheng [16, 1991] shows that the process α which we have used in the definition of the Brownian bridge does not belong to $\mathcal{L}^2([0,T])$, on the implicit assumption that it does belong to $\mathcal{L}^1([0,T])$.

Rogers [78, 1995] was a useful source for the analysis of the conditionally Gaussian one-factor processes.

It appears that Uhlenbeck and Ornstein [86, 1930] proposed their process as a model of the physical phenomenon of Brownian motion. Ornstein–Uhlenbeck processes were introduced in finance by Vasicek [87, 1977].

An Ornstein–Uhlenbeck process with $a > 0$ and $b = 0$ is also called an *elastic random walk*. The corresponding stochastic differential equation,

$$dr(t) = -ar(t)\,dt + \sigma\,dW(t)$$

is called the *Langevin equation*. In physics, it describes the movement of a particle which is subject to friction.

4

SECURITIES AND TRADING STRATEGIES

This and the following chapter develop the theory of valuation and replication of contingent claims in continuous-time dynamic models, with an emphasis on the case of dynamically complete markets.

We focus on the pricing and replication of contingent claims that pay a random payoff at a fixed future point in time but do not pay dividends before that time. Zero-coupon bonds, forward contracts, and European-style options are examples of such claims. They are replicated by self-financing trading strategies.

The story starts with a number of basic securities which are traded in the market. Traders initially buy a position in these securities, revise their holdings dynamically over time through trading, and end up with a random payoff equal to the value of their holdings at some future time. By trading back and forth in response to new information that they receive, they can make their payoff highly contingent on the state of the world, even if there is only a moderate number of basic securities.

In order to calculate the values of contingent claims, we first identify a so-called state price process. Its drift is minus the interest rate, and its dispersion is minus the vector of so-called prices of risk. A state price process has the property that the value process of a trading strategy, multiplied by the state price process, is an Itô process with zero drift.

As we shall see in the next chapter, many models have dynamically complete markets, which means that the payoff to virtually any contingent claim can be replicated by an admissible trading strategy. In this case, we can use the martingale property of the state price process to compute the value process of the trading strategy, and, hence, the value process of the claim. It simply comes down to computing the conditional expectation of the state price process multiplied by the payoff to the claim. This is the martingale valuation principle.

An arbitrage strategy is a trading strategy which creates value out of nothing. It is important to recognize that arbitrage strategies do exist, even in a model as simple as the Black–Scholes model. This implies that it may be possible to replicate a contingent claim by two different trading strategies with different value processes. However, if we consider only trading strategies that are admissible, then this problem goes away. A trading strategy is said to be admissible if its value multiplied by the state price process is not only an Itô process with zero drift but a martingale.

It is often useful to change the unit of account in which the prices of basic securities and the values of contingent claims are expressed. This may change the state price process, but the class of admissible trading strategies will not change.

The securities market lives on a time interval $\mathcal{T}$ which may be either bounded or unbounded, $\mathcal{T} = [0, T]$ or $\mathcal{T} = [0, \infty)$. Uncertainty is represented by an underlying probability space $(\Omega, \mathcal{F}, P)$, which is assumed to be complete. The probability measure P represents the common probability beliefs held by all investors or traders. The arrival of information is represented by an augmented filtration $F = \{\mathcal{F}_t\}_{t \in \mathcal{T}}$. This information structure allows the investors or traders to observe a K-dimensional process W, which is defined on $(\Omega, \mathcal{F}, P)$ and $\mathcal{T}$ and is a Wiener process relative to F.

4.1 Elements of the Model

There are $N + 1$ basic long-lived securities. Their prices per unit (or per share) are given by the basic securities *price process*. It is an $(N + 1)$-dimensional Itô process $\bar{S}$:

$$\bar{S}(t) = \bar{S}(0) + \int_0^t \bar{\mu}\, ds + \int_0^t \bar{\sigma}\, dW$$

where $\bar{\mu}$ is a vector process in $\mathcal{L}^1$ of dimension $N + 1$ and $\bar{\sigma}$ is a matrix-valued process in $\mathcal{L}^2$ of dimension $(N + 1) \times K$. In differential form,

$$d\bar{S} = \bar{\mu}\, dt + \bar{\sigma}\, dW$$

Example 4.1 *Continuation of Examples 1.7, 1.15, 2.3, 2.14, 2.20, and 2.28.* In the Black–Scholes model, there is a money market account and one stock. Prices are given by

$$\bar{S} = \begin{pmatrix} M \\ S \end{pmatrix}$$

where

$$dM = Mr\, dt$$

and

$$dS = S\mu\, dt + S\sigma\, dW$$

so that

$$d\bar{S} = \begin{pmatrix} dM \\ dS \end{pmatrix} = \begin{pmatrix} Mr \\ S\mu \end{pmatrix} dt + \begin{pmatrix} 0 \\ S\sigma \end{pmatrix} dW$$

Hence,

$$\bar{\mu} = \begin{pmatrix} Mr \\ S\mu \end{pmatrix}$$

and

$$\bar{\sigma} = \begin{pmatrix} 0 \\ S\sigma \end{pmatrix}$$

□

We do not at this point make any assumption that the basic securities prices are positive. Such an assumption would be fairly harmless, although it would rule out forward contracts and swaps as basic securities. However, it would not do much to simplify the theory either.

A *trading strategy* is an adapted, measurable $(N+1)$-dimensional row-vector-valued process $\bar{\Delta}$. The interpretation is that $\bar{\Delta}(t)$ is the position held at time t: at each state of the world ω, and for each security $n = 0, \ldots, N$, $\bar{\Delta}_n(\omega, t)$ is the number of units of security n held in that state.

The *value process* of a trading strategy $\bar{\Delta}$ in the price system $\bar{S}$ is the process

$$\bar{\Delta}\bar{S} = \bar{\Delta}_0 \bar{S}_0 + \cdots + \bar{\Delta}_N \bar{S}_N$$

The set of trading strategies $\bar{\Delta}$ such that $\bar{\Delta}\bar{\mu} \in \mathcal{L}^1$ and $\bar{\Delta}\bar{\sigma} \in \mathcal{L}^2$ will be denoted by $\mathcal{L}(\bar{S})$.

If $\bar{\Delta}$ is a trading strategy in $\mathcal{L}(\bar{S})$, then the *cumulative gains process* of $\bar{\Delta}$ (with respect to $\bar{S}$) is the process $\mathcal{G}(\bar{\Delta}; \bar{S})$ defined by

$$\mathcal{G}(\bar{\Delta}; \bar{S})(t) = \bar{\Delta}(0)\bar{S}(0) + \int_0^t \bar{\Delta}\, d\bar{S}$$

$$= \bar{\Delta}(0)\bar{S}(0) + \int_0^t \bar{\Delta}\bar{\mu}\, ds + \int_0^t \bar{\Delta}\bar{\sigma}\, dW$$

for all $t \in \mathcal{T}$. This definition of the cumulative gains process presumes that the basic long-lived securities do not pay dividends. It says that the cumulative gains equal the initial value of the trading strategy plus the sum (integral) of capital gains and losses made over the instants in the intervening time interval.

The trading strategies in $\mathcal{L}(\bar{S})$ are exactly those adapted measurable processes for which the stochastic integral in the definition of the cumulative gains process is well defined.

Expressed in differential form,

$$d\mathcal{G}(\bar{\Delta}; \bar{S}) = \bar{\Delta}\, d\bar{S} = \bar{\Delta}_0\, d\bar{S}_0 + \cdots + \bar{\Delta}_N\, d\bar{S}_N$$

This means that the instantaneous gain during an instant of time equals the sum over the various securities of the number of shares you hold of that security times the instantaneous change in the price of the security.

A trading strategy $\bar{\Delta}$ in $\mathcal{L}(\bar{S})$ is *self-financing* if it satisfies the *instantaneous budget constraint*:

$$\bar{\Delta}\bar{S} = \mathcal{G}(\bar{\Delta}; \bar{S})$$

which is equivalent to the *intertemporal budget constraint*:

$$\bar{\Delta}(t)\bar{S}(t) = \bar{\Delta}(0)\bar{S}(0) + \int_0^t \bar{\Delta}\, d\bar{S}$$

for all t. The budget constraint is to be understood to say that the value process and the cumulative gains process are indistinguishable. Expressed in differential form, $\bar{\Delta}$ is self-financing if and only if

$$d\left(\bar{\Delta}\bar{S}\right) = \bar{\Delta}\,d\bar{S}$$

In interpreting the budget constraint, it is useful to imagine that securities trading happens in a securities account dedicated to that purpose. After the initial investment of $\bar{\Delta}(0)\bar{S}(0)$ into the account, all new purchases of securities are financed by sales of other securities inside the account, there is no net new investment or withdrawal from the securities account, and all changes in the value of the holdings come about because of capital gains and losses.

Note that the value process of a self-financing trading strategy is an Itô process (even though the trading strategy itself is not an Itô process). On the other hand, if a trading strategy is not self-financing, then its value process will not in general be an Itô process. In particular, it may not be a continuous process. If, for example, money is taken out of the securities account or invested in the account at discrete dates, then the value of the account will jump down or up on those dates.

Changes in the value of the securities account arise only from changes in prices of the securities, not from net new investments or withdrawals.

A *buy-and-hold strategy* is a trading strategy $\bar{\Delta}$ which is constant. Every buy-and-hold strategy is in $\mathcal{L}(\bar{S})$, so that the budget constraint is well defined, and every buy-and-hold strategy is self-financing.

Example 4.2 *Continuation of Examples 1.7, 1.15, 2.3, 2.14, 2.20, 2.28, and 4.1.* Whether a trading strategy is self-financing is not only a question of its value process. It is possible that two trading strategies have the same value process, and yet one is self-financing while the other is not.

In the Black–Scholes model of Example 4.1, consider the trading strategies

$$\bar{\Delta} = \left(\frac{S}{M}, 0\right)$$

and

$$\bar{\Theta} = (0, 1)$$

The trading strategy $\bar{\Delta}$ involves holding S/M units of the money market account and no stock, while $\bar{\Theta}$ is a buy-and-hold strategy which consists in holding one unit of stock. They have the same value process, since

$$\bar{\Delta}\bar{S} = \left(\frac{S}{M}, 0\right)\bar{S} = \frac{S}{M}M + 0 \cdot S = S$$

and

$$\bar{\Theta}\bar{S} = (0, 1)\bar{S} = 0 \cdot M + 1 \cdot S = S$$

The trading strategy $\bar{\Theta}$ is self-financing since it is a buy-and-hold strategy. The trading strategy $\bar{\Delta}$ is not self-financing, since

$$\bar{\Delta}\,d\bar{S} = \left(\frac{S}{M}, 0\right)\begin{pmatrix} rM \\ S\mu \end{pmatrix} dt + \left(\frac{S}{M}, 0\right)\begin{pmatrix} 0 \\ S\sigma \end{pmatrix} dW$$

$$= Sr\,dt + 0\,dW$$
$$\neq S\mu\,dt + S\sigma\,dW$$
$$= d\left(\bar{\Delta}\bar{S}\right)$$

□

If $\bar{\Delta}$ is a trading strategy in $\mathcal{L}(\bar{S})$ which is not necessarily self-financing, then the *cumulative dividend process* or the *cumulative net withdrawal process* of $\bar{\Delta}$ in the price system $\bar{S}$ is the process $\mathcal{D}(\bar{\Delta};\bar{S})$ defined by

$$\bar{\Delta}\bar{S} + \mathcal{D}(\bar{\Delta};\bar{S}) = \mathcal{G}(\bar{\Delta};\bar{S})$$

or

$$\bar{\Delta}(t)\bar{S}(t) + \mathcal{D}(\bar{\Delta};\bar{S})(t) - \bar{\Delta}(0)\bar{S}(0) = \int_0^t \bar{\Delta}\,d\bar{S}$$

Note that $\mathcal{D}(\bar{\Delta};\bar{S})(0) = 0$, $\mathcal{D}(\bar{\Delta};\bar{S})$ is adapted and measurable, and that $\bar{\Delta}$ is self-financing if and only if $\mathcal{D}(\bar{\Delta};\bar{S}) = 0$. If $\bar{\Delta}$ is self-financing, then the cumulative gains process is identical to the value process.

The term "dividend" should be interpreted with some caution, since we are not really talking about dividends in the sense of dividends on stocks. The term "net withdrawal" better represents what is going on. Imagine that the trading strategy is executed in a brokerage account. If at some point in time, sales of securities exceed new purchases of other securities, then the net revenue is paid out from the brokerage account to the investor. If new purchases of securities exceed sales, then the investor has to deposit additional money into the brokerage account. The cumulative net withdrawal process or cumulative dividend process measures the cumulative value of these withdrawals and net new investments over time. If at all times, all new purchases of securities are financed by sales of other securities, then the trading strategy is self-financing, and the cumulative dividend process is zero.

A *numeraire* for $\bar{S}$ is a self-financing trading strategy $\bar{b}$ such that $\bar{b}\bar{S} = 1$. The securities price process $\bar{S}$ is said to be *normalized* if there exists a numeraire for $\bar{S}$.

If $\bar{S}$ is normalized, then the cumulative dividend process has a simple interpretation. We can imagine that the net withdrawals from the trading strategy $\bar{\Delta}$ are invested in the numeraire as they are received. The cumulative dividend process then measures the number of units of the numeraire that have been accumulated. The total holdings will be $\bar{\Delta}$ plus the accumulated dividends. The gains process will indicate the value of the total holdings, measured in units of the numeraire.

If $\bar{S}$ is not normalized, then the cumulative dividends process still gives information about the net withdrawals, because it measures the total net withdrawals that have been made up to any point in time. However, these withdrawals have been added up in nominal units, without taking into account the time value of money or the returns they could have earned if reinvested.

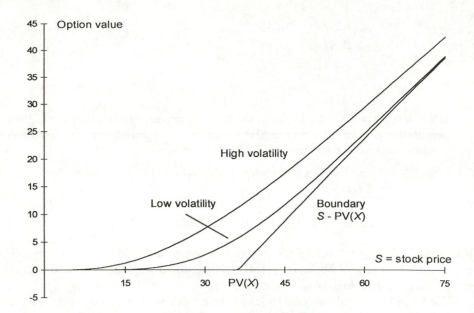

FIG. 4.1. Value of a standard call option

Example 4.3 *Continuation of Examples 1.7, 1.15, 2.3, 2.14, 2.20, 2.28, 4.1, and 4.2.* We use the Black–Scholes model to preview the theory of pricing and replication that will be developed in the following chapters.

A *standard call option* on the stock, with *exercise price* $X > 0$ and maturity T, has a payoff which is paid at time T and equals

$$Y = \max\{0, S(T) - X\} = \begin{cases} S(T) - X & \text{if } S(T) \geq X \\ 0 & \text{otherwise} \end{cases}$$

Based on the theory of pricing and replication, we shall show in Chapter 6 that the value of the option at a time $0 \leq t \leq T$ is given by the *Black–Scholes formula*:

$$C = SN(d_1) - e^{-r(T-t)} X N(d_2)$$

Here N is the cumulative standard normal distribution function, and the processes d_1 and d_2 are defined by

$$d_1 = \frac{\ln S - \ln X + \left(r + \frac{1}{2}\sigma^2\right)(T - t)}{\sigma\sqrt{T - t}}$$

and

$$d_2 = \frac{\ln S - \ln X + \left(r - \frac{1}{2}\sigma^2\right)(T - t)}{\sigma\sqrt{T - t}} = d_1 - \sigma\sqrt{T - t}$$

Figure 4.1 shows the value of the call option for two different levels of volatility, as functions of the value of the underlying. The value of the underlying is on the horizontal axis, and the call value is measured along the vertical axis. The higher curve corresponds to a volatility of $\sigma = 0.8$, and the lower curve corresponds to a volatility of $\sigma = 0.4$. The exercise price is $X = 40$, the time to maturity is $T - t = 1$, and the interest rate is $r = 0.1$. The 45 degree line which is also plotted in the figure intersects the horizontal axis at the present value $PV(X) = e^{-r(T-t)}X$ of the exercise price. It represents a lower boundary and a limit of the call option value.

We shall construct a self-financing trading strategy $\bar{\Delta} = (\Delta_0, \Delta)$ whose value at time T equals the payoff to the option:

$$\Delta_0(T)M(T) + \Delta(T)S(T) = Y = \max\{0, S(T) - X\}$$

The holdings Δ of the stock will be given by

$$\Delta = N(d_1)$$

for $t \in (0, T)$, while the holdings Δ_0 of the money market account will be

$$\Delta_0 = (C - \Delta S)/M$$

It turns out that Δ is the derivative of the Black–Scholes formula with respect to the stock price S. This looks a bit implausible at first, because it appears that we have forgotten that the value of the call option depends on S not only directly because the first term of the formula has S as a factor, but also indirectly because d_1 and d_2 are functions of S. It is nevertheless true, as will be demonstrated in Chapter 6.

Figure 4.2 shows Δ, the delta of the call option, for the same two levels of volatility as in Fig. 4.1. The value of the underlying is on the horizontal axis, and Δ is measured along the vertical axis. The curve which starts out higher corresponds to a volatility of $\sigma = 0.8$, and the curve which starts out lower corresponds to a volatility of $\sigma = 0.4$. As in Fig. 4.1, the exercise price is $X = 40$, the time to maturity is $T - t = 1$, and the interest rate is $r = 0.1$.

The value of the stock holdings prescribed by the trading strategy $\bar{\Delta}$ is

$$\Delta S = S N(d_1)$$

which is the first component of the Black–Scholes formula. The value of the debt (the negative holdings of the money market account) is

$$\Delta_0 M = C - \Delta S = -e^{-r(T-t)}X N(d_2)$$

which is the second part of the Black–Scholes formula.

The value process of the trading strategy is the same as the value process of the option:

$$\bar{\Delta}\bar{S} = \Delta_0 M + \Delta S$$

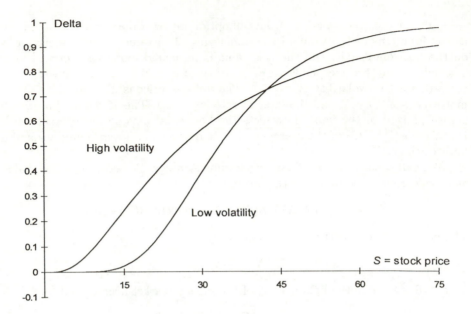

FIG. 4.2. Delta of a standard call option

$$= -e^{-r(T-t)} X N(d_2) + S N(d_1)$$
$$= C$$

Indeed, the way we value a contingent claim like the standard call option is in principle this: construct a self-financing trading strategy whose payoff at time T equals the payoff to the claim; the value process of the claim will then be the same as the value process of the trading strategy.

The logic behind this is that no riskless arbitrage is possible in the market. If the value of the trading strategy were less than the value of the claim, we could short-sell the claim and engage in the trading strategy. This would give a net profit up front, and there would be no net liability in the future, because the payoff to the trading strategy will exactly cover any liability resulting from the sold claim. Conversely, if the value of the trading strategy were more than the value of the claim, we could short-sell the trading strategy and buy the claim. Again, this would give a net profit up front. Any future negative payoff to the short-sold trading strategy would be covered by the payoff from the bought claim.

Unfortunately, this account of the valuation of contingent claims and the logic behind it is not strictly correct. Riskless arbitrage is indeed possible in the Black–Scholes model, even when no mispriced contingent claims are available but only the stock and the money market account are traded. This will be touched upon in the next section and explained more fully in Section 4.6. □

4.2 (*) Almost Simple Trading Strategies

In this section, we shall study a particular class of trading strategies called almost simple trading strategies. Their main characteristic is that there is trade only at a finite number of dates, although this number may be random and thus depend on the state of the world. It may be that there is no upper limit to the number of trading dates which applies across all states of the world. If there is such an upper limit, then the trading strategy is called simple. The so-called "doubling strategy" of Harrison and Kreps [43, 1979] is an example of an almost simple trading strategy.

If a trading strategy is simple or almost simple, then the intertemporal budget constraint and the instantaneous budget constraint can be simplified. The cumulative gains process and the cumulative dividend process can be written as a sum rather than an integral, and, hence, the intertemporal budget constraint can also be expressed in terms of a sum rather than an integral. The instantaneous budget constraint says that at each of the finitely or countably many potential trading dates, the value of the securities held immediately before trading equals the value of those held immediately after trading.

A disturbing fact about almost simple trading strategies is that they can be used to create value out of nothing. Using almost simple trading strategies, it is possible to create a riskless arbitrage strategy. An example is the doubling strategy of Harrison and Kreps [43, 1979], which will be discussed in Section 4.7 below, whose initial value is zero and whose final value is greater than one with probability one.

Riskless arbitrage in real life is a nice thing, but riskless arbitrage in a theoretical model indicates that there is a problem with the model. Harrison and Kreps [43, 1979] sidestepped the problem by considering only simple trading strategies. As we shall see later, in Exercise 4.1, it is normally not possible to create a riskless arbitrage strategy using only a simple trading strategy. Following Harrison and Pliska [44, 1981], we shall deal with the possibility of riskless arbitrage by requiring trading strategies to be "admissible." This will be discussed in Section 4.6 below.

Set $t_0 = 0$, and let (t_n) be a strictly increasing sequence of points in time:

$$0 = t_0 < t_1 < \cdots < t_n < \ldots$$

These points in time are the *potential trading dates*.

Let p be a random variable whose values are non-negative integers. Its interpretation will be that all actual trade happens at or before time t_p. Assume that for each non-negative integer n,

$$A(n) = \{\omega \in \Omega : p(\omega) \leq n\} \in \mathcal{F}_{t_n}$$

This means that it is known at each time t_n whether or not there will be more trade later. The set $A(n)$ represents the event that all trade happens no later than at time t_n.

Let

$$\bar{\Delta} : \Omega \times T \to I\!\!R^{N+1}$$

be a function such that for every $\omega \in \Omega$, the path $\bar{\Delta}(\omega, \cdot)$ is constant on each of the intervals $[t_i, t_{i+1})$, $0 \le i < p(\omega)$, and on $[t_{p(\omega)}, \infty) \cap T$.

The function $\bar{\Delta}$ will be an adapted stochastic process if the random variable $\bar{\Delta}(t_n)$ is measurable with respect to $\mathcal{F}_{t_n}$ for each n. Assume that this is the case.

The process $\bar{\Delta}$ is measurable, by Proposition 1.8, because it is right-continuous. Therefore $\bar{\Delta}$ is a trading strategy.

Following the terminology of Harrison and Kreps [43, 1979], a trading strategy of this form will be called *almost simple*. Its main characteristic is that there is trade only at a finite number of dates, although this number may be random. It may be that there is no uniform bound on this number across paths.

If the maximum number p of active trading dates can be chosen independently of ω, then the trading strategy would, in this context, be called *simple*. Note that this definition of a simple trading strategy differs slightly from the definition of a simple process used in the development of the stochastic integral, because the time subintervals used here are closed to the left and open to the right.

Let us show that $\bar{\Delta}$ belongs to $\mathcal{L}(\bar{S})$, so that it can be integrated up against $\bar{S}$.

Let $(\omega, t) \in \Omega \times T$. If $t_n < t$ for all n, pick n such that $p(\omega) \le n$. Otherwise, pick n such that $t_n \le t < t_{n+1}$. In either case,

$$\int_0^t |\bar{\Delta}(\omega, s)\bar{\mu}(\omega, s)| \, ds = \sum_{0 \le i < n} \int_{t_i}^{t_{i+1}} |\bar{\Delta}(\omega, s)\bar{\mu}(\omega, s)| \, ds$$

$$+ \int_{t_n}^t |\bar{\Delta}(\omega, s)\bar{\mu}(\omega, s)| \, ds$$

$$\le \sum_{0 \le i < n} \|\bar{\Delta}(\omega, t_i)\| \int_{t_i}^{t_{i+1}} \|\bar{\mu}(\omega, s)\| \, ds$$

$$+ \|\bar{\Delta}(\omega, t_n)\| \int_{t_n}^t \|\bar{\mu}(\omega, s)\| \, ds$$

$$< \infty$$

and

$$\int_0^t \|\bar{\Delta}(\omega, s)\bar{\sigma}(\omega, s)\|^2 \, ds = \sum_{0 \le i < n} \int_{t_i}^{t_{i+1}} \|\bar{\Delta}(\omega, s)\bar{\sigma}(\omega, s)\|^2 \, ds$$

$$+ \int_{t_n}^t \|\bar{\Delta}(\omega, s)\bar{\sigma}(\omega, s)\|^2 \, ds$$

$$\le \sum_{0 \le i < n} \|\bar{\Delta}(\omega, t_i)\|^2 \int_{t_i}^{t_{i+1}} \|\bar{\sigma}(\omega, s)\|^2 \, ds$$

$$+ \|\bar{\Delta}(\omega, t_n)\|^2 \int_{t_n}^{t} \|\bar{\sigma}(\omega, s)\|^2 \, ds$$
$$< \infty$$

It follows from these equations and inequalities that $\bar{\Delta}\bar{\mu} \in \mathcal{L}^1$ and $\bar{\Delta}\bar{\sigma} \in \mathcal{L}^2$, and, hence, $\bar{\Delta} \in \mathcal{L}(\bar{S})$.

We can now calculate the cumulative gains process $\mathcal{G}(\bar{\Delta}; \bar{S})(t)$ and the cumulative dividend process $\mathcal{D}(\bar{\Delta}; \bar{S})(t)$.

Again let $t \in \mathcal{T}$. If there exists a non-negative integer n such that $t_n \leq t < t_{n+1}$, then

$$
\begin{aligned}
\mathcal{G}(\bar{\Delta}; \bar{S})(t) - \bar{\Delta}(0)\bar{S}(0) &= \int_0^t \bar{\Delta} \, d\bar{S} \\
&= \sum_{0 \leq i < n} \int_{t_i}^{t_{i+1}} \bar{\Delta} \, d\bar{S} + \int_{t_n}^{t} \bar{\Delta} \, d\bar{S} \\
&= \sum_{0 \leq i < n} \bar{\Delta}(t_i) \int_{t_i}^{t_{i+1}} d\bar{S} + \bar{\Delta}(t_n) \int_{t_n}^{t} d\bar{S} \\
&= \sum_{0 \leq i < n} \bar{\Delta}(t_i)(\bar{S}(t_{i+1}) - \bar{S}(t_i)) \\
&\quad + \bar{\Delta}(t_n)(\bar{S}(t) - \bar{S}(t_n))
\end{aligned}
$$

This result says that the cumulative gains equal the value of the initial position plus the sum over the "holding periods" $[t_i, t_{i+1})$ and $[t_n, t)$ of the gain (or loss) made during that period, which equals the position during the period multiplied by the change in securities prices over the period.

If, alternatively, $t_n < t$ for all n, then the calculation becomes a bit more technical. The complications have to do with the fact that unlike the time integrals that we calculated above, the stochastic integral that defines the cumulative gains process is not calculated pathwise. Instead of calculating the cumulative gains process conditionally on each individual $\omega \in \Omega$, we have to calculate it conditionally on each of the events $A(n)$. Recall that

$$A(n) = \{\omega \in \Omega : p(\omega) \leq n\} \in \mathcal{F}_{t_n}$$

Now,

$$
\begin{aligned}
1_{A(n)} \int_{t_n}^{t} \bar{\Delta} \, d\bar{S} &= \int_{t_n}^{t} 1_{A(n)} \bar{\Delta} \, d\bar{S} \\
&= \int_{t_n}^{t} 1_{A(n)} \bar{\Delta}(t_n) \, d\bar{S} \\
&= 1_{A(n)} \bar{\Delta}(t_n)(\bar{S}(t) - \bar{S}(t_n))
\end{aligned}
$$

where we have used Corollary 2.9 and the fact that $1_{A(n)}$ and $1_{A(n)} \bar{\Delta}(t_n)$ are measurable with respect to $\mathcal{F}_{t_n}$. Hence,

$$1_{A(n)}[\mathcal{G}(\bar{\Delta}; \bar{S})(t) - \bar{\Delta}(0)\bar{S}(0)] = 1_{A(n)} \int_0^t \bar{\Delta} \, d\bar{S}$$

$$= 1_{A(n)} \sum_{0 \leq i < n} \int_{t_i}^{t_{i+1}} \bar{\Delta} \, d\bar{S}$$

$$+ 1_{A(n)} \int_{t_n}^t \bar{\Delta} \, d\bar{S}$$

$$= 1_{A(n)} \sum_{0 \leq i < n} \bar{\Delta}(t_i)(\bar{S}(t_{i+1}) - \bar{S}(t_i))$$

$$+ 1_{A(n)}\bar{\Delta}(t_n)(\bar{S}(t) - \bar{S}(t_n))$$

We can express this result by saying that on $A(n)$,

$$\mathcal{G}(\bar{\Delta}; \bar{S})(t) - \bar{\Delta}(0)\bar{S}(0) = \sum_{0 \leq i < n} \bar{\Delta}(t_i)(\bar{S}(t_{i+1}) - \bar{S}(t_i))$$

$$+ \bar{\Delta}(t_n)(\bar{S}(t) - \bar{S}(t_n))$$

The interpretation of this equation is the same as before.

It turns out that the cumulative dividend process can be expressed as follows. Let $t \in \mathcal{T}$. If there exists a non-negative integer n such that $t_n \leq t < t_{n+1}$, then

$$\mathcal{D}(\bar{\Delta}; \bar{S})(t) = \sum_{0 \leq i < n} (\bar{\Delta}(t_i) - \bar{\Delta}(t_{i+1}))\bar{S}(t_{i+1})$$

Alternatively, if $t_n < t$ for all n, then the same equation holds on $A(n)$.

This is shown by induction, as follows. If $n = 0$ and $0 = t_0 \leq t < t_1$, then

$$\bar{\Delta}(t) = \bar{\Delta}(0)$$

and

$$\mathcal{G}(\bar{\Delta}; \bar{S})(t) - \bar{\Delta}(0)\bar{S}(0) = \bar{\Delta}(0)(\bar{S}(t) - \bar{S}(0))$$

and hence

$$\mathcal{D}(\bar{\Delta}; \bar{S})(t) = \mathcal{G}(\bar{\Delta}; \bar{S})(t) - \bar{\Delta}(t)\bar{S}(t) = 0$$

as required. If $n = 1$ and $t_1 \leq t < t_2$, then

$$\bar{\Delta}(t) = \bar{\Delta}(t_1)$$

and

$$\mathcal{G}(\bar{\Delta}; \bar{S})(t) - \bar{\Delta}(0)\bar{S}(0) = \bar{\Delta}(0)(\bar{S}(t_1) - \bar{S}(t_0)) + \bar{\Delta}(t_1)(\bar{S}(t) - \bar{S}(t_1))$$

and hence

$$\begin{aligned}\mathcal{D}(\bar{\Delta}; \bar{S})(t) &= \mathcal{G}(\bar{\Delta}; \bar{S})(t) - \bar{\Delta}(t)\bar{S}(t) \\ &= \bar{\Delta}(0)\bar{S}(t_1) + \bar{\Delta}(t_1)(\bar{S}(t) - \bar{S}(t_1)) - \bar{\Delta}(t)\bar{S}(t) \\ &= (\bar{\Delta}(0) - \bar{\Delta}(t_1))\bar{S}(t_1)\end{aligned}$$

as required.

Finally, suppose we have shown for a particular n that

$$\mathcal{D}(\bar{\Delta};\bar{S})(t_n) = \sum_{0 \le i < n} (\bar{\Delta}(t_i) - \bar{\Delta}(t_{i+1}))\bar{S}(t_{i+1})$$

If $t_{n+1} \le t < t_{n+2}$, then

$$\bar{\Delta}(t) = \bar{\Delta}(t_{n+1})$$

and

$$\begin{aligned}
\mathcal{G}(\bar{\Delta};\bar{S})(t) &= \bar{\Delta}(0)\bar{S}(0) + \sum_{0 \le i < n+1} \bar{\Delta}(t_i)(\bar{S}(t_{i+1}) - \bar{S}(t_i)) \\
&\quad + \bar{\Delta}(t_{n+1})(\bar{S}(t) - \bar{S}(t_{n+1})) \\
&= \bar{\Delta}(0)\bar{S}(0) + \sum_{0 \le i < n} \bar{\Delta}(t_i)(\bar{S}(t_{i+1}) - \bar{S}(t_i)) \\
&\quad + \bar{\Delta}(t_n)(\bar{S}(t_{n+1}) - \bar{S}(t_n)) + \bar{\Delta}(t_{n+1})(\bar{S}(t) - \bar{S}(t_{n+1})) \\
&= \mathcal{G}(\bar{\Delta};\bar{S})(t_n) + \bar{\Delta}(t_n)(\bar{S}(t_{n+1}) - \bar{S}(t_n)) \\
&\quad + \bar{\Delta}(t_{n+1})(\bar{S}(t) - \bar{S}(t_{n+1}))
\end{aligned}$$

So,

$$\begin{aligned}
\mathcal{D}(\bar{\Delta};\bar{S})(t) &= \mathcal{G}(\bar{\Delta};\bar{S})(t) - \bar{\Delta}(t)\bar{S}(t) \\
&= \mathcal{G}(\bar{\Delta};\bar{S})(t_n) + (\mathcal{G}(\bar{\Delta};\bar{S})(t) - \mathcal{G}(\bar{\Delta};\bar{S})(t_n)) \\
&\quad - \bar{\Delta}(t_n)\bar{S}(t_n) - (\bar{\Delta}(t)\bar{S}(t) - \bar{\Delta}(t_n)\bar{S}(t_n)) \\
&= \mathcal{D}(\bar{\Delta};\bar{S})(t_n) + \bar{\Delta}(t_n)(\bar{S}(t_{n+1}) - \bar{S}(t_n)) \\
&\quad + \bar{\Delta}(t_{n+1})(\bar{S}(t) - \bar{S}(t_{n+1})) - \bar{\Delta}(t)\bar{S}(t) + \bar{\Delta}(t_n)\bar{S}(t_n) \\
&= \mathcal{D}(\bar{\Delta};\bar{S})(t_n) + (\bar{\Delta}(t_n) - \bar{\Delta}(t_{n+1}))\bar{S}(t_{n+1}) \\
&= \sum_{0 \le i < n} (\bar{\Delta}(t_i) - \bar{\Delta}(t_{i+1}))\bar{S}(t_{i+1}) + (\bar{\Delta}(t_n) - \bar{\Delta}(t_{n+1}))\bar{S}(t_{n+1}) \\
&= \sum_{0 \le i < n+1} (\bar{\Delta}(t_i) - \bar{\Delta}(t_{i+1}))\bar{S}(t_{i+1})
\end{aligned}$$

as required.

Alternatively, if $t_n < t$ for all n, then a virtually identical inductive argument will show that

$$1_{A(n)}\mathcal{D}(\bar{\Delta};\bar{S})(t) = 1_{A(n)} \sum_{0 \le i < n} (\bar{\Delta}(t_i) - \bar{\Delta}(t_{i+1}))\bar{S}(t_{i+1})$$

for every n.

The equation for the cumulative dividend process says that the cumulative net withdrawals equal the sum over the trading dates t_{i+1} of the net withdrawal generated on that date. The net withdrawal generated on date t_{i+1} equals the difference between the values, on that date, of the position held just before that date and the position held on and immediately after that date.

The trading strategy $\bar{\Delta}$ is self-financing if and only if the cumulative dividend process is zero, which is the case if and only if

$$(\bar{\Delta}(t_n) - \bar{\Delta}(t_{n+1}))\bar{S}(t_{n+1}) = 0$$

or

$$\bar{\Delta}(t_n)\bar{S}(t_{n+1}) = \bar{\Delta}(t_{n+1})\bar{S}(t_{n+1})$$

for all n. This is an *instantaneous budget constraint*, which says that on each potential trading date t_{n+1}, the value of the position held on and immediately after that date has to equal the value of the position held just before that date.

The instantaneous budget constraint holds at n if and only if the value process $\bar{\Delta}\bar{S}$ is continuous at t_{n+1}. To see this, first note that the value process of an almost simple trading strategy, as we have defined it, will always be continuous from the right. Secondly, if $t_n \le t < t_{n+1}$, then

$$\bar{\Delta}(t)\bar{S}(t) = \bar{\Delta}(t_n)\bar{S}(t) \rightarrow \bar{\Delta}(t_n)\bar{S}(t_{n+1})$$

as $t \rightarrow t_{n+1}$. Hence, the value process is continuous from the left at t_{n+1} if and only if

$$\bar{\Delta}(t_n)\bar{S}(t_{n+1}) = \bar{\Delta}(t_{n+1})\bar{S}(t_{n+1})$$

The instantaneous budget constraint holds at every n if and only if the value process $\bar{\Delta}\bar{S}$ is continuous.

4.3   State Prices

A *state price process* or *pricing kernel* for $\bar{S}$ is a positive one-dimensional Itô process Π such that $\Pi\bar{S}$ has zero drift.

Stated slightly differently, if we change the unit of account and use $\Pi\bar{S}$ as securities price process instead of $\bar{S}$, then the basic security prices have zero drift.

Requiring $\Pi\bar{S}$ to have zero drift is not quite the same thing as requiring it to be a martingale. If $\Pi\bar{S}$ is a martingale, then it has zero drift, but the converse is not true. Indeed, we shall not assume that $\Pi\bar{S}$ is a martingale.

Being a positive Itô process, a state price process must have the form $\Pi = \Pi(0)\eta[-r, -\lambda]$ for some $\Pi(0) > 0$ and processes $r \in \mathcal{L}^1$ and $\lambda \in \mathcal{L}^2$:

$$\Pi(t) = \Pi(0)\exp\left[\int_0^t \left(-r - \frac{1}{2}\lambda\lambda^\top\right)ds - \int_0^t \lambda\,dW\right]$$

and

$$\frac{d\Pi}{\Pi} = -r\,dt - \lambda\,dW$$

Given the state price process Π for $\bar{S}$, we refer to the processes r and λ as the (instantaneously riskless) *interest rate* and the *prices of risk*, respectively. This terminology will be explained in the following section.

If Π is a state price process for $\bar{S}$, and if $\bar{\Delta} \in \mathcal{L}(\bar{S})$ is a self-financing trading strategy, then the product of Π and the value process of $\bar{\Delta}$ has zero drift:

$$d(\Pi\bar{\Delta}\bar{S}) = \Pi\,d(\bar{\Delta}\bar{S}) + \bar{\Delta}\bar{S}\,d\Pi - \Pi\bar{\Delta}\bar{\sigma}\lambda^\top dt$$
$$= \Pi\bar{\Delta}\,d\bar{S} + \bar{\Delta}\bar{S}\,d\Pi - \Pi\bar{\Delta}\bar{\sigma}\lambda^\top dt$$
$$= \bar{\Delta}\,d(\Pi\bar{S})$$

Since $\Pi\bar{S}$ has zero drift, so does $\Pi\bar{\Delta}\bar{S}$.

4.4   The Interest Rate and the Prices of Risk

If $\bar{b}$ is a self-financing trading strategy whose value process is positive and instantaneously riskless (has zero dispersion), then we call $\bar{b}$ a *money market account* and denote its value process by M: $M = \bar{b}\bar{S}$.

It may be that the money market account is identical to one of the basic securities, for example security zero. In this case, the trading strategy $\bar{b}$ would be a buy-and-hold strategy. However, it is also possible that none of the basic securities is a money market account, but a money market account can be created by trading in the basic securities. In the Black–Scholes model, the basic securities are a money market account and one stock. As hinted in Example 4.3, we can create a call option by a trading strategy involving the money market account and the stock. We could alternatively use the stock and the option as basic securities and create the money market account by a trading strategy involving the stock and the option.

If $\bar{b}$ is a money market account, then $\bar{b}\bar{\sigma} = 0$. Hence, existence of a money market account requires that the $[(N+1) \times K]$-dimensional matrix $\bar{\sigma}$ have rank at most N.

If M is the value process of a money market account, then it must have the form $M = M(0)\eta[\alpha, 0]$ for some process $\alpha \in \mathcal{L}^1$ and some $M(0) > 0$. Then

$$\Pi M = \Pi(0)M(0)\eta[-r, -\lambda]\eta[\alpha, 0] = \Pi(0)M(0)\eta[\alpha - r, -\lambda]$$

Since Π is a state price process and M is the value process of a self-financing trading strategy, the drift of ΠM is zero. So, $\alpha - r = 0$, $\alpha = r$, and

$$M(t) = M(0)\eta[r, 0](t) = M(0)\exp\left[\int_0^t r\,ds\right]$$

$$\frac{dM}{M} = r\,dt$$

Hence, r has the interpretation of the unique candidate for the instantaneous rate of return on a money market account.

We shall use the notation M for a process of the form $M = M(0)\eta[r, 0]$ even if there does not exist a money market account in the economy; that is, even if there is no self-financing trading strategy $\bar{b}$ with $\bar{b}\bar{S} = M$.

By Itô's lemma, the drift of $\Pi \bar{S}$ is

$$\Pi\left[\bar{\mu} - r\bar{S} - \bar{\sigma}\lambda^{\top}\right]$$

So, $\Pi = \Pi(0)\eta[-r, -\lambda]$ is a state price process for $\bar{S}$ if and only if

$$\bar{\mu} - r\bar{S} = \bar{\sigma}\lambda^{\top}$$

This equation is the reason for calling the vector process λ the prices of risk. It says that the excess instantaneous return on each security, excess over the return to the same amount invested in a money market account, is a linear combination of the security's dispersion coefficients with respect to the various underlying Wiener processes, where the weights in the linear combination are the prices of risk.

The squared volatility of Π is $\lambda\lambda^{\top}$. So, large prices of risk mean large volatility of the state price process.

If $\bar{\Delta}$ is a security or a self-financing trading strategy, then its instantaneous expected excess dollar return is

$$\bar{\Delta}\bar{\mu} - r\bar{\Delta}\bar{S} = \bar{\Delta}(\bar{\mu} - r\bar{S}) = \bar{\Delta}\bar{\sigma}\lambda^{\top}$$

It equals the negative of the covariance of the instantaneous dollar return with the rate of change in the state price process. So, securities or self-financing trading strategies with large negative covariance with the state price process have high expected excess return.

Notice that

$$\Pi = \Pi(0)M(0)\frac{\eta[0, -\lambda]}{M}$$

and

$$\frac{\Pi(T)}{\Pi(t)} = \frac{\eta[0, -\lambda](T)/\eta[0, -\lambda](t)}{M(T)/M(t)}$$

The state prices adjust for the time value of money and for risk. Dividing by M corresponds to discounting at the rolled-over instantaneous interest rate, and multiplying by $\eta[0, -\lambda]$ is a risk adjustment.

The so-called "risk-adjusted probabilities," which we shall discuss in the next chapter, will be created from the state price process essentially by incorporating the risk adjustment into the probabilities.

If $\bar{S}$ is a normalized securities price process, then the instantaneously riskless interest rate for $\bar{S}$ is zero. In other words, measured in terms of a numeraire, the instantaneous interest rate is zero. Hence, a process Π is a state price process for $\bar{S}$ if and only if it has the form

$$\Pi = \Pi(0)\eta[0, -\lambda]$$

where λ is a system of prices of risk for $\bar{S}$, a process $\lambda \in \mathcal{L}^2$ such that

$$\bar{\mu} = \bar{\sigma}\lambda^{\top}$$

4.5   Existence and Uniqueness of Prices of Risk

Given the securities price process $\bar{S}$, the existence and uniqueness of a state price process are a question of the existence and uniqueness of processes $r \in \mathcal{L}^1$ and $\lambda \in \mathcal{L}^2$ such that

$$\bar{\mu} - r\bar{S} = \bar{\sigma}\lambda^\top$$

If there exists a money market account, then r has to be the interest rate on that account.

Recall that existence of a money market account requires that the $[(N+1) \times K]$-dimensional matrix $\bar{\sigma}$ have rank at most N. There is not much more to be said about it in general.

Given the interest rate process r, the existence and uniqueness of a state price process are equivalent to the existence and uniqueness of a process $\lambda \in \mathcal{L}^2$ solving the equation above.

Existence of λ requires that the matrices $\bar{\sigma}$ and $(\bar{\mu} - r\bar{S}, \bar{\sigma})$ have the same rank almost everywhere. They have dimension $(N+1) \times K$ and $(N+1) \times (K+1)$, respectively.

The rank condition is not sufficient, however. It ensures that at every (or almost every) (ω, t), there exists a vector $\lambda(\omega, t)$ which solves the equation, but it does not ensure that they fit together to form a process which is in $\mathcal{L}^2$.

If $\bar{\sigma}$ has rank K almost everywhere, then there is at most one system λ of prices of risk and hence at most one state price process.

Proposition 4.4 *Suppose $\bar{\sigma}$ has rank $N + 1$. Let $r \in \mathcal{L}^1$. Set*

$$\lambda^* = (\bar{\mu} - r\bar{S})^\top \left(\bar{\sigma}\bar{\sigma}^\top\right)^{-1} \bar{\sigma}$$

There exists a vector of prices of risk if and only if $\lambda^* \in \mathcal{L}^2$. If so, then λ^* is a vector of prices of risk, and

$$\lambda^*\lambda^{*\top} \leq \lambda\lambda^\top$$

for every vector λ of prices of risk.

Proof Set

$$A = \bar{\sigma}^\top \left(\bar{\sigma}\bar{\sigma}^\top\right)^{-1} \bar{\sigma}$$

If λ is a process which solves the equation

$$\bar{\mu} - r\bar{S} = \bar{\sigma}\lambda^\top$$

then

$$\begin{aligned}
\lambda A \lambda^\top &= \lambda\bar{\sigma}^\top \left(\bar{\sigma}\bar{\sigma}^\top\right)^{-1} \bar{\sigma}\lambda^\top \\
&= (\bar{\mu} - r\bar{S})^\top \left(\bar{\sigma}\bar{\sigma}^\top\right)^{-1} (\bar{\mu} - r\bar{S}) \\
&= (\bar{\mu} - r\bar{S})^\top \left(\bar{\sigma}\bar{\sigma}^\top\right)^{-1} \bar{\sigma}\bar{\sigma}^\top \left(\bar{\sigma}\bar{\sigma}^\top\right)^{-1} (\bar{\mu} - r\bar{S})
\end{aligned}$$

$$= \lambda^* \lambda^{*\top}$$

Observe that $AA = A$, $A^\top = A$, and $(I - A)(I - A)^\top = I - A$, where I is the identity matrix. Hence,

$$\begin{aligned}
\lambda\lambda^\top &= \lambda[A + (I - A)]\lambda^\top \\
&= \lambda A \lambda^\top + \lambda(I - A)\lambda^\top \\
&= \lambda^* \lambda^{*\top} + \lambda(I - A)[\lambda(I - A)]^\top \\
&\geq \lambda^* \lambda^{*\top}
\end{aligned}$$

If λ is a vector of prices of risk, then $\lambda \in \mathcal{L}^2$, which implies that $\lambda^* \in \mathcal{L}^2$. Since λ^* does solve the equation

$$\bar{\mu} - r\bar{S} = \bar{\sigma}\lambda^{*\top}$$

it follows that λ^* is a vector of market prices of risk if it is in $\mathcal{L}^2$.   □

We may call the process λ^* from Proposition 4.4 the *minimal vector of prices of risk*. It is minimal in the sense that it has minimal length. Notice that it is a linear combination of the rows of the matrix $\bar{\sigma}$. We may call the corresponding state price process the *minimal state price process*. It is minimal in the sense that it has minimal volatility.

The matrix

$$A = \bar{\sigma}^\top \left(\bar{\sigma}\bar{\sigma}^\top\right)^{-1} \bar{\sigma}$$

which appears in the proof of Proposition 4.4 can be interpreted as the matrix of the orthogonal projection in $\mathbb{R}^K$ onto the linear subspace spanned by the rows of $\bar{\sigma}$. If $x \in \mathbb{R}^K$, then

$$x = xA + x(I - A)$$

where xA is a linear combination of the rows of $\bar{\sigma}$, while $x(I - A)$ is orthogonal to the rows of $\bar{\sigma}$:

$$x(I - A)\bar{\sigma}^\top = x\left(\bar{\sigma}^\top - A\bar{\sigma}^\top\right) = x\left(\bar{\sigma}^\top - \bar{\sigma}^\top\right) = 0$$

If λ is a vector of prices of risk, then $\lambda A = \lambda^*$, and

$$\lambda = \lambda A + \lambda(I - A) = \lambda^* + \tilde{\lambda}$$

where $\tilde{\lambda} = \lambda(I - A)$ is in $\mathcal{L}^2$ and is orthogonal to the rows of $\bar{\sigma}$. Conversely, if $\tilde{\lambda}$ is any process in $\mathcal{L}^2$ which is orthogonal to the rows of $\bar{\sigma}$, then $\lambda = \lambda^* + \tilde{\lambda}$ is a vector of prices of risk.

Most of the time, we shall assume that security zero is a money market account. This means that the price process (price per share) of security zero has the form

$$S_0(t) = M(t) = M(0)\exp\left[\int_0^t r\,ds\right]$$

for some $M(0) > 0$ and some process $r \in \mathcal{L}^1$, the interest rate. In differential form,

$$\frac{dM}{M} = r\,dt$$

Write

$$\bar{S} = \begin{pmatrix} M \\ S \end{pmatrix}$$

where S is the N-dimensional column vector of prices of the instantaneously risky securities. Write

$$\tilde{\mu} = \begin{pmatrix} \tilde{\mu}_1 \\ \vdots \\ \tilde{\mu}_N \end{pmatrix}$$

and

$$\tilde{\sigma} = \begin{pmatrix} \bar{\sigma}_{1-} \\ \vdots \\ \bar{\sigma}_{N-} \end{pmatrix}$$

where $\bar{\sigma}_{i-}$ is the ith row of the matrix $\bar{\sigma}$. Then

$$\bar{\mu} = \begin{pmatrix} Mr \\ \tilde{\mu} \end{pmatrix}$$

and

$$\bar{\sigma} = \begin{pmatrix} 0 \\ \tilde{\sigma} \end{pmatrix}$$

The equation

$$\bar{\mu} - r\bar{S} = \bar{\sigma}\lambda^\top$$

is equivalent to

$$\begin{pmatrix} Mr \\ \tilde{\mu} \end{pmatrix} - r\begin{pmatrix} M \\ S \end{pmatrix} = \begin{pmatrix} 0 \\ \tilde{\sigma} \end{pmatrix}\lambda^\top$$

and to

$$\tilde{\mu} - rS = \tilde{\sigma}\lambda^\top$$

If $\tilde{\sigma}$ has rank N, then so does $\bar{\sigma}$, whereas Proposition 4.4 requires $\bar{\sigma}$ to have rank $N+1$. Even so, the following proposition says that there is a unique minimal vector of prices of risk λ^*, which can be calculated from $\tilde{\sigma}$ and $\tilde{\mu}$ by a formula which is similar to the one in Proposition 4.4.

Proposition 4.5 *Suppose the zeroth security is a money market account with interest rate $r \in \mathcal{L}^1$, and suppose $\tilde{\sigma}$ has rank N. Set*

$$\lambda^* = (\tilde{\mu} - rS)^\top \left(\tilde{\sigma}\tilde{\sigma}^\top\right)^{-1}\tilde{\sigma}$$

There exists a vector of prices of risk if and only if $\lambda^* \in \mathcal{L}^2$. If so, then λ^* is a vector of prices of risk, and

$$\lambda^*\lambda^{*\top} \leq \lambda\lambda^\top$$

for every vector λ of prices of risk.

Proof   Identical to the proof of Proposition 4.4.   □

Like the process λ^* from Proposition 4.4, the process λ^* from Proposition 4.5 may also be called the *minimal vector of prices of risk*, because it has minimal length. It is a linear combination of the rows of the matrix $\tilde{\sigma}$. The corresponding state price process may be called the *minimal state price process*, because it has minimal volatility.

In the context of Proposition 4.5, the matrix

$$A = \tilde{\sigma}^{\top} \left(\tilde{\sigma}\tilde{\sigma}^{\top}\right)^{-1} \tilde{\sigma}$$

is the matrix of the orthogonal projection in $\mathbb{R}^K$ onto the linear subspace spanned by the rows of $\tilde{\sigma}$, which is the same as the linear subspace spanned by the rows of $\bar{\sigma}$. As before, if λ is a vector of prices of risk, then $\lambda A = \lambda^*$, and

$$\lambda = \lambda A + \lambda(I - A) = \lambda^* + \tilde{\lambda}$$

where $\tilde{\lambda} = \lambda(I - A)$ is in $\mathcal{L}^2$ and is orthogonal to the rows of $\tilde{\sigma}$. Conversely, if $\tilde{\lambda}$ is any process in $\mathcal{L}^2$ which is orthogonal to the rows of $\tilde{\sigma}$, then $\lambda = \lambda^* + \tilde{\lambda}$ is a vector of prices of risk.

Consider next the case where all the basic securities prices are positive. For each $i = 0, \ldots, N$, there exist processes $\mu_i \in \mathcal{L}^1$ and σ_{i-} of dimension one and $1 \times K$, respectively, such that

$$\bar{S}_i = \bar{S}_i(0)\eta[\mu_i, \sigma_{i-}]$$

In differential form,

$$\frac{d\bar{S}_i}{\bar{S}_i} = \mu_i\, dt + \sigma_{i-}\, dW$$

Stack the μ_i, $i = 0, \ldots, N$, on top of each other to form an $(N+1)$-dimensional column vector $\hat{\mu}$:

$$\hat{\mu} = \begin{pmatrix} \mu_0 \\ \mu_1 \\ \vdots \\ \mu_N \end{pmatrix}$$

and stack the σ_{i-}, $i = 0, \ldots, N$, on top of each other to form an $[(N+1) \times K]$-dimensional matrix $\hat{\sigma}$:

$$\hat{\sigma} = \begin{pmatrix} \sigma_{0-} \\ \sigma_{1-} \\ \vdots \\ \sigma_{N-} \end{pmatrix}$$

In matrix notation, the differential of the securities prices is

$$d\bar{S} = \mathcal{D}(\bar{S})\left[\hat{\mu}\, dt + \hat{\sigma}\, dW\right]$$

where $\mathcal{D}(\bar{S})$ is the diagonal matrix with the vector $\bar{S}$ along the diagonal. So,

$$\bar{\mu} = \mathcal{D}(\bar{S})\hat{\mu}$$

and

$$\bar{\sigma} = \mathcal{D}(\bar{S})\hat{\sigma}$$

The vector $\hat{\mu}$ is the *relative* (or percentage) *drift* vector and the matrix $\hat{\sigma}$ is the *relative* (or percentage) *dispersion* matrix of the securities price processes. Alternatively, we call them the vector of *expected instantaneous rates of return* and the *dispersion matrix* of the instantaneous rates of return.

The $[(N+1) \times K]$-dimensional matrices $\hat{\sigma}$ and $\bar{\sigma} = \mathcal{D}(\bar{S})\hat{\sigma}$ have the same rank. Hence, existence of a money market account requires that $\hat{\sigma}$ have rank at most N.

The equation

$$\bar{\mu} - r\bar{S} = \bar{\sigma}\lambda^{\top}$$

now takes the form

$$\mathcal{D}(\bar{S})\hat{\mu} - r\mathcal{D}(\bar{S})\iota = \mathcal{D}(\bar{S})\hat{\sigma}\lambda^{\top}$$

or

$$\hat{\mu} - r\iota = \hat{\sigma}\lambda^{\top}$$

where ι is an $(N+1)$-dimensional column vector all of whose entries are one.

If $\hat{\sigma}$ has rank $N+1$ almost everywhere, then so does $\bar{\sigma}$, and the minimal vector of prices of risk λ^* from Proposition 4.4 is

$$\begin{aligned}
\lambda^* &= (\bar{\mu} - r\bar{S})^{\top}\left(\bar{\sigma}\bar{\sigma}^{\top}\right)^{-1}\bar{\sigma} \\
&= \left[\mathcal{D}(\bar{S})(\hat{\mu} - r\iota)^{\top}\right]\left(\mathcal{D}(\bar{S})\hat{\sigma}\hat{\sigma}^{\top}\mathcal{D}(\bar{S})\right)^{-1}\mathcal{D}(\bar{S})\hat{\sigma} \\
&= (\hat{\mu} - r\iota)^{\top}\left(\hat{\sigma}\hat{\sigma}^{\top}\right)^{-1}\hat{\sigma}
\end{aligned}$$

Example 4.6 *Continuation of Examples 1.17 and 2.21.* This is an example of a market where there is no money market account, the process r is essentially arbitrary, and the process λ is not unique. However, λ is unique once r has been chosen.

There are two risky securities whose price processes are correlated geometric Brownian motions.

Let A be a $(2 \times K)$-dimensional matrix with

$$AA^{\top} = \begin{pmatrix} 1 & \rho \\ \rho & 1 \end{pmatrix}$$

Then $Z = AW$ is a two-dimensional correlated Wiener process with increment correlation coefficient ρ. The financial price processes are

$$S_1 = S_1(0)\eta[\mu_1, (\sigma_1, 0)A]$$

and

$$S_2 = S_2(0)\eta[\mu_2, (0, \sigma_2)A]$$

where $S_1(0) > 0$, $S_2(0) > 0$, μ_1, μ_2, $\sigma_1 > 0$, and $\sigma_2 > 0$ are constants. Then

$$\frac{dS_1}{S_1} = \mu_1\,dt + (\sigma_1, 0)A\,dW = \mu_1\,dt + \sigma_1\,dZ_1$$

$$\frac{dS_2}{S_2} = \mu_2\,dt + (0, \sigma_2)A\,dW = \mu_2\,dt + \sigma_2\,dZ_2$$

Hence,

$$\hat{\mu} = \begin{pmatrix} \mu_1 \\ \mu_2 \end{pmatrix}$$

and

$$\hat{\sigma} = \begin{pmatrix} \sigma_1 & 0 \\ 0 & \sigma_2 \end{pmatrix} A$$

Since $\hat{\sigma}$ has rank two, so does the (2×3)-dimensional matrix $(\hat{\mu}, \hat{\sigma})$. Hence, there does not exist a money market account.

The processes r and λ must satisfy

$$\hat{\mu} - r\iota = \hat{\sigma}\lambda^{\mathsf{T}}$$

which is equivalent to

$$\begin{pmatrix} \mu_1 - r \\ \mu_2 - r \end{pmatrix} = \begin{pmatrix} \sigma_1 & 0 \\ 0 & \sigma_2 \end{pmatrix} A\lambda^{\mathsf{T}}$$

Since we require $\lambda \in \mathcal{L}^2$, this equation implies that $r \in \mathcal{L}^2$. On the other hand, given $r \in \mathcal{L}^2$, the process λ is uniquely determined by the equation above, whose solution is

$$\lambda^{\mathsf{T}} = A^{-1} \begin{pmatrix} \frac{1}{\sigma_1} & 0 \\ 0 & \frac{1}{\sigma_2} \end{pmatrix} \begin{pmatrix} \mu_1 - r \\ \mu_2 - r \end{pmatrix} = A^{-1} \begin{pmatrix} \frac{\mu_1 - r}{\sigma_1} \\ \frac{\mu_2 - r}{\sigma_2} \end{pmatrix}$$

If A is the matrix from Example 1.16, then

$$\lambda^{\mathsf{T}} = A^{-1} \begin{pmatrix} \frac{\mu_1 - r}{\sigma_1} \\ \frac{\mu_2 - r}{\sigma_2} \end{pmatrix}$$

$$= \frac{1}{\sqrt{1 - \rho^2}} \begin{pmatrix} \sqrt{\frac{1-\rho}{2}} & \sqrt{\frac{1-\rho}{2}} \\ \sqrt{\frac{1+\rho}{2}} & -\sqrt{\frac{1+\rho}{2}} \end{pmatrix} \begin{pmatrix} \frac{\mu_1 - r}{\sigma_1} \\ \frac{\mu_2 - r}{\sigma_2} \end{pmatrix}$$

$$= \frac{1}{\sqrt{1 - \rho^2}} \begin{pmatrix} \sqrt{\frac{1-\rho}{2}} \left(\frac{\mu_1 - r}{\sigma_1} + \frac{\mu_2 - r}{\sigma_2} \right) \\ \sqrt{\frac{1+\rho}{2}} \left(\frac{\mu_1 - r}{\sigma_1} - \frac{\mu_2 - r}{\sigma_2} \right) \end{pmatrix}$$

$$= \begin{pmatrix} \frac{1}{\sqrt{2(1+\rho)}} \left(\frac{\mu_1 - r}{\sigma_1} + \frac{\mu_2 - r}{\sigma_2} \right) \\ \frac{1}{\sqrt{2(1-\rho)}} \left(\frac{\mu_1 - r}{\sigma_1} - \frac{\mu_2 - r}{\sigma_2} \right) \end{pmatrix}$$

The associated state price process has differential

$$\frac{d\Pi}{\Pi} = -r\,dt - \lambda\,dW$$

$$= -r\,dt - \frac{1}{\sqrt{2(1+\rho)}} \left(\frac{\mu_1 - r}{\sigma_1} + \frac{\mu_2 - r}{\sigma_2} \right) dW_1$$

$$- \frac{1}{\sqrt{2(1-\rho)}} \left(\frac{\mu_1 - r}{\sigma_1} - \frac{\mu_2 - r}{\sigma_2} \right) dW_2$$

To express this differential in terms of dZ, first calculate

$$(A^{-1})^{\mathsf{T}} A^{-1} = \frac{1}{1-\rho^2} \begin{pmatrix} \sqrt{\frac{1-\rho}{2}} & \sqrt{\frac{1+\rho}{2}} \\ \sqrt{\frac{1-\rho}{2}} & -\sqrt{\frac{1+\rho}{2}} \end{pmatrix} \begin{pmatrix} \sqrt{\frac{1-\rho}{2}} & \sqrt{\frac{1-\rho}{2}} \\ \sqrt{\frac{1+\rho}{2}} & -\sqrt{\frac{1+\rho}{2}} \end{pmatrix}$$

$$= \frac{1}{1-\rho^2} \begin{pmatrix} 1 & -\rho \\ -\rho & 1 \end{pmatrix}$$

and

$$(A^{-1})^{\mathsf{T}} \lambda^{\mathsf{T}} = (A^{-1})^{\mathsf{T}} A^{-1} \begin{pmatrix} \frac{\mu_1 - r}{\sigma_1} \\ \frac{\mu_2 - r}{\sigma_2} \end{pmatrix}$$

$$= \frac{1}{1-\rho^2} \begin{pmatrix} 1 & -\rho \\ -\rho & 1 \end{pmatrix} \begin{pmatrix} \frac{\mu_1 - r}{\sigma_1} \\ \frac{\mu_2 - r}{\sigma_2} \end{pmatrix}$$

$$= \frac{1}{\sigma_1 \sigma_2 (1-\rho^2)} \begin{pmatrix} \sigma_2(\mu_1 - r) - \sigma_1 \rho(\mu_2 - r) \\ -\sigma_2 \rho(\mu_1 - r) + \sigma_1(\mu_2 - r) \end{pmatrix}$$

Now,

$$\frac{d\Pi}{\Pi} = -r\,dt - \lambda\,dW$$

$$= -r\,dt - \lambda A^{-1} A\,dW$$

$$= -r\,dt - \lambda A^{-1}\,dZ$$

$$= -r\,dt - \frac{\sigma_2(\mu_1 - r) - \sigma_1 \rho(\mu_2 - r)}{\sigma_1 \sigma_2 (1-\rho^2)}\,dZ_1$$

$$- \frac{-\sigma_2 \rho(\mu_1 - r) + \sigma_1(\mu_2 - r)}{\sigma_1 \sigma_2 (1-\rho^2)}\,dZ_2$$

$\square$

Example 4.7 (*) *The Ball–Torous [5, 1983] model. Continuation of Section 3.3.*
The Ball–Torous [5, 1983] model has two basic securities, which are zero-coupon

bonds with face value one and maturity dates T_1 and T_2, where $0 < T_1 < T_2$. The model was designed to price an option on the bond which matures at T_2 (the "long bond"). The option expires at T_1, and the bond which matures at T_1 (the "short bond") is used essentially to discount the option payoff. Cheng [16, 1991] argued that the model is not arbitrage free. Here we shall show that there exists no state price process on the life span $[0, T_1]$ of the short bond.

As I understand the model, each of the two bonds has a price process which is built from a different Brownian bridge process. These Brownian bridge processes are driven by two different Wiener processes, which may be correlated with each other.

Let Z be a two-dimensional correlated Wiener process with correlation coefficient ρ, where $-1 < \rho < 1$. Specifically, $Z = AW$, where W is a two-dimensional standard Wiener process and A is a (2×2)-dimensional matrix with

$$AA^{\mathsf{T}} = \begin{pmatrix} 1 & \rho \\ \rho & 1 \end{pmatrix}$$

Define processes α_1 and α_2 on $[0, T_1)$ and $[0, T_2)$, respectively, by

$$\alpha_i(t) = \int_0^t \frac{1}{T_i - s}\, dZ_i(s)$$

for $0 \le t < T_i$, $i = 1, 2$.

Define the Brownian bridge processes Y_1 and Y_2 on $[0, T_1]$ and $[0, T_2]$, respectively, by

$$Y_i(t) = \begin{cases} (T_i - t)\alpha_i(t) & \text{for } 0 \le t < T_i \\ 0 & \text{for } t = T_i \end{cases}$$

for $0 \le t < T_i$, $i = 1, 2$.

Finally, define two correlated zero-coupon bond price processes S_1 and S_2 on $[0, T_1]$ and $[0, T_2]$, respectively, by

$$S_i(t) = S_i(0) \exp[R_i t + \sigma_i Y_i(t)]$$

for $0 \le t < T_i$, $i = 1, 2$, where $S_i(0) > 0$ is a deterministic initial value, $\sigma_i > 0$ is a constant, and R_i is a constant related to $S_i(0)$ by

$$S_i(0) \exp(R_i T_i) = 1$$

Note that R_i is the yield on bond i at time zero:

$$R_i = \frac{1}{T_i} \ln\left(\frac{1}{S_i(0)}\right)$$

The price processes S_i have the property that $S_i(T_i) = 1$, which is desirable since the value of the zero-coupon bond at maturity must be one.

Recall that

$$Y_i(t) = -\int_0^t \alpha_i \, ds + Z_i(t)$$

for $0 \le t \le T_i$.

The zero-coupon bond price processes can be written as

$$S_i(t) = S_i(0) \exp[R_i t + \sigma_i Y_i(t)] = S_i(0) \exp\left[R_i t - \int_0^t \sigma_i \alpha_i \, ds + \sigma_i Z_i(t)\right]$$

The stochastic differential is

$$\frac{dS_i}{S_i} = R_i - \sigma_i \alpha_i + \frac{1}{2}\sigma_i^2 = \mu_i \, dt + \sigma_i \, dZ_i$$

where

$$\mu_i = R_i - \sigma_i \alpha_i + \frac{1}{2}\sigma_i^2$$

In terms of the underlying uncorrelated two-dimensional Wiener process W,

$$\frac{dS_1}{S_1} = \mu_1 \, dt + \sigma_1 \, dZ_1 = \mu_1 \, dt + (\sigma_1, 0)\, A \, dW$$

and

$$\frac{dS_2}{S_2} = \mu_2 \, dt + \sigma_2 \, dZ_2 = \mu_2 \, dt + (0, \sigma_2)\, A \, dW$$

On $[0, T_1]$, the two-dimensional price process

$$\bar{S} = \begin{pmatrix} S_1 \\ S_2 \end{pmatrix}$$

is an Itô process with differential

$$d\bar{S} = \mathcal{D}(\bar{S}) \left[\hat{\mu} \, dt + \hat{\sigma} \, dW\right]$$

where

$$\hat{\mu} = \begin{pmatrix} \mu_1 \\ \mu_2 \end{pmatrix} = \begin{pmatrix} R_1 - \sigma_1 \alpha_1 + \frac{1}{2}\sigma_1^2 \\ R_2 - \sigma_2 \alpha_2 + \frac{1}{2}\sigma_2^2 \end{pmatrix}$$

and

$$\hat{\sigma} = \begin{pmatrix} \sigma_1 & 0 \\ 0 & \sigma_2 \end{pmatrix} A$$

Since $\hat{\sigma}$ has rank two, so does the (2×3)-dimensional matrix $(\hat{\mu}, \hat{\sigma})$. Hence, there does not exist a money market account.

The processes r and λ must satisfy

$$\hat{\mu} - r\hat{S} = \hat{\sigma}\lambda^\top$$

which is equivalent to

$$\begin{pmatrix} R_1 - \sigma_1 \alpha_1 + \frac{1}{2}\sigma_1^2 - r \\ R_2 - \sigma_2 \alpha_2 + \frac{1}{2}\sigma_2^2 - r \end{pmatrix} = \begin{pmatrix} \sigma_1 & 0 \\ 0 & \sigma_2 \end{pmatrix} A\lambda^\top$$

Now here is the problem. We require that the process λ be in $\mathcal{L}^2([0, T_1])$ in order for the state price process to be well defined on $[0, T_1]$. But then the equation above implies that the processes $\sigma_1\alpha_1 + r$ and $\sigma_2\alpha_2 + r$ are in $\mathcal{L}^2([0,T_1])$. Since $\alpha_2 \in \mathcal{L}^2([0,T_1])$, it follows that $r \in \mathcal{L}^2([0,T_1])$, and hence $\alpha_1 \in \mathcal{L}^2([0,T_1])$. This is a contradiction, since we have shown in Section 3.3 that α_1 is not in $\mathcal{L}^2([0,T_1])$ because it exhibits extreme behavior near T_1.

The Ball–Torous model has become unfashionable, probably for two reasons. One is the Cheng [16, 1991] charge that it is not arbitrage free. The other is that it does not really model the entire term structure of interest rates. It models only a selection of zero-coupon bond prices, each of them driven by a different Wiener process. So the Ball–Torous model seems to require as many Wiener processes as there are maturity dates for zero-coupon bonds. By contrast, term structure models such as that of Vasicek [87, 1977] represent the entire continuous spectrum of zero-coupon bonds, and they do so on the basis of a finite and actually very small number of Wiener processes. See Chapter 7.   □

Now consider the case where all basic securities prices are positive and security zero is a money market account.

Stack the μ_i, $i = 1,\ldots,N$, on top of each other to form an N-dimensional column vector μ:

$$\mu = \begin{pmatrix} \mu_1 \\ \vdots \\ \mu_N \end{pmatrix}$$

and stack the σ_{i-}, $i = 1,\ldots,N$, on top of each other to form an $(N \times K)$-dimensional matrix σ:

$$\sigma = \begin{pmatrix} \sigma_{1-} \\ \vdots \\ \sigma_{N-} \end{pmatrix}$$

Then

$$\hat{\mu} = \begin{pmatrix} r \\ \mu_1 \\ \vdots \\ \mu_N \end{pmatrix} = \begin{pmatrix} r \\ \mu \end{pmatrix}$$

and

$$\hat{\sigma} = \begin{pmatrix} \sigma_{0-} \\ \sigma_{1-} \\ \vdots \\ \sigma_{N-} \end{pmatrix} = \begin{pmatrix} 0 \\ \sigma \end{pmatrix}$$

The differential of the risky securities price processes is

$$dS = \mathcal{D}(S)\mu\,dt + \mathcal{D}(S)\sigma\,dW$$

The equation

$$\hat{\mu} - r\iota = \hat{\sigma}\lambda^{\mathsf{T}}$$

is equivalent to

$$\begin{pmatrix} r \\ \mu \end{pmatrix} - r\begin{pmatrix} 1 \\ \iota \end{pmatrix} = \begin{pmatrix} 0 \\ \sigma \end{pmatrix}\lambda^{\mathsf{T}}$$

and to

$$\mu - r\iota = \sigma\lambda^{\mathsf{T}}$$

where ι now is the N-dimensional column vector all of whose entries are one.

We can also relate μ and σ to $\tilde{\mu}$ and $\tilde{\sigma}$:

$$\tilde{\mu} = \mathcal{D}(S)\mu$$

and

$$\tilde{\sigma} = \mathcal{D}(S)\sigma$$

If σ has rank N, then so do $\tilde{\sigma}$, $\hat{\sigma}$, and $\bar{\sigma}$. In that case, the minimal vector of prices of risk λ^* from Proposition 4.5 is

$$
\begin{aligned}
\lambda^* &= (\tilde{\mu} - rS)^{\mathsf{T}}\left(\tilde{\sigma}\tilde{\sigma}^{\mathsf{T}}\right)^{-1}\tilde{\sigma} \\
&= (\mathcal{D}(S)\mu - r\mathcal{D}(S)\iota)^{\mathsf{T}}\left(\mathcal{D}(S)\sigma\tilde{\sigma}^{\mathsf{T}}\mathcal{D}(S)^{\mathsf{T}}\right)^{-1}\mathcal{D}(S)\sigma \\
&= (\mu - r\iota)^{\mathsf{T}}\left(\sigma\sigma^{\mathsf{T}}\right)^{-1}\sigma
\end{aligned}
$$

and the matrix A is

$$
\begin{aligned}
A &= \tilde{\sigma}^{\mathsf{T}}\left(\tilde{\sigma}\tilde{\sigma}^{\mathsf{T}}\right)^{-1}\tilde{\sigma} \\
&= \left(\mathcal{D}(S)\sigma^{\mathsf{T}}\right)\left(\mathcal{D}(S)\sigma\sigma^{\mathsf{T}}\mathcal{D}(S)^{\mathsf{T}}\right)^{-1}\mathcal{D}(S)\sigma \\
&= \sigma^{\mathsf{T}}\left(\sigma\sigma^{\mathsf{T}}\right)^{-1}\sigma
\end{aligned}
$$

Example 4.8 *Continuation of Examples 1.7, 1.15, 2.3, 2.14, 2.20, 2.28, 4.1, 4.2, and 4.3.* In the Black–Scholes model, there exists a money market account and one stock. The price dynamics are given by

$$\frac{dM}{M} = r\,dt$$

and

$$\frac{dS}{S} = \mu\,dt + \sigma\,dW$$

where r, μ, and σ are constant. The price of risk λ is given by

$$\mu - r = \sigma\lambda$$

Provided that $\sigma > 0$, there is a unique solution, which is given by

$$\lambda = \frac{\mu - r}{\sigma}$$

$\square$

Example 4.9 (*) *The Ball–Torous [5, 1983] model. Continuation of Section 3.3 and Example 4.7.* Let us place the B zero-coupon bond price process in an economy where there is a money market account. It turns out that if the interest rate on the money market account is constant, then there exist no price of risk and no state price process. If, on the other hand, we want a constant price of risk, then the variance of the interest rate at a future time has to go to infinity as that time approaches the maturity of the bond.

Assume that W is a one-dimensional Wiener process, and let $T > 0$. Define a process α on $[0, T)$ by

$$\alpha(t) = \int_0^t \frac{1}{T - s} \, dW(s)$$

for $0 \le t < T$.

Define the Brownian bridge processes Y on $[0, T]$ by

$$Y(t) = \begin{cases} (T - t)\alpha(t) & \text{for } 0 \le t < T \\ 0 & \text{for } t = T \end{cases}$$

for $0 \le t < T$.

Finally, define the zero-coupon bond price process S on $[0, T]$ by

$$S(t) = S(0) \exp[Rt + \sigma Y(t)]$$

for $0 \le t < T$, where $S(0) > 0$ is a deterministic initial value, $\sigma > 0$ is a constant, and R is the yield on the bond at time zero:

$$R = \frac{1}{T} \ln \left(\frac{1}{S(0)} \right)$$

Recall that

$$Y(t) = - \int_0^t \alpha \, ds + W(t)$$

for $0 \le t \le T$.

The zero-coupon bond price process can be written as

$$S(t) = S(0) \exp[Rt + \sigma Y(t)] = S(0) \exp \left[Rt - \int_0^t \sigma \alpha \, ds + \sigma W(t) \right]$$

The stochastic differential is

$$\frac{dS}{S} = \left(R - \sigma \alpha + \frac{1}{2} \sigma^2 \right) dt + \sigma \, dW = \mu \, dt + \sigma \, dW$$

where

$$\mu = R - \sigma \alpha + \frac{1}{2} \sigma^2$$

In addition to the single zero-coupon bond with maturity T, there is a money market account with interest rate process $r \in \mathcal{L}^1[0,T]$ and price process

$$M = M(0)\eta[r,0]$$

The price of risk $\lambda \in \mathcal{L}^2([0,T])$ has to satisfy

$$R + \frac{1}{2}\sigma^2 - \sigma\alpha - r = \sigma\lambda$$

which requires that

$$\sigma\alpha + r \in \mathcal{L}^2([0,T])$$

Since α does not belong to $\mathcal{L}^2([0,T])$, the interest rate r cannot belong to $\mathcal{L}^2([0,T])$ either. For example, if the interest rate r is constant on all of $[0,T]$, then no price of risk process λ exists and no state price process exists on $[0,T]$.

For any process $\zeta \in \mathcal{L}^2([0,T])$, we can choose the interest rate process

$$r = \zeta - \sigma\alpha \in \mathcal{L}^1([0,T])$$

and set

$$\lambda = \frac{R + \frac{1}{2}\sigma^2 - \zeta}{\sigma} \in \mathcal{L}^2([0,T])$$

If we want a constant λ, then ζ has to be constant, which implies that

$$\mathrm{var}(r(t)) = \sigma^2\mathrm{var}(\alpha(t)) \to \infty$$

as $t \to T$. $\square$

4.6 Arbitrage and Admissibility

An arbitrage strategy is a trading strategy which creates some value out of nothing. Formally, a *self-financing arbitrage strategy* is a self-financing trading strategy $\bar{\Delta} \in \mathcal{L}(\bar{S})$ such that

- either $\bar{\Delta}(0)\bar{S}(0) < 0$ and for some t, $\bar{\Delta}(t)\bar{S}(t) \geq 0$,
- or else $\bar{\Delta}(0)\bar{S}(0) \leq 0$ and for some t,

$$\bar{\Delta}(t)\bar{S}(t) \geq 0 \quad \text{and} \quad P(\bar{\Delta}(t)\bar{S}(t) > 0) > 0$$

Later on, we shall define a more general concept of arbitrage strategies which may not be self-financing.

It will be shown in Section 4.7 below that self-financing arbitrage strategies do exist. Specifically, we shall construct a self-financing trading strategy in the Black–Scholes model (the so-called "doubling strategy" of Harrison and Kreps) whose initial value is zero and whose final value is greater than one with probability one.

The idea comes from the "doubling strategy" played in a casino. At a roulette table, one thing you can do is put your money on red or on black. The wheel spins, and if your color comes out, you get double your money back. If the other color comes out, you get nothing.

Begin by borrowing one dollar and put it on red. If red comes out, you receive two dollars, use one to pay back your debt, and quit with one dollar. If black comes out, borrow two more dollars and put them on red. If red comes out, you receive four dollars, use three of them to pay back your debt, and quit with one dollar. Otherwise, borrow four dollars, put them on red, etc.

After n attempts, if you have not quit yet, you owe

$$1 + 2 + 2^2 + \cdots + 2^{n-1} = 2^n - 1$$

dollars, and you borrow another 2^n dollars, to a total of $2^{n+1} - 1$ dollars. If you win, you receive 2^{n+1}, pay back your debt, and you are left with one dollar.

The probability that you will eventually win, after a finite but random number of attempts, is

$$2^{-1} + 2^{-2} + \cdots + 2^{-n} + \ldots = 1$$

To be able to implement this strategy, you would need unlimited credit and time, which in practice you do not have, of course.

In the theoretical context of the Black–Scholes model, it is possible to construct a trading strategy similar to the doubling strategy, because trade can happen infinitely many times in a finite time interval and credit is unlimited.

Because of the existence of trading strategies such as the doubling strategy, the set of self-financing trading strategies has to be restricted. It has to be restricted so as to rule out arbitrage, but on the other hand the more it is restricted, the smaller will be the set of "marketed contingent claims" that can be "replicated" by trading the basic long-lived securities. So the set of self-financing trading strategies should be restricted, but not too much.

The restriction that we shall adopt here is that self-financing trading strategies have to be what we call "admissible." In Propositions 4.11 and 5.1, we shall consider alternative restrictions in the form of "financing constraints."

A self-financing trading strategy $\bar{\Delta} \in \mathcal{L}(\bar{S})$ will be said to be *admissible* (for the securities price process $\bar{S}$ and the state price process Π) if $\Pi\bar{\Delta}\bar{S}$ is a martingale. Later on, we shall define admissibility also for trading strategies that are not self-financing.

Whether $\Pi\bar{S}$ is a martingale is a question of whether buy-and-hold strategies are admissible. In the general development of the theory, it is not necessary to assume that they are.

Requiring self-financing trading strategies to be admissible does achieve the objective of ruling out self-financing arbitrage strategies. If $\bar{\Delta}$ is a self-financing arbitrage strategy, then

$$E\left(\Pi(t)\bar{\Delta}(t)\bar{S}(t)\right) > \Pi(0)\bar{\Delta}(0)\bar{S}(0)$$

Hence, $\Pi\bar{\Delta}\bar{S}$ cannot be a martingale, and $\bar{\Delta}$ cannot be admissible. So, there are no self-financing arbitrage strategies among the admissible self-financing trading strategies.

Exercise 4.1 *Simple self-financing trading strategies are admissible provided that all buy-and-hold strategies are admissible. Recall that a trading strategy* $\bar{\Delta}$ *is simple if and only if there exists a finite, strictly increasing sequence of points in time*

$$0 = t_0 < t_1 < \cdots < t_m$$

interpreted as potential trading dates, such that for every $\omega \in \Omega$, *the path* $\bar{\Delta}(\omega, \cdot)$ *is constant on each of the intervals* $[t_i, t_{i+1})$, $0 \leq i < m$, *and on* $[t_m, \infty) \cap \mathcal{T}$. *Assume that the simple trading strategy* $\bar{\Delta}$ *is self-financing, which means that it satisfies the instantaneous budget constraint:*

$$\bar{\Delta}(t_n)\bar{S}(t_{n+1}) = \bar{\Delta}(t_{n+1})\bar{S}(t_{n+1})$$

for all $n < m$. *Assume that all buy-and-hold strategies are admissible. Show that* $\bar{\Delta}$ *is admissible.*

The set of admissible self-financing trading strategies is obviously a linear space.

Example 4.10 *Continuation of Examples 1.7, 1.15, 2.3, 2.14, 2.20, 2.28, 4.1, 4.2, 4.3, and 4.8.* In the Black–Scholes model, the buy-and-hold strategies are admissible. For the stock,

$$\Pi S = \Pi(0)S(0)\eta[-r, -\lambda]\eta[\mu, \sigma] = \Pi(0)S(0)\eta[0, \sigma - \lambda]$$

Since $\sigma - \lambda$ is constant, it follows from Example 2.25 that $\eta[0, \sigma - \lambda]$ is a martingale. For the money market account,

$$\Pi M = \Pi(0)M(0)\eta[-r, -\lambda]\eta[r, 0] = \Pi(0)M(0)\eta[0, -\lambda]$$

Again, it follows from Example 2.25 that $\eta[0, -\lambda]$ is a martingale.   □

We shall show later that requiring self-financing trading strategies to be admissible, as defined above, is not too much of a restriction. The argument will be that so long as there are as many risky securities as there are Wiener processes, virtually any "contingent claim" which is contingent only on the information generated by the Wiener process W can be replicated by an admissible self-financing trading strategy.

To sum up, the definition of the state price process Π requires that $\Pi\bar{S}$ have zero drift, which implies that for every self-financing trading strategy $\bar{\Delta}$, $\Pi\bar{\Delta}\bar{S}$ has zero drift. This almost makes $\Pi\bar{\Delta}\bar{S}$ a martingale, but not quite. The additional assumption of admissibility says that $\Pi\bar{\Delta}\bar{S}$ is a martingale. We impose this assumption in order to rule out arbitrage. While zero drift is a consequence of the definition of Π, admissibility is a property of the trading strategy $\bar{\Delta}$.

Imposing admissibility on the trading strategies is one way to rule out arbitrage. Another way is to impose a restriction which can be interpreted as a financing constraint.

One possible restriction on a self-financing trading strategy $\bar{\Delta}$ is that its value process $\bar{\Delta}\bar{S}$ should be non-negative. This means that the trader must make sure that his or her wealth never becomes negative in any state of the world. This requirement obviously has the disadvantage that it allows replication only of non-negative claims.

A less restrictive requirement is that the process $\Pi\bar{\Delta}\bar{S}$ should be bounded below. This will of course be the case if the value process $\bar{\Delta}\bar{S}$ is non-negative. However, the process $\Pi\bar{\Delta}\bar{S}$ may well be bounded below even if $\bar{\Delta}\bar{S}$ is unbounded below and, in particular, even if $\bar{\Delta}\bar{S}$ takes negative values.

Proposition 4.11 *Let Π be a state price process for $\bar{S}$. There exists no self-financing arbitrage strategy $\bar{\Delta}$ such that $\Pi\bar{\Delta}\bar{S}$ is bounded below.*

Proof Let $\bar{\Delta}$ be a self-financing arbitrage strategy such that $\Pi\bar{\Delta}\bar{S}$ is bounded below. Choose a constant K such that with probability one, $\Pi(t)\bar{\Delta}(t)\bar{S}(t) > K$ for all t. The process $\Pi\bar{\Delta}\bar{S} - K$ is a positive Itô process with zero drift, and hence it is a supermartingale, by Proposition 2.23. This implies that $\Pi\bar{\Delta}\bar{S}$ is a supermartingale. However, since $\bar{\Delta}$ is a self-financing arbitrage strategy, there is some t such that

$$E\left(\Pi(t)\bar{\Delta}(t)\bar{S}(t)\right) > \Pi(0)\bar{\Delta}(0)\bar{S}(0)$$

Hence, $\Pi\bar{\Delta}\bar{S}$ cannot be a supermartingale, a contradiction. □

4.7   (*) The Doubling Strategy

The formal construction of the doubling strategy is carried out as follows. At time zero, make an investment in the stock, financed by borrowing. If at time t_1 the value of the position is at least one, then sell the stock and hold everything in the money market account until time $T = 1$. Otherwise, at time t_1, invest even more in the stock, financed by further borrowing. At time t_2, follow the same principle. If the value of the position is at least one, liquidate it and hold all your wealth in the money market account until time $T = 1$. Otherwise, borrow more money and invest more in the stock, etc.

If the amounts invested in the stock market period by period are chosen appropriately, then with probability one, you will exit after a finite number of periods with wealth greater than one.

Notice that in the stock-market-based doubling strategy, you do not liquidate and stop betting the first time your wealth is positive but the first time your wealth is at least one. In the casino, there is no such distinction. You stop betting the first time you win, at which time your wealth is one.

To describe this trading strategy formally, let S and M be the stock price process and the value process for the money market account in the Black–Scholes model:

$$\frac{dS}{S} = \mu\,dt + \sigma\,dW$$

$$\frac{dM}{M} = r\,dt$$

where $S(0) > 0$, $M(0) > 0$, μ, $\sigma > 0$, and $r \geq 0$ are constant numbers.

Set $T = 1$, $t_0 = 0$, and let (t_n) be an infinite strictly increasing sequence in $(0, 1)$:

$$0 = t_0 < t_1 < \cdots < t_n < \cdots < 1$$

such that $t_n \to 1$ as $n \to \infty$. These points in time will be potential trading dates.

The trading strategy will be denoted

$$\bar{\Delta} = (\Delta_0, \Delta)$$

where Δ is the number of shares of stock and Δ_0 is the number of units of the money market account held.

Suppose that during the entire closed time interval $[t_n, t_{n+1}]$ we hold $\Delta(t_n) \geq 0$ shares of stock, financed by borrowing at the rolled-over interest rate. This corresponds to short-selling $-\beta$ units of the money market account, where

$$\Delta(t_n)S(t_n) + \beta M(t_n) = 0$$

or

$$\beta = -\Delta(t_n)\frac{S(t_n)}{M(t_n)}$$

The value of the position at t_{n+1} will be

$$\Delta(t_n)S(t_{n+1}) + \beta M(t_{n+1})$$

We shall argue that there exist small positive numbers $a, \epsilon > 0$, independent of n, such that with probability at least ϵ, the value of the position at t_{n+1} is at least $\Delta(t_n)S(t_n)a$.

In order to simplify the following expressions, set

$$\tau_n = t_{n+1} - t_n$$

and

$$U_n = W(t_{n+1}) - W(t_n)$$

The value of the position at t_{n+1} will be

$$\Delta(t_n)S(t_{n+1}) + \beta M(t_{n+1}) = \Delta(t_n)\left(S(t_{n+1}) - \frac{S(t_n)}{M(t_n)}M(t_{n+1})\right)$$

$$= \Delta(t_n)S(t_n)\left\{\exp\left[\left(\mu - \frac{1}{2}\sigma^2\right)\tau_n + \sigma U_n\right] - e^{r\tau_n}\right\}$$

This value will be positive if and only if

$$\exp\left[\left(\mu - \frac{1}{2}\sigma^2\right)\tau_n + \sigma U_n\right] - e^{r\tau_n} > 0$$

that is, if and only if the stock price grows by a larger factor than the value of the money market account. This is equivalent to

$$\frac{\mu - r - \frac{1}{2}\sigma^2}{\sigma}\sqrt{\tau_n} > -\frac{1}{\sqrt{\tau_n}}U_n$$

Since the right hand side of the last inequality follows a standard normal distribution, the probability that the inequality holds, or the probability that the value of the position will be positive, is

$$N\left(\frac{\mu - r - \frac{1}{2}\sigma^2}{\sigma}\sqrt{\tau_n}\right)$$

where N is the standard normal distribution function. If

$$\mu - r - \frac{1}{2}\sigma^2 > 0$$

then this probability is at least one-half. Otherwise, it is at least

$$N\left(\frac{\mu - r - \frac{1}{2}\sigma^2}{\sigma}\right)$$

In any case, we can choose some small positive number $\epsilon > 0$ such that the probability is at least 2ϵ, independently of n.

It follows that there exists a small positive constant $a > 0$ such that

$$\exp\left[\left(\mu - \frac{1}{2}\sigma^2\right)\tau_n + \sigma U_n\right] - e^{r\tau_n} > a$$

with probability at least ϵ, independently of n. Hence, the value of the position at t_{n+1} exceeds $\Delta(t_n)S(t_n)a$ with probability at least ϵ.

Now construct the trading strategy $\bar{\Delta}$. It will be pathwise constant on the time intervals $[t_n, t_{n+1})$, and it will be an almost simple trading strategy. Choose the holdings $\Delta(t_n)$ and $\Delta_0(t_n)$ inductively as follows.

Initially, when $n = 0$ and $t_n = t_0 = 0$, choose $\Delta(0) = \Delta(t_0)$ so large that

$$\Delta(0)S(0)a \geq 1$$

Buy $\Delta(0)$ shares of stock, and finance it by borrowing. That means put

$$\Delta_0(0) = -\Delta(0)\frac{S(0)}{M(0)}$$

so that

$$\Delta_0(0)M(0) + \Delta(0)S(0) = 0$$

Set

$$V(t_1) = \Delta_0(0)M(t_1) + \Delta(0)S(t_1)$$

This is the value of the position at time t_1 assuming that there would be no trade at t_1. With probability at least ϵ, $V(t_1)$ will exceed one.

Next let $1 \leq n$ and suppose that $\bar{\Delta}(t_i)$ has been chosen for $0 \leq i < n$, and in particular, $\bar{\Delta}(t_{n-1})$ has been chosen such that

$$V(t_n) = \Delta_0(t_{n-1})M(t_n) + \Delta(t_{n-1})S(t_n)$$

exceeds one with probability at least ϵ.

At time t_n, if $V(t_n) \geq 1$, invest everything in the money market account. That means put

$$\Delta(t_n) = 0$$

and

$$\Delta_0(t_n) = \frac{V(t_n)}{M(t_n)}$$

so that

$$\Delta_0(t_n)M(t_n) = V(t_n)$$

This ensures that the instantaneous budget constraint holds at time t_n. Keep this position unchanged up to and including time $T = 1$. Indeed, given that $r \geq 0$, the value of the position will stay above one until $T = 1$.

At time t_n, if $V(t_n) < 1$, choose $\Delta(t_n)$ such that

$$\Delta(t_n)S(t_n)a \geq 1 - V(t_n)e^{rr_n}$$

Buy $\Delta(t_n)$ shares of stock and finance it as necessary by borrowing. That means put

$$\beta = -\Delta(t_n)\frac{S(t_n)}{M(t_n)}$$

and

$$\Delta_0(t_n) = \beta + \frac{V(t_n)}{M(t_n)}$$

so that

$$\Delta_0(t_n)M(t_n) + \Delta(t_n)S(t_n) = V(t_n)$$

This again ensures that the instantaneous budget constraint is satisfied at time t_n.

The value at t_{n+1} of the stock and the financing β of the stock is

$$\Delta(t_n)S(t_{n+1}) + \beta M(t_{n+1})$$

which, as we have argued, will be greater than $\Delta(t_n)S(t_n)a$ with probability at least ϵ. Therefore,

$$V(t_{n+1}) = \Delta_0(t_n)M(t_{n+1}) + \Delta(t_n)S(t_{n+1})$$

will be greater than

$$\Delta(t_n)S(t_n)a + V(t_n)e^{rr_n} \geq 1$$

with probability at least ϵ.

Given $\omega \in \Omega$, if $V(\omega, t_n) \geq 1$ for some n, then $\Delta(\omega, t)$ is well defined for all $t \in [0, 1]$. Otherwise, we have defined it only for $t < 1$. Arbitrarily define $\Delta(\omega, 1) = 0$.

It is clear that $\bar{\Delta}$ is adapted. Since it is right-continuous, it follows that it is measurable.

Let us show that $\bar{\Delta}$ is an almost simple trading strategy. The probability that the value at time t_1 is less than one is

$$P(\bar{\Delta}(t_1)\bar{S}(t_1) < 1) \leq 1 - \epsilon$$

and the probability that the value at time t_{n+1} is less than one is

$$P(\bar{\Delta}(t_{n+1})\bar{S}(t_{n+1}) < 1) \leq P(\bar{\Delta}(t_n)\bar{S}(t_n))(1 - \epsilon)$$

Hence, by induction,

$$P(\bar{\Delta}(t_n)\bar{S}(t_n) < 1) \leq (1 - \epsilon)^n \to 0$$

as $n \to \infty$, and

$$P(\bar{\Delta}(t_n)\bar{S}(t_n) < 1 \text{ for all } n) = 0$$

Thus, the trading strategy $\bar{\Delta}$ is almost simple.

Indeed, define the random variable p by

$$p(\omega) = \min\{i : \bar{\Delta}(t_i) = \bar{\Delta}(t_j) \text{ for all } j \geq i\}$$

Then

$$A(n) = \{\omega \in \Omega : p(\omega) \leq n\} = \{\bar{\Delta}(t_n)\bar{S}(t_n) \geq 1\} \in \mathcal{F}_{t_n}$$

and the path $\bar{\Delta}(\omega, \cdot)$ is constant on each of the intervals $[t_i, t_{i+1})$, $0 \leq i < p(\omega)$, and on $[p(\omega), 1]$.

It follows that with probability one,

$$\bar{\Delta}(1)\bar{S}(1) \geq 1$$

So, the final value is at least one, even though the initial cost is zero. The trading strategy $\bar{\Delta}$ is a self-financing arbitrage trading strategy.

4.8 Changing the Unit of Account

It is often useful to change the unit of account in which prices are expressed. For example, one may wish to express prices in units of foreign currency, or to normalize them by expressing them in units of a numeraire (a security or a self-financing trading strategy). The numeraire will often be the money market account, but it may sometimes be convenient to use another security as numeraire.

Suppose E is a positive Itô process:

$$E(t) = E(0)\eta[\mu_E, \sigma_E](t)$$

where μ_E is a one-dimensional process in $\mathcal{L}^1$ and σ_E is a K-dimensional row vector process in $\mathcal{L}^2$. In differential form,

$$\frac{dE}{E} = \mu_E dt + \sigma_E dW$$

We interpret E as the price of the new unit of account in terms of the old unit of account. The generic example is an exchange rate: E is the price of a unit of foreign currency in units of home currency. If E is an exchange rate, then μ_E can be interpreted as the *expected instantaneous rate of appreciation* of the foreign currency, while σ_E is a vector of *instantaneous foreign exchange risks*.

By Itô's formula,

$$d\left(\frac{\bar{S}}{E}\right) = \frac{1}{E}\left[\bar{\mu} + \bar{S}\left(-\mu_E + \sigma_E\sigma_E^\top\right) - \bar{\sigma}\sigma_E^\top\right] dt + \frac{1}{E}\left[\bar{\sigma} - \bar{S}\sigma_E\right] dW$$

$$= \frac{1}{E}\left[\bar{\mu} - \bar{S}\mu_E - \left(\bar{\sigma} - \bar{S}\sigma_E\right)\sigma_E^\top\right] dt + \frac{1}{E}\left[\bar{\sigma} - \bar{S}\sigma_E\right] dW$$

If we imagine that the securities prices $\bar{S}$ are expressed in home currency units, and E is an exchange rate, then $\bar{S}/E$ is the securities price processes in terms of foreign currency.

Suppose we change the unit of account by using $\bar{S}/E$ as price process instead of $\bar{S}$. The following proposition shows that such a change does not affect the set of self-financing trading strategies.

Proposition 4.12 *Let E be a positive Itô process. A trading strategy $\bar{\Delta}$ is self-financing with respect to $\bar{S}$ if and only if it is self-financing with respect to $\bar{S}/E$.*

Proof Assume that $\bar{\Delta}$ is self-financing with respect to $\bar{S}$. Observe that

$$\bar{\Delta}\frac{1}{E}\left[\bar{\mu} - \bar{S}\mu_E - \left(\bar{\sigma} - \bar{S}\sigma_E\right)\sigma_E^\top\right] = \frac{1}{E}\left[\bar{\Delta}\bar{\mu} - \bar{\Delta}\bar{S}\mu_E - \left(\bar{\Delta}\bar{\sigma} - \bar{\Delta}\bar{S}\sigma_E\right)\sigma_E^\top\right]$$

This process is in $\mathcal{L}^1$ because $1/E$ is continuous, $\bar{\Delta}\bar{\mu} \in \mathcal{L}^1$, $\bar{\Delta}\bar{S}$ is continuous because $\bar{\Delta}$ is self-financing, μ_E is in $\mathcal{L}^1$, and $\bar{\Delta}\bar{\sigma}$ and σ_E are in $\mathcal{L}^2$. The fact that $\bar{\Delta}\bar{\sigma}$ and σ_E are in $\mathcal{L}^2$ implies that $\bar{\Delta}\bar{S}\sigma_E\sigma_E^\top$ is in $\mathcal{L}^1$ by Proposition 1.28 or directly by the Cauchy–Schwartz inequality. Furthermore,

$$\bar{\Delta}\frac{1}{E}\left[\bar{\sigma} - \bar{S}\sigma_E\right] = \frac{1}{E}\left[\bar{\Delta}\bar{\sigma} - \bar{\Delta}\bar{S}\sigma_E\right]$$

This process is in $\mathcal{L}^2$ because $1/E$ is continuous, $\bar{\Delta}\bar{\sigma} \in \mathcal{L}^2$, $\bar{\Delta}\bar{S}$ is continuous because $\bar{\Delta}$ is self-financing, and σ_E is in $\mathcal{L}^2$. Hence, $\bar{\Delta} \in \mathcal{L}(\bar{S}/E)$. The fact that $\bar{\Delta}$ is self-financing with respect to $\bar{S}/E$ is shown by the following calculation:

$$d\left(\bar{\Delta}\frac{\bar{S}}{E}\right) = d\left(\frac{1}{E}(\bar{\Delta}\bar{S})\right)$$

$$= \frac{1}{E} d(\bar{\Delta}\bar{S}) + \bar{\Delta}\bar{S} d\left(\frac{1}{E}\right) - \frac{1}{E}\bar{\Delta}\bar{\sigma}\sigma_E^{\top} dt$$

$$= \frac{1}{E}\bar{\Delta} d\bar{S} + \bar{\Delta}\bar{S} d\left(\frac{1}{E}\right) - \frac{1}{E}\bar{\Delta}\bar{\sigma}\sigma_E^{\top} dt$$

$$= \bar{\Delta} d\left(\frac{\bar{S}}{E}\right)$$

Conversely, if $\bar{\Delta}$ is self-financing with respect to $\bar{S}/E$, then the above argument applied to $1/E$ instead of E shows that $\bar{\Delta}$ is also self-financing with respect to $\bar{S}$. □

Exercise 4.2 *In the Black–Scholes model of Examples 4.1 and 4.2, let Δ be the deterministic process given by*

$$\Delta(t) = \begin{cases} t & \text{if } t \text{ is rational} \\ 1 & \text{if } t \text{ is irrational} \end{cases}$$

for $t \geq 0$. Find a process Δ_0 such that $\bar{\Delta} = (\Delta_0, \Delta)$ is a self-financing trading strategy with initial value zero. Is Δ_0 unique? What is the value process of $\bar{\Delta}$? Is $\bar{\Delta}$ admissible?

It is easily seen that Π is a state price process for $\bar{S}$ if and only if ΠE is a state price process for $\bar{S}/E$.

A self-financing trading strategy $\bar{\Delta}$ is admissible for $\bar{S}$ and Π if and only if it is admissible for $\bar{S}/E$ and ΠE. In both cases, the criterion is that

$$\Pi\bar{\Delta}\bar{S} = (\Pi E)\bar{\Delta}\bar{S}/E$$

should be a martingale.

In general, changing the unit of account changes the state price process, and, hence, it changes the interest rate and the prices of risk. If E has zero dispersion, then the change of unit of account does not change λ, but it does change r. For example, dividing by the value of a money market account sets the interest rate to zero but leaves the prices of risk unchanged. Dividing by the value process of a self-financing trading strategy which is not instantaneously riskless not only sets the interest rate to zero but will also change the prices of risk.

Suppose we express prices in terms of the value of a self-financing trading strategy $\bar{b}$ such that $\bar{b}\bar{S}$ is positive. Set $E = \bar{b}\bar{S}$. The sets of self-financing trading strategies with respect to $\bar{S}$ and $\bar{S}/(\bar{b}\bar{S})$ are identical. In particular, $\bar{b}$ is a self-financing trading strategy with respect to $\bar{S}/(\bar{b}\bar{S})$. The value process of $\bar{b}$ with respect to $\bar{S}/(\bar{b}\bar{S})$ is $\bar{b}\bar{S}/(\bar{b}\bar{S}) = 1$, so $\bar{S}/(\bar{b}\bar{S})$ is normalized with $\bar{b}$ as numeraire.

If $\bar{b}$ is a money market account, then we set $M = \bar{b}\bar{S}$. The dynamics of the basic securities price processes, remeasured in terms of the money market account, look like this:

$$d\left(\frac{\bar{S}}{M}\right) = \frac{1}{M} d\bar{S} - \bar{S}\frac{r}{M} dt = \frac{1}{M}(\bar{\mu} - r\bar{S}) dt + \frac{1}{M}\bar{\sigma} dW$$

Example 4.13 *Two risky securities whose price processes are correlated geometric Brownian motions. Continuation of Examples 2.21 and 4.6.* Let A be a $(2 \times K)$-dimensional matrix with

$$AA^{\mathsf{T}} = \begin{pmatrix} 1 & \rho \\ \rho & 1 \end{pmatrix}$$

Then $Z = AW$ is a two-dimensional correlated Wiener process with increment correlation coefficient ρ. The financial price processes are

$$S_1 = S_1(0)\eta[\mu_1, (\sigma_1, 0)A]$$

and

$$S_2 = S_2(0)\eta[\mu_2, (0, \sigma_2)A]$$

where $S_1(0) > 0$, $S_2(0) > 0$, μ_1, μ_2, $\sigma_1 > 0$, and $\sigma_2 > 0$ are constants.

In this model, as shown in Example 4.6, the process r can be chosen arbitrarily in $\mathcal{L}^2$. Given r, the vector process λ of prices of risk is uniquely determined by

$$\begin{pmatrix} \mu_1 \\ \mu_2 \end{pmatrix} - \begin{pmatrix} r \\ r \end{pmatrix} = \begin{pmatrix} \sigma_1 & 0 \\ 0 & \sigma_2 \end{pmatrix} A \lambda^{\mathsf{T}}$$

As seen in Example 2.21,

$$\frac{S_2}{S_1} = \frac{S_2(0)}{S_1(0)} \eta[\mu_2 - \mu_1 + \sigma_1^2 - \rho\sigma_1\sigma_2, (-\sigma_1, \sigma_2)A]$$

Assume that the increment correlation ρ satisfies $-1 < \rho < 1$. Set

$$\sigma = \sqrt{\sigma_1^2 + \sigma_2^2 - 2\rho\sigma_1\sigma_2}$$

Recall that the process

$$\tilde{W} = \frac{1}{\sigma}(-\sigma_1 Z_1 + \sigma_2 Z_2)$$

is a standard Wiener process relative to F, and that S_2/S_1 can be expressed as a stochastic exponential with respect to $\tilde{W}$:

$$\begin{aligned} d\left(\frac{S_2}{S_1}\right) &= \frac{S_2}{S_1}\left[(\mu_2 - \mu_1 + \sigma_1^2 - \rho\sigma_1\sigma_2)\, dt + (-\sigma_1, \sigma_2)A\, dW\right] \\ &= \frac{S_2}{S_1}\left[(\mu_2 - \mu_1 + \sigma_1^2 - \rho\sigma_1\sigma_2)\, dt - \sigma_1\, dZ_1(t) + \sigma_2\, dZ_2(t)\right] \\ &= \frac{S_2}{S_1}\left[(\mu_2 - \mu_1 + \sigma_1^2 - \rho\sigma_1\sigma_2)\, dt + \sigma\, d\tilde{W}\right] \end{aligned}$$

Now the only instantaneously risky security in the model is driven by the single, one-dimensional Wiener process $\tilde{W}$. We can define a price of risk $\tilde{\lambda}$ with respect to $\tilde{W}$ in the new price system by

$$\mu_2 - \mu_1 + \sigma_1^2 - \rho\sigma_1\sigma_2 = \sigma\tilde{\lambda}$$

or

$$\tilde{\lambda} = \frac{\mu_2 - \mu_1 + \sigma_1^2 - \rho\sigma_1\sigma_2}{\sigma}$$

The corresponding state price process $\tilde{\Pi}$ in the new price system (which is unique except for its initial value) will have differential

$$\frac{d\tilde{\Pi}}{\tilde{\Pi}} = -\tilde{\lambda}\, d\tilde{W} = -\frac{\tilde{\lambda}}{\sigma}(-\sigma_1\, dZ_1 + \sigma_2\, dZ_2) = -\frac{\tilde{\lambda}}{\sigma}(-\sigma_1, \sigma_2) A\, dW$$

$\square$

Exercise 4.3 *In Example 4.13, the process $\Pi = \tilde{\Pi}/S_1$ will be a state price process for the original price system. It will correspond to a specific choice of the (otherwise arbitrary) interest rate process r in the original price system. Calculate this interest rate process.*

4.9   Summary

We began this chapter by setting up a general model of trading in securities markets. There are a number of basic securities, whose price processes are Itô processes. These securities are assumed not to pay any distributions, dividends, or other cash flows before the horizon date. Typically they include a money market account plus a number of risky securities. In most applications to pricing and hedging of derivatives, there will be one, two, or maybe three risky basic securities. For example, the risky basic securities may be one or two stocks, or a stock and a foreign deposit, or one or two long-dated bonds. In the Black–Scholes model, there is just one stock plus the money market account. In a few applications, there will be no money market account.

A trading strategy is a multi-dimensional stochastic process which tells us at each point in time and in each state of the world how many units of the various basic securities to hold at that time and in that state of the world. It maps out a complete contingent plan for how to trade and what to hold at each future time and in each contingency, as it depends on the development of securities prices or other information up to that time.

The principle of pricing a contingent claim is the following. The future payoff to the claim, on its maturity date, is generally not known in advance and therefore random. In order to find its value before maturity, we try to construct a trading strategy which replicates the payoff in the sense that in every possible future scenario, its value on the maturity date will equal the payoff to the claim. The value of our holdings will be random, because the basic securities prices move randomly and because we may trade in response to these random fluctuations. But in every possible scenario, the value of the holdings should be equal to the payoff to the claim.

We also want the trading strategy to be self-financing and satisfy an admissibility condition which is imposed in order to rule out the possibility of arbitrage.

If such a replicating trading strategy can be found, then the current price of the claim should be equal to the initial amount of money needed to start off the trading strategy.

A trading strategy is self-financing if it satisfies an instantaneous budget constraint which says that the instantaneous change in the value of the holdings equals the sum across securities of the number of units held times the instantaneous change in the value of the security. Formally, the budget constraint is expressed as an integral equation. Intuitively, it is useful to think of it in terms of a securities account. Initially, you deposit money and take a position in securities in the account. Over time, you trade inside the account, but you do not take money out of the account or deposit more money in it. New securities purchases are financed by sales of other securities, or by borrowing, which is represented as holding a negative position in the money market account. This is the sense in which the trading strategy has to be self-financing.

We illustrated trading, pricing, and replication by the Black–Scholes formula, which we will actually not derive formally until Chapter 6. This formula gives the value of a European call option on a stock that does not pay any dividends before maturity of the option. The stock price is assumed to follow a geometric Brownian motion, and the interest rate is assumed to be constant.

The Black–Scholes formula tells us not only what will be the value of the option but also, indirectly, what will be the composition of a replicating trading strategy. The option price is a function of the current stock price, and the derivative with respect to the stock price, which is called the delta of the option, is the number of shares of stock that is to be included in the replicating trading strategy. These shares will be partially financed by borrowing, and we can calculate how much to borrow by using the fact that the total net value of the holdings must equal the value of the option. The difference between the value of the shares and the value of the option represents borrowed money. As we shall see in Chapter 6, a trading strategy constructed this way will indeed replicate the payoff to the option.

In order to illustrate the instantaneous budget constraint and prepare for the discussion of the doubling strategy, we analyzed simple and almost simple trading strategies in some detail. Simple trading strategies involve trading only at a finite and non-random number of prespecified points in time. Almost simple trading strategies also involve trading only at a finite number of dates, but this number may be random. Across states of the world, there may be a countably infinite number of potential trading dates. The doubling strategy is an example of an almost simple trading strategy.

If a trading strategy is simple or almost simple, then the budget constraint says that at each of the finitely or countably many potential trading dates, the value of the securities held immediately before trading equals the value of those held immediately after trading.

A state price process is a positive Itô process whose products with the basic securities prices have zero drift. Since a state price process is a positive Itô process, it is a stochastic exponential, and so it is characterized by a relative drift process and a relative dispersion process (plus an irrelevant initial value). By setting the drift of the product of the state price process and the value of the money market account equal to zero, we find that the relative drift of the state price process must be the negative of the instantaneous interest rate. We usually get the interest rate from the specification of the money market account, if there is one among the basic securities. Otherwise, we have to check whether it is possible to trade in the basic securities in such a way as to replicate a money market account.

By setting the drift of the product of the state price process and each of the securities prices equal to zero, we get an equation linking the relative dispersion of the state price process, the drift and dispersion of the securities prices, the interest rate, and the securities prices themselves.

On the basis of this equation, we interpret the negative of the relative dispersion of the state price process as a vector of prices of risk. The equation says that the excess instantaneous dollar return on a security, excess over the dollar return on the same amount of money invested in the money market account, is a sum across the underlying Wiener processes of the instantaneous covariance of the security with the Wiener process times a price of risk specific to the Wiener process. If, for example, a security has a positive and large instantaneous covariance with the first Wiener process, and if the price of risk for the first Wiener process is also positive and large, then this contributes to a high instantaneous excess dollar return for the security.

The equation also allows us to calculate the prices of risk. It is a linear equation which may have no solution, infinitely many solutions, or one unique solution.

If the rank of the dispersion matrix of the securities prices equals the number of basic securities, or if it equals the number of instantaneously risky basic securities in the case where one of the basic securities is a money market account, then we can write down a unique candidate for a vector of prices of risk which is a linear combination of the rows of the dispersion matrix of the basic securities. If this candidate process satisfies the appropriate integrability condition, then it is indeed a vector of prices of risk. It is the minimal vector of prices of risk in the sense that it has smaller length than any other vector of prices of risk. Any arbitrary vector of prices of risk is the sum of the minimal vector of prices of risk and a process which is orthogonal to the rows of the dispersion matrix, and any such sum is a vector of prices of risk, provided that it satisfies the required integrability condition.

The state price process which corresponds to the minimal vector of prices of risk is the minimal state price process in the sense that it has smaller volatility than any other state price process.

If the rank of the relative dispersion matrix of the securities prices equals the number of Wiener processes, then there is at most one vector of prices of risk and at most one state price process. However, even if there is a solution for the prices of risk at each time and in each state of the world, it is necessary to check that these solutions fit together to form a process which can be integrated up against the Wiener processes.

Given the interest rate, the existence and uniqueness of a state price process are equivalent to the existence and uniqueness of a vector of prices of risk.

In the case where all the basic securities prices are positive, their dynamics can be expressed in terms of a relative drift vector and a relative dispersion matrix. The equation which determines the prices of risk can be formulated in terms of these relative parameters. The equation now says that the excess instantaneous rate of return on a security, excess over the instantaneous interest rate, is a sum across the underlying Wiener processes of the instantaneous covariance of the rate of return to the security with the Wiener process times the price of risk for that Wiener process. If the zeroth security is a money market account, then the equation only needs to be verified for the remaining, instantaneously risky, securities.

The Ball–Torous [5, 1983] model has two basic securities, which are zero-coupon bonds with face value one and with different maturity dates. The model was designed to price an option on the long bond. We showed in Example 4.7 that there exists no state price process on the life span of the short bond.

In Example 4.8, we calculated the price of risk, and hence the state price process, in the Black–Scholes model.

Example 4.9 was a variation of the Ball–Torous [5, 1983] model, where there was a money market account but only one zero-coupon bond. We found that if the interest rate on the money market account is constant, then there exist no price of risk and no state price process. If, on the other hand, we want a constant price of risk, then the variance of the interest rate at a future time has to go to infinity as that time approaches the maturity of the bond.

A self-financing arbitrage strategy is a self-financing trading strategy which creates some value out of nothing. It is an unfortunate fact about our model that self-financing arbitrage strategies do exist. Specifically, we constructed the doubling strategy, which is a self-financing trading strategy in the Black–Scholes model whose initial value is zero and whose final value is greater than one with probability one.

Arbitrage strategies such as the doubling strategy are not due to mispricing of derivative securities, because they involve only the basic securities. Although they cannot be implemented in the real world, they can be implemented within the model, and so they are an embarrassment for the model builder.

Because of the existence of arbitrage strategies, we adopted the restriction that self-financing trading strategies have to be admissible, which means that the product of their value process and the state price process is a martingale. This does achieve the objective of ruling out arbitrage, because there are no self-financing arbitrage strategies among the admissible self-financing trading strategies.

Since each basic security price multiplied by the state price process has zero drift, the same is true of the value process of a self-financing trading strategy. That is almost the same as saying that the value process multiplied by the state price process is a martingale, but not quite. The admissibility requirement says that this product should indeed be a martingale.

Exercise 4.1 shows that simple self-financing trading strategies are admissible provided that all buy-and-hold strategies are admissible. Example 4.10 shows that in the Black–Scholes model, the buy-and-hold strategies are admissible.

Imposing admissibility on the trading strategies is one way to rule out arbitrage. Another way is to impose financing constraints, such as requiring the value process of a self-financing trading strategy to be non-negative, or requiring the product of the value process and the state price process to be bounded below. Proposition 4.11 says that the latter restriction does succeed in ruling out arbitrage.

It is often useful to change the unit of account in which prices are expressed. For example, one may wish to express prices in units of foreign currency, or to normalize them by expressing them in units of a self-financing trading strategy or a security such as the money market account. Even if there is no money market account in the original price system, there may be one in the new prices.

Proposition 4.12 shows that a change of the unit of account does not affect the set of self-financing trading strategies. It follows easily that it does not affect the set of admissible self-financing trading strategies either.

In general, changing the unit of account changes the state price process, and, hence, it changes the interest rate and the prices of risk. For example, if we express prices in terms of the value of a self-financing trading strategy with positive value process, then this trading strategy becomes a money market account in the new price system, and the interest rate in the new price system will be zero. The prices of risk will also change, unless the trading strategy was already a money market account in the original price system. We illustrated this in Example 4.13, which has two instantaneously risky securities whose price processes are correlated geometric Brownian motions. When prices are expressed in units of one of these securities, that security becomes a money market account with zero interest rate, and the prices of risk change.

4.10   (*) Notes

Our general trading model is similar to those of Merton [68, 1971], Merton [69, 1973], Harrison and Pliska [44, 1981], Bensoussan [7, 1984], and Pliska [76, 1986].

Merton [68, 1971], [69, 1973], and a number of other authors, assume that the price processes are functions of a Markovian vector of state variables.

Some authors, including Harrison and Pliska [44, 1981], Harrison and Pliska [45, 1983], Bensoussan [7, 1984], Jarrow and Madan [60, 1991], and Karatzas [62, 1997], require the price processes of the basic securities to be positive. This is not necessary. It is useful when the model is used for optimal portfolio management, but it does not seem to give any particular benefits when the model is used for pricing and hedging of derivatives. It is even undesirable, because we may want to hedge or replicate a derivative by trading securities whose value processes can become negative, such as forward contracts or swaps.

Some papers, such as Huang [50, 1985], [51, 1985], assume that trading strategies are bounded. In the context of pricing and hedging of derivative securities, the problem with bounded trading strategies is that their spanning properties are limited and unclear. In other words, there is no convenient version of the complete markets theorem (Theorem 5.6) for bounded trading strategies.

Some authors impose integrability conditions on trading strategies which are stricter than the requirement $\bar{\Delta} \in \mathcal{L}(\bar{S})$, which we have imposed here in order to be able to calculate the cumulative gains process as a stochastic integral with respect to the vector of price processes.

Harrison and Pliska [44, 1981], [45, 1983] used basic price processes that were more general than (positive) Itô processes, and they therefore had to impose a "local integrability" condition on their trading strategies in order for the stochastic integral that defines the cumulative gains process and the budget constraint to make sense. In the case of Itô processes, using our notation, their restriction says the following. There exists an increasing sequence of non-negative stopping times T_n which converges to T with probability one, such that

$$E_Q \left(\int_0^{T_n} \left\| \frac{1}{M} \bar{\Delta} \bar{\sigma} \right\|^2 ds \right)^{\frac{1}{2}} < \infty$$

for all n, where Q is the "risk-adjusted probability measure" or "equivalent martingale measure" (to be introduced in Chapter 5).

In the case where the basic securities price processes are Itô processes, the local integrability restriction of Harrison and Pliska [44, 1981] implies that each component of the trading strategy can be integrated up against the corresponding securities price process. See Example 2.8 and the discussion in Jarrow and Madan [60, 1991] of the distinction between "component self-financing trading strategies" and "vector self-financing trading strategies." With a restricted set of trading strategies, markets will not be dynamically complete except under a set of assumptions that are stronger than those in Theorem 5.6. See Müller [73, 1989] and Jarrow and Madan [60, 1991].

Other authors, including Duffie and Huang [32, 1985], Duffie [29, 1986], Huang [52, 1987], Duffie and Zame [33, 1989], and Duffie [30, 1992], have imposed a square integrability requirement on the trading strategies which, in our notation, says that

$$E_P \int_0^T \| \bar{\Delta} \bar{\sigma} \|^2 ds < \infty$$

Notice that the expectation is calculated under the original probability measure P, while the expectation in the condition of Harrison and Pliska [44, 1981] is calculated under the risk-adjusted probability measure. In Duffie [29, 1986] and Duffie and Zame [33, 1989], however, there is no distinction between the two measures. Duffie and Huang [32, 1985] and Huang [52, 1987] assume that the risk-adjusted probability measure is uniformly absolutely continuous with respect to the original measure, which means that the density is bounded above and below away from zero. This is a strong assumption which is not satisfied if, for example, the prices of risk are constant, as in the Black–Scholes model. The assumption implies that when the square integrability condition holds under the original probability measure, it also holds under the risk-adjusted probability measure. All four papers work with normalized prices, and the square integrability condition has the effect of making the normalized value processes of the trading strategies martingales under the risk-adjusted probability measure. It implies that the trading strategies are admissible.

Dothan [28, 1990], in his analysis of the Black–Scholes model, imposed an integrability requirement which corresponds to the one above, but with the expectation calculated under the risk-adjusted probabilities:

$$E_Q \int_0^T \|\Delta \sigma S\|^2 \, ds < \infty$$

He showed that the claims that can be replicated by such trading strategies (when the filtration is generated by the Wiener process) are those that are measurable with respect to the final sigma-algebra in the filtration and square integrable with respect to Q. However, he chose to consider only claims that are also square integrable under P.

Cox and Huang [23, 1989] imposed an integrability requirement on the trading strategies which, in our notation, says that

$$E_Q \int_0^T \left(\left\| \frac{1}{M} \bar{\Delta} \bar{\sigma} \right\|^2 ds \right)^{p/2} < \infty$$

for some $p > 1$. This again has the effect of making the normalized value processes of the trading strategies martingales under the risk-adjusted probability measure, and hence making the trading strategies admissible.

The main problem with these various integrability conditions is that they are not invariant under a change of unit of account, unless the deflator is bounded above and below away from zero. This means that the space of self-financing trading strategies will depend on the unit of account. This is so even if you just discount by a rolled-over instantaneously riskless interest rate, unless this rate is bounded. But in all the standard models of the term structure of interest rates, the interest rate is unbounded.

Some authors assume that the drift and dispersion coefficients of the prices, including the interest rate, are bounded. Examples include Bensoussan [7, 1984], Karatzas, Lehoczky, and Shreve [63, 1987], and Karatzas and Shreve [64, 1988].

The budget constraint in continuous time may have been originally formulated by Merton [67, 1969]. The term "self-financing" is from Harrison and Kreps [43, 1979].

The Black–Scholes formula was originally derived in Black and Scholes [10, 1973].

Harrison and Kreps [43, 1979] studied simple and almost simple trading strategies. They did not allow continuous trading. They assumed that the normalized (discounted) securities price processes form a Markovian vector of Itô processes and are square integrable under the original probabilities P. They required an equivalent martingale measure Q to have a positive square integrable density and to make the discounted price process a martingale. The purpose of requiring square integrability of the density appears to be to ensure that any process which is square integrable with respect to the original probability measure P will be integrable with respect to the risk-adjusted measure Q. They showed that arbitrage is not possible with simple trading strategies, and they described the doubling strategy as an example of arbitrage when almost simple trading strategies are allowed.

The state price process or pricing kernel is intimately related to the Arrow–Debreu securities and Arrow–Debreu prices. An Arrow–Debreu security is a contingent claim that will pay off only at a particular point in time in the future, contingent on a particular state of the world. Today's prices of Arrow–Debreu securities are called Arrow–Debreu prices. See the last chapter of Debreu [26, 1959].

The concept of a state price process or pricing kernel has been implicit in the continuous-time finance literature for a long time. Its central role in specifying a model was argued by Constantinides [21, 1992]. Duffie [30, 1992] also used this concept quite explicitly. Most of the literature downplays the state price process and relies instead on the concept of an equivalent martingale measure or risk-adjusted probability measure. We shall introduce the risk-adjusted probability measure in the next chapter.

The concept of a vector of prices of risk, although not the name, goes all the way back to Harrison and Kreps [43, 1979]. The minimal vector of prices of risk can be found in He and Pearson [46, 1991], who also showed how any vector of prices of risk can be written as the sum of the minimal vector of prices of risk and a vector which is orthogonal to the rows of the dispersion matrix of the basic securities.

The inequalities in Propositions 4.4 and 4.5 are continuous-time versions of the *volatility bound* of Hansen and Jagannathan [41, 1991]. See also Campbell, Lo, and MacKinlay [13, 1997, Chapter 8, Section 1].

We avoid arbitrage trading strategies, such as the doubling strategy of Harrison and Kreps [43, 1979], by the requirement that the value processes of admissible trading strategies, multiplied by the state price process, be martingales under the risk-adjusted probability measure. This is the natural extension of the requirement in Harrison and Pliska [44, 1981] and Pliska [76, 1986] that the normalized value processes of admissible self-financing trading strategies be martingales under the risk-adjusted probability measure.

As noted above, a number of authors have chosen instead to impose strict integrability conditions on the trading strategies, with the unfortunate implication that the space of self-financing trading strategies is not invariant under a change of unit of account.

Harrison and Pliska [44, 1981] suggested a different way of avoiding arbitrage trading strategies, which is to require trading strategies to have non-negative value processes. In that case, the product of the state price process and the value process will be a supermartingale under the original probabilities, and the value process itself will be a supermartingale under the risk-adjusted probabilities. This implies that arbitrage is impossible, as seen in Proposition 4.11.

However, suicide strategies continue to be possible. A *suicide strategy* is a self-financing trading strategy whose value process starts out positive but is zero with probability one at the horizon date. It can be constructed by making a deposit in the money market account and going short in a doubling strategy. The existence of suicide strategies implies that a claim which can be replicated does not have a unique value process: the same claim can be replicated by several different self-financing trading strategies with different value processes, all of which are non-negative. Harrison and Pliska [44, 1981] abandoned the idea for that reason.

Duffie [31, 1996] has a result which is similar to Proposition 4.11.

Karatzas, Lehoczky, and Shreve [63, 1987], Dybvig and Huang [34, 1988], and Karatzas and Shreve [64, 1988] generalized the idea of Harrison and Pliska [44, 1981] to a model with dividends on the basic securities and with consumption over time rather than just a payoff at the horizon date.

5

THE MARTINGALE VALUATION PRINCIPLE

This chapter continues the development of the theory of valuation of contingent claims. It defines the martingale value process of a claim, investigates the situations in which markets are dynamically complete, and introduces the concept of risk-adjusted probabilities.

We define the martingale value process of a contingent claim by the requirement that the product of the state price process and the value process should be a martingale. This definition is justified by the fact that if the claim can be replicated by an admissible self-financing trading strategy, then the value of the trading strategy equals the martingale value of the claim.

In many models, it is possible to replicate virtually any contingent claim by an admissible self-financing trading strategy. A model is said to have dynamically complete markets if every contingent claim can be replicated by an admissible self-financing trading strategy, provided that the claim is contingent only on the information generated by the Wiener processes, and provided that the product of the final value of the state price process and the payoff to the claim is integrable.

The complete markets theorem, Theorem 5.6, says that if there exists a money market account, then markets are dynamically complete if and only if there are at least as many instantaneously risky securities as there are sources of risk, and these securities are not instantaneously perfectly correlated.

The risk-adjusted probability measure is a probability measure over states of the world which arises from the original measure by reallocating probability mass according to a particular density function. The density of the risk-adjusted probability measure is the final value of a stochastic exponential whose drift is zero and whose relative dispersion is the negative of the prices of risk.

The risk-adjusted probabilities have the property that they make the discounted value process of any admissible trading strategy a martingale. Girsanov's theorem tells us that by adding a time integral to the original Wiener process, we can construct a process which is a Wiener process under the risk-adjusted probabilities. It may be possible to simplify the calculation of the martingale value of a claim when its payoff can be expressed as a function of this new risk-adjusted Wiener process.

5.1 Replication of Claims

A nice property of the admissible trading strategies is that if a "contingent claim" can be "replicated" by several different admissible self-financing trading strategies, then the value processes of those trading strategies are identical. This means that when we consider only admissible self-financing trading strategies, every "marketed contingent claim" has a unique value process. It is time to define these terms.

A *contingent claim* is simply a random variable Y, interpreted as a claim which has payoff $Y(\omega)$ in each state $\omega \in \Omega$.

A self-financing trading strategy $\bar{\Delta}$ is said to *replicate* a contingent claim Y at time T in the price system $\bar{S}$ if $\bar{\Delta}(T)\bar{S}(T) = Y$. This of course requires that Y be measurable with respect to $\mathcal{F}_T$.

A contingent claim Y is said to be *marketed* at time T with respect to $\bar{S}$ and Π if it is replicated at time T in the price system $\bar{S}$ by some self-financing trading strategy $\bar{\Delta}$ which is admissible for $\bar{S}$ and Π.

Since $\Pi(T)\bar{\Delta}(T)\bar{S}(T) = \Pi(T)Y$ and $\Pi\bar{\Delta}\bar{S}$ is a martingale, $\Pi(T)Y$ has to be integrable (have finite expectation).

If $\bar{\Delta}$ is a self-financing admissible trading strategy which replicates a contingent claim Y at time T, then for $t \leq T$, because of the martingale property,

$$\bar{\Delta}(t)\bar{S}(t) = \frac{1}{\Pi(t)}E[\Pi(T)Y \mid \mathcal{F}_t]$$

It follows from this equation that we can think of the values of $\Pi(T)/\Pi(t)$ as Arrow–Debreu state prices at time t, per unit of probability, for state-contingent payoffs to be received at time T.

It also follows from the equation that if two admissible self-financing trading strategies replicate the same contingent claim at time T, then their value processes are identical up to time T.

If Y is any claim such that $\Pi(T)Y$ is integrable, define its *value* process or, for emphasis, its *martingale value* process with respect to Π as the process $V(Y;\Pi)$ given by

$$V(Y;\Pi)(t) = \frac{1}{\Pi(t)}E[\Pi(T)Y \mid \mathcal{F}_t]$$

for $0 \leq t \leq T$. We refer to this valuation procedure as the *martingale method*.

If Y happens to be replicated at time T in the price system $\bar{S}$ by a self-financing strategy $\bar{\Delta}$ which is admissible for $\bar{S}$ and Π, then

$$V(Y;\Pi) = \bar{\Delta}\bar{S}$$

In particular, $V(Y;\Pi)$ is an Itô process.

If Y is not marketed, then we do not in general know that the martingale value process is an Itô process. However, if $F = F^W$, then since $\Pi V(Y;\Pi)$ is a martingale, it follows from the martingale representation theorem that $\Pi V(Y;\Pi)$ is an Itô process, and, hence, so is $V(Y;\Pi)$.

The martingale value process is the unique process V (unique up to stochastic equivalence) such that ΠV is a martingale and

$$\Pi(T)V(T) = E[\Pi(T)Y \mid \mathcal{F}_T]$$

If Y is measurable with respect to $\mathcal{F}_T$, then this equation simply says that $V(T) = Y$. If $V(Y;\Pi)$ is an Itô process, then it is the unique Itô process (unique up to indistinguishability) such that ΠV is a martingale and the equation above holds.

The function V is linear in Y and homogeneous of degree zero in Π. Specifically, if Y and Z are random variables such that $\Pi(T)Y$ and $\Pi(T)Z$ are integrable, and if a, b, and $c > 0$ are constants, then

$$V(aY + bZ;\Pi) = aV(Y;\Pi) + bV(Z;\Pi)$$

and

$$V(Y;c\Pi) = V(Y;\Pi)$$

One possible justification for requiring self-financing trading strategies to be admissible and for pricing contingent claims by the martingale method is the following proposition. It says that the martingale price is the lowest price at which a claim can be replicated, provided that the claim can indeed be replicated by an admissible trading strategy, and provided that the value processes of the replicating trading strategies multiplied by the state price process have to be bounded below.

Proposition 5.1 *Let Y be a claim which is replicated by two self-financing trading strategies $\bar{\Delta}$ and $\bar{\Theta}$ such that $\bar{\Delta}$ is admissible for $\bar{S}$ and Π and $\Pi\bar{\Theta}\bar{S}$ is bounded below. Then $\Pi\bar{\Delta}\bar{S}$ is bounded below, and with probability one,*

$$\bar{\Delta}(t)\bar{S}(t) \le \bar{\Theta}(t)\bar{S}(t) \quad \text{for all } t$$

Proof Choose a constant C such that with probability one,

$$\Pi(t)\bar{\Theta}(t)\bar{S}(t) > C \quad \text{for all } t$$

The process $\Pi\bar{\Theta}\bar{S} - C$ is a positive Itô process with zero drift, and hence it is a supermartingale, by Proposition 2.23. This implies that $\Pi\bar{\Theta}\bar{S}$ is a supermartingale. Now, for each t, with probability one,

$$\Pi(t)\bar{\Theta}(t)\bar{S}(t) \ge E[\Pi(T)Y \mid \mathcal{F}_t] = \Pi(t)\bar{\Delta}(t)\bar{S}(t)$$

Hence, with probability one, $\Pi(t)\bar{\Theta}(t)\bar{S}(t) \ge \Pi(t)\bar{\Delta}(t)\bar{S}(t)$ for all times t which are rational numbers. Since the process $\Pi\bar{\Theta}\bar{S}$ and $\Pi\bar{\Delta}\bar{S}$ are continuous, this implies that with probability one,

$$\bar{\Delta}(t)\bar{S}(t) \le \bar{\Theta}(t)\bar{S}(t) \quad \text{for all } t$$

Since

$$\Pi(T)Y = \Pi(T)\bar{\Theta}(T)\bar{S}(T) > C$$

with probability one, it follows that for every t,

$$\Pi(t)\bar{\Delta}(t)\bar{S}(t) = E[\Pi(T)Y \mid \mathcal{F}_t] > E[C \mid \mathcal{F}_t] = C$$

with probability one. Hence, with probability one, $\Pi(t)\bar{\Delta}(t)\bar{S}(t) > C$ for all times t which are rational numbers. As above, since $\Pi\bar{\Delta}\bar{S}$ is a continuous process, this implies that with probability one, the inequality holds for all t. $\square$

5.2   Delta Hedging

The concept of dynamic hedging or delta hedging of a claim is virtually the same as the concept of replication. Suppose you own a claim Y such that $\Pi(T)Y$ is integrable. This claim will have martingale value $V(Y;\Pi)$. *Delta hedging* (or dynamic hedging) of the claim means engaging in a *hedging strategy*, a trading strategy $\bar{H}$ such that the total value process $V(Y;\Pi) + \bar{H}\bar{S}$ is instantaneously riskless. We may also want $\bar{H}$ to be self-financing and have initial value zero.

Suppose $\bar{\Delta}$ is an admissible self-financing trading strategy which replicates Y. Then $\bar{\Delta}\bar{S} = V(Y;\Pi)$, and the total value process of both Y and the hedging strategy is

$$V(Y;\Pi) + \bar{H}\bar{S} = \bar{\Delta}\bar{S} + \bar{H}\bar{S}$$

For this value process to be instantaneously riskless requires that

$$\bar{H}\bar{\sigma} = -\bar{\Delta}\bar{\sigma}$$

This can obviously be achieved by setting $\bar{H} = -\bar{\Delta}$. Delta hedging is achieved by selling (possibly short-selling) the replicating trading strategy. Hence the choice of the notation $\bar{\Delta}$ for the generic trading strategy.

If security zero is a money market account, write $\bar{H} = (H_0, H)$ and $\bar{\Delta} = (\Delta_0, \Delta)$. In this case, for the total value process to be instantaneously riskless, it suffices that

$$H\hat{\sigma} = -\Delta\hat{\sigma}$$

If $\hat{\sigma}$ has rank K, then the only solution is $H = -\Delta$.

The net result will be that everything is invested in the money market account.

5.3   Making a Trading Strategy Self-financing

In this section, we shall do some preparatory analysis which will be useful in Section 5.4, in proving Theorem 5.6, the complete markets theorem. A part of that theorem says that if the filtration is generated by the Wiener process, if the dispersion matrix has rank equal to the dimension of the Wiener process, and if there is a money market account, then every contingent claim Y which is measurable with respect to $\mathcal{F}_T$, and such that $\Pi(T)Y$ is integrable, can be replicated by an admissible self-financing trading strategy.

The strategy of proof will be the following. Use the martingale valuation principle to calculate the martingale value process V of the claim Y. Show that the value process V is an Itô process, and find a trading strategy $\bar{\gamma}$ whose dispersion equals the dispersion b_V of V: $\bar{\gamma}\bar{\sigma} = b_V$. Make this trading strategy self-financing by reinvesting any dividends in the money market account, and then adjust the initial holdings so as to give it the appropriate initial value. If all this is done correctly, then the resulting trading strategy will be admissible and will replicate the claim Y.

One of the steps is to make the trading strategy self-financing by reinvesting any dividends in the money market account. That is the procedure which we shall study in this section.

First, the following proposition says that any trading strategy that involves only the money market account has constant normalized gains process. This is not surprising. Since the normalized value of the money market account is constant, if you only hold shares of the money market account, you do not make any gains or losses.

Proposition 5.2 *Let $\bar{b}$ be a money market account with value process M. Then*

$$\alpha\bar{b} \in \mathcal{L}(\bar{S}/M)$$

and

$$\mathcal{G}(\alpha\bar{b}; \bar{S}/M) = \alpha(0)$$

for every one-dimensional trading strategy α.

Proof Since
$$\bar{b}\,d(\bar{S}/M) = d\mathcal{G}(\bar{b}; \bar{S}/M) = d(\bar{b}\bar{S}/M) = 0$$

it follows that
$$\alpha\bar{b}\,d(\bar{S}/M) = 0$$

and, hence,
$$\alpha\bar{b} \in \mathcal{L}(\bar{S}/M)$$

Since
$$d\mathcal{G}(\alpha\bar{b}; \bar{S}/M) = \alpha\bar{b}\,d(\bar{S}/M) = 0$$

it follows that
$$\mathcal{G}(\alpha\bar{b}; \bar{S}/M) = \mathcal{G}(\alpha\bar{b}; \bar{S}/M)(0) = \alpha(0)\bar{b}(0)\bar{S}(0)/M(0) = \alpha(0)$$

$\square$

Let $\bar{\gamma}$ be a trading strategy in $\mathcal{L}(\bar{S})$ which is not necessarily self-financing. The next proposition constructs a trading strategy $\bar{\Delta}$ which is self-financing and has the same initial value and the same dispersion as $\bar{\gamma}$. This is done by holding $\bar{\gamma}$ and reinvesting the net withdrawals in the money market account. The number of units of the money market account that have been thus accumulated at any time t is $\mathcal{D}(\bar{\gamma}; \bar{S}/M)(t)$.

Proposition 5.3 *Let $\bar{b}$ be a money market account with value process M. Suppose $\bar{\gamma}$ is a trading strategy in $\mathcal{L}(\bar{S}/M)$ (not necessarily self-financing). Then the trading strategy*

$$\bar{\Delta} = \bar{\gamma} + \mathcal{D}(\bar{\gamma}; \bar{S}/M)\bar{b}$$

is self-financing and has initial value $\bar{\Delta}(0)\bar{S}(0) = \bar{\gamma}(0)\bar{S}(0)$ and dispersion $\bar{\Delta}\bar{\sigma} = \bar{\gamma}\bar{\sigma}$.

Proof We will show that $\bar{\Delta}$ is self-financing with respect to the price system $\bar{S}/M$. First, we have to show that $\bar{\Delta} \in \mathcal{L}(\bar{S}/M)$. For notational convenience, set

$$D = \mathcal{D}(\bar{\gamma}; \bar{S}/M)$$

It follows from Proposition 5.2 that

$$D\bar{b} \in \mathcal{L}(\bar{S}/M)$$

and

$$\mathcal{G}(D\bar{b}; \bar{S}/M) = D(0) = 0$$

Hence,

$$\bar{\Delta} = \bar{\gamma} + D\bar{b} \in \mathcal{L}(\bar{S}/M)$$

The value and cumulative gains processes of $\bar{\Delta}$, in the price system $\bar{S}/M$, are

$$\bar{\Delta}\bar{S}/M = \bar{\gamma}\bar{S}/M + \mathcal{D}(\bar{\gamma}; \bar{S}/M) = \mathcal{G}(\bar{\gamma}; \bar{S}/M)$$

and

$$\mathcal{G}(\bar{\Delta}; \bar{S}/M)(t) = \mathcal{G}(\bar{\gamma}; \bar{S}/M) + \mathcal{G}(D\bar{b}; \bar{S}/M) = \mathcal{G}(\bar{\gamma}; \bar{S}/M)$$

Hence, the cumulative dividend process is zero:

$$\mathcal{D}(\bar{\Delta}; \bar{S}/M) = 0$$

which implies that $\bar{\Delta}$ is self-financing.

The initial value of $\bar{\Delta}$ in the price system $\bar{S}/M$ is

$$\bar{\Delta}(0)\bar{S}(0)/M(0) = \mathcal{G}(\bar{\gamma}; \bar{S}/M)(0) = \bar{\gamma}(0)\bar{S}(0)/M(0)$$

and hence the initial value in the price system $\bar{S}$ is

$$\bar{\Delta}(0)\bar{S}(0) = \bar{\gamma}(0)\bar{S}(0)$$

The dispersion of $\bar{\Delta}$ is

$$\bar{\Delta}\bar{\sigma} = \bar{\gamma}\bar{\sigma} + \mathcal{D}(\bar{\gamma}; \bar{S}/M)\bar{b}\bar{\sigma} = \bar{\gamma}\bar{\sigma}$$

$\square$

Exercise 5.1 *Let $\bar{b}$ be a money market account with value process M. Suppose $\bar{\gamma} \in \mathcal{L}(\bar{S}/M)$ is a trading strategy (not necessarily self-financing) such that*

1. *$\mathcal{G}(\bar{\gamma}; \bar{S}/M) > 0$, $\bar{\gamma}\bar{\sigma} = 0$, and $\bar{\gamma}(\bar{\mu} - r\bar{S}) \geq 0$ almost everywhere,*
2. *$\bar{\gamma}(\bar{\mu} - r\bar{S}) > 0$ on a subset of $\Omega \times [0, T]$ with positive measure (this is not possible if there exists a vector of prices of risk).*

Show that there exists a self-financing arbitrage strategy $\bar{\theta}$ such that

1. *with probability one, $\bar{\theta}(0)\bar{S}(0) = 0$ and $\bar{\theta}(t)\bar{S}(t) \geq 0$ for all $t \in [0, T]$,*
2. *$\bar{\theta}(T)\bar{S}(T) > 0$ with positive probability.*

Proposition 5.3 constructs a self-financing trading strategy $\bar{\Delta}$ with a prescribed initial value and a prescribed dispersion, but it does not say to what extent this trading strategy is unique.

In fact, the value process of $\bar{\Delta}$ is unique. If V is the value process of another self-financing trading strategy which has the same initial value and the same dispersion as $\bar{\Delta}$, then V equals the value process of $\bar{\Delta}$. This will follow from the next proposition.

In general, if V is an Itô process and $\bar{\Delta} \in \mathcal{L}(\bar{S})$ is a self-financing trading strategy, then V is the value process of $\bar{\Delta}$ if and only if the processes V and $\bar{\Delta}\bar{S}$ have the same initial value and the same drift and dispersion coefficients.

The following proposition says that instead of verifying that these processes have the same drift, it suffices to check that ΠV has zero drift, where Π is a state price process for $\bar{S}$.

In preparation, we make the following observation. If X is an Itô process with

$$dX = a\,dt + b\,dW$$

and if $\lambda \in \mathcal{L}^2$, then the drift of $\eta[0, -\lambda]X$ is

$$\eta[0, -\lambda]\left[a - b\lambda^\top\right]$$

Hence, $\eta[0, -\lambda]X$ has zero drift if and only if

$$a = b\lambda^\top$$

that is, if and only if the drift of X equals its dispersion multiplied by $\lambda^\top$.

Proposition 5.4 *Let Π be a state price process for $\bar{S}$. Let V be an Itô process, and let $\bar{\Delta} \in \mathcal{L}(\bar{S})$ be a self-financing trading strategy. Then V is the value process of $\bar{\Delta}$ if and only if*

1. *ΠV has zero drift,*
2. *$\bar{\Delta}(0)\bar{S}(0) = V(0)$, and*
3. *the dispersion coefficient of V equals $\bar{\Delta}\bar{\sigma}$ (almost everywhere).*

Proof It is clear that if V is the value process of $\bar{\Delta}$, then 1–3 hold.

Conversely, suppose 1–3 hold. Since V is an Itô process, it has the form

$$dV = a_V\,dt + b_V\,dW$$

for processes $a_V \in \mathcal{L}^1$ and $b_V \in \mathcal{L}^2$, while

$$d(\bar{\Delta}\bar{S}) = \bar{\Delta}\bar{\mu}\,dt + \bar{\Delta}\bar{\sigma}\,dW$$

Since the process

$$\eta[0, -\lambda]V/M = \frac{\Pi V}{\Pi(0)M(0)}$$

has zero drift, the drift of the process V/M is $b_V\lambda^\top/M$. Since the process

$$\eta[0, -\lambda]\bar{\Delta}\bar{S}/M = \frac{\Pi\bar{\Delta}\bar{S}}{\Pi(0)M(0)}$$

has zero drift, the drift of $\bar{\Delta}\bar{S}/M$ is $\bar{\Delta}\bar{\sigma}\lambda^\top/M$.

By 3, $b_V = \bar{\Delta}\bar{\sigma}$. Hence,

$$b_V \lambda^\top / M = \bar{\Delta}\bar{\sigma}\lambda^\top / M$$

By 2, $\bar{\Delta}(0)\bar{S}(0) = V(0)$. It follows that the processes V/M and $\bar{\Delta}\bar{S}/M$ have the same initial value and the same drift and dispersion coefficients. Hence, they are indistinguishable, and so the processes V and $\bar{\Delta}\bar{S}$ are indistinguishable. $\qquad \square$

5.4   Dynamically Complete Markets

We say that markets are *dynamically complete* with respect to $\bar{S}$ and Π if every contingent claim Y which is measurable with respect to $\mathcal{F}_T$, and such that $\Pi(T)Y$ is integrable, is marketed at time T with respect to $\bar{S}$ and Π.

Recall that a contingent claim Y is said to be marketed at time T with respect to $\bar{S}$ and Π if there exists self-financing trading strategy $\bar{\Delta}$, admissible for $\bar{S}$ and Π, which replicates Y at time T in the price system $\bar{S}$.

If markets are dynamically complete with respect to $\bar{S}$ and Π, then in fact a claim Y is marketed at time T with respect to $\bar{S}$ and Π if and only if Y is measurable with respect to $\mathcal{F}_T$ and $\Pi(T)Y$ is integrable.

Theorem 5.6, the complete markets theorem, says that if the filtration is the augmented filtration generated by the Wiener process, and if there is a money market account, then markets are dynamically complete if and only if there are at least as many instantaneously risky securities as there are sources of risk, and these securities are not instantaneously perfectly correlated.

Before stating and proving the complete markets theorem, we need Proposition 5.5. It says that if there exists a money market account, and if the dispersion matrix $\bar{\sigma}$ of the basic price processes has rank equal to the number of sources of uncertainty (the dimension of the Wiener process), then any Itô process V such that ΠV has zero drift is the value process of some self-financing trading strategy.

To construct such a trading strategy, we shall first find a trading strategy whose value process has the same dispersion coefficient as V and the same initial value. This trading strategy might not be self-financing, so we make it self-financing by investing its dividends in the money market account (this is why we shall need to assume that there exists a money market account).

Proposition 5.5 *Assume that there is a money market account. Let V be an Itô process such that ΠV has zero drift.*

1. *If $\bar{\sigma}$ has rank K almost everywhere, then V is the value process of a self-financing trading strategy.*

2. *If, in addition, $N = K$, then the trading strategy is unique.*

Proof   Since V is an Itô process, it has the form

$$dV = a_V \, dt + b_V \, dW$$

for processes $a_V \in \mathcal{L}^1$ and $b_V \in \mathcal{L}^2$.

Let $\bar{b} \in \mathcal{L}(\bar{S})$ be a money market account: a self-financing trading strategy such that $\bar{b}\bar{S} = M$.

1: To show that V is the value process of a self-financing trading strategy, set

$$\bar{\gamma} = b_V \left(\bar{\sigma}^\top \bar{\sigma}\right)^{-1} \bar{\sigma}^\top$$

Then $\bar{\gamma} \in \mathcal{L}(\bar{S}/M)$ because

$$\bar{\gamma}\bar{\sigma}/M = b_V/M \in \mathcal{L}^2$$

and

$$\bar{\gamma}(\bar{\mu} - r\bar{S})/M = \bar{\gamma}\bar{\sigma}\lambda^\top/M \in \mathcal{L}^1$$

The trading strategy $\bar{\gamma} + \mathcal{D}(\bar{\gamma}; \bar{S}/M)\bar{b}$ arises from $\bar{\gamma}$ by reinvesting the net withdrawals in the money market account. By Proposition 5.3, it is self-financing and has the same initial value and the same dispersion as $\bar{\gamma}$. Adjust the initial value to be equal to that of V by setting

$$\bar{\Delta} = \bar{\gamma} + \mathcal{D}(\bar{\gamma}; \bar{S}/M)\bar{b} + \left(V(0)/M(0) - \bar{\gamma}(0)\bar{S}(0)/M(0)\right)\bar{b}$$

This is the self-financing trading strategy that arises from $\bar{\gamma}$ by reinvesting the net withdrawals in the money market account and adjusting the initial holdings of the money market account so that $\bar{\Delta}(0)\bar{S}(0) = V(0)$.

Now

$$\bar{\Delta}\bar{\sigma} = \bar{\gamma}\bar{\sigma} = b_V \left(\bar{\sigma}^\top \bar{\sigma}\right)^{-1} \bar{\sigma}^\top \bar{\sigma} = b_V$$

It follows from Proposition 5.4 that V is the value process of $\bar{\Delta}$.

2: To show uniqueness, let $\bar{\Delta}$ and $\bar{\Theta}$ be two self-financing trading strategies in $\mathcal{L}(\bar{S})$ with $\bar{\Delta}\bar{S} = \bar{\Theta}\bar{S}$. Since $\bar{b}\bar{S} = M > 0$ and $\bar{b}\bar{\sigma} = 0$, the matrix $(\bar{S}, \bar{\sigma})$ has rank $K + 1$. Hence, $(\bar{\Delta} - \bar{\Theta})\bar{S} = 0$ and $(\bar{\Delta} - \bar{\Theta})\bar{\sigma} = 0$ imply $\bar{\Delta} - \bar{\Theta} = 0$. □

Note that uniqueness of the trading strategy in Proposition 5.5 means uniqueness almost everywhere with respect to $P \otimes \lambda$.

Theorem 5.6 The complete markets theorem. *Assume that $F = F^W$. Assume that there is a money market account, and let Π be a state price process for $\bar{S}$. Then markets are dynamically complete with respect to $\bar{S}$ and Π if and only if $\bar{\sigma}$ has rank K almost everywhere.*

Proof First, suppose that $\bar{\sigma}$ has rank K almost everywhere. Let Y be a contingent claim such that $Y \in \mathcal{F}_T$ and $\Pi(T)Y$ is integrable. The process

$$X(t) = E[\Pi(T)Y \mid \mathcal{F}_t]$$

is a martingale. By Theorem 1.39 (the martingale representation theorem), X is an Itô process. Define a process V by

$$V = \frac{X}{\Pi}$$

Then V is an Itô process, which implies that ΠV is an Itô process. Since $\Pi V = X$ and X is a martingale, ΠV has zero drift. So, by Proposition 5.5, V is the value process of a self-financing trading strategy $\bar{\Delta}$. Since $\Pi V = X$ is a martingale, $\bar{\Delta}$ is admissible. Since

$$\Pi(T)V(T) = X(T) = E[\Pi(T)Y \mid \mathcal{F}_T] = \Pi(T)Y$$

it follows that

$$Y = V(T) = \bar{\Delta}(T)\bar{S}(T)$$

and so Y is marketed at time T.

Conversely, suppose markets are dynamically complete with respect to $\bar{S}$ and Π. For each $k = 1, \ldots, K$, let e^k be the K-dimensional row vector with one in entry k and zero in all other entries. Set

$$V_k = \eta[r + \lambda\lambda^\top + \lambda_k, \lambda + e^k]$$

Then

$$\begin{aligned}
\Pi V_k &= \Pi(0)\eta[-r, -\lambda]\eta[r + \lambda\lambda^\top + \lambda_k, \lambda + e^k] \\
&= \eta[-r + r + \lambda\lambda^\top + \lambda_k - (\lambda + e^k)\lambda^\top, -\lambda + \lambda + e^k] \\
&= \Pi(0)\eta[0, e^k]
\end{aligned}$$

Set

$$V_0 = \eta[r + \lambda\lambda^\top, \lambda]$$

Then

$$\begin{aligned}
\Pi V_0 &= \Pi(0)\eta[-r, -\lambda]\eta[r + \lambda\lambda^\top, \lambda] \\
&= \eta[-r + r + \lambda\lambda^\top - \lambda\lambda^\top, -\lambda + \lambda] \\
&= \Pi(0)
\end{aligned}$$

For each $k = 0, 1, \ldots, K$, since $\Pi(T)V_k(T)$ is integrable and markets are assumed to be dynamically complete, $V_k(T)$ is replicated by an admissible self-financing trading strategy $\bar{\Delta}^k$. Since ΠV_k is a martingale, V_k is the value process of $\bar{\Delta}^k$. Hence, the dispersion coefficient of V_k equals that of $\bar{\Delta}^k \bar{S}$:

$$V_0\lambda = \bar{\Delta}^0 \bar{\sigma}$$

and for $k > 0$,

$$V_k(\lambda + e^k) = \bar{\Delta}^k \bar{\sigma}$$

In matrix notation,

$$\begin{pmatrix} V_0 & 0 & \cdots & 0 \\ 0 & V_1 & \cdots & 0 \\ \vdots & \vdots & \ddots & \vdots \\ 0 & 0 & \cdots & V_K \end{pmatrix} \begin{pmatrix} \lambda \\ \iota\lambda + I \end{pmatrix} = \begin{pmatrix} \bar{\Delta}^0 \\ \bar{\Delta}^1 \\ \vdots \\ \bar{\Delta}^K \end{pmatrix} \bar{\sigma}$$

Here, ι is a K-dimensional column vector all of whose entries are one, and I is the $K \times K$ identity matrix. It is easily seen that the matrix on the left hand side of the equation has rank K. Hence, so does $\bar{\sigma}$. $\qquad\square$

The proof of Theorem 5.6 actually shows the following. If $F = F^W$, and if every *positive* contingent claim $Y > 0$ which is measurable with respect to $\mathcal{F}_T$ and such that $\Pi(T)Y$ is integrable, is marketed at time T with respect to $\bar{S}$ and Π, then $\bar{\sigma}$ has rank K almost everywhere, and hence markets are dynamically complete with respect to $\bar{S}$ and Π.

Notice that even if $Y \in \mathcal{F}_T$ and $\Pi(T)Y$ is integrable, so that there exists an admissible replicating trading strategy for Y, it may be that there exists another replicating trading strategy which is not admissible and whose value process is different.

To sum up, the space of admissible self-financing trading strategies consists of those self-financing trading strategies whose value processes become martingales when multiplied by the state price process Π. The space of admissible self-financing trading strategies is sufficiently restricted to ensure that it admits no arbitrage. It is large enough, however, to yield dynamically complete markets when all information is generated by the Wiener process and there are enough instantaneously risky basic securities.

Exercise 5.2 *Consider the model from Examples 2.21, 4.6, and 4.13. There are two securities with price processes S_1 and S_2. Change the unit of account by dividing by S_1. This yields two new securities price processes 1 and S_2/S_1. Let $\tilde{\Pi}$ be the state price process for the new price system identified in Example 4.13. Let $\Pi = \tilde{\Pi}/S_1$ be the corresponding state price process for the original price system. Show that a claim Y is marketed at time T with respect to S_1, S_2, and Π if and only if $\Pi(T)Y$ is integrable and Y satisfies a particular informational (measurability) constraint. Which informational constraint?*

5.5 How to Replicate

Very often, we shall calculate the value process of a claim first and then look for a replicating trading strategy. Most of the time, it turns out that the value process is path independent, in the sense that it is a function of time and of the prices of the risky basic securities. If so, then we can identify a replicating trading strategy by differentiating this function with respect to the securities prices.

By Itô's lemma, the dispersion vector of the value process equals the vector of derivatives multiplied by the dispersion matrix of the basic securities prices. The number of shares of each instantaneously risky basic security required in the replicating position will equal the partial derivative of the function with respect to the price of that security. This way, we ensure that the trading strategy we construct does indeed have the same dispersion as the value process we are trying to replicate.

We finance these holdings of the risky securities by borrowing or lending at the instantaneously riskless rate, as necessary, and we adjust the initial holdings of the money market account so that the trading strategy has the correct initial value.

Proposition 5.7 spells out a set of specific conditions under which this procedure will work.

Proposition 5.7 *Suppose*

1. *Security zero is a money market account.*
2. V *is the value process of a self-financing trading strategy on* $[0, T]$.
3. $\mathcal{O} \subset I\!\!R^N$ *is an open subset such that with probability one,* $S(t) \in \mathcal{O}$ *for all* $t \in (0, T)$.
4. $\Phi : \mathcal{O} \times (0, T) \rightarrow I\!\!R : (S, t) \mapsto \Phi(S, t)$ *is a function which is twice continuously differentiable with respect to* S *and once continuously differentiable
   with respect to* t.
5. *With probability one,* $V(t) = \Phi(S(t), t)$ *for all* $t \in (0, T)$.
6. $\bar{\Delta} = (\Delta_0, \Delta)$ *is a process such that*
   - $\Delta(t) = \Phi_S(S(t), t)$ *for* $t \in (0, T)$
   - $\Delta(0)$ *is measurable with respect to* $\mathcal{F}_0$ *and* $\Delta(T)$ *is measurable with
     respect to* $\mathcal{F}_T$
   - $\Delta_0(t) = (V(t) - \Delta(t)S(t))/M(t)$ *for* $t \in [0, T]$.

Then $\bar{\Delta}$ *is a self-financing trading strategy in* $\mathcal{L}(\bar{S})$, *and* V *is the value process
of* $\bar{\Delta}$ *on* $[0, T]$.

Proof First, it is clear that $\bar{\Delta}$ is adapted. It is also measurable, because it is
measurable on each of the subsets $\Omega \times \{0\}$, $\Omega \times \{T\}$, and $\Omega \times (0, T)$ of $\Omega \times [0, T]$.

By assumption, V is the value process of some self-financing trading strategy
$\bar{\theta} \in \mathcal{L}(\bar{S})$: $V = \bar{\theta}\bar{S}$. It is therefore an Itô process with

$$dV = d(\bar{\theta}\bar{S}) = \bar{\theta}\bar{\mu} \, dt + \bar{\theta}\bar{\sigma} \, dW$$

By construction,

$$\bar{\Delta}\bar{S} = \Delta_0 M + \Delta S = V = \bar{\theta}\bar{S}$$

Apply Itô's lemma to the function $V(t) = \Phi(S(t), t)$. For $t \in (0, T)$, since the
first row of $\bar{\sigma}$ is zero,

$$\bar{\theta}(t)\bar{\sigma}(t) = (0, \Phi_S(S(t), t))\bar{\sigma}(t) = (0, \Delta(t))\bar{\sigma}(t) = \bar{\Delta}(t)\bar{\sigma}(t)$$

Hence, $\bar{\theta}\bar{\sigma} = \bar{\Delta}\bar{\sigma}$ almost everywhere on $\Omega \times [0, T]$, and so $\bar{\Delta}\bar{\sigma} \in \mathcal{L}^2$. Furthermore,

$$\begin{aligned}
\bar{\theta}\bar{\mu} &= r\bar{\theta}\bar{S} + \bar{\theta}\bar{\sigma}\lambda^{\mathsf{T}} \\
&= rV + \bar{\Delta}\bar{\sigma}\lambda^{\mathsf{T}} \\
&= r\bar{\Delta}\bar{S} + \bar{\Delta}\bar{\sigma}\lambda^{\mathsf{T}} \\
&= \bar{\Delta}\bar{\mu}
\end{aligned}$$

almost everywhere, and, hence, $\bar{\Delta}\bar{\mu} \in \mathcal{L}^1$. So, $\bar{\Delta} \in \mathcal{L}(\bar{S})$.

Since $\bar{\theta}\bar{\sigma} = \bar{\Delta}\bar{\sigma}$ and $\bar{\theta}\bar{\mu} = \bar{\Delta}\bar{\mu}$, the trading strategies $\bar{\theta}$ and $\bar{\Delta}$ have the same
cumulative gains process. Since they have the same value process and the same
cumulative gains process, and $\bar{\theta}$ is self-financing, it follows that $\bar{\Delta}$ is self-financing.
□

If the process V in Proposition 5.7 is the value process of some admissible self-financing trading strategy, then the trading strategy $\bar{\Delta}$ constructed in the proposition will be admissible.

The proposition makes no assumption about the rank of $\bar{\sigma}$ and does not rule out redundancy among the basic securities. It is possible that two different admissible self-financing trading strategies have the same value process V.

Because of Proposition 5.7, we shall refer to the function Φ_S as the *delta function* of the claim $V(T)$.

The role of the set $\mathcal{O}$ in Proposition 5.7, like the set D in Itô's lemma (Theorem 2.2), is this. It may be that the value function Φ is defined only for risky basic securities prices in a subset of $I\!\!R^N$ and cannot be extended to a continuous and sufficiently smooth function of securities prices everywhere in $I\!\!R^N$. For example, in the Black–Scholes model, the value function will be defined only for positive prices of the stock.

The function Φ is assumed to be defined and appropriately differentiable only on $\mathcal{O} \times (0,T)$, not on $\mathcal{O} \times [0,T]$. There is a technical reason for this, which is that Itô's lemma requires the domain of the function Φ to be an open set—the set D in Itô's lemma (Theorem 2.2) corresponds to $\mathcal{O} \times (0,T)$ here. But there is also a more substantial reason, which is that even if Φ can be extended to a continuous function on $\mathcal{O} \times [0,T]$, the extension will often not be differentiable at $t = T$; and sometimes Φ cannot even be extended in a continuous manner to $\mathcal{O} \times [0,T]$.

The value process of a standard call option in the Black–Scholes model will be an example of the former: as a function of the price of the underlying security, it is not differentiable at $t = T$, because the payoff to the option is a function of the final price of the security, but not a differentiable function. The value process of a cash-or-nothing option will be an example of the latter: as a function of the price of the underlying security, it is not even continuous at $t = T$, because the payoff to the option is a discontinuous function of the final price of the security.

In Section 6.2, in the specific context of the Black–Scholes model, we shall show that path-independent claims do indeed have value functions and path-independent value processes as in Proposition 5.7. A claim will be called path independent if its payoff is a function of the final stock price only.

5.6   Example: Cash-or-nothing Options

In this section, we shall price a cash-or-nothing call option within the Black–Scholes model. This example will illustrate the dynamic completeness of markets and the notion of martingale pricing using the state price process.

The calculations will be elementary but somewhat long. Later on, we shall see that they can be simplified if we make use of the so-called risk-adjusted probabilities.

Let $K = 1$, and let

$$M = M(0)\eta[r,0]$$

and

$$S = S(0)\eta[\mu, \sigma]$$

be the price processes in the Black–Scholes model, where r, μ, and $\sigma > 0$ are constants. The price of risk is

$$\lambda = \frac{\mu - r}{\sigma}$$

and the state price process is

$$\Pi = \Pi(0)\eta[-r, -\lambda]$$

Let $0 \le t \le T$. The payoff to the *cash-or-nothing call option* happens at time T and equals

$$Y = 1_{S(T) \ge X} = \begin{cases} 1 & \text{if } S(T) \ge X \\ 0 & \text{otherwise} \end{cases}$$

where X is a non-negative *trigger price*. So, the option pays one dollar at maturity if the value of the underlying stock equals or exceeds the trigger price X, otherwise it expires worthless.

We want to value the cash-or-nothing call option at time t, and we do it using the state price process.

First, we verify that $\Pi(T)Y$ is integrable. This is obvious since $\Pi(T)$ is lognormally distributed (see below) and Y is bounded.

Let $C_{CN}(t)$ denote the martingale value of the option at time t. Then

$$\Pi(t)C_{CN}(t) = E[\Pi(T)Y \mid \mathcal{F}_t] = E\left[\Pi(T)1_{S(T) \ge X} \mid \mathcal{F}_t\right]$$

It is not too difficult to calculate this conditional expectation, because given the information at time t, both $\Pi(T)$ and $S(T)$ are functions of $W(T) - W(t)$, which follows a known normal distribution. Specifically,

$$\ln S(T) = \ln S(t) + \left(\mu - \frac{1}{2}\sigma^2\right)(T - t) + \sigma(W(T) - W(t))$$

$$= \ln S(t) + \left(r + \sigma\lambda - \frac{1}{2}\sigma^2\right)(T - t) + \sigma(W(T) - W(t))$$

and

$$\ln \Pi(T) = \ln \Pi(t) - \left(r + \frac{1}{2}\lambda^2\right)(T - t) - \lambda(W(T) - W(t))$$

So, given the information available at time t, $\Pi(T)$ is lognormally distributed, and $\ln \Pi(T)$ is normally distributed with mean

$$E[\ln \Pi(T) \mid \mathcal{F}_t] = \ln \Pi(t) - \left(r + \frac{1}{2}\lambda^2\right)(T - t)$$

and variance

$$\text{var}(\ln \Pi(T) \mid \mathcal{F}_t) = \lambda^2(T - t)$$

Furthermore, given information at time t, the random variables $\ln \Pi(T)$ and $\ln S(T)$ are random only through their dependence on the increment $W(T) - W(t)$

of the Wiener process. Therefore, the restriction $S(T) \geq X$ can be rewritten in the form $\Pi(T) \leq Z$ for an appropriately defined value of Z.

To see this and to calculate Z, first define a variable d_2 by

$$d_2 = \frac{\ln S(t) - \ln X + \left(r - \frac{1}{2}\sigma^2\right)(T - t)}{\sigma\sqrt{T - t}}$$

This variable appears in the Black–Scholes formula, where it is usually denoted d_2, like here.

Observe that $S(T) \geq X$ if and only if

$$W(T) - W(t) \geq \frac{\ln X - \ln S(t) - \left(r - \frac{1}{2}\sigma^2\right)(T - t)}{\sigma} - \lambda(T - t)$$

$$= -d_2\sqrt{T - t} - \lambda(T - t)$$

which is true if and only if

$$\ln \Pi(T) \leq \ln \Pi(t) - \left(r + \frac{1}{2}\lambda^2\right)(T - t) + \lambda d_2\sqrt{T - t} + \lambda^2(T - t)$$

$$= \ln \Pi(t) - \left(r - \frac{1}{2}\lambda^2\right)(T - t) + \lambda d_2\sqrt{T - t}$$

$$= \ln Z$$

where the last line defines Z. Hence, what we need to calculate is

$$\Pi(t)C_{CN}(t) = E\left[\Pi(T)1_{S(T)\geq X} \mid \mathcal{F}_t\right] = E\left[\Pi(T)1_{\Pi(T)\leq Z} \mid \mathcal{F}_t\right]$$

This is the expectation of a truncated lognormally distributed variable. We calculated such an expectation in Proposition 2.29.

In this particular application, the parameters in Proposition 2.29 are as follows: $U = \ln \Pi(T)$, $U_0 = \ln Z$,

$$m = E[\ln \Pi(T) \mid \mathcal{F}_t] = \ln \Pi(t) - \left(r + \frac{1}{2}\lambda^2\right)(T - t)$$

$$s^2 = \operatorname{var}(\ln \Pi(T) \mid \mathcal{F}_t) = \lambda^2(T - t)$$

$$U_0 - m - s^2 = \ln \Pi(t) - \left(r - \frac{1}{2}\lambda^2\right)(T - t) + \lambda d_2\sqrt{T - t}$$

$$- \ln \Pi(t) + \left(r + \frac{1}{2}\lambda^2\right)(T - t) - \lambda^2(T - t)$$

$$= \lambda d_2\sqrt{T - t}$$

and

$$d = \frac{U_0 - m - s^2}{s} = \frac{\lambda d_2\sqrt{T - t}}{\sqrt{\lambda^2(T - t)}} = d_2$$

We find

$$m + s^2/2 = \ln \Pi(t) - \left(r + \frac{1}{2}\lambda^2\right)(T - t) + \frac{1}{2}\lambda^2(T - t)$$

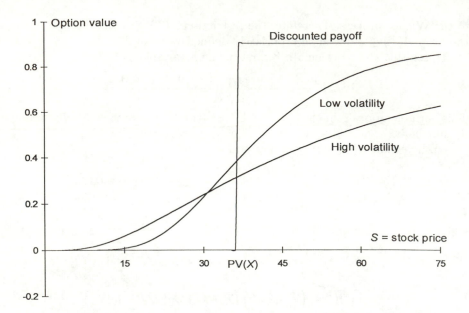

FIG. 5.1. Value of a cash-or-nothing call option

$$= \ln \Pi(t) - r(T - t)$$

With the above value of d,

$$\Pi(t)C_{CN}(t) = \exp\left(m + \frac{1}{2}s^2\right) N(d) = \Pi(t)e^{-r(T-t)}N(d_2)$$

and the value of the cash-or-nothing call option is

$$C_{CN} = e^{-r(T-t)}N(d_2)$$

Figure 5.1 shows the value of the cash-or-nothing call option for two different levels of volatility, as functions of the value of the underlying. The value of the underlying is on the horizontal axis, and the option value is measured along the vertical axis. The flatter curve corresponds to a volatility of $\sigma = 0.8$, and the steeper curve corresponds to a volatility of $\sigma = 0.4$. The potential payoff is one, the trigger price is $X = 40$, the time to maturity is $T - t = 1$, and the interest rate is $r = 0.1$. The step function which is also plotted in the figure is zero up to the discounted value of the trigger price, $e^{-r(T-t)}X$, and thereafter it equals the discounted value of the payoff of one. It represents an upper boundary and a limit of the option value.

Note that

$$E\left[\Pi(T)1_{S(T)>X} \mid \mathcal{F}_t\right] = E\left[\Pi(T)1_{S(T)\geq X} \mid \mathcal{F}_t\right]$$

because $P(S(T) = X) = 0$. Hence, the value of a claim with payoff $1_{S(T)>X}$ will be the same as the value of a claim with payoff $1_{S(T)\geq X}$.

Next, we shall show how to replicate the cash-or-nothing call option by a trading strategy involving positions in the stock and the money market account.

Write the martingale value of the option as a function of (S, t):

$$C_{CN} = \Phi(S, t) = e^{-r(T-t)} N(d_2(S, t))$$

where

$$d_2(S, t) = \frac{\ln S - \ln X + \left(r - \frac{1}{2}\sigma^2\right)(T - t)}{\sigma\sqrt{T - t}}$$

The function Φ is defined (at least) for $(S, t) \in (0, \infty) \times (0, T)$, and on this domain it is twice continuously differentiable with respect to S and once continuously differentiable with respect to t, with

$$\Phi_S(S, t) = e^{-r(T-t)} N'(d_2(S, t)) \frac{1}{S\sigma\sqrt{T - t}} > 0$$

where the derivative N' of the cumulative standard normal distribution function N is of course the standard normal density function:

$$N'(d) = \frac{1}{\sqrt{2\pi}} \exp(-d^2/2)$$

It follows from Proposition 5.7 that the cash-or-nothing call option will be replicated by any trading strategy $\bar{\Delta} = (\Delta_0, \Delta)$ where

$$\Delta(t) = \Phi_S(S(t), t) = e^{-r(T-t)} N'(d_2(S(t), t)) \frac{1}{S(t)\sigma\sqrt{T - t}}$$

for $t \in (0, T)$, while $\Delta(0)$ and $\Delta(T)$ are chosen arbitrarily subject only to the constraint that they be measurable with respect to $\mathcal{F}_0$ and $\mathcal{F}_T$, respectively, and the holdings Δ_0 of the money market account are given by

$$\Delta_0(t) = \frac{C_{CN}(t) - \Delta(t)S(t)}{M(t)}$$

for $t \in [0, T]$.

In simplified notation,

$$\Delta = \Phi_S(S, t) = e^{-r(T-t)} N'(d_2) \frac{1}{S\sigma\sqrt{T - t}}$$

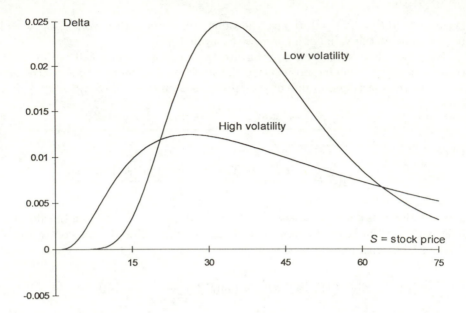

FIG. 5.2. Delta of a cash-or-nothing call option

Figure 5.2 shows Δ, the delta of the cash-or-nothing option, for the same two levels of volatility as in Fig. 5.1. The value of the underlying is on the horizontal axis, and Δ is measured along the vertical axis. The lower curve corresponds to a volatility of $\sigma = 0.8$, and the higher curve corresponds to a volatility of $\sigma = 0.4$. As in Fig. 5.1, the potential payoff is one, the trigger price is $X = 40$, the time to maturity is $T - t = 1$, and the interest rate is $r = 0.1$.

5.7   The State Price Process as a Primitive

The logic of the development so far has been to start from the $(N+1)$-dimensional vector $\bar{S}$ of price processes of the basic securities and then derive a state price process Π from $\bar{S}$. Once we know the state price process Π, we can value claims by the martingale method. To do this, we do not need $\bar{S}$ any more. All the relevant information is contained in the state price process.

To replicate or hedge a contingent claim, we still need to know the basic securities price processes, because replication involves trading in those securities.

There are other ways to specify a model. Instead of starting from the basic securities prices and deriving the state prices, we can start by specifying the state price process. Given the state price process, we can value any contingent claim. We can then pick a set of claims, designate their price processes as basic securities price processes, and use them to replicate and hedge other claims.

Given any positive Itô process Π, interpreted as a state price process, and any invertible $(K \times K)$-dimensional matrix-valued process $\hat{\sigma} \in \mathcal{L}^2$, we shall construct a K-dimensional vector S of positive price process with relative dispersion matrix $\hat{\sigma}$, such that if we define the price process M by

$$M = M(0)\eta[r, 0]$$

then Π is a state price process for

$$\bar{S} = \begin{pmatrix} M \\ S \end{pmatrix}$$

and M is a money market account.

Start with the state price process Π, given by

$$\Pi = \Pi(0)\eta[-r, -\lambda]$$

where $r \in \mathcal{L}^1$ has dimension one and $\lambda \in \mathcal{L}^2$ takes values which are row vectors of dimension K.

Let $\hat{\sigma} \in \mathcal{L}^2$ be any invertible $(K \times K)$-dimensional matrix-valued process, such as for example $\hat{\sigma} = I$, the constant $K \times K$ identity matrix. Set $N = K$ and construct an N-dimensional vector S of price processes of (risky) basic securities, as follows. Write

$$\hat{\sigma} = \begin{pmatrix} \hat{\sigma}_{1-} \\ \vdots \\ \hat{\sigma}_{K-} \end{pmatrix}$$

where $\hat{\sigma}_{k-}$ is the kth row of $\hat{\sigma}$, $k = 1, \ldots, K$. Set

$$\hat{\mu} = r\iota + \hat{\sigma}\lambda^{\mathsf{T}}$$

where ι is a K-dimensional column vector all of whose entries are one. Then $\hat{\mu} \in \mathcal{L}^1$.

Choose initial prices $M(0) > 0$, $S_1(0) > 0$, $\ldots, S_K(0) > 0$, and define

$$M = M(0)\eta[r, 0]$$

and

$$S_k = S_k(0)\eta[\hat{\mu}_k, \hat{\sigma}_{k-}]$$

for $k = 1, \ldots, K$. Write

$$S = \begin{pmatrix} S_1 \\ \vdots \\ S_K \end{pmatrix}$$

and

$$\bar{S} = \begin{pmatrix} M \\ S \end{pmatrix}$$

Then

$$dM = Mr\,dt$$

and

$$dS_k = S_k\hat{\mu}_k\,dt + S_k\hat{\sigma}_{k-}\,dW$$

for $k = 1, \ldots, K$. The equations

$$\hat{\mu} = r\iota + \hat{\sigma}\lambda^{\top}$$

and

$$dM = Mr\,dt$$

ensure that Π is a state price process for $\bar{S}$. Since $\hat{\sigma}$ is assumed to be invertible, Π is in fact the unique state price process for $\bar{S}$ (up to an arbitrary positive initial value), and markets are dynamically complete, provided that the filtration is the augmented filtration $F = F^W$ generated by the Wiener process.

5.8 Risk-adjusted Probabilities

Let Π be a state price process for $\bar{S}$, with interest rate process r and prices of risk λ.

As we have observed before, the state prices adjust for the time value of money and for risk. If $V = \bar{\Delta}\bar{S}$ is the value process of an admissible self-financing trading strategy $\bar{\Delta}$, then ΠV is a martingale, and so

$$V(t) = \frac{1}{\Pi(t)}E[\Pi(T)V(T) \mid \mathcal{F}_t]$$

for $0 \le t \le T$. Recall that

$$\Pi = \Pi(0)M(0)\frac{\eta[0, -\lambda]}{M}$$

This equation splits the state price process into two separate effects, discounting and risk adjustment. In the previous equation, dividing $V(T)$ by $M(T)$ corresponds to discounting at the rolled-over instantaneous interest rate, and multiplying by $\eta[0, -\lambda](T)$ is a risk adjustment.

The idea of risk-adjusted probabilities is to put the risk adjustment into the probabilities, so that we are left only with the discounting. We create a new probability measure Q with the property that the conditional expectation of any discounted random payoff X, computed under Q, is the same as the conditional expectation of the discounted and risk-adjusted random payoff, computed under the original probabilities P.

Specifically, if Y is a random payoff (happening at time T), and if $0 \le t \le T$, then the payoff discounted back from T to t is

$$X = \frac{M(t)}{M(T)}Y$$

We want the new probability measure Q to have the property that

$$E_Q[X \mid \mathcal{F}_t] = E\left[\frac{\eta[0,-\lambda](T)}{\eta[0,-\lambda](t)} X \;\Big|\; \mathcal{F}_t\right]$$

(provided that the expectations make sense). Here E_Q will denote expectation with respect to Q, and the expectation on the right hand side is computed using the original probabilities P. On the left hand side, we discount and compute the conditional expectation under Q. On the right hand side, we discount, adjust for risk, and compute the conditional expectation under P.

Here is how the risk-adjusted probability measure Q is defined. Let $\mathcal{T} = [0, T]$. Define the *risk-adjusted probability measure* Q (on the horizon T) as the measure on $(\Omega, \mathcal{F})$ which has density $\eta[0, -\lambda](T)$ with respect to P.

For this definition to make sense, we need to assume that

$$E\eta[0, -\lambda](T) = 1$$

so that $\eta[0, -\lambda](T)$ is indeed the density of a probability measure. We know from Proposition 2.24 that this is so if and only if $\eta[0, -\lambda]$ is a martingale (under the original probabilities).

If there is a money market account in the economy, then $\eta[0, -\lambda]$ is a martingale if and only if the trading strategy which consists in buying and holding the money market account is admissible. To see this, note that the value process of this trading strategy is M, and so the trading strategy is admissible if and only if

$$\Pi M = \Pi(0)M(0)\eta[0, -\lambda]$$

is a martingale.

We call $\eta[0, -\lambda]$ the *density process* of the risk-adjusted probability measure or the *likelihood process*.

So, the use of risk-adjusted probabilities requires the assumption that $\eta[0, -\lambda]$ is a martingale. It is not a particularly objectionable assumption, because it is equivalent to saying that the strategy of buying and holding the money market account is admissible. However, it may be painful to have to check in specific situations whether it is true or not. Note that the more fundamental theory of state price processes does not require this assumption.

It follows from Proposition 1.9 and the definition of Q that a random variable X (interpreted as a discounted payoff) is integrable under Q if and only if $\eta[0, -\lambda](T)X$ is integrable under P, in which case

$$E_Q[X \mid \mathcal{F}_t] = E\left[\frac{\eta[0,-\lambda](T)}{\eta[0,-\lambda](t)} X \;\Big|\; \mathcal{F}_t\right]$$

which is what we wanted.

Better yet, we can express admissibility of a self-financing trading strategy and derive a valuation formula in terms of the risk-adjusted probabilities.

If $V = \bar{\Delta}\bar{S}$ is the value process of a self-financing trading strategy $\bar{\Delta}$, then the trading strategy is admissible if and only if V/M is a martingale with respect to Q. This follows from the fact that, by definition, $\bar{\Delta}$ is admissible if and only if

$$\Pi V = \Pi(0)M(0)\frac{\eta[0,-\lambda]}{M}V$$

is a martingale with respect to P, and by Proposition 1.9, $\eta[0,-\lambda]V/M$ is a martingale with respect to P if and only if V/M is a martingale with respect to Q.

If $\bar{\Delta}$ is admissible and replicates a contingent claim Y at time T, then for $0 \le t \le T$, because of the martingale property,

$$\frac{\bar{\Delta}(t)\bar{S}(t)}{M(t)} = E_Q\left[\frac{Y}{M(T)} \mid \mathcal{F}_t\right]$$

This is an alternative to the valuation formula which uses the state price process:

$$\Pi(t)\bar{\Delta}(t)\bar{S}(t) = E[\Pi(T)Y \mid \mathcal{F}_t]$$

Often, it is easier to calculate the conditional expectation based on the risk-adjusted probabilities. This will be illustrated in Example 5.10 below.

If Y is a claim such that $\Pi(T)Y$ is integrable (under the original probabilities P), recall that we have defined the martingale value $V(Y;\Pi)$ of Y with respect to Π by

$$V(Y;\Pi)(t) = \frac{1}{\Pi(t)}E_P[\Pi(T)Y \mid \mathcal{F}_t]$$

Now observe that $\eta[0,-\lambda]$ is a state price process for $\bar{S}/M$, that is for prices measured in units of the money market account. The payoff measured in these units is $Y/M(T)$, which is integrable under Q because $\Pi(T)Y$ is integrable under P. Applying the definition of the martingale value to $Y/M(T)$ and $\eta[0,-\lambda]$, we find

$$V(Y/M(T);\eta[0,-\lambda])(t) = \frac{1}{\eta[0,-\lambda](t)}E\left[\eta[0,-\lambda](T)\frac{Y}{M(T)} \mid \mathcal{F}_t\right]$$

$$= E_Q\left[\frac{Y}{M(T)} \mid \mathcal{F}_t\right]$$

This process is a martingale under Q.

If we know the risk-adjusted probability measure Q, then we do not need to know the prices of risk in order to calculate the value of the claim in units of the money market account. Therefore, it is useful to introduce the notation

$$V(Y/M(T);Q)(t) = V(Y/M(T);\eta[0,-\lambda])(t) = E_Q\left[\frac{Y}{M(T)} \mid \mathcal{F}_t\right]$$

The relation between the two value processes (in units of the money market account and in nominal units, respectively) is

$$V(Y/M(T); Q) = V(Y; \Pi)/M$$

In general, the interest rate r and the prices of risk λ depend on the price system (the unit of account). If we change the price system, then r and λ usually change. If λ changes, so does the risk-adjusted probability measure Q. So, Q depends on the price system as well.

As noted earlier in connection with our discussion of Girsanov's theorem, the risk-adjusted probability measure Q is equivalent to the original probability measure P, which means that Q and P have the same null sets. In particular, the probability space $(\Omega, \mathcal{F}, Q)$ is complete since $(\Omega, \mathcal{F}, P)$ is assumed to be complete, and the filtration F is augmented with respect to Q since it is assumed to be augmented with respect to P. The spaces $\mathcal{L}^1$ and $\mathcal{L}^2$ do not depend on whether we are using P or Q.

When performing calculations based on the risk-adjusted probability measure Q, it is often useful to express the relevant processes in terms of the process W^λ instead of the process W.

Recall that the K-dimensional process W^λ is defined by

$$W^\lambda(t) = \int_0^t \lambda^\top du + W(t)$$

This process is adapted to F. It is an Itô process with

$$dW^\lambda = \lambda^\top dt + dW$$

According to Girsanov's theorem (Theorem 2.26), W^λ is a Wiener process with respect to F and the probability measure Q, provided that $\eta[0, -\lambda]$ is a martingale. In that case, we may as well call W^λ the *risk-adjusted Wiener process*.

Here is how to rewrite an Itô process in terms of W^λ. If X is an Itô process with

$$dX = a\, dt + b\, dW$$

then we can write the differential with respect to W^λ as

$$\begin{aligned} dX &= a\, dt + b\, dW \\ &= a\, dt + b\, dW^\lambda - b\lambda^\top dt \\ &= \left(a - b\lambda^\top\right) dt + b\, dW^\lambda \end{aligned}$$

We have already observed that the drift of $\eta[0, -\lambda]X$ is zero if and only if $a = b\lambda^\top$. We now see that this is so if and only if dX has the form $dX = b\, dW^\lambda$.

In particular, if $\bar{S}$ is normalized, then $\bar{\mu} = \bar{\sigma}\lambda^\top$ and

$$d\bar{S} = \bar{\sigma}\, dW^\lambda$$

If $\bar{S}$ is not necessarily normalized, then $\bar{\mu} - r\bar{S} = \bar{\sigma}\lambda^\top$, and we can write $\bar{S}/M$ in terms of W^λ as follows:

$$d(\bar{S}/M) = \frac{1}{M}\, d\bar{S} - \bar{S}\frac{r}{M}\, dt$$

$$= \frac{1}{M}(\bar{\mu} - r\bar{S})\,dt + \frac{1}{M}\bar{\sigma}\,dW$$

$$= \frac{1}{M}\bar{\sigma}\,dW^{\lambda}$$

Consequently, if $\bar{\Delta}$ is a self-financing trading strategy in $\mathcal{L}(\bar{S}/M)$, then

$$d(\bar{\Delta}\bar{S}/M) = \frac{1}{M}\bar{\Delta}\bar{\sigma}\,W^{\lambda}$$

In what follows, whenever statements are made about the risk-adjusted probabilities, it is implicitly or explicitly assumed that $\eta[0, -\lambda]$ is a martingale. By contrast, statements about the state price process Π, or about $\eta[0, -\lambda]$ itself, or about W^{λ}, do not implicitly assume that $\eta[0, -\lambda]$ is a martingale. They assume this only if it is explicitly stated.

When there is a risk-adjusted probability measure, it is possible to rule out arbitrage by imposing a requirement on self-financing trading strategies which can be interpreted as a credit constraint and is analogous to the financing constraint imposed in Propositions 4.11 and 5.1. This requirement says that the discounted value process $\bar{\Delta}\bar{S}/M$ should be bounded below.

Proposition 5.8 *Suppose there is a risk-adjusted probability measure Q. Then there exists no self-financing arbitrage strategy $\bar{\Delta}$ such that $\bar{\Delta}\bar{S}/M$ is bounded below.*

Proof The proof is analogous to the proof of Proposition 4.11. In fact, Proposition 5.8 is a special case of Proposition 4.11, applied to the price system $\bar{S}/M$, the probability measure Q, and the Wiener process W^{λ}. In a sense, the constant one is a state price process for $\bar{S}/M$ under Q. $\square$

The following proposition is analogous to Proposition 5.1. It says that when there exists a risk-adjusted probability measure, the martingale price is the lowest price at which a claim can be replicated, provided that the claim can indeed be replicated by an admissible trading strategy, and provided that the discounted value processes of the replicating trading strategies are bounded below.

Proposition 5.9 *Let Y be a claim which is replicated by two self-financing trading strategies $\bar{\Delta}$ and $\bar{\Theta}$ such that $\bar{\Delta}$ is admissible for $\bar{S}$ and Π and $\bar{\Theta}\bar{S}/M$ is bounded below. Then $\bar{\Delta}\bar{S}/M$ is bounded below, and with probability one,*

$$\bar{\Delta}(t)\bar{S}(t) \le \bar{\Theta}(t)\bar{S}(t) \quad \text{for all } t$$

Proof The proof is analogous to the proof of Proposition 5.1. In fact, Proposition 5.9 is a special case of Proposition 5.1, applied to the price system $\bar{S}/M$, the probability measure Q and the Wiener process W^{λ}. $\square$

Example 5.10 *Continuation of Examples 1.7, 1.15, 2.3, 2.14, 2.20, 2.28, 4.1, 4.2, 4.3, 4.8, and 4.10, and Exercise 4.2.* This example recalculates the martingale value of a cash-or-nothing call option in the Black–Scholes model. It illustrates the methodology of valuing claims by using the risk-adjusted probability measure Q, the process W^λ, and Girsanov's theorem. Notice that this calculation is simpler than the one performed earlier using the state price process. In particular, it does not require the use of Proposition 2.29 (the formula for the expectation of a truncated lognormal distribution).

Let $K = 1$, and let
$$M = M(0)\eta[r, 0]$$
and
$$S = S(0)\eta[\mu, \sigma]$$

be the price processes in the Black–Scholes model, where r, μ, and $\sigma > 0$ are constants. The price of risk is
$$\lambda = \frac{\mu - r}{\sigma}$$

Let $0 \le t \le T$, and let Q be the risk-adjusted probability measure, which has density $\eta[0, -\lambda](T)$ with respect to P.

Consider a cash-or-nothing call option on the stock, whose payoff happens at time T and equals
$$Y = 1_{S(T) \ge X} = \begin{cases} 1 & \text{if } S(T) \ge X \\ 0 & \text{otherwise} \end{cases}$$

where X is a non-negative trigger price.

We want to value the option at time t, and we do it using the risk-adjusted probability measure.

First, we verify that the option is indeed marketed. According to Theorem 5.6, all we need to check is that $\Pi(T)Y$ is integrable under P, or equivalently, that $Y/M(T)$ is integrable under Q. This is obvious since $M(T)$ is positive and nonrandom and Y is bounded.

Let $C_{CN}(t)$ denote the martingale value of the option at time t. Then

$$C_{CN}(t) = M(t)E_Q\left[\frac{Y}{M(T)} \,\Big|\, \mathcal{F}_t\right]$$
$$= \frac{M(t)}{M(T)}E_Q\left[1_{S(T) \ge X} \,\big|\, \mathcal{F}_t\right]$$
$$= e^{-r(T-t)}Q\left[S(T) \ge X \,\big|\, \mathcal{F}_t\right]$$

It is not too difficult to calculate this conditional probability, because given the information at time t, $S(T)$ is a function of $W^\lambda(T) - W^\lambda(t)$, which follows a known normal distribution under Q.

Specifically,
$$\frac{dS}{S} = \mu\,dt + \sigma\,dW$$
$$= \mu\,dt + \sigma(dW^\lambda - \lambda\,dt)$$

$$= r\,dt + \sigma\,dW^\lambda$$

so that

$$S(T) = S(t)\exp\left[\left(r - \frac{1}{2}\sigma^2\right)(T-t) + \sigma(W^\lambda(T) - W^\lambda(t))\right]$$

and, taking logs,

$$\ln S(T) = \ln S(t) + \left(r - \frac{1}{2}\sigma^2\right)(T-t) + \sigma(W^\lambda(T) - W^\lambda(t))$$

So, given information at time t, $S(T)$ follows a lognormal distribution under Q, and $\ln S(T)$ follows a normal distribution with mean

$$\ln S(t) + \left(r - \frac{1}{2}\sigma^2\right)(T-t)$$

and variance

$$\sigma^2(T-t)$$

The corresponding standardized random variable is

$$U = \frac{\ln S(T) - \ln S(t) - \left(r - \frac{1}{2}\sigma^2\right)(T-t)}{\sigma\sqrt{T-t}}$$

It is standardized in the sense that it follows a standard normal distribution under Q.

Observe that $S(T) \geq X$ if and only if $U \geq -d$, where

$$d = d_2 = \frac{\ln S(t) - \ln X + \left(r - \frac{1}{2}\sigma^2\right)(T-t)}{\sigma\sqrt{T-t}}$$

Hence,

$$Q[S(T) \geq X \mid \mathcal{F}_t] = 1 - N(-d_2) = N(d_2)$$

where, again, N is the cumulative standard normal distribution function. In other words, $N(d_2)$ is the risk-adjusted probability that the option will finish in the money.

The value of the cash-or-nothing call option is

$$C_{CN} = e^{-r(T-t)}Q[S(T) \geq X \mid \mathcal{F}_t] = e^{-r(T-t)}N(d_2)$$

which is the same as we found earlier using the state price process. $\qquad\square$

5.9 Summary

If a contingent claim is replicated by an admissible self-financing trading strategy, then the value process of the trading strategy can be calculated as a conditional expectation. Specifically, the product of the value process and the state price process at each point in time equals the conditional expectation, given the information available at that time, of the product of the payoff to the claim and the final value of the state price process. This equation can be solved for the value of the trading strategy.

We can now price a derivative security in a very simple way. If the derivative is replicated by an admissible trading strategy, then its current value equals the conditional expectation, given current information, of state prices times payoff, normalized by today's state prices. In general, we use this equation to define the martingale value of the claim, and we call this valuation procedure the martingale method. The equation suggests that we can interpret the ratio between the final and the current value of the state price process as Arrow–Debreu state prices per unit of probability.

In many cases, the conditional expectation can be calculated fairly explicitly, because we know the probability distributions that are involved. For example, the payoff and the final value of the state price process are often functions of the final value of the Wiener process, which is normally distributed.

Our main foundation for the martingale valuation method is the assumption that the claim can be replicated by an admissible trading strategy. Proposition 5.1 provides an alternative justification for the martingale method, based on a financing constraint. The proposition says that the martingale price of a claim is the lowest price at which the claim can be replicated, provided that it can indeed be replicated by an admissible trading strategy, and provided that the value processes of replicating trading strategies multiplied by the state price process are required to be bounded below.

Delta hedging of a contingent claim means engaging in a hedging strategy, which is a trading strategy such that the total of its value and the value of the claim is instantaneously riskless. We may also want the hedging strategy to be self-financing and have initial value zero.

If a trading strategy is not self-financing, then it can be made self-financing by reinvesting the net withdrawals in the money market account. The result will be a trading strategy which is self-financing and has the same initial value and the same dispersion as the original one.

Proposition 5.4 gives a criterion for checking whether a given Itô process is the value process of a given self-financing trading strategy. The criterion says that the Itô process should have the same initial value and the same dispersion as the trading strategy, and its product with the state price process should have zero drift.

Proposition 5.5 says that if there exists a money market account, and if the dispersion matrix of the basic price processes has rank equal to the dimension of the Wiener process, then any Itô process whose product with the state price process has zero drift is the value process of some self-financing trading strategy. This trading strategy will be unique if the rank of the dispersion matrix equals the number of instantaneously risky securities.

To construct such a trading strategy, we first find a trading strategy whose value process has the same dispersion coefficient and the same initial value as the Itô process in question, and then we make it self-financing by investing its net withdrawals in the money market account.

We say that markets are dynamically complete if every contingent claim which is contingent only on the information generated by the Wiener processes and whose product with the final value of the state price process is integrable, can be replicated by an admissible self-financing trading strategy.

The information generated by the Wiener processes consists, at each point in time, in knowing, or having observed or inferred, the total movement of each of the Wiener processes up to that point in time. That often corresponds to knowing the paths of the securities prices up to that point in time. In the case of dynamically complete markets, if the derivative security depends at most on that information, then it can be replicated and priced. On the other hand, if it depends on more information than that, then there is no presumption that it can be replicated.

The surprising and powerful complete markets theorem, Theorem 5.6, says that markets are very often dynamically complete. Specifically, provided that there exists a money market account, markets are dynamically complete if and only if there are at least as many instantaneously risky securities as there are sources of risk, and these securities are not instantaneously perfectly correlated.

If there are ten sources of risk, meaning ten Wiener processes driving the system, then complete markets requires that there are at least ten risky basic securities. If there are fewer than that, then there is not enough flexibility to trade and to replicate the derivative. Furthermore, we require that there not be any perfect instantaneous correlation among the basic securities. If one of them is equivalent to a combination of the others, then effectively there is one fewer risky basic security, and then there are not enough of them.

The complete markets theorem holds when the securities prices are Itô processes, but in general it does not hold if they are not Itô processes. That is one of the main reasons why we stick to Itô processes in this book.

The value process of a claim often turns out to be a function of time and of the prices of the risky basic securities. If so, then we can identify a replicating trading strategy by differentiating this function with respect to the securities prices. The derivative with respect to the price of a particular basic security will be the delta with respect to that security. It tells us the number of shares of that security to hold in the replicating trading strategy. These holdings are financed by borrowing or lending at the instantaneously riskless rate, as necessary. The initial holdings of the money market account are chosen so that the trading strategy has the correct initial value.

We illustrated the martingale valuation principle by an example where we found a formula for the value of a cash-or-nothing option. The point of this example was to show that the calculation is feasible, although it is somewhat complicated. In particular, we needed to use the formula for the expected value of a truncated lognormally distributed variable. It is easier to implement the martingale method on the basis of the risk-adjusted probabilities, as we illustrated in Example 5.10. There, the calculation simply came down to finding the risk-adjusted probability of the event that the option will be in the money.

So far, we have described our trading and valuation model by positing the dynamics of some basic securities price processes. An alternative way of specifying a model would be to start by specifying the state price process. Given the state price process, we can value any contingent claim, provided that we can specify its payoff. We can go from there to a model with basic securities by picking an appropriate set of claims and using their martingale values as price processes of basic securities.

Apart from some irrelevant multiplicative constants, the state price process is the ratio between the so-called likelihood process and the value of the money market account. This means that when we multiply the payoff to a derivative security by the state prices, the effect is to adjust for risk and for the time value of money. Multiplying by the likelihood process is a risk adjustment, and dividing by the value of the money market account corresponds to discounting at the rolled-over instantaneous interest rate.

The idea behind the risk-adjusted probabilities is to incorporate the risk adjustment in the probabilities, so that we are left only with the discounting. The risk-adjusted probability measure has the property that the conditional expectation of any discounted random payoff equals the conditional expectation of the risk-adjusted and discounted payoff, computed under the original probabilities.

Given a fixed horizon date, the risk-adjusted probability measure is defined by the requirement that its density with respect to the original probabilities should be the final value of the likelihood process. For this definition to make sense, we need to assume that the final value of the likelihood process has expectation one, or equivalently, that the likelihood process is a martingale. This is not a particularly objectionable assumption, because it is equivalent to saying that the strategy of buying and holding the money market account is admissible. However, it may be annoying to have to check in specific situations whether it is true or not.

We now have a version of the martingale method which uses the risk-adjusted probabilities instead of the state price process. The current martingale value of the derivative will be the conditional expectation, given current information and based on the risk-adjusted probabilities, of the payoff to the derivative discounted back to the present at the rolled-over instantaneous rate. The state prices have disappeared, the risk adjustment has gone into the probabilities, but the discounting remains.

When there is a risk-adjusted probability measure, it is possible to rule out arbitrage by requiring that the discounted value processes of self-financing trading strategies should be bounded below. This requirement can be interpreted as a credit constraint and is analogous to the financing constraint mentioned in the previous chapter. Furthermore, the martingale value of a claim is the lowest price at which the claim can be replicated, provided that it can indeed be replicated by an admissible trading strategy, and provided that the discounted value processes of the replicating trading strategies have to be bounded below.

To get some benefit from the risk-adjusted probabilities in the form of simpler calculations, we need to use Girsanov's theorem. We introduce a new process by taking the original Wiener process and adding a drift to it which is equal to the prices of risk. Girsanov's theorem says that this new process is a Wiener process under the risk-adjusted probabilities. We call it the risk-adjusted Wiener process.

For the purpose of calculating the martingale values of claims, it is often useful to express the relevant processes, including the basic securities price processes, in terms of the risk-adjusted Wiener process. This is what we did in Example 5.10, where we recalculated the value of the cash-or-nothing option in the Black–Scholes model.

The new Wiener process helps explain why prices are martingales under the risk-adjusted probabilities. What happens is that when we express the price processes in terms of the new Wiener process, their drifts get replaced by the riskless rate. This is true both of the basic securities prices and of the value processes of self-financing trading strategies. The drift of a discounted security price becomes zero. Risk adjustment replaces the drift by the riskless rate, whereas discounting deducts the riskless rate. The combination of the two removes the drift entirely. This helps make discounted prices into martingales under the risk-adjusted probabilities.

5.10   (*) Notes

The fundamental insight behind dynamic market completeness in continuous time goes back to Black and Scholes [10, 1973]. They constructed a trading strategy that replicates a call option by exploiting the fact that the payoff to the option is a function of the final stock price. The general concept of dynamically complete markets in continuous time was introduced by Harrison and Pliska [44, 1981]. They proved the completeness of a model where the interest rate is constant and the risky securities follow correlated geometric Brownian motions with a regular relative dispersion matrix. They stated that these conditions could be generalized, but they conjectured that it would be necessary to assume a deterministic interest rate.

Bensoussan [7, 1984] generalized the completeness result to a model where the prices are still positive and the relative dispersion matrix σ is regular, but where the relative drift and dispersion coefficients, including the interest rate, may be random processes, so long as they are bounded. He assumed that the volatilities or instantaneous return variances of the risky securities are bounded below away from zero. This assumption ensures that the unique solution to the

equation for the vector of prices of risk is in $\mathcal{L}^2$. In Theorem 5.6, we have simply
assumed that there exists a state price process.

Duffie [31, 1996] has a complete markets result where he assumes that the
interest rate process is bounded and that there exists a risk-adjusted probability
measure whose density has finite variance.

Theorem 0.3.5 of Karatzas [62, 1997] is essentially the same as Theorem 5.6,
except that Karatzas assumes that there exists a risk-adjusted probability measure and that the basic securities prices are positive.

Theorem 5.6 is quite general. It does not assume that prices are positive
or impose boundedness on the coefficient processes. The marketed claims are
not limited to those that are square integrable under either the original or the
risk-adjusted probabilities. It is not assumed that there exists a risk-adjusted
probability measure, and in particular, nothing like the Novikov condition is
needed.

Risk-adjusted probability measures, also called "risk-neutral probability measures" or "equivalent martingale measures," seem to have been invented by Cox
and Ross [24, 1976] and Harrison and Kreps [43, 1979].

Harrison and Kreps [43, 1979] brought both the martingale representation
theorem and Girsanov's theorem into their analysis.

Proposition 5.8 corresponds to (ii) of Theorem 0.2.4 of Karatzas [62, 1997],
which, however, assumes that the basic securities prices are non-negative.

Karatzas [62, 1997] considers only non-negative contingent claims and positive basic securities price processes. He defines the "upper hedging price" of a
claim as the lowest initial cost at which the claim can be replicated (or at which
a larger claim can be replicated, but in a complete market that distinction does
not matter) by a self-financing trading strategy whose discounted value process
is bounded below. His Theorem 1.2.1 says, among other things, that in the complete markets case, if a risk-adjusted probability measure exists, then the upper
hedging price of a non-negative claim whose discounted value is integrable under the risk-adjusted probabilities will be equal to the martingale value. That
corresponds to Proposition 5.9.

Karatzas [62, 1997] also defines the "lower hedging price" of a claim. The
definition is equivalent to saying that the lower hedging price is the highest
initial cost at which the claim can be replicated (or at which a smaller claim can
be replicated, but in a complete market that distinction does not matter) by a
self-financing trading strategy whose discounted value process is a submartingale
under the risk-adjusted probabilities. In the complete markets case, the lower
hedging price, the upper hedging price, and the martingale price of a contingent
claim are the same.

Recall that in this book, we do not require the basic securities prices to be
martingales under the risk-adjusted probabilities, although it would make little
difference if we did. Such a requirement is equivalent to assuming that all buy-
and-hold strategies are admissible. In other words, admissibility is a property of
trading strategies and not of the basic securities price processes.

In a model where the basic securities price processes are given in advance, the state price process is a more fundamental concept than the risk-adjusted probabilities. The risk-adjusted probabilities are mainly a computational device. The computational aspect is brought out in the two alternative calculations of the value of the cash-or-nothing option in Section 5.6 and in Example 5.10. The value can well be calculated without any use of the risk-adjusted probabilities. It is a matter of calculating the expectation of a truncated lognormal variable. However, when the calculations are based on the risk-adjusted probabilities, they become considerably simpler. This is so because Girsanov's theorem is used in an essential way. The fact that W^λ is a Wiener process under the risk-adjusted probability measure reduces the problem to that of calculating a conditional probability rather than a conditional expectation.

By contrast, Girsanov's theorem does not play any essential role in proving the absence of arbitrage or the dynamic completeness of markets. Therefore, the general theory of trading, pricing, and hedging is better developed in terms of the state price process and without use of risk-adjusted probabilities.

6

THE BLACK–SCHOLES MODEL

This chapter investigates the Black–Scholes model in detail. What we call the Black–Scholes model is not the formula for the value of a standard call option, but rather the economy consisting of a money market account with a constant interest rate and a risky security which does not pay dividends and whose price follows a geometric Brownian motion.

We study the value function of a contingent claim whose payoff is a fairly general function of the final price of the stock. It is shown that the value function is infinitely often differentiable and satisfies the Black–Scholes partial differential equation.

As examples of contingent claims, we consider cash-or-nothing options, asset-or-nothing options, and standard options. We compute and analyze their value functions and delta functions. The value function of a standard call option, which is given by the Black–Scholes formula, as well as the value function of a standard put option, are analyzed in detail. We compute the so-called "Greeks," that is the partial derivatives of the value functions.

Finally, we consider the problem of identifying the value function of a claim by solving the Black–Scholes partial differential equation subject to a terminal condition which says that the final value of the claim equals its payoff. This is how Black and Scholes [10, 1973] originally derived their formula. It turns out that one has to be careful in imposing the terminal condition in an appropriate way. Once that is done, the main issue is to show that there is a unique solution to the equation subject to the terminal condition. This requires that some additional restriction be imposed on the solution function.

6.1   Review of the Black–Scholes Economy

We introduced the Black–Scholes model in Example 1.7, and we have studied it further in Examples 1.15, 2.3, 2.14, 2.20, 2.28, 4.1, 4.2, 4.3, 4.8, 4.10, and 5.10, and in Exercise 4.2. It has a money market account and one instantaneously risky security, driven by a one-dimensional Wiener process W. Hence, $N = 1$ and $K = 1$.

The money market account has price process

$$M(t) = M(0)\eta[r, 0](t) = M(0)e^{rt}$$

where $M(0) > 0$ and the interest rate r is constant. In differential form:

$$dM = Mr\, dt$$

The instantaneously risky security, normally conceived to be a stock, has the price process

$$S(t) = S(0)\eta[\mu, \sigma](t) = S(0)\exp\left[\left(\mu - \frac{1}{2}\sigma^2\right)t + \sigma W(t)\right]$$

where $S(0) > 0$, and μ and $\sigma > 0$ are constant numbers. In differential form:

$$\frac{dS}{S} = \mu \, dt + \sigma \, dW$$

These differential forms were calculated in Example 2.3, using Itô's formula.

The specification implies that $S(t)$ follows a lognormal distribution. Specifically,

$$\ln S(t) = \ln S(0) + \left(\mu - \frac{1}{2}\sigma^2\right)t + \sigma W(t)$$

is a generalized Wiener process, and the conditional distribution of $\ln S(T)$ given $S(t)$ is normal with mean

$$\ln S(t) + \left(\mu - \frac{1}{2}\sigma^2\right)(T - t)$$

and variance $\sigma^2(T - t)$.

In Example 2.14, we found that the differential of the stock price, measured in units of the money market account, or discounted at the rolled-over instantaneous interest rate r, is

$$d\left(\frac{S}{M}\right) = \left(\frac{S}{M}\right)[(\mu - r)\,dt + \sigma \, dW]$$

Like $S(t)$, $S(t)/M(t)$ follows a lognormal distribution.

A price of risk λ must satisfy the equation

$$\mu - r = \sigma\lambda$$

so λ is the constant number given by

$$\lambda = \frac{\mu - r}{\sigma}$$

The state price process is

$$\Pi(t) = \eta[-r, -\lambda](t)$$

$$= \exp\left[\int_0^t \left(-r - \frac{1}{2}\lambda^2\right)ds - \int_0^t \lambda \, dW(s)\right]$$

$$= \exp\left[\left(-r - \frac{1}{2}\lambda^2\right)t - \lambda W(t)\right]$$

In Example 2.28, we used the price of risk to obtain the risk-adjusted probabilities. Since λ is a constant, the associated process

$$\eta[0, -\lambda](t) = \exp\left(-\frac{1}{2}\int_0^t \lambda^2 ds - \int_0^t \lambda dW(s)\right) = \exp\left(-\frac{1}{2}\lambda^2 t - \lambda W(t)\right)$$

is a martingale. The risk-adjusted probability measure Q has density $\eta[0, -\lambda](T)$ with respect to P. By Girsanov's theorem, the process W^λ defined by

$$W^\lambda(t) = \lambda t + W(t)$$

is a Wiener process with respect to F and Q. The differential of W^λ can be expressed as

$$dW^\lambda = \lambda\, dt + dW$$

In terms of dW^λ, the differential of the stock price is

$$\frac{dS}{S} = r\, dt + \sigma\, dW^\lambda$$

and the differential of S/M is

$$d\left(\frac{S}{M}\right) = \frac{S}{M}\sigma\, dW^\lambda$$

For notational compactness, set

$$\gamma = r - \frac{1}{2}\sigma^2$$

since this expression will appear very often in the analysis of this model.

Both $S(t)$ and $S(t)/M(t)$ follow a lognormal distribution under Q. Specifically,

$$\ln S(t) = \ln S(0) + \left(r - \frac{1}{2}\sigma^2\right)t + \sigma W^\lambda(t) = \ln S(0) + \gamma t + \sigma W^\lambda(t)$$

is a generalized Wiener process, and the conditional distribution under Q of $\ln S(T)$ given $S(t)$ is normal with mean

$$\ln S(t) + \left(r - \frac{1}{2}\sigma^2\right)(T - t) = \ln S(t) + \gamma(T - t)$$

and variance $\sigma^2(T - t)$.

We know from Theorem 5.6 that the model has dynamically complete markets.

In Section 5.6, we calculated the value of a cash-or-nothing call option, using the state price process. We also calculated delta. In Example 5.10, we recalculated the value using the risk-adjusted probabilities. The payoff to the cash-or-nothing call option happens at time T and equals

$$Y = 1_{S(T)\geq X} = \begin{cases} 1 & \text{if } S(T) \geq X \\ 0 & \text{otherwise} \end{cases}$$

where X is a non-negative trigger price. We found that the value is

$$C_{CN} = e^{-r(T-t)}N(d_2) = \Phi(S,t)$$

where

$$d_2 = \frac{\ln S - \ln X + \left(r - \frac{1}{2}\sigma^2\right)(T-t)}{\sigma\sqrt{T-t}} = \frac{\ln S - \ln X + \gamma(T-t)}{\sigma\sqrt{T-t}}$$

The value was plotted in Fig. 5.1.

In Section 5.6, we found that the delta of the cash-or-nothing call option is

$$\Delta = \Phi_S(S,t) = e^{-r(T-t)}N'(d_2)\frac{1}{S\sigma\sqrt{T-t}} > 0$$

where N' is the standard normal density function:

$$N'(d) = \frac{1}{\sqrt{2\pi}}\exp(-d^2/2)$$

Delta was plotted in Fig. 5.2.

It is remarkable that the instantaneous expected rate of return μ to the stock does not enter into the formula for the value of the cash-or-nothing call option. One might think that the higher the expected rate of return to the stock, the higher the value of the option. We shall return to this point below, in a more general setting.

For now, we observe that we actually do not need to assume that μ is a constant. Henceforth, we shall assume instead that μ has the form

$$\mu = \sigma\lambda + r$$

for some $\lambda \in \mathcal{L}^2$ such that $E_P\eta[0,-\lambda](T) = 1$. We continue to assume that r is constant and that σ is a positive constant.

As before, the risk-adjusted probability measure Q has density $\eta[0,-\lambda](T)$ with respect to P. By Girsanov's theorem, the process W^λ defined by

$$W^\lambda(t) = \int_0^t \lambda\,ds + W(t)$$

is a Wiener process with respect to F and Q. Note that λ is not necessarily constant any more. The process W^λ and the probability measure Q depend on

λ and on μ, but in any case W^λ is a Wiener process relative to F under Q. The differential of W^λ can be expressed as

$$dW^\lambda = \lambda\,dt + dW$$

In terms of dW^λ, the differentials of the stock price $S(t)$ and the normalized stock price $S(t)/M(t)$ are the same as before. This implies that the conditional and unconditional distributions under Q of $S(t)$ and $S(t)/M(t)$ are the same as before. Specifically, the conditional distribution under Q of $\ln S(T)$ given $S(t)$ is normal with mean

$$\ln S(t) + \left(r - \frac{1}{2}\sigma^2\right)(T - t) = \ln S(t) + \gamma(T - t)$$

and variance $\sigma^2(T - t)$.

In Example 5.10, we calculated the value of the cash-or-nothing call option as

$$C_{CN}(t) = e^{-r(T-t)}Q[S(T) \geq X \mid S(t)] = \Phi(S(t), t)$$

where Φ is the function defined above. These equations continue to hold, because the conditional distribution of $S(T)$ given $S(t)$ is unaffected by the fact that we no longer assume μ to be constant.

6.2   The Value Function

A cash-or-nothing call option with trigger price X has payoff

$$Y = 1_{S(T) \geq X}$$

and value process

$$V(t) = \Phi(S(t), t)$$

where $\Phi : (0, \infty) \times (0, T) \to I\!R$ is the function given by

$$\Phi(S, t) = e^{-r(T-t)}N(d_2) = e^{-r(T-t)}N\left(\frac{\ln S - \ln X + \gamma(T - t)}{\sigma\sqrt{T - t}}\right)$$

The claim is *path independent* in the sense that the payoff depends only on the final stock price $S(T)$, not on the path of the stock price before T. The value process is also *path independent*, in the sense that the value at any time $t < T$ is a function Φ of the stock price $S(t)$ at that time (and of time itself) but not a function of the path of the stock price. The function Φ is infinitely often differentiable, and in particular, it satisfies the differentiability requirements of Itô's lemma.

We shall now consider general path-independent contingent claims or derivative securities. The cash-or-nothing call option is a special case, but so are cash-or-nothing put options, asset-or-nothing call and put options, standard call and put options, and many other claims.

We assume that the payoff at time T is a function of the stock price $S(T)$ at T. We shall show that there exists a value function Φ which is a function of the current stock price and of time. Furthermore, the value function Φ is infinitely often differentiable and solves a partial differential equation called the Black–Scholes partial differential equation.

Heuristically, we could define the function Φ by the formula

$$\Phi(S,t) = e^{-r(T-t)}E_Q[g(S(T)) \mid S(t) = S]$$

For this definition to be successful, we need to impose some regularity on the function g to ensure that the conditional expectation makes sense. We also need to demonstrate that $\Phi(S(t),t) = V(t)$, or in other words, that the conditional expectation of $g(S(T))$ given the current value of $S(t)$ is the same as the conditional expectation given all information available at time t. This is in fact true, and it is a consequence of the fact that the conditional distribution of $S(T)$ given the current value of $S(t)$ is the same as the conditional distribution of $S(T)$ given all information available at time t. Finally, we need to demonstrate that Φ is infinitely often differentiable, or at least sufficiently differentiable to apply Itô's lemma.

The actual definition of Φ will be somewhat different, but we shall show that it is equivalent to the heuristic definition outlined above.

For each $t \in [0, T]$, define a function $h[t] : I\!R \to (0, \infty)$ by

$$h[t](x) = S(0)e^{\gamma t + \sigma x}$$

It is strictly increasing, with $h[t](I\!R) = (0, \infty)$. The inverse function $h[t]^{-1} : (0, \infty) \to I\!R$ is given by

$$h[t]^{-1}(S) = \frac{1}{\sigma}(\ln S - \ln S(0) - \gamma t)$$

The usefulness of the function $h[t]$ stems from the fact that it maps the value of the risk-adjusted Wiener process into the price of the stock:

$$h[t](W^\lambda(t)) = S(t)$$

and

$$h[t]^{-1}(S(t)) = W^\lambda(t)$$

Let $g : (0, \infty) \to I\!R$ be a function whose interpretation will be that $g(S(T))$ is the random payoff to a contingent claim.

Define a function $f[g] : I\!R \to I\!R$ by $f[g] = g \circ h[T]$, or

$$f[g](x) = g\left(S(0)e^{\gamma T + \sigma x}\right)$$

This function expresses the payoff as a function of $W^\lambda(T)$:

$$f[g](W^\lambda(T)) = g\{h[T](W^\lambda(T))\} = g(S(T))$$

We shall make the following assumptions about the functions g and $f[g]$:

1. g is locally integrable, and

2. $f[g] \in G_0(a)$ for some $a > 0$ such that $T < 1/(2a)$.

As in Appendix C, Section C.1, if α is a constant, let $G_0(\alpha)$ denote the set of functions $f : I\!\!R \to I\!\!R$ which satisfy the following *growth condition*: there exist positive constants κ and C such that

$$|f(y)| \le C \exp\left(ay^2\right)$$

for almost all $y \in I\!\!R$ with $|y| \ge \kappa$.

Since the function $h[T]$ is continuously differentiable with positive derivative, it follows from Proposition B.24 that $f[g]$ is locally integrable if and only if g is locally integrable.

Proposition 6.1 *A sufficient condition for $f[g]$ to be in $G_0(\alpha)$ for all $\alpha > 0$ is that g satisfies a* polynomial growth condition: *for some $\beta > 0$, $y_0 \ge 0$,*

$$|g(y)| \le 1 + y^\beta$$

for all $y \in (y_0, \infty)$.

Proof We find

$$
\begin{aligned}
|f[g](x)| &= |g(h[T](x))| \\
&\le 1 + h[T](x)^\beta \\
&= 1 + S(0)^\beta \exp\left(\gamma T + \sigma x\right)^\beta \\
&= 1 + S(0)^\beta \exp\left(\beta\gamma T + \beta\sigma x\right) \\
&\le \exp\left(\alpha x^2\right)
\end{aligned}
$$

where both inequalities hold when $|x|$ is sufficiently large. □

In order to define the value function of the claim $g(S(T))$, we first express the value as a function of the Wiener process. This allows us to use some of the results from the probabilistic analysis of the heat equation in Appendix C, Section C.1. We then transform by the family of functions $h[t]^{-1}$ in order to express the value of the claim as a function of the stock price.

Define a function

$$p : I\!\!R \times (0, \infty) \to (0, \infty)$$

by

$$p(x, \tau) = \frac{1}{\sqrt{2\pi\tau}} \exp\left(-\frac{x^2}{2\tau}\right)$$

It is the density function of a normal distribution with mean zero and variance τ. It is also the fundamental solution of the heat equation, cf. Appendix C, Section C.1.

Define a function $v : \mathbb{R} \times [0, T) \to \mathbb{R}$ by

$$v(x, \tau) = \int_{-\infty}^{\infty} f[g](y) p(y - x, \tau) \, dy = E f[g](x + W(\tau))$$

It follows from Proposition C.2 that this function is well defined. By Proposition C.3, it is infinitely often differentiable. Moreover,

$$
\begin{aligned}
v(x, T - t) &= E_Q f[g](x + W^\lambda(T) - W^\lambda(t)) \\
&= E_Q[f[g](W^\lambda(T)) \mid W^\lambda(t) = x]
\end{aligned}
$$

for $x \in \mathbb{R}$ and $t \in (0, T)$, and

$$
\begin{aligned}
v(W^\lambda(t), T - t) &= E_Q[f[g](W^\lambda(t) + (W^\lambda(T) - W^\lambda(t))) \mid \mathcal{F}_t] \\
&= E_Q[f[g](W^\lambda(T)) \mid \mathcal{F}_t] \\
&= E_Q[g(S(T)) \mid \mathcal{F}_t] \\
&= e^{r(T-t)} V(t)
\end{aligned}
$$

for $t \in (0, T)$. This shows that the function v expresses the value of the claim as a function of $(W^\lambda(t), T - t)$ and as a future value rather than a present value.

To define the value function, we simply need to discount v and express it as a function of the stock price $S(t)$ and calendar time t instead of as a function of the value of the Wiener process $W^\lambda(t)$ and time to maturity $T - t$.

Accordingly, define the function Φ on $(0, \infty) \times [0, T)$ by

$$
\begin{aligned}
\Phi(S, t) &= e^{-r(T-t)} v(h[t]^{-1}(S), T - t) \\
&= e^{-r(T-t)} v\left(\frac{1}{\sigma}[\ln S - \ln S(0) - \gamma t], T - t\right)
\end{aligned}
$$

for $S \in (0, \infty)$ and $t \in (0, T)$.

Since v is infinitely often differentiable, so is Φ. In fact, Φ is also infinitely often differentiable if it is considered to be a function of (S, t, r, σ).

The function Φ is indeed the *value function* of the claim. In other words, for $t \in (0, T)$,

$$\Phi(S(t), t) = V(t)$$

where V is the martingale value process of the claim. This is shown by the following calculation:

$$
\begin{aligned}
\Phi(S(t), t) &= e^{-r(T-t)} v(h[t]^{-1}(S(t)), T - t) \\
&= e^{-r(T-t)} v(W^\lambda(t), T - t) \\
&= e^{-r(T-t)} E_Q[g(S(T)) \mid \mathcal{F}_t] \\
&= V(t)
\end{aligned}
$$

We can verify that the function Φ corresponds to the initial heuristic definition that we started out with:

$$\Phi(S, t) = e^{-r(T-t)} v(h[t]^{-1}(S), T - t)$$

$$= e^{-r(T-t)} E_Q f[g][h[t]^{-1}(S) + W^\lambda(T) - W^\lambda(t)]$$
$$= e^{-r(T-t)} E_Q[f[g](W^\lambda(T)) \mid W^\lambda(t) = h[t]^{-1}(S)]$$
$$= e^{-r(T-t)} E_Q[g(S(T)) \mid S(t) = S]$$

for $(S,t) \in (0,\infty) \times (0,T)$.

A function

$$\Psi : (0,\infty) \times (0,T) \to I\!R : (S,t) \mapsto \Psi(S,t)$$

is said to be a *solution of the Black–Scholes partial differential equation* if it is twice continuously differentiable with respect to S and once continuously differentiable with respect to t, and

$$rS\Psi_S + \Psi_t + \frac{1}{2}\sigma^2 S^2 \Psi_{SS} = r\Psi$$

or

$$rS\Psi_S(S,t) + \Psi_t(S,t) + \frac{1}{2}\sigma^2 S^2 \Psi_{SS}(S,t) = r\Psi(S,t)$$

for all $(S,t) \in (0,\infty) \times (0,T)$.

Proposition 6.2 *Assume that the function*

$$\Psi : (0,\infty) \times (0,T) \to I\!R : (S,t) \mapsto \Psi(S,t)$$

is twice continuously differentiable with respect to S and once continuously differentiable with respect to t. Then Ψ is a solution of the Black–Scholes partial differential equation if and only if the process $e^{-rt}\Psi(S(t),t)$ has zero drift under Q.

Proof By Itô's formula, the absolute drift of the process $e^{-rt}\Psi(S(t),t)$ is

$$e^{-rt}\left[rS(t)\Psi_S - r\Psi + \Psi_t + \frac{1}{2}S(t)^2\sigma^2\Psi_{SS}\right]$$

where it is understood that Ψ and its derivatives are evaluated at $(S(t),t)$. If Ψ solves the Black–Scholes partial differential equation, then this drift is zero.

Conversely, suppose the drift is zero almost everywhere in $\Omega \times (0,T)$. For almost all $t \in (0,T)$, the equation

$$rS(t)\Psi_S(S(t),t) + \Psi_t(S(t),t) + \frac{1}{2}S(t)^2\sigma^2\Psi_{SS}(S(t),t) = r\Psi(S(t),t)$$

holds with probability one. Since $S(t)$ follows a lognormal distribution, which has positive density with respect to Lebesgue measure on $(0,\infty)$, the Black–Scholes partial differential equation

$$rS\Psi_S(S,t) + \Psi_t(S,t) + \frac{1}{2}S^2\sigma^2\Psi_{SS}(S,t) = r\Psi(S,t)$$

holds for almost all $(S,t) \in (0,\infty) \times [0,T)$, with respect to Lebesgue measure. Since the derivatives of Ψ are continuous, it follows that the Black–Scholes partial differential equation holds everywhere in that set. $\square$

Corollary 6.3 *The value function* Φ *solves the Black–Scholes partial differential equation*

$$rS\Phi_S + \Phi_t + \frac{1}{2}\sigma^2 S^2 \Phi_{SS} = r\Phi$$

Proof Since $\Phi(S(t), t)$ is the martingale value process of the claim, the process

$$e^{-rt}\Phi(S(t), t) = E_Q[e^{-rT}g(S(T)) \mid \mathcal{F}_t]$$

is a martingale under Q. Therefore, it has zero drift. By Proposition 6.3, Φ solves the Black–Scholes partial differential equation. $\qquad\square$

The *delta* of the claim is the process

$$\Delta(t) = \Phi_S(S(t), t)$$

and the *delta function* of the claim is the function Φ_S.

The delta measures the sensitivity of the claim value to small changes in the price of the stock. It also measures the number of shares of stock in the replicating trading strategy. It follows from Proposition 5.7 that the claim will be replicated by any trading strategy $\bar{\Delta} = (\Delta_0, \Delta)$ where $\Delta(t) = \Phi_S(S(t), t)$ is the delta of the claim for $t \in (0, T)$, while $\Delta(0)$ and $\Delta(T)$ are chosen arbitrarily subject only to the constraint that they be measurable with respect to $\mathcal{F}_0$ and $\mathcal{F}_T$, respectively, and the holdings Δ_0 of the money market account are given by

$$\Delta_0(t) = (V(t) - \Delta(t)S(t))/M(t)$$

for $t \in [0, T]$.

Proposition 6.4 *If the payoff function g is non-decreasing but not constant, then $\Delta > 0$. If g is convex but not affine, then*

$$\Phi(S, t) > e^{-r(T-t)}g\left(Se^{r(T-t)}\right)$$

Exercise 6.1 *Prove Proposition 6.4*

The *gamma* of the claim is the process

$$\Gamma(t) = \Phi_{SS}(S(t), t)$$

and the *gamma function* of the claim is the function Φ_{SS}. Gamma measures the sensitivity of delta to small changes in the price of the stock.

The *theta* of the claim is the process

$$\Theta(t) = \Phi_t(S(t), t)$$

and the *theta function* of the claim is the function Φ_t. Theta measures how fast the value of the claim changes as time goes by, if the stock price does not change.

In terms of the Greek-letter names of the derivatives of the value function, the Black–Scholes partial differential equation says that

$$Sr\Delta + \Theta + \frac{1}{2}\sigma^2 S^2 \Gamma = r\Phi$$

The *elasticity or eta* of the claim is the elasticity of the claim's value with respect to S:

$$\eta = \Phi_S(S,t)\frac{S}{V} = \Delta\frac{S}{V}$$

Eta measures the percentage sensitivity of the value V of the claim to small percentage changes in S. Eta is sometimes called lambda.

Since the value of the holdings of the money market account in the replicating trading strategy is

$$\Delta_0 M = V - \Delta S$$

the debt-to-equity ratio of the replicating trading strategy is

$$-\frac{\Delta_0 M}{V}$$

The eta of the claim can be written as

$$\eta = \Delta\frac{S}{V} = \frac{V - \Delta_0 M}{V} = 1 - \frac{\Delta_0 M}{V}$$

So, eta is a measure of leverage of the replicating trading strategy in the sense that it equals one plus the debt-to-equity ratio.

The dispersion of the claim price is $\Delta S\sigma$. The relative dispersion is

$$\frac{\Delta S\sigma}{V} = \eta\sigma$$

Since it is positive, it is also equal to the volatility of the claim. The relative drift of the claim value under the risk-adjusted probabilities is r. Hence, the risk-adjusted dynamics of the claim value is

$$\frac{dV}{V} = r\,dt + \eta\sigma\,dW^\lambda$$

The instantaneous expected excess rate of return to the claim is eta times the instantaneous expected excess rate of return to the stock:

$$\eta\sigma\lambda = \eta\sigma\frac{\mu - r}{\sigma} = \eta(\mu - r)$$

The relative drift of the claim value under the original probabilities is

$$\eta\sigma\lambda + r = \eta(\mu - r) + r = \eta\mu + (1 - \eta)r$$

Hence, the dynamics of the claim value in the original probabilities is

$$\frac{dV}{V} = [\eta(\mu - r) + r]\,dt + \eta\sigma\,dW$$

$$= [\eta\mu + (1 - \eta)r]\, dt + \eta\sigma\, dW$$

The covariance between the instantaneous rates of return to the claim and to the stock is $\eta\sigma^2$, and the volatility of the claim value is $\eta\sigma$. Hence, the correlation between the instantaneous rates of return to the claim and to the stock is one. Every contingent claim of the form considered here is instantaneously perfectly correlated with the stock.

Recall that Φ was defined by

$$\Phi(S,t) = e^{-r(T-t)}v\left(\frac{1}{\sigma}\left[\ln S - \ln S(0) - \gamma t\right], T - t\right)$$

where v is the function

$$v(x,\tau) = \int_{-\infty}^{\infty} f[g](y)p(y - x,\tau)\, dy$$

Observe that the instantaneous expected rate of return μ to the stock does not enter into these formulas. We noted above that the value of a cash-or-nothing call option does not depend on μ, and now we can see that this is a general property of contingent claims in the Black–Scholes model.

Mathematically, the reason why μ does not enter the formulas is that μ gets replaced by the interest rate r when we go from the original probability measure P and the original Wiener process W to the risk-adjusted probability measure Q and the risk-adjusted Wiener process W^λ.

To understand the result intuitively, remember that we are valuing the claim for a given price of the stock. The expected future value of the stock is reflected in the current value of the stock. The expected rate of return to the stock affects the expected rate of return of the claim but not its value. If the claim has a high expected rate of return, its future value is discounted at a high rate, so its current value is not high. Also note that μ does not affect Δ, the number of shares needed to replicate the claim.

6.3 Cash-or-nothing Options Revisited

Recall that the value of the cash-or-nothing call option is

$$C_{CN} = \Phi(S,t) = e^{-r(T-t)}N(d_2)$$

and the delta is

$$\Delta = \Phi_S(S,t) = e^{-r(T-t)}N'(d_2)\frac{1}{S\sigma\sqrt{T-t}} > 0$$

Set

$$d_1 = \frac{\ln S - \ln X + \left(r + \frac{1}{2}\sigma^2\right)(T - t)}{\sigma\sqrt{T - t}}$$

(because this is how this variable is usually denoted in the Black–Scholes formula). Set

$$S^* = X \exp\left[-\left(r + \frac{1}{2}\sigma^2\right)(T - t)\right]$$

According to Proposition 6.5 below, S^* is the maximum point of the delta function. Note that

$$\frac{\ln S - \ln S^*}{\sigma\sqrt{T-t}} = \frac{\ln S - \ln X + \left(r + \frac{1}{2}\sigma^2\right)(T-t)}{\sigma\sqrt{T-t}} = d_1$$

Hence, $S = S^*$ if and only if $d_1 = 0$, and $S > S^*$ if and only if $d_1 > 0$.

The value function and the delta function of the cash-or-nothing call option were plotted in Fig. 5.1 and Fig. 5.2. The following propositions spell out some qualitative features of these two functions.

Proposition 6.5 *For fixed $t \in [0, T)$, the delta function $\Delta = \Phi_S(S, t)$ is strictly increasing as a function of S on $(0, S^*]$, reaches a maximum at $S = S^*$, and is strictly decreasing on $[S^*, \infty)$. Its limits are*

$$\Phi_S(S, t) \to 0 \quad as \quad S \to \infty$$

$$\Phi_S(S, t) \to 0 \quad as \quad S \to 0$$

and, for fixed $S \in (0, \infty)$,

$$\Phi_S(S, t) \to \begin{cases} 0 & \text{if } S > X \\ +\infty & \text{if } S = X \\ 0 & \text{if } S < X \end{cases}$$

as $t \to T$.

Exercise 6.2 *Prove Proposition 6.5.*

Proposition 6.6 *For fixed $t \in [0, T)$, the value function Φ is a strictly increasing function of S. It is convex on $(0, S^*]$ and concave on $[S^*, \infty)$. Its limits are*

$$\Phi(S, t) \to 0 \quad as \quad S \to 0$$

$$\Phi(S, t) \to e^{-r(T-t)} \quad as \quad S \to \infty$$

and, for fixed $S \in (0, \infty)$,

$$\Phi(S, t) \to \begin{cases} 1 & \text{if } S > X \\ \frac{1}{2} & \text{if } S = X \\ 0 & \text{if } S < X \end{cases}$$

as $t \to T$.

Exercise 6.3 *Prove Proposition 6.6.*

Notice, in Propositions 6.5 and 6.6, that the limits of both the value function and the delta function, as $t \to T$, are discontinuous as functions of S.

The limiting behavior of $\Phi_S(S,t)$ as $t \to T$ implies that when the cash-or-nothing option is at the money and has a short time to maturity, its delta (the holdings of the stock in the replicating position) varies a lot with S. This implies that a large volume of trading is necessary in order to implement the replicating trading strategy, and in practice (but not in theory), it may in fact be impossible to replicate the option by a trading strategy using the underlying stock and the money market account.

A *cash-or-nothing put option* is a claim which pays one dollar at maturity if the value of the underlying stock equals or is less than (rather than exceeds) the trigger price X, and otherwise expires worthless. The payoff to the cash-or-nothing put option is

$$Y = 1_{S(T)<X} = \begin{cases} 0 & \text{if } S(T) \geq X \\ 1 & \text{otherwise} \end{cases}$$

As in the case of the cash-or-nothing call option, it does not matter for the value of the cash-or-nothing put option whether we specify the payoff using weak or sharp inequalities.

The payoff above is identical to the payoff to a combination of $e^{-r(T-t)}$ invested in the money market account and a short position in the cash-or-nothing call option. Hence, the value of the put option is

$$\begin{aligned} P_{CN}(t) &= e^{-r(T-t)} - e^{-r(T-t)}N(d_2) \\ &= e^{-r(T-t)}(1 - N(d_2)) \\ &= e^{-r(T-t)}N(-d_2) \end{aligned}$$

The sum of the payoffs to the cash-or-nothing call option and the cash-or-nothing put option is one. Hence, the sum of the values of these two options is $e^{-r(T-t)}$:

$$C_{CN} + P_{CN} = e^{-r(T-t)}$$

This is *put–call parity* for cash-or-nothing options.

Write the value of the put option as a function of (S,t):

$$P_{CN} = \Phi(S,t) = e^{-r(T-t)}N(-d_2)$$

The delta of the put option is

$$\begin{aligned} \Delta &= \Phi_S(S,t) \\ &= -e^{-r(T-t)}N'(-d_2)\frac{1}{S\sigma\sqrt{T-t}} \\ &= -e^{-r(T-t)}N'(d_2)\frac{1}{S\sigma\sqrt{T-t}} \\ &< 0 \end{aligned}$$

The sum of the deltas of the cash-or-nothing call option and the cash-or-nothing put option is zero. This also follows directly from put–call parity.

6.4 Asset-or-nothing Options

An *asset-or-nothing call option* on the stock is a claim whose payoff happens at time T and equals

$$Y = S(T)1_{S(T) \geq X} = \begin{cases} S(T) & \text{if } S(T) \geq X \\ 0 & \text{otherwise} \end{cases}$$

where X is a non-negative *trigger price*. The payoff equals the price of the stock if this price at expiration is no less than the trigger price X, and otherwise the payoff is zero.

We want to value the asset-or-nothing call option at time t, and we do it using the risk-adjusted probability measure.

First, we verify that the option is indeed marketed. According to Theorem 5.6, all we need to check is that $\Pi(T)Y$ is integrable under P, or equivalently, that $Y/M(T)$ is integrable under Q. This is obvious since $M(T)$ is positive and non-random and Y follows a truncated lognormal distribution.

Let $C_{AN}(t)$ denote the value of the option at time t. Then

$$C_{AN}(t) = M(t)E_Q[Y/M(T) \mid \mathcal{F}_t] = \frac{M(t)}{M(T)}E_Q[S(T)1_{S(T) \geq X} \mid \mathcal{F}_t]$$

We know from Example 5.10 that given information at time t, $S(T)$ follows a lognormal distribution under Q, and $\ln S(T)$ follows a normal distribution with mean

$$m = \ln S(t) + \left(r - \frac{1}{2}\sigma^2 \right)(T - t)$$

and variance

$$s^2 = \sigma^2(T - t)$$

We can use Proposition 2.29 to calculate the conditional expectation. In this application, $U = \ln S(T)$, $U_0 = \ln X$, m and s^2 are as above, and

$$\begin{aligned} d &= \frac{U_0 - m - s^2}{s} \\ &= \frac{\ln X - \ln S(t) - \left(r - \frac{1}{2}\sigma^2 \right)(T - t) - \sigma^2(T - t)}{\sigma\sqrt{T - t}} \\ &= \frac{\ln X - \ln S(t) - \left(r + \frac{1}{2}\sigma^2 \right)(T - t)}{\sigma\sqrt{T - t}} \\ &= -d_1 \end{aligned}$$

where

$$d_1 = \frac{\ln S(t) - \ln X + \left(r + \frac{1}{2}\sigma^2 \right)(T - t)}{\sigma\sqrt{T - t}}$$

as before. Now,

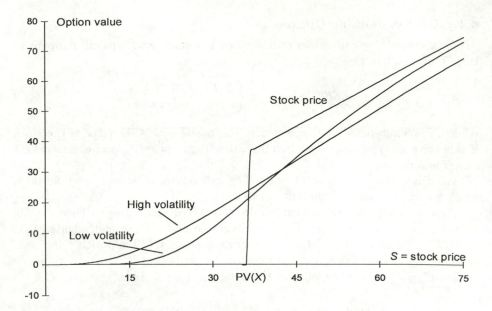

FIG. 6.1. Value of an asset-or-nothing call option

$$m + s^2/2 = \ln S(t) + r(T - t)$$

and

$$E_Q[S(T)1_{S(T)\geq X} \mid \mathcal{F}_t] = \exp(m + s^2/2)N(-d) = S(t)e^{r(T-t)}N(d_1)$$

Hence, the value is

$$C_{AN} = e^{-r(T-t)}E_Q[S(T)1_{S(T)\leq X} \mid \mathcal{F}_t] = S(t)N(d_1)$$

Figure 6.1 shows the value of the asset-or-nothing call option for two different levels of volatility, as functions of the value of the underlying. The value of the underlying is on the horizontal axis, and the option value is measured along the vertical axis. The flatter curve corresponds to a volatility of $\sigma = 0.8$, and the steeper curve corresponds to a volatility of $\sigma = 0.4$. The trigger price is $X = 40$, the time to maturity is $T - t = 1$, and the interest rate is $r = 0.1$. The discontinuous function which is also plotted in the figure is zero up to the discounted value of the trigger price, $e^{-r(T-t)}X$, and thereafter it equals the value of the underlying. It represents an upper boundary and a limit of the option value.

Exercise 6.4 Alternative valuation of an asset-or-nothing option. *Change the price system by using the stock as a numeraire. Express the payoff to the asset-or-nothing call option in the new numeraire. Calculate d_2 in the new price system. Calculate the value of the asset-or-nothing call option in the new price system.*

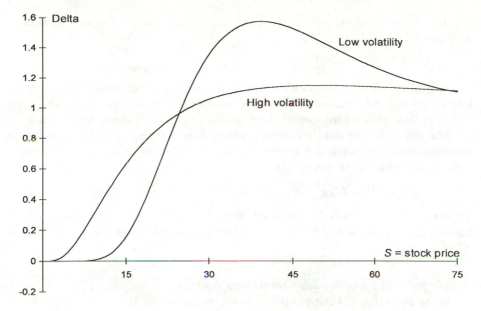

FIG. 6.2. Delta of an asset-or-nothing option

Translate this value into the original price system, and verify that the resulting value equals the value already calculated above.

Write the value of the option as a function of (S, t):

$$C_{AN} = \Phi(S, t) = SN(d_1)$$

where

$$d_1 = \frac{\ln S - \ln X + \left(r + \frac{1}{2}\sigma^2\right)(T - t)}{\sigma\sqrt{T - t}}$$

The delta function of the option is

$$\Delta = \Phi_S(S, t) = N(d_1) + SN'(d_1)\frac{1}{S\sigma\sqrt{T - t}} = N(d_1) + N'(d_1)\frac{1}{\sigma\sqrt{T - t}}$$

Figure 6.2 shows Δ, the delta of the asset-or-nothing call option, for the same two levels of volatility as in Fig. 6.1. The value of the underlying is on the horizontal axis, and Δ is measured along the vertical axis. The curve with the low peak corresponds to a volatility of $\sigma = 0.8$, and the curve with the high peak corresponds to a volatility of $\sigma = 0.4$. As in Fig. 6.1, the trigger price is $X = 40$, the time to maturity is $T - t = 1$, and the interest rate is $r = 0.1$.

An *asset-or-nothing put option* is a claim whose payoff happens at time T and equals

$$Y = S(T)1_{S(T)<X} = \begin{cases} 0 & \text{if } S(T) \geq X \\ S(T) & \text{otherwise} \end{cases}$$

The payoff equals the price of the stock if this price at expiration is less than the trigger price X, and otherwise the payoff is zero. It does not matter for the value of the option whether we specify the payoff using weak or sharp inequalities.

The payoff to the asset-or-nothing put option is identical to the payoff to a combination of the stock and a short position in the asset-or-nothing call option. Hence, the value of the put option is

$$P_{AN} = S - C_{AN} = S - SN(d_1) = S(1 - N(d_1)) = SN(-d_1)$$

The sum of the payoffs to the asset-or-nothing call option and the asset-or-nothing put option is $S(T)$. The sum of the present values of the two options is $S(t)$:

$$C_{AN} + P_{AN} = S$$

This is *put–call parity* for asset-or-nothing options.

Write the value of the put option as a function of (S, t):

$$P_{AN} = \Phi(S, t) = SN(-d_1)$$

The delta function is

$$\Delta = \Phi_S(S, t)$$
$$= N(-d_1) - SN'(-d_1)\frac{1}{S\sigma\sqrt{T-t}}$$
$$= N(-d_1) - N'(d_1)\frac{1}{\sigma\sqrt{T-t}}$$

6.5   Standard Call Options

We can now derive the Black–Scholes formula for the value of a *standard call option* on the stock, with *exercise price* $X > 0$ and maturity T. The results were previewed in Example 4.3.

The payoff to the option happens at T and equals

$$Y = \max\{0, S(T) - X\} = \begin{cases} S(T) - X & \text{if } S(T) \geq X \\ 0 & \text{otherwise} \end{cases}$$

This payoff is the same as the payoff to a combination of an asset-or-nothing option with trigger price X and a short position in X cash-or-nothing options (with trigger price X as well). Hence, we can compute the value of the standard call option as the difference between the value of an asset-or-nothing option and the value of X cash-or-nothing options:

$$C = C_{AN} - XC_{CN}$$

The various payoffs are shown in Fig. 6.3.

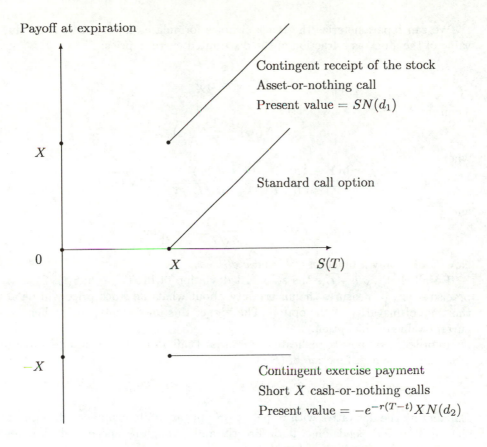

FIG. 6.3. Payoff to the call and its components

The value will be given by the *Black–Scholes formula*:

$$C = SN(d_1) - e^{-r(T-t)}XN(d_2)$$

where d_1 and d_2 are defined as above:

$$d_1 = \frac{\ln S - \ln X + \left(r + \frac{1}{2}\sigma^2\right)(T-t)}{\sigma\sqrt{T-t}}$$

and

$$d_2 = \frac{\ln S - \ln X + \left(r - \frac{1}{2}\sigma^2\right)(T-t)}{\sigma\sqrt{T-t}} = d_1 - \sigma\sqrt{T-t}$$

The value was plotted in Fig. 4.1.

We can reparameterize the Black–Scholes formula as follows. Let Y be the value of the stock as a fraction of the discounted exercise price:

$$Y = \frac{S}{e^{-r(T-t)}X}$$

Then

$$\frac{C}{S} = N(d_1) - \frac{1}{Y}N(d_2)$$

where

$$d_1 = \frac{\ln Y + \frac{1}{2}\sigma^2(T-t)}{\sigma\sqrt{T-t}} = \frac{\ln Y}{\sigma\sqrt{T-t}} + \frac{1}{2}\sigma\sqrt{T-t}$$

and

$$d_2 = d_1 - \sigma\sqrt{T-t} = \frac{\ln Y}{\sigma\sqrt{T-t}} - \frac{1}{2}\sigma\sqrt{T-t}$$

Now C/S is only a function of Y and $\sigma\sqrt{T-t}$.

Recall that $\sigma\sqrt{T-t}$ is the standard deviation of $\ln S(T) - \ln S(t)$. In that precise sense, it measures the uncertainty about what the stock price will be at the time of maturity of the option. The higher this uncertainty, the higher the current value of the option.

In order to see how to replicate the standard call option by a trading strategy, write the value as a function of (S, t):

$$\Phi(S,t) = C = SN(d_1) - e^{-r(T-t)}XN(d_2)$$

Calculating the derivative with respect to S appears quite complicated, because the function Φ depends on S both directly and through d_1 and d_2, which enter into the normal distribution function N.

Since the value equals the value of an asset-or-nothing option minus the value of X cash-or-nothing options, the derivative with respect to S equals the derivative of the asset-or-nothing value minus X times the derivative of the cash-or-nothing value, which we have already computed:

$$\Delta = \Phi_S(S,t) = N(d_1) + N'(d_1)\frac{1}{\sigma\sqrt{T-t}} - e^{-r(T-t)}XN'(d_2)\frac{1}{S\sigma\sqrt{T-t}}$$

However, the expression can be simplified.

The following trick will be useful not only for calculating (and simplifying) the derivative of the Black–Scholes formula with respect to S, but also for calculating the derivatives with respect to other parameters.

Consider the Black–Scholes value of the call option as a function of the variables $(S, t, d_1, X, r, \sigma)$:

$$\hat{C}(S,t,d_1,X,r,\sigma) = SN(d_1) - e^{-r(T-t)}XN(d_1 - \sigma\sqrt{T-t}) = \Phi(S,t)$$

Then the partial derivative of $\hat{C}$ with respect to d_1 is zero:

$$\hat{C}_{d_1} = 0$$

To see this, observe that

$$\hat{C}_{d_1} = SN'(d_1) - e^{-r(T-t)}XN'(d_1 - \sigma\sqrt{T-t})$$

and apply the following proposition.

Proposition 6.7

$$SN'(d_1) = e^{-r(T-t)}XN'(d_1 - \sigma\sqrt{T-t}) = e^{-r(T-t)}XN'(d_2)$$

Proof The equation can be verified by calculating the natural logarithm of the ratio:

$$
\begin{aligned}
\ln\left(\frac{SN'(d_1)}{e^{-r(T-t)}XN'(d_1 - \sigma\sqrt{T-t})}\right) \\
= \ln S + \ln N'(d_1) + r(T-t) - \ln X - \ln N'(d_1 - \sigma\sqrt{T-t}) \\
= \ln S - d_1^2/2 + r(T-t) - \ln X + (d_1 - \sigma\sqrt{T-t})^2/2 \\
= \ln S - d_1^2/2 + r(T-t) - \ln X + d_1^2/2 - d_1\sigma\sqrt{T-t} + \sigma^2(T-t)/2 \\
= \ln S - \ln X + \left(r + \frac{1}{2}\sigma^2\right)(T-t) - d_1\sigma\sqrt{T-t} \\
= 0
\end{aligned}
$$

$\square$

Now, the partial derivative of the call value Φ with respect to S is simply equal to the corresponding derivative of $\hat{C}$:

$$\Delta = \Phi_S(S,t) = \hat{C}_S(S,t,d_1) = N(d_1)$$

Delta was plotted in Fig. 4.2.

Note that $0 < \Delta < 1$. This means that C increases as S increases, but C increases less than S in absolute amounts.

One interpretation of the Black–Scholes formula comes directly from our derivation. The first term in the formula, $SN(d_1)$, is the value of the asset-or-nothing call option. The second term, $-e^{-r(T-t)}XN(d_2)$, is the value of a short position in X cash-or-nothing call options.

A second interpretation is a restatement of the first in terms of risk-adjusted probabilities. The risk-adjusted probability that the option will be in the money at time T is $N(d_2)$. If the option ends up in the money, then the option holder will make an exercise payment of X and will receive the stock. The risk-adjusted expected exercise payment is $XN(d_2)$, and hence $e^{-r(T-t)}XN(d_2)$ is the discounted risk-adjusted expected exercise payment. The risk-adjusted expected value of the stock to be received is $SN(d_1)e^{r(T-t)}$, and, hence, the discounted risk-adjusted expected value of the stock is $SN(d_1)$.

The present value of contingent receipt of the stock is not equal to but larger than the current stock price multiplied by $N(d_2)$, the risk-adjusted probability of exercise. The reason for this is that the event of exercise is not independent of the future stock price. If exercise were completely random and unrelated to the stock price, then indeed the present value of contingent receipt of the stock would be the current stock price multiplied by $N(d_2)$. Actually the present value is larger than this, since exercise is dependent on the future stock price and indeed happens when the stock price is high.

Finally, the formula can be interpreted in terms of the replicating trading strategy. We have seen that $\Delta = N(d_1)$ is the number of shares of stock in the replicating trading strategy. Hence, the first term in the formula, $SN(d_1)$, is the value of the shares of stock held in the replicating trading strategy. Since the option is replicated by holding some stock and partially financing it by borrowing, the second term in the formula, $-e^{-r(T-t)}XN(d_2)$, must be the value of the debt in the replicating trading strategy.

The gamma of the standard call option is

$$\Gamma = \frac{\partial \Delta}{\partial S} = \frac{1}{S\sigma\sqrt{T-t}}N'(d_1) > 0$$

The fact that gamma is positive implies that when the stock price goes up, you rebalance the replicating position by buying some more stock, financed by additional borrowing. When the stock price goes down, you sell some stock and use the revenue to pay back some of the debt.

Figure 6.4 shows Γ, the gamma of the standard call option, for the same two levels of volatility as in Fig. 4.1 and Fig. 4.2. The value of the underlying is on the horizontal axis, and Γ is measured along the vertical axis. The curve with the lower peak corresponds to a volatility of $\sigma = 0.8$, and the curve with the higher peak corresponds to a volatility of $\sigma = 0.4$. As in Fig. 4.1 and Fig. 4.2, the exercise price is $X = 40$, the time to maturity is $T - t = 1$, and the interest rate is $r = 0.1$.

Notice that the gamma of the standard call option resembles the delta of the cash-or-nothing call option.

Set

$$S^{**} = X \exp\left[-\left(r + \frac{3}{2}\sigma^2\right)(T-t)\right]$$

According to Proposition 6.8 below, S^{**} is the maximum point of the gamma function. Note that

$$\frac{\ln S - \ln S^{**}}{\sigma\sqrt{T-t}} = \frac{\ln S - \ln X + \left(r + \frac{3}{2}\sigma^2\right)(T-t)}{\sigma\sqrt{T-t}}$$

$$= \frac{\ln S - \ln X + \left(r + \frac{1}{2}\sigma^2\right)(T-t) + \sigma^2(T-t)}{\sigma\sqrt{T-t}}$$

$$= \sigma\sqrt{T-t} + \frac{\ln S - \ln X + \left(r + \frac{1}{2}\sigma^2\right)(T-t)}{\sigma\sqrt{T-t}}$$

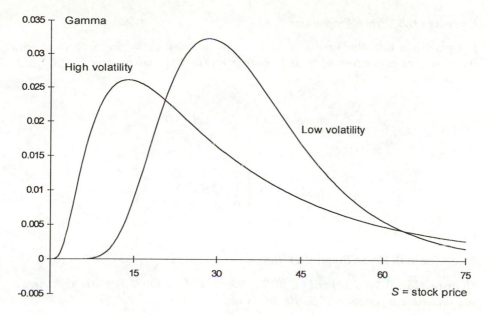

FIG. 6.4. Gamma of a standard call option

$$= \sigma\sqrt{T-t} + d_1$$

Hence, $S = S^{**}$ if and only if

$$\sigma\sqrt{T-t} + d_1 = 0$$

and $S > S^{**}$ if and only if

$$\sigma\sqrt{T-t} + d_1 < 0$$

The value, delta, and gamma of the standard call option were plotted in Fig. 4.1, Fig. 4.2, and Fig. 6.4. The following propositions spell out some qualitative features of these functions.

Proposition 6.8 *For fixed $t \in [0, T)$, the function $\Gamma = \Phi_{SS}$ is strictly increasing on $(0, S^{**}]$, reaches a maximum at $S = S^{**}$, and is strictly decreasing on $[S^{**}, \infty)$. Its limits are*

$$\Phi_{SS}(S, t) \to 0 \quad as \quad S \to \infty$$

$$\Phi_{SS}(S, t) \to 0 \quad as \quad S \to 0$$

and, for fixed $S \in (0, \infty)$,

$$\Phi_{SS}(S, t) \to \begin{cases} 0 & \text{if } S > X \\ +\infty & \text{if } S = X \\ 0 & \text{if } S < X \end{cases}$$

as $t \to T$.

Exercise 6.5 *Prove Proposition 6.8.*

Proposition 6.9 *For fixed $t \in [0, T)$, the function $\Delta = \Phi_S(S, t)$ is strictly increasing as a function of S. It is convex on $(0, S^{**}]$ and concave on $[S^{**}, \infty)$. Its limits are*

$$\Phi_S(S, t) \to 1 \quad as \quad S \to \infty$$

$$\Phi_S(S, t) \to 0 \quad as \quad S \to 0$$

and, for fixed $S \in (0, \infty)$,

$$\Phi_S(S, t) \to \begin{cases} 1 & if\ S > X \\ \frac{1}{2} & if\ S = X \\ 0 & if\ S < X \end{cases}$$

as $t \to T$.

Exercise 6.6 *Prove Proposition 6.9.*

Proposition 6.10 *For fixed $t \in [0, T)$, the value function Φ is a strictly increasing and convex function of S. Its limits are*

$$\Phi(S, t) \to 0 \quad as \quad S \to 0$$

$$\Phi(S, t) - \left[S - e^{-r(T-t)} X \right] \to 0 \quad as \quad S \to \infty$$

For fixed $S_T \in (0, \infty)$,

$$\Phi(S, t) \to \max\{S_T - X, 0\}$$

as $t \to T$, $t < T$, $S \to S_T$.

Exercise 6.7 *Prove Proposition 6.10.*

A *forward contract* on the stock with *delivery price* X has a payoff which happens at time T and equals $S(T) - X$. The value of the contract at time $t < T$ is

$$V(t) = M(t) E_Q \left[\frac{S(T) - X}{M(T)} \,\Big|\, \mathcal{F}_t \right]$$

$$= M(t) \left[\frac{S(t)}{M(t)} - \frac{X}{M(T)} \right]$$

$$= S(t) - e^{-r(T-t)} X$$

The contract can be replicated by holding the stock and borrowing the present value of the delivery price through a short position in the money market account.

The limit, $S - X e^{-r(T-t)}$, of the value of the call option as $S \to \infty$ equals the value of the forward contract. When the stock price is very high, it is very likely that it will be exercised, in which case its payoff will be the same as the payoff to the forward contract.

The elasticity or eta of the standard call option is

$$\eta = \Phi_S(S,t)\frac{S}{\Phi(S,t)} = \Delta\frac{S}{C} = \frac{SN(d_1)}{C}$$

Recall that eta equals one plus the debt–equity ratio of the replicating trading strategy. In the case of the standard call option, the debt in the replicating trading strategy is $e^{-r(T-t)}XN(d_2)$. So,

$$\begin{aligned}
\eta &= \Delta\frac{S}{C} \\
&= \frac{SN(d_1)}{C} \\
&= \frac{C + e^{-r(T-t)}XN(d_2)}{C} \\
&= 1 + \frac{e^{-r(T-t)}XN(d_2)}{C} \\
&> 1
\end{aligned}$$

The fact that $\eta > 1$ implies that C has higher volatility than S. In this specific sense, the option is more risky than the underlying asset.

In order to investigate the influence of parameters other than S and t, write the Black–Scholes value of the call option as a function of the variables (S,t,X,r,σ) or (S,t,d_1,X,r,σ):

$$\begin{aligned}
C(S,t,X,r,\sigma) &= \hat{C}(S,t,d_1,X,r,\sigma) \\
&= SN(d_1) - e^{-r(T-t)}XN(d_1 - \sigma\sqrt{T-t})
\end{aligned}$$

where

$$d_1 = \frac{\ln S - \ln X + \left(r + \frac{1}{2}\sigma^2\right)(T-t)}{\sigma\sqrt{T-t}}$$

We have observed that

$$\hat{C}_{d_1} = 0$$

which implies that all the partial derivatives of C are equal to the corresponding partial derivatives of $\hat{C}$. We used this observation to calculate delta and gamma. We shall now use it to calculate the remaining partial derivatives of C.

The *vega* of the call option is the derivative with respect to σ:

$$\begin{aligned}
\text{vega} &= C_\sigma(S,t,X,r,\sigma) \\
&= \hat{C}_\sigma(S,t,d_1,X,r,\sigma) \\
&= e^{-r(T-t)}XN'(d_1 - \sigma\sqrt{T-t})\sqrt{T-t} \\
&= e^{-r(T-t)}XN'(d_2)\sqrt{T-t}
\end{aligned}$$

$$= SN'(d_1)\sqrt{T-t}$$
$$> 0$$

Vega is sometimes called kappa.

Since vega is positive, the value of the option is an increasing function of the volatility of the stock. The intuitive reason for this is the following. We know from Example 1.7 that the conditional expected value of the stock at time T, given information at time t and calculated under the risk-adjusted probabilities, is $e^{-r(T-t)}S(t)$. It is independent of volatility. Thus, an increase in volatility does not change the risk-adjusted expectation of the future stock price, but it does increase the variance around the expectation. Both the upside potential and the downside risk become larger. The option payoff is affected only by the upside potential, and therefore the value of the option goes up.

In the figures illustrating the value, delta, and gamma of various options, we have generally plotted two curves, one for high volatility of the stock and one for lower volatility. In particular, in Fig. 4.1, which illustrates the value of the standard call option, the curve which corresponds to high volatility is above the curve which corresponds to low volatility. This is consistent with the fact that the vega of the option is positive, which means that the option value is a strictly increasing function of the volatility of the stock. The following proposition says that the option value approaches the lower boundary in Fig. 4.1 as volatility goes to zero, while it approaches the stock price as volatility goes to infinity.

Proposition 6.11 *For fixed (S, t, X, r), the value function $C(S, t, X, r, \sigma)$ is a strictly increasing function of $\sigma > 0$ with limits*

$$C(S, t, X, r, \sigma) \to \max\left\{0, S - e^{-r(T-t)}X\right\} \qquad as \qquad \sigma \to 0$$

and

$$C(S, t, X, r, \sigma) \to S \qquad as \qquad \sigma \to \infty$$

Furthermore,

$$N(d_2) \to 0 \qquad as \qquad \sigma \to \infty$$

Exercise 6.8 *Prove Proposition 6.11.*

The limiting behavior of the call price as the volatility goes to zero is easily explained. If the stock price is below the discounted exercise price and volatility is low, then the stock price will, with high risk-adjusted probability, be below the exercise price at maturity, and hence the current value of the option is close to zero. If the stock price is above the discounted exercise price and volatility is low, then it will, with high risk-adjusted probability, be above the exercise price at maturity, and hence the current value of the option is close to the value of the forward contract.

The limiting behavior of the call price as the volatility goes to infinity is one of the most curious features of the Black–Scholes formula. It is particularly strange that the value of the call approaches the current stock price, while at the same time the probability that the call will be exercised goes to zero. Here is an attempt at an explanation.

The logarithm of the stock price at expiration, $\ln S(T)$, is normally distributed with standard deviation $\sigma\sqrt{T-t}$, which is proportional to σ, and with risk-adjusted conditional expectation

$$\ln S + \left(r - \frac{1}{2}\sigma^2\right)(T-t) = \ln S + r(T-t) - \frac{1}{2}\sigma^2(T-t)$$

As σ increases, the expectation of $\ln S(T)$ decreases with the square of σ, while the standard deviation is proportional to σ itself. This implies that the probability of exercise of the option goes to zero. Moreover, for any $\epsilon > 0$, the risk-adjusted probability that $S(T) \geq \epsilon$ goes to zero and the probability that $S(T) < \epsilon$ goes to one.

Recall that the standard call option corresponds to a combination of a short position in X cash-or-nothing call options with trigger price X and a long position in an asset-or-nothing call option, also with trigger price X. By put–call parity for asset-or-nothing options, the asset-or-nothing call option is equivalent to a long position in the stock combined with a short position in an asset-or-nothing put option with trigger price X. Hence, the standard call option corresponds to a short position in X cash-or-nothing call options, a long position in the stock, and a short position in an asset-or-nothing put option.

Since the probability that $S(T) \geq X$ goes to zero, the value of the cash-or-nothing options goes to zero. Since for every $\epsilon > 0$, the probability that $S(T) < \epsilon$ goes to one, the value of the asset-or-nothing put option goes to zero. What is left is the long position in the stock. Hence the value of the standard call option approaches the value of the stock as σ goes to infinity.

In particular, note that the value of the asset-or-nothing call option approaches the value of the stock as σ goes to infinity. The probability that this option gives any payoff at all will go to zero, but the conditional distribution of the payoff given that it occurs will become very favorable.

The *theta* of the call option is

$$\begin{aligned}
\Theta &= \Phi_t(S,t) \\
&= C_t(S,t,X,r,\sigma) \\
&= \hat{C}_t(S,t,d_1,X,r,\sigma) \\
&= -re^{-r(T-t)}XN(d_1 - \sigma\sqrt{T-t}) \\
&\quad - e^{-r(T-t)}XN'(d_1 - \sigma\sqrt{T-t})\frac{\sigma}{2\sqrt{T-t}}
\end{aligned}$$

It was shown in Proposition 6.7 that

$$e^{-r(T-t)}XN'(d_1 - \sigma\sqrt{T-t}) = SN'(d_1)$$

Hence,

$$\Theta = -re^{-r(T-t)}XN(d_2) - \frac{S\sigma}{2\sqrt{T-t}}N'(d_1) < 0$$

The fact that theta is negative implies that the value of the option declines as time goes by, if the price of the stock stays constant. There are two reasons for this, related to the two terms in the expression for theta above. The first is the pure effect of discounting. As time goes forward, the discounted value of the exercise price increases, because the time to maturity decreases. The second reason is a variance effect. Wherever the volatility enters into the Black–Scholes formula, it is multiplied by the square root of the time to maturity. A shorter time to maturity has the same effect as a lower volatility on the risk-adjusted conditional distribution of the stock price at maturity. A shorter time to maturity does not affect the mean but lowers the variance. Both the upside potential and the downside risk become smaller, but since the option payoff is affected only by the upside potential, the value of the option goes down.

The *rho* of the call option is the partial derivative with respect to the interest rate r:

$$\begin{aligned}
\rho &= C_r(S, t, X, r, \sigma) \\
&= \hat{C}_r(S, t, d_1, X, r, \sigma) \\
&= (T-t)Xe^{-r(T-t)}N(d_1 - \sigma\sqrt{T-t}) \\
&= (T-t)Xe^{-r(T-t)}N(d_2) \\
&> 0
\end{aligned}$$

Since ρ is positive, the value of the option is an increasing function of the interest rate. This is a consequence of the fact that exercise of the option involves future payment of the exercise price. The higher the interest rate, the lower is the present value of the exercise payment.

Exercise 6.9 *Suppose the price processes of the money market account and the stock are*

$$M = M(0)\eta[r, 0]$$

and

$$S = S(0)\eta[\mu, \sigma]$$

where $r \in \mathcal{L}^1$ and $\sigma \in \mathcal{L}^2$ are deterministic processes, and μ has the form

$$\mu = \sigma\lambda + r$$

for some deterministic process $\lambda \in \mathcal{L}^2$.

1. *Show that the value of a standard call option expiring at time T is*

$$\Phi(S(t), t) = C(S(t), t, X, \tilde{r}(t), \tilde{\sigma}(t))$$

where

$$\tilde{r}(t) = \frac{1}{T-t} \int_t^T r \, ds$$

and

$$\tilde{\sigma}^2(t) = \frac{1}{T-t} \int_t^T \sigma^2 \, ds$$

2. *Calculate delta, gamma, and theta of the option.*
3. *Does the value function* Φ *satisfy the Black–Scholes partial differential equation?*

6.6 Standard Put Options

Consider a *standard put option* on the stock, with *exercise price* $X > 0$ and maturity T. It gives the owner the right, but not the obligation, to sell the stock at maturity for a price of X.

The payoff to the option happens at T and equals

$$Y = \max\{0, X - S(T)\} = \begin{cases} X - S(T) & \text{if } S(T) \le X \\ 0 & \text{otherwise} \end{cases}$$

The payoff to the put is identical to the payoff to a combination of a standard call option, $e^{-r(T-t)}X$ invested in the money market account, and a short position in the stock. Hence, the value of the put option satisfies the relation

$$P = C + e^{-r(T-t)}X - S$$

This is *put–call parity* for standard options.

Using put–call parity and the Black–Scholes formula for the value of the call option, we find a formula for the value function Φ of the put option:

$$\begin{aligned}
\Phi(S,t) &= P \\
&= C + e^{-r(T-t)}X - S \\
&= SN(d_1) - e^{-r(T-t)}XN(d_2) + e^{-r(T-t)}X - S \\
&= S(N(d_1) - 1) - e^{-r(T-t)}X(N(d_2) - 1) \\
&= -SN(-d_1) + e^{-r(T-t)}XN(-d_2)
\end{aligned}$$

This is the Black–Scholes formula for a put option.

Figure 6.5 shows the value of a standard put option for two different levels of volatility, as functions of the value of the underlying. The value of the underlying is on the horizontal axis, and the put value is measured along the vertical axis. The higher curve corresponds to a volatility of $\sigma = 0.8$, and the lower curve corresponds to a volatility of $\sigma = 0.4$. The exercise price is $X = 40$, the time to maturity is $T - t = 1$, and the interest rate is $r = 0.1$. The 45 degree line which is also plotted in the figure intersects both the vertical and the horizontal axis at the present value $\text{PV}(X) = e^{-r(T-t)}X$ of the exercise price. It represents a lower boundary and a limit of the put option value.

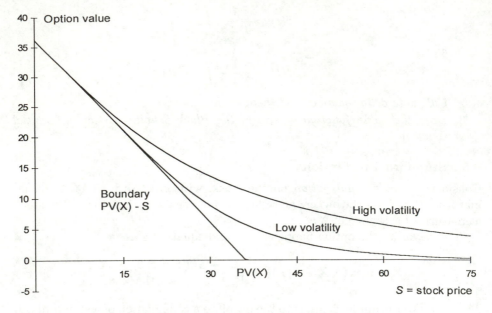

FIG. 6.5. Value of a standard put option

From put–call parity, it is clear that the delta of the put option is

$$\Delta = N(d_1) - 1 = -N(-d_1)$$

Note that $-1 < \Delta < 0$. This means that P decreases as S increases, but P decreases less than S in absolute amounts.

One interpretation of the Black–Scholes formula for a put option comes from the observation that the payoff to the option equals the payoff to a combination consisting of a long position in X cash-or-nothing put options with trigger price X and a short position in an asset-or-nothing put option with trigger price X. The first term in the formula, $-SN(-d_1)$, is the value of the short position in the asset-or-nothing option. The second term, $-e^{-r(T-t)}XN(d_2)$, is the value of the long position in X cash-or-nothing put options.

A second interpretation is a restatement of the first in terms of risk-adjusted probabilities. The risk-adjusted probability that the option will be in the money at time T is $1 - N(d_2) = N(-d_2)$. If the option ends up in the money, then the option holder will receive the exercise payment of X and hand over the stock. The risk-adjusted expected exercise payment is $XN(-d_2)$, and hence $e^{-r(T-t)}XN(-d_2)$ is the discounted risk-adjusted expected exercise payment. The risk-adjusted expected value of the stock is $-SN(-d_1)e^{r(T-t)}$, and, hence, the discounted risk-adjusted expected value of the stock is $-SN(-d_1)$.

Finally, the formula can be interpreted in terms of the replicating trading strategy. We have seen that $\Delta = -N(-d_1)$ is the number of shares of stock in the replicating trading strategy. This is a negative number: the replicating portfolio involves short-selling the stock. The first term in the formula, $-SN(-d_1)$, is the value of the shares of stock sold short in the replicating trading strategy. The second term in the formula, $e^{-r(T-t)}XN(-d_2)$, is the value of the holdings of the money market account in the replicating trading strategy.

Proposition 6.12 *For fixed $t \in [0, T)$, the value function Φ is a strictly decreasing and convex function of S. Its limits are*

$$\Phi(S, t) \to 0 \quad as \quad S \to \infty$$

$$\Phi(S, t) \to e^{-r(T-t)}X \quad as \quad S \to 0$$

For fixed $S_T \in (0, \infty)$,

$$\Phi(S, t) \to \max\{0, X - S_T\}$$

as $t \to T$, $t < T$, $S \to S_T$.

Proof Follows from Proposition 6.10 combined with put–call parity. □

The gamma of the put option is the same as the gamma of the call option.

The fact that gamma is positive implies that when the stock price goes up, you rebalance the replicating position by buying back some of the stock that was sold short, financed by reducing your holding of the money market account. When the stock price goes down, you short-sell some more stock and invest the revenue in the money market account.

The elasticity or eta of the put option is

$$\eta = \Phi_S(S, t)\frac{S}{\Phi(S, t)} = \Delta\frac{S}{P} = \frac{-SN(-d_1)}{P} < 0$$

The vega of the put option is the same as the vega of the call option. Since vega is positive, the value of the put option is an increasing function of the volatility of the stock, just like the value of the call option. The intuitive reason for this is the same as for the call option. An increase in volatility does not change the risk-adjusted expectation of the future stock price, but it does increase the variance around the expectation. Both the upside risk and the downside potential become larger, but the option payoff is affected only by the downside potential. Therefore the value of the option goes up.

In Fig. 6.5, which illustrates the value of the standard put option, the curve which corresponds to high volatility is above the curve which corresponds to low volatility. This is consistent with the fact that the vega of the option is positive, which means that the option value is a strictly increasing function of the volatility of the stock. The following proposition says that the option value approaches the lower boundary in Fig. 6.5 as volatility goes to zero, while it approaches the discounted exercise price as volatility goes to infinity.

Proposition 6.13 *For fixed* (S, t, X, r), *the value function* $P(S, t, X, r, \sigma)$ *of the put option is a strictly increasing function of* $\sigma > 0$ *with limits*

$$P(S, t, X, r, \sigma) \to \max\left\{0, e^{-r(T-t)}X - S\right\} \quad as \quad \sigma \to 0$$

and

$$P(S, t, X, r, \sigma) \to e^{-r(T-t)}X \quad as \quad \sigma \to \infty$$

Proof Follows from Proposition 6.11 combined with put–call parity.   □

The reason why the put price approaches the discounted exercise price as volatility goes to infinity is that the stock price at maturity goes to zero with probability one.

The theta of the put option can be calculated from the theta of the call option, using put–call parity:

$$\begin{aligned}
\Theta_P &= \Theta_C + re^{-r(T-t)}X \\
&= -re^{-r(T-t)}XN(d_2) - \frac{S\sigma}{2\sqrt{T-t}}N'(d_1) + re^{-r(T-t)}X \\
&= re^{-r(T-t)}X(1 - N(d_2)) - \frac{S\sigma}{2\sqrt{T-t}}N'(d_1)
\end{aligned}$$

Theta may be positive or negative. The first term in the formula is positive and represents the pure effect of discounting. As time goes forward, the discounted value of the exercise price increases, because the time to maturity decreases. The second term is negative and represents a variance effect. A shorter time to maturity lowers the variance of the stock price at maturity, which in turn lowers the value of the put option.

The rho of the put option can be calculated from the rho of the call option, again using put–call parity:

$$\begin{aligned}
\rho_P &= \rho_C - (T-t)e^{-r(T-t)}X \\
&= (T-t)e^{-r(T-t)}XN(d_2) - (T-t)e^{-r(T-t)}X \\
&= (T-t)e^{-r(T-t)}X(N(d_2) - 1) \\
&< 0
\end{aligned}$$

Since ρ is negative, the value of the put option is a decreasing function of the interest rate. The higher the interest rate, the lower is the present value of the exercise payment to be received.

6.7   (*) Black–Scholes and the Heat Equation

Throughout this chapter, we have considered claims whose payoff is a function $g(S(T))$ of the stock price at some expiration date T. Every such claim has a value function $\Phi(S, t)$, which gives the value of the claim at time $t < T$ as a function of the stock price S at that time. The value function was calculated by the martingale valuation principle. We saw in Corollary 6.3 that the value function Φ solves the Black–Scholes partial differential equation. According to Proposition 6.2, any sufficiently differentiable function $\Psi : (0, \infty) \times (0, T)$ solves the Black–Scholes PDE if and only if the process $e^{-rt}\Psi(S(t), t)$ has zero drift.

The goal now will be to identify the value function of a claim in an alternative way, by solving the Black–Scholes PDE subject to a terminal condition. In other words, we want to identify the function Φ from the fact that it solves the Black–Scholes PDE and from knowledge of the payoff function g.

This problem turns out to be quite similar to the problem of finding a solution to the heat equation from physics, subject to an initial value condition. The heat equation is discussed in detail in Appendix C. The main technique that we shall use in order to study the Black–Scholes PDE is to transform it into the heat equation and then use results from the appendix.

Determining the precise sense in which a solution Ψ of the Black–Scholes PDE should have terminal value g is a non-trivial matter. It is natural to consider the extension

$$\hat{\Psi} : (0, \infty) \times (0, T] \to I\!R : (S, t) \to \hat{\Psi}(S, t)$$

of Ψ defined on the extended domain $(0, \infty) \times (0, T]$ (including $t = T$) by

$$\hat{\Psi}(S, t) = \begin{cases} g(S) & \text{if } t = T \\ \Psi(S, t) & \text{if } t < T \end{cases}$$

One idea would be to require $\hat{\Psi}$ to be twice continuously differentiable with respect to S and once continuously differentiable with respect to t also at $t = T$ and to satisfy the PDE in the entire extended domain. However, no solution can satisfy this requirement if the payoff function g is not differentiable, which is very often the case. The payoffs to standard call and put options, as well as to cash-or-nothing options and asset-or-nothing options, are not differentiable.

A second idea is to require the extended solution function $\hat{\Psi}$ to be continuous on the extended domain, including $t = T$. Indeed, this works well when the payoff function g is continuous, as in the case of standard calls and puts. However, no solution can satisfy this requirement if g is not continuous, as in the case of cash-or-nothing options or asset-or-nothing options. For this reason, we shall need also to consider other ways of imposing the terminal condition. These issues are studied below in Section 6.8.

Not only do we want to find a solution Ψ of the Black–Scholes PDE with terminal value g, we also want to know that it is the unique such solution, and, therefore, that it equals the value function Φ. Unfortunately, it is not true that there is a unique solution to the Black–Scholes PDE with given terminal data, even if the terminal data are imposed in an appropriate way. This follows directly from a corresponding result for the heat equation. For this reason, we shall need to impose an additional restriction on the solution function in order to make it unique. We shall consider three different restrictions: an integrability condition, a non-negativity condition, and a growth condition. These restrictions will be studied in Section 6.9.

We start by making explicit the link between the Black–Scholes PDE and the heat equation.

As explained in Appendix C, Section C.1, a function

$$u : I\!\!R \times (0, T) \to I\!\!R : (x, \tau) \mapsto u(x, \tau)$$

is said to be a *solution of the heat equation* if it is twice continuously differentiable with respect to x and once continuously differentiable with respect to τ, and

$$u_\tau = u_{xx}$$

or

$$u_\tau(x, \tau) = u_{xx}(x, \tau)$$

for all $(x, \tau) \in I\!\!R \times (0, T)$.

We establish the correspondence between solutions of the Black–Scholes PDE and solutions of the heat equation as follows. Recall that we have defined a function $h[t] : I\!\!R \to (0, \infty)$, for each $t \in [0, T]$, by

$$h[t](x) = S(0)e^{\gamma t + \sigma x}$$

As before, we use the notation

$$\gamma = r - \frac{1}{2}\sigma^2$$

If $u : I\!\!R \times (0, T) \to I\!\!R$ is a function, define a function $\Psi[u] : (0, \infty) \times (0, T) \to I\!\!R$ by

$$\Psi[u](S, t) = e^{-r(T-t)}u(h[t]^{-1}(S), T - t)$$
$$= e^{-r(T-t)}u\left(\frac{1}{\sigma}\left[\ln S - \ln S(0) - \gamma t\right], T - t\right)$$

for $S \in (0, \infty)$ and $t \in (0, T)$.

If $\Psi : (0, \infty) \times (0, T) \to I\!\!R$ is a function, define a function $u[\Psi] : I\!\!R \times (0, T) \to I\!\!R$ by

$$u[\Psi](x, \tau) = e^{r\tau}\Psi(h[T - \tau](x), T - \tau)$$
$$= e^{r\tau}\Psi\left(S(0)e^{\gamma(T-\tau)+\sigma x}, T - \tau\right)$$

The mappings $\Psi \mapsto u[\Psi]$ and $u \mapsto \Psi[u]$ are inverses of each other. In other words, if $u : I\!\!R \times (0, T) \to I\!\!R$ and $\Psi : (0, \infty) \times (0, T) \to I\!\!R$ are two functions, then $u[\Psi] = u$ if and only if $\Psi[u] = \Psi$. This can be seen as follows:

$$u[\Psi[u]](x, \tau) = e^{r\tau}\Psi[u](h[T - \tau](x), T - \tau)$$
$$= e^{r\tau}e^{-r\tau}u(h[T - \tau]^{-1}(h[T - \tau](x)), \tau)$$

$$= u(x, \tau)$$

and

$$
\begin{aligned}
\Psi[u[\Psi]](S, t) &= e^{-r(T-t)} u[\Psi] \left(h[t]^{-1}(S), T - t \right) \\
&= e^{-r(T-t)} e^{r(T-t)} \Psi(h[t](h[t]^{-1}(S)), t) \\
&= \Psi(S, t)
\end{aligned}
$$

Proposition 6.14 *A function* $\Psi : (0, \infty) \times (0, T) \to I\!R$ *is a solution of the Black–Scholes PDE if and only if* $u[\Psi]$ *is a solution of the heat equation.*

Proof According to Proposition 6.2, Ψ is a solution of the Black–Scholes PDE if and only if it is twice continuously differentiable with respect to S and once continuously differentiable with respect to t and the process $e^{-rt}\Psi(S(t), t)$ has zero drift. According to Proposition C.1, $u[\Psi]$ is a solution of the heat equation if and only if it is twice continuously differentiable with respect to x and once continuously differentiable with respect to τ and the process $u(W^\lambda(t), T - t)$ has zero drift. Observe that Ψ is twice continuously differentiable with respect to S and once continuously differentiable with respect to t if and only if $u[\Psi]$ is twice continuously differentiable with respect to x and once continuously differentiable with respect to τ, and that

$$e^{rT} e^{-rt} \Psi(S(t), t) = u(W^\lambda(t), T - t)$$

$\square$

Exercise 6.10 *Prove Proposition 6.14 directly by calculating the partial derivatives of* Ψ *and of* $u[\Psi]$.

6.8   (*) The Black–Scholes PDE: Terminal Data

In this section, we shall consider three different ways of imposing the terminal condition on the solution function: adjusted local convergence in mean, double convergence, and convergence almost everywhere. They correspond to three ways of imposing an initial condition on solutions to the heat equation.

As in Appendix C, if $f : I\!R \to I\!R$ is a locally integrable function, then a function

$$u : I\!R \times (0, T) \to I\!R : (x, \tau) \mapsto u(x, \tau)$$

has *initial data* f in the *sense of local convergence in mean* if u is locally integrable with respect to x for each $\tau \in (0, T)$, and if

$$\int_b^c |u(x, \tau) - f(x)| \, dx \to 0 \quad \text{as} \quad \tau \to 0$$

whenever $b, c \in I\!R$, $b < c$.

If $g : (0, \infty) \to I\!R$ is a locally integrable function, then a function

$$\Psi : (0, \infty) \times (0, T) \to I\!R : (S, t) \mapsto \Psi(S, t)$$

has *terminal data g* in the *sense of adjusted local convergence in mean* if Ψ is locally integrable with respect to S for each $t \in (0, T)$, and if for all $b, c \in I\!R$ with $b < c$,

$$\int_b^c \left| \Psi\left(S e^{-\gamma(T-t)}, t\right) - g(S) \right| dS \to 0$$

as $t \to T$.

Proposition 6.15 *Let* $g : (0, \infty) \to I\!R$ *be a locally integrable function, and let* $\Psi : (0, \infty) \times (0, T) \to I\!R$ *be a function such that* Ψ *is locally integrable with respect to* S *for each* $t \in (0, T)$. *Then* Ψ *has terminal data* g *in the sense of adjusted local convergence in mean if and only if for all* $b, c \in I\!R$ *with* $b < c$,

$$\int_b^c \left| e^{r(T-t)} \Psi\left(S e^{-\gamma(T-t)}, t\right) - g(S) \right| dS \to 0$$

as $t \to T$.

Proof Suppose Ψ has terminal data g in the sense of adjusted local convergence in mean. Let $b, c \in I\!R$, $b < c$. For $t > 0$ sufficiently close to T,

$$\int_b^c \left| \Psi\left(S e^{-\gamma(T-t)}, t\right) - g(S) \right| dS < 1$$

and, hence,

$$\int_b^c \left| \Psi\left(S e^{-\gamma(T-t)}, t\right) \right| dS \leq \int_b^c \left| \Psi\left(S e^{-\gamma(T-t)}, t\right) - g(S) \right| dS + \int_b^c |g(S)| \, dS$$

$$< 1 + \int_b^c |g(S)| \, dS$$

Now,

$$\int_b^c \left| e^{r(T-t)} \Psi\left(S e^{-\gamma(T-t)}, t\right) - g(S) \right| dS$$

$$\leq \int_b^c \left| e^{r(T-t)} \Psi\left(S e^{-\gamma(T-t)}, t\right) - \Psi\left(S e^{-\gamma(T-t)}, t\right) \right| dS$$

$$+ \int_b^c \left| \Psi\left(S e^{-\gamma(T-t)}, t\right) - g(S) \right| dS$$

$$= \left(e^{r(T-t)} - 1 \right) \int_b^c \left| \Psi\left(S e^{-\gamma(T-t)}, t\right) \right| dS$$

$$+ \int_b^c \left| \Psi\left(S e^{-\gamma(T-t)}, t\right) - g(S) \right| dS$$

$$\to 0$$

as $t \to T$.

The converse implication is analogous. $\square$

Proposition 6.16 *A function* $\Psi : (0, \infty) \times (0, T) \to I\!\!R$ *has terminal data g in the sense of adjusted local convergence in mean if and only if* $u[\Psi]$ *has initial data* $f[g]$ *in the sense of local convergence in mean.*

Proof Observe that

$$h[t]^{-1}\left(Se^{-\gamma(T-t)}\right)$$

$$= \frac{1}{\sigma}\left[\ln\left(Se^{-\gamma(T-t)}\right) - \gamma t - \ln S(0)\right]$$

$$= \frac{1}{\sigma}\left[\ln S - \gamma(T-t) - \gamma t - \ln S(0)\right]$$

$$= \frac{1}{\sigma}\left[\ln S - \gamma T - \ln S(0)\right]$$

$$= h[T]^{-1}(S)$$

It follows that

$$\int_{h[T](b)}^{h[T](c)} \left| e^{r(T-t)}\Psi\left(Se^{-\gamma(T-t)}, t\right) - g(S)\right| \, dS$$

$$= \int_{h[T](b)}^{h[T](c)} \left| u[\Psi]\left(h[T]^{-1}(S), T-t\right) - f[g]\left(h[T]^{-1}(S)\right)\right| \, dS$$

$$= \int_{b}^{c} \left| u[\Psi](x, T-t) - f[g](x)\right| \sigma S(0) e^{\sigma x + \gamma T} \, dx$$

where we have made the substitution

$$x = h[T]^{-1}(S) = \frac{1}{\sigma}\left[\ln S - \gamma T - \ln S(0)\right]$$

$$S = h[T](x) = S(0)e^{\sigma x + \gamma T}$$

$$dS = \sigma S(0)e^{\sigma x + \gamma T}\, dx$$

Since the function $\sigma S(0)e^{\sigma x + \gamma T}$, as a function of x, is bounded above and below away from zero on the interval $[b, c]$, the last integral converges to zero as $t \to T$ if and only if

$$\int_{b}^{c} \left| u[\Psi](x, T-t) - f[g](x)\right| \, dx \to 0 \quad \text{as} \quad t \to 0$$

Hence, Ψ has terminal data g in the sense of adjusted local convergence in mean if and only if $u[\Psi]$ has initial data $f[g]$ in the sense of local convergence in mean. $\square$

Proposition 6.17 *The value function* Φ *has terminal data g in the sense of adjusted local convergence in mean.*

Proof By Proposition C.5, $u[\Phi] = v$ has initial data $f[g]$ in the sense of local convergence in mean. It then follows from Proposition 6.16 that Φ has terminal data g in the sense of adjusted local convergence in mean. $\square$

Let $\Psi : (0, \infty) \times (0, T) \to I\!R$ and $g : (0, \infty) \to I\!R$ be functions. Say that Ψ has *terminal data g* in the sense of *double convergence* if for all $z \in I\!R$,

$$\Psi(y, t) \to g(z) \quad \text{as} \quad (y, t) \to (z, T), \quad t < T$$

Observe that Ψ has terminal data g in the sense of double convergence if and only if for all $z \in I\!R$,

$$\Psi\left(y \, e^{-\gamma(T-t)}, t\right) \to g(z) \quad \text{as} \quad (y, t) \to (z, T), \quad t < T$$

and if and only if for all $x \in I\!R$,

$$e^{r(T-t)} \Psi\left(y \, e^{-\gamma(T-t)}, t\right) \to g(z) \quad \text{as} \quad (y, t) \to (z, T), \quad t < T$$

Proposition 6.18 *A function $\Psi : (0, \infty) \times (0, T) \to I\!R$ has terminal data g in the sense of double convergence if and only if $u[\Psi]$ has initial data $f[g]$ in the sense of double convergence.*

Proof Suppose Ψ has terminal data g in the sense of double convergence. Recall that

$$u[\Psi](y, \tau) = e^{r\tau} \Psi(h[T - \tau](y), T - \tau)$$

for $(y, \tau) \in I\!R \times (0, T)$, and

$$f[g](x) = g(h[T](x))$$

for $x \in I\!R$. Note that

$$(h[T - \tau](y), T - \tau) \to (h[T](x), T) \quad \text{as} \quad (y, \tau) \to (x, 0), \quad 0 < \tau$$

Hence,

$$u[\Psi](y, \tau) = e^{r\tau} \Psi(h[T - \tau](y), T - \tau) \to g(h[T](x)) = f[g](x)$$

as $(y, \tau) \to (x, 0)$, $0 < \tau$. This shows that $u[\Psi]$ has initial data $f[g]$ in the sense of double convergence.

Conversely, suppose $u[\Psi]$ has initial data $f[g](x)$ in the sense of double convergence. Note that

$$\Psi(y, t) = e^{-r(T-t)} u[\Psi]\left(h[t]^{-1}(y), T - t\right)$$

for $(y, t) \in (0, \infty) \times (0, T)$ and

$$g(z) = f[g]\left(h[T]^{-1}(z)\right)$$

for $z \in (0, \infty)$, and that

$$\left(h[t]^{-1}(y), T - t\right) \to \left(h[T]^{-1}(z), 0\right) \quad \text{as} \quad (y, t) \to (z, T), \quad t < T$$

Hence,

$$\Psi(y, t) = e^{-r(T-t)} u[\Psi] \left(h[t]^{-1}(y), T - t\right) \to f[g] \left(h[T]^{-1}(z)\right) = g(z)$$

as $(y, t) \to (z, T)$, $t < T$. This shows that Ψ has terminal data g in the sense of double convergence. □

Proposition 6.19 *Let Ψ be a solution of the Black–Scholes PDE. If g is continuous, then Ψ has terminal data g in the sense of double convergence if and only if the function*

$$\hat{\Psi} : (0, \infty) \times (0, T] \to I\!\!R : (S, t) \mapsto \hat{\Psi}(S, t)$$

defined by

$$\hat{\Psi}(S, t) = \begin{cases} g(S) & \text{if } t = T \\ \Psi(S, t) & \text{if } t < T \end{cases}$$

is continuous.

Proof Obvious. □

Proposition 6.20 *If g is continuous, then the value function Φ has terminal data g in the sense of double convergence.*

Proof This follows from Propositions 6.18 and C.7. □

Proposition 6.21 *Let Ψ be a solution of the Black–Scholes PDE. If g is continuous, and if Ψ has terminal data g in the sense of double convergence, then Ψ has terminal data g in the sense of adjusted local convergence in mean.*

Proof By Proposition 6.18, $u[\Psi]$ has initial data $f[g]$ in the sense of double convergence. Since g is continuous, so is $f[g]$, and therefore it follows from Proposition C.8 that $u[\Psi]$ has initial data $f[g]$ in the sense of local convergence in mean. By Proposition 6.18, Ψ has terminal data g in the sense of adjusted local convergence in mean. □

As in Appendix C, if $f : I\!\!R \to I\!\!R$ is a function, then a function $u : I\!\!R \times (0, T) \to I\!\!R$ has *initial data f* in the *sense of convergence almost everywhere* if for almost all $x \in I\!\!R$,

$$u(x, \tau) \to f(x) \quad \text{as} \quad \tau \to 0$$

Say that a function $\Psi : (0, \infty) \times (0, T) \to I\!\!R$ has *terminal data g* in the *sense of adjusted convergence almost everywhere* if for almost all $y \in (0, \infty)$,

$$\Psi\left(y\, e^{-\gamma(T-t)}, t\right) \to g(y) \quad \text{as} \quad t \to T$$

Observe that Ψ has terminal data g in the sense of adjusted convergence almost everywhere if and only if for almost all $y \in (0, \infty)$,

$$e^{r(T-t)} \Psi\left(y\, e^{-\gamma(T-t)}, t\right) \to g(y) \quad \text{as} \quad t \to T$$

Proposition 6.22 *A function* $\Psi : (0,\infty) \times (0,T) \to \mathbb{R}$ *has terminal data* g *in the sense of adjusted convergence almost everywhere if and only if* $u[\Psi]$ *has initial data* $f[g]$ *in the sense of convergence almost everywhere.*

Proof As in the proof of Proposition 6.16, observe that for every $y \in (0,\infty)$,

$$h[t]^{-1}\left(y\,e^{-\gamma(T-t)}\right) = h[T]^{-1}(y)$$

Hence,

$$e^{r(T-t)}\Psi\left(y\,e^{-\gamma(T-t)},t\right) = u[\Psi]\left(h[T]^{-1}(y),T-t\right)$$

Since

$$g(y) = f[g]\left(h[T]^{-1}(y)\right)$$

it follows that

$$e^{r(T-t)}\Psi\left(y\,e^{-\gamma(T-t)},t\right) \to g(y) \quad \text{as} \quad t \to T$$

if and only if

$$u[\Psi]\left(h[T]^{-1}(y),T-t\right) \to f[g]\left(h[T]^{-1}(y)\right) \quad \text{as} \quad t \to T$$

$\square$

As in Appendix C, if α is a constant, let $G(\alpha)$ denote the set of functions $f : \mathbb{R} \to \mathbb{R}$ which satisfy the following strong exponential *growth condition*: there exists a positive constant C such that

$$|f(y)| \le C\exp\left(\alpha y^2\right)$$

for almost all $y \in \mathbb{R}$.

The difference between $G(\alpha)$ and $G_0(\alpha)$ is that the functions in $G_0(\alpha)$ are required to satisfy the inequality above only for y with sufficiently large absolute value. Observe that $G(\alpha) \subset G_0(\alpha)$ and that all measurable functions in $G(\alpha)$ are locally integrable.

Proposition 6.23 *Let* $T > 0$, *and let* $\Psi : (0,\infty) \times (0,T) \to \mathbb{R}$ *be a function. A sufficient condition for* $u[\Psi](\cdot,\tau)$ *to be in* $G(\alpha)$ *for all* $\alpha > 0$ *and all* $\tau \in (0,T)$ *is that* Ψ *satisfies a* polynomial growth condition: *for some* $\beta > 0$, $C > 0$,

$$|\Psi(y,t)| \le C(1 + y^\beta)$$

for all $y \in (0,\infty)$, $t \in (0,T)$.

Proof We find

$$|u[\Psi](x,\tau)| = e^{r\tau}\Psi(h[T-\tau](x),T-\tau)$$
$$\le e^{rT}C(1 + h[T-\tau](x)^\beta)$$

$$= e^{rT}C(1 + S(0)^\beta \exp[\gamma(T - \tau) + \sigma x]^\beta)$$
$$= e^{rT}C(1 + S(0)^\beta \exp[\beta\gamma(T - \tau) + \beta\sigma x])$$
$$= C_1 + C_2 e^{\beta\sigma x}$$

where

$$C_1 = e^{rT}C$$

and

$$C_2 = e^{rT}CS(0)^\beta e^{\beta\gamma(T-\tau)}$$

Suppose $x \geq \beta\sigma/\alpha$. Then $\alpha x^2 \geq \beta\sigma x$ and $e^{\beta\sigma x} \geq 1$. Hence,

$$C_1 + C_2 e^{\beta\sigma x} \leq (C_1 + C_2)e^{\beta\sigma x} \leq (C_1 + C_2)e^{\alpha x^2}$$

Alternatively, suppose $x < \beta\sigma/\alpha$. Then $\beta\sigma x < \beta^2\sigma^2/\alpha$, and

$$C_1 + C_2 e^{\beta\sigma x} < C_1 + C_2 e^{\beta^2\sigma^2/\alpha} = C_3$$

where the last equality defines C_3. In both cases,

$$|u[\Psi](x,\tau)| \leq C_1 + C_2 e^{\beta\sigma x} \leq (C_1 + C_2 + C_3)e^{\alpha x^2}$$

$\square$

We have already seen in Proposition 6.21 that if g is continuous, then terminal data g in the sense of double convergence implies terminal data g in the sense of local convergence in mean. The next proposition says that the same is true if for some α, $u[\Psi](\cdot, \tau) \in G(\alpha)$ for all $\tau \in (0, T)$.

Proposition 6.24 *Let Ψ be a solution of the Black–Scholes PDE. Assume that for some α, $u[\Psi](\cdot, \tau) \in G(\alpha)$ for all $\tau \in (0, T)$. If Ψ has terminal data g in the sense of adjusted convergence almost everywhere, then Ψ has terminal data g in the sense of adjusted local convergence in mean.*

Proof By Proposition 6.22, $u[\Psi]$ has initial data $f[g]$ in the sense of convergence almost everywhere. By Proposition C.9, $u[\Psi]$ has initial data $f[g]$ in the sense of local convergence in mean. By Proposition 6.16, Ψ has terminal data g in the sense of adjusted local convergence in mean. $\square$

6.9   (*) The Black–Scholes PDE: Integrability

This and the following section investigate the conditions under which the value function Φ is the unique solution of the Black–Scholes PDE. Uniqueness requires that we impose a terminal condition on the solution, and that we restrict in some way the set of functions that are admissible as solutions.

This section considers how to restrict the set of admissible solution functions. The main restriction is an integrability condition. It turns out that non-negative functions automatically satisfy the integrability condition. An alternative restriction is a growth condition, which turns out to imply the integrability condition. The analysis is similar to the analysis of the heat equation in Section C.4.

Let $T > 0$. A function

$$\Psi : (0,\infty) \times (0,T) \to I\!\!R : (S,t) \mapsto \Psi(S,t)$$

is *conditionally integrable* with respect to the process S if it is measurable with respect to S for each $t \in (0,T)$ and if for all $y \in (0,\infty)$ and all s,t with $0 < s < t < T$,

$$E_Q\left|\Psi\left(y\exp\left[\gamma(t-s)+\sigma W^\lambda(t-s)\right],T-s\right)\right| < \infty$$

This is equivalent to

$$E_Q\left|\Psi\left(y\frac{S(t)}{S(s)},T-s\right)\right| < \infty$$

since

$$\frac{S(t)}{S(s)} = \exp\left[\gamma(t-s)+\sigma\left(W^\lambda(t)-W^\lambda(s)\right)\right]$$

As in Appendix C, say that a function

$$u : I\!\!R \times (0,T) \to I\!\!R : (x,\tau) \mapsto u(x,\tau)$$

is *integrable* with respect to p if it is measurable as a function of x for each fixed τ, and if

$$\int |u(y,s)|p(y-x,t-s)\,dy < \infty$$

for all $s,t \in (0,T)$ with $s < t$ and all $x \in I\!\!R$. Equivalently,

$$E_Q|u(x+W^\lambda(t)-W^\lambda(s),s)| = E_Q|u(x+W^\lambda(t-s),s)| < \infty$$

for all $x \in I\!\!R$ and all $s,t \in (0,T)$ with $s < t$.

Proposition 6.25 *A function* $\Psi : (0,\infty)\times(0,T)$ *is conditionally integrable with respect to the process* S *if and only if* $u[\Psi]$ *is integrable with respect to* p.

Proof Make the substitution

$$y = S(0)e^{\gamma(T-t)+\sigma x}$$

Then

$$y\exp[\gamma(t-s)+\sigma W^\lambda(t-s)] = S(0)\exp\{\gamma(T-s)+\sigma[x+W^\lambda(t-s)]\}$$

and

$$e^{-rs}u[\Psi](x+W(t-s),s)$$
$$= \Psi(S(0)\exp\{\gamma(T-s)+\sigma[x+W^\lambda(t-s)]\},T-s)$$

$$= \Psi(y \exp[\gamma(t-s) + \sigma W^\lambda(t-s)], T-s)$$

Hence,

$$E_Q |u[\Psi](x + W(t-s), s)| < \infty$$

for all $x \in I\!\!R$ if and only if

$$E_Q |\Psi(y \exp[\gamma(t-s) + \sigma W^\lambda(t-s)], T-s)| < \infty$$

for all $y \in (0, \infty)$. $\qquad\square$

Proposition 6.26 *The value function Φ is conditionally integrable with respect to the process S, with*

$$e^{r(t-s)} \Phi(y, T-t) = E_Q \Phi(y \exp[\gamma(t-s) + \sigma W^\lambda(t-s)], T-s)$$

for all $y \in (0, \infty)$ and all $s, t \in (0, T)$ with $s < t$.

Proof By Proposition C.13 the function $v = u[\Phi]$ is integrable with respect to p, with

$$Ev(x + W(t-s), s) = v(x, t)$$

for all $x \in I\!\!R$ and all $s, t \in (0, 1/(2a))$ with $s < t$.

Make the substitution

$$y = S(0) e^{\gamma(T-t) + \sigma x}$$

Then

$$u[\Phi](x, t) = e^{rt} \Phi\left(S(0) e^{\gamma(T-t) + \sigma x}, T-t\right) = e^{rt} \Phi(y, T-t)$$

and

$$
\begin{aligned}
u[\Phi]&(x + W^\lambda(t-s), s) \\
&= e^{rs} \Phi(S(0) \exp(\gamma(T-s) + \sigma[x + W^\lambda(t-s)]), T-s) \\
&= e^{rs} \Phi(y \exp[\gamma(t-s) + \sigma W^\lambda(t-s)], T-s)
\end{aligned}
$$

Hence,

$$e^{rt} \Phi(y, T-t) = e^{rs} E_Q \Phi\left(y \exp[\gamma(t-s) + \sigma W^\lambda(t-s)], T-s\right)$$

$\qquad\square$

Proposition 6.27 *If $\Psi : (0, \infty) \times (0, T) \to I\!\!R$ is a non-negative solution of the Black–Scholes PDE, then Ψ is conditionally integrable with respect to the process S, with*

$$e^{r(t-s)} \Psi(y, T-t) \geq E_Q \Psi(y \exp[\gamma(t-s) + \sigma W^\lambda(t-s)], T-s)$$

for all $y \in (0, \infty)$ and all $s, t \in (0, T)$ with $s < t$.

Proof By Proposition 6.14, $u[\Psi]$ is a solution of the heat equation. Since it is non-negative, it is integrable with respect to p, by Proposition C.12, and

$$E_Q u[\Psi](x + W^\lambda(t - s), s) \leq u[\Psi](x, t)$$

for all $x \in I\!\!R$ and all $s, t \in (0, T)$ with $s < t$. By Proposition 6.25, Ψ is conditionally integrable with respect to the process S.

As in the proof of Proposition 6.26, make the substitution

$$y = S(0)e^{\gamma(T-t)+\sigma x}$$

Then
$$u[\Psi](x, t) = e^{rt}\Psi\left(S(0)e^{\gamma(T-t)+\sigma x}, T - t\right) = e^{rt}\Psi(y, T - t)$$

and
$$
\begin{aligned}
&u[\Psi](x + W^\lambda(t - s), s) \\
&= e^{rs}\Psi(S(0)\exp\{\gamma(T - s) + \sigma[x + W^\lambda(t - s)]\}, T - s) \\
&= e^{rs}\Psi(y\exp[\gamma(t - s) + \sigma W^\lambda(t - s)], T - s)
\end{aligned}
$$

Hence,

$$e^{rt}\Psi(y, T - t) \geq e^{rs}E_Q\Psi(y\exp[\gamma(t - s) + \sigma W^\lambda(t - s)], T - s)$$

$\square$

We know from Proposition C.14 that for each $T \in (0, 1/(2a))$, there exists α such that $u[\Phi](\cdot, \tau) = v(\cdot, \tau)$ is in $G(\alpha)$ for all $\tau \in (0, T)$.

Proposition 6.28 *Let $T > 0$, $0 < \alpha \leq 1/(2T)$, and let $\Psi : (0, \infty) \times (0, T) \to I\!\!R$ be a solution of the Black–Scholes PDE such that $u[\Psi](\cdot, \tau) \in G_0(\alpha)$ for each $\tau \in (0, T)$. Then Ψ is conditionally integrable with respect to the process S.*

Proof By Proposition C.15, $u[\Psi]$ is integrable with respect to p. By Proposition 6.25, Ψ is conditionally integrable with respect to the process S. $\square$

6.10 (*) The Black–Scholes PDE: Uniqueness

Theorem 6.29 *Let $0 < T < 1/(2a)$, and let $\Psi : (0, \infty) \times (0, T) \to I\!\!R$ be a solution of the Black–Scholes PDE which is conditionally integrable with respect to the process S. If Ψ has terminal data g in the sense of adjusted local convergence in mean, then $\Psi = \Phi$ on $(0, \infty) \times (0, T)$.*

Proof It follows from Proposition 6.14 that $u[\Psi]$ is a solution of the heat equation, it follows from Proposition 6.25 that $u[\Psi]$ is integrable with respect to p, and it follows from Proposition 6.16 that $u[\Psi]$ has initial data $f[g]$ in the sense of local convergence in mean. Hence, $u[\Psi] = v = u[\Phi]$ on $I\!\!R \times (0, T)$, by Theorem C.17. This implies that $\Psi = \Phi$ on $I\!\!R \times (0, T)$. $\square$

Corollary 6.30 *Let $0 < T < 1/(2a)$, and let $\Psi : (0, \infty) \times (0, T) \to \mathbb{R}$ be a solution of the Black–Scholes PDE which is conditionally integrable with respect to the process S. If Ψ has terminal data g in the sense of double convergence, and if g is continuous, then $\Psi = \Phi$ on $(0, \infty) \times (0, T)$.*

Proof It follows from Proposition 6.21 that Ψ has terminal data g in the sense of adjusted local convergence in mean. It then follows from Theorem 6.29 that $\Psi = \Phi$ on $(0, \infty) \times (0, T)$.   □

Corollary 6.31 *Let $0 < T < 1/(2a)$, and let $\Psi : (0, \infty) \times (0, T) \to \mathbb{R}$ be a non-negative solution of the Black–Scholes PDE. If Ψ has terminal data g in the sense of adjusted local convergence in mean, then $\Psi = \Phi$ on $(0, \infty) \times (0, T)$, and $g(y) \geq 0$ for almost all $y \in \mathbb{R}$.*

Proof Follows from Proposition 6.27 and Theorem 6.29.   □

Corollary 6.32 *Let $0 < T < 1/(2a)$, and let $\Psi : (0, \infty) \times (0, T) \to \mathbb{R}$ be a non-negative solution of the Black–Scholes PDE. If Ψ has terminal data g in the sense of double convergence, and if g is continuous, then $\psi = \Phi$ on $(0, \infty) \times (0, T)$, and $g(z) \geq 0$ for all $z \in (0, \infty)$.*

Proof It follows from Proposition 6.21 that Ψ has terminal data g in the sense of adjusted local convergence in mean. It then follows from Corollary 6.31 that $\Psi = \Phi$ on $(0, \infty) \times (0, T)$.

For every $z \in \mathbb{R}$,

$$\Psi(z, t) \to g(z) \quad \text{as} \quad t \to T, \quad t < T$$

and $\Psi(z, t) \geq 0$ for all $t \in (0, T)$. Hence, $g(z) \geq 0$.   □

We know from Proposition C.14 that there exists α such that

$$u[\Phi](\cdot, \tau) = v(\cdot, \tau) \in G(\alpha)$$

for all $\tau \in (0, T)$.

Corollary 6.33 *Let $0 < T < 1/(2a)$, and let $\Psi : (0, \infty) \times (0, T) \to \mathbb{R}$ be a solution of the Black–Scholes PDE such that for some α, $u[\Psi](\cdot, \tau) \in G_0(\alpha)$ for all $\tau \in (0, T)$. If Ψ has terminal data g in the sense of adjusted local convergence in mean, then $\Psi = \Phi$ on $(0, \infty) \times (0, T)$.*

Proof By Proposition 6.28, Ψ is conditionally integrable with respect to the process S. Theorem 6.29 then implies that $\Psi = \Phi$ on $(0, \infty) \times (0, T)$.   □

Corollary 6.34 *Let $0 < T < 1/(2a)$, and let $\Psi : (0, \infty) \times (0, T) \to \mathbb{R}$ be a solution of the Black–Scholes PDE such that for some α, $u[\Psi](\cdot, \tau) \in G_0(\alpha)$ for all $\tau \in (0, T)$. If Ψ has terminal data g in the sense of double convergence, and if g is continuous, then $\Psi = \Phi$ on $(0, \infty) \times (0, T)$.*

Proof By Proposition 6.28, Ψ is conditionally integrable with respect to the process S. Corollary 6.30 then implies that $\Psi = \Phi$ on $(0, \infty) \times (0, T)$.   □

Corollary 6.35 *Let* $0 < T < 1/(2a)$, *and let* $\Psi : (0, \infty) \times (0, T) \to I\!R$ *be a solution of the Black–Scholes PDE such that for some* α, $u[\Psi](\cdot, \tau) \in G(\alpha)$ *for all* $\tau \in (0, T)$. *If* Ψ *has terminal data* g *in the sense of adjusted convergence almost everywhere, then* $\Psi = \Phi$ *on* $(0, \infty) \times (0, T)$.

Proof By Proposition 6.24, Ψ has terminal data g in the sense of adjusted local convergence in mean. It then follows from Corollary 6.33 that $\Psi = \Phi$ on $(0, \infty) \times (0, T)$. $\square$

6.11   Summary

In earlier chapters, we used the Black–Scholes model systematically as a source of examples, and in this chapter we began by a review of that material. It included the basic securities price processes and their stochastic differentials, the distribution of the stock price, the price of risk and the state price process, the risk-adjusted probabilities and the risk-adjusted Wiener process, and the valuation of a cash-or-nothing call option.

We then studied the valuation of general path-independent claims within the Black–Scholes model. The payoff to a path-independent claim is random only through its dependence on the final stock price. Cash-or-nothing calls and puts, asset-or-nothing calls and puts, and standard calls and puts are all examples of such claims. We showed that a path-independent claim has a path-independent value process, in the sense that the martingale value of the claim at any point in time is a function only of time and of the stock price at that time. We call that function the value function of the claim.

In order to construct the value function, we assumed that the payoff function is locally integrable. We then rewrote the payoff function as a function of the final value of the risk-adjusted Wiener process rather than the final stock price. The transformed payoff function that arises in this way inherits the local integrability property from the original payoff function. We furthermore required it to satisfy an exponential growth condition near infinity. A sufficient condition for this would be that the original payoff function satisfies a polynomial growth condition.

Under these assumptions, we defined a transformed value function which is a function of the Wiener process rather than the stock price, and which expresses the future rather than the present value of the claim. It is defined by integrating the transformed payoff function up against a normal probability density function. The transformed value function will be infinitely often differentiable, even if the payoff function or the transformed payoff function are not differentiable, because any non-differentiability gets smoothed out in the integration process.

By rewriting the transformed value function as a function of the stock price and discounting it back to the present, we arrived at the value function of the claim. An implication of this construction is that the value function itself is infinitely often differentiable, which is good to know when applying Itô's lemma.

The value function solves the Black–Scholes PDE. We showed this by exploiting the fact that the value function discounted back to time zero has zero drift. In fact, any sufficiently differentiable function of time and of the stock price solves the Black–Scholes PDE if and only if it has zero drift when discounted back to zero. This is seen by calculating the drift by Itô's formula and setting it equal to zero.

For path-independent claims, we defined the delta, gamma, and theta as partial derivatives of the value function. Delta is the first derivative with respect to the stock price, gamma is the second derivative, and theta is the derivative with respect to calendar time.

Delta measures the sensitivity of the claim value to small changes in the price of the stock. It also measures the number of shares of stock in the replicating trading strategy. Gamma measures the sensitivity of delta to small changes in the price of the stock. Theta measures how fast the value of the claim changes as time goes by, if the stock price does not change.

We also defined the elasticity or eta of the claim. It measures the percentage sensitivity of the value of the claim to small percentage changes in the stock price. It also measures the leverage of the replicating trading strategy in the sense that it equals one plus the debt–equity ratio. Eta can be used to calculate the volatility of the claim as well as its instantaneous expected excess rate of return under the original probabilities. The volatility of the claim equals eta times the volatility of the stock, and the instantaneous expected excess rate of return to the claim equals eta times the instantaneous expected excess rate of return to the stock.

It is well known that the Black–Scholes formula for the value of a standard call option does not depend on the expected rate of return to the stock. This result extends to other claims as well. We showed in general that the instantaneous expected rate of return to the stock does not enter into the formulas that define the value function. Mathematically, the reason is that the expected rate of return gets replaced by the interest rate when we go from the original probabilities to the risk-adjusted probabilities. Intuitively, the expected future value of the stock is reflected in the current value of the stock. The expected rate of return to the stock affects the expected rate of return to the claim but not its value. If the claim has a high expected rate of return, its future value will be discounted at a high rate, and so its current value will not be high. The expected rate of return does not affect delta, the number of shares needed to replicate the claim.

After investigating the value functions of path-independent claims in general, we studied cash-or-nothing options, asset-or-nothing options, and standard options in detail.

We analyzed the value function and the delta function of a cash-or-nothing call option, derived a put–call parity relation for cash-or-nothing options, used it to value a cash-or-nothing put option, and calculated the delta of a cash-or-nothing put option.

We then calculated the value of an asset-or-nothing option. Using risk-adjusted probabilities, this came down to calculating the expectation of a truncated log-normal distribution. In Exercise 6.4, we saw an alternative method which consisted in changing the price system by using the stock as a numeraire, valuing the option in the new price system, and then translating the value back into the original price system. In the new price system, the option was in effect a cash-or-nothing option, which we had already valued.

From the value function of the asset-or-nothing option, we calculated the delta. We then derived a put–call parity relation for asset-or-nothing options, used it to value an asset-or-nothing put option, and calculated the delta of an asset-or-nothing put option.

A standard call option can be interpreted as a combination of an asset-or-nothing option and a short position in a number of cash-or-nothing options. We used this observation to derive the Black–Scholes formula from the formulas for the values of the cash-or-nothing option and the asset-or-nothing option.

When the value of the standard call option is expressed as a fraction of the stock price, it is a function only of two variables: the stock price as a fraction of the discounted exercise price, and the conditional standard deviation of the logarithm of the stock price.

It can be somewhat tedious to calculate the partial derivatives of the Black–Scholes formula, because of the indirect effects of the various parameters through the variables d_1 and d_2. There is a trick, however, which simplifies the calculations. The trick is to write the Black–Scholes call price as a function not only of the exogenous parameters but also separately of the variable d_1. It turns out that the partial derivative with respect to d_1 is zero, and therefore many of the indirect effects disappear.

We calculated the delta and gamma functions of the standard call option and analyzed their shapes and limit behavior as well as those of the value function.

Delta equals $N(d_1)$. This leads to an attractive interpretation of the Black–Scholes formula as representing the value of the replicating trading strategy. The first term in the formula is the value of the shares of stock held in the replicating trading strategy, and the second term is the value of the debt.

We also calculated the vega, theta, and rho of the standard call option. Vega is the derivative with respect to the volatility parameter, and rho is the derivative with respect to the interest rate.

Vega is positive, which implies that the value of the option is an increasing function of the volatility of the stock. The intuitive reason is that an increase in volatility increases both the upside potential and the downside risk, but the option payoff is affected only by the upside potential, and therefore the value of the option goes up.

The value of the standard call option approaches the value of a forward contract as volatility goes to zero, and it approaches the stock price as volatility goes to infinity. The latter is particularly remarkable because the probability that the option will be exercised goes to zero. A way to understand it is to look at the option as a combination of a short position in a number of cash-or-nothing call options, a long position in the stock, and a short position in an asset-or-nothing put option. The value of the cash-or-nothing call options goes to zero, the value of the asset-or-nothing put option goes to zero, and what is left is the long position in the stock.

Theta is negative, which implies that the value of the option declines over time if the stock price stays constant. This is partly because the discounted value of the exercise price increases, and partly because the conditional variance of the logarithm of the final stock price decreases.

Rho is positive, which implies that the value of the option is an increasing function of the interest rate. This is because the higher the interest rate, the lower is the present value of the exercise payment.

Using put–call parity and the Black–Scholes formula for the value of the call option, we found the value function of a standard put option.

We analyzed the value function and computed the delta, gamma, eta, vega, theta, and rho of the put. The delta of the put equals the delta of the call minus one. The gamma and the vega of the put are the same as the gamma and the vega of the call. The theta of the put may be positive or negative, because there is a discounting effect and a variance effect which work in opposite directions. The rho of the put is negative, because the higher the interest rate is, the lower is the present value of the exercise payment to be received.

As mentioned, we showed at the beginning of the chapter that a path-independent claim has a value function, which can be calculated by the martingale valuation principle. We also showed that the value function solves the Black–Scholes PDE. In the process, we defined a transformed value function which is a function of the Wiener process rather than of the stock price, and which expresses the future rather than the present value of the claim. The transformed function solves the heat equation.

Towards the end of the chapter, we returned to the Black–Scholes PDE in order to use it to identify the value function in an alternative way. The idea was that under appropriate conditions, the value function will be the unique solution of the Black–Scholes PDE subject to a terminal condition given by the payoff function.

For this purpose, we observed that any function of the stock price and of time can be subjected to the same transformation as the value function, so that it becomes a function of the Wiener process rather than of the stock price. The function itself solves the Black–Scholes PDE if and only if the transformed function solves the heat equation. The transformation implies that uniqueness of the solution to the Black–Scholes PDE is equivalent to uniqueness of the solution of the heat equation.

Mathematically, it is not entirely simple to impose the terminal condition. The issue is analogous to the question of how to impose the initial condition on solutions of the heat equation. We imposed the terminal data on solutions of the Black–Scholes PDE in three ways.

The most general formulation is terminal data in the sense of adjusted local convergence in mean, which corresponds to initial data for the heat equation in the sense of local convergence in mean. The value function does satisfy the terminal condition in this sense.

When the payoff function is continuous, it makes sense to impose the terminal condition in the sense of double convergence, because the value function will converge to the payoff function in this sense, and because terminal data in the sense of double convergence will imply terminal data in the sense of adjusted local convergence in mean. Terminal data in the sense of double convergence are equivalent to initial data in the sense of double convergence for the corresponding solution of the heat equation.

Finally, for solutions that satisfy a certain strong growth condition, the terminal condition can be imposed in the sense of adjusted convergence almost everywhere, because under the growth condition, adjusted convergence almost everywhere implies adjusted local convergence in mean. Terminal data in the sense of adjusted convergence almost everywhere are equivalent to initial data in the sense of convergence almost everywhere for the corresponding solution of the heat equation.

The adjustment involved in adjusted local convergence in mean and adjusted convergence almost everywhere consists in letting the convergence happen along exponential paths for the stock price.

Even when the terminal condition is properly imposed, the solution of the Black–Scholes PDE is in fact not unique. This phenomenon corresponds to the observation that the solution of the heat equation is not unique. To ensure uniqueness, it is necessary to restrict the set of functions that are admissible as solutions.

The main restriction we imposed was that the solution function should be conditionally integrable with respect to the stock price process. This means that conditionally on the price of the stock at any time before maturity, the value of the solution at any later time before maturity is integrable. The value function does indeed have this property.

It turns out that non-negative solutions of the Black–Scholes PDE automatically are conditionally integrable with respect to the stock price process. An alternative sufficient condition is an exponential growth condition imposed on the transformed function near infinity. If the solution itself satisfies a polynomial growth condition, then the transformed function will satisfy this exponential growth condition.

The main uniqueness result is Theorem 6.29. It says that the value function is the only solution of the Black–Scholes PDE which is conditionally integrable with respect to the stock price process and has terminal data equal to the payoff function in the sense of adjusted local convergence in mean.

A number of corollaries follow from this theorem. If the payoff function is continuous, then the value function is the only solution which is conditionally integrable and has terminal data equal to the payoff function in the sense of double convergence. If the payoff function is non-negative, then the value function is the only solution which is non-negative and has terminal data equal to the payoff function in the sense of adjusted local convergence in mean. If the payoff function is both continuous and non-negative, then the value function is the only solution which is non-negative and has terminal data equal to the payoff function in the sense of double convergence.

The value function is the only solution whose transformed function satisfies the exponential growth condition near infinity and which has terminal data equal to the payoff function in the sense of adjusted local convergence in mean. If the payoff function is continuous, then the value function is the only solution whose transformed function satisfies the exponential growth condition near infinity and which has terminal data equal to the payoff function in the sense of double convergence.

The value function is the only solution whose transformed function satisfies the strong version of the exponential growth condition and which has terminal data equal to the payoff function in the sense of adjusted convergence almost everywhere.

6.12   (*) Notes

The present derivation of the Black–Scholes formula follows Dothan [28, 1990] and Nielsen [74, 1993].

Put–call parity (for commodity options) has been known at least since de Pinto [25, 1771]. João Amaro de Matos showed me this reference.

As mentioned in the notes to Appendix C, Karatzas and Shreve [64, 1988, Chapter 4, Corollary 3.7] strengthen Proposition C.12 by showing that the inequality is actually an equality. It follows that Proposition 6.27 can be strengthened in a similar manner. The inequality

$$e^{r(t-s)}\Psi(y, T-t) \geq E_Q\Psi(y\exp[\gamma(t-s) + \sigma W^\lambda(t-s)], T-s)$$

is actually an equality, for all $y \in (0, \infty)$ and all $s, t \in (0, T)$ with $s < t$.

Black and Scholes [10, 1973] derived their formula as follows. They assumed from the outset that the price of the option was a function of the stock price and of time. They formed a portfolio from the stock and the option by holding one of them long and the other short in a proportion such that the portfolio has zero delta. This portfolio will be instantaneously riskless, and therefore it follows either from the instantaneous version of the capital asset pricing model or from an instantaneous no-arbitrage argument that it must earn the riskless interest rate. They calculated its expected instantaneous rate of return using Itô's lemma and set it equal to the interest rate. This led to the Black–Scholes PDE.

Note that the portfolio described does not amount to a self-financing trading strategy. This is immaterial, however, because the trading strategy can easily be made self-financing by borrowing and lending using the money market account.

Black and Scholes stated that there is only one formula or function that satisfies the partial differential equation subject to the terminal condition that the final option price should equal the payoff to the option. To find that function, they transformed the equation into a version of the heat equation and referred to Churchill [19, 1963, p. 155] for the solution.

It is easy to verify that the formula they obtained is indeed a solution. However, to establish that the option price must be given by the Black–Scholes formula, it was necessary to argue that the solution is unique. Unfortunately, the reference to Churchill does not suffice to establish uniqueness. Churchill [19, 1963] and Churchill and Brown [20, 1987, Chapter 7, Section 69] assume that the initial data are given by a bounded function, while Black and Scholes' initial data for the heat equation are given by a function which grows as an exponential, except in the unlikely case where $r < \sigma^2/2$.

Black and Scholes used a transformation which is different from the one employed in this book. Their transformation assumes that $r \neq \sigma^2/2$, while no such assumption is necessary for the transformation used here.

Note that Black and Scholes did not impose any boundary conditions on the solution function other than the terminal condition (or the initial condition for the heat equation). For example, they did not impose a condition that said that the value of the option should be zero (or should go to zero) when the price of the stock is zero (or goes to zero).

The no-arbitrage argument is attributed to Robert C. Merton. He used it in Merton [70, 1973]. He argued that it is not necessary to use the capital asset pricing model, because the partial differential equation can be derived from an assumption of absence of arbitrage. This assumption has to be interpreted carefully because, as Harrison and Kreps [43, 1979] have shown, there is always an arbitrage possibility in the Black–Scholes model. Their doubling strategy is an arbitrage which can be implemented by trading the stock and the money market account, even if there is no option available.

Merton [70, 1973] effectively assumed the absence of what could be called instantaneous arbitrage. An instantaneous arbitrage would be a portfolio with zero instantaneous risk but with an instantaneous expected rate of return strictly greater than the interest rate.

Both Black and Scholes [10, 1973] and Merton [70, 1973] relied on the assumption that the option price was a function of the stock price and of calendar time, and that this function was sufficiently smooth to apply Itô's lemma. Merton [71, 1977] set out to prove this rather than assume it. For this purpose, he relied on an assumption of no arbitrage, or no "intertemporal arbitrage," as opposed to an assumption of no instantaneous arbitrage. Therefore, it seems that his argument has been invalidated by Harrison and Kreps [43, 1979].

The partial differential equations methodology was very influential in the early literature on derivative securities pricing. Today, it is still important as a computational technique, but it is less important in theoretical investigations.

7

GAUSSIAN TERM STRUCTURE MODELS

This chapter studies one-factor Gaussian models of the term structure of interest rates. They are all special cases of the generalized Vasicek model.

In the generalized Vasicek model, which is the subject of Section 7.7, the interest rate follows a general one-factor Gaussian process. The model has three time-dependent parameters. It can, in principle, be calibrated so as to be consistent with initially given cross-sectional term structure data. One of the time-dependent parameters may be chosen so as to reflect a view of the future standard deviation of the interest rate. The two remaining ones can be chosen so as to fit exactly the initial term structure of forward rates and their standard deviations, or the initial term structure of zero-coupon bond yields and their standard deviations.

In the simplified Hull–White model and the continuous-time Ho–Lee model, to be studied in Sections 7.8 and 7.9, respectively, there is only one time-dependent parameter. It can be used to fit exactly the initial term structure of forward rates or the initial term structure of zero-coupon bond yields.

In the Vasicek model and the Merton model, to be studied in Sections 7.2–7.5 and 7.6, respectively, there are no time-dependent parameters. Therefore, it is not possible to fit the initial term structures exactly. These models impose their own shapes of the forward rate curves and yield curves. In the Vasicek model, the interest rate follows an Ornstein–Uhlenbeck process, while in the Merton model, it follows a generalized Wiener process.

In the Gaussian term structure models, the interest rate, the instantaneous forward rates, and the yields on zero-coupon bonds are normally distributed. For this reason, it is possible to calculate closed form pricing and hedging formulas for a large number of interest rate derivative securities. We shall calculate only the prices of zero-coupon bonds.

We begin, in Section 7.1, by introducing in general terms the concepts of zero-coupon bond prices and yields, forward contracts for bonds, forward rates, and instantaneous forward rates.

7.1 Zero-coupon Bonds and Forward Rates

A default-free *zero-coupon bond* (or *discount bond*) with maturity t and face value one is a claim which has a non-random payoff of one for sure at time t and no payoff at other times.

For $0 \leq s \leq t$, let $P(s; t)$ denote the price (the martingale value) at time s of a zero-coupon bond which matures at time t and has payoff or face value one.

Assume that $P(s;t) > 0$.

Notational convention regarding semicolons: For various functions and processes that will be introduced in this chapter, a maturity date such as t in $P(s;t)$ will be separated from the other arguments by a semicolon.

The continuously compounded *yield* on the bond is

$$R(s;t) = \frac{1}{t-s} \ln\left(\frac{1}{P(s;t)}\right) = -\frac{1}{t-s} \ln P(s;t)$$

Observe that $R(s;t) > 0$ if and only if $P(s;t) < 1$. The price of the zero-coupon bond can be calculated from its yield by

$$P(s;t) = \exp[-(t-s)R(s;t)]$$

The zero-coupon *yield curve* or *term structure of interest rates* at time s is the function

$$\tau \to R(s;s+\tau) : [0,\infty) \to \mathbb{R}$$

which maps the time to maturity τ into the yield (at time s) of the zero-coupon bond with that maturity τ.

Example 7.1 Suppose the interest rate r is constant. Then

$$P(s;t) = E_Q\left[\exp\left(-\int_s^t r\,du\right)\bigg|\mathcal{F}_s\right] = e^{-r(t-s)}$$

$$R(s;t) = -\frac{1}{t-s}\ln P(s;t) = r$$

and

$$\frac{dP(\cdot;t)}{P(\cdot;t)} = r\,ds$$

□

A *forward contract* with maturity t is a contract to buy a specified underlying asset on date t at a fixed price X, called the *delivery price*.

If the random value of the underlying asset at t is $A(t)$, then the random payoff to the forward contract on that date is $A(t) - X$. If A is the martingale value process of a marketed claim, then the forward contract can be replicated by going short in X zero-coupon bonds and engaging in a trading strategy which replicates A. Therefore, the value at time s of the forward contract is

$$A(s) - P(s;t)X$$

On the day the forward contract is entered into, the delivery price is set in such a way that the value of the contract is zero. The value $F(s) = X$ of the delivery price that achieves this is the *forward price* of the asset at time s. It is given by

$$F(s) = \frac{A(s)}{P(s;t)}$$

For example, if the interest rate r is constant, then

$$F(s) = e^{r(t-s)}A(s)$$

Let $0 \le s \le t \le u$. A forward contract for the zero-coupon bond with maturity u and face value one, with delivery price X and maturity t, is a contract to buy the zero-coupon bond at time t for a price of X. The payoff to the contract is $P(t;u) - X$ at time t.

The value of the forward contract at time s is

$$P(s;u) - P(s;t)X$$

The payoff to the forward contract can be replicated by buying one discount bond maturing at time u and selling X discount bonds maturing at time t.

Let $F(s;t;u)$ denote the forward price. Then

$$P(s;u) = F(s;t;u)P(s;t)$$

or

$$F(s;t;u) = \frac{P(s;u)}{P(s;t)}$$

In particular, $F(s;t;t) = 1$ and $F(s;s;u) = P(s;u)$. Note that $F(s;t;u) < 1$ if and only if $P(s;u) < P(s;t)$.

In the expression $F(s;t;u)$, both t and u are maturity dates—t for the forward contract and u for the underlying bond. That is why, notationally, both are separated from the other arguments by semicolons.

If $0 \le s \le t \le u \le v$, then

$$F(s;t;u)F(s;u;v) = \frac{P(s;u)P(s;v)}{P(s;t)P(s;u)} = \frac{P(s;v)}{P(s;t)} = F(s;t;v)$$

The *forward yield* for the time interval $[t,u]$, in effect at time s, where $0 \le s \le t < u$, is the yield at time t on a zero-coupon bond which matures at time u, assuming that at time t it has price $F(s;t;u)$:

$$f(s;t;u) = \frac{1}{u-t}\ln\left(\frac{1}{F(s;t;u)}\right) = -\frac{1}{u-t}\ln F(s;t;u)$$

Note that $f(s;t;u) > 0$ if and only if $F(s;t;u) < 1$. The forward price can be calculated from the forward yield by

$$F(s;t;u) = \exp[-(u-t)f(s;t;u)]$$

From the relation

$$P(s;u) = F(s;t;u)P(s;t)$$

it follows that

$$(u-s)R(s;u) = (u-t)f(s;t;u) + (t-s)R(s;t)$$

or

$$R(s;u) = \frac{t-s}{u-s}R(s;t) + \frac{u-t}{u-s}f(s;t;u)$$

Assume that the function $P(s;t)$ is continuously differentiable as a function of the maturity date t. Then so is the function $\ln P(s;t)$. Now, for $0 \leq s \leq t \leq u$,

$$\begin{aligned}
f(s;t;u) &= -\frac{1}{u-t}\ln F(s;t;u) \\
&= -\frac{1}{u-t}[\ln P(s;u) - \ln P(s;t)] \\
&\to -\frac{\partial}{\partial t}\ln P(s;t)
\end{aligned}$$

as $u \to t$. We denote this limit by $f(s;t)$ and call it the *instantaneous forward rate* for time t:

$$f(s;t) = -\frac{\partial}{\partial t}\ln P(s;t)$$

So,

$$\ln P(s;u) = -\int_s^u f(s;t)\,dt$$

$$P(s;u) = \exp\left(-\int_s^u f(s;t)\,dt\right)$$

and

$$R(s;u) = -\frac{1}{u-s}\ln P(s;u) = \frac{1}{u-s}\int_s^u f(s;t)\,dt$$

The yield on a zero-coupon bond is the average of the instantaneous forward rates over the life of the bond.

Example 7.2 *Continuation of Example 7.1.* When the interest rate r is constant, all the forward rates will be constant and equal to r. The price of a zero-coupon bond is

$$P(s;t) = e^{-r(t-s)}$$

Hence,

$$\ln P(s;t) = -r(t-s)$$

and the instantaneous forward rates are

$$f(s;t) = -\frac{\partial}{\partial t}\ln P(s;t) = r$$

$\square$

Note that

$$f(s;t) = -\frac{P_t(s;t)}{P(s;t)}$$

and that $f(s;t) > 0$ if and only if $P_t(s;t) < 0$. Furthermore, since

$$\ln P(s;t) = -(t-s)R(s;t)$$

when $s < t$,

$$f(s;t) = R(s;t) + (t-s)R_t(s;t)$$

The forward price of a bond and the forward yield over a time interval $[u,t]$ can be recovered from the instantaneous forward rates, as follows:

$$\ln F(s;t;u) = \ln P(s;u) - \ln P(s;t)$$
$$= -\int_s^u f(s;v)\,dv + \int_s^t f(s;v)\,dv$$
$$= -\int_t^u f(s;v)\,dv$$

Hence,

$$F(s;t;u) = \exp\left(-\int_t^u f(s;v)\,dv\right)$$

and

$$f(s;t;u) = -\frac{1}{u-t}\ln F(s;t;u) = \frac{1}{u-t}\int_t^u f(s;v)\,dv$$

The forward yield over the time interval $[u,t]$ equals the average of the instantaneous forward rates over that interval.

7.2 The Vasicek Model

In the Vasicek model, the interest rate follows an Ornstein–Uhlenbeck process. It is one of the earliest and simplest continuous-time models of the term structure of interest rates.

We use the Vasicek model to illustrate how to set up a model by specifying the state price process, which amounts to specifying the interest rate and the price of risk. In the next section, we show how to specify the model directly in the risk-adjusted probabilities.

Let $K = 1$, and let W be a one-dimensional Wiener process relative to the filtration F. Let r_0, $a > 0$, b, and $\sigma > 0$ be constants.

In the *Vasicek model*, the instantaneous interest rate r is assumed to follow the Ornstein–Uhlenbeck process with differential

$$dr = a(b-r)\,dt + \sigma\,dW$$

and with constant initial value $r(0) = r_0$. It follows from Proposition 3.8 that these conditions are satisfied by a unique Itô process r.

The market price of risk λ is assumed to be a positive constant. The interest rate process r and the market price of risk λ determine the state price process Π (up to an arbitrary positive initial value):

$$\Pi = \Pi(0)\eta[-r, -\lambda]$$

Consider a finite time interval $\mathcal{T} = [0, T]$. Since λ is a deterministic constant, it follows as in Example 2.25 that there exists a risk-adjusted probability measure Q, with density $\eta[0, -\lambda](T)$ with respect to the original probability measure P. The process

$$W^\lambda(t) = W(t) + \lambda t$$

is a Wiener process under Q.

Set

$$\bar{r} = b - \sigma\lambda/a$$

Then

$$\sigma\lambda = a(b - \bar{r})$$

and

$$\begin{aligned}
dr &= a(b - r)\, dt + \sigma\, dW \\
&= a(b - r)\, dt + \sigma\left(dW^\lambda - \lambda\, dt\right) \\
&= [a(b - r) - a(b - \bar{r})]\, dt + \sigma\, dW^\lambda \\
&= a(\bar{r} - r)\, dt + \sigma\, dW^\lambda
\end{aligned}$$

The differential of the interest rate under the risk-adjusted probability measure comes about by replacing b by $\bar{r}$ and W by W^λ. The interest rate follows an Ornstein–Uhlenbeck process under Q, with the same dispersion coefficient σ and the same speed-of-adjustment coefficient a as under P, but with a different mean-reversion level: $\bar{r}$ instead of b.

Unlike securities price processes, the interest rate process r does not have zero drift when its differential is expressed in terms of W^λ.

Note that $\bar{r} < b$: the mean reversion level is less under Q than under P. What is going on? Recall from Example 2.27 that when going from the original probability measure P to the risk-adjusted measure Q, probability mass is shifted downwards onto the lower paths of W. At the same time, the lower paths of the interest rate process r also become more likely relative to the higher paths. As a result, the mean reversion level is lower under Q than under P.

Using the results from the section on Ornstein–Uhlenbeck processes,

$$r(t) = \bar{r} + e^{-a(t-s)}(r(s) - \bar{r}) + \sigma\int_s^t e^{-a(t-u)}\, dW^\lambda(u)$$

The value of the money market account is

$$M(t) = \exp\left[\int_0^t r(u)\,du\right]$$

If $0 \le s \le t \le T$, set

$$I(s;t) = \int_s^t r(u)\,du$$

Then

$$M(t) = M(s)\exp[I(s;t)]$$

and

$$\frac{M(s)}{M(t)} = \exp[-I(s;t)]$$

Suppose Y is a contingent claim which is measurable with respect to $\mathcal{F}_t$. Assume that $Y/M(t)$ is integrable under Q. Then the martingale value process of Y is

$$V(s) = E_Q\left(Y\frac{M(s)}{M(t)}\ \Big|\ \mathcal{F}_s\right) = E_Q(Y\exp[-I(s;t)]\mid \mathcal{F}_s)$$

We can calculate $V(s)$ if we know the conditional joint distribution of Y and $I(s;t)$, given information at time s, under the risk-adjusted probabilities.

In particular, the martingale value of a zero-coupon bond maturing at time t is

$$P(s;t) = E_Q\left(\frac{M(s)}{M(t)}\ \Big|\ \mathcal{F}_s\right) = E_Q(\exp[-I(s;t)]\mid \mathcal{F}_s)$$

provided that $1/M(t)$ is integrable under Q.

In order to calculate $P(s;t)$, we shall first calculate $I(s;t)$ for $0 \le s \le t \le T$.

Proposition 7.3 *For $0 \le s \le t$,*

$$I(s;t) = (t-s)\bar{r} + \frac{1}{a}\left(1 - e^{-a(t-s)}\right)(r(s) - \bar{r})$$

$$+ \frac{\sigma}{a}\int_s^t \left(1 - e^{-a(t-v)}\right)dW^\lambda(v)$$

Exercise 7.1 *Prove Proposition 7.3.*

It follows from Proposition 7.3 that given information at time s, $I(s;t)$ is normally distributed under Q.

The conditional mean of $I(s;t)$ is

$$E_Q[I(s;t)\mid \mathcal{F}_s] = (t-s)\bar{r} + \frac{1}{a}\left(1 - e^{-a(t-s)}\right)(r(s) - \bar{r}) = m(r(s), t-s)$$

where m is the function

$$m(r,\tau) = \tau\bar{r} + \frac{1}{a}\left(1 - e^{-a\tau}\right)(r - \bar{r})$$

The conditional variance of $I(s;t)$ is

$$\text{var}_Q[I(s;t)\mid \mathcal{F}_s] = \frac{\sigma^2}{a^2}\int_s^t \left(1 - e^{-a(t-v)}\right)^2 dv$$

$$= \frac{\sigma^2}{a^2} \int_s^t \left(1 + e^{-2a(t-v)} - 2e^{-a(t-v)}\right) dv$$

$$= \frac{\sigma^2}{a^2} \left[v + \frac{1}{2a}e^{-2a(t-v)} - \frac{2}{a}e^{-a(t-v)}\right]_{v=s}^{t}$$

$$= \frac{\sigma^2}{a^2} \left[(t-s) + \frac{1}{2a}\left(1 - e^{-2a(t-s)}\right) - \frac{2}{a}\left(1 - e^{-a(t-s)}\right)\right]$$

$$= \frac{\sigma^2}{2a^3} \left(4e^{-a(t-s)} - e^{-2a(t-s)} + 2a(t-s) - 3\right)$$

$$= v(t-s)$$

where v is the function

$$v(\tau) = \frac{\sigma^2}{2a^3} \left(4e^{-a\tau} - e^{-2a\tau} + 2a\tau - 3\right)$$

We have shown that given information at time s, $I(s;t)$ is normally distributed under Q with mean $m(r(s), t-s)$ and variance $v(t-s)$.

Let $0 \le s \le t \le T$. Using Proposition 2.29 we find that the value at time s of the zero-coupon bond maturing at t is

$$P(s;t) = E_Q(\exp[-I(s;t)] \mid \mathcal{F}_s)$$

$$= \exp\left[-m(r(s), t-s) + \frac{1}{2}v(t-s)\right]$$

$$= P(r(s), t-s)$$

where P is the function

$$P(r, \tau) = \exp\left[-m(r, \tau) + \frac{1}{2}v(\tau)\right]$$

Through this formula, the model gives a complete description of the term structure of zero-coupon bond prices

$$\tau \to P(r(s), \tau) : [0, \infty) \to \mathbb{R}$$

at any given point in time s, as it depends on the instantaneous interest rate at that time.

In $P(r, \tau)$, τ is not the maturity date but the time to maturity. That is why notationally it is not separated from r by a semicolon but by a comma.

Define functions A and B by

$$B(\tau) = \frac{1}{a}\left(1 - e^{-a\tau}\right)$$

and

$$A(\tau) = (\tau - B(\tau))\bar{r} - \frac{1}{2}v(\tau)$$

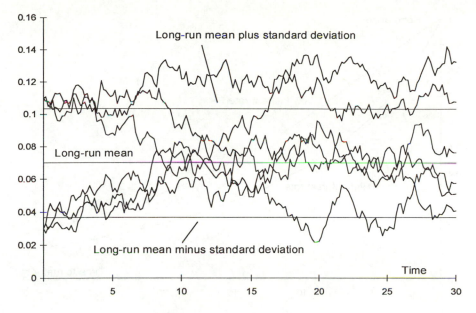

FIG. 7.1. Interest rate paths

Then

$$-m(r, \tau) + \frac{1}{2}v(\tau) = -A(\tau) - B(\tau)r$$

$$P(r, \tau) = \exp[-A(\tau) - B(\tau)r]$$

and the value of the bond at time s is

$$P(r(s), t - s) = \exp[-A(t - s) - B(t - s)r(s)]$$

In several of our illustrations, we shall use the following parameters of the interest rate process. The long-run mean is $\bar{r} = 0.07$. The speed of adjustment a and the standard deviation parameter σ have the values estimated by Chan, Karolyi, Longstaff, and Sanders [15, 1992]: $a = 0.18$ and $\sigma = 0.02$. The corresponding long-run standard deviation of the interest rate is

$$\sqrt{\frac{\sigma^2}{2a}} = \frac{\sigma}{\sqrt{2a}} = 0.033$$

This implies that the 66 percent confidence interval around the long-run mean is

$$\left[\bar{r} - \frac{\sigma}{\sqrt{2a}}, \bar{r} + \frac{\sigma}{\sqrt{2a}} \right] = [0.037, 0.103]$$

Figure 7.1 shows six sample paths of the process r, simulated under the risk-adjusted probabilities. It is analogous to Fig. 3.3 but has a time horizon of 30

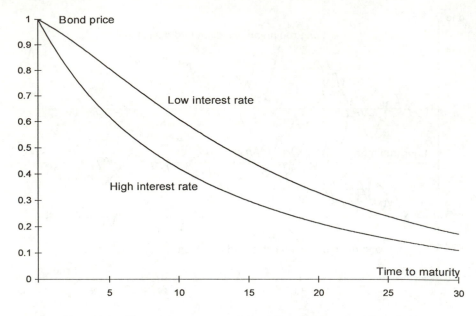

FIG. 7.2. Two price curves with $r(0) = 0.11$ and $r(0) = 0.03$

years instead of 6 years and different speed of adjustment and standard deviation. Three of the paths are conditional on the initial value $r(0) = 0.03$, and three are conditional on the initial value $r(0) = 0.11$. The three horizontal lines show the long-run mean and the long-run mean plus/minus one standard deviation.

Figure 7.2 shows two bond price curves conditional on the two different initial interest rates, $r(0) = 0.03$ and $r(0) = 0.11$. The lower curve corresponds to an initial interest rate of $r(0) = 0.11$, and the higher curve corresponds to $r(0) = 0.03$. Time to maturity, τ, is on the horizontal axis, and the price of a zero-coupon bond with that time to maturity and with face value one is measured along the vertical axis. The parameters $\bar{r}$, a, and σ are the same as in Fig. 7.1.

Figure 7.2 illustrates the fact that the model satisfies *pull-to-par*, the phenomenon that the price of a zero-coupon bond approaches its face value as the time to maturity approaches zero:

$$P(r, t - s) \to 1 \quad \text{as} \quad s \to t$$

for fixed r, and with probability one,

$$P(r(s), t - s) \to 1 \quad \text{as} \quad s \to t$$

This can be immediately verified by looking at the formula for $P(r, \tau)$.

Since $r(t)$ is normally distributed, the price $P(r(t), T - t)$ of the zero-coupon bond is lognormally distributed, both under the risk-adjusted probabilities and under the original probabilities.

Consider the price process $P(r(s), t - s)$ of a bond that matures at a fixed time t, with s as the time variable, $0 \le s \le t \le T$. The differential of the logarithm of the bond price is

$$d \ln P(r(s), t - s) = d[-A(t - s) - B(t - s)r(s)]$$
$$= -dA(t - s) - B(t - s)\, dr(s) - r(s)\, dB(t - s)$$

The dispersion coefficient of the logarithm of the bond price with respect to W^λ is

$$-B(t - s)\sigma = -\frac{\sigma}{a}\left(1 - e^{-a(t-s)}\right)$$

This is equal to the relative dispersion coefficient of the bond price itself. Since the relative drift coefficient of the bond price under the risk-adjusted probabilities must be the interest rate,

$$\frac{dP(r(s), t - s)}{P(r(s), t - s)} = r(s)\, ds - B(t - s)\sigma\, dW^\lambda(s)$$

The differential of the bond price under the original probabilities is

$$\frac{dP(r(s), t - s)}{P(r(s), t - s)} = r(s)\, ds - B(t - s)\sigma\, dW^\lambda(s)$$
$$= r(s)\, ds - B(t - s)\sigma\, (dW(s) + \lambda\, ds)$$
$$= (r(s) - a(b - \bar{r})B(t - s))\, ds - B(t - s)\sigma\, dW(s)$$

The percentage dispersion coefficient is negative: a positive shock to W makes the interest rate go up and the bond price go down.

The volatility of the bond price is

$$\frac{\sigma}{a}\left(1 - e^{-a(t-s)}\right)$$

It is a deterministic function of s, and it goes to zero as s approaches t. It is independent of the current interest rate $r(s)$ and of the mean reversion level $\bar{r}$.

Figure 7.3 shows the zero-coupon bond price volatilities as they depend on time to maturity, for two levels of the standard deviation parameter σ. The lower curve corresponds to $\sigma = 0.02$, and the higher curve corresponds to $\sigma = 0.06$. Time to maturity, τ, is on the horizontal axis, and the bond price volatility is measured along the vertical axis. The parameter a is as in the previous figures, $a = 0.18$.

Observe that the bond price volatility is an increasing function of time to maturity τ, and that it converges to zero as $\tau \to 0$ and to σ/a as $\tau \to \infty$. This is reflected in Fig. 7.3, where the two horizontal lines show the limiting volatilities $\sigma/a = 0.1111$ and $\sigma/a = 0.3333$ for long maturities in the two cases $\sigma = 0.02$ and $\sigma = 0.06$, respectively.

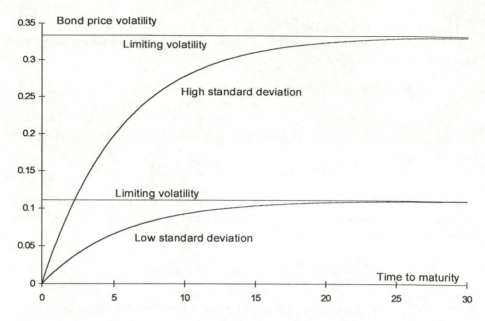

FIG. 7.3. Two bond volatility curves with $\sigma = 0.02$ and $\sigma = 0.06$

Alternatively, consider the price process $P(r(s), \tau)$ of a bond that has a fixed time τ to maturity, with s as the time variable, $0 \le s \le T - \tau$:

$$P(r(s), \tau) = \exp[-A(\tau) - B(\tau)r(s)]$$

The differential of the logarithm of the price is

$$
\begin{aligned}
d \ln P(r(s), \tau) &= d[-A(\tau) - B(\tau)r(s)] \\
&= -B(\tau)\, dr(s) \\
&= -B(\tau)a(\bar{r} - r(s))\, ds - B(\tau)\sigma\, dW^\lambda(s)
\end{aligned}
$$

The dispersion coefficient of the logarithm of the bond price with respect to W^λ is

$$-B(\tau)\sigma = -\frac{\sigma}{a}\left(1 - e^{-a\tau}\right)$$

This is the same as the relative dispersion coefficient of the bond price itself. Hence, the volatility of the bond price is

$$B(\tau)\sigma = \frac{\sigma}{a}\left(1 - e^{-a\tau}\right)$$

which is the same as the volatility we found above for a bond with fixed maturity time $t = s + \tau$.

When the time to maturity τ is fixed, we are no longer looking at the price process of a fixed claim, and the relative drift coefficient of the bond price under the risk-adjusted probabilities is not the interest rate. The relative drift of the bond price equals the relative drift of the logarithm of the bond price plus a half times the square of the relative dispersion:

$$-B(\tau)a(\bar{r} - r(s)) + \frac{1}{2}B(\tau)^2\sigma^2$$

Hence,

$$\frac{dP(r(s),\tau)}{P(r(s),\tau)} = \left[-B(\tau)a(\bar{r} - r(s)) + \frac{1}{2}B(\tau)^2\sigma^2 \right] ds - B(\tau)\sigma\, dW^\lambda(s)$$

The differential of the bond price under the original probabilities is

$$\frac{dP(r(s),\tau)}{P(r(s),\tau)} = \left[-B(\tau)a(\bar{r} - r(s)) + \frac{1}{2}B(\tau)^2\sigma^2 \right] ds - B(\tau)\sigma\, dW^\lambda(s)$$

$$= \left[-B(\tau)a(\bar{r} - r(s)) + \frac{1}{2}B(\tau)^2\sigma^2 \right] ds - B(\tau)\sigma\, (dW(s) + \lambda\, ds)$$

$$= \left[-B(\tau)a(b - r(s)) + \frac{1}{2}B(\tau)^2\sigma^2 \right] ds - B(\tau)\sigma\, dW(s)$$

7.3   The Risk-adjusted Dynamics as Primitives

In the development of the Vasicek model above, we started with the dynamics of the interest rate in terms of a process W which is a Wiener process under the true probability measure P. We added information about the price of risk λ, and specifically we assumed λ to be a constant. This corresponds to taking the state price process under the true probabilities as a primitive.

Based on this information, we used Girsanov's theorem to construct a risk-adjusted probability measure Q and a process W^λ which is a Wiener process under Q. We expressed the dynamics of the interest rate in terms of W^λ and proceeded to calculate the prices of zero-coupon bonds as conditional risk-adjusted expectations of their discounted payoff. All the calculations were done in terms of Q and W^λ except towards the end where we wanted to calculate the dynamics of the bond prices under the true probabilities. At that point, we reintroduced the original Wiener process W.

It is common to specify models of the term structure of interest rates in a different way, by starting from the risk-adjusted dynamics. You specify the dynamics of the interest rate in terms of a process $\hat{W}$ which is assumed already to be a Wiener process under the risk-adjusted probabilities (and which corresponds to W^λ above). Then you calculate the prices of zero-coupon bonds and other claims by calculating the conditional risk-adjusted expectations of their discounted payoff. You do not need any information about the prices of risk λ in order to do this.

In the Vasicek model, you would specify the interest rate process directly as

$$r(t) = \bar{r} + e^{-at}(r_0 - \bar{r}) + \sigma e^{-at} \int_0^t e^{au} \, d\hat{W}(u)$$

or

$$dr = a(\bar{r} - r) \, dt + \sigma \, d\hat{W}$$

with initial condition $r(0) = r_0$. The formula for the price $P(r(s), t - s)$ of a zero-coupon bond maturing at a fixed time t can be calculated solely on the basis of this information. Its risk-neutral dynamics will be

$$\frac{dP(r(s), t - s)}{P(r(s), t - s)} = r(s) \, ds - \sigma B(t - s) \, d\hat{W}(s)$$

Similarly, the risk-neutral dynamics of the price $P(r(s), \tau)$ of a bond with a fixed time τ to maturity will be

$$\frac{dP(r(s), \tau)}{P(r(s), \tau)} = \left[-B(\tau)a(\bar{r} - r(s)) + \frac{1}{2}B(\tau)^2\sigma^2 \right] ds - B(\tau)\sigma \, d\hat{W}(s)$$

However, if you now want to calculate the dynamics of prices under the true probabilities, then you need the prices of risk λ. Let us assume that λ is a constant. Then the process W defined by

$$W(t) = \hat{W}^{-\lambda}(t) = \hat{W}(t) - \lambda t$$

is a Wiener process under the true probability measure P (corresponding to the process W above). Define the parameter b by

$$b = \bar{r} + \sigma\lambda/a$$

Then the differential of the price of a bond maturing at a fixed time t will be

$$\frac{dP(r(s), t - s)}{P(r(s), t - s)} = (r(s) - a(b - \bar{r})B(t - s)) \, ds - \sigma B(t - s) \, dW(s)$$

and the differential of the price of a bond maturing with a fixed time τ to maturity will be

$$\frac{dP(r(s), \tau)}{P(r(s), \tau)} = \left[-B(\tau)a(b - r(s)) + \frac{1}{2}B(\tau)^2\sigma^2 \right] ds - B(\tau)\sigma \, dW(s)$$

Often, models of the term structure of interest rates are used mainly for pricing purposes, and the values of their parameters are inferred from a procedure of calibration to currently observed prices rather than from statistical estimation. This is one reason why it is common to express such models directly in terms of the risk-neutral dynamics without specifying the prices of risk.

For the rest of this chapter, we shall take the point of view of specifying the models directly in terms of a risk-adjusted Wiener process $\hat{W}$.

The parameter $\bar{r}$ will be treated as an exogenous parameter. This implies that we can perform comparative statics analyses of changes in $\bar{r}$.

One of the most remarkable results of such analyses is that the risk-adjusted stochastic differential of the bond price with fixed maturity date t is unaffected by the risk-adjusted mean reversion level $\bar{r}$. The mean reversion level does affect the distribution of the initial value $P(r(s), s; t)$ of the bond at time s, but given this value, it does not affect the relative drift and dispersion of the bond price. The mean reversion level affects the distribution of interest rates well into the future, but because the bond has a fixed maturity date, no new interest rates are taken into account as calendar time goes forward.

Recall that in the Black–Scholes model, the risk-adjusted dynamics of the stock price are unaffected by the relative drift μ of the stock price under the original probabilities, and, hence, the prices of contingent claims are independent of μ. This phenomenon is not analogous to the one we are considering here, because here we are already working with the risk-adjusted probabilities.

Unlike a bond with a fixed maturity date t, a bond with a fixed time τ to maturity has a risk-adjusted stochastic differential which is affected by $\bar{r}$:

$$\frac{dP(r(s), \tau)}{P(r(s), \tau)} = \left[-B(\tau)a(\bar{r} - r(s)) + \frac{1}{2}B(\tau)^2\sigma^2 \right] ds - B(\tau)\sigma \, d\hat{W}(s)$$

The higher the mean reversion level, the lower will be the drift of the bond. As calendar time s goes forward by an instant, a new interest rate occurring at time $s + \tau$ from now will affect the bond price. The higher $\bar{r}$ is, the higher will $r(s + \tau)$ tend to be, and the lower will be the drift of the bond price.

7.4   The Vasicek Model: Forward Rates

The functions

$$B(\tau) = \frac{1}{a}\left(1 - e^{-a\tau}\right)$$

$$v(\tau) = \frac{\sigma^2}{2a^3}\left(4e^{-a\tau} - e^{-2a\tau} + 2a\tau - 3\right)$$

and

$$A(\tau) = (\tau - B(\tau))\bar{r} - \frac{1}{2}v(\tau)$$

are continuously differentiable with

$$B'(\tau) = e^{-a\tau}$$

$$v'(\tau) = \frac{\sigma^2}{2a^3}\left(-4ae^{-a\tau} + 2ae^{-2a\tau} + 2a\right)$$

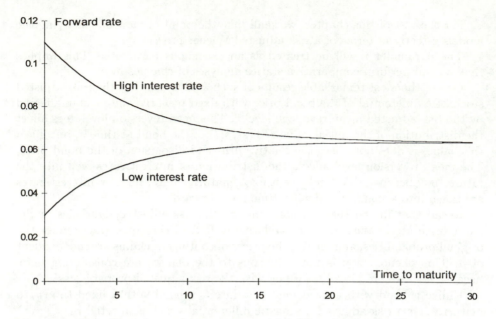

FIG. 7.4. Two forward rate curves with $r(0) = 0.11$ and $r(0) = 0.03$

$$= \frac{\sigma^2}{a^2} \left(-2e^{-a\tau} + e^{-2a\tau} + 1\right)$$
$$= B(\tau)^2 \sigma^2$$

and

$$A'(\tau) = \left(1 - e^{-a\tau}\right) \bar{r} - \frac{1}{2}v'(\tau) = \left(1 - e^{-a\tau}\right) \bar{r} - \frac{1}{2}B(\tau)^2 \sigma^2$$

Hence, the bond price function $P(s;t)$ is continuously differentiable with respect to t. The instantaneous forward rates are

$$f(s;t) = -\frac{\partial}{\partial t} \ln P(s;t)$$
$$= A'(t - s) + B'(t - s)r(s)$$
$$= \left(1 - e^{-a(t-s)}\right) \bar{r} - \frac{1}{2}v'(t - s) + e^{-a(t-s)}r(s)$$
$$= f(r(s), t - s)$$

where $f(r, \tau)$ is the function

$$f(r, \tau) = \left(1 - e^{-a\tau}\right) \bar{r} - \frac{1}{2}v'(\tau) + e^{-a\tau} r$$

The forward rate is an affine function of the interest rate, and it is normally distributed.

Figure 7.4 shows the forward rate curves corresponding to the price curves in Fig. 7.2. The parameters are the same in the two figures. The lower forward rate curve corresponds to an initial interest rate of $r(0) = 0.11$, and the higher curve corresponds to $r(0) = 0.03$. Time to maturity, τ, is on the horizontal axis, and the instantaneous forward rate with that time to maturity and with face value one is measured along the vertical axis.

Recall that the risk-adjusted conditional expectation of the future interest rate is

$$E_Q(r(t) \mid \mathcal{F}_s) = e^{-a(t-s)}r(s) + \left(1 - e^{-a(t-s)}\right)\bar{r}$$

Hence,

$$f(s;t) = E_Q(r(t) \mid \mathcal{F}_s) - \frac{1}{2}v'(t-s)$$

or

$$E_Q(r(t) \mid \mathcal{F}_s) = f(s;t) + \frac{1}{2}v'(t-s)$$

The term

$$\frac{1}{2}v'(t-s) = \frac{\sigma^2}{2a^2}\left(-2e^{-a(t-s)} + e^{-2a(t-s)} + 1\right) = \frac{1}{2}B(t-s)^2\sigma^2$$

can be interpreted as a *forward rate risk premium*. Because the future interest rate is random, its expectation exceeds the forward rate, which is known, by this forward rate risk premium.

Note that we define the forward rate risk premium as the difference between the expected interest rate and the forward rate, where the expected interest rate is calculated using the risk-adjusted probabilities. A risk premium calculated using the true probabilities would be a different concept.

The forward rate risk premium is an increasing function of the instantaneous standard deviation σ of the interest rate. It is also an increasing function of the time to maturity, with the following limits:

$$\frac{1}{2}B(\tau)^2\sigma^2 \to 0 \quad \text{as} \quad \tau \to 0$$

and

$$\frac{1}{2}B(\tau)^2\sigma^2 \to \frac{\sigma^2}{2a^2} \quad \text{as} \quad \tau \to \infty$$

These limits are independent of the initial interest rate. In Fig. 7.4, the risk premia in the long forward rates converge to

$$\frac{\sigma^2}{2a^2} = \frac{0.02^2}{2 \times 0.18^2} = 0.0062$$

The forward rate is a decreasing function of σ. The partial derivative of the forward rate with respect to σ is

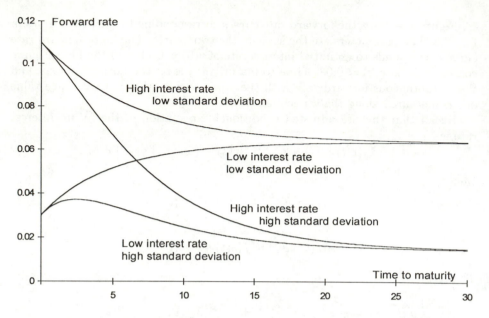

FIG. 7.5. Four forward rate curves with $\sigma = 0.02$ or $\sigma = 0.06$

$$\frac{\partial f(r,\tau)}{\partial \sigma} = -\sigma B(t-s)^2 = -\frac{\sigma}{a^2}\left(-2e^{-a\tau} + e^{-2a\tau} + 1\right)$$

which is negative for $\tau > 0$. It is a decreasing function of τ (meaning that it becomes more and more negative as τ gets larger).

When considering the effect of σ on the forward rates, recall that the risk-adjusted mean reversion parameter $\bar{r}$ is taken as exogenous. Hence, it is unaffected by changes in σ.

The effect of σ is illustrated in Fig. 7.5. It shows four forward rate curves conditional on two different initial interest rates, $r(0) = 0.03$ and $r(0) = 0.11$, and two different standard deviations, $\sigma = 0.02$ and $\sigma = 0.06$. For each value of the initial interest rate, the higher curve corresponds to $\sigma = 0.02$ and the lower curve corresponds to $\sigma = 0.06$. The figure is similar to Fig. 7.4, except that the latter shows forward rate curves for only one standard deviation, $\sigma = 0.2$. The other parameters are the same in the two figures. In particular, the risk-adjusted mean reversion level for the interest rate is in all cases $\bar{r} = 0.07$.

The limits of the forward rate as a function of time to maturity are

$$f(r,\tau) \to r \quad \text{as} \quad \tau \to 0$$

and

$$f(r,\tau) \to \bar{r} - \frac{\sigma^2}{2a^2} \quad \text{as} \quad \tau \to \infty$$

In Fig. 7.4, the long forward rates converge to

$$\lim_{\tau \to \infty} f(r,\tau) = \bar{r} - \frac{\sigma^2}{2a^2} = 0.07 - 0.0062 = 0.0638$$

which is just a little bit below the risk-adjusted mean reversion level $\bar{r} = 0.07$ of the interest rate.

The effects of $\bar{r}$ and r on the forward rates $f(r,\tau)$ are described by the following partial derivatives and limits:

$$\frac{\partial f(r,\tau)}{\partial \bar{r}} = 1 - e^{-a\tau} > 0$$

$$\frac{\partial^2 f(r,\tau)}{\partial \tau \partial \bar{r}} = ae^{-a\tau} > 0$$

$$\frac{\partial f(r,\tau)}{\partial \bar{r}} \to 1 \quad \text{as} \quad \tau \to \infty$$

$$\frac{\partial f(r,\tau)}{\partial \bar{r}} \to 0 \quad \text{as} \quad \tau \to 0$$

$$\frac{\partial f(r,\tau)}{\partial r} = e^{-a\tau} > 0$$

$$\frac{\partial^2 f(r,\tau)}{\partial \tau \partial r} = -ae^{-a\tau} < 0$$

$$\frac{\partial f(r,\tau)}{\partial r} \to 0 \quad \text{as} \quad \tau \to \infty$$

$$\frac{\partial f(r,\tau)}{\partial r} \to 1 \quad \text{as} \quad \tau \to 0$$

It is clear that

$$\frac{\partial f(r,\tau)}{\partial \bar{r}} + \frac{\partial f(r,\tau)}{\partial r} = 1$$

and

$$\frac{\partial^2 f(r,\tau)}{\partial \tau \partial \bar{r}} + \frac{\partial^2 f(r,\tau)}{\partial \tau \partial r} = 0$$

An increase in $\bar{r}$ raises all the forward rates. The effect is larger the longer the maturity, it is almost one-for-one for very long maturities, and it is almost zero for very short maturities. An increase in the initial interest rate r will also raise all the forward rates. This effect will be stronger for shorter maturities, it will be almost one-for-one for very short maturities, and it will be almost zero for very long maturities. An equal increase or decrease in both r and $\bar{r}$ will make all forward rates move up or down by the same amount. The forward curve will shift up or down in a parallel manner.

Since the interest rate is normally distributed, it has a positive probability of becoming negative at any point in time. This is a significant drawback of the Vasicek model which it shares with the other Gaussian models of the interest rate. In practice, it may not be too much of a concern so long as a reasonable range of

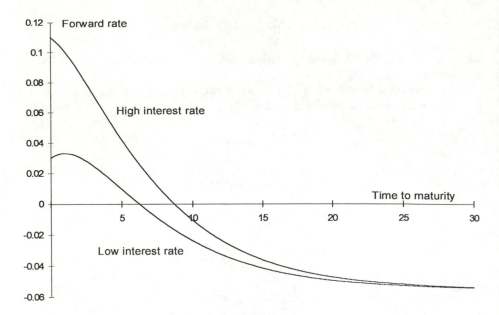

FIG. 7.6. Two forward rate curves with high σ

parameter values are chosen. For example, the forward rate curves shown in Fig. 7.4 and Fig. 7.5 look reasonable enough. However, if the standard deviation σ increases, then the forward rates will decrease, and eventually they will become negative. This is illustrated in Fig. 7.6.

Figure 7.6, like Fig. 7.4, shows two forward rate curves conditional on two different initial interest rates, $r(0) = 0.03$ and $r(0) = 0.11$. The figures are identical except for the value of σ: it is $\sigma = 0.09$ in Fig. 7.6 versus $\sigma = 0.02$ in Fig. 7.4.

Negative forward rates are equivalent to a bond price that is increasing as a function of the time to maturity. Figure 7.7 shows the bond prices that correspond to the forward rates in Fig. 7.6. The parameters in Fig. 7.7 are the same as in Fig. 7.6.

The reason why forward rates can become negative when the standard deviation is high is that the probability of negative interest rates is high. Figure 7.8 illustrates that for some parameter values, and in particular for high values of σ, there is a significant probability that the interest rate will become negative.

Figure 7.8 shows six sample paths of the process r. It is analogous to Fig. 7.1. The speed of adjustment is $a = 0.18$ and the long-run mean is $\bar{r} = 0.07$ as in Fig. 7.1, but the standard deviation parameter is $\sigma = 0.09$ in Fig. 7.8, compared to $\sigma = 0.02$ in Fig. 7.1. The three horizontal lines show the long-run mean and the long-run mean plus/minus one long-run standard deviation.

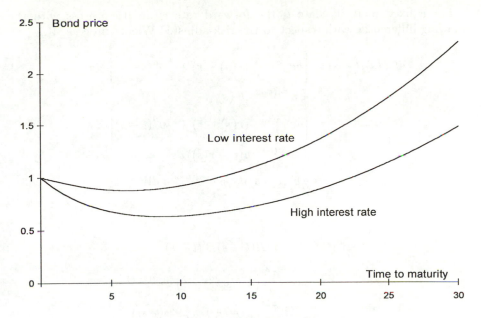

FIG. 7.7. Two price curves with high σ

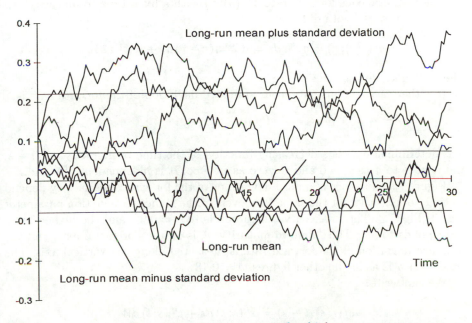

FIG. 7.8. Interest rate paths: high σ

For a fixed maturity date t, the forward rate is an Itô process with the following differential with respect to the risk-adjusted Wiener process $\hat{W}$:

$$df(r(s), t-s) = \left[ae^{-a(t-s)}(r(s) - \bar{r}) + \frac{1}{2}v''(t-s) \right] ds$$
$$+ e^{-a(t-s)} dr(s)$$
$$= \left[ae^{-a(t-s)}(r(s) - \bar{r}) + \frac{1}{2}v''(t-s) \right] ds$$
$$+ e^{-a(t-s)} a(\bar{r} - r(s)) ds + e^{-a(t-s)} \sigma d\hat{W}$$
$$= \frac{1}{2}v''(t-s) ds + e^{-a(t-s)} \sigma d\hat{W}$$

The drift is

$$\frac{1}{2}v''(t-s) = \sigma^2 B(t-s) B'(t-s)$$
$$= \frac{\sigma^2}{a} \left(1 - e^{-a(t-s)} \right) e^{-a(t-s)}$$
$$= \frac{\sigma^2}{a} \left(e^{-a(t-s)} - e^{-2a(t-s)} \right)$$

Note that it is independent of $\bar{r}$.

The instantaneous forward rate $f(r(s), \tau)$ with a fixed time to maturity τ is also an Itô process, with differential

$$df(r(s), \tau) = e^{-a\tau} dr = e^{-a\tau} a(r - \bar{r}) ds + e^{-a\tau} \sigma d\hat{W}$$

The drift does depend on $\bar{r}$.

In either case, the instantaneous standard deviation of the forward rate is

$$e^{-a(t-s)} \sigma = e^{-a\tau} \sigma$$

It is deterministic. It is a decreasing function of the time to maturity $\tau = t - s$, and it goes to σ as $\tau \to 0$ and to zero as $\tau \to \infty$. It is independent of r and $\bar{r}$.

Figure 7.9 shows the standard deviations of the forward rates as they depend on time to maturity, for the same two levels of the standard deviation parameter σ as in Fig. 7.3. The lower curve corresponds to $\sigma = 0.02$, and the higher curve corresponds to $\sigma = 0.06$. Time to maturity, τ, is on the horizontal axis, and the standard deviation of the forward rate is measured along the vertical axis. The parameter a is as in the other figures, $a = 0.18$.

We can write

$$df(r(s), t-s) = \alpha^f(s; t) ds + \beta^f(s; t) d\hat{W}$$

where the drift is

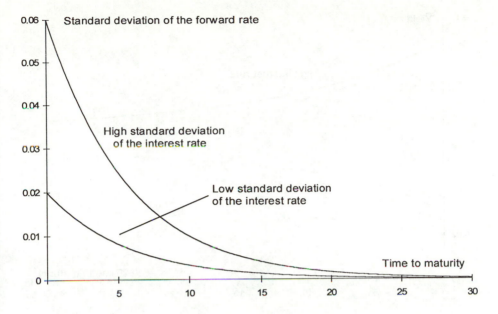

FIG. 7.9. Standard deviations of the forward rates

$$\alpha^f(s;t) = \frac{\sigma^2}{a}\left(e^{-a(t-s)} - e^{-2a(t-s)}\right)$$

and the dispersion coefficient is

$$\beta^f(s;t) = e^{-a(t-s)}\sigma$$

The general result of Heath, Jarrow, and Morton [47, 1989], [48, 1992] says that

$$\alpha^f(s;t) = \beta^f(s;t)\int_s^t \beta^f(s;v)\,dv$$

This can easily be verified in the Vasicek model:

$$\beta^f(s;t)\int_s^t \beta^f(s;v)\,dv = \sigma e^{-a(t-s)}\int_s^t \sigma e^{-a(v-s)}\,dv$$

$$= \frac{\sigma^2}{a}e^{-a(t-s)}\left[-e^{-a(v-s)}\right]_{v=s}^t$$

$$= \frac{\sigma^2}{a}e^{-a(t-s)}\left(-e^{-a(t-s)} + 1\right)$$

$$= \frac{\sigma^2}{a}\left(e^{-a(t-s)} - e^{-2a(t-s)}\right)$$

$$= \alpha^f(s;t)$$

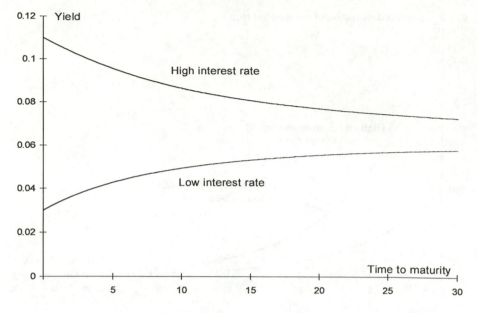

FIG. 7.10. Two yield curves with $r(0) = 0.11$ and $r(0) = 0.03$

7.5   The Vasicek Model: Yields

The continuously compounded *yield* at time s of the zero-coupon bond maturing at t is

$$R(s;t) = \frac{1}{t-s} \ln\left(\frac{1}{P(r(s), t-s)}\right)$$
$$= \frac{1}{t-s}[A(t-s) + B(t-s)r(s)]$$
$$= R(r(s), t-s)$$

where R is the function

$$R(r,\tau) = \frac{1}{\tau}\ln\left(\frac{1}{P(r,\tau)}\right) = \frac{1}{\tau}\left[m(r,\tau) - \frac{1}{2}v(\tau)\right] = \frac{1}{\tau}[A(\tau) + B(\tau)r]$$

The yield at time s is an affine function of the interest rate $r(s)$ at time s, and it is normally distributed.

Figure 7.10 shows the yield curves corresponding to the bond prices in Fig. 7.2 and the forward rates in Fig. 7.4. The parameters are the same in all three figures. The higher yield curve corresponds to an initial interest rate of $r(0) = 0.11$, and the lower yield curve corresponds to $r(0) = 0.03$. Time to maturity, τ, is on the horizontal axis, and the yield on zero-coupon bonds with that time to maturity is measured along the vertical axis.

The yield can be related to the expectation of the average of the future interest rate over the life of the bond. The average future interest rate over the time interval $[s, t]$ is

$$r_a = \frac{1}{t-s} \int_s^t r(u)\, du = \frac{1}{t-s} I(s; t)$$

It equals the continuously compounded rate of return on the money market account:

$$\frac{1}{t-s} \ln\left(\frac{M(t)}{M(s)}\right) = \frac{1}{t-s} I(s; t) = r_a$$

It is normally distributed conditionally on information at time s, with mean

$$E_Q(r_a \mid \mathcal{F}_s) = \frac{1}{t-s} E_Q(I(s; t) \mid \mathcal{F}_s) = \frac{1}{t-s} m(t-s)$$

and variance

$$\mathrm{var}_Q(r_a \mid \mathcal{F}_s) = \frac{1}{(t-s)^2} \mathrm{var}_Q(I(s; t) \mid \mathcal{F}_s) = \frac{1}{(t-s)^2} v(t-s)$$

Hence,

$$R(r, t-s) = -\frac{1}{t-s}\left[-m(r, t-s) + \frac{1}{2}v(t-s)\right]$$

$$= E_Q(r_a \mid \mathcal{F}_s) - \frac{1}{2(t-s)} v(t-s)$$

or

$$E_Q(r_a \mid \mathcal{F}_s) = R(r, t-s) + \frac{1}{2(t-s)} v(t-s)$$

The term

$$\frac{1}{2(t-s)} v(t-s) = \frac{t-s}{2} \mathrm{var}_Q(r_a \mid \mathcal{F}_s)$$

$$= \frac{\sigma^2}{4a^3(t-s)}\left(4e^{-a(t-s)} - e^{-2a(t-s)} + 2a(t-s) - 3\right)$$

can be interpreted as a *yield risk premium*. Because the rate of return on the money market account is random, the expectation of the average return exceeds the yield on the bond, which is known, by this yield risk premium. The yield risk premium is an increasing function of the instantaneous standard deviation σ of the interest rate.

Recall that the yield equals the average forward rate:

$$R(s;t) = \frac{1}{t-s} \int_s^t f(s;u)\,du$$

and that each forward rate differs from the risk-adjusted expectation of the corresponding future interest rate by a forward rate risk premium:

$$f(s;u) = E_Q(r(u) \mid \mathcal{F}_s) - \frac{1}{2}B(u-s)^2\sigma^2 = E_Q(r(u) \mid \mathcal{F}_s) - \frac{1}{2}v'(u-s)$$

Accordingly, the yield risk premium equals the average of the forward rate risk premia over the life of the bond:

$$\frac{1}{2(t-s)}v(t-s) = \frac{1}{t-s}\int_s^t \frac{1}{2}v'(u-s)\,du$$

The yield risk premium is in a sense an effect of Jensen's inequality and the convexity of the exponential function. Since r_a is normally distributed,

$$\begin{aligned}
\exp[-(t-s)R(t;s)] &= P(t;s) \\
&= E_Q[\exp[-(t-s)r_a] \mid \mathcal{F}_s] \\
&= \exp\left[-(t-s)E_Q(r_a \mid \mathcal{F}_s) + \frac{(t-s)^2}{2}\mathrm{var}_Q(r_a \mid \mathcal{F}_s)\right] \\
&> \exp[-(t-s)E_Q(r_a \mid \mathcal{F}_s)]
\end{aligned}$$

and hence

$$R(t;s) = E_Q(r_a \mid \mathcal{F}_s) - \frac{t-s}{2}\mathrm{var}_Q(r_a \mid \mathcal{F}_s) < E_Q(r_a \mid \mathcal{F}_s)$$

We have seen that bonds are not priced in such a way that their yield equals the risk-adjusted expected average future interest rate or the risk-adjusted expected continuously compounded rate of return on the money market account.

One might conjecture, alternatively, that bonds are priced in such a way that equal values invested in a bond and in the money market account would be expected to grow to the same future value, when expectations are calculated using the risk-adjusted probabilities. In other words, the expected growth factor for the bond would equal the expected growth factor for the money market account, or the discretely compounded yield on the bond would equal the expected discretely compounded rate of return on the money market account.

However, this is not true. Since

$$P(r(s), t-s) = \exp\left[-m(r(s), t-s) + \frac{1}{2}v(t-s)\right]$$

the expected factor by which the value of the bond will grow is

$$\frac{1}{P(r(s), t-s)} = \exp\left[m(r(s), t-s) - \frac{1}{2}v(t-s)\right]$$

The expected factor by which the value of the money market account will grow over the life of the bond is

$$E_Q\left(\frac{M(t)}{M(s)} \mid \mathcal{F}_s\right) = E_Q(\exp I(s; t) \mid \mathcal{F}_s)$$

$$= \exp\left[E_Q(I(s; t) \mid \mathcal{F}_s) + \frac{1}{2}\text{var}_Q(I(s; t) \mid \mathcal{F}_s)\right]$$

$$= \exp\left[m(r(s), t-s) + \frac{1}{2}v(t-s)\right]$$

$$= \frac{1}{P(r(s), t-s)} e^{v(t-s)}$$

The expected growth factor for the money market account over the life of the bond is larger than the expected growth factor for the bond. This is so because over this time period, the money market account is a risky asset, while the bond is riskless. Instantaneously, the bond and the money market account will have the same expected rate of return r, but over discrete time periods, their risk-adjusted expected rates of return differ.

Proposition 7.4 *The function $B(\tau)/\tau$ is a strictly decreasing function of τ with limits*

$$\frac{B(\tau)}{\tau} \to 1 \quad as \quad \tau \to 0$$

and

$$\frac{B(\tau)}{\tau} \to 0 \quad as \quad \tau \to \infty$$

The function $v(\tau)/\tau$ is a strictly increasing function of τ with limits

$$\frac{v(\tau)}{\tau} \to 0 \quad as \quad \tau \to 0$$

and

$$\frac{v(\tau)}{\tau} \to \frac{\sigma^2}{a^2} \quad as \quad \tau \to \infty$$

Exercise 7.2 *Prove Proposition 7.4.*

It follows from Proposition 7.4 that the yield risk premium is a strictly increasing function of time to maturity, with limits

$$\frac{1}{2\tau}v(\tau) \to 0 \quad as \quad \tau \to 0$$

and

$$\frac{1}{2\tau}v(\tau) \to \frac{\sigma^2}{2a^2} \quad as \quad \tau \to \infty$$

These limits of the yield risk premium are the same as the limits of the forward rate risk premium.

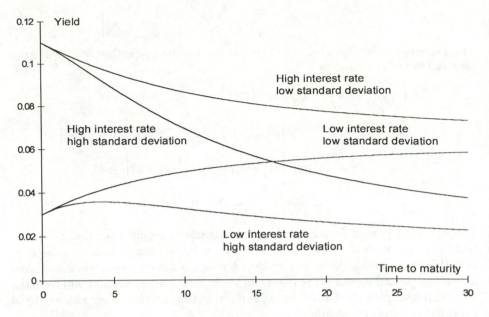

FIG. 7.11. Four yield curves with $\sigma = 0.02$ or $\sigma = 0.06$

The standard deviation σ affects the yields of all zero-coupon bonds and not only the limiting yield at very long maturities. Keeping $\bar{r}$ fixed, the partial derivative is

$$\frac{\partial R}{\partial \sigma} = -\frac{1}{2\tau}\frac{\partial v(\tau)}{\partial \sigma} = -\frac{1}{2\tau}\frac{2\sigma}{2a^3}\left(4e^{-a\tau} - e^{-2a\tau} + 2a\tau - 3\right) = -\frac{1}{\tau\sigma}v(\tau)$$

which is negative for $\tau > 0$ and is a strictly decreasing function of τ. This effect is illustrated in Fig. 7.11.

Figure 7.11 shows four yield curves conditional on two different initial interest rates, $r(0) = 0.03$ and $r(0) = 0.11$, and two different standard deviations, $\sigma = 0.02$ and $\sigma = 0.06$. For each value of the initial interest rate, the higher curve corresponds to $\sigma = 0.02$ and the lower curve corresponds to $\sigma = 0.06$. The figure is similar to Fig. 7.10, except that the latter shows yield curves for only one standard deviation, $\sigma = 0.2$. The other parameters are the same in the two figures. In particular, the risk-adjusted mean reversion level for the interest rate is in all cases $\bar{r} = 0.07$.

It follows from the limits of the yield risk premium that the limits of $R(r, \tau)$, for fixed r, are

$$R(r, \tau) \to r \quad \text{as} \quad \tau \to 0, \tau > 0$$

and

$$R(r, \tau) \to \bar{r} - \frac{\sigma^2}{2a^2} \quad \text{as} \quad \tau \to \infty$$

Now let us turn to the effect of r and $\bar{r}$ on bond yields. The relevant partial derivatives and limits are computed in Exercise 7.3 below. An increase in $\bar{r}$ raises the yield and lowers the price of a zero-coupon bond. The impact on the yield is larger the longer the maturity of the bond, it is almost one-for-one for very long bonds, and it is close to zero for very short bonds.

Think of the yield as the expected average interest rate over the life of the bond less an adjustment for the variance. The variance is unaffected by an increase in $\bar{r}$, but the expectation increases. The expected interest rate far in the future increases more than the expected interest rate in the near future, and so the expected average interest rate over a long period of time increases more than the expected average over a short period.

An increase in the initial interest rate r will raise the yields on all zero-coupon bonds. This effect will be stronger for bonds with shorter maturities, it will be close to zero for very long bonds, and it will be close to one-for-one for very short bonds.

Again, this makes sense because the expected average interest rate over the life of the bond goes up while the variance is unchanged. The expected average interest rate over a short time period goes up more than the expected average over a long period.

An equal increase or decrease in both r and $\bar{r}$ will make all zero-coupon yields move up or down by the same amount. The yield curve will shift up or down in a parallel manner.

These effects are similar to the effects of $\bar{r}$ and r on the bond yields.

Exercise 7.3 *Calculate the following partial derivatives of the zero-coupon bond yield and verify the signs and limits:*

$$\frac{\partial R(r,\tau)}{\partial \bar{r}} > 0$$

$$\frac{\partial^2 R(r,\tau)}{\partial \tau \partial \bar{r}} > 0$$

$$\frac{\partial R(r,\tau)}{\partial \bar{r}} \to 1 \quad as \quad \tau \to \infty$$

$$\frac{\partial R(r,\tau)}{\partial \bar{r}} \to 0 \quad as \quad \tau \to 0$$

$$\frac{\partial R(r,\tau)}{\partial r} > 0$$

$$\frac{\partial^2 R(r,\tau)}{\partial \tau \partial r} < 0$$

$$\frac{\partial R(r,\tau)}{\partial r} \to 0 \quad as \quad \tau \to \infty$$

$$\frac{\partial R(r,\tau)}{\partial r} \to 1 \quad as \quad \tau \to 0$$

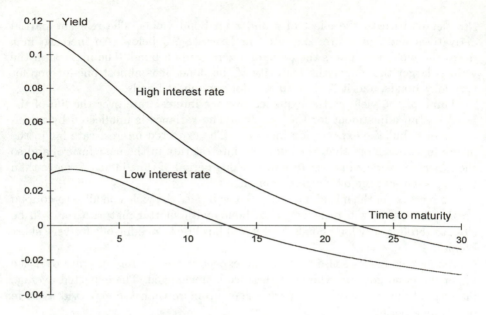

FIG. 7.12. Two yield curves with high σ

Also verify that

$$\frac{\partial R(r,\tau)}{\partial \bar{r}} + \frac{\partial R(r,\tau)}{\partial r} = 1$$

and

$$\frac{\partial^2 R(r,\tau)}{\partial \tau \partial \bar{r}} + \frac{\partial^2 R(r,\tau)}{\partial \tau \partial r} = 0$$

Just like negative forward rates are possible in the Vasicek model, so are negative yields. Figure 7.12 shows the yield curves corresponding to the forward rate curves in Fig. 7.6 and the price curves in Fig. 7.7. The parameters are the same in all three figures.

Consider the yield $R(r(s), t - s)$ on a zero-coupon bond that matures at a fixed time t, with s as the time variable, $0 \leq s \leq t$. By Itô's lemma, the dispersion of the process $R(r(s), t - s)$ equals the negative of the dispersion of the process $P(r(s), t - s)$ divided by $t - s$, or

$$\frac{B(t - s)\sigma}{t - s} = \frac{\sigma}{a(t - s)}\left(1 - e^{-a(t-s)}\right)$$

Since this is positive, it is equal to the instantaneous standard deviation of the yield $R(r(s), t - s)$. It is independent of the current interest rate $r(s)$ and of the mean reversion level $\bar{r}$.

Figure 7.13 shows the instantaneous standard deviations of the zero-coupon yields as they depend on time to maturity, for the same two levels of the standard

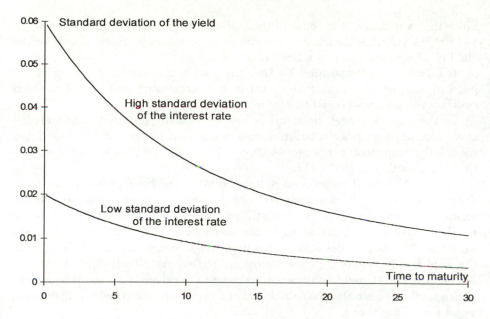

FIG. 7.13. Standard deviations of the bond yields

deviation parameter σ as in Fig. 7.3. The lower curve corresponds to $\sigma = 0.02$, and the higher curve corresponds to $\sigma = 0.06$. Time to maturity, τ, is on the horizontal axis, and the standard deviation of the yield is measured along the vertical axis. The parameter a is as in the other figures, $a = 0.18$.

It will follow from Exercise 7.9 in Section 7.7 that the stochastic differential of the process $R(r(s), t - s)$ is

$$
\begin{aligned}
& dR(r(s), t - s) \\
& = \frac{R(r(s), t - s) + \frac{1}{2}B(t - s)^2\sigma^2 - r(s)}{t - s}\, ds + \frac{B(t - s)\sigma}{t - s}\, d\hat{W}(s)
\end{aligned}
$$

Alternatively, consider the yield $R(r(s), \tau)$ on a zero-coupon bond with a fixed time τ to maturity. The differential of the process

$$
R(r(s), \tau) = \frac{1}{\tau}[A(\tau) + B(\tau)r(s)]
$$

is

$$
dR(r(s), \tau) = \frac{B(\tau)}{\tau}\, dr(s) = \frac{B(\tau)}{\tau}a(\bar{r} - r(s))\, ds + \frac{B(\tau)}{\tau}\sigma\, d\hat{W}(s)
$$

The dispersion is

$$
\frac{B(\tau)\sigma}{\tau} = \frac{\sigma}{a\tau}\left(1 - e^{-a\tau}\right)
$$

Since this is positive, it is equal to the instantaneous standard deviation of the yield $R(r(s), \tau)$. It is the same as the standard deviation we found above for the yield of a bond maturing at a fixed time $t = s + \tau$.

It follows from Proposition 7.4 that the standard deviation $\sigma B(\tau)/\tau$ of the yield of a bond with time τ to maturity is a decreasing function of τ which converges to σ as $\tau \to 0$ and to zero as $\tau \to \infty$.

In the Vasicek model, bond prices are lognormally distributed and always stay positive. Bond price volatilities make sense, and we have in fact calculated the relative dispersion of the process $P(r(t), T - t)$ as $-B(T - t)\sigma$, which implies that the volatility is $B(T - t)\sigma$.

On the other hand, interest rates, forward rates, and bond yields are normally distributed and may become negative. This implies that interest rate volatilities, forward rate volatilities, or yield volatilities do not make sense. Volatility is the absolute value of the relative dispersion coefficient. The volatility of the yield would be the standard deviation of the percentage change in the yield. But since the yield may be zero or negative, it does not make sense to calculate its percentage change, and therefore it does not make sense to calculate its volatility either. Instead, we calculate the absolute dispersion coefficients or standard deviations, as we have done above.

7.6   The Merton Model

In the Vasicek model, changes in the current interest rate move short forward rates and yields more than long forward rates and yields because of mean reversion.

In this section, we shall build the simplest possible model which has no mean reversion. Changes in the interest rate in this model will lead to parallel shifts in the forward rate curve and in the yield curve. The model will be parameterized by just two parameters.

Let $K = 1$, and let $\hat{W}$ be a one-dimensional Wiener process relative to a filtration F. We interpret $\hat{W}$ as a Wiener process under the risk-adjusted probabilities Q. Let r_0, α, and $\sigma > 0$ be constants.

In the *Merton model*, the interest rate process is assumed to be the generalized Wiener process given by

$$r(t) = r_0 + \alpha t + \sigma \hat{W}(t)$$

In differential form,

$$dr = \alpha \, dt + \sigma \, d\hat{W}$$

If $0 \leq s \leq t$, then

$$r(t) = r(s) + \alpha(t - s) + \sigma(\hat{W}(t) - \hat{W}(s))$$

The distribution of $r(t)$ given information at time s is normal with mean $r(s) + \alpha(t - s)$ and variance $\sigma^2(t - s)$. It is a function only of $r(s)$ and $t - s$.

The value of the money market account is

$$M(t) = \exp\left[\int_0^t r(u)\,du\right]$$

If $0 \le s \le t$, set

$$I(s;t) = \int_s^t r(u)\,du$$

Then

$$
\begin{aligned}
I(s;t) &= \int_s^t r(u)\,du \\
&= \int_s^t [r(s) + \alpha(u - s) + \sigma(\hat{W}(u) - \hat{W}(s)]\,du \\
&= r(s)(t - s) + \frac{1}{2}\alpha(t - s)^2 + \sigma\int_s^t (\hat{W}(u) - \hat{W}(s))\,du
\end{aligned}
$$

The integral term has conditional expectation zero. This can be seen by using the conditional Fubini theorem (Theorem B.28):

$$E\left[\int_s^t (\hat{W}(u) - \hat{W}(s))\,du \mid \mathcal{F}_s\right] = \int_s^t E[\hat{W}(u) - \hat{W}(s) \mid \mathcal{F}_s]\,du = 0$$

The integral term can be rewritten like this:

$$
\begin{aligned}
\int_s^t (\hat{W}(u) - \hat{W}(s))\,du &= \int_0^t \hat{W}(u)\,du - \int_0^s \hat{W}(u)\,du - (t - s)\hat{W}(s) \\
&= \int_0^t (t - u)\,d\hat{W}(u) - \int_0^s (s - u)\,d\hat{W}(u) - (t - s)\hat{W}(s)
\end{aligned}
$$

Given information at time s, $I(s;t)$ is normally distributed with conditional mean

$$E_Q[I(s;t) \mid \mathcal{F}_s] = r(s)(t - s) + \frac{1}{2}\alpha(t - s)^2$$

and conditional variance

$$
\begin{aligned}
\text{var}_Q[I(s;t) \mid \mathcal{F}_s] &= \sigma^2 \text{var}_Q\left(\int_0^t (t - u)\,d\hat{W}(u) \mid \mathcal{F}_s\right) \\
&= \sigma^2 \int_s^t (t - u)^2\,du \\
&= \frac{\sigma^2}{3}(t - s)^3
\end{aligned}
$$

Let $0 \le s \le t$. Since $-I(s;t)$ is normally distributed, we can use the formula for the expectation of a lognormally distributed random variable (Proposition 2.29) to calculate the value at time s of a zero-coupon bond maturing at time t:

$$P(s;t) = E_Q[\exp[-I(s;t)]|\mathcal{F}_s]$$

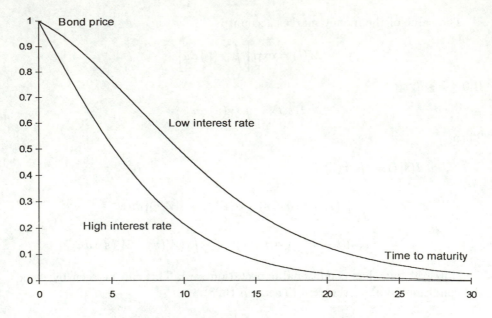

FIG. 7.14. Two bond price curves with $\sigma = 0.02$

$$= \exp\left[-r(s)(t-s) - \frac{1}{2}\alpha(t-s)^2 + \frac{\sigma^2}{6}(t-s)^3\right]$$
$$= P(r(s), t-s)$$

where P is the function

$$P(r, \tau) = \exp\left[-r\tau - \frac{1}{2}\alpha\tau^2 + \frac{\sigma^2}{6}\tau^3\right]$$

Define a function A by

$$A(\tau) = \frac{1}{2}\alpha\tau^2 - \frac{\sigma^2}{6}\tau^3$$

Then

$$P(r, \tau) = \exp[-A(\tau) - \tau r]$$

and the value at time s of a bond maturing at time t is

$$P(r(s), t-s) = \exp[-A(t-s) - (t-s)r]$$

Figures 7.14 and 7.15 each show two bond price curves corresponding to two initial interest rates $r(0) = 0.03$ and $r(0) = 0.11$. Time to maturity is measured along the horizontal axis, and the bond prices are measured along the vertical axis. The difference between the two figures is that the value of the standard deviation parameter is $\sigma = 0.02$ in Fig. 7.14 but $\sigma = 0.04$ in Fig. 7.15. In both figures, the drift parameter is $\alpha = 0.01$.

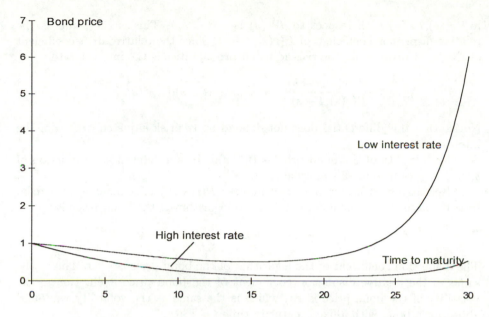

FIG. 7.15. Two bond price curves with $\sigma = 0.04$

The bond price curves in Fig. 7.14 seem plausible, but those in Fig. 7.15 do not. In Fig. 7.15, the bond price is not a decreasing function of time to maturity, and the curve corresponding to an initial interest rate of $r = 0.03$ even goes way above one.

In principle, the curves in Fig. 7.14 also have these unfortunate features, except that they are not visible because they occur only at times to maturity greater than 30 years. The model has the annoying feature that

$$P(r, \tau) \to \infty \quad \text{as} \quad \tau \to \infty$$

which implies that the prices of long zero-coupon bonds will always be above par. It appears from the figures that for some configurations of the parameters, and in particular for low values of σ, this may not be a serious problem.

The model of course satisfies *pull-to-par*:

$$P(r, t - s) \to 1 \quad \text{as} \quad s \to t$$

for fixed r, which is also evident from the figures, and with probability one,

$$P(r(s), t - s) \to 1 \quad \text{as} \quad s \to t$$

Since $r(s)$ is normally distributed, the price $P(r(s), t - s)$ of a zero-coupon bond is lognormally distributed.

Consider the price process $P(r(s), t - s)$ of a bond which matures at a fixed time t, with s as time parameter, $0 \le s \le t$. The dispersion coefficient of

$\ln P(r(s), t-s)$ with respect to $d\hat{W}(s)$ is $-(t-s)\sigma$. This is the same as the relative dispersion coefficient of $P(r(s), t-s)$. Since the relative drift coefficient of the bond price under the risk-adjusted probabilities is the interest rate,

$$\frac{dP(r(s), t-s)}{P(r(s), t-s)} = r(s)\,ds - (t-s)\sigma\,d\hat{W}(s)$$

Notice that this differential does not depend on the risk-adjusted drift α of the interest rate.

The volatility of the bond price is $(t-s)\sigma$. It is a deterministic function of s, and it goes to zero as s approaches t.

Alternatively, consider the price process $P(r(s), \tau)$ of a bond with a fixed time to maturity τ. The differential of the logarithm of the bond price is

$$d\ln P(r, \tau) = -\tau\,dr = -\tau\alpha\,ds - \tau\sigma\,d\hat{W}$$

The dispersion coefficient of the logarithm of the bond price is $-\tau\sigma$. This is the same as the relative dispersion coefficient of the bond price itself. Hence, the volatility of the bond price is $\tau\sigma$, which is the same as the volatility we found above for a bond with a fixed maturity time $t = s + \tau$.

The relative drift of the bond price equals the drift of the logarithm of the bond price plus a half times the square of the relative dispersion:

$$-\tau\alpha + \frac{1}{2}\tau^2\sigma^2$$

Hence,

$$\frac{dP(r, \tau)}{P(r, \tau)} = \left[-\tau\alpha + \frac{1}{2}\tau^2\sigma^2\right]ds - \tau\sigma\,d\hat{W}$$

As in the Vasicek model, the percentage dispersion coefficient is negative: a positive shock to $\hat{W}$ makes the interest rate go up and the bond price go down.

The function A is continuously differentiable with

$$A'(\tau) = \alpha\tau - \frac{1}{2}\sigma^2\tau^2$$

Hence, the function

$$\ln P(s; t) = \ln P(r(s), t-s) = -A(t-s) - (t-s)r(s)$$

is continuously differentiable. The forward rates are

$$\begin{aligned}f(s; t) &= -\frac{\partial}{\partial t}\ln P(s; t)\\ &= A'(t-s) + r(s)\\ &= r(s) + \alpha(t-s) - \frac{1}{2}\sigma^2(t-s)^2\end{aligned}$$

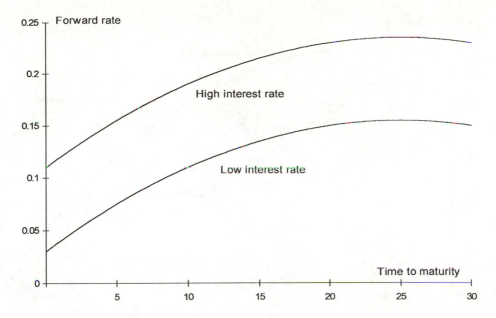

FIG. 7.16. Two forward rate curves with $\sigma = 0.02$

$$= f(r(s), t - s)$$

where $f(r, \tau)$ is the function

$$f(r, \tau) = r + \alpha\tau - \frac{1}{2}\sigma^2\tau^2$$

The forward rate is a quadratic function of the interest rate, and it is normally distributed. The coefficient of the interest rate is one, and, in particular, it is independent of the time τ to maturity. A change in the interest rate will make the forward rates at all maturities go up or down by the same amount. In other words, the forward rate curve shifts in a parallel manner.

Figures 7.16 and 7.17 show the forward rate curves corresponding to the bond price curves in Fig. 7.14 and Fig. 7.15, respectively. The standard deviation parameter is $\sigma = 0.02$ in Fig. 7.16 and $\sigma = 0.04$ in Fig. 7.17. The other parameters are the same in all four figures.

The risk-adjusted conditional expectation of the future interest rate is

$$E_Q(r(t) \mid \mathcal{F}_s) = r(s) + \alpha(t - s)$$

Hence,

$$f(s; t) = E_Q(r(t) \mid \mathcal{F}_s) - \frac{1}{2}\sigma^2(t - s)^2$$

or

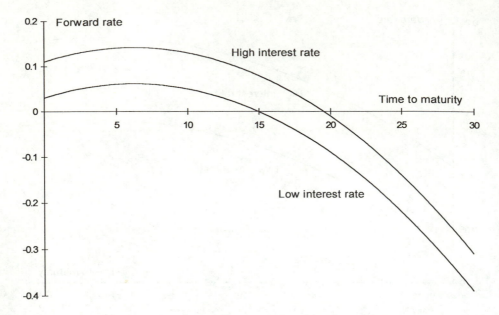

FIG. 7.17. Two forward rate curves with $\sigma = 0.04$

$$E_Q(r(t) \mid \mathcal{F}_s) = f(s;t) + \frac{1}{2}\sigma^2(t-s)^2$$

The *forward rate risk premium* is

$$\frac{1}{2}\sigma^2(t-s)^2$$

It is an increasing, parabolic function of the time to maturity $\tau = t - s$ of the forward contract. It goes to zero as the time to maturity $t - s$ goes to zero, and it goes to infinity as the time to maturity goes to infinity.

An increase in σ lowers all the forward rates. The effect is stronger at longer maturities. The partial derivative with respect to σ is

$$\frac{\partial f(r,\tau)}{\partial \sigma} = -\sigma\tau^2$$

It is negative, and it is a decreasing function of τ.

The forward rate converges to the initial interest rate as the time to maturity goes to zero, and it goes to minus infinity as time to maturity goes to infinity:

$$f(r,\tau) \to r \quad \text{as} \quad \tau \to 0$$

and

$$f(r,\tau) \to -\infty \quad \text{as} \quad \tau \to \infty$$

In particular, the forward rates will always be negative at very long maturities.

By contrast, in the Vasicek model, there is a range of configurations of the parameters (including the current interest rate) such that the forward rates will be positive at all maturities. The reason for this difference between the two models is as follows. In both models, the forward rate is negatively affected by the variance of the future interest rate, and the variance of the future interest rate is an increasing function of the distance in time. However, in the Merton model, it goes linearly to infinity, while in the Vasicek model, it grows to a finite limit. Therefore, the variance effect is more powerful in the Merton model, and it forces the forward rates to be negative at long maturities.

For fixed t, the forward rate $f(r(s), t-s)$ is an Itô process with

$$df(r(s), t-s) = dr - \alpha \, ds + \sigma^2(t-s) \, ds = \sigma^2(t-s) \, ds + \sigma \, d\hat{W}$$

This differential does not depend on the risk-adjusted drift α of the interest rate. The instantaneous standard deviation is σ.

For a fixed time to maturity τ, the forward rate $f(r(s), \tau)$ is also an Itô process, with differential

$$df(r(s), \tau) = dr = \alpha \, ds + \sigma \, d\hat{W}$$

As before, the instantaneous standard deviation is σ.

We can write

$$df(r(s), t-s) = \alpha^f(s; t) \, ds + \beta^f(s; t) \, d\hat{W}$$

where the drift is

$$\alpha^f(s; t) = \sigma^2(t-s)$$

and the dispersion coefficient is

$$\beta^f(s; t) = \sigma$$

The result of Heath, Jarrow, and Morton [47, 1989], [48, 1992] that

$$\alpha^f(s; t) = \beta^f(s; t) \int_s^t \beta^f(s; v) \, dv$$

can easily be verified:

$$\begin{aligned} \beta^f(s; t) \int_s^t \beta^f(s; v) \, dv &= \sigma \int_s^t \sigma \, dv \\ &= \sigma^2(t-s) \\ &= \alpha^f(s; t) \end{aligned}$$

The continuously compounded yield at time s of the zero-coupon bond maturing at t is

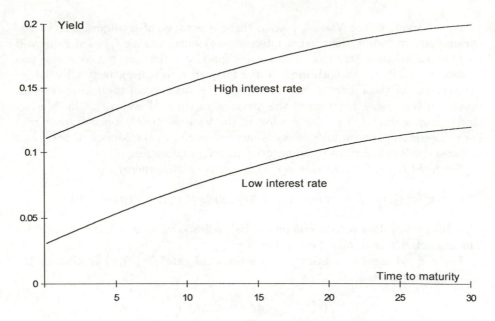

FIG. 7.18. Two yield curves with $\sigma = 0.02$

$$R(s;t) = \frac{1}{t-s} \ln \left(\frac{1}{P(r(s), t-s)} \right) = \frac{1}{t-s} A(t-s) + r(s) = R(r(s), t-s)$$

where R is the function

$$R(r, \tau) = \frac{1}{\tau} A(\tau) + r = \frac{1}{2} \alpha \tau - \frac{\sigma^2}{6} \tau^2 + r$$

The yield at time s is an affine function of the interest rate $r(s)$, and it is normally distributed. The coefficient of the interest rate is one, and, in particular, it is independent of the time τ to maturity of the bond. A change in the interest rate will make the yields at all maturities go up or down by the same amount. In other words, the yield curve shifts in a parallel manner.

Figures 7.18 and 7.19 show the zero-coupon yield curves corresponding to the bond price curves in Fig. 7.14 and Fig. 7.15 and the forward rate curves in Fig. 7.4 and Fig. 7.5, respectively. The standard deviation parameter is $\sigma = 0.02$ in Fig. 7.18 and $\sigma = 0.04$ in Fig. 7.19. The other parameters are the same in all six figures.

The average future interest rate over the time interval $[s, t]$ is

$$r_a = \frac{1}{t-s} \int_s^t r(u) \, du = \frac{1}{t-s} I(s;t)$$

It is normally distributed conditionally on information at time s, with mean

$$E_Q(r_a \mid \mathcal{F}_s) = \frac{1}{t-s} E_Q(I(s;t) \mid \mathcal{F}_s)$$

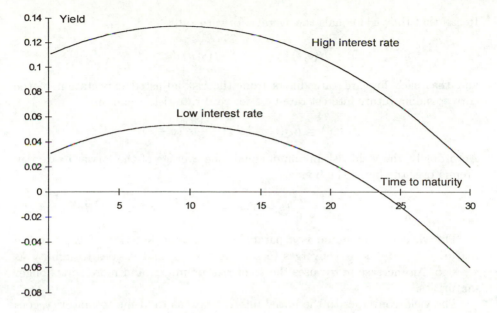

FIG. 7.19. Two yield curves with $\sigma = 0.04$

$$= \frac{1}{t-s}\left[r(s)(t-s) + \frac{1}{2}\alpha(t-s)^2\right]$$

$$= r(s) + \frac{1}{2}\alpha(t-s)$$

and variance

$$\mathrm{var}_Q(r_a \mid \mathcal{F}_s) = \frac{1}{(t-s)^2}\mathrm{var}_Q(I(s;t) \mid \mathcal{F}_s)$$

$$= \frac{1}{(t-s)^2}\frac{\sigma^2}{3}(t-s)^3$$

$$= \frac{\sigma^2}{3}(t-s)$$

Hence,

$$R(r, t-s) = E_Q(r_a \mid \mathcal{F}_s) - \frac{\sigma^2}{6}(t-s)^2$$

or

$$E_Q(r_a \mid \mathcal{F}_s) = R(r, t-s) + \frac{\sigma^2}{6}(t-s)^2$$

The *yield risk premium* is

$$\frac{\sigma^2}{6}(t-s)^2 = \frac{t-s}{2}\mathrm{var}_Q(I(s;t) \mid \mathcal{F}_s)$$

Recall that the yield equals the average forward rate:

$$R(s;t) = \frac{1}{t-s} \int_s^t f(s;u)\, du$$

and that each forward rate differs from the risk-adjusted expectation of the corresponding future interest rate by a forward rate risk premium:

$$f(s;u) = E_Q(r(u)\mid \mathcal{F}_s) - \frac{1}{2}\sigma^2(u-s)^2$$

Accordingly, the yield risk premium equals the average of the forward rate risk premia over the life of the bond:

$$\frac{\sigma^2}{6}(t-s)^2 = \frac{1}{t-s}\frac{\sigma^2}{6}(t-s)^3 = \frac{1}{(t-s)}\int_s^t \frac{1}{2}\sigma^2(u-s)^2\, du$$

The yield risk premium is a parabolic, increasing function of the time to maturity $\tau = t - s$. It converges to zero as $\tau \to 0$, and it goes to infinity as $\tau \to \infty$. An increase in σ raises the yield risk premium, and more so at longer maturities.

The yield converges to the initial interest rate as the time to maturity goes to zero, and it goes to minus infinity as time to maturity goes to infinity:

$$R(r,\tau) \to r \quad \text{as} \quad \tau \to 0$$

and

$$R(r,\tau) \to -\infty \quad \text{as} \quad \tau \to \infty$$

In particular, the yields will always be negative at very long maturities.

The yield is a parabolic function of the time to maturity.

Exercise 7.4 *Given the current interest rate r, calculate the maximum points $(\tau^*, f(r,\tau^*))$ and $(\tau^{**}, R(r,\tau^{**}))$ of the forward rate curve and the yield curve.*

An increase in the instantaneous standard deviation σ or a decrease in the instantaneous mean increment α of the interest rate lowers the yield at all maturities. The effect is stronger at longer maturities.

Consider the yield

$$R(r(s), t-s) = \frac{1}{2}\alpha(t-s) - \frac{\sigma^2}{6}(t-s)^2 + r(s)$$

on a zero-coupon bond that matures at a fixed time t, with s as the time variable, $0 \le s \le t$. It is an Itô process with differential

$$dR(r(s), t-s) = \left[-\frac{1}{2}\alpha + \frac{\sigma^2}{3}(t-s)\right] ds + dr(s)$$

$$= \left[\frac{1}{2}\alpha + \frac{\sigma^2}{3}(t-s)\right] ds + \sigma\, d\hat{W}(s)$$

The dispersion and the instantaneous standard deviation of the yield is σ.

The yield
$$R(r(s), \tau) = \frac{1}{2}\alpha\tau - \frac{\sigma^2}{6}\tau^2 + r(s)$$

on a zero-coupon bond with a fixed time τ to maturity is also an Itô process, with differential
$$dR(r(s), \tau) = dr(s) = \alpha\, ds + \sigma\, dW(s)$$

Again, the instantaneous standard deviation is σ.

7.7   The Extended Vasicek Model

Let r_0 be a constant, and let α, a, and σ be functions of time, or deterministic processes with $\sigma \in \mathcal{L}^2$, $\alpha, a \in \mathcal{L}^1$.

In the *extended Vasicek model*, the interest rate follows a process with differential
$$dr = (\alpha - ar)\, dt + \sigma\, d\hat{W}$$

and with initial value $r(0) = r_0$. This interest rate process is a general conditionally Gaussian one-factor process with constant initial value.

The model is also called the *general Hull–White model*. The *simplified Hull–White model* is the special case where a and σ are constant and $a \neq 0$. The *Ho–Lee model* has $a = 0$ and σ constant.

The Merton model and the Vasicek model are also special cases of the extended Vasicek model. The Merton model has $a = 0$ and α constant. The Vasicek model has $a \neq 0$ constant, $\alpha = a\bar{r}$, where $\bar{r}$ is constant, and σ constant.

We know from Proposition 3.7 that
$$r(t) = e^{-K(t))}\left[r_0 + \int_0^t e^K \alpha\, ds + \int_0^t e^K \sigma\, d\hat{W}\right]$$

where the process K is defined by
$$K(t) = \int_0^t a\, ds$$

Recall that for $0 \leq s \leq t$,
$$r(t) = e^{K(t)}\left[e^{K(s)}r(s) + \int_s^t e^K \alpha\, ds + \int_s^t e^K \sigma\, d\hat{W}\right]$$

In order to calculate the prices of zero-coupon bonds, we begin by calculating the integral
$$I(s; t) = \int_s^t r\, du$$

for $0 \leq s \leq t$. Define a function B by
$$B(s; t) = \int_s^t e^{K(u)+K(s)}\, du = e^{K(s)}\int_s^t e^{-K}\, du$$

Proposition 7.5 *For* $0 \leq s \leq t$,

$$I(s;t) = B(s;t)r(s) + \int_s^t e^{-K(u)} \int_s^u e^K \alpha \, dx \, du + \int_s^t \sigma(x)B(x;t) \, d\hat{W}(x)$$

Exercise 7.5 *Prove Proposition 7.5.*

Define functions $m(r, s; t)$ and $v(s; t)$, for $r \in \mathbb{R}$ and $0 \leq s \leq t$, by

$$m(r, s; t) = B(s;t)r + \int_s^t e^{K-K(u)} \int_s^u e^K \alpha \, dx \, du$$

and

$$v(s;t) = \int_s^t \sigma(x)^2 B(x;t)^2 \, dx$$

The process $m(r(s), s; t)$, with s as the time variable, is Gaussian. The function $v(s;t)$ is deterministic. It follows from Proposition 7.5 that conditionally on information at time s, $I(s;t)$ is normally distributed with mean $m(r(s), s; t)$ and with variance $v(s;t)$.

The price of a bond will be

$$
\begin{aligned}
P(s;t) &= E_Q[\exp[-I(s;t)] \mid \mathcal{F}_s] \\
&= \exp\left[-m(r(s), s; t) + \frac{1}{2}v(s;t)\right] \\
&= P(r(s), s; t)
\end{aligned}
$$

where $P(r, s; t)$ is the function

$$P(r(s), s; t) = \exp\left[-m(r, s; t) + \frac{1}{2}v(s;t)\right]$$

Since $m(r(s), s; t)$ is normally distributed, the bond price is lognormally distributed.

Define a function $A(s; t)$ by

$$A(s;t) = \int_s^t e^{-K(u)} \int_s^u e^K \alpha \, dx \, du - \frac{1}{2}v(s;t)$$

Then

$$P(r, s; t) = \exp\left[-m(r, s; t) + \frac{1}{2}v(s;t)\right] = \exp[-A(s;t) - B(s;t)r]$$

The price function is in general not stationary: the price $P(r, s; s+\tau)$ at time s of a bond with time τ to maturity is a function not only of $r(s)$ and τ but also separately of s.

Proposition 7.6 *The functions m and v satisfy the formulas*

$$m(r(s), s; t) = \int_s^t E(r(u) \mid \mathcal{F}_s) \, du$$

and

$$v(s; t) = 2 \int_s^t \int_s^y \int_s^u \sigma(x)^2 \exp^{2K(x) - K(y) - K(u)} \, dx \, du \, dy$$

$$= \int_s^t \int_s^t \text{cov}(r(u), r(y) \mid \mathcal{F}_s) \, du \, dy$$

Exercise 7.6 *Prove Proposition 7.6.*

It follows from Proposition 7.6 that

$$v(s; t) \to 0 \quad \text{as} \quad s \to t$$

Hence,

$$A(s; t) \to 0 \quad \text{as} \quad s \to t$$

and it is easily seen that

$$B(s; t) \to 0 \quad \text{as} \quad s \to t$$

It follows that the model satisfies *pull-to-par*:

$$P(r, s; t) \to 1 \quad \text{as} \quad s \to t$$

for fixed r, and with probability one,

$$P(r(s), s; t) \to 1 \quad \text{as} \quad s \to t$$

Consider the price process $P(r(s), s; t)$ of a bond which matures at a fixed time t, with s as the time variable, $0 \le s \le t$. The differential of the logarithm of the price is

$$d \ln P(s; t) = d[-B(s; t) r(s) - A(s; t)]$$
$$= -B(s; t) \, dr(s) - r(s) \, dB(s; t) - dA(s; t)$$

Hence, the dispersion coefficient with respect to $\hat{W}$ is $-B(s; t)\sigma(s)$. Since the relative drift coefficient of the bond price under the risk-adjusted probabilities must be the interest rate,

$$\frac{dP(s; t)}{P(s; t)} = r(s) \, ds - B(s; t)\sigma(s) \, d\hat{W}(s)$$

This stochastic differential is not affected by α. The reason for this is the same as the reason why the risk-adjusted mean reversion level $\bar{r}$ has no effect on the stochastic differential of the bond price in the Vasicek model. The time-dependent parameter α does affect the distribution of the initial value $P(r(s), s; t)$ of the bond at time s, but given this value, it does not affect the relative drift and dispersion of the bond price. It affects the distribution of future interest rates, but because the bond has a fixed maturity date, no new interest rates are taken into account as calendar time goes forward.

The relative dispersion coefficient is negative: a positive shock to $\hat{W}$ makes the interest rate go up and the bond price go down. The volatility of the bond price is $B(s; t)\sigma(s)$. It is a deterministic function of s. It goes to zero as s approaches t, provided that σ is continuous at t.

The differential of the bond price is consistent with what we found for the Vasicek model and the Merton model. In those models, $B(s; t) = B(t - s)$ and $B(s; t) = t - s$, respectively.

By Proposition 7.6, the function $v(s; t)$ is continuously differentiable with respect to t, with

$$v_t(s; t) = 2e^{-K(t)} \int_s^t \int_s^u \sigma(x)^2 e^{2K(x)-K(u)} \, dx \, du$$

$$= 2e^{-K(t)} \int_s^t \int_x^t \sigma(x)^2 e^{2K(x)-K(u)} \, du \, dx$$

$$= 2\int_s^t \sigma(x)^2 \left(\int_x^t e^{-K(u)+K(x)} \, du \right) e^{-K(t)+K(x)} \, dx$$

$$= 2\int_s^t \sigma(x)^2 B(x; t) B_t(x; t) \, dx$$

The functions $B(s; t)$ and $A(s; t)$ are also continuously differentiable functions of t, with

$$B_t(s; t) = e^{-K(t)+K(s)}$$

and

$$A_t(s; t) = e^{-K(t)} \int_s^t e^K \alpha \, dx - \frac{1}{2}v_t(s; t)$$

$$= \int_s^t B_t(x; t)e^K \alpha(x) \, dx - \frac{1}{2}v_t(s; t)$$

Therefore, the function

$$\ln P(s; t) = -A(s; t) - B(s; t)r(s)$$

is continuously differentiable as a function of t. The forward rates are

$$f(s; t) = -\frac{\partial}{\partial t} \ln P(s; t)$$

$$= A_t(s; t) + B_t(s; t)r(s)$$

$$= e^{-K(t)} \int_s^t e^K \alpha \, dx - \frac{1}{2} v_t(s;t) + e^{-K(t)+K(s)} r(s)$$
$$= f(r(s), s; t)$$

where $f(r, s; t)$ is the function

$$f(r, s; t) = e^{-K(t)} \int_s^t e^K \alpha \, dx - \frac{1}{2} v_t(s;t) + e^{-K(t)+K(s)} r$$

The forward rate is an affine function of the instantaneous interest rate, and it is normally distributed.

Like the bond price function, the forward rate function is not stationary: the forward rate $f(r, s; s + \tau)$ at time s with time τ to maturity is a function not only of $r(s)$ and τ but also separately of s.

The expression for the forward rates is consistent with what we found in the Vasicek model and in the Merton model. In the Vasicek model, $A(s; t) = A(t-s)$,

$$A_t(s; t) = A'(t - s) = \bar{r} \left(1 - e^{-a(t-s)}\right) - \frac{1}{2} B(t - s)^2 \sigma^2$$

$B(t; s) = B(t - s)$,

$$B_t(t; s) = B'(t - s) = e^{-a(t-s)}$$

and

$$A_t(s; t) + B_t(s; t) r(s) = \bar{r} \left(1 - e^{-a(t-s)}\right) - \frac{1}{2} B(t - s)^2 \sigma^2 + e^{-a(t-s)} r(s)$$

In the Merton model, $A(s; t) = A(t - s)$,

$$A_t(s; t) = A'(t - s) = \mu(t - s) - \frac{1}{2} \sigma^2 (t - s)^2$$

$B(t; s) = t - s$, $B_t(t - s) = 1$, and

$$A_t(s; t) + B_t(s; t) r(s) = \mu(t - s) - \frac{1}{2} \sigma^2 (t - s)^2 + r(s)$$

In the extended Vasicek model, the risk-adjusted conditional expectation of the future interest rate is

$$E_Q(r(t) \mid \mathcal{F}_s) = e^{-K(t)+K(s)} r(s) + e^{-K(t)} \int_s^t e^K \alpha \, dx$$

Hence,

$$f(s; t) = E_Q(r(t) \mid \mathcal{F}_s) - \frac{1}{2} v_t(s;t)$$

or

$$E_Q(r(t) \mid \mathcal{F}_s) = f(s; t) + \frac{1}{2} v_t(s;t)$$

The *forward rate risk premium* is

$$\frac{1}{2} v_t(s;t)$$

For a fixed maturity date t, consider the process $f(r(s), s; t)$ with s as time variable.

If the function a is continuous, then the function $B_t(s;t)$, as a function of s, is a (deterministic) Itô process. To see this, note that the function is differentiable as a function of s, with

$$B_{st}(s;t) = K'(s)e^{-K(t)+K(s)} = a(s)e^{-K(t)+K(s)} = B_t(s;t)a(s)$$

If a is continuous, then this function is a continuous function of s. By the fundamental theorem of calculus (Theorem B.22), which requires continuity of the derivative,

$$B_t(s;t) = B_t(0;t) + \int_0^s B(x;t)a(x)\,dx$$

Hence, $B_t(s;t)$ is a (deterministic) Itô process with

$$dB_t(s;t) = B(s;t)a(s)\,ds$$

The function $v_t(s;t)$ is continuously differentiable as a function of s, with

$$v_{st}(s;t) = -2\sigma(s)^2 B(s;t)B_t(s;t)$$

and so $v_t(s;t)$ is an Itô process. If α is a continuous function, then $A_t(s;t)$ is continuously differentiable as a function of s, with

$$A_{st}(s;t) = -e^{-K(t)}e^{K(s)}\alpha(s) - \frac{1}{2}v_{st}(s;t) = -B_t(s;t)\alpha(s) - \frac{1}{2}v_{st}(s;t)$$

which implies that $A_t(s;t)$ is also an Itô process.

Hence, for fixed t, if a and α are continuous, then the forward rate $f(r(s), s;t)$ is an Itô process with differential

$$
\begin{aligned}
df(r(s), s;t) &= d[A_t(s;t) + B_t(s;t)r(s)] \\
&= dA_t(s;t) + r(s)\,dB_t(s;t) + B_t(s;t)dr(s) \\
&= [A_{st}(s;t) + r(s)B_{st}(s;t)]\,ds + B_t(s;t)dr(s) \\
&= [A_{st}(s;t) + r(s)B_{st}(s;t)]\,ds + B_t(s;t)(\alpha(s) - a(s)r(s))\,ds \\
&\quad + B_t(s;t)\sigma(s)\,d\hat{W}(s) \\
&= \left[-B_t(s;t)\alpha(s) - \frac{1}{2}v_{st}(s;t) + B_t(s;t)a(s)r(s)\right]\,ds \\
&\quad + B_t(s;t)(\alpha(s) - a(s)r(s))\,ds + B_t(s;t)\sigma(s)\,d\hat{W}(s) \\
&= -\frac{1}{2}v_{st}(s;t)\,ds + B_t(s;t)\sigma(s)\,d\hat{W}(s)
\end{aligned}
$$

The differential of the forward rate is not affected by α.

We assumed continuity of a and α in this derivation, but in fact the same result holds even if a and α are not continuous. This is stated in the following proposition.

Proposition 7.7 *The forward rate $f(r(s), s; t)$ is an Itô process with differential*

$$df(r(s), s; t) = -\frac{1}{2}v_{st}(s; t)\, ds + B_t(s; t)\sigma(s)\, d\hat{W}(s)$$

Exercise 7.7 *Prove Proposition 7.7.*

We can write

$$df(s; t) = \alpha^f(s; t)\, ds + \beta^f(s; t)\, d\hat{W}$$

where the drift is

$$\alpha^f(s; t) = -\frac{1}{2}v_{st}(s; t)$$

and the dispersion coefficient is

$$\beta^f(s; t) = B_t(s; t)\sigma(s)$$

The general result of Heath, Jarrow, and Morton [47, 1989], [48, 1992], which says that

$$\alpha^f(s; t) = \beta^f(s; t) \int_s^t \beta^f(s; u)\, du$$

can easily be verified in the extended Vasicek model:

$$\begin{aligned}
\beta^f(s; t) \int_s^t \beta^f(s; u)\, du &= B_t(s; t)\sigma(s) \int_s^t B_u(s; u)\, du \\
&= B_t(s; t)\sigma(s)B(s; t) \\
&= -\frac{1}{2}v_{st}(s; t) \\
&= \alpha^f(s; t)
\end{aligned}$$

Proposition 7.8 *If a and α are continuous, then*

$$a(t) = -\frac{B_{tt}(s; t)}{B_t(s; t)}$$

and

$$\alpha(t) = a(t)A_t(s; t) + A_{tt}(s; t) + e^{-2K(t)} \int_s^t \sigma^2 e^{2K}\, dx$$

for $0 \leq s \leq t$.

Exercise 7.8 *Prove Proposition 7.8.*

The function

$$a(t) = -\frac{B_{tt}(s; t)}{B_t(s; t)}$$

is a measure of the curvature of the bond price volatility $B(s; t)\sigma(s)$ as a function of the maturity date t. It is analogous to the Arrow–Pratt absolute risk aversion of a utility function, see Pratt [77, 1964], Arrow [2, 1965].

Alternatively, $a(t)$ can be interpreted as the fractional decrease in the standard deviation $B_t(s;t)\sigma(s)$ of the instantaneous forward rate $f(r(s), s; t)$ as the time to maturity t increases.

If the deterministic processes α and a are time integrals, then they are, in particular, Itô processes, and then so is the drift $\alpha(t) - a(t)r(t)$ of the interest rate. The instantaneous covariance between the drift $\alpha(t) - a(t)r(t)$ and the level $r(t)$ of the interest rate is $-a(t)\sigma(t)^2$.

If $a(t)$ is positive, then shocks to the interest rate will tend to be reversed because of the drift term. If $a(t)$ is large, then this effect will be strong. The bond price volatility $B(s;t)\sigma(s)$ will increase only slowly as the maturity date t moves forward, whereas the standard deviation $B_t(s;t)\sigma(s)$ of the forward rate $f(r(s), s; t)$ will decrease fast.

The extended Vasicek model can in principle be calibrated on the basis of the forward rates, using Proposition 7.8. Suppose that at time s, we know the following:

- the interest rate $r(s)$
- the standard deviation $\sigma(t)$ of the interest rate, for $t \geq s$
- the instantaneous forward rates

$$f(r(s), s; t) = A_t(s; t) + B_t(s; t)r(s)$$

  for $t \geq s$
- the standard deviations $B_t(s;t)\sigma(s)$ of the instantaneous forward rates for $t \geq s$.

Suppose the instantaneous forward rates and their standard deviations are given in a form such that we also know or can calculate their first derivatives with respect to t.

From the standard deviations $B_t(s;t)\sigma(s)$ of the instantaneous forward rates and the standard deviation $\sigma(s)$ of the current interest rate, we can calculate $B_t(s;t)$ for $t \geq s$. From knowledge of $B_t(s;t)$, we can in principle calculate its derivative $B_{tt}(s;t)$, and then, using the first formula in Proposition 7.8, we can calculate $a(t)$ for $t \geq s$.

From the current interest rate $r(s)$, the forward rates, and the function $B_t(s;t)$, we can then calculate $A_t(s;t)$ for $t \geq s$. From knowledge of $A_t(s;t)$, we can in principle calculate its derivative $A_{tt}(s;t)$. From knowledge of $a(t)$, $A_t(s;t)$, $A_{tt}(s;t)$, and $\sigma(t)$ for $t \geq s$, using the second formula in Proposition 7.8, we can finally calculate $\alpha(t)$ for $t \geq s$.

According to this procedure, the time-dependent parameter a is used to match the initially given standard deviations of the forward rates, while the time-dependent parameter α is used to match the forward rates themselves.

The continuously compounded *yield* at time s of the zero-coupon bond maturing at t is

$$R(s;t) = \frac{1}{t-s}\left[m(r(s), s; t) - \frac{1}{2}v(s; t)\right]$$

$$= \frac{1}{t-s} \ln \left(\frac{1}{P(s;t)} \right)$$

$$= \frac{1}{t-s} (A(s;t) + B(s;t)r(s))$$

$$= R(r(s), s; t)$$

where R is the function

$$R(r, s; t) = \frac{1}{t-s} (A(s;t) + B(s;t)r)$$

The yield at time s is an affine function of the interest rate $r(s)$ at time s, and it is normally distributed. The yield curve function is not stationary: the yield $R(r, s; s+\tau)$ on a bond with time τ to maturity is a function not only of r and τ but also of s.

The average future interest rate over the time interval $[s, t]$ is

$$r_a = \frac{1}{t-s} \int_s^t r(u)\, du = \frac{1}{t-s} I(s;t)$$

It is normally distributed conditionally on information at time s, with mean

$$E_Q(r_a \mid \mathcal{F}_s) = \frac{1}{t-s} E_Q(I(s;t) \mid \mathcal{F}_s) = \frac{1}{t-s} m(r(s), s; t)$$

and variance

$$\mathrm{var}_Q(r_a \mid \mathcal{F}_s) = \frac{1}{(t-s)^2} \mathrm{var}_Q(I(s;t) \mid \mathcal{F}_s) = \frac{1}{(t-s)^2} v(s;t)$$

Hence,

$$R(r, s; t) = \frac{1}{t-s} \left[m(r, s; t) - \frac{1}{2} v(s;t) \right]$$

$$= E_Q(r_a \mid \mathcal{F}_s) - \frac{1}{2(t-s)} v(s;t)$$

or

$$E_Q(r_a \mid \mathcal{F}_s) = R(r, s; t) + \frac{1}{2(t-s)} v(s;t)$$

The term

$$\frac{1}{2(t-s)} v(s;t) = \frac{t-s}{2} \mathrm{var}_Q(r_a \mid \mathcal{F}_s)$$

can be interpreted as a *yield risk premium*. Because the rate of return on the money market account is random, the expectation of the average return exceeds the yield on the bond, which is known, by this yield risk premium.

Recall that the yield equals the average forward rate:

$$R(s;t) = \frac{1}{t-s} \int_s^t f(s;u)\,du$$

and that each forward rate differs from the risk-adjusted expectation of the corresponding future interest rate by a forward rate risk premium:

$$f(s;u) = E_Q(r(u) \mid \mathcal{F}_s) - \frac{1}{2}v_u(s;u)$$

Accordingly, the yield risk premium equals the average of the forward rate risk premia over the life of the bond:

$$\frac{1}{2(t-s)}v(s;t) = \frac{1}{2(t-s)} \int_s^t v_u(s;u)\,du$$

For a fixed maturity date t, the yield $R(r(s),s;t)$ is an Itô process with dispersion

$$\frac{B(s;t)\sigma(s)}{t-s}$$

Since this is positive, it is also equal to the instantaneous standard deviation of the yield.

Exercise 7.9 *Show that the differential of the process $R(r(s),s;t)$ is*

$$dR(r(s),s;t)$$
$$= \frac{R(r(s),s;t) + \frac{1}{2}B(s;t)^2\sigma(s)^2 - r(s)}{t-s}\,ds + \frac{B(s;t)\sigma(s)}{t-s}\,dW(s)$$

Proposition 7.8 can in principle be used for calibrating the model's parameters on the basis of the yields.

The model can in principle be calibrated on the basis of the yields, as follows. Suppose that at time s, we know the following:

- the interest rate $r(s)$
- the standard deviation $\sigma(t)$ of the interest rate, for $t \geq s$
- the yields

$$R(r(s),s;t) = \frac{1}{t-s}[A(s;t) + B(s;t)r(s)]$$

  for $t \geq s$
- the instantaneous standard deviations

$$\frac{B(s;t)\sigma(s)}{t-s}$$

  of the yields for $t \geq s$.

Suppose the yields and their instantaneous standard deviations are given in a form such that we also know or can calculate their two first derivatives with respect to t.

From the instantaneous standard deviations $B(s;t)\sigma(s)/(t-s)$ of the yields and the standard deviation $\sigma(s)$ of the current interest rate, we can calculate $B(s;t)$ for $t \geq s$. From knowledge of the function $B(s;t)$, we can then in principle calculate its derivatives $B_t(s;t)$ and $B_{tt}(s;t)$. Using the first formula in Proposition 7.8, we can then calculate $a(t)$ for $t \geq s$.

From the current interest rate $r(s)$, the yields, and the function $B(s;t)$, we can calculate $A(s;t)$ for $t \geq s$. From knowledge of the function $A(s;t)$, we can in principle calculate its derivatives $A_t(s;t)$ and $A_{tt}(s;t)$. From knowledge of $a(t)$, $A_t(s;t)$, $A_{tt}(s;t)$, and $\sigma(t)$ for $t \geq s$, using the second formula in Proposition 7.8, we can then calculate $\alpha(t)$ for $t \geq s$.

According to this procedure, the time-dependent parameter a is used to match the initially given standard deviations of the yields, while the time-dependent parameter α is used to match the yields themselves.

In practice, the initial data will be known precisely only for a discrete set of maturity times t. They will have to be interpolated between those dates. If the model is calibrated on the basis of the yields, then the functions $A(s;t)$ and $B(s;t)$ are backed out from the yield data and the interpolation procedure. They need to be differentiated twice, which is problematic because of the interpolation.

If the model is calibrated on the basis of the forward rates rather than the yields, then the first derivatives $A_t(s;t)$ and $B_t(s;t)$ are backed out from the forward rate data and the interpolation procedure, and it is only necessary to differentiate them once. On the other hand, the data will correspond to forward rates over discrete time intervals, and they will have to be converted into data for instantaneous forward rates.

7.8 The Simplified Hull–White Model

In the *simplified Hull–White model*, the interest rate follows a process of the form

$$dr = (\alpha - ar)\,dt + \sigma\,d\hat{W}$$

where $\alpha \in \mathcal{L}^1$ is a deterministic process, a and σ are constants, and $a \neq 0$. Indeed, it is the special case of the extended Vasicek model where a and σ are constant and $a \neq 0$.

We can write the interest rate process as

$$r(t) = e^{-at}\left[r_0 + \int_0^t e^{as}\alpha(s)\,ds + \sigma\int_0^t e^{as}\,d\hat{W}(s)\right]$$

and, for $0 \leq s \leq t$,

$$r(t) = e^{-at}\left[e^{as}r(s) + \int_s^t e^{as}\alpha(s)\,ds + \sigma\int_s^t e^{au}\,d\hat{W}(u)\right]$$

The function $B(s;t)$ is given by

$$
\begin{aligned}
B(s;t) &= e^{as} \int_s^t e^{-au}\, du \\
&= e^{as} \frac{1}{a} \left[-e^{-au} \right]_s^t \\
&= e^{as} \frac{1}{a} \left(-e^{-at} + e^{-as} \right) \\
&= \frac{1}{a} \left(1 - e^{-a(t-s)} \right)
\end{aligned}
$$

Since it is a function of (s,t) only through $t-s$, we will write, by a slight abuse of notation,

$$
B(s;t) = B(t-s)
$$

where the function $B(\tau)$ is the same as in the Vasicek model:

$$
B(\tau) = \frac{1}{a} \left(1 - e^{-a\tau} \right)
$$

The functions $m(r,s;t)$ and $v(s;t)$, for $r \in \mathbb{R}$ and $0 \le s \le t$, are given by

$$
m(r,s;t) = \frac{1}{a} \left(1 - e^{-a(t-s)} \right) r + \int_s^t e^{-au} \int_s^u e^{ax} \alpha(x)\, dx\, du
$$

and

$$
\begin{aligned}
v(s;t) &= \frac{\sigma^2}{a^2} \int_s^t \left(1 - e^{-a(t-x)} \right)^2 dx \\
&= \frac{\sigma^2}{a^2} \int_s^t \left(1 + e^{-2a(t-x)} - 2e^{-a(t-x)} \right)^2 dx \\
&= \frac{\sigma^2}{a^2} \left[(t-s) + \frac{1}{2a} \left(1 - e^{-2a(t-s)} \right) - \frac{2}{a} \left(1 - e^{-a(t-s)} \right) \right] \\
&= \frac{\sigma^2}{2a^3} \left(4e^{-a(t-s)} - e^{-2a(t-s)} + 2a(t-s) - 3 \right)
\end{aligned}
$$

Since v is a function of (s,t) only through $t-s$, we will write, with a slight abuse of notation,

$$
v(s;t) = v(t-s)
$$

where the function $v(\tau)$ is the same as in the Vasicek model:

$$
v(\tau) = \frac{\sigma^2}{2a^3} \left(4e^{-a\tau} - e^{-2a\tau} + 2a\tau - 3 \right)
$$

Conditionally on information at time s, $I(s;t)$ is normally distributed with mean $m(r(s),s;t)$ and with variance $v(t-s)$.

The price of a bond will be

$$P(r(s), s; t) = E_Q[\exp[-I(s;t)] \mid \mathcal{F}_s] = \exp\left[-m(r(s), s; t) + \frac{1}{2}v(t-s)\right]$$

The function $A(s;t)$ is given by

$$A(s;t) = \int_s^t e^{-au} \int_s^u e^{ax}\alpha(x)\,dx\,du - \frac{1}{2}v(t-s)$$

We can express the bond price by means of the functions A and B as follows:

$$P(r(s), s; t) = \exp\left[-m(r(s), s; t) + \frac{1}{2}v(t-s)\right]$$
$$= \exp[-A(s;t) - B(t-s)r(s)]$$

The stochastic differential of the bond value, for a fixed maturity date t, is

$$\frac{dP(s;t)}{P(s;t)} = r(s)\,ds - B(t-s)\sigma\,d\hat{W}(s)$$

This is the same as in the Vasicek model. As in general in the extended Vasicek model, the time-dependent parameter α does not affect the dynamics of the bond price. It does, however, affect the initial bond price curve. Indeed, α can be chosen so as to fit any given initial bond price curve.

The volatility of the bond price is also the same as in the Vasicek model.

The forward rates are

$$f(s;t) = f(r(s), s; t)$$

where $f(r, s; t)$ is the function

$$f(r, s; t) = e^{-K(t)} \int_s^t e^K \alpha\,dx - \frac{1}{2}v_t(s;t) + e^{-K(t)+K(s)}r$$
$$= e^{-at} \int_s^t e^{ax}\alpha(x)\,dx - \frac{1}{2}v'(t-s) + e^{-a(t-s)}r$$

The forward rate risk premium is

$$\frac{1}{2}v'(t-s) = \frac{\sigma^2}{2a^2}\left(-2e^{-a(t-s)} + e^{-2a(t-s)} + 1\right) = \frac{1}{2}B(t-s)^2\sigma^2$$

as in the Vasicek model.

The effects of σ and r on the forward rate are similar to what happens in the Vasicek model.

For a fixed maturity date t, the forward rate $f(r(s), s; t)$ is an Itô process with differential

$$df(r(s), s; t) = -\frac{1}{2} v_{st}(s; t)\, ds + B_t(s; t)\sigma\, d\hat{W}(s)$$

$$= \frac{1}{2} v''(t - s)\, ds + e^{-a(t-s)}\sigma\, d\hat{W}(s)$$

This differential is not affected by α. It is the same as in the Vasicek model. The time-dependent parameter α affects the initial forward rate curve, but it does not affect the dynamics of the forward rates.

The instantaneous standard deviation of the forward rate is also the same as in the Vasicek model.

The simplified Hull–White model can in principle be calibrated on the basis of the forward rates, as follows. Suppose that at time s, we know the following:

- the parameters σ and a
- the interest rate $r(s)$
- the instantaneous forward rates

$$f(r(s), s; t) = e^{-at} \int_s^t e^{ax} \alpha(x)\, dx - \frac{1}{2} v'(t - s) + e^{-a(t-s)} r(s)$$

for $t \geq s$.

Suppose the instantaneous forward rates are given in a form such that we also know or can calculate their first derivative with respect to t.

Rearranging the equation for the forward rate, we find

$$e^{at} f(s; t) + \frac{1}{2} v'(t - s) - e^{-a(t-s)} r(s) = \int_s^t e^{ax} \alpha(x)\, dx$$

From knowledge of σ, a, and the function $f(s; t)$, we can calculate the left hand side of this equation, as well as its first derivative with respect to t, which equals $e^{at}\alpha(t)$. Since e^{at} is known, we can then calculate $\alpha(t)$, for $t \geq s$.

According to this procedure, the time-dependent parameter α is used to match the forward rates.

The continuously compounded yield at time s of the zero-coupon bond maturing at t is

$$R(s; t) = R(r(s), s; t)$$

where the function R is given by

$$R(r, s; t) = \frac{1}{t - s}\left[m(r, s; t) - \frac{1}{2} v(t - s) \right] = \frac{1}{t - s}[A(s; t) + B(t - s)r]$$

The yield risk premium is

$$\frac{1}{2(t - s)} v(t - s)$$

as in the Vasicek model.

The effects of σ and r on the yield are similar to what happens in the Vasicek model.

For fixed t, the dispersion of the yield $R(r(s), s; t)$, and the instantaneous standard deviation, is

$$\frac{B(t-s)\sigma}{t-s} = \frac{\sigma}{a(t-s)}\left(1 - e^{-a(t-s)}\right)$$

as in the Vasicek model.

The model can in principle be calibrated on the basis of the yields, as follows. Suppose that at time s, we know the following:

- the parameters a and σ
- the interest rate $r(s)$
- the yields

$$R(r(s), s; t) = \frac{1}{t-s}[A(s; t) + B(t-s)r(s)]$$

for $t \geq s$.

Suppose the yields are given in a form such that we also know or can calculate the two first derivatives with respect to t.

From a, we can calculate $B(t-s)$ for $t \geq s$. From the current interest rate $r(s)$, the yields, and the function $B(t-s)$, we can calculate $A(s; t)$ for $t \geq s$. From knowledge of the function $A(s; t)$, we can in principle calculate its derivatives $A_t(s; t)$ and $A_{tt}(s; t)$. From knowledge of a, σ, and $A_t(s; t)$ and $A_{tt}(s; t)$, for $t \geq s$, using the second formula in Proposition 7.8, we can then calculate $\alpha(t)$ for $t \geq s$.

According to this procedure, the time-dependent parameter α is used to match the yields.

7.9 The Continuous-time Ho–Lee Model

In the *Ho–Lee model*, or rather, the continuous-time version of the Ho–Lee model, the interest rate follows a process of the form

$$dr = \alpha \, dt + \sigma \, d\hat{W}$$

where $\alpha \in \mathcal{L}^1$ is a deterministic process, and σ is a constant. Indeed, it is the special case of the extended Vasicek model where σ is constant and $a = 0$. It is like the Merton model, except that we now allow the parameter α to be a deterministic function of time. This will allow us to fit the initial yield curve.

The interest rate process is given by

$$r(t) = r(0) + \int_0^t \alpha \, ds + \sigma \hat{W}(t)$$

and, for $0 \leq s \leq t$,

$$r(t) = r(s) + \int_s^t \alpha \, du + \sigma(\hat{W}(t) - \hat{W}(s))$$

The function $B(s;t)$ is given by

$$B(s;t) = t - s$$

as in the Merton model.

The functions $m(r,s;t)$ and $v(s;t)$ are given by

$$m(r,s;t) = (t-s)r + \int_s^t \int_s^u \alpha \, dx \, du$$

and

$$v(s;t) = \int_s^t \sigma^2(t-x)^2 \, dx = \sigma^2 \left[-\frac{1}{3}(t-x)^3 \right]_{x=s}^t = \frac{\sigma^2}{3}(t-s)^3$$

Since v is a function of (s,t) only through $t-s$, we will write, with a slight abuse of notation,

$$v(s;t) = v(t-s)$$

where the function $v(\tau)$ is the same as in the Merton model:

$$v(\tau) = \frac{\sigma^2}{3}\tau^3$$

Conditionally on information at time s, $I(s;t)$ is normally distributed with mean $m(r(s),s;t)$ and with variance $v(t-s)$.

The price of a bond will be

$$P(s;t) = E_Q[\exp[-I(s;t)] \mid \mathcal{F}_s]$$

$$= \exp\left[-m(r(s),s;t) + \frac{1}{2}v(t-s) \right]$$

$$= \exp\left[-r(s)(t-s) - \int_s^t \int_s^u \alpha \, dv \, du + \frac{\sigma^2}{6}(t-s)^3 \right]$$

The function $A(s;t)$ is given by

$$A(s;t) = \int_s^t \int_s^u \alpha \, dx \, du - \frac{1}{2}v(t-s) = \int_s^t \int_s^u \alpha \, dx \, du - \frac{\sigma^2}{6}(t-s)^3$$

In terms of this function, the bond price is

$$P(r(s),s;t) = \exp[A(s,t) - r(s)(t-s)]$$

The stochastic differential of the bond value, for a fixed maturity date t, is

$$\frac{dP(s;t)}{P(s;t)} = r(s) \, ds - (t-s)\sigma \, d\hat{W}(s)$$

This is the same as in the Merton model. As in general in the extended Vasicek model, and in the special case of the simplified Hull–White model, the time-dependent parameter α does not affect the dynamics of the bond price, but it does affect the initial bond price curve.

The volatility of the bond price is also the same as in the Merton model. The forward rates are

$$f(s;t) = f(r(s),s;t)$$

where $f(r,s;t)$ is the function

$$f(r,s;t) = e^{-K(t)} \int_s^t e^K \alpha \, dx - \frac{1}{2} v_t(s;t) + e^{-K(t)+K(s)} r$$

$$= \int_s^t \alpha \, dx - \frac{\sigma^2}{2}(t-s)^2 + r$$

The forward rate risk premium is

$$\frac{1}{2} v_t(s;t) = \frac{1}{2} v'(t-s) = \frac{\sigma^2}{2}(t-s)^2$$

as in the Merton model.

The effects of σ and r on the forward rate are similar to what happens in the Vasicek model.

For a fixed maturity date t, the forward rate $f(r(s),s;t)$ is an Itô process with

$$df(f(s),s;t) = dr(s) - \alpha(s) \, ds + \sigma^2(t-s) \, ds = \sigma^2(t-s) \, ds + \sigma \, d\hat{W}$$

This differential is not affected by α. It is the same as in the Merton model. The time-dependent parameter α affects the initial forward rate curve, but it does not affect the dynamics of the forward rates.

The instantaneous standard deviation of the forward rate is also the same as in the Merton model.

The continuous-time Ho–Lee model can in principle be calibrated on the basis of the forward rates, as follows. Suppose that at time s, we know the following:

- the parameter σ
- the interest rate $r(s)$
- the instantaneous forward rates

$$f(r(s),s;t) = \int_s^t \alpha \, dx - \frac{\sigma^2}{2}(t-s)^2 + r(s)$$

for $t \geq s$.

Suppose the instantaneous forward rates are given in a form such that we also know or can calculate their first derivative with respect to t.

By rearranging the equation for the forward rate and differentiating with respect to t, we can find

$$\alpha(t) = f_t(s;t) + \sigma^2(t-s)$$

which allows direct calculation of $\alpha(t)$ for $t \geq s$.

According to this procedure, the time-dependent parameter α is used to match the forward rates.

The continuously compounded yield at time s of the zero-coupon bond maturing at t is

$$R(s;t) = \frac{1}{t-s} \ln\left(\frac{1}{P(s;t)}\right) = -\frac{1}{t-s} A(s,t) + r(s) = R(r(s), s, t)$$

where R is the function

$$R(r, s, t) = \frac{1}{t-s} \ln\left(\frac{1}{P(r,t,s)}\right)$$

$$= -\frac{1}{t-s} A(s,t) + r$$

$$= \frac{1}{t-s} \int_s^t \int_s^u \alpha\, dv\, du - \frac{\sigma^2}{6}(t-s)^2 + r$$

The function α deterministically determines how the yield curve, as a function of the current interest rate, changes over time. Indeed,

$$R(r, t, t+\tau) - R(r, s, s+\tau) = \frac{1}{\tau}\left(\int_t^{t+\tau} \int_t^u \alpha\, dv\, du - \int_s^{s+\tau} \int_s^u \alpha\, dv\, du\right)$$

The yield risk premium is

$$\frac{1}{2(t-s)} v(s;t) = \frac{\sigma^2}{6}(t-s)^2$$

as in the Merton model.

The effects of σ and r on the yield are similar to what happens in the Vasicek model.

The model can in principle be calibrated on the basis of the yields, as follows. Suppose that at time s, we know the following:

- the parameters a and σ
- the interest rate $r(s)$
- the yields

$$R(r(s), s; t) = \frac{1}{t-s} \int_s^t \int_s^u \alpha\, dv\, du - \frac{\sigma^2}{6}(t-s)^2 + r(s)$$

for $t \geq s$.

Suppose the yields are given in a form such that we also know or can calculate the two first derivatives with respect to t.

Rearranging the equation for the yields gives

$$\int_s^t \int_s^u \alpha \, dv \, du = (t-s)R(r(s), s; t) + \frac{\sigma^2}{6}(t-s)^3 - r(s)(t-s)$$

Differentiating with respect to t, we find

$$\int_s^t \alpha \, dv = R(r(s), s; t) + (t-s)R_t(r(s), s; t) + \frac{\sigma^2}{2}(t-s)^2 - r(s)$$

Differentiating again gives

$$\alpha(t) = R_t(r(s), s; t) + R_t(r(s), s; t) + (t-s)R_{tt}(r(s), s; t) + \sigma^2(t-s)$$

This equation allows direct calculation of $\alpha(t)$ for $t \geq s$.

According to this procedure, the time-dependent parameter α is used to match the yields.

7.10 Summary

In this chapter, we have analyzed the one-factor Gaussian models of the term structure of interest rates.

To specify a term structure model, it is not necessary to posit the dynamics of a set of basic securities price processes. It suffices to describe the state price process, or the interest rate process and the prices of risk. From there, one can pass to the risk-adjusted probabilities and calculate the prices of zero-coupon bonds. This is how we initially derived the Vasicek model. We could have gone from there to a model with basic securities by picking an appropriate set of claims and using their martingale values as price processes of basic securities.

The rest of the models in this chapter were specified in an even simpler manner: by describing the interest rate process directly under the risk-adjusted probabilities, without worrying about the prices of risk. This gave enough information to calculate the prices of zero-coupon bonds and the forward rates and yields, as well as their dynamics under the risk-adjusted probabilities. To find the dynamics under the original probabilities, however, it would be necessary to specify the prices of risk.

All the models in this chapter are special cases of the extended Vasicek model, which has three potentially time-dependent parameters.

We started by analyzing the Vasicek and Merton models, where the parameters are assumed to be constant. These two models impose their own shapes of the forward rate curve or the yield curve and their corresponding standard deviation curves. By contrast, the extended Vasicek model can accommodate any predetermined shapes of these curves. The simplified Hull–White model and the continuous-time Ho–Lee model can accommodate any predetermined shapes of the forward rate curve or the yield curve, but they impose the same shapes of the standard deviation curves as the Vasicek and Merton models, respectively.

Here, we shall reverse the order and start with the extended Vasicek model, which incorporates the other models as special cases. Everything we say about the extended Vasicek model also applies to the other models, if properly interpreted. We shall then move progressively to the more specialized cases.

Two things happen when we move from a more general to a more specialized model. First, we can do comparative statics with respect to those parameters that are assumed to be constant in the specialized model. Secondly, certain functions that characterize the model become stationary in the sense that they are functions of time to maturity and possibly of the current interest rate, but they are not functions of calendar time. This makes it possible to analyze the shapes of these functions when they are plotted against time to maturity.

In the extended Vasicek model, the interest rate follows a general conditionally Gaussian one-factor process.

The price of a zero-coupon bond equals the risk-adjusted conditional expectation of the discounting factor. Since the discounting factor is the exponential of minus the time integral of the interest rate, we calculated this time integral and determined its distribution. It turned out to be normally distributed, because it is essentially a sum of normally distributed interest rates at various points in time. Its mean is an affine function of the current interest rate, with deterministic parameters, and its variance is deterministic.

Using the formula for the expectation of a lognormally distributed random variable, we then calculated the price of the zero-coupon bond. It is the exponential of an affine function of the current interest rate, with deterministic parameters. Since the interest rate is normally distributed, the bond price is lognormally distributed.

The bond price satisfies pull-to-par. Because of the time-dependent parameters, the price function will not necessarily be stationary: the price of a bond with a fixed time to maturity will change over time, even if the interest rate happens to stay constant.

The price of a bond with a fixed maturity date is an Itô process. The relative drift is the interest rate, and the dispersion is deterministic. It turns out that the dispersion is affected by only two of the three time-dependent parameters.

As explained in Section 7.1, the instantaneous forward rate curve is a convenient representation of the information in the term structure. The yield or forward yield on a zero-coupon bond equals the average of the instantaneous forward rates, and the price or forward price equals the exponential of the negative of the integral of the instantaneous forward rates.

We calculated the forward rates in the extended Vasicek model by differentiating the logarithm of the bond price. Each forward rate is an affine function of the current interest rate, with deterministic parameters, and it is normally distributed. Like the bond price function, the forward rate function will not necessarily be stationary.

The forward rate differs from the expected future interest rate by a forward rate risk premium, which is deterministic.

The forward rate for a given maturity date is an Itô process. It has a deterministic drift and a deterministic dispersion coefficient.

Like the forward rates, the yields on zero-coupon bonds are affine functions of the current interest rate, and they are normally distributed. Like the bond price and forward rate functions, the yield function will not necessarily be stationary.

The yield on a zero-coupon bond differs from the expected average interest rate over the life of the bond by a yield risk premium which, like the forward risk premium, is deterministic. The yield risk premium equals the average of the forward rate risk premia over the life of the bond.

The yield on a bond with a fixed maturity date is an Itô process. Like the forward rate, it has a deterministic dispersion coefficient.

The model can be calibrated so as to match either the initial forward rates and their standard deviations, or the initial bond yields and their standard deviations.

Since the interest rate in the extended Vasicek model is normally distributed, it has a positive probability of becoming negative at any point in time. The same is true of the forward rates and the yields. This implies that interest rate volatilities, forward rate volatilities, or yield volatilities do not make sense. The bond prices always stay positive, and so bond price volatilities do make sense.

In the simplified Hull–White model, two of the three parameters of the interest rate process are assumed to be constant, and one of those constants is assumed to be non-zero. The drift of the interest rate equals a deterministic function of time minus a non-zero constant times the interest rate, and the dispersion is constant.

Several variance-related deterministic functions that characterize this model are stationary, in the sense that they are functions only of time to maturity, not of calendar time. This is true of the variance of the integral of the interest rate, the volatility of the bond price, the drift and dispersion of the forward rate, and the dispersion of the bond yield. The forward rate risk premium and the yield risk premium are also stationary.

The volatility of the bond price is an increasing, deterministic function of time to maturity. It goes to zero as time to maturity goes to zero, and it goes to a finite limit as time to maturity goes to infinity.

The forward rate risk premium is an increasing function of the standard deviation of the interest rate and of the time to maturity. Like the volatility of the bond price, it goes to zero as the time to maturity goes to zero, and to a finite limit as the time to maturity goes to infinity.

The forward rate itself is a decreasing function of the standard deviation of the interest rate. This effect of the standard deviation on forward rates is stronger at longer maturities.

An increase in the initial interest rate r will raise all the forward rates. This effect will be stronger for shorter maturities, it will be almost one-for-one for very short maturities, and it will be almost zero for very long maturities.

The instantaneous standard deviation of the forward rate is a decreasing function of the time to maturity. It approaches the standard derivation of the interest rate as the time to maturity goes to zero, and it declines exponentially towards zero as the time to maturity goes to infinity.

The yield risk premium is an increasing function of the standard deviation of the interest rate. It is a strictly increasing function of the time to maturity. It goes to zero as time to maturity goes to zero, and it goes to a finite limit as time to maturity goes to infinity.

The yield itself is a decreasing function of the standard deviation of the interest rate. This effect of the standard deviation on yields is stronger at longer maturities.

An increase in the initial interest rate r will raise the yields on all zero-coupon bonds. This effect will be stronger for bonds with shorter maturities, it will be close to zero for very long bonds, and it will be close to one-for-one for very short bonds.

The instantaneous standard deviation of the bond yield is a strictly decreasing function of time to maturity. It goes to zero as time to maturity goes to infinity, and it approaches the standard deviation of the interest rate as time to maturity goes to zero.

The model can be calibrated so as to match either the initial forward rates or the initial bond yields.

The Vasicek model is the special case of the simplified Hull–White model where all the three parameters of the interest rate process are constant. The interest rate process is an Ornstein–Uhlenbeck process, which implies that it exhibits mean reversion. Mean reversion means that the interest rate has a tendency to revert to a long-run mean. If at some point in time it happens to be below the long-run mean, then it will have a tendency to be pulled up. If it is above the long-run mean, then it will have a tendency to go down over time.

The variance of the future interest rate does not go to infinity as we look further and further into the future. The variance grows, but with a finite bound, because it will be limited by the mean reversion phenomenon. In the long run, the interest rate will get pulled towards its long-run mean, and so it will be distributed around the long-run mean with a finite variance. This contrasts with the behavior of the stock price in the Black–Scholes model, where the variance of the logarithm of the stock price is proportional to time.

When we described the model in terms of the original probabilities, we posited a constant price of risk. One effect of this is that the interest rate continues to follow an Ornstein–Uhlenbeck process under the risk-adjusted probabilities, but with a mean reversion level which is less than what it was under the original probabilities. Intuitively, this is because in order to pass from the original Wiener process to the new risk-adjusted one, we push its paths down, and so the paths of the interest rate also get pushed down.

The mean of the integral of the interest rate over the life of a zero-coupon bond is stationary in the sense that it depends only on the current interest rate and the time to maturity. It is a linear function of the current interest rate and the long-run interest rate, with deterministic coefficients.

The zero-coupon bond price function, the forward rate function, and the bond yield function are also stationary.

We calculated the differential of the price of a bond in two ways, assuming either a fixed maturity date or a fixed time to maturity. The dispersion is the same in the two cases, but the drift is different. For a fixed maturity date, the drift equals the interest rate, but for a fixed maturity time, it is a function of time to maturity and of the difference between the current and the long-run interest rate.

As the time to maturity goes to infinity, the forward rates converge to a level below the long-run risk-adjusted mean reversion level of the instantaneous interest rate. This limiting forward rate depends on the standard deviation of the interest rate, and it is lower the higher the standard deviation. The forward rates for very short maturities approach the current interest rate as the time to maturity approaches zero.

An increase in the risk-adjusted long-run mean of the interest rate raises all the forward rates. The effect is larger the longer the maturity. An equal increase in both the initial and the long-run interest rates will make the forward rate curve shift up in a parallel manner.

Whether we consider a fixed maturity date or a fixed time to maturity, the forward rate is an Itô process. The dispersion is the same in the two cases, but the drift is different. For a fixed maturity date, the drift is a deterministic function of the time to maturity, but for a fixed maturity time, it is a function both of time to maturity and of the difference between the current and the long-run interest rate.

As the time to maturity goes to infinity, the yield on long bonds converges to a level below the long-run risk-adjusted mean reversion level of the instantaneous interest rate. This limiting yield on long bonds depends on the standard deviation of the interest rate, and it is lower the higher the standard deviation. The yield on very short bonds approaches the current interest rate as the time to maturity approaches zero.

An increase in the risk-adjusted long-run mean of the interest rate raises the yield and lowers the price of a zero-coupon bond. This happens because the expected future interest rate goes up, which makes the money market account more attractive as an investment and the bond relatively less attractive. The impact on the price and yield of the bond is stronger the longer the maturity of the bond, because the effect on the expected interest rate in the far future is more pronounced than the effect on the expected interest rate in the near future.

An increase in the current interest rate will raise the yields on all zero-coupon bonds. This effect will be stronger for bonds with shorter maturities. An equal increase in both the initial and the long-run interest rates will make the yield curve shift up in a parallel manner.

Whether we consider a bond with a fixed maturity date or with a fixed time to maturity, the yield is an Itô process. The dispersion is the same in the two cases, but the drift is different.

In the continuous-time Ho–Lee model, the same two parameters of the interest rate process are assumed to be constant as in the simplified Hull–White model, but in addition, one of those constants is assumed to be zero. The drift of the interest rate equals a deterministic function of time, and the dispersion is constant.

The same variance-related functions that are stationary in the simplified Hull–White model are also stationary in the Ho–Lee model: the variance of the integral of the interest rate, the volatility of the bond price, the drift and dispersion of the forward rate, and the dispersion of the bond yield. As in the simplified Hull–White model, the forward rate risk premium and the yield risk premium are also stationary.

The volatility of the bond price is proportional to the standard deviation of the interest rate and to the time to maturity. It goes to zero as time to maturity goes to zero, and it goes to infinity as time to maturity goes to infinity.

The forward rate risk premium is proportional to the instantaneous variance of the interest rate and to the square of the time to maturity. Like the volatility of the bond price, it goes to zero as the time to maturity goes to zero, and to infinity as the time to maturity goes to infinity.

The forward rate itself is a decreasing function of the standard deviation of the interest rate. This effect of the standard deviation on forward rates is stronger at longer maturities.

A change in the initial interest rate r will change all the forward rates by the same amount. The entire forward rate curve shifts up or down in a parallel manner.

The instantaneous standard deviation of the forward rate equals the instantaneous standard deviation of the interest rate.

The yield risk premium, like the forward rate risk premium, is proportional to the instantaneous variance of the interest rate and to the square of the time to maturity.

The yield itself is a decreasing function of the standard deviation of the interest rate. This effect of the standard deviation on yields is stronger at longer maturities.

A change in the initial interest rate r will raise the yields on all zero-coupon bonds by the same amount. Like the forward rate curve, the yield curve shifts up or down in a parallel manner.

The instantaneous standard deviation of the bond yield equals the instantaneous standard deviation of the interest rate.

The model can be calibrated so as to match either the initial forward rates or the initial bond yields.

The Merton model is the special case of the Ho–Lee model where all the three parameters of the interest rate process are constant (and one of them is zero). The interest rate process is a generalized Wiener process. This implies that the variance of the future interest rate goes to infinity as we look further and further into the future.

As in the Vasicek model, the mean of the integral of the interest rate over the life of a zero-coupon bond is stationary. It is a linear function of the current interest rate and it is a quadratic function of the time to maturity. As in the Vasicek model, the zero-coupon bond price function, the forward rate function, and the bond yield function are also stationary.

We calculated the differential of the price of a bond both assuming a fixed maturity date and assuming a fixed time to maturity. The dispersion is the same in the two cases, but the drift is different. For a fixed maturity date, the drift equals the interest rate, but for a fixed maturity time, it is a quadratic function of time to maturity.

The forward rate is a quadratic function of the time to maturity. As the time to maturity goes to infinity, the forward rate goes to minus infinity. The forward rates for very short maturities approach the current interest rate as the time to maturity approaches zero.

Whether we consider a fixed maturity date or a fixed time to maturity, the forward rate is an Itô process. For a fixed maturity date, the drift is proportional to the time to maturity, while the dispersion is the same as that of the interest rate. For a fixed maturity time, both the drift and the dispersion are the same as those of the interest rate.

The zero-coupon bond yield, like the forward rate, is a quadratic function of the time to maturity. Like the forward rate, it goes to minus infinity as the time to maturity goes to infinity, and it goes to zero as the time to maturity goes to zero.

A change in the current interest rate will change the yields on all zero-coupon bonds by the same amount. Like the forward rate curve, the yield curve will shift up or down in a parallel manner.

Whether we consider a bond with a fixed maturity date or with a fixed time to maturity, the yield is an Itô process. The dispersion is the same in the two cases, but the drift is different.

7.11 (*) Notes

The Vasicek model of the term structure of interest rates was described by Vasicek [87, 1977]. It appears to have been the first term structure model based on the theory of derivative securities pricing. In fact, Vasicek developed a more general theory of the term structure with the instantaneous interest rate as a state variable, where prices of zero-coupon bonds are functions of the instantaneous interest rate. He recognized that the money market account plus one zero-coupon bond span the term structure, in the sense that any other zero-coupon bond can be replicated by a trading strategy. What is known as the Vasicek model is the particular parameterized example that we have developed here. Within this example, Vasicek found the formulas for the prices of discount bonds by solving a partial differential equation.

The idea of specifying a term structure model by specifying the state price process may be due to Constantinides [21, 1992].

Chan et al. [15, 1992] estimated and compared a number of different specifications of the dynamics of the short interest rate. We used their estimates in the analysis of the Vasicek term structure. There is a growing literature on the subject. See Campbell, Lo, and MacKinlay [13, 1997, Chapter 11].

Jamshidian [57, 1989] showed how to value a European option on a bond in the Vasicek model. Many interest rate derivatives have closed form pricing formulas in the Gaussian term structure models.

The Merton model is named after Merton [70, 1973], see also [72, 1990]. The process for the interest rate, as well as the formulas for the bond price and bond price volatility, were in a footnote. The formulation in Merton's main text was more general and actually also included the simplified Hull–White model. Merton did not intend the model as a term structure model but as a component of an option pricing model with a stochastic interest rate.

The extended Vasicek model was studied by Hull and White [53, 1990], Jamshidian [58, 1990], and Jamshidian [59, 1991]. Rogers [78, 1995] is a useful source.

Carverhill [14, 1995] and Hull and White [54, 1995] discuss relative merits of various models including the extended Vasicek model and the simplified Hull–White model.

The Ho–Lee model was originally formulated as a binomial model by Ho and Lee [49, 1986]. Hull and White [53, 1990] and Jamshidian [59, 1991] noted that the model has the continuous-time limit that we have described here.

APPENDIX A

MEASURE AND PROBABILITY

This and the following appendix give a brief introduction to measure, probability, and integration. They cover sigma-algebras and measures, including the important special case of Borel sigma-algebras and Lebesgue measure in Euclidean spaces, measurable mappings, Lebesgue integration, product measure and Fubini's theorem about interchanging the order of integration, L^p-spaces, convergence of random variables, densities, conditional expectations and probabilities, and stochastic independence.

I aim to define all concepts and state all results in a precise and rigorous manner. This implies the need for a fair amount of conceptual development.

On the other hand, I have skipped some proofs. While it is necessary to know and be able to apply a number of mathematical concepts and results, I do not think it is necessary to know all the proofs. Whenever I leave out a proof completely, I give an authoritative reference to the literature.

It is not only proofs but also some technical concepts that are left out. One example is the so-called outer measure. It is normally used in the proofs of various results about construction of measures, but since we leave out those proofs we can also leave out the concept of outer measure.

For readers who are drawn by the inherent beauty of the subject, or who need more measure theory as they go into finance theory beyond this book, I strongly recommend Billingsley [8, 1986].

For readers who feel a need or a desire to brush up or develop their knowledge of mathematical analysis and set theory, I recommend Rudin [81, 1976] and Royden [80, 1968].

A.1 Sigma-algebras

Let Ω be any non-empty set. A *sigma-algebra* or sigma-field on Ω is a class $\mathcal{F}$ of subsets of Ω with the following three properties:

1. $\Omega \in \mathcal{F}$.

2. If (A_n) is a finite or infinite sequence of sets in $\mathcal{F}$, then

$$\bigcup A_n \in \mathcal{F}$$

3. If $A \in \mathcal{F}$ then $A^c \in \mathcal{F}$.

It is very important to notice that property 2 is only assumed to apply to sequences of sets. It is not assumed that the union of any collection of sets from a sigma-algebra is an element of the sigma-algebra. This is assumed only of collections of sets which can be enumerated in a sequence.

In property 3, A^c denotes the *complement* of A in Ω:

$$A^c = \{\omega \in \Omega : \omega \notin A\}$$

Sigma-algebras are often used to represent information structures. In probability theory and in decision theory, we think of points $\omega \in \Omega$ as *states of the world* or *histories of the world*. We imagine that there is one particular state or history of the world which is the true one, but we do not know exactly which one it is. If our information is represented by a sigma-algebra $\mathcal{F}$, then the interpretation is that for every set $A \in \mathcal{F}$, we know whether or not the true state or history of the world is in A.

Another important role of sigma-algebras is that they serve as the domains of definition of measures. As we shall see below, a measure is a certain kind of function μ which assigns to each set A in a sigma-algebra a number $\mu(A)$, to be interpreted as the measure or size or probability of A.

The set of all subsets of Ω is a sigma-algebra on Ω, and so is the set $\{\Omega, \emptyset\}$. The set of all subsets of Ω is the largest possible sigma-algebra on Ω, in the sense that all other sigma-algebras are contained in it. When interpreted as an information set, it represents full information. The set $\{\Omega, \emptyset\}$ is the smallest possible sigma-algebra on Ω, in the sense that it is contained in any other sigma-algebra. As an information set, it represents zero information.

Usually, we are interested in "medium-sized" sigma-algebras which contain more sets than just Ω and $\emptyset$ but do not contain all subsets of Ω. These sigma-algebras can be used to represent the information of individuals who are not fully informed but who, on the other hand, are not completely uninformed either.

There is also a more technical reason for studying "medium-sized" sigma-algebras, which has to do with the properties of measures. As we shall see, many important measures can be defined only on sigma-algebras which do not contain all subsets of Ω. Notably, this is true of the so-called Lebesgue measures.

Example A.1 Suppose $\Omega = \{1, 2, 3, 4\}$ and

$$\mathcal{G} = \{\Omega, \emptyset, \{1\}, \{2\}, \{1, 3, 4\}, \{2, 3, 4\}\}$$

Then $\mathcal{G}$ is not a sigma-algebra, because

$$\{1, 2\} = \{1\} \cup \{2\} \notin \mathcal{G}$$

Let

$$\begin{aligned} \mathcal{F} &= \mathcal{G} \cup \{\{1, 2\} \cup \{3, 4\}\} \\ &= \{\Omega, \emptyset, \{1\}, \{2\}, \{1, 2\}, \{3, 4\}, \{1, 3, 4\}, \{2, 3, 4\}\} \end{aligned}$$

The $\mathcal{F}$ is a sigma-algebra, but it is strictly smaller than the sigma-algebra consisting of all subsets of Ω.   □

A *measurable space* is a pair $(\Omega, \mathcal{F})$ of a non-empty set Ω and a sigma-algebra $\mathcal{F}$ of subsets of Ω. In the context of a measurable space $(\Omega, \mathcal{F})$, a *measurable* set is a set in $\mathcal{F}$.

Proposition A.2 *Properties of sigma-algebras. Let $(\Omega, \mathcal{F})$ be a measurable space. Then*

1. $\emptyset \in \mathcal{F}$.
2. *If A_n is a finite or infinite sequence of sets in $\mathcal{F}$, then*

$$\bigcap_n A_n \in \mathcal{F}$$

3. *If $A \in \mathcal{F}$ and $B \in \mathcal{F}$, then $A \setminus B \in \mathcal{F}$.*

The following two exercises will give you an initial familiarity with sigma-algebras.

Exercise A.1 *Prove Proposition A.2.*

Recall that a set A is *countable* if either it is finite or else its elements can be enumerated in an infinite sequence. The empty set is, in particular, considered to be finite and hence also countable. An infinite *sequence* (a_n) of elements of A is a mapping

$$n \mapsto a_n : I\!N \to A$$

So A is *countable* if either it is finite or else there exists an infinite sequence (a_n) which exhausts A in the sense that

$$A = \{a_n : n \in I\!N\}$$

In fact, even if A is finite, there exists an infinite sequence (a_n) which exhausts A. Simply let $a_n = a_N$ for $n \geq N$, where N is the number of elements of A.

The set $I\!N$ of natural numbers (positive integers), the set $\mathcal{Z}$ of integers, and the set $\mathcal{Q}$ of rational numbers are countable. A non-empty interval on the real line is uncountable.

Exercise A.2 *Let Ω be a set, and let $\mathcal{A}$ be the set of all subsets $A \subset \Omega$ such that A or A^c is countable. Show that $\mathcal{A}$ is a sigma-algebra.*

The following is a seemingly abstract but very useful and frequently encountered way of defining particular sigma-algebras.

Let $\mathcal{A}$ be a class of subsets of Ω. Define $\sigma(\mathcal{A})$, the *sigma-algebra generated by $\mathcal{A}$*,

$$\sigma(\mathcal{A}) = \bigcap \{\mathcal{F} : \ \mathcal{F} \text{ is a sigma-algebra on } \Omega \text{ with } \mathcal{A} \subset \mathcal{F}\}$$

It is easily verified that $\sigma(\mathcal{A})$ is a sigma-algebra; indeed it is the smallest sigma-algebra containing $\mathcal{A}$: any other sigma-algebra which contains $\mathcal{A}$ must contain $\sigma(\mathcal{A})$.

If $\mathcal{F}$ is a sigma-algebra and $\mathcal{A}$ is a class of subsets of Ω, we say that $\mathcal{A}$ *generates* the sigma-algebra $\mathcal{F}$ if $\sigma(\mathcal{A}) = \mathcal{F}$.

Notice that there is a sort of hierarchy of points or states of the world, sets, sets of sets, etc. At the most elementary level we have the points $\omega \in \Omega$. The next level up is subsets A of Ω. Next we have sets of subsets of Ω. For example, a sigma-algebra is a set of subsets of Ω, and when we consider a class $\mathcal{A}$ of subsets of Ω which generates a sigma-algebra $\sigma(\mathcal{A})$, both the class $\mathcal{A}$ and the sigma-algebra $\sigma(\mathcal{A})$ are sets of subsets of Ω. We have even encountered sets of sets of subsets of Ω, because when we defined $\sigma(\mathcal{A})$ above, we wrote it as the intersection of a set of sigma-algebras or, in other words, the intersection of a set of sets of subsets of Ω. Such an intersection results in a set of subsets, which happens to be a sigma-algebra also. It is imperative to distinguish this level of intersection from intersections like the one in statement 2 of Proposition A.2, which is an intersection simply of subsets of Ω and which results in a subset of Ω.

So $\sigma(\mathcal{A})$ is defined by taking the intersection of all the sigma-algebras that contain $\mathcal{A}$. This definition implies that $\sigma(\mathcal{A})$ contains all complements of sets in $\mathcal{A}$, all countable unions and countable intersections of such sets, all complements, countable unions, and countable intersections of such complements, unions, and intersections, etc. However, be aware that we cannot *define* $\sigma(\mathcal{A})$ by repeatedly taking complements, countable unions, and countable intersections, starting with the sets in $\mathcal{A}$.

Specifically, if $\mathcal{H}$ is a class of subsets of a set Ω, let $\mathcal{H}^*$ denote the set of sets from $\mathcal{H}$, complements of such sets, and countable unions of such sets. Then $\mathcal{H}^*$ also contains all countable intersections of sets from $\mathcal{H}$.

Given a class $\mathcal{A}$ of subsets of Ω, define a sequence $(\mathcal{A}_n)$ of classes of sets of subsets of Ω like this: set $\mathcal{A}_1 = \mathcal{A}$, and define the following classes inductively by $\mathcal{A}_{n+1} = \mathcal{A}_n^*$. Then

$$\bigcup_{n=1}^{\infty} \mathcal{A}_n \subset \sigma(\mathcal{A})$$

and the conjecture would be that equality holds. The thing to note is that this turns out to be untrue, at least not true in general, cf. Example A.13 below.

In the special case where $\mathcal{A}$ is a countable partition, we can describe $\sigma(\mathcal{A})$ in a simple way. A set $\mathcal{A}$ of subsets of Ω is called a *partition* of Ω if the sets in $\mathcal{A}$ are non-empty and mutually disjoint, and their union is Ω. A partition is finite (respectively, countable) if it consists of finitely (respectively, countably) many sets.

Proposition A.3 *If $\mathcal{A}$ is a countable partition of Ω, then $\sigma(\mathcal{A})$ consists of all unions of sets from $\mathcal{A}$.*

Proof Let $\mathcal{F}$ be the set of all unions of sets from $\mathcal{A}$. We have to show that $\mathcal{F} = \sigma(\mathcal{A})$.

Since $\mathcal{A}$ is countable, every set in $\mathcal{F}$ is a countable union of sets from $\mathcal{A}$, and therefore it is in $\sigma(\mathcal{A})$. Hence, $\mathcal{F}$ is contained in $\sigma(\mathcal{A})$.

Observe that $\mathcal{F}$ is a sigma-algebra. First, $\Omega \in \mathcal{F}$ since Ω is the union of all the sets in $\mathcal{A}$. Secondly, any union of countably many sets from $\mathcal{F}$ is a union of sets from $\mathcal{A}$, and, hence, it is in $\mathcal{F}$. Thirdly, if $B \in \mathcal{F}$, then B is a union of some of the sets in $\mathcal{A}$. But then B^c is the union of the rest of the sets from $\mathcal{A}$, and so $B^c \in \mathcal{F}$. This shows that $\mathcal{F}$ is a sigma-algebra.

Since $\mathcal{F}$ is a sigma-algebra which contains $\mathcal{A}$, it contains $\sigma(\mathcal{A})$.

Hence, $\mathcal{F} = \sigma(\mathcal{A})$.   □

The definition of product sigma-algebras is an example of the procedure of defining a sigma-algebra as the sigma-algebra generated by a given class of sets.

Let $(\Omega^i, \mathcal{F}^i)$, $i = 1, \ldots, n$, be a finite sequence of measurable spaces. Define the *product sigma-algebra* $\mathcal{F}^1 \otimes \cdots \otimes \mathcal{F}^n$ on $\Omega^1 \times \cdots \times \Omega^n$ as the sigma-algebra generated by products of measurable sets:

$$\mathcal{F}^1 \otimes \cdots \otimes \mathcal{F}^n = \sigma\left(\{B_1 \times \cdots \times B_n : B_i \in \mathcal{F}^i \text{ for } i = 1, \ldots, n\}\right)$$

If for each $i = 1, \ldots, n$, $\mathcal{A}^i$ is a class of subsets of Ω^i (but not necessarily a sigma-algebra), set

$$\mathcal{A}^1 \square \cdots \square \mathcal{A}^n = \{B_1 \times \cdots \times B_n : B_i \in \mathcal{A}^i \text{ for } i = 1, \ldots, n\}$$

This is a class of subsets of $\Omega^1 \times \cdots \times \Omega^n$. We can think of it as the set of "rectangles" where each "side" B_i is in $\mathcal{A}^i$.

By definition,

$$\mathcal{F}^1 \otimes \cdots \otimes \mathcal{F}^n = \sigma\left(\mathcal{F}^1 \square \cdots \square \mathcal{F}^n\right)$$

Here is a very common and very useful procedure for showing that all the sets in a given sigma-algebra $\mathcal{F}$ have a certain property. Find a class $\mathcal{A}$ of sets that have the property and which generates $\mathcal{F}$: $\sigma(\mathcal{A}) = \mathcal{F}$; and show that the class of all sets that have the property in question is a sigma-algebra. This class contains $\mathcal{A}$, and therefore it contains the smallest sigma-algebra which contains $\mathcal{A}$. In other words, the class of all sets with the property in question contains $\sigma(\mathcal{A})$. But since $\sigma(\mathcal{A}) = \mathcal{F}$, it follows that all sets in $\mathcal{F}$ have the property in question.

The next proposition says that if each of the sigma-algebras $\mathcal{F}^i$ is generated by a class of sets $\mathcal{A}^i$, then the product sigma-algebra $\mathcal{F}^1 \otimes \cdots \otimes \mathcal{F}^n$ is generated by the "rectangles" where each "side" B_i is in $\mathcal{A}^i$.

We include the proof of this proposition because it contains several instructive examples of how to handle the sigma-algebra generated by a class of subsets and how to prove that all the sets in a given sigma-algebra have a certain property.

Proposition A.4 *Let $(\Omega^i, \mathcal{F}^i)$, $i = 1, \ldots, n$, be a finite sequence of measurable spaces, and for each i, let $\mathcal{A}^i$ be a subset of $\mathcal{F}^i$ such that $\sigma(\mathcal{A}^i) = \mathcal{F}^i$. Assume that for each i, Ω^i can be covered by a sequence of sets $C_i(m) \in \mathcal{A}^i$:*

$$\Omega^i = \bigcup_{m=1}^{\infty} C_i(m)$$

Then

$$\sigma\left(\mathcal{A}^1 \square \cdots \square \mathcal{A}^n\right) = \mathcal{F}^1 \otimes \cdots \otimes \mathcal{F}^n$$

Proof Since $\mathcal{F}^1 \otimes \cdots \otimes \mathcal{F}^n$ is a sigma-algebra which contains $\mathcal{A}^1 \square \cdots \square \mathcal{A}^n$, and since $\sigma\left(\mathcal{A}^1 \square \cdots \square \mathcal{A}^n\right)$ is the smallest sigma-algebra that contains $\mathcal{A}^1 \square \cdots \square \mathcal{A}^n$, it is clear that

$$\sigma\left(\mathcal{A}^1 \square \cdots \square \mathcal{A}^n\right) \subset \mathcal{F}^1 \otimes \cdots \otimes \mathcal{F}^n$$

Conversely, consider the set

$$\mathcal{G} = \left\{ B_1 \in \mathcal{F}^1 : \{B_1\} \square \mathcal{A}^2 \square \cdots \square \mathcal{A}^n \subset \sigma\left(\mathcal{A}^1 \square \cdots \square \mathcal{A}^n\right) \right\}$$

This set $\mathcal{G}$ is a sigma-algebra. To see that $\Omega \in \mathcal{G}$, use the fact that Ω can be covered by a sequence of sets $C_i(m)$ from $\mathcal{A}^1$. If $B_i \in \mathcal{A}^i$ for $i = 2, \ldots, n$, then

$$\Omega \times B_2 \times \cdots \times B_n = \left(\bigcup_{m=1}^{\infty} C_1(m) \right) \times B_2 \times \cdots \times B_n$$

$$= \bigcup_{m=1}^{\infty} \left(C_1(m) \times B_2 \times \cdots \times B_n \right)$$

$$\subset \sigma\left(\mathcal{A}^1 \square \cdots \square \mathcal{A}^n\right)$$

since

$$C_1(m) \times B_2 \times \cdots \times B_n \in \mathcal{A}^1 \square \cdots \square \mathcal{A}^n$$

for all m. It is now easily seen that $\mathcal{G}$ allows the formation of complements and countable unions, and hence $\mathcal{G}$ is a sigma-algebra. Since it contains $\mathcal{A}^1$ and is contained in $\mathcal{F}^1$, it equals $\mathcal{F}^1$. Hence,

$$\mathcal{F}^1 \square \mathcal{A}^2 \square \cdots \square \mathcal{A}^n \subset \sigma\left(\mathcal{A}^1 \square \cdots \square \mathcal{A}^n\right)$$

By applying this argument successively to $\mathcal{A}^2, \ldots, \mathcal{A}^n$, it follows that

$$\mathcal{F}^1 \square \mathcal{F}^2 \square \cdots \square \mathcal{F}^n \subset \sigma\left(\mathcal{A}^1 \square \cdots \square \mathcal{A}^n\right)$$

But then

$$\mathcal{F}^1 \otimes \cdots \otimes \mathcal{F}^n = \sigma\left(\mathcal{F}^1 \square \mathcal{F}^2 \square \cdots \square \mathcal{F}^n\right) \subset \sigma\left(\mathcal{A}^1 \square \cdots \square \mathcal{A}^n\right)$$

$$\square$$

Example A.5 In Proposition A.4, the assumption that each Ω^i can be covered by a sequence of sets from $\mathcal{A}^i$ is important. Let $n = 2$,

$$\Omega^1 = \Omega^2 = \{0, 1\}$$

and

$$\mathcal{A}^1 = \mathcal{A}^2 = \{\{0\}\}$$

Then $\mathcal{F}^1 = \sigma(\mathcal{A}^1)$ and $\mathcal{F}^2 = \sigma(\mathcal{A}^2)$ consist of all subsets of $\{0, 1\}$:

$$\mathcal{F}^1 = \mathcal{F}^2 = \{\emptyset, \{0\}, \{1\}, \{0, 1\}\}$$

The product is

$$\Omega^1 \times \Omega^2 = \{(0, 0), (1, 0), (0, 1), (1, 1)\}$$

and the product sigma-algebra $\mathcal{F}^1 \otimes \mathcal{F}^2$ consists of all subsets. However,

$$\mathcal{A}^1 \square \mathcal{A}^2 = \{\{(0, 0)\}\}$$

so that

$$\sigma\left(\mathcal{A}^1 \square \mathcal{A}^2\right)$$
$$= \{\emptyset, \{(0, 0)\}, \{(1, 0), (0, 1), (1, 1)\}, \{(0, 0), (1, 0), (0, 1), (1, 1)\}\}$$
$$\neq \mathcal{F}^1 \otimes \mathcal{F}^2$$

$\square$

A.2 Measures and Measure Spaces

Let $(\Omega, \mathcal{F})$ be a measurable space. A *measure* on $(\Omega, \mathcal{F})$ is a function $\mu : \mathcal{F} \to [0, \infty]$ with the following two properties:

1. $\mu(\emptyset) = 0$.
2. Countable additivity: if (A_n) is a finite or infinite sequence of disjoint sets in $\mathcal{F}$, then

$$\mu\left(\bigcup_n A_n\right) = \sum_n \mu(A_n)$$

A *probability measure* on $(\Omega, \mathcal{F})$ is a measure P such that $P(\Omega) = 1$.

A *measure space* is a triple $(\Omega, \mathcal{F}, \mu)$ consisting of a measurable space $(\Omega, \mathcal{F})$ and a measure μ on $(\Omega, \mathcal{F})$. A *probability space* is a measure space $(\Omega, \mathcal{F}, P)$ where P is a probability measure.

Examples of measure spaces are numerous. Because the concept of a measure space is so abstract and general, it can be applied in a wide variety of situations.

Measures derive their name from the idea that we somehow want to interpret the value $\mu(A)$ of a measure μ on a set $A \in \mathcal{F}$ as the measure or size of A. We shall soon encounter the Lebesgue measure λ^k in the Euclidean space $\mathbb{R}^k$. In dimension $k = 1$, the measure $\lambda(A)$ that it assigns to a measurable set A is understood to be its length, in dimension $k = 2$ it is the area, and in dimension $k = 3$, $\lambda(A)$ is the volume of A.

In probability theory, where we think of points $\omega \in \Omega$ as states of the world, sets in the sigma-algebra $\mathcal{F}$ are called *events*: a set $A \in \mathcal{F}$ is interpreted as the event that the state of the world is in A. If P is a probability measure on $(\Omega, \mathcal{F})$, then we interpret the measure $P(A)$ of an event $A \in \mathcal{F}$ as the probability of A. It quantifies our belief about how likely it is that the true state is in A.

Example A.6 Let $(\Omega, \mathcal{F})$ be a measurable space. When $A \in \mathcal{F}$, let $\mu(A)$ be the number of elements in A (if A is infinite then $\mu(A) = \infty$). Then μ is a measure on $(\Omega, \mathcal{F})$, called *counting measure*. To see that it is a measure, note that the number of elements in the empty set is zero, and the number of elements in a union of disjoint sets equals the sum of the number of elements in each of the sets. □

Exercise A.3 *Consider the set $I\!N$ of natural numbers with the sigma-algebra $\mathcal{F}$ that consists of all subsets of $I\!N$. Let (p_n) be a sequence of non-negative numbers with $\sum_n p_n = 1$. Define $\nu(A) = \sum_{i \in A} p_i$ for $A \subset I\!N$. Show that ν is a probability measure on $(I\!N, \mathcal{F})$.*

The following proposition states the most important elementary properties of measures.

Proposition A.7 *Properties of measures. Let $(\Omega, \mathcal{F}, \mu)$ be a measure space.*

1. *If $A \in \mathcal{F}$, $B \in \mathcal{F}$, and $A \subset B$, then $\mu(A) \leq \mu(B)$.*
2. *If (A_n) is a sequence of sets in $\mathcal{F}$ which is increasing in the sense that $A_n \subset A_{n+1}$ for all n, then*

$$\mu(A_n) \rightarrow \mu\left(\bigcup_{k=1}^{\infty} A_k\right)$$

as $n \rightarrow \infty$.

3. *If (A_n) is a sequence of sets in $\mathcal{F}$ which is decreasing in the sense that $A_n \supset A_{n+1}$ for all n, and if $\mu(A_1) < \infty$, then*

$$\mu(A_n) \rightarrow \mu\left(\bigcap_{k=1}^{\infty} A_k\right)$$

as $n \rightarrow \infty$.

4. *If (A_n) is a sequence of sets in $\mathcal{F}$, then*

$$\mu\left(\bigcup_k A_k\right) \leq \sum_k \mu(A_k)$$

Proof We prove only 1 and 2. The proof of 3 and 4 will be an exercise.

1: $\mu(B) = \mu(A) + \mu(B \setminus A) \geq \mu(A)$.

2: Define a new sequence (B_n) of events by $B_1 = A_1$, $B_2 = A_2 \setminus A_1$, and, in general, $B_{n+1} = A_{n+1} \setminus A_n$. Then the events B_n are pairwise disjoint, $\cup_{j=1}^n B_j = A_n$ for all n, and $\cup_{n=1}^{\infty} B_n = \cup_{n=1}^{\infty} A_n$. So,

$$\mu(A_n) = \mu\left(\bigcup_{j=1}^{n} A_j\right)$$

$$= \mu\left(\bigcup_{j=1}^{n} B_n\right)$$

$$= \sum_{j=1}^{n} \mu(B_n)$$

$$\to \sum_{n=1}^{\infty} \mu(B_n)$$

$$= \mu\left(\bigcup_{n=1}^{\infty} B_n\right)$$

$$= \mu\left(\bigcup_{n=1}^{\infty} A_n\right)$$

□

Exercise A.4 *Prove statements 3 and 4 of Proposition A.7.*

The reason for the inequality in statement 4 of Proposition A.7 is that there may be double counting on the right hand side. If the sequence is disjoint, then there is no double counting, and we get an equality, as in the definition of a measure.

In Proposition A.7, statement 3, the assumption that $\mu(A_1) < \infty$ is important. More specifically, it is important that for some n, $\mu(A_n) < \infty$, as indicated by the following counterexample.

Example A.8 Let $\Omega = I\!N$, let $\mathcal{F}$ be the set of all subsets of $I\!N$, and let μ be the counting measure. Set

$$A_n = \{k \in I\!N : k \geq n\}$$

Then (A_n) is a decreasing sequence of sets in $\mathcal{F}$ with $\mu(A_n) = \infty$ for all n, and so $\mu(A_n) \to \infty$; but

$$\mu\left(\bigcap_n A_n\right) = \mu(\emptyset) = 0$$

□

If μ and ν are measures on $(\Omega, \mathcal{F})$, we can define their sum $\mu+\nu : \mathcal{F} \to [0, \infty]$ by

$$(\mu + \nu)(A) = \mu(A) + \nu(A)$$

for $A \in \mathcal{F}$. It is easily seen that $\mu + \nu$ is a measure.

If μ is a measure on $(\Omega, \mathcal{F})$ and $k \geq 0$ is a constant, define $k\mu : \mathcal{F} \to [0, \infty]$ by

$$(k\mu)(A) = k\mu(A)$$

for $A \in \mathcal{F}$. It is easily seen that $k\mu$ is a measure.

A measure space $(\Omega, \mathcal{F}, \mu)$ is said to be *sigma-finite* if there exists a sequence of measurable sets $A_n \in \mathcal{F}$ such that $\mu(A_n) < \infty$ for all n and $\Omega = \cup_n A_n$.

Many constructions involving measures assume that the measures are sigma-finite. Fortunately, most of the measures that you come across in practice are sigma-finite. But not all measures are sigma-finite, as illustrated in the following example.

Example A.9 Not all measures are sigma-finite. Let $\mathcal{F}$ be the sigma-algebra on $I\!R$ consisting of all subsets of $I\!R$. Let μ be the counting measure on $(I\!R, \mathcal{F})$, cf. Example A.6. Then μ or $(I\!R, \mathcal{F}, \mu)$ is not sigma-finite. If $A_n \in \mathcal{F}$ is a sequence of sets with $\mu(A_n) < \infty$, then each A_n is finite, and their union is countable. Since $I\!R$ is not countable, the union cannot be $I\!R$.   □

If μ and ν are sigma-finite measures on $(\Omega, \mathcal{F})$, then the measure $\mu + \nu$ is also sigma-finite. To see this, let (A_n) and (B_m) be sequences of measurable sets $A_n, B_m \in \mathcal{F}$ such that $\mu(A_n) < \infty$ and $\nu(B_m) < \infty$ for all n, m and

$$\Omega = \bigcup_n A_n = \bigcup_m B_m$$

Then $(\mu + \nu)(A_n \cap B_m) < \infty$ for all n, m, and $\Omega = \cup_{n,m}(A_n \cap B_m)$. It now suffices to order the sets $A_n \cap B_m$ in a sequence.

If μ is a sigma-finite measure on $(\Omega, \mathcal{F})$ and $k \geq 0$ is a constant, then it is easily seen that the measure $k\mu$ is sigma-finite.

Proposition A.10 *Let $(\Omega^i, \mathcal{F}^i, \mu^i)$, $i = 1, \ldots, n$, be a finite sequence of sigma-finite measure spaces. Then there exists a unique measure*

$$\mu = \mu^1 \otimes \cdots \otimes \mu^n$$

on the product measurable space

$$(\Omega^1 \times \cdots \times \Omega^n, \mathcal{F}^1 \otimes \cdots \otimes \mathcal{F}^n)$$

such that

$$\mu(A_1 \times \cdots \times A_n) = \mu^1(A_1) \cdot \cdots \cdot \mu^n(A_n)$$

whenever $A_i \in \mathcal{F}^i$ for each $i = 1, \ldots, n$.

Proof A simple generalization of Billingsley [8, 1986, Theorem 18.2].   □

A product of non-negative but possibly infinite factors, like

$$\mu^1(A_1) \cdot \cdots \cdot \mu^n(A_n)$$

is understood to be infinite if at least one of the factors is infinite and no factor is zero. If at least one of the factors is zero, then the product is zero.

The measure identified in the proposition is called the *product measure*.

The reason why sigma-finiteness is required in Proposition A.10 has to do with the uniqueness of the product measure. We shall illuminate it later on in connection with Tonelli's and Fubini's theorems, in Example B.11.

The product of measures is *associative*. This means that if $(\Omega^i, \mathcal{F}^i, \mu^i)$, $i = 1, 2, 3$, are sigma-finite measure spaces, then

$$\mu^1 \otimes (\mu^2 \otimes \mu^3) = (\mu^1 \otimes \mu^2) \otimes \mu^3$$

This is easily seen from the uniqueness property in Proposition A.10.

Let $(\Omega, \mathcal{F}, \mu)$ be a measure space. A *null set* is a set in $\mathcal{F}$ which has measure zero. Let $\mathcal{N}$ be the set of null sets in $\mathcal{F}$:

$$\mathcal{N} = \{A \in \mathcal{F} : \mu(A) = 0\}$$

A sigma-algebra $\mathcal{G} \subset \mathcal{F}$ is said to be *augmented* (with respect to $\mathcal{F}$) if it contains all the null sets: $\mathcal{N} \subset \mathcal{G}$.

If $\mathcal{A} \subset \mathcal{F}$, which means that $\mathcal{A}$ is a class of sets from $\mathcal{F}$, define $\tilde{\sigma}(\mathcal{A})$, the *augmented sigma-algebra generated by* $\mathcal{A}$, as the sigma-algebra generated by $\mathcal{A}$ and $\mathcal{N}$:

$$\tilde{\sigma}(\mathcal{A}) = \sigma(\mathcal{A} \cup \mathcal{N})$$

It is the smallest augmented sigma-algebra contained in $\mathcal{F}$ which contains $\mathcal{A}$: it is augmented, and any other augmented sigma-algebra which contains $\mathcal{A}$ must contain $\tilde{\sigma}(\mathcal{A})$.

Define the *symmetric difference* $A \triangle B$ between two sets A and B by

$$A \triangle B = (A \cup B) \setminus (A \cap B)$$

This operation has the following nice properties, which go a long way in explaining its name. If A, B, and C are sets, then

1. $A \triangle B = (A \setminus B) \cup (B \setminus A) = B \triangle A$
2. $(A \triangle B)^c = (A^c \triangle B) = (A \triangle B^c)$
3. $A = B \triangle C$ if and only if $C = A \triangle B$ and if and only if $B = C \triangle A$.

Proposition A.11 *If $\mathcal{G}$ is a sigma-algebra, then the augmented sigma-algebra generated by $\mathcal{G}$ is*

$$\tilde{\sigma}(\mathcal{G}) = \{A \triangle N : A \in \mathcal{G} \text{ and } N \in \mathcal{N}\}$$
$$= \{D \in \mathcal{F} : D \triangle A \in \mathcal{N} \text{ for some } A \in \mathcal{G}\}$$
$$= \{D \in \mathcal{F} : N \triangle D \in \mathcal{G} \text{ for some } N \in \mathcal{N}\}$$

Exercise A.5 *Prove Proposition A.11.*

A measure space $(\Omega, \mathcal{F}, \mu)$ is said to be *complete* if every subset of a null set is measurable: $A \in \mathcal{F}$ whenever there is $N \in \mathcal{N}$ such that $A \subset N$.

Note well the distinction between an augmented sigma-algebra and a complete measure space. Augmentedness is a property of a sigma-algebra, in the context of a given measure space. Completeness is a property of the measure space itself. Augmentedness of $\mathcal{G}$ (with respect to $\mathcal{F}$) means that $\mathcal{G}$ contains all those sets which are in $\mathcal{F}$ and happen to have zero measure. Completeness of $(\Omega, \mathcal{F}, \mu)$ means that every subset of Ω which is contained in a measurable set of measure zero is itself measurable, and, hence, has measure zero.

It turns out that every measure space $(\Omega, \mathcal{F}, \mu)$ can be embedded in a complete measure space, in the sense that the sigma-algebra $\mathcal{F}$ can be enlarged a bit to a sigma-algebra $\hat{\mathcal{F}}$, and the measure μ can be extended to a measure $\hat{\mu}$ on $\hat{\mathcal{F}}$, in such a way that $(\Omega, \hat{\mathcal{F}}, \hat{\mu})$ is complete.

If $(\Omega, \mathcal{F}, \mu)$ is a measure space, define

$$\hat{\mathcal{F}} = \{A \triangle B : A \in \mathcal{F} \text{ and there exists } N \in \mathcal{N} \text{ such that } B \subset N\}$$

By the general properties of the symmetric difference operator,

$$\begin{aligned}
\hat{\mathcal{F}} &= \{A \triangle B : A \in \mathcal{F} \text{ and there exists } N \in \mathcal{N} \text{ such that } B \subset N\} \\
&= \{D \subset \Omega : \text{ there exists } N \in \mathcal{N} \text{ and } A \in \mathcal{F} \text{ such that } D \triangle A \subset N\} \\
&= \{D \subset \Omega : \text{ there exists } N \in \mathcal{N} \text{ and } B \subset N \text{ such that } B \triangle D \in \mathcal{F}\}
\end{aligned}$$

Define a function $\hat{\mu} : \hat{\mathcal{F}} \to [0, \infty]$ by $\hat{\mu}(D) = \mu(A)$, where $A \in \mathcal{F}$ is chosen such that $D \triangle A \subset N$ for some null set N.

Proposition A.12 $\hat{\mathcal{F}}$ *is a sigma-algebra with* $\mathcal{F} \subset \hat{\mathcal{F}}$, *the function* $\hat{\mu}$ *is well defined,* $\hat{\mu}(A) = \mu(A)$ *for* $A \in \mathcal{F}$, *and* $(\Omega, \hat{\mathcal{F}}, \hat{\mu})$ *is a complete measure space.*

Exercise A.6 *Prove Proposition A.12. Warning: This exercise is long and complicated. However, it does provide some practice in using the elementary properties of sigma-algebras and measures.*

The complete measure space $(\Omega, \hat{\mathcal{F}}, \hat{\mu})$ constructed above is called the *completion* of the measure space $(\Omega, \mathcal{F}, \mu)$.

A.3   Borel Sigma-algebras and Lebesgue Measures

In this section, we shall introduce the so-called Lebesgue measure, which is a natural and very important measure on the real line $I\!\!R$ and on the higher-dimensional spaces $I\!\!R^k$. In dimension one, the Lebesgue measure can be interpreted as a measure of length, and in higher dimensions, it can be interpreted as a measure of area or volume. The Borel sigma-algebras on the real line $I\!\!R$ and on $I\!\!R^k$ are the sigma-algebras where the Lebesgue measure is defined.

If $a, b \in I\!\!R^k$, the expression $a \ll b$ means that $a_i < b_i$ for every $i = 1, \ldots, n$. A *rectangle* in $I\!\!R^k$ is a set of the form

$$(a, b] = \{x \in I\!\!R^k : a_i < x_i \le b_i \text{ for } i = 1, \ldots, k\}$$

where $a \in I\!\!R^k$ and $b \in I\!\!R^k$. Of course, $(a, b]$ is the empty set unless $a \ll b$.

The *Borel sigma-algebra* $\mathcal{B}(\mathbb{R}^k)$ on $\mathbb{R}^k$ is the sigma-algebra generated by the rectangles.

For $k = 1$, a rectangle in $\mathbb{R}$ is a bounded interval in $\mathbb{R}$ which is open to the left and closed to the right (or the empty set). So, the Borel sigma-algebra $\mathcal{B}(\mathbb{R})$ on $\mathbb{R}$ is the sigma-algebra generated by the intervals of the form $(a, b]$, where $a, b \in \mathbb{R}$.

Let $\bar{\mathbb{R}}$ denote the *extended real line*:

$$\bar{\mathbb{R}} = [-\infty, \infty] = \mathbb{R} \cup \{-\infty, +\infty\}$$

The elements of $\bar{\mathbb{R}}$ are called *extended real numbers*.

It will be useful to consider functions whose values are extended real numbers. This is done not in order to achieve greater generality but in order to streamline the exposition of the theory of Lebesgue integration.

The *Borel sigma-algebra* $\mathcal{B}(\bar{\mathbb{R}})$ on the extended real line is the sigma-algebra generated by the sets of the form $(a, b]$ where $a, b \in \bar{\mathbb{R}}$. It consists of all unions of a set from $\mathcal{B}(\mathbb{R})$ with a subset of $\{-\infty, +\infty\}$.

Example A.13 If we let $\mathcal{A}$ denote the set of rectangles (intervals of the form $(a, b]$) in $\mathbb{R}$, then the Borel sigma-algebra is defined by $\mathcal{B}(\mathbb{R}) = \sigma(\mathcal{A})$. Recall that we defined $\mathcal{A}^*$ to be the set of sets from $\mathcal{A}$, complements of such sets, and countable unions of such sets; and that we defined the sequence $(\mathcal{A}_n)$ of classes of subsets of $\mathbb{R}$ inductively by setting $\mathcal{A}_1 = \mathcal{A}$, and $\mathcal{A}_{n+1} = \mathcal{A}_n^*$. In this case, where $\mathcal{A}$ denotes the set of rectangles in $\mathbb{R}$, it can be shown that

$$\bigcup_{n=1}^{\infty} \mathcal{A}_n \neq \sigma(\mathcal{A})$$

This means that there exist Borel sets that cannot be constructed from the rectangles by any finite sequence of set-theoretic operations. See Billingsley [8, 1986, pp. 26–28 and Problems 2.22 and 2.23]. □

We shall always assume that $\mathbb{R}^k$ is equipped with the Borel sigma-algebra unless some other sigma-algebra is explicitly specified.

Proposition A.14 $\mathcal{B}(\mathbb{R})$ *contains all intervals.*

Proof $\mathcal{B}(\mathbb{R})$ contains all intervals of the form (a, ∞) or $[a, \infty)$ because

$$(a, \infty) = \bigcup_n (a, a + n]$$

and

$$[a, \infty) = \bigcap_n (a - 1/n, \infty)$$

It also contains all intervals of the form $(-\infty, b]$ or $(-\infty, b)$, because their complements have one of the forms above. Any bounded interval is an intersection of two intervals of the forms exhibited, so $\mathcal{B}(\mathbb{R})$ contains all intervals. □

Recall that a set $G \subset I\!R^k$ is *open* if for every point in $x \in G$ there is a little ball around x which is contained in G. Formally, for every $x \in G$ there exists a (small) $\epsilon > 0$ such that

$$\{y \in I\!R^k : \|y - x\| < \epsilon\} \subset G$$

Proposition A.15 *The Borel sigma-algebra $\mathcal{B}(I\!R^k)$ is generated by either of these two classes of sets:*

1. *The open subsets of $I\!R^k$.*
2. *The class*

$$\mathcal{A} = \{(-\infty, d_1] \times \cdots \times (-\infty, d_k] : d \in \mathcal{Q}^k\}$$

   ($\mathcal{Q}$ is the set of rational numbers).

Proof This proof combines the elementary properties of sigma-algebras with specific properties of $I\!R^k$.

Let $\mathcal{G}$ be the sigma-algebra generated by the open subsets of $I\!R^k$, and let $\mathcal{E}$ be the sigma-algebra generated by the rectangles whose end-points have rational coordinates. We want to show that

$$\mathcal{G} = \mathcal{E} = \mathcal{B}(I\!R^k)$$

If $G \subset I\!R^k$ is an open set, and if $x \in G$, then there exist vectors a and b in G with rational coordinates such that $a \ll b$ and $x \in (a, b] \subset G$. Hence,

$$G = \bigcup (a, b]$$

where the union is over pairs a, b of vectors in G with rational coordinates. This is a countable union. Hence, every open set G belongs to $\mathcal{E}$, and so $\mathcal{G} \subset \mathcal{E}$.

Since the rectangles with rational end-points are in $\mathcal{B}(I\!R^k)$, it is clear that $\mathcal{E} \subset \mathcal{B}(I\!R^k)$.

To show that $\mathcal{B}(I\!R^k) \subset \mathcal{G}$, observe that $\mathcal{G}$ contains every rectangle $(a, b]$ (whether the end-points a and b have rational coordinates or not), since

$$(a, b] = \bigcap_n (a_1, b_1 + 1/n) \times \cdots \times (a_k, b_k + 1/n)$$

which is a countable intersection of open sets. $\square$

Proposition A.16 Properties of Borel sigma-algebras.

1. $\mathcal{B}(I\!R^k) = \mathcal{B}(I\!R) \otimes \cdots \otimes \mathcal{B}(I\!R)$.
2. *Translation invariance: if $A \in \mathcal{B}(I\!R^k)$ and $x \in I\!R^k$, then*

$$A + x \in \mathcal{B}(I\!R^k)$$

3. *If $A \subset I\!R^k$ is countable (in particular, if it is finite), then $A \in \mathcal{B}(I\!R^k)$.*

Exercise A.7 *Prove Proposition A.16.*

Theorem A.17 *There exists a unique measure λ^k on $(\mathbb{R}^k, \mathcal{B}(\mathbb{R}^k))$ such that the measure of every rectangle equals its volume:*

$$\lambda^k((a, b]) = \prod_i (b_i - a_i)$$

whenever $a, b \in \mathbb{R}^k$ and $a \ll b$.

Proof A consequence of Billingsley [8, 1986, Theorem 12.5]. □

The measure λ^k on $(\mathbb{R}^k, \mathcal{B}(\mathbb{R}^k))$ identified in Theorem A.17 is called the *Lebesgue measure*. Let $\lambda = \lambda^1$ be the Lebesgue measure on the real line. As we have noted before, in dimension $k = 1$, the measure $\lambda(A) = \lambda^1(A)$ of a set A is interpreted as the length of A, in dimension $k = 2$ it is the area, and in dimension $k = 3$, $\lambda(A)$ is the volume of A.

Theorem A.17 and its proof are by no means trivial. Uniqueness of the Lebesgue measure is a consequence of "Dynkin's π-λ theorem," see Billingsley [8, 1986, Theorem 3.2]. The proof of existence of the Lebesgue measure relies on the theory of "outer measure," see Billingsley [8, 1986, Section 11]. Because we skip a number of proofs in the present development of measure theory, we need neither Dynkin's π-λ theorem nor the theory of "outer measure."

Proposition A.18 Properties of Lebesgue measures.

1. $\lambda^k = \lambda \otimes \cdots \otimes \lambda$.
2. *Translation invariance: if $A \in \mathcal{B}(\mathbb{R}^k)$ and $x \in \mathbb{R}^k$, then*

$$\lambda^k(A + x) = \lambda^k(A)$$

3. *If $A \subset \mathbb{R}^k$ is countable (in particular, if it is finite) then $\lambda^k(A) = 0$.*

Exercise A.8 *Prove Proposition A.18.*

We are now in a position to explain why we need the concept of sigma-algebras. There are two main reasons for this.

The first reason is that we need sigma-algebras as the domains of definition of measures. The obvious alternative would be to have the measures defined on all subsets of Ω rather than only on those subsets that belong to $\mathcal{F}$. Unfortunately, this will not work, because in many situations, the measures we are interested in cannot be defined on all subsets of Ω, for reasons of a technical mathematical nature.

Example A.19 The one-dimensional Lebesgue measure λ has been defined on the Borel sigma-algebra $\mathcal{B}(\mathbb{R})$ in such a way as to represent the notion of length. By definition, it is the unique measure on $\mathcal{B}(\mathbb{R})$ such that the measure of every interval $(a, b]$ equals its length: $\lambda((a, b]) = b - a$. According to Proposition A.18, λ is also translation invariant: if $A \in \mathcal{B}$ and $x \in \mathbb{R}$, then $\lambda(A + x) = \lambda(A)$. It turns out that on the sigma-algebra of all subsets of the real line, there exists no measure with these two properties. See Royden [80, 1968, Chapter 3]. Hence, in the definition of the Lebesgue measure, it is important that the domain of definition be the Borel sigma-algebra and not the sigma-algebra of all subsets of the real line. It also follows that the Borel sigma-algebra is different from the sigma-algebra consisting of all subsets. In other words, there exist subsets of the real line that are not Borel measurable.   □

Example A.20 Let $(\mathbb{R}, \hat{\mathcal{B}}(\mathbb{R}), \hat{\lambda})$ be the completion of $(\mathbb{R}, \mathcal{B}(\mathbb{R}), \lambda)$. The sets in $\hat{\mathcal{B}}(\mathbb{R})$ are called *Lebesgue measurable* sets. There do exist Lebesgue measurable sets that are not Borel measurable. See Billingsley [8, 1986, Problem 3.14 and Example 31.4]. Since $\hat{\lambda}$ and λ take the same value on the Borel sets, the measure $\hat{\lambda}$ on $\hat{\mathcal{B}}(\mathbb{R})$ has the property that $\hat{\lambda}((a,b]) = b - a$ for all $a, b \in \mathbb{R}$ with $a < b$. It is also translation invariant, cf. Exercise A.9 below. Since no measure on the sigma-algebra of all subsets of $\mathbb{R}$ has these two properties, cf. Example A.19 above, this implies that the sigma-algebra $\hat{\mathcal{B}}(\mathbb{R})$ of Lebesgue measurable sets is strictly smaller than the sigma-algebra of all subsets of $\mathbb{R}$. In other words, there do exist sets that are not Lebesgue measurable.   □

Exercise A.9 *Let $(\mathbb{R}^k, \hat{\mathcal{B}}(\mathbb{R}^k), \hat{\lambda}^k)$ be the completion of $(\mathbb{R}^k, \mathcal{B}(\mathbb{R}^k), \lambda^k)$. Show that the measure $\hat{\lambda}^k$ on $\hat{\mathcal{B}}(\mathbb{R}^k)$ is translation invariant: if $A \in \hat{\mathcal{B}}(\mathbb{R}^k)$ and $x \in \mathbb{R}^k$, then $\hat{\lambda}^k(A + x) = \hat{\lambda}^k(A)$.*

The second reason for introducing sigma-algebras is that they serve to represent information structures in probability theory. If $(\Omega, \mathcal{F}, P)$ is a probability space, then sets $A \in \mathcal{F}$ are events that can be assigned probabilities. But an individual may have some information that tells him whether some events occur or not. Such information will be represented by a sigma-algebra $\mathcal{G} \subset \mathcal{F}$, which will typically be considerably smaller than $\mathcal{F}$. The interpretation is that if $A \in \mathcal{G}$, then the individual knows whether the true state is in A. We shall see below, in Section B.5, how to calculate conditional expectations and conditional probabilities given such an information sigma-algebra. We shall also see why, in general, it is not sufficient to consider information structures that can be represented by partitions of Ω rather than sigma-algebras in Ω.

We showed in Proposition A.18 that countable subsets of $\mathbb{R}^k$ have Lebesgue measure zero. It is not true, conversely, that sets with measure zero have to be countable. The set $\mathbb{R} \times \{0\} \subset \mathbb{R}^2$, for example, is uncountable but has Lebesgue measure zero. Even in dimension one there exist uncountable Borel sets with Lebesgue measure zero, as illustrated in the following example.

Example A.21 *Cantor's set.* Cantor's set C is an uncountable subset of $[0, 1]$ which has Lebesgue measure zero.

Define a sequence A_n of subsets of $[0, 1]$ by

$$A_1 = [0/3, 1/3] \cup [2/3, 3/3]$$

$$A_2 = [0/9, 1/9] \cup [2/9, 3/9] \cup [4/9, 5/9] \cup [6/9, 7/9] \cup [8/9, 9/9]$$

and, in general,

$$A_n = \bigcup_{i=0}^{(3^n-1)/2} [2i3^{-n}, (2i+1)3^{-n}]$$

Set

$$C_m = \bigcap_{n=1}^{m} A_n$$

Described in words, the set C_m results from successively removing the open middle third from intervals, starting with $[0, 1]$, repeating the operation m times.

The set C defined by

$$C = \bigcap_{m=1}^{\infty} C_m = \bigcap_{n=1}^{\infty} A_n$$

is *Cantor's set*.

It is clear that C is a Borel set. Since the sequence (A_n) is decreasing, and the Lebesgue measure of A_n is $\lambda(A_n) = (2/3)^n$, it follows from Proposition A.7 that

$$\lambda(C) = \lambda\left(\bigcap_{n=1}^{\infty} A_n\right) = \lim_n \lambda(A_n) = \lim_n (2/3)^n = 0$$

Hence, $\lambda(C) = 0$. To see that C is uncountable, argue as follows. Whenever (a_i), $i = 1, 2, \ldots$, is a sequence of digits $a_i \in \{0, 2\}$, the sum of the series

$$\frac{a_1}{3} + \frac{a_2}{3^2} + \ldots = \sum_{i=1}^{\infty} \frac{a_i}{3^i}$$

belongs to C. A sequence (a_i) is said to be non-terminating if for every i there exists a $j > i$ such that $a_j \neq a_i$. Any two distinct non-terminating sequences give rise to series with distinct sums and, hence, correspond to two different points in C. The set of non-terminating sequences of elements from $\{0, 2\}$ is uncountable; hence so is C. To see that the set of non-terminating sequences of elements from $\{0, 2\}$ is uncountable, observe that it has the same number of elements (the same cardinality) as the set of non-terminating sequences of elements from $\{0, 1\}$. The latter has the same number of elements (the same cardinality) as $(0, 1]$, and hence is uncountable, because every number $x \in (0, 1]$ has a unique non-terminating binary expansion. In other words, there exists a unique sequence (b_i) of elements of $\{0, 1\}$ such that

$$x = \frac{b_1}{2} + \frac{b_2}{2^2} + \ldots = \sum_{i=1}^{\infty} \frac{b_i}{2^i}$$

□

A.4   Measurable Mappings

This section defines and studies the concept of a measurable mapping from one measure space to another. Apart from the fact that the definition of a measurable mapping is natural and appealing, we shall see that this class of mappings is important because integrable functions are measurable, and because random variables are measurable functions.

If $(\Omega', \mathcal{F}')$ and $(\Omega, \mathcal{F})$ are measurable spaces, and $f : \Omega \to \Omega'$ is a mapping, then f is said to be *measurable* if $f^{-1}(B) \in \mathcal{F}$ for all $B \in \mathcal{F}'$.

Recall that if nothing else is explicitly specified, then $I\!R^k$ is equipped with the Borel sigma-algebra. Hence, a mapping $f : \Omega \to I\!R^k$ is said to be measurable if $f^{-1}(B) \in \mathcal{F}$ for all $B \in \mathcal{B}(I\!R^k)$.

Similarly, if nothing else is explicitly specified, then the extended real line $\bar{I\!R}$ is equipped with the Borel sigma-algebra. Hence, a mapping $f : \Omega \to \bar{I\!R}$ is said to be measurable if $f^{-1}(B) \in \mathcal{F}$ for all $B \in \mathcal{B}(\bar{I\!R})$.

If $A \subset \Omega$, then the *indicator function* of A is the function

$$1_A : \Omega \to I\!R$$

defined by

$$1_A(\omega) = \begin{cases} 1 & \text{if } \omega \in A \\ 0 & \text{if } \omega \in \Omega \setminus A \end{cases}$$

Example A.22 If $(\Omega, \mathcal{F})$ is a measurable space and $A \subset \Omega$, then the indicator function 1_A is measurable if and only if A is measurable $(A \in \mathcal{F})$.   □

It is important to notice that measurability of a mapping $f : \Omega \to \Omega'$ does not necessarily imply that the images $f(A)$ of measurable subsets $A \subset \Omega$ are measurable subsets of Ω'. Measurability is a statement about the inverse images $f^{-1}(B)$ of measurable subsets $B \subset \Omega'$.

Example A.23 If $\mathcal{F}' = \{\emptyset, \Omega'\}$, then every mapping $f : \Omega \to \Omega'$ is measurable, no matter which sigma-algebra $\mathcal{F}$ is. Suppose f is injective (one-to-one). Then $f(A) \in \mathcal{F}'$ if and only if $A = \emptyset$ or $A = \Omega$. So, $f(A) \in \mathcal{F}'$ for all $A \in \mathcal{F}$ if and only if $\mathcal{F} = \{\emptyset, \Omega\}$.   □

Example A.24 Suppose $(\Omega, \mathcal{F})$ and $(\Omega', \mathcal{F}')$ are measurable spaces, $\mathcal{A} \subset \mathcal{F}$ is a countable partition of Ω, and $f : \Omega \to \Omega'$ is a mapping. Assume that $\{\omega'\} \in \mathcal{F}$ for all $\omega' \in \Omega'$. Then f is measurable with respect to $\sigma(\mathcal{A})$ if and only if f is constant on every cell $A \in \mathcal{A}$. To see this, argue as follows. If f is constant on every $A \in \mathcal{A}$, then

$$f^{-1}(B') = \bigcup \{A \in \mathcal{A} : A \cap f^{-1}(B) \neq \emptyset\} \in \sigma(\mathcal{A})$$

for every $B' \in \mathcal{F}'$. Hence, f is measurable with respect to $\sigma(\mathcal{A})$. Conversely, suppose f is measurable with respect to $\sigma(\mathcal{A})$. Let $A \in \mathcal{A}$, $A \neq \emptyset$. Pick $\omega' \in f(A)$. Since $\{\omega'\} \in \mathcal{F}'$, $f^{-1}(\{\omega'\}) \in \sigma(\mathcal{A})$. Hence, $f^{-1}(\{\omega'\})$ is a union of sets from $\mathcal{A}$. Since $A \cap f^{-1}(\{\omega'\}) \neq \emptyset$, it must be that $A \subset f^{-1}(\{\omega'\})$. Hence, $f(\omega) = \omega'$ for all $\omega \in A$, which means that f is constant on A.   □

Let $(\Omega', \mathcal{F}')$ be a measurable space, Ω a non-empty set, and H a set of mappings $f : \Omega \to \Omega'$. Define $\sigma(H)$, the *sigma-algebra generated by H*, as the smallest sigma-algebra on Ω such that all the mappings $f \in H$ are measurable:

$$\sigma(H) = \sigma\left(\{f^{-1}(A') : A' \in \mathcal{F}', f \in H\}\right)$$

If $\mathcal{F}$ is a sigma-algebra on Ω and $\sigma(H) = \mathcal{F}$, we say that H *generates* the sigma-algebra $\mathcal{F}$.

Proposition A.25 *Let $(\Omega, \mathcal{F})$ and $(\Omega', \mathcal{F}')$ be measurable spaces, H a set of mappings $f : \Omega \to \Omega'$, $\mathcal{A}'$ a class of subsets of Ω', and*

$$\mathcal{A} = \{f^{-1}(A') : A' \in \mathcal{A}', f \in H\}$$

1. *If $\mathcal{A}'$ generates the sigma-algebra $\mathcal{F}'$, then $\mathcal{A}$ generates the sigma-algebra $\sigma(H)$.*
2. *All the mappings $f \in H$ are measurable if and only if $\mathcal{A} \subset \mathcal{F}$.*

Exercise A.10 *Prove Proposition A.25.*

In particular, if $f : \Omega \to \Omega'$ is a mapping, define $\sigma(f)$, the *sigma-algebra generated by f*, as the smallest sigma-algebra on Ω such that f is measurable. In fact,

$$\sigma(f) = \{f^{-1}(A') : A' \in \mathcal{F}'\}$$

If $\mathcal{F}$ is a sigma-algebra on Ω and f is a mapping, we say that f *generates* the sigma-algebra $\mathcal{F}$ if $\sigma(f) = \mathcal{F}$.

Corollary A.26 *Let $(\Omega, \mathcal{F})$ and $(\Omega', \mathcal{F}')$ be measurable spaces, $f : \Omega \to \Omega'$ a mapping, $\mathcal{A}'$ a class of subsets of Ω', and*

$$\mathcal{A} = \{f^{-1}(A') : A' \in \mathcal{A}'\}$$

1. *If $\mathcal{A}'$ generates the sigma-algebra $\mathcal{F}'$, then $\mathcal{A}$ generates the sigma-algebra $\sigma(f)$.*
2. *The mapping f is measurable if and only if $\mathcal{A} \subset \mathcal{F}$.*

Proof Follows directly from Proposition A.25.   □

Corollary A.27 *Suppose $\Omega \subset \Omega'$.*

1. *If $\mathcal{F}'$ is a sigma-algebra on Ω', then*

$$\mathcal{F} = \{A' \cap \Omega : A' \in \mathcal{F}'\}$$

   is a sigma-algebra on Ω.
2. *If $\mathcal{A}'$ is a class of subsets of Ω' which generates the sigma-algebra $\mathcal{F}'$, then*

$$\mathcal{A} = \{A' \cap \Omega : A' \in \mathcal{A}'\}$$

   generates the sigma-algebra $\mathcal{F}$.

Proof Follows directly from Corollary A.26 applied to the inclusion mapping $f : \Omega \to \Omega'$. □

If $(\Omega', \mathcal{F}')$ is a measurable space and $\Omega \subset \Omega'$, then the sigma-algebra $\mathcal{F}$ on Ω defined as in Corollary A.27 by

$$\mathcal{F} = \{A' \cap \Omega : A' \in \mathcal{F}'\}$$

will be called the sigma-algebra *induced* or *inherited* from $\mathcal{F}'$.

If $(\Omega', \mathcal{F}')$ and $(\Omega'', \mathcal{F}'')$ are measurable spaces, Ω is a subset of Ω', and $f : \Omega' \to \Omega''$ is a mapping, then we say that f is *measurable on* Ω if the restriction of f to $\Omega \subset \Omega'$ is measurable with respect to the sigma-algebra $\mathcal{F}$ inherited from $\mathcal{F}'$.

If there exists a measurable mapping $g : \Omega' \to \Omega''$ such that the restriction of g to Ω equals the restriction of f to Ω, then f is measurable on Ω. Conversely, if f is measurable on Ω and Ω is measurable, then there exists a measurable mapping $g : \Omega' \to \Omega''$ such that the restriction of g to Ω equals the restriction of f to Ω.

Proposition A.28 *Let $(\Omega, \mathcal{F})$ and $(\Omega', \mathcal{F}')$ be measurable spaces and let $f : \Omega \to \Omega'$ be a mapping. Suppose (Ω_n) is a finite or countable sequence of measurable subsets of Ω such that*

$$\Omega = \bigcup_n \Omega_n$$

Then f is measurable if and only if it is measurable on Ω_n for every n.

Proof It is clear that if f is measurable, then it is measurable on Ω_n for every n. Conversely, suppose f is measurable on Ω_n for every n. If $A' \in \mathcal{F}'$, then for each n, $f^{-1}(A') \cap \Omega_n$ is measurable in the induced sigma-algebra on Ω_n, which means that there exists $A_n \in \mathcal{F}$ such that $f^{-1}(A') \cap \Omega_n = A_n \cap \Omega_n$. Hence,

$$f^{-1}(A') = \bigcup_n \left(f^{-1}(A') \cap \Omega_n\right) = \bigcup_n (A_n \cap \Omega_n) \in \mathcal{F}$$

which implies that f is measurable. □

If $C \subset \mathbb{R}^k$, then $\mathcal{B}(C)$, the *Borel sigma-algebra* on C, is the sigma-algebra induced by $\mathcal{B}(\mathbb{R}^k)$ in the manner of Corollary A.27:

$$\mathcal{B}(C) = \{A \cap C : A \in \mathcal{B}\left(\mathbb{R}^k\right)\}$$

It then follows from the corollary that whenever $\mathcal{A}$ is a class of subsets of $\mathbb{R}^k$ that generates the Borel sigma-algebra $\mathcal{B}(\mathbb{R}^k)$ on $\mathbb{R}^k$, the Borel sigma-algebra $\mathcal{B}(C)$ on C is generated by the sets of the form $A \cap C$, where $A \in \mathcal{A}$. For example, according to Proposition A.16, the Borel sigma-algebra on $\mathbb{R}^k$ is generated by the open subsets of $\mathbb{R}^k$. Hence, the Borel sigma-algebra on C is generated by the sets of the form $A \cap C$, where A ranges over the open subsets of $\mathbb{R}^k$.

The Borel sigma-algebra $\mathcal{B}(\mathbb{R})$ on $\mathbb{R}$ is the sigma-algebra induced by $\mathcal{B}(\bar{\mathbb{R}})$ in the manner of Corollary A.27:

$$\mathcal{B}(\mathbb{R}) = \{A \cap \mathbb{R} : A \in \mathcal{B}(\bar{\mathbb{R}})\}$$

Proposition A.29 *Properties of measurable mappings. Let* $(\Omega, \mathcal{F})$ *and* $(\Omega^i, \mathcal{F}^i)$, $i = 1, \ldots, n$, *be measurable spaces. Equip the product space* $\Omega^1 \times \cdots \times \Omega^n$ *with the product sigma-algebra* $\mathcal{F}^1 \otimes \cdots \otimes \mathcal{F}^n$.

1. *The projection mappings*

$$(\omega_1, \ldots, \omega_n) \mapsto \omega_i : \Omega^1 \times \cdots \times \Omega^n \to \Omega^i$$

   $i = 1, \ldots, n$, *are measurable.*

2. *If* $\omega_i \in \Omega^i$, $i = 1, \ldots, n$, *then the injection mappings*

$$\omega \mapsto (\omega_1, \ldots, \omega_{j-1}, \omega, \omega_{j+1}, \ldots \omega_n) : \Omega^j \to \Omega^1 \times \cdots \times \Omega^n$$

   are measurable.

3. *If* $f : \Omega \to \Omega^1$ *and* $f^1 : \Omega^1 \to \Omega^2$ *are measurable, then the composition* $f^1 \circ f : \Omega \to \Omega^2$ *is measurable.*

4. *If* f_i, $i = 1, \ldots, n$, *are mappings* $\Omega \to \Omega^i$, *and if* $f = (f_1, \ldots, f_k) : \Omega \to \Omega^1 \times \cdots \times \Omega^k$, *then* f *is measurable if and only if all the* f_i *are measurable.*

5. *Any continuous function* $f : \mathbb{R}^k \to \mathbb{R}$ *is measurable.*

Exercise A.11 *Prove Proposition A.29.*

It follows from Proposition A.29 that if $(\Omega, \mathcal{F})$ is a measurable space and f_i, $i = 1, \ldots, n$, are measurable functions $\Omega \to \mathbb{R}$, then the product

$$f_1 \cdots \cdots f_n$$

the sum

$$f_1 + \cdots + f_n$$

the maximum

$$\bar{f}(\omega) = \max\{f_1(\omega), \ldots, f_n(\omega)\}$$

the minimum

$$\underline{f}(\omega) = \min\{f_1(\omega), \ldots, f_n(\omega)\}$$

and any linear combination

$$a_1 f_1 + \cdots + a_n f_n$$

with coefficients $a_1, \ldots, a_n \in \mathbb{R}$ are measurable functions $\Omega \to \mathbb{R}$.

Proposition A.30 *If* C *is a subset of* $\mathbb{R}$ *endowed with its Borel sigma-algebra* $\mathcal{B}(C)$, *and if* $f : C \to \mathbb{R}$ *is increasing, then* f *is measurable.*

A word on terminology: throughout this book, the words *increasing* and *decreasing* are understood to mean non-decreasing and non-increasing, respectively. So, an increasing function may be constant, or it may be constant on some parts of its domain; and a decreasing function may similarly be constant on all or part of its domain.

Exercise A.12 *Prove Proposition A.30.*

A concave function f defined on an interval I on the real line is measurable. This follows from the fact that f is continuous, and hence measurable, on the interior of I, and it is also measurable on the set consisting of any end-points of I.

Proposition A.31 *Limits of measurable functions. Let $(\Omega, \mathcal{F})$ be a measurable space, f an extended real function on Ω, and (f_n) a sequence of measurable extended real functions on Ω.*

1. *The set $\{\omega \in \Omega : f_n(\omega)$ converges$\}$ is measurable.*
2. *If $f_n(\omega) \to f(\omega)$ for every $\omega \in \Omega$, then f is measurable.*
3. *If f is measurable, then the set $\{\omega \in \Omega : f_n(\omega) \to f(\omega)\}$ is measurable.*

Proof   Billingsley [8, 1986, Theorem 13.4].   □

Example A.22 and Propositions A.29 and A.31 together provide the facts most often needed when checking whether a particular mapping is measurable. They imply that virtually every real-valued function that comes up in practice is measurable.

Example A.32 There do exist real-valued functions that are not measurable. Let $A \subset I\!\!R$, and consider the indicator function $1_A : I\!\!R \to I\!\!R$, cf. Example A.22. If A is not Borel measurable, cf. Example A.19, then 1_A is not measurable as a mapping

$$(I\!\!R, \mathcal{B}(I\!\!R)) \to (I\!\!R, \mathcal{B}(I\!\!R))$$

If A is not Lebesgue measurable, cf. Example A.20, then 1_A is not measurable as a mapping

$$(I\!\!R, \hat{\mathcal{B}}(I\!\!R)) \to (I\!\!R, \mathcal{B}(I\!\!R))$$

□

If $(\Omega, \mathcal{F}, \mu)$ is a measure space, $(\Omega', \mathcal{F}')$ is a measurable space, and $X : (\Omega, \mathcal{F}) \to (\Omega', \mathcal{F}')$ is a measurable mapping, then a measure $X[\mu]$ on $(\Omega', \mathcal{F}')$ is defined by

$$X[\mu](A') = \mu(X^{-1}(A'))$$

If $\mu = P$ is a probability measure, then so is $X[P]$.

Example A.33 Even if μ is sigma-finite, the transformed measure $X[\mu]$ is not necessarily sigma-finite. Let $(\Omega, \mathcal{F}, \mu) = (I\!\!R^2, \mathcal{B}(I\!\!R^2), \lambda^2)$, where λ^2 is the two-dimensional Lebesgue measure, which is sigma-finite. Let $X : I\!\!R^2 \to I\!\!R$ be the coordinate projection mapping $(x, y) \mapsto x$. The transformed measure $X[\mu]$ is given by

$$X[\mu](A) = \lambda^2(A \times I\!\!R) = \begin{cases} 0 & \text{if } \lambda(A) = 0 \\ +\infty & \text{if } \lambda(A) > 0 \end{cases}$$

for $A \in \mathcal{B}(I\!\!R)$. This measure is not sigma-finite. □

If $(\Omega, \mathcal{F}, P)$ is a probability space, then a measurable mapping $X : (\Omega, \mathcal{F}) \to (I\!\!R^k, \mathcal{B}(I\!\!R^k))$ is called a *random vector*, or, if $k = 1$, a *random variable*. The probability measure $X[P]$ on $I\!\!R^k$ (or on $I\!\!R$) is called the *distribution* or *probability distribution* of the random vector (or variable).

Normally, two random vectors or random variables are identified if they are equal with probability one.

Let $(\Omega, \mathcal{F}, \mu)$ be a measure space. Somewhat loosely speaking, a property is said to hold *almost everywhere* (or *almost surely*, or *with probability one* in the case where $\mu = P$ is a probability measure) if it holds outside a set of measure zero.

For example, if X and Y are mappings defined on Ω, then $X = Y$ almost everywhere if there exists a set $N \in \mathcal{F}$ such that $\mu(N) = 0$ and $X(\omega) = Y(\omega)$ for all $\omega \in \Omega \setminus N$.

Suppose X is a random vector defined on $(\Omega, \mathcal{F})$. The information content of X is represented by the sigma-algebra $\sigma(X)$ generated by X. The following proposition says that any random variable Y which depends only on the information in $\sigma(X)$ is in fact a (measurable) function of X.

Proposition A.34 *Suppose $X : (\Omega, \mathcal{F}) \to (I\!\!R^k, \mathcal{B}(I\!\!R^k))$ is a measurable mapping, and $Y : \Omega \to I\!\!R$ is a mapping. Then Y is measurable with respect to $\sigma(X)$ if and only if there exists a measurable mapping $f : I\!\!R^k \to I\!\!R$ such that $Y = f(X)$.*

Proof Billingsley [8, 1986, Theorem 20.1]. □

Let $(\Omega, \mathcal{F}, \mu)$ be a measure space, $(\Omega', \mathcal{F}')$ a measurable space, $\mathcal{G} \subset \mathcal{F}$ a sigma-algebra contained in $\mathcal{F}$, and let $f : \Omega \to \Omega'$ a mapping. Say that f is *almost everywhere measurable* with respect to $\mathcal{G}$ if there exists a null set $N \in \mathcal{F}$ such that f is measurable on $\Omega \setminus N$. Recall that this means that the restriction of f to $\Omega \setminus N$ is measurable with respect to the sigma-algebra on $\Omega \setminus N$ inherited from $\mathcal{G}$.

Proposition A.35 *Let $(\Omega, \mathcal{F}, \mu)$ be a measure space, $\mathcal{G} \subset \mathcal{F}$ a sigma-algebra contained in $\mathcal{F}$, $(\Omega', \mathcal{F}')$ a measurable space, and f a mapping $\Omega \to \Omega'$.*

1. *If there exists a mapping $g : \Omega \to \Omega'$ which is measurable with respect to $\mathcal{G}$ and such that $f = g$ almost everywhere, then f is almost everywhere measurable with respect to $\mathcal{G}$.*

2. *If f is almost everywhere measurable with respect to $\mathcal{G}$ and $\mathcal{G}$ is augmented, then there exists a mapping $g : \Omega \to \Omega'$ which is measurable with respect to $\mathcal{G}$ and such that $f = g$ almost everywhere.*
3. *If $(\Omega, \mathcal{F}, \mu)$ is a complete measure space, then f is measurable with respect to $\mathcal{F}$ if and only if it is measurable almost everywhere with respect to $\mathcal{F}$.*

Exercise A.13 *Prove Proposition A.35.*

The following theorem is sometimes useful for showing that if a set H of functions has a given property, then all functions (or all bounded functions) measurable with respect to $\sigma(H)$ also have that property.

Theorem A.36 *Let Ω be a set, and let B and H be two sets of functions $f : \Omega \to \mathbb{R}$. Assume the following:*

1. *All functions in B are bounded.*
2. *If $f, g \in B$ and $k \in \mathbb{R}$, then $f + g \in B$ and $kf \in B$.*
3. *If $f : \Omega \to \mathbb{R}$ is a function, and if (f_n) is a bounded sequence of functions in B such that $f_n(\omega) \to f(\omega)$ for all $\omega \in \Omega$, then $f \in B$.*
4. *If $f, g \in H$, then $fg \in H$.*
5. *B contains H and all constant functions.*

Then B contains all bounded functions measurable with respect to $\sigma(H)$.

Proof Dynkin and Yushkevich [35, 1979, Appendix 5, Lemma 1]. □

A.5 Convergence in Probability

Let $(\Omega, \mathcal{F}, P)$ be a probability space.

If (X_n) is a sequence of random variables defined on $(\Omega, \mathcal{F}, P)$, then X_n is said to *converge in probability* to zero if for every $\epsilon > 0$,

$$P\left(\{\omega \in \Omega : |X_n(\omega)| \geq \epsilon\}\right) \to 0$$

as $n \to \infty$.

If X is a random variable defined on $(\Omega, \mathcal{F}, P)$, then X_n is said to *converge in probability* to X if $X_n - X$ converges to zero in probability.

Recall that if (x_n) is a sequence, then a *subsequence* of (x_n) is any sequence that arises from (x_n) by omitting some of the elements. Formally, a subsequence is a sequence of the form $(x_{n_m}) : m \mapsto x_{n_m}$, where (n_m) is an increasing sequence of integers.

Proposition A.37 *Let X be a random variable and (X_n) a sequence of random variables.*

1. *If X_n converges to X with probability one, then X_n converges to X in probability.*
2. *If X_n converges to X in probability, then every subsequence of (X_n) has a subsequence which converges to X with probability one.*

Proof Billingsley [8, 1986, Theorem 20.5].   □

It follows from Proposition A.37 that a limit in probability is unique in the following sense. If X and Y are random variables, if X_n converges to X in probability, and if X_n also converges to Y in probability, then $X = Y$ with probability one.

It also follows from Proposition A.37 that convergence in probability is preserved under continuous transformations, in this sense: let I be an interval and $f : I \to \mathbb{R}$ a continuous function; if (X_n) is a sequence of random variables with values in an interval I, if X is a random variable with values in I, and if X_n converges to X in probability, then $f(X_n)$ converges to $f(X)$ in probability.

Example A.38 This example shows that a sequence of random variables that converge in probability does not necessarily converge with probability one; in fact, it may not converge at any state of the world. Let I_n be the nth dyadic subinterval of $(0,1]$: the nth interval in the following sequence:

$$
\begin{array}{llll}
(0,1] & & & \\
(0,1/2] & (1/2,1] & & \\
(0,1/4] & (1/4,2/4] & (2/4,3/4] & (3/4,1] \\
\quad\vdots & \quad\vdots & \quad\vdots & \quad\vdots \\
(0,1/2^k] & (1/2^k,2/2^k] & \cdots & \cdots & \cdots & ((2^k-1)/2^k,1] \\
\quad\vdots & \quad\vdots & \quad\vdots & \quad\vdots & \cdots & \quad\vdots & \cdots
\end{array}
$$

Let $(\Omega, \mathcal{F}, P) = ((0,1], \mathcal{B}((0,1]), \lambda)$, where λ is (the restriction of) the Lebesgue measure, and let $X_n = 1_{I_n}$ for each n. Then for $0 < \epsilon < 1$,

$$
P(|X_n| \geq \epsilon) = \lambda(I_n) \to 0
$$

so that $X_n \to 0$ in probability, but $X_n(\omega)$ does not converge to zero for any $\omega \in (0,1]$.   □

A.6   Measures and Distribution Functions

Proposition A.39 *If $F : \mathbb{R} \to \mathbb{R}$ is an increasing and right-continuous function, then there exists a unique measure μ_F on $(\mathbb{R}, \mathcal{B}(\mathbb{R}))$ such that*

$$
\mu_F((a,b]) = F(b) - F(a)
$$

for all $a, b \in \mathbb{R}$ with $a < b$.

Proof Follows from Billingsley [8, 1986, Theorem 12.5].   □

A function $F : \mathbb{R} \to \mathbb{R}$ is a *cumulative distribution function* if it is right-continuous and increasing, and if $F(t) \to 1$ for $t \to +\infty$ and $F(t) \to 0$ for $t \to -\infty$.

If $F : I\!R \to I\!R$ is an increasing and right-continuous function, then F is a cumulative distribution function if and only if μ_F is a probability measure and

$$F(t) = \mu_F(\{y \in I\!R : y \le t\})$$

for all $t \in I\!R$.

If μ is a measure on $I\!R$, then we can define an associated function F_μ by

$$F_\mu(t) = \mu((-\infty, t])$$

It is right-continuous and increasing. If the values of F_μ are finite, then μ is the measure associated with F_μ.

If p is a probability measure on $I\!R$ then the function F_p is a distribution function, since the associated measure p is a probability measure. The function is called the cumulative *distribution function* of p.

A function F is a distribution function if and only if it has the form F_p for some probability measure p.

We define the distribution function of a random variable on the basis of its distribution. So, if X is a random variable, defined on an underlying probability space with probability measure P, then the cumulative *distribution function* of X is the function $F_X : I\!R \to I\!R$ defined by

$$F_X(t) = P(X \le t) = X[P]((-\infty, t])$$

A.7 Stochastic Independence

Let $(\Omega, \mathcal{F}, P)$ be a probability space.

A (possibly infinite) collection $\{A_i : i \in I\}$ of events A_i in $\mathcal{F}$ is said to be stochastically *independent* if for every finite subset $J \subset I$,

$$P\left(\bigcap_{i \in J} A_i\right) = \prod_{i \in j} P(A_i)$$

For example, for three events A_1, A_2, and A_3 to be independent requires that

$$P(A_1 \cap A_2) = P(A_1)P(A_2)$$

$$P(A_1 \cap A_3) = P(A_1)P(A_3)$$

$$P(A_2 \cap A_3) = P(A_2)P(A_3)$$

and

$$P(A_1 \cap A_2 \cap A_3) = P(A_1)P(A_2)P(A_3)$$

On the basis of independence of events, we can define independence of classes of events: a (possibly infinite) collection $\{\mathcal{A}^i : i \in I\}$ of classes of events $\mathcal{A}^i \subset \mathcal{F}$ is said to be stochastically *independent* if every collection $\{A_i : i \in I\}$ of events

A_i such that $A_i \in \mathcal{A}^i$ for all $i \in I$ is independent (according to the previous definition).

Clearly, a collection $\{\mathcal{A}^i : i \in I\}$ is independent if and only if $\{\mathcal{A}^i : i \in J\}$ is independent for every finite $J \subset I$.

If $\{\mathcal{A}^i : i \in I\}$ is an independent collection of events, and if $\{\mathcal{B}^i : i \in I\}$ is a collection of events such that $\mathcal{B}^i \subset \mathcal{A}^i$ for all $i \in I$, then the collection $\{\mathcal{B}^i : i \in I\}$ is independent.

Proposition A.40 *If a collection* $\{\mathcal{A}^i : i \in I\}$ *of classes* $\mathcal{A}^i \subset \mathcal{F}$ *of events is independent, and if each* $\mathcal{A}^i$ *is stable with respect to the formation of finite intersections, then the collection* $\{\sigma(\mathcal{A}^i) : i \in I\}$ *is independent.*

Proof   Billingsley [8, 1986, Corollary 1, p. 50].   □

Stochastic independence of random variables or vectors is defined on the basis of the sigma-algebras they generate. For example, two random vectors X and Y are stochastically *independent* if $\sigma(X)$ and $\sigma(Y)$ are independent. A collection $\{X_i : i \in I\}$ of random vectors is stochastically *independent* if the collection $\{\sigma(X_i) : i \in I\}$ of sigma-algebras is independent.

Clearly, a collection $\{X_i : i \in I\}$ of random vectors is independent if and only if $\{X_i : i \in J\}$ is independent for every finite $J \subset I$.

A random vector X and a sigma-algebra $\mathcal{G}$ are stochastically *independent* if $\sigma(X)$ and $\mathcal{G}$ are independent.

If a random vector is independent of a sigma-algebra $\mathcal{G}$, then each of its components is independent of $\mathcal{G}$. The converse is not necessarily true, as illustrated in the following example.

Example A.41   Consider the probability space $(\Omega, \mathcal{F}, P)$ where

$$\Omega = \{1, 2, 3, 4\}$$

$\mathcal{F}$ is the set of all subsets of Ω, and P is given by

$$P(1) = P(2) = P(3) = P(4) = 1/4$$

Let $\mathcal{G}_1$, $\mathcal{G}_2$, and $\mathcal{G}_3$ be the sigma-algebras given by

$$\mathcal{G}_1 = \{\emptyset, \Omega, \{1, 4\}, \{2, 3\}\}$$

$$\mathcal{G}_2 = \{\emptyset, \Omega, \{2, 4\}, \{1, 3\}\}$$

and

$$\mathcal{G}_3 = \{\emptyset, \Omega, \{3, 4\}, \{1, 2\}\}$$

Any two of these sigma-algebras are mutually independent, but the three sigma-algebras taken together are not independent, because

$$P(\{1, 4\} \cap \{2, 4\} \cap \{3, 4\}) = p(\{1\}) = 1/4$$

while
$$P(\{1,4\})P(\{2,4\})P(\{3,4\}) = (1/2)^3 = 1/8$$

Let X and Y be the random variables defined by

$$X(1) = X(4) = 0$$

$$X(2) = X(3) = 1$$

$$Y(2) = Y(4) = 0$$

and

$$Y(1) = Y(3) = 1$$

Then $\sigma(X) = \mathcal{G}_1$ and $\sigma(Y) = \mathcal{G}_2$, so that both X and Y are independent of $\mathcal{G}_3$. However, the random vector (X, Y) is not independent of $\mathcal{G}_3$ because $\sigma(X, Y) = \mathcal{F}$.   □

Say that a collection $\{X_i : i \in I\}$ of random variables is *Gaussian* if, for every finite subset $J \subset I$, the random variables $\{X_i : i \in J\}$ follow a joint normal distribution.

Exercise A.14 *Show that a Gaussian family $\{X_i : i \in I\}$ of random variables is independent if and only if any two of the random variables are independent: X_i and X_j are independent whenever $i, j \in I$, $i \neq j$.*

Proposition A.42 *A finite sequence $(\mathcal{G}^i)_{i=1}^N$ of sigma-algebras is independent if and only if for each $n = 1, \ldots, N-1$, the sigma-algebra $\mathcal{G}^{n+1}$ is independent of the sigma-algebra*

$$\sigma\left(\mathcal{G}^1 \bigcup \cdots \bigcup \mathcal{G}^n\right)$$

Proof First, suppose the sequence $(\mathcal{G}^i)_{i=1}^N$ of sigma-algebras is independent. Let $1 \leq n \leq N-1$. Let $\mathcal{A}$ be the set of intersections of an event from each of the sigma-algebras $\mathcal{G}^i$, $i = 1, \ldots, n$:

$$\mathcal{A} = \{A_1 \cap \cdots \cap A_n : A_i \in \mathcal{G}^i \text{ for } i = 1, \ldots, n\}$$

The classes of events $\mathcal{A}$ and $\mathcal{G}^{n+1}$ are independent. To see this, let $A_i \in \mathcal{G}^i$ for $i = 1, \ldots, n+1$. It has to be shown that

$$P((A_1 \cap \cdots \cap A_n) \cap A_{n+1}) = P(A_1 \cap \cdots \cap A_n)P(A_{n+1})$$

But this follows from the independence of the sigma-algebras $\mathcal{G}^i$, $i = 1, \ldots, n+1$:

$$P((A_1 \cap \cdots \cap A_n) \cap A_{n+1}) = P(A_1) \cdot \cdots \cdot P(A_n)P(A_{n+1})$$

$$= P(A_1 \cap \cdots \cap A_n)P(\cap A_{n+1})$$

Both $\mathcal{A}$ and $\mathcal{G}^{n+1}$ are stable under the formation of finite intersections. Hence, from Proposition A.40, $\sigma(\mathcal{A})$ and $\mathcal{G}^{n+1}$ are independent. But

$$\sigma(\mathcal{A}) = \sigma\left(\mathcal{G}^1 \bigcup \cdots \bigcup \mathcal{G}^n\right)$$

Conversely, suppose that for each $n = 1, \ldots, N-1$, the sigma-algebra $\mathcal{G}^{n+1}$ is independent of the sigma-algebra

$$\sigma\left(\mathcal{G}^1 \bigcup \cdots \bigcup \mathcal{G}^n\right)$$

It has to be shown that the sequence $(\mathcal{G}^i)_{i=1}^N$ of sigma-algebras is independent.

It will be shown by induction over n that the sigma-algebras $\mathcal{G}^1, \ldots, \mathcal{G}^n$ are independent, for each $n = 1, \ldots, N$. The statement is clearly true for $n = 1$ and $n = 2$. Suppose it is true of $n < N-1$. Then it is also true of $n+1$. To see this, let $A_i \in \mathcal{G}^i$ for $i = 1, \ldots n+1$. Then

$$P(A_1 \cap \cdots \cap A_n \cap A_{n+1}) = P(A_1 \cap \cdots \cap A_n)P(A_{n+1})$$
$$= P(A_1) \cdot \cdots \cdot P(A_n)P(A_{n+1})$$

$\square$

APPENDIX B

LEBESGUE INTEGRALS AND EXPECTATIONS

This appendix continues the previous one by introducing the Lebesgue integral and some of its applications in probability theory.

Also in this appendix I have compressed the material by skipping a number of proofs. Some of those proofs are suggested as exercises, for others, I give a citation to an authoritative source. I have continued my attempt to define all concepts and state all results in a completely precise and rigorous manner.

B.1 Lebesgue Integration

Introductory calculus courses most often rely on the so-called Riemann integral. Here, we shall introduce and study the Lebesgue integral, which is more general and more convenient to work with than the Riemann integral.

The Lebesgue integral is more general because it can be used to integrate functions defined on any measure space, whereas the Riemann integral is defined only for functions whose domains are (subsets of) $I\!R$ or $I\!R^k$. And even on those domains, the class of Lebesgue integrable functions is larger than the class of Riemann integrable functions.

The Lebesgue integral is more convenient than the Riemann integral because there exist very nice rules for "integrating to the limit:" the monotone convergence theorem and the dominated convergence theorem. They say that under reasonable conditions, if a sequence of functions converges to a limit function in some appropriate sense, then the sequence of integrals of the functions converges to the integral of the limit function.

Fortunately, the Lebesgue integral and the Riemann integral are identical in those situations where both are defined.

For information on the Riemann integral and its relation to the Lebesgue integral, see Billingsley [8, 1986, Section 17].

Recall that $\bar{I\!R}$ is the extended real line:

$$\bar{I\!R} = [-\infty, \infty] = I\!R \cup \{-\infty, +\infty\}$$

In this appendix, a "function" will mean a mapping with extended real values, unless otherwise specified or qualified. Infinite values are allowed in order to streamline the theory. The advantage of this is that any increasing sequence of functions converges everywhere to some function with extended real values.

Let $(\Omega, \mathcal{F}, \mu)$ be a measure space.

A function $f : \Omega \to \bar{\mathbb{R}}$ is *simple* if it takes only a finite number of values: $f(\Omega)$ is a finite set. If $\mu = P$ is a probability measure, then we call f a simple random variable.

If $f : \Omega \to \bar{\mathbb{R}}$ is a non-negative, simple measurable function, its integral is defined as

$$\int f \, d\mu = \sum_{x \in f(\Omega)} x \mu(f^{-1}(\{x\}))$$

This means that the integral of f is the weighted sum of its values, where the weight given to each value is the measure of the set where f takes that value. If $\mu = P$ is a probability measure, so that f is a simple random variable, then the integral will be interpreted as an expectation. It is the weighted sum of the values of the random variable, where the weight of each value equals its probability.

If $f : \Omega \to \bar{\mathbb{R}}$ is a non-negative measurable function which is not necessarily simple, then it can be approximated by simple functions in the following way: there exists a sequence of simple, finite-valued functions $f_n : \Omega \to \mathbb{R}$ such that $0 \leq f_n(\omega) \leq f_{n+1}(\omega)$ and $f_n(\omega) \to f(\omega)$ for all $\omega \in \Omega$. To see this, define a sequence (ψ_n) of functions $\psi_n : [0, \infty] \to [0, \infty)$ by

$$\psi_n(x) = \begin{cases} (k-1)2^{-n} & \text{if } (k-1)2^{-n} \leq x \leq k2^{-n} \\ n & \text{if } n \leq x \leq +\infty \end{cases}$$

and set $f_n(\omega) = \psi_n(f(\omega))$, $\omega \in \Omega$.

If $f : \Omega \to \bar{\mathbb{R}}$ is non-negative and measurable, its integral is defined as

$$\int f \, d\mu = \sup \int h \, d\mu$$

where the supremum is taken over non-negative, simple measurable functions h such that $h \leq f$ almost everywhere. Notice that this integral may well be infinite.

Recall the definition of the supremum, or least upper bound, and the infimum, or greatest lower bound: if A is a subset of the extended real line, then $b \in \bar{\mathbb{R}}$ is an *upper bound* for A if $b \geq a$ for all $a \in A$, and b is a *lower bound* for A if $b \leq a$ for all $a \in A$. An upper bound c for A is a *supremum* of A if $c \leq b$ for all upper bounds b for A. A lower bound c of A is an *infimum* of A if $c \geq b$ for all lower bounds b for A. A supremum is unique if it exists, and it is denoted $\sup A$. An infimum is likewise unique if it exists. It is denoted $\inf A$.

A fundamental property of the real numbers, indeed one of the axioms that characterize the real numbers, is that every non-empty set of real numbers which has a finite upper bound has a supremum (which must then be finite). It follows from this property that every subset A of the extended real line $\bar{\mathbb{R}}$ has a supremum. If A is empty, then $\sup A = -\infty$, and if A is not empty but has no finite upper bound, then $\sup A = +\infty$.

Similarly, every subset A of the extended real line $\bar{\mathbb{R}}$ has an infimum. If A is empty, then $\inf A = +\infty$, and if A is not empty but has no finite lower bound, then $\inf A = -\infty$.

If $f : \Omega \to \bar{I\!R}$ is a measurable function which is not necessarily non-negative, define its positive part f^+ and its negative part f^- by

$$f^+(\omega) = \max\{f(\omega), 0\}$$

and

$$f^-(\omega) = -\min\{f(\omega), 0\}$$

Then f^+ and f^- are non-negative measurable functions with

$$f^+ - f^- = f$$

and

$$f^+ + f^- = |f|$$

If f^+ has finite integral, then we say that f is *integrable above*. If f^- has finite integral, then we say that f is *integrable below*. If at least one of these functions has finite integral, define the *integral* or *Lebesgue integral* of f by

$$\int f \, d\mu = \int f^+ d\mu - \int f^- d\mu$$

If both have finite integral, then the integral of f is also finite, and f is said to be *integrable*. This will be the case if and only if $|f|$ has finite integral.

Proposition B.1 Properties of the integral. *Suppose f and g are non-negative measurable functions.*

1. *If $f \leq g$ almost everywhere, then*

$$\int f \, d\mu \leq \int g \, d\mu$$

2. *$\int f \, d\mu = 0$ if and only if $f = 0$ almost everywhere.*
3. *If $\int f \, d\mu < \infty$ then $f < \infty$ almost everywhere.*

Exercise B.1 *Prove Proposition B.1.*

Proposition B.2 *Suppose f and g are non-negative measurable functions and a and b are non-negative numbers. Then*

$$\int (af + bg) \, d\mu = a \int f \, d\mu + b \int g \, d\mu$$

Proof   See Billingsley [8, 1986, Theorem 15.1].   □

Proposition B.3 Properties of the integral. *Suppose f and g are measurable functions.*

1. *If f and g are both integrable above (or both integrable below), and if $f \leq g$ almost everywhere, then*

$$\int f \, d\mu \leq \int g \, d\mu$$

and the integrals are equal if and only if $f = g$ almost everywhere.

2. *If f and g are both integrable above (or both integrable below), then $f + g$ is integrable above (below) and*

$$\int (f + g) \, d\mu = \int f \, d\mu + \int g \, d\mu$$

3. *If f is integrable above (or below), then $-f$ is integrable below (above), and*

$$\int (-f) d\mu = - \int f d\mu$$

4. *If f is integrable above (or below), and if $a \geq 0$ is a scalar, then af is integrable above (below), and*

$$\int af \, d\mu = a \int f \, d\mu$$

Exercise B.2 *Prove Proposition B.3. Hint: Use Propositions B.1 and B.2.*

If x_n is a sequence in $\bar{I\!R}$, recall that its *limit inferior* $\liminf_n x_n$ is defined by

$$\liminf_n x_n = \liminf_n \{x_m : m \geq n\}$$

Observe that $\inf\{x_m : m \geq n\}$ is increasing in n and hence does have a (possibly infinite) limit.

If f_n is a sequence of functions on Ω with values in $\bar{I\!R}$, then we define the function $\liminf_n f_n$ pointwise:

$$\left(\liminf_n f_n \right) (\omega) = \liminf_n f_n(\omega)$$

The following theorem contains the major results about limits of sequences of Lebesgue integrals. These are the results that make the Lebesgue integral superior to the Riemann integral even when the domain is $I\!R$ or $I\!R^k$.

Theorem B.4 Convergence of the integral. *Let f be a measurable function, and let (f_n) be a sequence of measurable functions.*

1. *The monotone convergence theorem: if for all n, $0 \leq f_n \leq f_{n+1}$ almost everywhere, and if $f_n \to f$ almost everywhere, then*

$$\int f_n \, d\mu \to \int f \, d\mu$$

2. *Fatou's lemma: if the functions f_n are non-negative, then*

$$\int \liminf_n f_n \, d\mu \le \liminf_n \int f_n \, d\mu$$

3. *The dominated convergence theorem: if g is an integrable function, if $|f_n| \le g$ almost everywhere for all n, and if $f_n \to f$ almost everywhere, then f and the f_n are integrable and*

$$\int f_n \, d\mu \to \int f \, d\mu$$

Proof Billingsley [8, 1986, Theorems 16.2, 16.3, and 16.4]. ☐

Fatou's lemma is normally used to derive the dominated convergence theorem, but apart from that, it does not seem to be used much in practice. It may come in handy in solving Exercise B.4 below.

Example B.5 *Billingsley [8, 1986, Example 16.6].* It is not always true that the limit of a sequence of Lebesgue integrals equals the integral of the limit function, and the inequality in Fatou's lemma may be strict. Consider $(\mathbb{R}, \mathcal{B}(\mathbb{R}), \lambda)$, the real line with the Borel sigma-algebra and Lebesgue measure. Define the functions f and f_n by $f = 0$ and

$$f_n(x) = \begin{cases} n^2 & \text{if } 0 < x \le 1/n \\ 0 & \text{otherwise} \end{cases}$$

Then $f_n(x) \to f(x) = 0$ for all x, but

$$\int f_n \, d\lambda = n \to \infty > \int f \, d\lambda = 0$$

☐

When $\mu = P$ is a probability measure and X is a random variable such that the integral $\int X \, dP$ is well defined, then the integral is also called the *mean* or *expectation* or the *expected value* of X and denoted

$$EX = E_P X = \int X \, dP$$

Proposition B.6 *If X and Y are independent, integrable random variables, then XY is integrable, and*

$$E(XY) = (EX)(EY)$$

Exercise B.3 *Prove Proposition B.6. Hint: Prove it first under the assumption that X and Y are simple.*

Exercise B.4 Convergence of the integral. *Let f and g be measurable functions, and let (f_n) be a sequence of measurable functions. Assume that g is integrable above, $f_n \leq g$ and $f_n^- \leq f^-$ almost everywhere for all n, and $f_n \to f$ almost everywhere. Show that f and the f_n are integrable above and that*

$$\int f_n \, d\mu \to \int f \, d\mu$$

Proposition B.7 *Let μ and ν be measures on $(\Omega, \mathcal{F})$, let $k \geq 0$ be a non-negative constant, and let f be a function on Ω.*

1. *If f is integrable above (below) with respect to μ and ν, then f is integrable above (below) with respect to $\mu + \nu$, and*

$$\int f \, d(\mu + \nu) = \int f \, d\mu + \int f \, d\nu$$

2. *If f is integrable above (below) with respect to μ, then f is integrable above (below) with respect to $k\mu$, and*

$$\int f \, d(k\mu) = k \int f \, d\mu$$

Proof If f is a non-negative simple function (integrable or not), then it is clear that

$$\int f \, d(\mu + \nu) = \int f \, d\mu + \int f \, d\nu$$

and

$$\int f \, d(k\mu) = k \int f \, d\mu$$

If f is non-negative but not necessarily simple, then choose a sequence (f_n) of simple non-negative functions such that $f_n \leq f_{n+1}$ for all n and $f_n(\omega) \to f(\omega)$ for all $\omega \in \Omega$. Then, by the monotone convergence theorem,

$$\int f \, d(\mu + \nu) = \lim_n \int f_n \, d(\mu + \nu)$$

$$= \lim_n \left(\int f_n \, d\mu + \int f_n \, d\nu \right)$$

$$= \lim_n \int f_n \, d\mu + \lim_n \int f_n \, d\nu$$

$$= \int f \, d\mu + \int f \, d\nu$$

and

$$\int f \, d(k\mu) = \lim_n \int f_n \, d(k\mu) = \lim_n k \int f_n \, d\mu = k \int f \, d\mu$$

If f is not necessarily non-negative but is integrable above with respect to $\mu + \nu$, then

$$\int f^+ \, d\mu + \int f^+ \, d\nu = \int f^+ \, d(\mu + \nu) < \infty$$

so f is integrable above with respect to μ and ν, and

$$\int f \, d\mu + \int f \, d\nu = \int f^+ \, d\mu - \int f^- \, d\mu + \int f^+ \, d\nu - \int f^- \, d\nu$$

$$= \int f^+ \, d(\mu + \nu) - \int f^- \, d(\mu + \nu)$$

$$= \int f \, d(\mu + \nu)$$

The proof is similar in the case where f is integrable below with respect to $\mu + \nu$.
    If f is integrable above with respect to μ, then

$$\int f^+ \, d(k\mu) = k \int f^+ \, d\mu < \infty$$

so f is integrable above with respect to $k\mu$, and

$$\int f \, d(k\mu) = \int f^+ \, d(k\mu) - \int f^- \, d(k\mu) = k \int f^+ \, d\mu - k \int f^- \, d\mu = k \int f \, d\mu$$

The proof is similar in the case where f is integrable below. □

    Recall that if A is a subset of Ω, then the indicator function 1_A is measurable if and only if $A \in \mathcal{F}$. In this case, if f is a non-negative or integrable measurable function, we write

$$\int_A f \, d\mu = \int 1_A f \, d\mu$$

Proposition B.8 Integration with respect to a transformed measure. *Suppose $(\Omega, \mathcal{F}, \mu)$ is a measure space, $(\Omega', \mathcal{F}')$ a measurable space, and*

$$X : (\Omega, \mathcal{F}) \to (\Omega', \mathcal{F}')$$

a measurable mapping. Let

$$f : \Omega' \to \bar{\mathbb{R}}$$

be a measurable function. Then f is integrable above (below) with respect to $X[\mu]$ if and only if $f \circ X$ is integrable above (below) with respect to μ. If f is integrable above or below, then

$$\int f \, d(X[\mu]) = \int f \circ X \, d\mu$$

Proof It follows from Billingsley [8, 1986, Theorem 16.12] that f is integrable with respect to $X[\mu]$ if and only if $f \circ X$ is integrable with respect to μ, and that if f is integrable, then

$$\int f \, d(X[\mu]) = \int f \circ X \, d\mu$$

Apply this result separately to f^+ and f^-.   □

The following is a version of Jensen's inequality, which has been expanded to handle variables that are integrable above or below but are not necessarily integrable.

Proposition B.9 *Let f be a concave (real-valued) function defined on an interval I on the real line, and let X be a random variable with values in I.*

1. *If X is integrable, then $f(X)$ is integrable above, and*

$$Ef(X) \leq f(EX)$$

2. *If f is strictly increasing on some subinterval of I and if $f(X)$ is integrable below, then X is integrable below.*
3. *If f is strictly increasing on some subinterval of I and if X is integrable above, then $f(X)$ is integrable above*

Proof The set of points under the graph of f,

$$\{(x, y) \in I \times \mathbb{R} : y \leq f(x)\}$$

is convex.

1: If EX is an end-point of I, then X is non-random, and there is nothing to prove. Otherwise, pick numbers a and b such that the line $x \mapsto a + bx$ is a tangent to the set of points under the graph, through the point $(EX, f(EX))$: $a + bx \geq f(x)$ for all $x \in I$ and $a + bEX = f(EX)$. Since

$$f(X) \leq a + bX$$

it follows that $f(X)$ is integrable above and that

$$Ef(X) \leq f(EX)$$

2 and 3: Again pick numbers a and b such that the line $x \mapsto a + bx$ is a tangent to the set of points under the graph, but this time through a point $(z, f(z))$, where z is in the interior of a subinterval of I on which f is strictly increasing. Then $b > 0$, $a + bx \geq f(x)$ for all $x \in I$. Since

$$f(X) \leq a + bX$$

it follows that $f(X)$ is integrable above if X is integrable above, and X is integrable below if $f(X)$ is integrable below.   □

Jensen's inequality is used very often in finance theory.

Let us introduce some frequently used notation.

If $(\Omega, \mathcal{F}, \mu)$ is a measure space and $f : \Omega \to \bar{I\!\!R}$ is a function which is integrable above or below, we write, interchangeably,

$$\int f \, d\mu = \int f(\omega) \, d\mu(\omega) = \int f(\omega) \mu(d\omega)$$

Let $f : I\!\!R \to \bar{I\!\!R}$ be a function with extended real values. If f is integrable above or below, then we write

$$\int f(t) \, dt = \int f \, d\lambda$$

where λ is the Lebesgue measure. If $a, b \in I\!\!R$, $a < b$, and $1_{(a,b]} f$ is integrable above or below, then we write

$$\int_a^b f(t) \, dt = \int_{(a,b]} f \, d\lambda$$

If $b \in I\!\!R$ and $1_{(-\infty,b]} f$ is integrable above or below, then we write

$$\int_{-\infty}^b f(t) \, dt = \int_{(-\infty,b]} f \, d\lambda$$

If $a \in I\!\!R$ and $1_{(a,\infty)} f$ is integrable above or below, then we write

$$\int_a^\infty f(t) \, dt = \int_{(a,\infty)} f \, d\lambda$$

Note that since $\lambda(\{a\}) = \lambda(\{b\}) = 0$, it does not matter whether the integration limits a and b are included or not included in the interval over which we integrate.

B.2   Tonelli's and Fubini's Theorems

Theorem B.10 Tonelli's theorem. *Let $(\Omega^i, \mathcal{F}^i, \mu^i)$ be measure spaces, $i = 1, 2$. Let f be a non-negative measurable function on $(\Omega^1 \times \Omega^2, \mathcal{F}^1 \otimes \mathcal{F}^2, \mu^1 \otimes \mu^2)$ with extended real values.*

1. *If $(\Omega^1, \mathcal{F}^1, \mu^1)$ is sigma-finite, then the function*

$$\omega_2 \mapsto \int_{\Omega^1} f(\omega_1, \omega_2) \mu^1(d\omega_1)$$

is measurable as a function of ω_2.

2. *If $(\Omega^2, \mathcal{F}^2, \mu^2)$ is sigma-finite, then the function*

$$\omega_1 \mapsto \int_{\Omega^2} f(\omega_1, \omega_2) \mu^2(d\omega_2)$$

is measurable as a function of ω_1.

3. *If both measure spaces are sigma-finite, then*

$$\int_{\Omega^2} \int_{\Omega^1} f(\omega_1, \omega_2) \mu^1(d\omega_1) \mu^2(d\omega_2) = \int_{\Omega^1 \times \Omega^2} f d(\mu^1 \otimes \mu^2)$$

$$= \int_{\Omega^1} \int_{\Omega^2} f(\omega_1, \omega_2) \mu^2(d\omega_2) \mu^1(d\omega_1)$$

Proof Follows from Billingsley [8, 1986, Theorem 18.3 and its proof]. Observe that in 1, only $(\Omega^1, \mathcal{F}^1, \mu^1)$ needs to be sigma-finite, and in 2, only $(\Omega^2, \mathcal{F}^2, \mu^2)$ needs to be sigma-finite.   □

Recall in connection with Theorem B.10 that according to Proposition A.29, $f(\omega_1, \omega_2)$ is measurable as a function of ω_1 for fixed ω_2, and it is measurable as a function of ω_2 for fixed ω_1.

The following example shows that if the measure spaces are not sigma-finite, then the formula for interchange of the order of integration in Theorem B.10 may fail, and the product measure may not be well defined.

Example B.11 Let

$$(\Omega^1, \mathcal{F}^1) = (\Omega^2, \mathcal{F}^2) = (\mathbb{R}, \mathcal{B}(\mathbb{R}))$$

let $\mu^1 = \lambda$ be the Lebesgue measure and μ^2 the counting measure on $(\mathbb{R}, \mathcal{B}(\mathbb{R}))$. Let $A \in \mathcal{B}(\mathbb{R}) \otimes \mathcal{B}(\mathbb{R})$. The function

$$y \mapsto \int 1_A(x, y) \, d\lambda(x)$$

is measurable because λ is sigma-finite. The function

$$x \mapsto \int 1_A(x, y) \, d\mu_2(y)$$

associates with x the number of y such that $(x, y) \in A$. It is measurable because it can take only countably many values. Define

$$\nu(A) = \iint 1_A(x, y) \, d\lambda(x) \, d\mu_2(y)$$

and

$$\pi(A) = \iint 1_A(x, y) \, d\mu_2(y) \, d\lambda(x)$$

These functions are easily seen to be measures on $(\Omega^1 \times \Omega^2, \mathcal{F}^1 \otimes \mathcal{F}^2)$. They coincide on products of measurable sets: if $B, C \in \mathcal{B}(\mathbb{R})$, then

$$\nu(B \times C) = \iint 1_{B \times C}(x, y) \, d\lambda(x) \, d\mu_2(y)$$

$$= \iint 1_B(x)1_C(y)\, d\lambda(x)\, d\mu_2(y)$$

$$= \int \lambda(B)1_C(y)\, d\mu_2(y)$$

$$= \lambda(B)\mu_2(C)$$

and

$$\pi(B \times C) = \iint 1_{B \times C}(x,y)\, d\mu_2(y)\, d\lambda(x)$$

$$= \iint 1_B(x)1_C(y)\, d\mu_2(y)\, d\lambda(x)$$

$$= \int 1_B(x)\mu_2(C)\, d\lambda(x)$$

$$= \lambda(B)\mu_2(C)$$

However, the measures ν and π are not identical. Let D be the diagonal in $I\!R^2$:

$$D = \{(x,y) \in I\!R^2 : x = y\}$$

Then

$$\int 1_D(x,y)\lambda(dx) = 0$$

and

$$\int 1_D(x,y)\mu^2(dy) = 1$$

but

$$\nu(D) = \iint 1_D(x,y)\lambda(dx)\mu^2(dy) = \int 0\mu^2(dy) = 0$$

while

$$\pi(D) = \iint 1_D(x,y)\mu^2(dy)\lambda(dx) = \int 1\lambda(dx) = \infty$$

Hence, the product measure $\lambda \otimes \mu_2$ is not well defined, and the formula for changing the order of integration does not hold.   □

Exercise B.5 *Let* $(\Omega, \mathcal{F}, \mu)$ *be a sigma-finite measure space, and let* $f : \Omega \to \bar{I\!R}$ *be a non-negative measurable function. Show that the integral of* f *equals the area under its graph:*

$$\int f\, d\mu = (\mu \otimes \lambda)(\{(\omega, t) : 0 \le t \le f(\omega)\})$$

where λ *is the Lebesgue measure.*

Theorem B.12 Fubini's theorem. *Suppose $(\Omega^i, \mathcal{F}^i, \mu^i)$ are sigma-finite measure spaces, $i = 1, 2$. Let f be a function on $(\Omega^1 \times \Omega^2, \mathcal{F}^1 \otimes \mathcal{F}^2, \mu^1 \otimes \mu^2)$ which is integrable above (below). Then the function*

$$\omega_1 \mapsto f(\omega_1, \omega_2)$$

is integrable above (below) with respect to $\mu^1(d\omega_1)$ for almost all ω_2, the function

$$\omega_2 \mapsto \int_{\Omega^1} f(\omega_1, \omega_2)\mu^1(d\omega_1)$$

is well defined μ^2-almost everywhere, measurable, and integrable above (below), the function

$$\omega_2 \mapsto f(\omega_1, \omega_2)$$

is integrable above (below) with respect to $\mu^2(d\omega_2)$ for almost all ω_1, the function

$$\omega_1 \mapsto \int_{\Omega^2} f(\omega_1, \omega_2)\mu^2(d\omega_2)$$

is well defined μ^1-almost everywhere, measurable, and integrable above (below), and

$$\int_{\Omega^2} \int_{\Omega^1} f(\omega_1, \omega_2)\mu^1(d\omega_1)\mu^2(d\omega_2) = \int_{\Omega^1 \times \Omega^2} f d(\mu^1 \otimes \mu^2)$$

$$= \int_{\Omega^1} \int_{\Omega^2} f(\omega_1, \omega_2)\mu^2(d\omega_2)\mu^1(d\omega_1)$$

Proof Assume f is integrable above (the case where f is integrable below is analogous).

By Tonelli's theorem, the function

$$\omega_2 \mapsto \int_{\Omega^1} f^+(\omega_1, \omega_2)\mu^1(d\omega_1)$$

is measurable, and

$$\int_{\Omega^2} \int_{\Omega^1} f^+(\omega_1, \omega_2)\mu^1(d\omega_1)\mu^2(d\omega_2) = \int_{\Omega^1 \times \Omega^2} f^+ d(\mu^1 \otimes \mu^2) < \infty$$

Set

$$A_+ = \left\{ \omega_2 \in \Omega_2 : \int_{\Omega^1} f^+(\omega_1, \omega_2)\mu^1(d\omega_1) < \infty \right\}$$

Then $\mu_2(\Omega \setminus A_+) = 0$, and the function

$$\omega_1 \mapsto f(\omega_1, \omega_2)$$

is integrable above with respect to $\mu^1(d\omega_1)$ for all $\omega_2 \in A_+$. Set

$$A_- = \left\{ \omega_2 \in \Omega_2 : \int_{\Omega^1} f^-(\omega_1, \omega_2) \mu^1(d\omega_1) < \infty \right\}$$

The function

$$\omega_2 \mapsto \int_{\Omega^1} f(\omega_1, \omega_2) \mu^1(d\omega_1)$$

$$= \int_{\Omega^1} f^+(\omega_1, \omega_2) \mu^1(d\omega_1) - \int_{\Omega^1} f^-(\omega_1, \omega_2) \mu^1(d\omega_1)$$

is well defined and measurable on $A_+ \cup A_-$, which is measurable, and it may be defined arbitrarily on the rest of Ω_2 so as to be measurable. It is integrable above because

$$\int_{\Omega^2} \left[\int_{\Omega^1} f(\omega_1, \omega_2) \mu^1(d\omega_1) \right]^+ \mu^2(d\omega_2) \le \int_{\Omega^2} \int_{\Omega^1} f^+(\omega_1, \omega_2) \mu^1(d\omega_1) \mu^2(d\omega_2) < \infty$$

since

$$\left[\int_{\Omega^1} f(\omega_1, \omega_2) \mu^1(d\omega_1) \right]^+ \le \int_{\Omega^1} f^+(\omega_1, \omega_2) \mu^1(d\omega_1)$$

for all ω_2.

Now,

$$\int_{\Omega^2} \int_{\Omega^1} f(\omega_1, \omega_2) \mu^1(d\omega_1) \mu^2(d\omega_2)$$

$$= \int_{\Omega^2} \left[\int_{\Omega^1} f^+(\omega_1, \omega_2) \mu^1(d\omega_1) - \int_{\Omega^1} f^-(\omega_1, \omega_2) \mu^1(d\omega_1) \right] \mu^2(d\omega_2)$$

$$= \int_{\Omega^2} \int_{\Omega^1} f^+(\omega_1, \omega_2) \mu^1(d\omega_1) \mu^2(d\omega_2) - \int_{\Omega^2} \int_{\Omega^1} f^-(\omega_1, \omega_2) \mu^1(d\omega_1) \mu^2(d\omega_2)$$

The proof of the rest of the theorem is analogous.   □

B.3   Densities and Absolute Continuity

Let $(\Omega, \mathcal{F}, \mu)$ be a measure space.

If f is a non-negative measurable function, then

$$\nu(A) = \int_A f \, d\mu \quad \text{for all } A \in \mathcal{F}$$

defines a measure ν on $(\Omega, \mathcal{F})$. We say that ν has *density* f with respect to μ.

A density is unique in the following sense.

Proposition B.13 *If the measure μ is sigma-finite, and if f and g are non-negative functions such that*

$$\int_A f \, d\mu = \int_A g \, d\mu$$

for all $A \in \mathcal{F}$, then $f = g$ μ-almost everywhere.

Proof Billingsley [8, 1986, p. 216]. $\square$

Example B.14 The conclusion of Proposition B.13 may fail if the measure μ is not sigma-finite. Indeed, let μ be the measure on $(\mathbb{R}, \mathcal{B}(\mathbb{R}))$ given by

$$\mu(A) = \begin{cases} 0 & \text{if } \lambda(A) = 0 \\ \infty & \text{if } \lambda(A) > 0 \end{cases}$$

where λ is the Lebesgue measure. Let $f = 1$ and $g = 2$. Then $f \neq g$ μ-almost everywhere, but

$$\int_A f \, d\mu = \int_A g \, d\mu$$

for all $A \in \mathcal{B}(\mathbb{R})$. $\square$

A class $\mathcal{A} \subset \mathcal{F}$ of sets is *stable with respect to the formation of finite intersections* if $B \cap C \in \mathcal{A}$ whenever $B \in \mathcal{A}$ and $C \in \mathcal{A}$.

Proposition B.15 *Let $\mathcal{A} \subset \mathcal{F}$ be a class of sets such that*

1. *$\mathcal{A}$ is stable with respect to the formation of finite intersections.*
2. *$\mathcal{A}$ generates $\mathcal{F}$: $\sigma(\mathcal{A}) = \mathcal{F}$.*
3. *Ω is a finite or countable union of sets from $\mathcal{A}$.*

If f and g are integrable functions such that

$$\int_A f \, d\mu = \int_A g \, d\mu$$

for all $A \in \mathcal{A}$, then $f = g$ almost everywhere.

Proof Billingsley [8, 1986, p. 216]. $\square$

Proposition B.16 Integration and densities. *Suppose ν has density δ with respect to μ, and let f be a measurable function. Then f is integrable above (below) with respect to ν if and only if $f\delta$ is integrable above (below) with respect to μ. If so, then*

$$\int f \, d\nu = \int f\delta \, d\mu$$

Proof It follows from Billingsley [8, 1986, Theorem 16.10] that f is integrable with respect to ν if and only if $f\delta$ is integrable with respect to μ, and that if f is integrable, then

$$\int f \, d\nu = \int f\delta \, d\mu$$

Apply this result separately to f^+ and f^-. $\square$

We say that ν is *absolutely continuous* with respect to μ, written $\nu \ll \mu$, if all null sets under μ are also null sets under ν: if $A \in \mathcal{F}$ and $\mu(A) = 0$, then $\nu(A) = 0$.

It is clear that if ν has a density with respect to μ, then ν is absolutely continuous with respect to μ. For sigma-finite measures, the converse is also true. This is stated in the following theorem.

Theorem B.17 The Radon–Nikodym theorem. *If μ and ν are sigma-finite measures such that ν is absolutely continuous with respect to μ, then ν has a density with respect to μ.*

Proof Billingsley [8, 1986, Theorem 32.2]. □

Example B.18 The conclusion of the Radon–Nikodym theorem may fail if μ is not sigma-finite. Let $\mathcal{F} \subset \mathcal{B}(I\!R)$ be the sigma-algebra consisting of sets $A \subset I\!R$ such that either A or A^c is countable, cf. Exercise A.2. Let μ be the counting measure on $(I\!R, \mathcal{F})$, and let ν be the measure on $(I\!R, \mathcal{F})$ given by

$$\nu(A) = \begin{cases} 0 & \text{if } A \text{ is countable} \\ 1 & \text{if } A^c \text{ is countable} \end{cases}$$

Then ν is absolutely continuous with respect to μ, but μ is not sigma-finite, and ν does not have a density with respect to μ. □

Two measures μ and ν are said to be *equivalent* if each is absolutely continuous with respect to the other. This will be the case if and only if the two measures have the same null sets.

Proposition B.19 *Two sigma-finite measures μ and ν are equivalent if and only if ν has a density δ with respect to μ which is positive μ-almost everywhere, in which case μ has density $1/\delta$ with respect to ν.*

Proof Suppose ν has density δ with respect to μ, where $\delta > 0$ μ-almost everywhere. If $A \in \mathcal{F}$, then

$$\mu(A) = \int_A 1 \, d\mu = \int_A (1/\delta)\delta \, d\mu = \int_A (1/\delta) \, d\nu$$

so μ has density $1/\delta$ with respect to ν. Hence, the measures are equivalent. Conversely, if the measures are equivalent, then ν has a density δ with respect to μ. Let

$$A = \{\omega \in \Omega : \delta(\omega) = 0\}$$

Then

$$\nu(A) = \int_A \delta \, d\mu = 0$$

so $\mu(A) = 0$, and δ is positive μ-almost everywhere. □

The following is a very commonly used result about change of variable.

Proposition B.20 Density of a transformed measure. *Let I be an open interval on the real line, let $g : I \to I\!R$ be a continuously differentiable, strictly increasing function, and let μ be the measure on $(I, \mathcal{B}(I))$ with density g' with respect to the Lebesgue measure λ. Then*

1. *the transformed measure $g[\mu]$ is the Lebesgue measure on $g(I)$, and*
2. *a function $f : g(I) \to \mathbb{R}$ is integrable above (below) if and only if $f \circ g$ is integrable above (below) with respect to μ, in which case*

$$\int f(t)\, dt = \int f\, d\lambda = \int f \circ g\, d\mu = \int (f \circ g)g'\, d\lambda = \int f(g(t))g'(t)\, dt$$

Proof 1: Billingsley [8, 1986, Sections 17 and 20]. 2: this follows from 1 combined with Propositions B.16 and B.8. □

Proposition B.21 *Let I be an interval and $F : I \to \mathbb{R}$ an increasing function. Then F is differentiable almost everywhere, the derivative $f = F'$ is measurable and non-negative, and*

$$\int_a^x f(t)\, dt \leq F(x) - F(a)$$

whenever $a, x \in I$.

Proof Billingsley [8, 1986, Theorem 31.2]. □

Observe that the derivative F' in Proposition B.21 may not be continuous. For comparison, we quote the so-called fundamental theorem of calculus:

Theorem B.22 *Let I be an interval and $f : I \to \mathbb{R}$ a continuous function. Let $a \in I$ and define a function F on I by*

$$F(x) = \int_a^x f(t)\, dt$$

Then F is continuously differentiable with $F' = f$. If G is a continuously differentiable function on I with $G' = f$, then $G - G(a) = F$.

Proof Billingsley [8, 1986, p. 227]. □

If the function f in Proposition B.21 is not continuous, then its integral may be strictly less than the increment of the function F (so that the inequality is not in fact an equality). Billingsley [8, 1986, Example 31.1] exhibits a function F, defined over the unit interval $[0, 1]$, which is strictly increasing and continuous, and yet has derivative $F' = f = 0$ almost everywhere.

Theorem B.23 *Let I be an interval and $f : I \to \bar{\mathbb{R}}$ an integrable function. Let $a \in I$ and define a function F on I by*

$$F(x) = \int_a^x f(t)\, dt$$

Then F is continuous and almost everywhere differentiable with $F' = f$.

Proof For non-negative integrable f, it follows from Billingsley [8, 1986, Theorem 31.1] that F is almost everywhere differentiable with $F' = f$. The case where f is not necessarily non-negative follows by considering f^+ and f^-.

Continuity of F can be seen as follows. If $y \in I$, then

$$1_{(a,x]}(t)f(t) \to 1_{(a,y]}(t)f(t)$$

as $x \to y$, for all $t \neq y$. Since $|1_{(-\infty,x]}(t)f(t)| \leq |f(t)|$ for all t, it follows from the dominated convergence theorem that

$$\int_a^x f(t)\,dt = \int 1_{(a,x]}(t)f(t)\,dt \to \int 1_{(a,y]}(t)f(t)\,dt = \int_a^y f(t)\,dt$$

as $x \to y$.   □

B.4   Locally Integrable Functions

If $I \subset \mathbb{R}$ is an interval, and $k : I \to \mathbb{R}$ is a measurable function, then k is said to be *locally integrable* if

$$\int_b^c |k(y)|\,dy < \infty$$

whenever $b, c \in I$, $b < c$.

Proposition B.24 *Let I and J be open intervals, let $k : I \to \mathbb{R}$ be a measurable function, and let $h : J \to I$ be a continuously differentiable function with positive derivative. Then $k \circ h$ is locally integrable if and only if k is locally integrable.*

Proof Suppose k is locally integrable. If $b, c \in J$, $b < c$, then there exists a constant C such that

$$\frac{1}{h'(y)} \leq C \quad \text{for } b \leq y \leq c$$

Now,

$$\int_b^c |k \circ h(x)|\,dx = \int_{h(b)}^{h(c)} |k(y)|\frac{1}{h'(y)}\,dy \leq C \int_{h(b)}^{h(c)} |k(y)|\,dy < \infty$$

where we have used the change of variables

$$y = h(x)$$

$$x = h^{-1}(y)$$

$$dx = \left(h^{-1}\right)'(y)\,dy = \frac{1}{h'(y)}\,dy$$

Hence, $k \circ h$ is locally integrable. Conversely, if $k \circ h$ is locally integrable, then the same argument shows that $k = (k \circ h) \circ h^{-1}$ is locally integrable.   □

B.5   Conditional Expectations and Probabilities

Let $(\Omega, \mathcal{F}, P)$ be a probability space, and let X be an integrable random variable. If $B \in \mathcal{F}$, $P(B) > 0$, define

$$E(X \mid B) = \frac{E(1_B X)}{P(B)}$$

The conditional expectation of X given an event B is simply a number. We now want to define the conditional expectation of X given an information structure. This conditional expectation will be a random variable, because it depends on the random piece of information received.

First, consider the case where the information structure is represented by a partition. Let $\mathcal{A} \subset \mathcal{F}$ be a partition of Ω into finitely many measurable sets (called cells), each of which has positive probability. The sigma-algebra $\sigma(\mathcal{A})$ consists of all unions of sets from $\mathcal{A}$. For each state $\omega \in \Omega$, let $A(\omega)$ denote the unique cell in $\mathcal{A}$ which contains ω: $\omega \in A(\omega) \in \mathcal{A}$. Define a function $E(X \mid \mathcal{A})$ on Ω by

$$E(X \mid \mathcal{A})(\omega) = E(X \mid A(\omega))$$

This function has the following crucial properties:

1. $E(X \mid \mathcal{A})$ is measurable with respect to $\sigma(\mathcal{A})$.
2. If $B \in \sigma(\mathcal{A})$, then

$$E[1_B E(X \mid \mathcal{A})] = E[1_B X]$$

Measurability follows from the fact that $E(X \mid \mathcal{A})$ is constant over each cell of $\mathcal{A}$. To show the second property, note that the set $B \in \sigma(\mathcal{A})$ can be written as a disjoint union $B = \cup_{j=1}^{k} A_j$ of cells $A_j \in \mathcal{A}$. Then

$$E[1_B E(X \mid \mathcal{A})] = E\left[\sum_{j=1}^{k} 1_{A_j} E(X \mid \mathcal{A})\right]$$

$$= \sum_{j=1}^{k} E[1_{A_j} E(X \mid A_j)]$$

$$= \sum_{j=1}^{k} P(A_j) E(X \mid A_j)$$

$$= \sum_{j=1}^{k} E(1_{A_j} X)$$

$$= E\left[\left(\sum_{j=1}^{k} 1_{A_j}\right) X\right]$$

$$= E(1_B X)$$

Not all information structures can be described by partitions of the underlying probability space. Let X be a random variable such that each of the events

$$B(x) = \{\omega \in \Omega : X(\omega) = x\}, \ x \in \mathbb{R}$$

have zero probability. For example, this will be the case if X is normally distributed. These events form a partition

$$\mathcal{B} = \{B(x) : x \in \mathbb{R}\}$$

of Ω. If the information contained in X were to be represented by a partition, then it would have to be this partition $\mathcal{B}$. However, one of the major uses of an information structure is to compute conditional expectations and conditional probabilities. No method exists for computing expectations and probabilities conditionally on a partition of Ω into events with zero probability (intuitively, it would involve dividing by zero). Instead, the information contained in X is represented by $\sigma(X)$, the sigma-algebra generated by X. As we shall see, one can indeed compute expectations and probabilities conditionally on a sigma-algebra.

Then why not use the sigma-algebra $\sigma(\mathcal{B})$ generated by the partition $\mathcal{B}$ instead of the sigma-algebra $\sigma(X)$ generated by X to represent the information contained in X? Because $\sigma(\mathcal{B})$ is too small to represent any information! The sigma-algebra $\sigma(\mathcal{B})$ consists of all countable unions of sets in $\mathcal{B}$ and all complements of such countable unions. It turns out that the conditional probability of an event given $\sigma(\mathcal{B})$ equals the unconditional probability of the event, and the conditional expectation of a random variable given $\sigma(\mathcal{B})$ equals the unconditional expectation of the random variable. So, $\sigma(\mathcal{B})$ represents essentially no information. See Exercise B.6 and the discussion after Proposition B.25 below.

Exercise B.6 *Let X be a random variable. Set*

$$B(x) = \{\omega \in \Omega : X(\omega) = x\}, \ x \in \mathbb{R}$$

Let $\mathcal{B}$ be the partition

$$\mathcal{B} = \{B(x) : x \in \mathbb{R}\}$$

of Ω.

1. *Show that the sigma-algebra $\sigma(\mathcal{B})$ generated by $\mathcal{B}$ consists of all countable unions of sets in $\mathcal{B}$ and all complements of such countable unions.*
2. *Assume that X is normally distributed. Show that the set $\{\omega \in \Omega : X(\omega) \leq 0\}$ is a union of sets in $\sigma(\mathcal{B})$ (in fact, a union of sets in $\mathcal{B}$) but is not itself in $\sigma(\mathcal{B})$.*

Consider the general case where the information structure is represented by a sigma-algebra $\mathcal{G} \subset \mathcal{F}$. The sigma-algebra $\mathcal{G}$ corresponds to $\sigma(\mathcal{A})$ above. In this case, properties 1–2 are taken as the definition of the random variable $E(X \mid G)$:

Proposition B.25 *Suppose $\mathcal{G} \subset \mathcal{F}$ is a sigma-algebra and X is an integrable random variable. Then there exists an integrable random variable Z such that Z is measurable with respect to $\mathcal{G}$, and for every $B \in \mathcal{G}$,*

$$E\left[1_B Z\right] = E\left[1_B X\right]$$

The variable Z is unique in the sense that if Z' is another random variable with these two properties, then $Z = Z'$ almost surely.

Proof   See Billingsley [8, 1986, p. 466].   □

The variable Z in Proposition B.25 is called the *conditional expectation* of X given $\mathcal{G}$ and is denoted $E(X \mid \mathcal{G}) = Z$.

Now go back to the situation above. Suppose X is a finite-valued random variable such that $P(X^{-1}(x)) = 0$ for all $x \in I\!R$, and let $\mathcal{B}$ be the partition of Ω into the cells $X^{-1}(x)$:

$$\mathcal{B} = \{X^{-1}(x) : x \in I\!R\}$$

There has to be an uncountably infinite number of cells, each with zero probability. The sigma-algebra $\sigma(\mathcal{B})$ consists of all countable unions of sets from $\mathcal{B}$ and all complements of such unions. Each of these events has probability either zero or one. Consequently, the conditional expectation of any integrable random variable Z given $\sigma(\mathcal{B})$ equals the unconditional expectation. This indicates that $\sigma(\mathcal{B})$ is too small to represent any information at all. For that reason, $\sigma(\mathcal{B})$ cannot be used to represent the information contained in X, and the sigma-algebra $\sigma(X)$ should be used instead.

Proposition B.26 Properties of conditional expectations. *Let X and Y be integrable random variables, and let $\mathcal{G} \subset \mathcal{F}$ be a sigma-algebra.*

1. *If $X \leq Y$ with probability one, then*

$$E(X \mid \mathcal{G}) \leq E(Y \mid \mathcal{G})$$

   with probability one.

2. *If a and b are numbers, then*

$$E(aX + bY \mid \mathcal{G}) = aE(X \mid \mathcal{G}) + bE(Y \mid \mathcal{G})$$

   with probability one.

3. *$|E(X \mid \mathcal{G})| \leq E(|X| \mid \mathcal{G})$ with probability one.*

4. *If X is measurable with respect to $\mathcal{G}$, and if Y and XY are integrable, then*

$$E(XY \mid \mathcal{G}) = XE(Y \mid \mathcal{G})$$

   with probability one.

5. *Iterated expectations: if X is integrable and if $\mathcal{G}$ and $\mathcal{H}$ are sigma-algebras with $\mathcal{G} \subset \mathcal{H} \subset \mathcal{F}$, then*

$$E[E(X \mid \mathcal{H}) \mid \mathcal{G}] = E(X \mid \mathcal{G})$$

   with probability one.

Proof Billingsley [8, 1986, Theorems 34.2, 34.3, and 34.4]. □

Proposition B.27 The conditional Bayes' rule. *Let Q be a probability measure with density $dQ/dP = \xi$ with respect to P. Let X be a random variable which is integrable with respect to Q, and let $\mathcal{G} \subset \mathcal{F}$ be a sigma-algebra. Then*

$$E(\xi X \mid \mathcal{G}) = E(\xi \mid \mathcal{G}) E_Q(X \mid \mathcal{G})$$

Proof The expression on the right hand side is $\mathcal{G}$-measurable. If $B \in \mathcal{G}$, then

$$\int_B E(\xi \mid \mathcal{G}) E_Q(X \mid \mathcal{G}) \, dP = \int_B E[\xi E_Q(X \mid \mathcal{G}) \mid \mathcal{G}] \, dP$$

$$= \int_B E_Q(X \mid \mathcal{G}) \xi \, dP$$

$$= \int_B E_Q(X \mid \mathcal{G}) \, dQ$$

$$= \int_B X \, dQ$$

$$= \int_B \xi X \, dP$$

□

Exercise B.7 *Show that if X is an integrable random variable which is independent of a sigma-algebra $\mathcal{G} \subset \mathcal{F}$, then $E[X \mid \mathcal{G}] = EX$ with probability one.*

Theorem B.28 The conditional Fubini theorem. *Let $(\Omega, \mathcal{F}, P)$ be a probability space, $\mathcal{T}$ a subset of the real line, with $\mathcal{B}(\mathcal{T})$ the Borel sigma-algebra on $\mathcal{T}$, μ a sigma-finite measure on $(\mathcal{T}, \mathcal{B}(\mathcal{T}))$,*

$$X : \Omega \times \mathcal{T} \to I\!R$$

a function which is measurable with respect to $\mathcal{B}(\mathcal{T}) \otimes \mathcal{F}$ and such that

$$\int E|X(t)| \, \mu(dt) < \infty$$

and let $\mathcal{G} \subset \mathcal{F}$ be a sigma-algebra. Then there exists a function

$$Y : \Omega \times \mathcal{T} \to I\!R$$

which is measurable with respect to $\mathcal{G} \otimes \mathcal{B}$ and such that

$$\int E|Y(t)| \, \mu(dt) < \infty$$

$$\int Y(t) \, \mu(dt)$$

is a version of

$$E\left[\int X(t)\,\mu(dt)\,\middle|\,\mathcal{G}\right]$$

and for all $t \in \mathcal{T}$, $Y(t)$ *is integrable with respect to* P *and is a version of* $E(X(t)\mid \mathcal{G})$.

Proof Ethier and Kurtz [36, 1986, Chapter 2, Proposition 4.6].   □

On the basis of Theorem B.28, we write

$$\int E[X(t)\mid\mathcal{G}]\,\mu(dt) = E\left[\int X(t)\,\mu(dt)\,\middle|\,\mathcal{G}\right]$$

The measure μ would often be the Lebesgue measure, and $t \in \mathcal{T}$ would be interpreted as time.

If $(\Omega, \mathcal{F}, P)$ is a probability space, $X : \Omega \to I\!\!R^k$ is a random vector, and $Z : \Omega \to I\!\!R$ is an integrable random variable, then the conditional expectation of Z given X is defined as the conditional expectation of Z given the sigma-algebra $\sigma(X)$ generated by X:

$$E[Z\mid X] = E[Z\mid\sigma(X)]$$

Since $E[Z\mid X]$ is measurable with respect to $\sigma(X)$, by Proposition A.34, there exists a measurable mapping $f : I\!\!R^k \to I\!\!R$ such that

$$E[Z\mid X] = f(X)$$

It is common to write

$$f(x) = E[Z\mid X = x]$$

for $x \in I\!\!R^k$.

B.6 L^p-spaces

Let $0 < p \le \infty$. Let $(\Omega, \mathcal{F}, \mu)$ be a measure space (not necessarily a probability space).

If $X : \Omega \to \bar{I\!\!R}$ is a measurable mapping (a random variable in the case where μ is a probability measure), define the *essential supremum* of X by

$$\operatorname{ess\,sup}X = \inf\{b \in I\!\!R : \mu(\{\omega \in \Omega : X(\omega) > b\}) = 0\}$$

Define $\|X\|_p$ by

$$\|X\|_p = \begin{cases} \left(\int |X|^p\,d\mu\right)^{1/p} & \text{for } 0 < p < \infty \\ \operatorname{ess\,sup}|X| & \text{for } p = \infty \end{cases}$$

Define

$$L^p(\mu) = \{X : \|X\|_p < \infty\}$$

where any two functions (random variables) that are equal μ-almost everywhere are identified.

When $1 \le p \le \infty$, the function $\|\cdot\|_p$ on $L^p(\mu)$ is called the *L^p-norm*. It has the following properties:

1. For all $X \in L^p(\mu)$, $\|X\|_p \geq 0$.
2. For all $X \in L^p(\mu)$, $\|X\|_p = 0$ if and only if $X = 0$.
3. For all $X \in L^p(\mu)$ and all scalars a, $\|aX\|_p = |a|\|X\|_p$.
4. The Minkowski inequality: for all $X, Y \in L^p(\mu)$,

$$\|X + Y\|_p \leq \|X\|_p + \|Y\|_p$$

Properties 1, 2, and 3 are simple to show. For a proof of 4, see Billingsley [9, 1995, Section 19].

Properties 3 and 4 imply that $L^p(\mu)$ is a linear space.

Proposition B.29 The Hölder inequality. *If $1 \leq p \leq \infty$, if q is defined by $(1/p) + (1/q) = 1$, and if $X \in L^p(\mu)$ and $Y \in L^q(\mu)$, then*

$$\int |XY| \, d\mu \leq \|X\|_p \|Y\|_q$$

In particular, $XY \in L^1(\mu)$.

Proof   See Billingsley [9, 1995, Section 19]. □

The definition of q in the proposition above is to be understood such that if $p = 1$ or $p = \infty$, then $q = \infty$ or $q = 1$, respectively.

The Hölder inequality for $p = q = 2$ is the Cauchy–Schwartz inequality.

Proposition B.30 The Liapounov inequality. *If $0 < r \leq s < \infty$, and if $\mu(\Omega)$ is finite, then*
$$\|X\|_r \leq \|X\|_s \mu(\Omega)^{\frac{1}{r} - \frac{1}{s}}$$

for all measurable functions X, and consequently $L^s(\mu) \subset L^r(\mu)$.

Proof   Set $p = s/r \geq 1$, and define q by $(1/p) + (1/q) = 1$. Then

$$\frac{1}{qr} = \frac{1}{r} - \frac{1}{pr} = \frac{1}{r} - \frac{1}{s}$$

By the Hölder inequality,

$$\int |X|^r \, d\mu \leq \||X|^r\|_p \|1\|_q = \left(\int |X|^s \, d\mu \right)^{r/s} \mu(\Omega)^{1/q}$$

and so

$$\|X\|_r \leq \|X\|_s \mu(\Omega)^{1/(qr)} = \|X\|_s \mu(\Omega)^{\frac{1}{r} - \frac{1}{s}}$$

□

Corollary B.31 The Liapounov inequality. *If $0 < r \leq s \leq \infty$, and if $\mu = P$ is a probability measure, then*
$$\|X\|_r \leq \|X\|_s$$

Proof This is clear if $s = \infty$. It follows from Proposition B.30 if $s < \infty$. □

Exercise B.8 *Show that if X is a random variable, then $\|X\|_p \to \|X\|_\infty$ as $p \to \infty$.*

In the following, assume that $1 \le p$.

If (X_n) is a sequence in $L^p(\mu)$ and $X \in L^p(\mu)$, then, by definition, X_n *converges in L^p* or *converges in p-norm* to X if $\|X_n - X\|_p \to 0$.

A limit in L^p is unique almost everywhere, in the following sense. If (X_n) is a sequence in $L^p(\mu)$, if $X, Y \in L^p(\mu)$, and if X_n converges both to X and to Y in $L^p(\mu)$, then $X = Y$ almost everywhere.

Exercise B.9 *Let $1 \le p < \infty$. Show that if X_n is a sequence in $L^p(\mu)$ which converges to X almost everywhere, and if there is some Y in $L^p(\mu)$ such that $|X_n| \le Y$ almost everywhere, for all n, then $X \in L^p(\mu)$ and X_n converges to X in $L^p(\mu)$.*

Exercise B.10 *Show that convergence in $L^\infty(\mu)$ implies convergence with probability one.*

For $1 \le p < \infty$, it is not in general true that convergence in $L^p(\mu)$ implies convergence almost everywhere, as is illustrated in the following counterexample.

Example B.32 Let I_n be the nth dyadic subinterval of $(0, 1]$: the nth interval in the following sequence:

$$(0, 1]$$
$$(0, 1/2] \quad (1/2, 1]$$
$$(0, 1/4] \quad (1/4, 2/4] \quad (2/4, 3/4] \quad (3/4, 1]$$
$$\vdots \qquad \vdots \qquad \vdots \qquad \vdots$$
$$(0, 1/2^k] \quad (1/2^k, 2/2^k] \quad \cdots \qquad \cdots \qquad \cdots ((2^k - 1)/2^k, 1]$$
$$\vdots \qquad \vdots \qquad \vdots \qquad \vdots \qquad \vdots \qquad \vdots$$

Let $(\Omega, \mathcal{F}, \mu) = ((0, 1], \mathcal{B}((0, 1]), \lambda)$, where λ is (the restriction of) the Lebesgue measure, and let $X_n = 1_{I_n}$ for each n. Then $X_n \to 0$ in L^p, because

$$\|X_n\|_p = (\lambda(I_n))^{1/p} \to 0$$

but $X_n(\omega)$ does not converge to zero for any $\omega \in (0, 1]$. □

If $\mu = P$ is a probability measure, and if $1 \le r \le p \le \infty$, then convergence in $L^p(P)$ implies convergence in $L^r(P)$. This follows from the Liapounov inequality.

Proposition B.33 *Let $1 \le p \le \infty$. If X_n is a sequence which converges to X in $L^p(P)$, then X_n converges to X in probability.*

Exercise B.11 *Prove Proposition B.33.*

APPENDIX C

THE HEAT EQUATION

The theory of heat diffusion is useful in finance because the problem of valuing a contingent claim in the Black–Scholes model can be transformed into a question of heat diffusion along an infinite rod. This transformation is carried out in the last sections of Chapter 6.

In physics, the diffusion of heat during a finite time interval $[0, T)$ along a rod of infinite length can be described by two functions

$$u : \mathbb{R} \times (0, T) \to \mathbb{R} : (x, \tau) \mapsto u(x, \tau)$$

and

$$f : \mathbb{R} \to \mathbb{R} : x \mapsto f(x)$$

The rod is represented by the real line. The interpretation of the functions is that $f(x)$ is the amount of heat at the point x on the rod at time zero, and $u(x, \tau)$ is the amount of heat at point x at time $\tau \in (0, T)$.

In the financial interpretation, x will be a potential value of the risk-adjusted Wiener process which drives the stock price, T will be the maturity date or the time when the holder of the claim receives his or her payoff, and $f(x)$ will be the payoff to the claim contingent on the Wiener process taking the value x at that time. The time variable τ will measure not calendar time but time to maturity. The quantity $u(x, \tau)$ will be the value of the claim expressed as a future value at time T, provided that the current value of the Wiener process is x and the currently remaining time to maturity is τ.

The issue is to identify the function u from knowledge of the function f. In other words, from knowledge of the distribution of heat at time zero, applying the laws of physics, we want to calculate the distribution of heat at any time up to T.

The relevant law of physics, according to the experts, is embodied in the heat equation. The function u is a solution of the *heat equation* if it is twice continuously differentiable with respect to x and once continuously differentiable with respect to τ, and

$$u_\tau(x, \tau) = k u_{xx}(x, \tau)$$

for all $(x, \tau) \in \mathbb{R} \times (0, T)$. Here, $k > 0$ is a dimensionless parameter called the *conductivity*.

The version that we study here corresponds to $k = 1/2$:

$$u_\tau = \frac{1}{2} u_{xx}$$

Observe that the constant k makes little difference, because it can be eliminated by a time change, as follows. If

$$\tilde{u} : I\!R \times (0,T) \to I\!R : (x,\tau) \to \tilde{u}(x,\tau)$$

is the function defined by $\tilde{u}(x,\tau) = u(x,k\tau)$, then $\tilde{u}$ solves the equation

$$\tilde{u}_\tau = k\tilde{u}_{xx}$$

if and only if u solves the equation

$$u_\tau = u_{xx}$$

This follows from the fact that $\tilde{u}_\tau = ku_\tau$ and $\tilde{u}_{xx} = u_{xx}$.

The problem now is to find a solution u of the heat equation on the time interval $(0,T)$ which in some sense has initial value f.

Determining the precise sense in which the solution function u should have initial value f is a non-trivial matter. In physics, some treatments assume that the initial heat distribution is continuous. If f is a continuous function, then it seems reasonable to require that the function

$$\hat{u} : I\!R \times [0,T) \to I\!R : (x,\tau) \to \hat{u}(x,\tau)$$

defined by

$$\hat{u}(x,\tau) = \begin{cases} f(x) & \text{if } \tau = 0 \\ u(x,\tau) & \text{if } \tau > 0 \end{cases}$$

should be continuous.

However, in applications in finance, f will often not be continuous, and therefore we shall need also to experiment with imposing the initial value in other ways. The initial data will correspond to the final payoff of a contingent claim or derivative security, and there is no theoretical reason why such a payoff should be continuous. Its shape is limited primarily by the imagination of its creator, and several actually existing claims or securities have discontinuous payoffs.

Not only do we want to find a solution u of the heat equation with initial value f, we also want to know that it is the unique such solution. Unfortunately, it is not true that there is a unique solution to the heat equation with a given initial value function, even if the initial data are imposed in an appropriate way. This is shown in DiBenedetto [27, 1995, Chapter V, Proposition 5.1].

Therefore, we shall need to impose an additional restriction on the solution function in order to make it unique. We shall consider three different restrictions: an integrability condition, a non-negativity condition, and a growth condition.

C.1   The Martingale Solution

Fix a one-dimensional Wiener process W relative to a filtration F on a probability space $(\Omega, \mathcal{F}, P)$.

The following proposition relates solutions of the heat equation to the Wiener process.

Proposition C.1 *Let $T > 0$, let*

$$u : \mathbb{R} \times (0, T) \to \mathbb{R} : (x, \tau) \mapsto u(x, \tau)$$

be a function which is twice continuously differentiable with respect to x and once continuously differentiable with respect to τ, and let $x_0 \in \mathbb{R}$. Then u solves the heat equation

$$u_\tau = \frac{1}{2} u_{xx}$$

if and only if the process $u(x_0 + W(t), T - t)$ has zero drift.

Proof By Itô's formula, the absolute drift of the process $u(x_0 + W(t), T - t)$ is

$$-u_t(x_0 + W(t), T - t) + \frac{1}{2} u_{xx}(x_0 + W(t), T - t)$$

If u solves the heat equation, then this drift is zero.

Conversely, suppose the drift is zero almost everywhere in $\Omega \times (0, T)$. For almost all $t \in (0, T)$, the equation

$$u_t(x_0 + W(t), T - t) = \frac{1}{2} u_{xx}(x_0 + W(t), T - t)$$

holds with probability one. Since $W(t)$ follows a normal distribution, which has positive density with respect to Lebesgue measure, the partial differential equation

$$u_\tau(x, T - t) = \frac{1}{2} u_{xx}(x, T - t)$$

holds for almost all $(x, t) \in \mathbb{R} \times (0, T)$, with respect to Lebesgue measure. Since the derivatives of u are continuous, it follows that the partial differential equation holds everywhere in $\mathbb{R} \times (0, T)$. $\square$

According to Proposition C.1, a function u is a solution of the heat equation if and only if there is some $x \in \mathbb{R}$ such that the process $u(x + W(t), T - t)$ has zero drift, in which case this process has zero drift for all $x \in \mathbb{R}$. We shall now show that given an initial value function f, there is a particular solution v such that for each $x \in \mathbb{R}$, the process $v(x + W(t), T - t)$ not only has zero drift but is a martingale and satisfies

$$v(x + W(t), T - t) = E\left[f(x + W(T)) \mid \mathcal{F}_t \right]$$

for all $t \in (0, T)$. This solution will be called the *martingale solution*.

The martingale solution will be constructed by integrating the function f up against the function

$$p : \mathbb{R} \times (0, \infty) \to (0, \infty)$$

defined by

$$p(x, \tau) = \frac{1}{\sqrt{2\pi\tau}} \exp\left[-\frac{x^2}{2\tau} \right]$$

For fixed τ, p is the density function of a normal distribution with mean zero and variance τ. For fixed (x, τ), the function $y \mapsto p(y - x, \tau)$ is the density function of a normal distribution with mean x and variance τ.

The function p is called the *diffusion kernel*, *Green's function* for the heat equation, or the *source function*, the *Gaussian*, the *propagator*, or the *fundamental solution* of the heat equation, see Strauss [83, 1992].

The function p is infinitely often differentiable, and it does indeed solve the heat equation

$$p_\tau = \frac{1}{2} p_{xx}$$

This is easily verified by direct calculation:

$$p_\tau(x,\tau) = -\frac{1}{2\tau\sqrt{2\pi\tau}} \exp\left[-\frac{x^2}{2\tau}\right] + \frac{x^2}{2\tau^2\sqrt{2\pi\tau}} \exp\left[-\frac{x^2}{2\tau}\right]$$

$$= \left(\frac{x^2}{2\tau^2} - \frac{1}{2\tau}\right) p(x,\tau)$$

$$p_x(x,\tau) = -\frac{x}{\tau\sqrt{2\pi\tau}} \exp\left[-\frac{x^2}{2\tau}\right] = -\frac{x}{\tau} p(x,\tau)$$

$$p_{xx}(x,\tau) = -\frac{1}{\tau} p(x,\tau) + \frac{x^2}{\tau} p(x,\tau) p(x,\tau) = \left(\frac{x^2}{\tau} - \frac{1}{\tau}\right) p(x,\tau)$$

In order to be sure we can integrate the initial value function f up against the function p, we shall impose the following *growth condition* on f.

If α is a constant, let $G_0(\alpha)$ denote the set of functions $f : \mathbb{R} \to \mathbb{R}$ such that there exist positive constants k and C such that

$$|f(y)| \le C \exp\left(\alpha y^2\right)$$

for almost all $y \in \mathbb{R}$ with $|y| \ge k$.

Proposition C.2 *Let $\alpha > 0$, let $f \in G_0(\alpha)$, and suppose f is locally integrable. Then*

$$\int |f(y)| p(y - x, \tau) \, dy < \infty$$

for all $(x, \tau) \in \mathbb{R} \times (0, 1/(2\alpha))$.

Proof Pick positive constants r and C such that

$$|f(y)| \le C \exp(\alpha y^2)$$

for almost all y with $|y| \ge r$. Set $\alpha_1 = 1/(2\tau)$. Since $\tau < 1/(2\alpha)$, it follows that $\alpha < \alpha_1$. Choose b such that

$$0 < b < \alpha_1 - \alpha$$

Set

$$h = \max\left\{r, \frac{2\alpha_1}{b}|x|\right\}$$

If $|y| \geq h$, then

$$|x| \leq \frac{b}{2\alpha_1}|y|$$

$$2\alpha_1 xy \leq 2\alpha_1 |x||y| \leq b|y|^2$$

$$\begin{aligned}
\alpha y^2 - \alpha_1(x-y)^2 &= \alpha y^2 - \alpha_1 x^2 - \alpha_1 y^2 + 2\alpha_1 xy \\
&\leq \alpha y^2 - \alpha_1 y^2 + by^2 \\
&= -(\alpha_1 - \alpha - b)\, y^2
\end{aligned}$$

and

$$\begin{aligned}
\sqrt{2\pi\tau}\,|f(y)|p(y-x,\tau) &= |f(y)|\exp\left[-\alpha_1(y-x)^2\right] \\
&\leq C\exp(\alpha y^2)\exp\left[-\alpha_1(y-x)^2\right] \\
&= C\exp\left[\alpha y^2 - \alpha_1(y-x)^2\right] \\
&\leq C\exp\left[-(\alpha_1 - \alpha - b)\,y^2\right]
\end{aligned}$$

Hence,

$$\begin{aligned}
\int_{|y|\geq h} |f(y)|p(y-x,\tau)\,dy &\leq \frac{C}{\sqrt{2\pi\tau}}\int \exp\left[-(\alpha_1 - \alpha - b)\,y^2\right]dy \\
&\leq \frac{C}{\sqrt{2\pi\tau}}\int \exp\left[-(\alpha_1 - \alpha - b)\,y^2\right]dy \\
&< \infty
\end{aligned}$$

Since for all y,

$$p(y-x,\tau) \leq \frac{1}{\sqrt{2\tau}}$$

and since f is locally integrable,

$$\int_{|y|\leq h} |f(y)|p(y-x,\tau)\,dy \leq \frac{1}{\sqrt{2\tau}}\int_{|y|\leq h}|f(y)|\,dy < \infty$$

This shows that

$$\int_{-\infty}^{\infty} |f(y)|p(y-x,\tau)\,dy < \infty$$

$\square$

From now on, let $a > 0$ and a locally integrable function $f \in G_0(a)$ be given. Define a function

$$v : \mathbb{R} \times (0, 1/(2a)) \to \mathbb{R}$$

by

$$v(x,\tau) = \int f(y)p(y-x,\tau)\,dy$$

It follows from Proposition C.2 that v is well defined.

Note that

$$v(x,\tau) = \int f(y)p(y-x,\tau)\,dy = Ef(x+W(\tau))$$

Proposition C.3 *The function v is infinitely often differentiable. For all non-negative integers m and n, and all $(x,\tau) \in \mathbb{R} \times (0, 1/(2a))$, the function*

$$y \mapsto f(y)\frac{\partial^{m+n}}{\partial\tau^m\partial x^n}p(y-x,\tau) : \mathbb{R} \to \mathbb{R}$$

is in $G_0(a)$, and

$$\frac{\partial^{m+n}}{\partial\tau^m\partial x^n}v(\tau,x) = \int f(y)\frac{\partial^{m+n}}{\partial t^m\partial x^n}p(y-x,\tau)\,dy$$

Proof The derivative of the function $f(y)p(y-x,\tau)$ with respect to x is

$$f(y)\frac{\partial}{\partial x}p(y-x,\tau) = f(y)\frac{x-y}{\tau}p(y-x,\tau)$$

For fixed (x,τ), the function

$$y \mapsto f(y)\frac{x-y}{\tau}$$

is in $G_0(a)$. Let us show that in a neighborhood of (x,τ) it is dominated uniformly by a function in $G_0(a)$. Let $0 < \tau_1 < \tau < 1/(2a)$ and $|x| < x_2$. Then

$$\left|\frac{x'-y}{\tau'}\right| \le \frac{|x'|+|y|}{\tau'} \le \frac{|x_2|}{\tau_1} + \frac{y}{\tau_1}$$

for all y, and all (x',τ') with $\tau_1 < \tau' < 1/(2a)$ and $|x'| < x_2$. Hence,

$$\left|f(y)\frac{x'-y}{\tau'}\right| \le |f(y)|\frac{x_2}{\tau_1} + |f(y)|\frac{|y|}{\tau_1}$$

for those (x',τ'). The function

$$y \mapsto |f(y)|\frac{x_2}{\tau_1} + |f(y)|\frac{|y|}{\tau_1}$$

is in $G_0(a)$. This implies that the function v is differentiable with derivative

$$v_x(x,\tau) = \int f(y)\frac{\partial}{\partial x}p(y-x,\tau)\,dy = \int f(y)\frac{x-y}{\tau}p(y-x,\tau)\,dy$$

The derivative of the function $f(y)p(y-x,\tau)$ with respect to τ is

$$f(y)\frac{\partial}{\partial x}p(y-x,\tau) = f(y)\left(\frac{1}{2\tau} - \frac{(y-x)^2}{2\tau^2}\right)p(y-x,\tau)$$

For fixed (x, τ), the function

$$y \mapsto f(y) \left(\frac{1}{2\tau} - \frac{(y-x)^2}{2\tau^2} \right) p(y - x, \tau)$$

is in $G_0(a)$. In a neighborhood of (x, τ) it is dominated uniformly by a function in $G_0(a)$. The proof is similar to the one above, relating to the derivative with respect to x. This implies that the function v is differentiable with derivative

$$v_\tau(x, \tau) = \int f(y) \frac{\partial}{\partial \tau} p(y - x, \tau) \, dy$$

$$= \int f(y) \left(\frac{1}{2\tau} - \frac{(y-x)^2}{2\tau^2} \right) p(y - x, \tau) \, dy$$

It now follows by repeated application of the results above that v is infinitely often differentiable with the indicated derivatives.   □

Proposition C.4 *If $0 < T < 1/(2a)$, then*

$$v(x + W(t), T - t) = E[f(x + W(T)) \mid \mathcal{F}_t]$$

for $(x, t) \in \mathbb{R} \times (0, T)$. In particular, the process $v(x + W(t), T - t)$ is a martingale, and v solves the heat equation

$$v_\tau = \frac{1}{2} v_{xx}$$

Proof For $(x, t) \in (0, T)$,

$$E[f(x + W(T)) \mid \mathcal{F}_t] = E[f(x + W(t) + (W(T) - W(t))) \mid \mathcal{F}_t]$$

$$= \int f(y) p(y - x - W(t), T - t) \, dy$$

$$= v(x + W(t), T - t)$$

Hence, the process $v(x + W(t), T - t)$ is a martingale on $(0, T)$. By Proposition C.3, the function v is infinitely often differentiable, and, in particular, it is sufficiently differentiable to apply Itô's lemma. By Itô's lemma, the process $v(x + W(t), T - t)$ is an Itô process, and since it is a martingale, it has zero drift. It now follows from Proposition C.1 that v solves the heat equation on $\mathbb{R} \times (0, T)$. Since $T < 1/(2a)$ is arbitrary, v solves the heat equation on $(0, 1/(2a))$.

Alternatively, the fact that v solves the heat equation follows directly from the fact that p solves the heat equation and from the expression for the partial derivatives in Proposition C.3.   □

Because of Proposition C.4, we shall call v the *martingale solution* to the heat equation with initial data f.

C.2   The Heat Equation: Initial Data

In this section, we shall consider three different ways of imposing the initial condition on the solution function. They correspond to three types of convergence: local convergence in mean, double convergence, and convergence almost everywhere.

Let $T > 0$, and let

$$u : \mathbb{R} \times (0, T) \to \mathbb{R} : (x, \tau) \mapsto u(x, \tau)$$

be a function. Let $f : \mathbb{R} \to \mathbb{R}$ be a locally integrable function. Say that u has *initial data f* in the *sense of local convergence in mean* if u is locally integrable with respect to x for each $\tau \in (0, T)$, and if

$$\int_b^c |u(x, \tau) - f(x)| \, dx \to 0 \quad \text{as} \quad \tau \to 0$$

whenever $b, c \in \mathbb{R}$, $b < c$.

Proposition C.5 *The function v has initial data f in the sense of local convergence in mean.*

Proof Follows from DiBenedetto [27, 1995, Chapter V, Theorem 6.1]. There appears to be a misprint in that theorem: the reference to (2.5) should be to (2.7). Note that DiBenedetto works with a conductivity parameter of one instead of one-half.   □

Let $u : \mathbb{R} \times (0, T) \to \mathbb{R}$ and $f : \mathbb{R} \to \mathbb{R}$ be functions. Say that u has *initial data f* in the sense of *double convergence* if for all $x \in \mathbb{R}$,

$$u(y, \tau) \to f(x) \quad \text{as} \quad (y, \tau) \to (x, 0), \quad \tau > 0$$

Proposition C.6 *Let u be a solution of the heat equation. If f is continuous, then u has initial data f in the sense of double convergence if and only if the function*

$$\hat{u} : \mathbb{R} \times [0, T) \to \mathbb{R} : (x, \tau) \to \hat{u}(x, \tau)$$

defined by

$$\hat{u}(x, \tau) = \begin{cases} f(x) & \text{if } \tau = 0 \\ u(x, \tau) & \text{if } \tau > 0 \end{cases}$$

is continuous.

Proof Obvious.   □

Proposition C.7 *If f is continuous, then v has initial data f in the sense of double convergence.*

Proof Widder [88, 1944], Karatzas and Shreve [64, 1988, Chapter 4, Problem 3.2].   □

Proposition C.8 *Let u be a solution of the heat equation. If f is continuous, and if u has initial data f in the sense of double convergence, then u has initial data f in the sense of local convergence in mean.*

Proof By Proposition C.7, the function

$$\hat{u} : I\!R \times [0, T) \to I\!R : (x, \tau) \to \hat{u}(x, \tau)$$

defined by

$$\hat{u}(x, \tau) = \begin{cases} f(x) & \text{if } \tau = 0 \\ u(x, \tau) & \text{if } \tau > 0 \end{cases}$$

is continuous. Let $b, c \in I\!R$, $b < c$, and choose $\epsilon \in (0, T)$. Since $\hat{u}$ is continuous, there exists a constant $K > 0$ such that

$$|\hat{u}(x, \tau)| \leq K$$

for all $(x, \tau) \in [b, c] \times [0, \epsilon]$. Since for all $x \in [b, c]$, $\hat{u}(x, \tau) \to f(x)$ as $\tau \to 0$, it follows from the dominated convergence theorem that

$$\int_b^c |\hat{u}(x, \tau) - f(x)| \, dx \to 0 \quad \text{as} \quad \tau \to 0$$

Hence,

$$\int_b^c |u(x, \tau) - f(x)| \, dx \to 0 \quad \text{as} \quad \tau \to 0, \ \tau > 0$$

which implies that u has initial data f in the sense of local convergence in mean.

□

Let $u : I\!R \times (0, T) \to I\!R$ and $f : I\!R \to I\!R$ be functions. Say that u has *initial data f* in the sense of *convergence almost everywhere* if for almost all $x \in I\!R$,

$$u(x, \tau) \to f(x) \quad \text{as} \quad \tau \to 0, \quad \tau > 0$$

Note that if u has initial data f in the sense of double convergence, then u also has initial data f in the sense of convergence almost everywhere.

If α is a constant, let $G(\alpha)$ denote the set of functions $h : I\!R \to I\!R$ which satisfy the following *growth condition*: there exists a positive constant C such that

$$|h(y)| \leq C \exp\left(\alpha y^2\right)$$

for almost all $y \in I\!R$.

Note the difference between $G(\alpha)$ and $G_0(\alpha)$: the functions in $G_0(\alpha)$ are required to satisfy the inequality above only for y with sufficiently large absolute value.

Note that $G(\alpha) \subset G_0(\alpha)$ and that all measurable functions in $G(\alpha)$ are locally integrable.

We have already seen in Proposition C.8 that if f is continuous, then initial data f in the sense of double convergence implies initial data f in the sense of local convergence in mean. The next proposition implies that the same is true if for some α, $u(\cdot, \tau) \in G(\alpha)$ for all $\tau \in (0, T)$.

Proposition C.9 *Let u be a solution of the heat equation. Assume that for some α, $u(\cdot, \tau) \in G(\alpha)$ for all $\tau \in (0, T)$. If u has initial data f in the sense of convergence almost everywhere, then u has initial data f in the sense of local convergence in mean.*

Proof Choose a positive constant C such that

$$|u(x, \tau)| \leq C \exp(\alpha x^2)$$

for all $(x, \tau) \in I\!\!R \times (0, T)$. Let $b, c \in I\!\!R$, $b < c$. Then for all $(x, \tau) \in I\!\!R \times (0, T)$,

$$\left| 1_{[b,c]} u(x, \tau) \right| \leq 1_{[b,c]} |u(x, \tau)| + 1_{[b,c]} |f(x)| \leq 1_{[b,c]} C \exp(\alpha x^2) + 1_{[b,c]} |f(x)|$$

The right hand side is integrable because f is locally integrable. It now follows from the dominated convergence theorem that

$$\int_b^c |u(x, \tau) - f(x)| \, dx \to 0 \quad \text{as} \quad \tau \to 0$$

$\square$

Example C.10 The fundamental solution p of the heat equation has initial data zero in the sense of convergence almost everywhere but not in the sense of local convergence in mean or in the sense of double convergence. There are no $T > 0$ and $\alpha > 0$ such that $p(\cdot, \tau) \in G(\alpha)$ for all $\tau \in (0, T)$. On the other hand, for every $T > 0$ and $\alpha > 0$, $p(\cdot, \tau) \in G(\alpha)$ for all $\tau \in (0, T)$.

First, if $x \neq 0$, then

$$\ln p(x, \tau) = -\ln \sqrt{2\pi} + \frac{1}{2} \ln \frac{1}{\tau} - \frac{1}{2} x^2 \frac{1}{\tau} \to -\infty$$

as $\tau \to 0$, and, hence, $p(x, \tau) \to 0$ as $\tau \to 0$. This shows that p has initial data zero in the sense of convergence almost everywhere.

Secondly, let Y be a random variable which follows a standard normal distribution. We denote the cumulative distribution function by N. The density function of $\sqrt{\tau} Y$ is $p(\cdot, \tau)$. Hence,

$$\int_{-1}^{1} p(x, \tau) \, dx = E\left[1_{[-1,1]} \left(\sqrt{\tau} Y \right) \right]$$

$$= E\left[1_{[-1/\sqrt{\tau}, 1/\sqrt{\tau}]} (Y) \right]$$

$$= N\left(\frac{1}{\sqrt{\tau}} \right) - N\left(-\frac{1}{\sqrt{\tau}} \right)$$

$$\to 1$$

as $\tau \to 0$. This implies that p does not have initial data zero in the sense of local convergence in mean. By Proposition C.8, p does not have initial data zero in the sense of double convergence either.

Thirdly, let T, α, and C be positive constants. When $|x| \leq \min\{\sqrt{2\tau}, 1/\sqrt{\alpha}\}$,

$$\frac{p(x,\tau)}{C\exp(\alpha x^2)} = \frac{1}{C\sqrt{2\pi\tau}} \exp\left(-\frac{x^2}{2\tau} - \alpha x^2\right)$$
$$\geq \frac{1}{C\sqrt{2\pi\tau}} \exp(-2)$$
$$> 1$$

for sufficiently small τ, and, hence,

$$p(x,\tau) > C\exp(\alpha x^2)$$

for sufficiently small τ. This shows that $p(\cdot,\tau)$ does not belong to $G(\alpha)$ for all $\tau \in (0,T)$.

Finally, let T and α be positive constants. For each $\tau \in (0,T)$,

$$\frac{p(x,\tau)}{\exp(\alpha x^2)} = \frac{1}{\sqrt{2\pi\tau}} \exp\left(-\frac{x^2}{2\tau} - \alpha x^2\right) < 1$$

for sufficiently large $|x|$, and, hence,

$$p(x,\tau) < \exp(\alpha x^2)$$

for sufficiently large $|x|$. So, $p(\cdot,\tau) \in G_0(\alpha)$ for each $\tau \in (0,T)$. $\square$

Example C.10 can easily be adapted so as to make the solution converge to zero not just almost everywhere but literally at every point. This is done in Example C.11 below.

Example C.11 Let $T > 0$ and define a function $u : \mathbb{R} \times (0,T) \to \mathbb{R}$ by

$$u(x,\tau) = \frac{x}{\tau} p(x,\tau)$$

Then u is a solution of the heat equation. It has initial data zero in the sense that for every $x \in \mathbb{R}$,

$$u(x,\tau) \to 0 \quad \text{as} \quad \tau \to 0, \quad \tau > 0$$

but it does not have initial data zero in the sense of local convergence in mean or in the sense of double convergence. There are no $\alpha > 0$ such that $u(\cdot,\tau) \in G(\alpha)$ for all $\tau \in (0,T)$. On the other hand, for every $T > 0$ and $\alpha > 0$, $u(\cdot,\tau) \in G(\alpha)$ for all $\tau \in (0,T)$.

First, let us verify that u is a solution of the heat equation. We make use of the formula

$$p_x(x, \tau) = -\frac{x}{\tau} p(x, \tau)$$

and the fact that p is a solution. The first derivative of u with respect to x is

$$u_x(x, \tau) = \frac{1}{\tau} \left[p(x, \tau) + x p_x(x, \tau) \right]$$

and the second derivative is

$$
\begin{aligned}
u_{xx}(x, \tau) &= \frac{1}{\tau} \left[p_x(x, \tau) + p_x(x, \tau) + x p_{xx}(x, \tau) \right] \\
&= \frac{2}{\tau} p_x(x, \tau) + \frac{x}{\tau} p_{xx}(x, \tau) \\
&= \frac{2}{\tau} p_x(x, \tau) + \frac{2x}{\tau} p_\tau(x, \tau) \\
&= -\frac{2x}{\tau^2} p(x, \tau) + \frac{2x}{\tau} p_\tau(x, \tau) \\
&= 2x \left[-\frac{1}{\tau^2} p(x, \tau) + \frac{1}{\tau} p_\tau(x, \tau) \right] \\
&= 2 u_\tau(x, \tau)
\end{aligned}
$$

which shows that, indeed, u is a solution.

Secondly, it was shown in Example C.10 that if $x \neq 0$, then $p(x, \tau) \to 0$ as $\tau \to 0$. This implies that $u(x, \tau) \to 0$ as $\tau \to 0$. If $x = 0$, then $u(x, \tau) = 0$ for all τ.

Thirdly, as in Example C.10, let Y be a random variable which follows a standard normal distribution. Since the variable $\sqrt{\tau} Y$ has density function $p(\cdot, \tau)$,

$$
\begin{aligned}
\int_{-1}^{1} |u(x, \tau)| \, dx &= \int_{-1}^{1} \frac{|x|}{\tau} p(x, \tau) \, dx \\
&= E \left[\frac{\sqrt{\tau} |Y|}{\tau} 1_{[-1,1]} \left(\sqrt{\tau} Y \right) \right] \\
&= \frac{1}{\sqrt{\tau}} E \left[|Y| 1_{[-1/\sqrt{\tau}, 1/\sqrt{\tau}]} (Y) \right]
\end{aligned}
$$

Since

$$E \left[|Y| 1_{[-1/\sqrt{\tau}, 1/\sqrt{\tau}]} (Y) \right] \to E|Y| > 0$$

as $\tau \to 0$, it follows that

$$\int_{-1}^{1} |u(x, \tau)| \, dx = \frac{1}{\sqrt{\tau}} E \left[|Y| 1_{[-1/\sqrt{\tau}, 1/\sqrt{\tau}]} (Y) \right] \to \infty$$

as $\tau \to 0$. This implies that u does not have initial data zero in the sense of local convergence in mean. By Proposition C.8, u does not have initial data zero in the sense of double convergence either.

Fourthly, let α and C be positive constants. When $|x| \leq \min\{\sqrt{2\tau}, 1/\sqrt{\alpha}\}$ and $x \neq 0$,

$$\frac{|u(x,\tau)|}{C\exp(\alpha x^2)} = \frac{|x|}{\tau}p(x,\tau)\frac{1}{x\exp(\alpha x^2)}$$

$$= \frac{|x|}{\tau C\sqrt{2\pi\tau}}\exp\left(-\frac{x^2}{2\tau} - \alpha x^2\right)$$

$$\geq \frac{|x|}{\tau C\sqrt{2\pi\tau}}\exp(-2)$$

$$> 1$$

for sufficiently small τ, and hence,

$$|u(x,\tau)| > C\exp(\alpha x^2)$$

for sufficiently small τ. This shows that $u(\cdot,\tau)$ does not belong to $G(\alpha)$ for all $\tau \in (0,T)$.

Finally, let T and α be positive constants. For each $\tau \in (0,T)$,

$$\frac{|u(x,\tau)|}{\exp(\alpha x^2)} = \frac{|x|}{\tau}p(x,\tau)\frac{1}{\exp(\alpha x^2)} = \frac{|x|}{\tau\sqrt{2\pi\tau}}\exp\left(-\frac{x^2}{2\tau} - \alpha x^2\right)$$

Hence,

$$\ln\left(\frac{|u(x,\tau)|}{\exp(\alpha x^2)}\right) = \ln|x| - \ln\left(\tau\sqrt{2\pi\tau}\right) - \frac{x^2}{2\tau} - \alpha x^2 \to -\infty$$

as $|x| \to \infty$, and

$$\frac{|u(x,\tau)|}{\exp(\alpha x^2)} \to 0 \quad \text{as} \quad |x| \to \infty$$

This shows that $u(\cdot,\tau) \in G_0(\alpha)$ for each $\tau \in (0,T)$. $\square$

C.3   The Heat Equation: Integrability

This and the following section investigate the conditions under which the martingale solution is the unique solution of the heat equation. Uniqueness requires that we impose an initial condition or initial data on the solution function, and that we restrict in some way the set of functions that are admissible as solutions.

This section considers how to restrict the set of admissible solution functions. The main restriction is an integrability condition. It turns out that non-negative functions automatically satisfy the integrability condition. An alternative restriction is a growth condition, which turns out to imply the integrability condition.

Let $T > 0$, and let

$$u : I\!R \times (0, T) \to I\!R : (x, \tau) \mapsto u(x, \tau)$$

be a function. Say that u is *integrable* with respect to p if it is measurable as a function of x for each fixed τ, and if

$$\int |u(y, s)| p(y - x, t - s) \, dy < \infty$$

or, equivalently,

$$E|u(x + W(t) - W(s), s)| = E|u(x + W(t - s), s)| < \infty$$

for all $x \in I\!R$ and all $s, t \in (0, T)$ with $s < t$.

If u is integrable with respect to p, then

$$\int u(y, s) p(y - x, t - s) \, dy = Eu(x + W(t) - W(s), s)$$
$$= Eu(x + W(t - s), s)$$

for all $x \in I\!R$ and all $s, t \in (0, T)$ with $s < t$.

Proposition C.12 *If $u : I\!R \times (0, T) \to I\!R$ is a non-negative solution of the heat equation, then u is integrable with respect to p, with*

$$Eu(x + W(t - s), s) \le u(x, t)$$

for all $x \in I\!R$ and all $s, t \in (0, T)$ with $s < t$.

Proof Given $(x, t) \in I\!R \times (0, T)$, consider the process $u(x + W(\tau), t - \tau)$ with $\tau \in [0, t)$ as time variable. It is a non-negative Itô process. Because u solves the heat equation, the drift is zero, by Proposition C.1. Hence, the process is a supermartingale. In particular,

$$Eu(x + W(\tau), t - \tau) \le u(x, t) < \infty$$

for $\tau \in (0, t)$. Hence, u is integrable with respect to p. Make the substitution $s = t - \tau$ to find that

$$Eu(x + W(t - s), s) \le u(x, t) < \infty$$

$\square$

Proposition C.13 *The function v is integrable with respect to p, with*

$$Ev(x + W(t - s), s) = v(x, t)$$

for all $x \in I\!R$ and all $s, t \in (0, 1/(2a))$ with $s < t$.

Proof First, assume that v is integrable with respect to p. Then

$$
\begin{aligned}
v(x,t) &= \int f(y)p(y-x,t)\,dy \\
&= Ef(x+W(t)) \\
&= E\left[E(f(x+(W(t)-W(s))+W(s)) \mid W(t)-W(s))\right] \\
&= Ev(x+W(t)-W(s),s) \\
&= Ev(x+W(t-s),s)
\end{aligned}
$$

Next, we shall show that v is indeed integrable with respect to p. Since $|f| \in G_0(a)$, we can define a function $\bar{v} : \mathbb{R} \times (0, 1/(2a)) \to \mathbb{R}$ by

$$
\bar{v}(x,\tau) = \int |f(y)|p(y-x,\tau)\,dy
$$

for $(x,\tau) \in \mathbb{R} \times (0, 1/(2a))$. Then $\bar{v}$ is non-negative, and by Proposition C.4, applied to $|f|$ and $\bar{v}$ instead of f and v, $\bar{v}$ is a solution of the heat equation. By Proposition C.12, $\bar{v}$ is integrable with respect to p. We find the following inequality:

$$
|v(x,\tau)| = \left| \int f(y)p(y-x,\tau)\,dy \right| \leq \int |f(y)|p(y-x,\tau)\,dy = \bar{v}(x,\tau)
$$

Using the formula that has already been proved,

$$
E|v(x+W(t-s),s)| \leq E\bar{v}(x+W(t-s),s) = \bar{v}(x,t) < \infty
$$

Hence, v is integrable with respect to p. □

Proposition C.14 *For each $T \in (0, 1/(2a))$, there exists α such that $v(\cdot,\tau) \in G(\alpha)$ for all $\tau \in (0,T)$.*

Proof Follows from DiBenedetto [27, 1995, Chapter V, Proposition 4.1]. □

Proposition C.15 *Let $T > 0$, $0 < \alpha \leq 1/(2T)$, and let $u : \mathbb{R} \times (0,T) \to \mathbb{R}$ be a solution of the heat equation such that $u(\cdot,\tau) \in G_0(\alpha)$ for each $\tau \in (0,T)$. Then u is integrable with respect to p.*

Proof Let $(x,t) \in \mathbb{R} \times (0,T)$ and $s \in (0,t)$. Then $u(\cdot,s) \in G_0(\alpha)$. Since $u(\cdot,s)$ is locally integrable and

$$
0 < t - s < t \leq 1/(2\alpha)
$$

it follows from Proposition C.2 that

$$
\int |u(y,s)|p(y-x,t-s)\,dy < \infty
$$

This shows that u is integrable with respect to p. □

C.4   The Heat Equation: Uniqueness

Proposition C.16 *Let* $u : \mathbb{R} \times (0,T) \to \mathbb{R}$ *be a solution of the heat equation which is integrable with respect to* p. *If* u *has initial data zero in the sense of local convergence in mean, then* $u = 0$.

Proof DiBenedetto [27, 1995, Chapter V, Theorem 14.1]. As mentioned before, DiBenedetto's conductivity parameter is one instead of one-half.   □

Theorem C.17 *Let* $0 < T < 1/(2a)$, *and let* $u : \mathbb{R} \times (0,T) \to \mathbb{R}$ *be a solution of the heat equation which is integrable with respect to* p. *If* u *has initial data* f *in the sense of local convergence in mean, then* $u = v$ *on* $\mathbb{R} \times (0,T)$.

Proof By Proposition C.5, v has initial data f in the sense of local convergence in mean. Hence, $u - v$ has initial data zero in the sense of local convergence in mean. By Proposition C.13, v is integrable with respect to p. Hence, $u - v$ is integrable with respect to p. Now apply Proposition C.16 to the function $u - v$.   □

Corollary C.18 *Let* $0 < T < 1/(2a)$, *and let* $u : \mathbb{R} \times (0,T) \to \mathbb{R}$ *be a solution of the heat equation which is integrable with respect to* p. *If* u *has initial data* f *in the sense of double convergence, and if* f *is continuous, then* $u = v$ *on* $\mathbb{R} \times (0,T)$.

Proof It follows from Proposition C.8 that u has initial data f in the sense of local convergence in mean. It then follows from Theorem C.17 that $u = v$ on $\mathbb{R} \times (0,T)$.   □

Corollary C.19 *Let* $0 < T < 1/(2a)$, *and let* $u : \mathbb{R} \times (0,T) \to \mathbb{R}$ *be a non-negative solution of the heat equation. If* u *has initial data* f *in the sense of local convergence in mean, then* $u = v$ *on* $\mathbb{R} \times (0,T)$, *and* $f(x) \geq 0$ *for almost all* $x \in \mathbb{R}$.

Proof It follows from Proposition C.12 that u is integrable with respect to p. It then follows from Theorem C.17 that $u = v$ on $\mathbb{R} \times (0,T)$. To show that f is non-negative almost everywhere, it suffices to show that for each $b > 0$, f is zero almost everywhere in $[-b, b]$. Since u has initial data f in the sense of local convergence in mean,

$$0 \leq - \int_{-b}^{b} 1_{f(x)<0} f(x) \, dx$$

$$\leq \int_{-b}^{b} 1_{f(x)\geq 0} |f(x) - u(x,\tau)| \, dx + \int_{-b}^{b} 1_{f(x)<0}(-f(x) + u(x,\tau)) \, dx$$

$$= \int_{-b}^{b} |f(x) - u(x,\tau)| \, dx$$

$$\to 0$$

as $\tau \to 0$. Hence,

$$\int_{-b}^{b} 1_{f(x)<0} f(x)\, dx = 0$$

which implies that f is zero almost everywhere in $[-b, b]$. □

Corollary C.20 *Let $0 < T < 1/(2a)$, and let $u : \mathbb{R} \times (0, T) \to \mathbb{R}$ be a non-negative solution of the heat equation. If u has initial data f in the sense of double convergence, and if f is continuous, then $u = v$ on $\mathbb{R} \times (0, T)$, and $f(x) \geq 0$ for all $x \in \mathbb{R}$.*

Proof It follows from Proposition C.8 that u has initial data f in the sense of local convergence in mean. It then follows from Corollary C.19 that $u = v$ on $\mathbb{R} \times (0, T)$, and $f(x) \geq 0$ for almost all $x \in \mathbb{R}$. Since f is continuous, this implies that $f(x) \geq 0$ for all $x \in \mathbb{R}$. □

Proposition C.21 *Let $0 < T$ and let $u : \mathbb{R} \times (0, T) \to \mathbb{R}$ be a solution of the heat equation such that for some $\alpha > 0$, $u(\cdot, \tau) \in G_0(\alpha)$ for all $\tau \in (0, T)$. If u has initial data zero in the sense of local convergence in mean, then $u = 0$.*

Proof Let $0 < T' < T$. We shall show that $u(x, \tau) = 0$ for all $(x, \tau) \in \mathbb{R} \times (0, T']$. Choose

$$0 = T_0 < T_1 < \cdots < T_n = T'$$

and $\epsilon > 0$ such that $\alpha < 1/(2(T_i + \epsilon - T_{i-1}))$ and $T_i + \epsilon < T$ for $i = 1, \ldots, n$.

For each i, consider the function

$$u[i] : \mathbb{R} \times (0, T_i + \epsilon - T_{i-1}) \to \mathbb{R} : (x, \tau) \mapsto u[i](x, \tau) = u(x, T_{i-1} + \tau)$$

$i = 1, \ldots, n-1$. It is a solution of the heat equation. We shall show by induction that $u[i] = 0$ for all $i = 1, \ldots, n$.

Observe that $u[i](\cdot, \tau) \in G_0(\alpha)$ for all $\tau \in (0, T_i + \epsilon - T_{i-1})$.

It follows from Proposition C.15 that $u[1]$ is integrable with respect to p. It then follows from Theorem C.17 that $u[1](x, \tau) = 0$ for all $(x, \tau) \in \mathbb{R} \times (0, T_1 + \epsilon)$.

Now suppose $1 < i \leq n$ and that the induction hypothesis has been shown for $i - 1$. Let us show that it holds for i also. Since u is continuous, it follows from Proposition C.8 that $u[i]$ has initial data zero in the sense of local convergence in mean. It follows from Proposition C.15 that $u[i]$ is integrable with respect to p. It then follows from Theorem C.17 that $u[i](x, \tau) = 0$ for all $(x, \tau) \in \mathbb{R} \times (0, T_i + \epsilon - T_{i-1})$, which implies that $u(x, \tau) = 0$ for all $(x, \tau) \in \mathbb{R} \times (T_{i-1}, T_i + \epsilon)$. □

Corollary C.22 *Let $0 < T < 1/(2a)$ and let $u : \mathbb{R} \times (0, T) \to \mathbb{R}$ be a solution of the heat equation such that for some α, $u(\cdot, \tau) \in G_0(\alpha)$ for all $\tau \in (0, T)$. If u has initial data f in the sense of local convergence in mean, then $u = v$ on $\mathbb{R} \times (0, T)$.*

Proof By Proposition C.5, v has initial data f in the sense of local convergence in mean. Hence, $u - v$ has initial data zero in the sense of local convergence in mean.

By Proposition C.14, there exists α' such that $v(\cdot, \tau) \in G(\alpha')$ for all $\tau \in (0, T)$. Hence there exists $\alpha'' > 0$ such that $u(\cdot, \tau) - v(\cdot, \tau) \in G_0(\alpha'')$ for all $\tau \in (0, T)$.

It now follows from Proposition C.21 that $u = v$ on $\mathbb{R} \times (0, T)$. $\qquad\square$

Examples C.10 and C.11 show that local convergence in mean cannot be replaced by convergence almost everywhere (or convergence everywhere) in Proposition C.21 or Corollary C.22.

Corollary C.23 *Let* $0 < T < 1/(2a)$ *and let* $u : \mathbb{R} \times (0, T) \to \mathbb{R}$ *be a solution of the heat equation such that for some* α, $u(\cdot, \tau) \in G_0(\alpha)$ *for all* $\tau \in (0, T)$. *If* u *has initial data* f *in the sense of double convergence, and if* f *is continuous, then* $u = v$ *on* $\mathbb{R} \times (0, T)$.

Proof By Proposition C.8, u has initial data f in the sense of local convergence in mean. It then follows from Corollary C.22 that $u = v$ on $\mathbb{R} \times (0, T)$. $\qquad\square$

Examples C.10 and C.11 show that double convergence cannot be replaced by convergence almost everywhere (or convergence everywhere) in Corollary C.23.

Corollary C.24 *Let* $0 < T < 1/(2a)$ *and let* $u : \mathbb{R} \times (0, T) \to \mathbb{R}$ *be a solution of the heat equation such that for some* α, $u(\cdot, \tau) \in G(\alpha)$ *for all* $\tau \in (0, T)$. *If* u *has initial data* f *in the sense of convergence almost everywhere, then* $u = v$ *on* $\mathbb{R} \times (0, T)$.

Proof By Proposition C.9, u has initial data f in the sense of local convergence in mean. By Corollary C.22, then $u = v$ on $\mathbb{R} \times (0, T)$. $\qquad\square$

Examples C.10 and C.11 are not counterexamples to Corollary C.24, because the solution p in Example C.10 and the solution u in Example C.11 do not satisfy the strong growth condition $G(\alpha)$ imposed in this corollary.

C.5   Notes

For the heat equation, we have relied mainly on DiBenedetto [27, 1995], supplemented by Karatzas and Shreve [64, 1988, Chapter 4, Section 3]. Curiously, few other books on partial differential equations proved to be useful.

Karatzas and Shreve [64, 1988, Chapter 4, Corollary 3.7] strengthen Proposition C.12 by showing that the inequality

$$Eu(x + W(t - s), s) \le u(x, t)$$

is actually an equality, for all $x \in \mathbb{R}$ and all $s, t \in (0, T)$ with $s < t$. In other words, given $(x, t) \in \mathbb{R} \times (0, T)$, the process $u(x + W(\tau), t - \tau)$, $\tau \in [0, t)$, is not only a supermartingale but a martingale.

Corollary C.20 (in the case $f = 0$) is the Widder uniqueness theorem (Karatzas and Shreve [64, 1988, Chapter 4, Exercise 3.8], Widder [88, 1944]).

Corollary C.23 (in the case $f = 0$) generalizes the Tychonoff uniqueness theorem (Tychonoff [85, 1935], Widder [88, 1944]). The rendering of this theorem in Karatzas and Shreve [64, 1988, Chapter 4, Theorem 3.3] imposes the stronger restriction $u(\cdot, \tau) \in G(\alpha)$ instead of $u(\cdot, \tau) \in G_0(\alpha)$. As seen in Corollary C.24, under this stronger restriction, the initial data can in fact be imposed in the sense of convergence almost everywhere instead of in the stronger sense of double convergence.

Widder [88, 1944] notes that one cannot replace double convergence by pointwise convergence in the Tychonoff uniqueness theorem (under the weak restriction $u(\cdot, \tau) \in G_0(\alpha)$). Therefore one cannot replace it by convergence almost everywhere either. Widder cites the solution u in Example C.11 as a counterexample.

The Feynman–Kac theorem or Feynman–Kac formula (Karatzas and Shreve [64, 1988, Chapter 4, Theorem 4.2], Feynman [37, 1948], Kac [61, 1949]) deals with a version of the heat equation where time runs backwards, and which is more general than the one studied here, because it includes a "potential" and a "Lagrangian." The Feynman–Kac theorem is a uniqueness result, not an existence result. Applied to our version of the heat equation, it says the following:

Theorem C.25 *Let $0 < T < 1/(2a)$ and let $u : I\!R \times (0, T) \to I\!R$ be a solution of the heat equation such that $u(\cdot, \tau) \in G(a)$ for all $\tau \in (0, T)$. If u has initial data f in the sense of double convergence, and if f is continuous, then $u = v$ on $I\!R \times (0, T)$.*

Proof Follows from Corollary C.23 or Corollary C.24 or Karatzas and Shreve [64, 1988, Chapter 4, Theorem 4.2]. □

Corollary C.23 is actually sharper than Theorem C.25. It imposes only the weak restriction $u(\cdot, \tau) \in G_0(\alpha)$, while Theorem C.25 imposes the strong restriction $u(\cdot, \tau) \in G(\alpha)$.

Corollary C.24 is also sharper than Theorem C.25. It does not assume f to be continuous, and it imposes the initial data only in the sense of convergence almost everywhere, rather than in the sense of double convergence.

Taylor [84, 1996, Chapter 3, Proposition 5.1] is representative of treatments of the heat equation based on functional analysis. He uses the Fourier transform to establish the uniqueness of the solution. He considers solutions which are "tempered distributions" and also requires the initial data to be given by a tempered distribution. If the initial data are given by a function f, then the requirement that f should be a tempered distribution is more stringent than the growth condition $f \in G_0(\alpha)$ imposed in Corollary C.22. For example, if $f = \exp$, then $f \in G_0(\alpha)$ for all $\alpha > 0$, but f is not a tempered distribution.

Virtually all of our analysis of the one-dimensional heat equation generalizes to higher dimensions.

APPENDIX D

SUGGESTED SOLUTIONS TO EXERCISES

D.1 Solutions for Chapter 1

Exercise 1.1 For any c, the process X starts at zero and has independent increments and continuous paths.

What matters is to find c such that when $0 \le t < s$, the increment $X(s) - X(t)$ is normally distributed with mean zero and variance $s - t$.

Since

$$X(s) - X(t) = c\left(W\left(\frac{s}{\sigma^2}\right) - W\left(\frac{t}{\sigma^2}\right)\right)$$

the increment has mean zero and variance

$$c^2\left(\frac{s}{\sigma^2} - \frac{t}{\sigma^2}\right)$$

The variance equals $s - t$ if $c = \sigma$.

Exercise 1.2 *Proof of Proposition 1.3.* First, suppose B is a K-dimensional standard Brownian motion. It is clear that each of the component processes B^k is a one-dimensional standard Brownian motion. What requires a bit of thought is the fact that they are independent. By Proposition 1.1, it is enough that the random vectors $(B^k_{t_0}, \ldots, B^k_{t_n})$, $k = 1, \ldots, K$, are independent whenever $0 \le t_0 < \cdots < t_n$. All the elements $B^k_{t_i}$, $k = 1, \ldots, K$, $i = 1, \ldots n$, are mutually uncorrelated. Since they are jointly normally distributed, it follows from Exercise A.14 that they are independent. But then the vectors are also independent.

Conversely, if the processes B^k are independent standard Brownian motions, it is easily checked that B is a K-dimensional standard Brownian motion.

Exercise 1.3 *Proof of Proposition 1.9.* Use Propositions B.16 and B.27. The process X is Q-integrable if and only if

$$E_Q\|X(t)\| < \infty$$

for all t. The process ηX is P-integrable if and only if

$$E\|\eta(t)X(t)\| < \infty$$

for all t. Since

$$E_Q\|X(t)\| = E(\xi\|X(t)\|)$$

$$= E(E(\xi \|X(t)\| \mid \mathcal{F}_t))$$
$$= E(E(\xi \mid \mathcal{F}_t)\|X(t)\|)$$
$$= E(\eta(t)\|X(t)\|)$$
$$= E\|\eta(t)X(t)\|$$

X is Q-integrable if and only if ηX is P-integrable.

If so, then

$$\eta(s)E_Q(X(t) \mid \mathcal{F}_s) = E(\xi \mid \mathcal{F}_s)E_Q(X(t) \mid \mathcal{F}_s)$$
$$= E(\xi X(t) \mid \mathcal{F}_s)$$
$$= E(E(\xi X(t) \mid \mathcal{F}_t) \mid \mathcal{F}_s)$$
$$= E(\eta(t)X(t) \mid \mathcal{F}_s)$$

where the second equation follows from Proposition B.27.

Exercise 1.4 For any constant c, the process

$$\tilde{W} = c\left(-\sigma_1 Z_1 + \sigma_2 Z_2\right) = c\left(-\sigma_1, \sigma_2\right) Z = c\left(-\sigma_1, \sigma_2\right) A W$$

is a one-dimensional generalized Wiener process relative to F with initial value $\tilde{W}(0) = 0$ and increment mean zero. So we just have to choose c such that the increment variance of $\tilde{W}(t)$ is one.

We know that the increment covariance matrix of

$$\begin{pmatrix} \sigma_1 Z_1(t) \\ \sigma_2 Z_2(t) \end{pmatrix}$$

is

$$\begin{pmatrix} \sigma_1 & 0 \\ 0 & \sigma_2 \end{pmatrix} \begin{pmatrix} 1 & \rho \\ \rho & 1 \end{pmatrix} \begin{pmatrix} \sigma_1 & 0 \\ 0 & \sigma_2 \end{pmatrix} = \begin{pmatrix} \sigma_1^2 & \rho\sigma_1\sigma_2 \\ \rho\sigma_1\sigma_2 & \sigma_2^2 \end{pmatrix}$$

Hence, the variance of $\tilde{W}(t)$ is

$$c\left(-1\ 1\right) \begin{pmatrix} \sigma_1^2 & \rho\sigma_1\sigma_2 \\ \rho\sigma_1\sigma_2 & \sigma_2^2 \end{pmatrix} \begin{pmatrix} -1 \\ 1 \end{pmatrix} ct = c^2 \left(\sigma_1^2 + \sigma_2^2 - 2\rho\sigma_1\sigma_2\right) t$$

This variance equals t if

$$c = \frac{1}{\sqrt{\sigma_1^2 + \sigma_2^2 - 2\rho\sigma_1\sigma_2}}$$

so that

$$\tilde{W} = \frac{1}{\sqrt{\sigma_1^2 + \sigma_2^2 - 2\rho\sigma_1\sigma_2}} \left(-\sigma_1 Z_1 + \sigma_2 Z_2\right)$$

Exercise 1.5 *Proof of Proposition 1.18.* Suppose X and Y are indistinguishable processes. Pick a set $N \in \mathcal{F}$ such that $P(N) = 0$ and

$$X(\omega, t) = Y(\omega, t) \text{ for all } \omega \in \Omega \setminus N \text{ and all } t \in T$$

Then for all $t \in T$, $X(\omega, t) = Y(\omega, t)$ for all $\omega \in \Omega \setminus N$, and, hence, $X(t) = Y(t)$ with probability one. So, X and Y are stochastically equivalent.

Set $M = N \times T$. Then

$$(P \times \lambda)(M) = P(N)\lambda(T) = 0$$

and

$$(\Omega \setminus N) \times T = (\Omega \times T) \setminus M$$

Hence,

$$X(\omega, t) = Y(\omega, t) \text{ for all } (\omega, t) \in (\Omega \times T) \setminus M$$

and X and Y are almost everywhere identical.

Exercise 1.6 *Proof of Proposition 1.20.* Suppose X and Y are measurable and stochastically equivalent. Then

$$(P \times \lambda)(\{(\omega, t) \in \Omega \times T : X(\omega, t) \neq Y(\omega, t)\})$$
$$= \int 1_{\{(\omega,t) \in \Omega \times T : X(\omega,t) \neq Y(\omega,t)\}}(\omega, t) \, d(P \times \lambda)$$
$$= \int \int 1_{\{(\omega,t) \in \Omega \times T : X(\omega,t) \neq Y(\omega,t)\}}(\omega, t) dP(\omega) \, d\lambda(t)$$
$$= \int \int 0 \, d\lambda = 0$$

Hence, X and Y are almost everywhere identical.

Exercise 1.7 Pick a set $M \in \mathcal{F} \otimes \mathcal{B}(T)$ such that $(P \times \lambda)(M) = 0$ and

$$X(\omega, t) = Y(\omega, t) \text{ for all } (\omega, t) \in (\Omega \times T) \setminus M$$

For each $\omega \in \Omega$, set
$$M(\omega) = \{t \in T : (\omega, t) \in M\}$$

Then, by Fubini's theorem, $M(\omega) \in \mathcal{B}(T)$. Set

$$N = \{\omega \in \Omega : \lambda(M(\omega)) = 0\}$$

Again by Fubini's theorem, $N \in \mathcal{F}$ and $P(N) = 0$.

Consider first case 1. Both X and Y are right-continuous, and if $T = [0, T]$ then $X(T) = Y(T)$ with probability one. In the latter case, set

$$N' = \{\omega \in \Omega : X(T) \neq Y(T)\}$$

If $T = [0, \infty)$, set $N' = \emptyset$. In any case $P(N') = 0$.

Let $\omega \in \Omega \setminus (N \cup N')$ and $t \in \mathcal{T}$. If $\mathcal{T} = [0, T]$, assume without loss of generality that $t < T$.

Since $\lambda(M(\omega)) = 0$, $M(\omega)$ does not contain any non-empty open interval. Hence, there is a sequence (t_n) of numbers $t_n \in (\mathcal{T} \setminus M(\omega))$ such that $t_n \geq t$ and $t_n \to t$. Since the paths $X(\omega, \cdot)$ and $Y(\omega, \cdot)$ are right-continuous, $X(t_n, \omega) \to X(t, \omega)$ and $Y(t_n, \omega) \to Y(t, \omega)$; but since $X(t_n, \omega) = Y(t_n, \omega)$ it follows that $X(t, \omega) = Y(t, \omega)$.

Hence, X and Y are indistinguishable.

The proof for case 2, where X and Y are left-continuous, is similar.

Exercise 1.8 *Proof of Proposition 1.24.* It suffices to prove this in the case $N = 1$. Let $t \in \mathcal{T}$. Since ϕ is continuous, almost all its paths are continuous and hence bounded on $[0, t]$. In other words, there exists an event $A \in \mathcal{F}$ with $P(A) = 0$ such that for each $\omega \in \Omega \setminus A$, there exists a constant $C(\omega)$ such that $|\phi(\omega, s)| \leq C(\omega)$ for all $s \in [0, t]$. Hence,

$$\int_0^t \|\phi(\omega, s)a(\omega, s)\| \, ds = \int_0^t |\phi(\omega, s)| \|a(\omega, s)\| \, ds$$

$$\leq C(\omega) \int_0^t \|a(\omega, s)\| \, ds$$

$$< \infty$$

for all $\omega \in \Omega \setminus A$, which implies that $\phi a \in \mathcal{L}^1$.

Exercise 1.9 Assume that

$$a(t) = \alpha 1_{\{0\}}(t) + \sum_{i=0}^{n-1} \alpha_i 1_{(t_i, t_{i+1}]}(t)$$

and

$$b(t) = \beta 1_{\{0\}}(t) + \sum_{i=0}^{n-1} \beta_i 1_{(t_i, t_{i+1}]}(t)$$

where $0 = t_0 < \cdots < t_n = t$, $\alpha, \beta \in \mathcal{F}_0$, and the random variables α_i, β_i are measurable with respect to $\mathcal{F}_{t_i}$. These random variables are bounded.

1: From

$$\gamma a(t) = \gamma \alpha_0 1_{\{0\}}(t) + \sum_{i=0}^{n-1} \gamma \alpha_i 1_{(t_i, t_{i+1}]}(t)$$

and

$$\delta b(t) = \delta \beta_0 1_{\{0\}}(t) + \sum_{i=0}^{n-1} \delta \beta_i 1_{(t_i, t_{i+1}]}(t)$$

it follows that

$$(\gamma a + \delta b)(t) = (\gamma \alpha_0 + \delta \beta_0) 1_{\{0\}}(t) + \sum_{i=0}^{n-1} (\gamma \alpha_i + \delta \beta_i) 1_{(t_i, t_{i+1}]}(t)$$

and

$$\int_0^t (\gamma a + \delta b)\, dW = \sum_{i=0}^{n-1} (\gamma \alpha_i + \delta \beta_i)(W(t_{i+1}) - W(t_i))$$

$$= \gamma \sum_{i=0}^{n-1} \alpha_i (W(t_{i+1}) - W(t_i)) + \delta \sum_{i=0}^{n-1} \beta_i (W(t_{i+1}) - W(t_i))$$

$$= \gamma \int_0^t a\, dW + \delta \int_0^t b\, dW$$

2:

$$E\left[\left(\int_0^t a\, dW\right)\left(\int_0^t b\, dW\right)\right] = E\left[\sum_{i=0}^{n-1} \alpha_i \beta_i (W(t_{i+1}) - W(t_i))^2\right]$$

$$= E\left[E\left(\sum_{i=0}^{n-1} \alpha_i \beta_i (W(t_{i+1}) - W(t_i))^2 \,\middle|\, \mathcal{F}_{t_i}\right)\right]$$

$$= E\left[\sum_{i=0}^{n-1} \alpha_i \beta_i E\left((W(t_{i+1}) - W(t_i))^2\right)\right]$$

$$= E\left[\sum_{i=0}^{n-1} \alpha_i \beta_i (t_{i+1} - t_i)^2\right]$$

$$= E\int_0^t a(t)b(t)\, dt$$

3: Supposing that $t_k \leq s \leq t_{k+1}$,

$$\int_0^s a\, dW = \sum_{i=0}^{k-1} \alpha_i (W(t_{i+1}) - W(t_i)) + \alpha_k (W(s) - W(t_i))$$

which is measurable with respect to $\mathcal{F}_s$. It is easily seen from this formula that the stochastic integral is continuous as a function of s.

Since the stochastic integral is a sum of products of bounded random variables with normally distributed random variables, it is square integrable. Let us show that it is a martingale.

Suppose that $t_k \leq s \leq t_{k+1}$, and $t_l \leq t \leq t_{l+1}$, $k \leq l$, $s \leq t$. Then

$$E[\alpha_k (W(t_{k+1}) - W(t_k)) \mid \mathcal{F}_s] = \alpha_k E[W(t_{k+1}) - W(t_k) \mid \mathcal{F}_s]$$
$$= \alpha_k (W(s) - W(t_k))$$

If $k < l$, then

$$E[\alpha_l (W(t) - W(t_l)) \mid \mathcal{F}_s] = E(E[\alpha_l (W(t) - W(t_l)) \mid \mathcal{F}_{t_l}] \mid \mathcal{F}_s)$$

$$= E(0 \mid \mathcal{F}_s)$$
$$= 0$$

and

$$E\left[\int_0^t a\,dW \;\middle|\; \mathcal{F}_s\right]$$

$$= \sum_{i=0}^{l-1} E[\alpha_i(W(t_{i+1}) - W(t_i)) \mid \mathcal{F}_s] + E[\alpha_l(W(t) - W(t_l)) \mid \mathcal{F}_s]$$

$$= \sum_{i=0}^{k-1} \alpha_i(W(t_{i+1}) - W(t_i)) + E[\alpha_k(W(t_{k+1}) - W(t_k)) \mid \mathcal{F}_s]$$
$$+ E[\alpha_l(W(t) - W(t_l)) \mid \mathcal{F}_s]$$

$$= \sum_{i=0}^{k-1} \alpha_i(W(t_{i+1}) - W(t_i)) + \alpha_k(W(s) - W(t_k))$$

$$= \int_0^s a\,dW$$

If $l = k$, then

$$E\left[\int_0^t a\,dW \;\middle|\; \mathcal{F}_s\right]$$

$$= \sum_{i=0}^{l-1} E[\alpha_i(W(t_{i+1}) - W(t_i)) \mid \mathcal{F}_s] + E[\alpha_l(W(t) - W(t_l)) \mid \mathcal{F}_s]$$

$$= \sum_{i=0}^{k-1} \alpha_i(W(t_{i+1}) - W(t_i)) + \alpha_k(W(s) - W(t_k))$$

$$= \int_0^s a\,dW$$

Exercise 1.10 *Proof of Proposition 1.28.* First, assume that $b \in \mathcal{L}^2$. Then each of the elements b_{ik}, $i = 1, \ldots, N$, $k = 1, \ldots, K$, is in $\mathcal{L}^2$. This means that there exists an event $A \in \mathcal{F}$ with $P(A) = 0$ such that for every $\omega \in \Omega \setminus A$ and every $i = 1, \ldots, N$ and $k = 1, \ldots, K$,

$$b_{ik}(\omega, \cdot) \in L^2([0, T], \mathcal{B}([0, T]), \lambda)$$

But then it follows from the Cauchy–Schwartz inequality (Proposition B.29) that for every $\omega \in \Omega \setminus A$ and every $i, j = 1, \ldots, N$ and $k, l = 1, \ldots, K$,

$$b_{ik}(\omega, \cdot)b_{j,l}(\omega, \cdot) \in L^1([0, T], \mathcal{B}([0, T]), \lambda)$$

Hence, $b_{ik}b_{jl} \in \mathcal{L}^1$ for all i, j, k, l. Since the elements of $bb^\top$ are

$$\left(bb^{\mathsf{T}}\right)_{ij} = \sum_{k=1}^{K} b_{ik}b_{jk}$$

each element of bb^{T} is in $\mathcal{L}^1$, and hence $bb^{\mathsf{T}} \in \mathcal{L}^1$.

Conversely, if $bb^{\mathsf{T}} \in \mathcal{L}^1$, then in particular the diagonal elements

$$\left(bb^{\mathsf{T}}\right)_{ii} = \sum_{k=1}^{K} b_{ik}^2$$

are in $\mathcal{L}^1$, $i = 1,\ldots,N$, which implies that $b_{ik} \in \mathcal{L}^2$ for every $i = 1,\ldots,N$, $k = 1,\ldots,K$, and hence $b \in \mathcal{L}^2$.

Exercise 1.11 *Proof of Proposition 1.29.* The elements of $b^{\mathsf{T}}\phi b$ are

$$\left(b^{\mathsf{T}}\phi b\right)_{kl} = \sum_{i,j=1}^{N} b_{ki}\phi_{ij}b_{jl}$$

By Proposition 1.28, $\phi_{ij}b_{jl} \in \mathcal{L}^2$. Hence, by Proposition 1.24, $b_{ki}\phi_{ij}b_{jl} \in \mathcal{L}^1$. This implies that the elements of $b^{\mathsf{T}}\phi b$ are in $\mathcal{L}^1$, and hence $b^{\mathsf{T}}\phi b$ itself is in $\mathcal{L}^1$.

Exercise 1.12 It is clear that $a, b \in \mathcal{H}^2$, so that we can use Proposition 1.37. For $0 \le s < 2$, $Ea(s)^2 = 1$. For $2 \le s \le 3$,

$$Ea(s)^2 = \frac{1}{2} \times 1 + \frac{1}{2} \times 4 = 2.5$$

Hence,

$$\begin{aligned}
\operatorname{var}\left(\int_0^3 a\,dW\right) &= \int_0^3 Ea(s)^2\,ds \\
&= \int_0^2 1\,ds + \int_2^3 2.5\,ds \\
&= 4.5
\end{aligned}$$

$$\begin{aligned}
\operatorname{var}\left(\int_1^3 a\,dW \,\Big|\, \mathcal{F}_1\right) &= \int_1^3 E\left[a(s)^2 \mid \mathcal{F}_1\right]\,ds \\
&= \int_1^2 1\,ds + \int_2^3 2.5\,ds \\
&= 3.5
\end{aligned}$$

For $0 \le s < 2$, $E(a(s)b(s)) = 1$. For $2 \le s \le 3$,

$$E(a(s)b(s)) = \frac{1}{4} \times 1 + \frac{1}{4} \times 2 + \frac{1}{4} \times 3 + \frac{1}{4} \times 6 = 2.5$$

Hence,

$$\operatorname{cov}\left(\int_0^3 a\,dW, \int_0^3 b\,dW\right) = \int_0^3 E(a(s)b(s))\,ds$$

$$= \int_0^2 1\,ds + \int_2^3 2.5\,ds$$
$$= 4.5$$

$$\mathrm{cov}\left(\int_1^3 a\,dW, \int_1^3 b\,dW \,\Big|\, \mathcal{F}_1\right) = \int_1^3 E(a(s)b(s)\mid \mathcal{F}_1)\,ds$$
$$= \int_1^2 1\,ds + \int_2^3 2.5\,ds$$
$$= 4.5$$

D.2   Solutions for Chapter 2

Exercise 2.1   The Wiener process W itself is an Itô process:

$$W(t) = W(0) + \int_0^t 0\,ds + \int_0^t 1\,dW$$

Time is an Itô process:

$$t = 0 + \int_0^t 1\,ds + \int 0\,dW$$

Consider the function

$$f : \mathbb{R}^2 \to \mathbb{R} : f(x,t) = xt$$

It is (at least) once continuously differentiable with respect to t and twice continuously differentiable with respect to x. The derivatives are

$$f_t(x,t) = x$$

$$f_x(x,t) = t$$

$$f_{xx}(x,t) = 0$$

By Itô's lemma, the process $f(W(t),t) = tW(t)$ is an Itô process, and the differential is

$$d(tW(t)) = W(t)\,dt + t\,dW(t)$$

Hence,

$$tW(t) = \int_0^t W(s)\,ds + \int_0^t s\,dW(s)$$

and

$$\int_0^t (t-s)\,dW(s) = \int_0^t W(s)\,ds$$

Exercise 2.2   The Wiener process W itself is an Itô process:

$$W(t) = W(0) + \int_0^t 0\, ds + \int_0^t 1\, dW_t$$

Consider the function f defined on the real line by $f(x) = x^3$. It is (at least) twice continuously differentiable. By Itô's lemma, the process $f(W(t)) = W(t)^3$ is an Itô process with differential

$$dW^3 = \left[f'(W) \times 0 + \frac{1}{2} f''(W) \times 1 \right] dt + [f'(W) \times 1]\, dW$$

$$= 3W\, dt + 3W^2\, dW$$

Hence,

$$W(t)^3 = \int_0^t 3W\, ds + \int_0^t 3W^2\, dW$$

and, using the result of Exercise 2.1,

$$\int_0^t W^2\, dW = \frac{1}{3} W(t)^3 - \int_0^t W\, ds = \frac{1}{3} W(t)^3 - tW(t) + \int_0^t s\, dW(s)$$

D.3   Solutions for Chapter 3

Exercise 3.1   Because the integrand is non-random, the integral

$$\int_s^t e^{au}\, dW(u)$$

is normally distributed and its mean is zero. So, the random variable

$$e^{-at} \int_s^t e^{au}\, dW(u)$$

is also normally distributed with mean zero. Its variance is calculated by using the formula for the variance of a stochastic integral of a non-random integrand:

$$\left(e^{-at}\right)^2 \int_s^t e^{2au}\, du = e^{-2at} \frac{1}{2a}\left(e^{2at} - e^{2as}\right) = \frac{1}{2a}\left(1 - e^{-2a(t-s)}\right)$$

D.4   Solutions for Chapter 4

Exercise 4.1   Let $s, t \in T$, $s \leq t$. We need to show that

$$E[\Pi(t)\bar{\Delta}(t)\bar{S}(t) \mid \mathcal{F}_s] = \Pi(s)\bar{\Delta}(s)\bar{S}(s)$$

We may assume without loss of generality that s and t are among the potential trading dates:

$$s, t \in \{t_0, t_1, \ldots, t_m\}$$

For every $n < m$,

$$E[\Pi(t_{n+1})\bar{\Delta}(t_{n+1})\bar{S}(t_{n+1}) \mid \mathcal{F}_{t_n}] = E[\Pi(t_{n+1})\bar{\Delta}(t_n)\bar{S}(t_{n+1}) \mid \mathcal{F}_{t_n}]$$

$$= \bar{\Delta}(t_n)E[\Pi(t_{n+1})\bar{S}(t_{n+1}) \mid \mathcal{F}_{t_n}]$$
$$= \bar{\Delta}(t_n)\Pi(t_n)\bar{S}(t_n)$$

where the first equation follows from the instantaneous budget constraint, and the third equation follows from the assumption that the buy-and-hold strategies are admissible. Hence, if $s \leq t_n$, then

$$E[\Pi(t_{n+1})\bar{\Delta}(t_{n+1})\bar{S}(t_{n+1}) \mid \mathcal{F}_s] = E[E[\Pi(t_{n+1})\bar{\Delta}(t_{n+1})\bar{S}(t_{n+1}) \mid \mathcal{F}_{t_n}] \mid \mathcal{F}_s]$$
$$= E[\bar{\Delta}(t_n)\Pi(t_n)\bar{S}(t_n) \mid \mathcal{F}_s]$$

By induction,

$$E[\Pi(t_{n+1})\bar{\Delta}(t_{n+1})\bar{S}(t_{n+1}) \mid \mathcal{F}_s] = E[\bar{\Delta}(s)\Pi(s)\bar{S}(s) \mid \mathcal{F}_s] = \bar{\Delta}(s)\Pi(s)\bar{S}(s)$$

for all $n < m$ with $s \leq t_n$. We now only have to pick n such that $t = t_{n+1}$.

Exercise 4.2 Normalize the price system by dividing by the value M of the money market account. In the new price system, the money market account has constant price equal to one, and the price of the stock is S/M. The normalized cumulative gains process of $\bar{\Delta}$ will be

$$\mathcal{G}\left(\bar{\Delta}; \bar{S}/M\right)(t) = \bar{\Delta}(0)\bar{S}(0)/M + \int_0^t \bar{\Delta}\, d(\bar{S}/M)$$
$$= \int_0^t \Delta_0\, d1 + \int_0^t \Delta\, d(S/M)$$
$$= \int_0^t d(S/M)$$
$$= S(t)/M(t) - S(0)/M(0)$$

Since the trading strategy has to be self-financing and have initial value zero, the value process in the normalized units must be

$$\bar{\Delta}(t)\bar{S}(t)/M(t) = \mathcal{G}\left(\bar{\Delta}; \bar{S}/M\right)(t) = S(t)/M(t) - S(0)/M(0)$$

and the nominal value process will be

$$\bar{\Delta}(t)\bar{S}(t) = S(t) - M(t)S(0)/M(0)$$

Therefore, the process Δ_0 must be given by

$$\Delta_0 M + \Delta S = S - MS(0)/M(0)$$

or

$$\Delta_0(t) = \frac{1}{M(t)}(1-t)S(t) - \frac{1}{M(0)}S(0)$$

for rational t, and

$$\Delta_0(t) = -\frac{1}{M(0)}S(0)$$

for irrational t. Therefore, Δ_0 is unique. Since

$$\Pi\bar{\Delta}\bar{S} = \Pi S - \Pi M S(0)/M(0)$$

and since both ΠS and ΠM are martingales according to Example 4.10, the trading strategy $\bar{\Delta} = (\Delta_0, \Delta)$ is indeed admissible.

Exercise 4.3 Since

$$\tilde{\Pi} = \tilde{\Pi}(0)\eta\left[0, -\frac{\tilde{\lambda}}{\sigma}(-\sigma_1, \sigma_2)A\right]$$

and

$$S_1 = S_1(0)\eta[\mu_1, (\sigma_1, 0)A]$$

the negative of the relative drift of $\tilde{\Pi}/S_1$ is

$$\mu_1 + \frac{\tilde{\lambda}}{\sigma}(-\sigma_1, \sigma_2)AA^{\mathsf{T}}(\sigma_1, 0)^{\mathsf{T}}$$

$$= \mu_1 + \frac{\tilde{\lambda}}{\sigma}(-\sigma_1, \sigma_2)\begin{pmatrix} 1 & \rho \\ \rho & 1 \end{pmatrix}\begin{pmatrix} \sigma_1 \\ 0 \end{pmatrix}$$

$$= \mu_1 + \frac{\tilde{\lambda}}{\sigma}(-\sigma_1^2 + \rho\sigma_1\sigma_2)$$

$$= \mu_1 + \frac{\mu_2 - \mu_1 + \sigma_1^2 - \rho\sigma_1\sigma_2}{\sigma_1^2 + \sigma_2^2 - \rho\sigma_1\sigma_2}(-\sigma_1^2 + \rho\sigma_1\sigma_2)$$

D.5   Solutions for Chapter 5

Exercise 5.1 As in Proposition 5.3, set

$$\bar{\Delta} = \bar{\gamma} + \mathcal{D}(\bar{\gamma}; \bar{S}/M)\bar{b}$$

Then $\bar{\Delta}$ is a self-financing trading strategy with dispersion $\bar{\Delta}\bar{\sigma} = \bar{\gamma}\bar{\sigma} = 0$ and initial value $\bar{\Delta}(0)\bar{S}(0) = \bar{\gamma}(0)\bar{S}(0)$. Observe that

$$\bar{\Delta}\bar{S} = \mathcal{G}(\bar{\Delta}; \bar{S}/M) = \mathcal{G}(\bar{\gamma}; \bar{S}/M) > 0$$

almost everywhere. Furthermore,

$$\bar{\Delta}\bar{\mu} - r\bar{\Delta}\bar{S} = \bar{\Delta}(\bar{\mu} - r\bar{S}) = \bar{\gamma}(\bar{\mu} - r\bar{S})$$

since

$$\bar{b}(\bar{\mu} - r\bar{S}) = Mr - Mr = 0$$

This implies that

$$\frac{\bar{\Delta}\bar{\mu}}{\bar{\Delta}\bar{S}} \geq r$$

almost everywhere, with strict inequality on a subset of $\Omega \times [0, T]$ with positive measure. Since

$$d(\bar{\Delta}\bar{S}) = \bar{\Delta}\bar{S} \frac{\bar{\Delta}\bar{\mu}}{\bar{\Delta}\bar{S}} \, dt$$

we know that

$$\bar{\Delta}\bar{S} = \bar{\Delta}(0)\bar{S}(0)\eta \left[\frac{\bar{\Delta}\bar{\mu}}{\bar{\Delta}\bar{S}}, 0 \right]$$

and

$$\begin{aligned}
\bar{\Delta}(t)\bar{S}(t) &= \bar{\Delta}(0)\bar{S}(0) \exp\left[\int_0^t \frac{\bar{\Delta}\bar{\mu}}{\bar{\Delta}\bar{S}} \, ds \right] \\
&\geq \bar{\Delta}(0)\bar{S}(0) \exp\left[\int_0^t r \, ds \right] \\
&= \frac{\bar{\Delta}(0)\bar{S}(0)}{M(0)} M(t)
\end{aligned}$$

for all $t \geq 0$, while a strict inequality holds for $t = T$ with positive probability. Set

$$\bar{\theta} = \bar{\Delta} - \frac{\bar{\Delta}(0)\bar{S}(0)}{M(0)} \bar{b}$$

Then $\bar{\theta}$ is a self-financing trading strategy. Its initial value is

$$\bar{\theta}(0)\bar{S}(0) = \bar{\Delta}(0)\bar{S}(0) - \frac{\bar{\Delta}(0)\bar{S}(0)}{M(0)} \bar{b}(0)\bar{S}(0) = 0$$

Its value process is

$$\bar{\theta}\bar{S} = \bar{\Delta}\bar{S} - \frac{\bar{\Delta}(0)\bar{S}(0)}{M(0)} \bar{b}\bar{S} = \bar{\Delta}\bar{S} - \frac{\bar{\Delta}(0)\bar{S}(0)}{M(0)} M$$

Therefore, with probability one, $\bar{\theta}(t)\bar{S}(t) \geq 0$ for all $t \in [0, T]$, and $\bar{\theta}(T)\bar{S}(T) > 0$ with positive probability.

Exercise 5.2 The answer is that a claim Y is marketed at time T with respect to S_1, S_2, and Π if and only if $\Pi(T)Y$ is integrable and Y is measurable with respect to $F_T^{\tilde{W}} = F_T^{S_2/S_1}$. Let us elaborate.

Recall that

$$\tilde{W} = \frac{1}{\sqrt{\sigma_1^2 + \sigma_2^2 - 2\rho\sigma_1\sigma_2}} (-\sigma_1 Z_1 + \sigma_2 Z_2)$$

is a standard Wiener process relative to F, and that

$$d\left(\frac{S_2}{S_1}\right) = \frac{S_2}{S_1}\left[\left(\mu_2 - \mu_1 + \sigma_1^2 - \rho\sigma_1\sigma_2\right)dt + \sigma\,d\tilde{W}(t)\right]$$

where

$$\sigma = \sqrt{\sigma_1^2 + \sigma_2^2 - 2\rho\sigma_1\sigma_2}$$

This implies, in particular, that the processes $\tilde{W}$ and S_2/S_1 generate the same augmented filtration:

$$F^{\tilde{W}} = F^{S_2/S_1}$$

The price of risk $\tilde{\lambda}$ with respect to $\tilde{W}$ in the new price system is

$$\tilde{\lambda} = \frac{\mu_2 - \mu_1 + \sigma_1^2 - \rho\sigma_1\sigma_2}{\sigma}$$

The differential of the process $\tilde{\Pi}$ is

$$\frac{d\tilde{\Pi}}{\tilde{\Pi}} = -\tilde{\lambda}\,d\tilde{W} = -\frac{\tilde{\lambda}}{\sigma}(-\sigma_1\,dZ_1 + \sigma_2\,dZ_2) = -\frac{\tilde{\lambda}}{\sigma}(-\sigma_1, \sigma_2)A\,dW$$

Let Y be a claim. A trading strategy $\bar{\Delta}$ is self-financing and admissible with respect to S_1, S_2, and Π if and only if it is self-financing and admissible with respect to the price processes 1 and S_2/S_1 and the state price process $\tilde{\Pi} = S_1\Pi$. It replicates the claim Y in the original price system if and only if it replicates the claim Y/S_1 in the new price system 1 and S_2/S_1. Hence, the claim Y is marketed at time T with respect to S_1, S_2, and Π if and only if the claim $Y/S_1(T)$ is marketed at time T with respect to 1, S_2/S_1, and $\tilde{\Pi}$.

By Theorem 5.6, markets are dynamically complete with respect to the new price system 1 and S_2/S_1 and the state price process $\tilde{\Pi}$. Hence, the claim $Y/S_1(T)$ is marketed at time T with respect to 1, S_2/S_1, and $\tilde{\Pi}$ if and only if it is measurable with respect to $F_T^{\tilde{W}} = F_T^{S_2/S_1}$ and $\tilde{\Pi}(T)Y/S_1(T) = \Pi(T)Y$ is integrable.

D.6   Solutions for Chapter 6

Exercise 6.1   Recall that

$$\Phi(S, t) = e^{-r(T-t)}v(h[t]^{-1}(S(t)), T - t)$$
$$= e^{-r(T-t)}\int_{-\infty}^{\infty} f(y)p(y - h[t]^{-1}(S), T - t)\,dy$$

where p is the fundamental solution of the heat equation.

For brevity of notation, write $k(S) = h[t]^{-1}(S)$.

If g is non-decreasing but not constant, then so is f. Hence,

$$\Delta = \Phi_S(S, t)$$
$$= e^{-r(T-t)}k'(S)\int_{-\infty}^{\infty} f(y)p_x\left(y - k(S), T - t\right)dy$$

$$= e^{-r(T-t)} \frac{1}{\sigma S} \int_{-\infty}^{\infty} f(y)(y - h(S)) p(y - k(S), T - t) \, dy$$

$$= e^{-r(T-t)} \frac{1}{\sigma S} \int_{-\infty}^{\infty} f(k(S) + z) \, zp(z, T - t) \, dz$$

$$= e^{-r(T-t)} \frac{1}{\sigma S} \int_0^{\infty} [f(k(S) + z) - f(k(S) - z)] \, zp(z, T - t) \, dz$$

$$> 0$$

Suppose g is convex but not affine. Let Z be a normally distributed random variable with mean zero and variance $T - t$. Then

$$\Phi(S, t) = e^{-r(T-t)} \int_{-\infty}^{\infty} f(y) p(y - k(S), T - t) \, dy$$

$$= e^{-r(T-t)} E f(k(S) + Z)$$

$$= e^{-r(T-t)} E g \left(S_0 \exp \left[\left(r - \frac{1}{2}\sigma^2 \right) T + \sigma \left(k(S) + Z \right) \right] \right)$$

$$= e^{-r(T-t)} E g \left(S \exp \left[\left(r - \frac{1}{2}\sigma^2 \right) (T - t) + \sigma Z \right] \right)$$

$$> e^{-r(T-t)} g \left(S E \exp \left[\left(r - \frac{1}{2}\sigma^2 \right) (T - t) + \sigma Z \right] \right)$$

$$= e^{-r(T-t)} g \left(S e^{r(T-t)} \right)$$

where the inequality follows from Jensen's inequality and the last equality follows from the formula for the mean of a lognormally distributed variable.

Exercise 6.2 Note that

$$N''(d) = -d \frac{1}{\sqrt{2\pi}} \exp(-d^2/2) = -d N'(d).$$

Let us calculate the gamma of the cash-or-nothing call option:

$$\Phi_{SS}(S, t) = e^{-r(T-t)} \left[N''(d_2(S, t)) \frac{1}{S^2 \sigma^2 (T - t)} - N'(d_2(S, t)) \frac{1}{S^2 \sigma \sqrt{T - t}} \right]$$

$$= -e^{-r(T-t)} N'(d_2(S, t)) \frac{1}{S^2 \sigma \sqrt{T - t}} \left[d_2(S, t) \frac{1}{\sigma \sqrt{T - t}} + 1 \right]$$

$$= -e^{-r(T-t)} N'(d_2(S, t)) \frac{\ln S - \ln X + \left(r + \frac{1}{2}\sigma^2 \right) (T - t)}{S^2 \sigma^3 (T - t)\sqrt{T - t}}$$

$$= -e^{-r(T-t)} N'(d_2) \frac{d_1}{S^2 \sigma^2 (T - t)}$$

It follows that $\Phi_{SS}(S, t) = 0$ if and only if $d_1 = 0$, and if and only if $S = S^*$. It also follows that $\Phi_{SS}(S, t) > 0$ if and only if $S < S^*$. Hence, the delta function

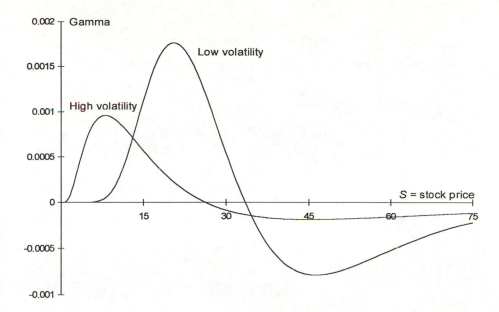

FIG. D.1. Gamma of a cash-or-nothing call option

$\Delta = \Phi_S$ is strictly increasing as a function of S on $(0, S^*]$, reaches a maximum at $S = S^*$, and is strictly decreasing on $[S^*, \infty)$.

Figure D.1 shows the gamma of the cash-or-nothing option for the same two levels of volatility as in Fig. 5.1 and Fig. 5.2. The value of the underlying is on the horizontal axis, and Γ is measured along the vertical axis. The curve with the lower peak corresponds to a volatility of $\sigma = 0.8$, and the curve with the higher peak corresponds to a volatility of $\sigma = 0.4$. As in Fig. 5.1 and Fig. 5.2, the potential payoff is one, the trigger price is $X = 40$, the time to maturity is $T - t = 1$, and the interest rate is $r = 0.1$.

It is clear that

$$\Phi_S(S, t) \to 0 \quad \text{as} \quad S \to \infty$$

To find the limit as $S \to 0$, observe that

$$\ln \Phi_S(S, t) = -r(T - t) - \ln \sqrt{2\pi} - d_2^2/2 - \ln S - \ln(\sigma \sqrt{T - t})$$

Since

$$d_2^2/2 + \ln S = \frac{\left(\ln S - \ln X + \left(r - \frac{1}{2}\sigma^2\right)(T - t)\right)^2}{\sigma^2(T - t)} + \ln S \to +\infty$$

as $S \to 0$, it follows that

$$\ln \Phi_S(S, t) \to -\infty \quad \text{as} \quad S \to 0$$

and hence

$$\Phi_S(S, t) \to 0 \quad \text{as} \quad S \to 0$$

Next, let us find the limit of Φ_S as t approaches T. Observe that

$$d_2^2/2 + \ln(\sigma\sqrt{T-t}) = \frac{\left(\ln S - \ln X + \left(r - \frac{1}{2}\sigma^2\right)(T-t)\right)^2}{2\sigma^2(T-t)} + \ln(\sigma\sqrt{T-t})$$

$$= \frac{(\ln S - \ln X)^2}{2\sigma^2(T-t)} + \frac{(\ln S - \ln X)\left(r - \frac{1}{2}\sigma^2\right)}{\sigma^2}$$

$$+ \frac{\left(r - \frac{1}{2}\sigma^2\right)^2(T-t)}{2\sigma^2} + \ln(\sigma\sqrt{T-t})$$

If $S = X$, then

$$d_2^2/2 + \ln(\sigma\sqrt{T-t}) \to -\infty \quad \text{as} \quad t \to T$$

and, hence,

$$\Phi_S(S, t) \to \infty$$

If $S \neq X$, then

$$\frac{(\ln S - \ln X)^2}{2\sigma^2(T-t)} + \ln(\sigma\sqrt{T-t}) = \frac{(\ln S - \ln X)^2}{2\sigma^2}y + \ln\sigma - \ln\sqrt{y} \to +\infty$$

as $t \to T$, where $y = 1/(T-t) \to +\infty$. Hence,

$$\Phi_S(S, t) \to 0 \quad \text{as} \quad t \to T$$

In brief,

$$\Phi_S(S, t) \to \begin{cases} 0 & \text{if } S > X \\ +\infty & \text{if } S = X \\ 0 & \text{if } S < X \end{cases}$$

as $t \to T$.

Exercise 6.3 Since Δ is positive, the value function Φ is strictly increasing as a function of S. Since Δ is strictly increasing as a function of S on $(0, S^*]$ and is strictly decreasing on $[S^*, \infty)$, the value function Φ is convex as a function of S on $(0, S^*]$ and concave on $[S^*, \infty)$.

It is clear that

$$\Phi(S, t) \to 0 \quad \text{as} \quad S \to 0$$

and

$$\Phi(S, t) \to e^{-r(T-t)} \quad \text{as} \quad S \to \infty$$

To find the limit as t approaches T, first look at the limit of d_2. Since

$$d_2 = d_2(S, t)$$

$$= \frac{\ln S - \ln X + \left(r - \frac{1}{2}\sigma^2\right)(T - t)}{\sigma\sqrt{T - t}}$$

$$= \frac{\ln S - \ln X}{\sigma\sqrt{T - t}} + \frac{r - \frac{1}{2}\sigma^2}{\sigma}\sqrt{T - t}$$

we find that

$$d_2 \to \begin{cases} +\infty & \text{if } S > X \\ 0 & \text{if } S = X \\ -\infty & \text{if } S < X \end{cases}$$

as $t \to T$. Hence,

$$\Phi(S, t) \to \begin{cases} 1 & \text{if } S > X \\ \frac{1}{2} & \text{if } S = X \\ 0 & \text{if } S < X \end{cases}$$

as $t \to T$.

Exercise 6.4 The payoff to the option is

$$\frac{Y}{S(T)} = \begin{cases} 1 & \text{if } \frac{M(T)}{X} \geq \frac{M(T)}{S(T)} \\ 0 & \text{otherwise} \end{cases}$$

This is the payoff to a cash-or-nothing put option on asset zero, with trigger price $M(T)/X$. Write d_2^* for the variable d_2 in the new price system. Notice that since the stock has constant price equal to one in the new price system, the interest rate in the new price system is zero. Hence,

$$d_2^* = \frac{\ln\left(\frac{M}{S}\right) - \ln\left(\frac{M(T)}{X}\right) - \frac{1}{2}\sigma^2(T - t)}{\sigma\sqrt{T - t}}$$

$$= \frac{\ln X - \ln S - \left(r + \frac{1}{2}\sigma^2\right)(T - t)}{\sigma\sqrt{T - t}}$$

$$= -d_1$$

where d_1 is calculated in the original price system.

The value of the asset-or-nothing call option, in the new price system, equals the value of the cash-or-nothing put option:

$$\frac{V}{S} = N(-d_2^*) = N(d_1)$$

In the original price system, the value of the option is

$$V = SN(d_1)$$

which is the same as we found earlier.

Exercise 6.5 The derivative of gamma with respect to S is

$$\frac{\partial}{\partial S}\Gamma = -\frac{1}{S^2\sigma\sqrt{T-t}}\frac{1}{\sqrt{2\pi}}\exp\left(-\frac{d_1^2}{2}\right)$$

$$-\frac{1}{S\sigma\sqrt{T-t}}\frac{1}{\sqrt{2\pi}}\frac{d_1}{S\sigma\sqrt{T-t}}\exp\left(-\frac{d_1^2}{2}\right)$$

$$= -\frac{1}{S^2\sigma\sqrt{T-t}}\frac{1}{\sqrt{2\pi}}\exp\left(-\frac{d_1^2}{2}\right)\left(1+\frac{d_1}{\sigma\sqrt{T-t}}\right)$$

This derivative is zero if and only if $\sigma\sqrt{T-t}+d_1 = 0$, which is equivalent to $S = S^{**}$. The derivative is positive if and only if $\sigma\sqrt{T-t}+d_1 < 0$, which is equivalent to $S < S^{**}$. We find

$$\sigma\sqrt{T-t}+d_1 = \sigma\sqrt{T-t}+\frac{\ln S - \ln X + \left(r+\frac{1}{2}\sigma^2\right)(T-t)}{\sigma\sqrt{T-t}}$$

$$= \frac{\ln S - \ln X + \left(r+\frac{1}{2}\sigma^2\right)(T-t)+\sigma^2(T-t)}{\sigma\sqrt{T-t}}$$

$$= \frac{\ln S - \ln X + \left(r+\frac{3}{2}\sigma^2\right)(T-t)}{\sigma\sqrt{T-t}}$$

$$= \frac{\ln S - \ln S^{**}}{\sigma\sqrt{T-t}}$$

Hence, the derivative of gamma is zero if and only if $S = S^{**}$ and positive if and only if $S < S^{**}$. This shows that Γ is strictly increasing on $(0, S^*]$, reaches a maximum at $S = S^{**}$, and is strictly decreasing on $[S^*, \infty)$.

The derivation of the limits of gamma is similar to the derivation of the limits of the delta of a cash-or-nothing call option in Proposition 6.5 and Exercise 6.2.

It is clear that

$$\Phi_{SS}(S,t) \to 0 \quad \text{as} \quad S \to \infty$$

To find the limit as $S \to 0$, observe that

$$\ln\Phi_{SS}(S,t) = -\ln\sqrt{2\pi} - d_1^2/2 - \ln S - \ln(\sigma\sqrt{T-t})$$

Since

$$d_1^2/2 + \ln S = \frac{\left(\ln S - \ln X + \left(r+\frac{1}{2}\sigma^2\right)(T-t)\right)^2}{\sigma^2(T-t)} + \ln S \to +\infty$$

as $S \to 0$, it follows that

$$\ln\Phi_{SS}(S,t) \to -\infty \quad \text{as} \quad S \to 0$$

and hence

$$\Phi_{SS}(S,t) \to 0 \quad \text{as} \quad S \to 0$$

Next, let us find the limit of Φ_{SS} as t approaches T. Observe that

$$d_1^2/2 + \ln(\sigma\sqrt{T-t}) = \frac{\left(\ln S - \ln X + \left(r+\frac{1}{2}\sigma^2\right)(T-t)\right)^2}{2\sigma^2(T-t)} + \ln(\sigma\sqrt{T-t})$$

$$= \frac{(\ln S - \ln X)^2}{2\sigma^2(T-t)} + \frac{(\ln S - \ln X)\left(r + \frac{1}{2}\sigma^2\right)}{\sigma^2}$$

$$+ \frac{\left(r + \frac{1}{2}\sigma^2\right)^2 (T-t)}{2\sigma^2} + \ln(\sigma\sqrt{T-t})$$

If $S = X$, then

$$d_1^2/2 + \ln(\sigma\sqrt{T-t}) \to -\infty \quad \text{as} \quad t \to T$$

and, hence,

$$\Phi_{SS}(S,t) \to \infty$$

If $S \neq X$, then

$$\frac{(\ln S - \ln X)^2}{2\sigma^2(T-t)} + \ln(\sigma\sqrt{T-t}) = \frac{(\ln S - \ln X)^2}{2\sigma^2}y + \ln\sigma - \ln\sqrt{y} \to +\infty$$

as $t \to T$, where $y = 1/(T-t) \to +\infty$. Hence,

$$\Phi_{SS}(S,t) \to 0 \quad \text{as} \quad t \to T$$

In brief,

$$\Phi_{SS}(S,t) \to \begin{cases} 0 & \text{if } S > X \\ +\infty & \text{if } S = X \\ 0 & \text{if } S < X \end{cases}$$

as $t \to T$.

Exercise 6.6 The function $\Delta = \Phi_S(S,t) = N(d_1)$ is strictly increasing as a function of S because Γ is positive. It is convex on $(0, S^{**}]$ because the derivative of Γ is positive there, and it is concave on $[S^{**}, \infty)$ because the derivative of Γ is negative there.

The limit

$$\Phi_S(S,t) \to 1 \quad \text{as} \quad S \to \infty$$

follows from the fact that $d_1 \to \infty$ and $N(d_1) \to 1$ as $S \to \infty$. The limit

$$\Phi_S(S,t) \to 0 \quad \text{as} \quad S \to 0$$

follows from the fact that $d_1 \to -\infty$ and $N(d_1) \to 0$ as $S \to -\infty$.

To find the limit as t approaches T, first note that

$$d_1 \to \begin{cases} +\infty & \text{if } S > X \\ 0 & \text{if } S = X \\ -\infty & \text{if } S < X \end{cases}$$

as $t \to T$. This can be demonstrated just like the corresponding limits of d_2 in Proposition 6.6 and Exercise 6.3. It follows that

$$\Phi_S(S,t) \to \begin{cases} 1 & \text{if } S > X \\ \frac{1}{2} & \text{if } S = X \\ 0 & \text{if } S < X \end{cases}$$

as $t \to T$.

Exercise 6.7 The function $\Phi(S,t)$ is strictly increasing and convex as a function of S because Δ is positive and strictly increasing.

The limit

$$\Phi(S,t) \to 0 \quad \text{as} \quad S \to 0$$

follows from the fact that $d_1 \to -\infty$ and $d_2 \to -\infty$, and, hence, $N(d_1) \to 0$ and $N(d_2) \to 0$, as $S \to 0$. The limit

$$\Phi(S,t) - \left(S - e^{-r(T-t)}X\right) \to 0 \quad \text{as} \quad S \to \infty$$

can be verified as follows:

$$\Phi(S,t) - \left(S - e^{-r(T-t)}X\right)$$
$$= SN(d_1) - e^{-r(T-t)}XN(d_2) - S + e^{-r(T-t)}X$$
$$= S(N(d_1) - 1) - e^{-r(T-t)}X(N(d_2) - 1)$$

It is clear that the last term goes to zero as $S \to \infty$. To show that the first term goes to zero, write it as

$$S(N(d_1) - 1) = \frac{N(d_1)}{1/S}$$

and use l'Hôpital's rule. The ratio of the derivatives of the numerator and the denominator is

$$\frac{\Phi_{SS}(S,t)}{-(1/S^2)} = -S^2 \Phi_{SS}(S,t)$$

We have to demonstrate that this ratio goes to zero as $S \to \infty$. Observe that

$$\ln\left(S^2 \Phi_{SS}(S,t)\right) = 2\ln S - \ln\sqrt{2\pi} - d_1^2/2 - \ln S - \ln(\sigma\sqrt{T-t})$$
$$= \ln S - \ln\sqrt{2\pi} - d_1^2/2 - \ln(\sigma\sqrt{T-t})$$

Since

$$\ln S - d_1^2/2 = \ln S - \frac{\left(\ln S - \ln X + \left(r + \frac{1}{2}\sigma^2\right)(T-t)\right)^2}{\sigma^2(T-t)} \to -\infty$$

as $S \to 0$, it follows that

$$\ln\left(S^2 \Phi_{SS}(S,t)\right) \to -\infty \quad \text{as} \quad S \to 0$$

and hence

$$-S^2 \Phi_{SS}(S,t) \to 0 \quad \text{as} \quad S \to 0$$

as was to be demonstrated.

If $S_T > X$, then $d_1 \to \infty$, $d_2 \to \infty$, $N(d_1) \to 1$, and $N(d_2) \to 1$, and hence

$$\Phi(S,t) \to S_T - X$$

as $t \to T$, $t < T$, $S \to S_T$.

If $S_T < X$, then $d_1 \to -\infty$, $d_2 \to -\infty$, $N(d_1) \to 0$, and $N(d_2) \to 0$, and hence

$$\Phi(S,t) \to 0$$

as $t \to T$, $t < T$, $S \to S_T$.

If $S_T = X$, then

$$\Phi(S,t) = SN(d_1) - e^{-r(T-t)}XN(d_2)$$
$$= (S - X)N(d_1) + X\left(1 - e^{-r(T-t)}\right)N(d_2) + X(N(d_1) - N(d_2))$$

Each of the three terms go to zero as $t \to T$, $t < T$, $S \to S_T$. The first term goes to zero because $S - X \to 0$ and $N(d_1)$ is bounded. The second term goes to zero because $X\left(1 - e^{-r(T-t)}\right) \to 0$ and $N(d_2)$ is bounded. To see that the third term goes to zero, note that by the mean value theorem, for each $t \in [0,T)$, there exists a number $h(t)$ such that

$$d_2 \le h(t) \le d_1$$

and such that

$$N(d_1) - N(d_2) = (d_1 - d_2)N'(h(t))$$

Since $N'(h(t))$ is bounded and

$$d_1 - d_2 = \sigma\sqrt{T-t} \to 0$$

it follows that

$$N(d_1) - N(d_2) \to 0$$

as $t \to T$, $t < T$, $S \to S_T$.

Exercise 6.8 If $S > Xe^{-r(T-t)}$, then $\ln S - \ln X + r(T-t) > 0$. This implies that $d_1 \to \infty$, $d_2 \to \infty$, $N(d_1) \to 1$, $N(d_2) \to 1$, and $C(S,t,X,r,\sigma) \to S - Xe^{-r\tau}$ as $\sigma \to 0$.

If $S < Xe^{-r(T-t)}$, then $\ln S - \ln X + r(T-t) < 0$. This implies that $d_1 \to -\infty$, $d_2 \to -\infty$, $N(d_1) \to 0$, $N(d_2) \to 0$, and $C(S,t,X,r,\sigma) \to 0$ as $\sigma \to 0$.

If $S = Xe^{-r(T-t)}$, then $\ln S - \ln X + r(T-t) = 0$. This implies that $d_1 \to 0$, $d_2 \to 0$, $N(d_1) \to 1/2$, $N(d_2) \to 1/2$, and $C(S,t,X,r,\sigma) \to 0$ as $\sigma \to 0$.

In any case, $d_1 \to \infty$, $d_2 \to 0$, $N(d_1) \to 1$, $N(d_2) \to 0$, and $C(S,t,X,r,\sigma) \to S$ as $\sigma \to \infty$.

Exercise 6.9 The value of the money market account is

$$M(t) = M(0)\eta[r,0](t) = M(0)\exp\left[\int_0^t r\,ds\right]$$

Hence,

$$\frac{M(t)}{M(T)} = \exp\left[-\int_t^T r\,ds\right] = e^{-(T-t)\bar{r}(t)}$$

This is the same expression for the discounting factor as in the general derivation, except that r has been replaced by $\bar{r}(t)$.

Since λ is deterministic, it follows from Example 2.25 that the process $\eta[0, -\lambda]$ is a martingale. Let Q be the risk-adjusted probability measure: it has density $\eta[0, -\lambda](T)$ with respect to the original probability measure P. Let W^λ be the risk-adjusted Wiener process:

$$W^\lambda(t) = W(t) + \int_0^t \lambda^\top \, dW$$

It is a standard Wiener process under Q. The dynamics of the stock price in terms of W^λ are

$$\frac{dS}{S} = r \, dt + \sigma \, dW^\lambda$$

Hence,

$$S(T) = S(t) \exp\left[\int_t^T \left(r - \frac{1}{2}\sigma^2 \right) ds + \int_t^T \sigma \, dW^\lambda \right]$$

$$= S(t) \exp\left[\left(\tilde{r}(t) - \frac{1}{2}\tilde{\sigma}^2(t) \right)(T - t) + \int_t^T \sigma \, dW^\lambda \right]$$

and

$$\ln S(T) = \ln S(t) + \left(\tilde{r}(t) - \frac{1}{2}\tilde{\sigma}^2(t) \right)(T - t) + \int_t^T \sigma \, dW^\lambda$$

The conditional distribution of $\ln S(T)$ given $S(t)$ is normal with mean

$$\ln S(t) + \left(\tilde{r}(t) - \frac{1}{2}\tilde{\sigma}^2(t) \right)(T - t)$$

and variance

$$\int_t^T \sigma^2 \, ds = \tilde{\sigma}^2(t)(T - t)$$

This is the same distribution as in the general derivation, except that r and σ have been replaced by $\tilde{r}(t)$ and $\tilde{\sigma}(t)$. Since the Black–Scholes formula has been calculated as a conditional expectation under this distribution, it follows that the value of the option is given by the Black–Scholes formula with r and σ replaced by $\tilde{r}(t)$ and $\tilde{\sigma}(t)$.

Specifically, let $g : (0, \infty) \to \mathbb{R}$ be the payoff function of the standard European call option:

$$g(S) = \max\{0, S - X\}$$

Then the value of the option at time t is

$$V = M(t) E_Q\left[\frac{g(S(T))}{M(T)} \,\Big|\, S(t) \right]$$

$$= E_Q\left[e^{-\tilde{r}(t)(T - t)} g(S(T)) \,|\, S(t) \right]$$

$$= C(S(t), t, X, \tilde{r}(t), \tilde{\sigma}(t))$$

The delta of the option is

$$\Delta = N(\tilde{d}_1)$$

$$\tilde{d}_1 = \frac{\ln S - \ln X + \left(\tilde{r}(t) + \frac{1}{2}\tilde{\sigma}^2(t)\right)(T-t)}{\tilde{\sigma}(t)\sqrt{T-t}}$$

The gamma of the option is the derivative of theta with respect to S:

$$\Gamma = \frac{\partial \Delta}{\partial S} = \frac{1}{S\tilde{\sigma}(t)\sqrt{T-t}} N'(\tilde{d}_1) > 0$$

Both delta and gamma are the same as when r and σ are constant, except that r and σ are replaced by $\tilde{r}(t)$ and $\tilde{\sigma}(t)$.

The theta of the option is

$$\begin{aligned}
\Theta &= \Phi_t(S,t) \\
&= C_t(S, t, X, \tilde{r}(t), \tilde{\sigma}(t)) \\
&= -r(t)e^{-\tilde{r}(t)(T-t)} X N(\tilde{d}_1 - \tilde{\sigma}(t)\sqrt{T-t}) \\
&\quad - e^{-\tilde{r}(t)(T-t)} X N'(\tilde{d}_1 - \tilde{\sigma}(t)\sqrt{T-t}) \frac{\sigma^2(t)}{2\tilde{\sigma}(t)\sqrt{T-t}}
\end{aligned}$$

where we have used the following calculation:

$$\frac{\partial \tilde{\sigma}(t)\sqrt{T-t}}{\partial t} = \frac{\partial}{\partial t}\sqrt{\int_t^T \sigma^2\,ds} = \frac{-\sigma^2(t)}{2\sqrt{\int_t^T \sigma^2\,ds}} = \frac{-\sigma^2(t)}{2\tilde{\sigma}(t)\sqrt{T-t}}$$

Since

$$e^{-\tilde{r}(t)(T-t)} X N'(\tilde{d}_1 - \tilde{\sigma}\sqrt{T-t}) = SN'(\tilde{d}_1)$$

we find

$$\begin{aligned}
\Theta &= -r(t)e^{-\tilde{r}(t)(T-t)} X N(\tilde{d}_1 - \tilde{\sigma}\sqrt{T-t}) \\
&\quad - e^{-\tilde{r}(t)(T-t)} X N'(\tilde{d}_1 - \tilde{\sigma}\sqrt{T-t}) \frac{\sigma^2(t)}{2\tilde{\sigma}(t)\sqrt{T-t}} \\
&= -r(t)e^{-\tilde{r}(t)(T-t)} X N(\tilde{d}_2) - SN'(\tilde{d}_1) \frac{\sigma^2(t)}{2\tilde{\sigma}(t)\sqrt{T-t}}
\end{aligned}$$

Note that theta is not simply the same as when r and σ are constant, with r and σ replaced by $\tilde{r}(t)$ and $\tilde{\sigma}(t)$.

The value function Φ does satisfy the Black–Scholes partial differential equation, except that the coefficients r and σ^2 are now deterministic functions of time rather than constants. This can be seen by direct substitution, using the expressions for Δ, Γ, and Θ found above. Alternatively, since

$$e^{\tilde{r}(t)(T-t)}C(S(t),t,X,\tilde{r}(t),\tilde{\sigma}(t)) = E_Q[g(S(T)) \mid S(t)]$$

is a martingale on $(0,T]$ under Q, its drift is zero on that interval. By Itô's lemma, when $0 < t \le T$, the drift is

$$e^{\tilde{r}(t)(T-t)}\left[rS(t)\Phi_S - r\Phi + \Phi_t + \frac{1}{2}S(t)^2\sigma^2\Phi_{SS}\right] = 0$$

which implies

$$rS(t)\Phi_S(S(t),t) + \Phi_t(S(t),t) + \frac{1}{2}S(t)^2\sigma^2\Phi_{SS}(S(t),t) = r\Phi(S(t),t)$$

This equation holds almost everywhere in $\Omega \times (0,T]$. Since $S(t)$ follows a lognormal distribution, we can argue as in the case of constant r and σ that the Black–Scholes partial differential equation

$$rS\Phi_S(S,t) + \Phi_t(S,t) + \frac{1}{2}S^2\sigma^2\Phi_{SS}(S,t) = r\Phi(S,t)$$

holds on $(0,\infty) \times (0,T]$.

Exercise 6.10 It is clear that $\Psi(S,t)$ is twice continuously differentiable with respect to S and once continuously differentiable with respect to t if and only if $u[\Psi](x,\tau)$ is twice continuously differentiable with respect to x and once continuously differentiable with respect to τ.

Write $u = u[\Psi]$. Then $\Psi = \Psi[u]$. Express the partial derivatives of Ψ in terms of the partial derivatives of u:

$$\Psi_S = \frac{e^{-r(T-t)}}{\sigma S}u_x$$

$$\Psi_{SS} = -\frac{e^{-r(T-t)}}{\sigma S^2}u_{xx} + \frac{e^{-r(T-t)}}{\sigma^2 S^2}u_{xx}$$

and

$$\Psi_t = re^{-r(T-t)}u - e^{-r(T-t)}\frac{r - \frac{1}{2}\sigma^2}{\sigma}u_x - e^{-r(T-t)}u_\tau$$

We find

$$rS\Psi_S + \Psi_t + \frac{1}{2}\sigma^2 S^2\Psi_{SS} - r\Psi$$

$$= rS\frac{e^{-r(T-t)}}{\sigma S}u_x + re^{-r(T-t)}u - e^{-r(T-t)}\frac{r - \frac{1}{2}\sigma^2}{\sigma}u_x - e^{-r(T-t)}u_\tau$$

$$+ \frac{1}{2}\sigma^2 S^2\left(-\frac{e^{-r(T-t)}}{\sigma S^2}u_x + \frac{e^{-r(T-t)}}{\sigma^2 S^2}u_{xx}\right) - re^{-r(T-t)}u$$

$$= -e^{-r(T-t)} \left(u_\tau - \frac{1}{2} u_{xx} \right)$$

Hence,

$$rS\Psi_S + \Psi_t + \frac{1}{2}\sigma^2 S^2 \Psi_{SS} - r\Psi = 0$$

if and only if

$$u_\tau - \frac{1}{2} u_{xx} = 0$$

D.7 Solutions for Chapter 7

Exercise 7.1 *Proof of Proposition 7.3.* Integrate each term in the equation

$$r(u) = \bar{r} + e^{-a(u-s)}(r(s) - \bar{r}) + \sigma \int_s^u e^{-a(u-v)} \, dW^\lambda(v)$$

separately. First,

$$\int_s^t \bar{r} \, du = (t-s)\bar{r}$$

Secondly,

$$\int_s^t e^{-a(u-s)} \left(r(s) - \bar{r} \right) du = \frac{1}{a} \left[-e^{-a(u-s)} \right]_{u=s}^t (r(s) - \bar{r})$$

$$= \frac{1}{a} \left(1 - e^{-a(t-s)} \right) (r(s) - \bar{r})$$

Thirdly,

$$\int_s^t \sigma \int_s^u e^{-a(u-v)} \, dW^\lambda(v) \, du = \sigma \int_s^t \int_s^u e^{-au} e^{av} \, dW^\lambda(v) \, du$$

$$= \sigma \int_s^t \int_v^t e^{-au} e^{av} \, du \, dW^\lambda(v)$$

$$= \sigma \int_s^t \int_v^t e^{-a(u-v)} \, du \, dW^\lambda(v)$$

$$= \frac{\sigma}{a} \int_s^t \left(1 - e^{-a(t-v)} \right) dW^\lambda(v)$$

where, in the second equation, we have taken the liberty of interchanging the order of integration, as in Proposition 2.17.

Adding these three terms,

$$I(s; t) = \int_s^t r(u) \, du$$

$$= (t-s)\bar{r} + \frac{1}{a} \left(1 - e^{-a(t-s)} \right) (r(s) - \bar{r}) + \frac{\sigma}{a} \int_s^t \left(1 - e^{-a(t-v)} \right) dW^\lambda(v)$$

Exercise 7.2 The function $\tau \mapsto -e^{-a\tau}$ has value minus one and derivative a at $\tau = 0$. Hence,

$$\frac{B(\tau)}{\tau} = \frac{1}{a} \frac{-e^{-a\tau} + 1}{\tau} \to \frac{1}{a} a = 1 \quad \text{as} \quad \tau \to 0$$

and

$$\begin{aligned}
\frac{v(\tau)}{\tau} &= \frac{\sigma^2}{2a^3} \frac{4e^{-a\tau} - e^{-2a\tau} + 2a\tau - 3}{\tau} \\
&= -\frac{\sigma^2}{2a^3} \left(4 \times \frac{-e^{-a\tau} + 1}{\tau} - \frac{-e^{-2a\tau} + 1}{\tau} - 2a \right) \\
&\to -\frac{\sigma^2}{2a^3} (4a - 2a - 2a) \\
&= 0
\end{aligned}$$

as $\tau \to 0$.

It is clear that

$$\frac{B(\tau)}{\tau} \to 0 \quad \text{as} \quad \tau \to \infty$$

and that

$$\begin{aligned}
\frac{v(\tau)}{\tau} &= -\frac{\sigma^2}{2a^3} \left(4 \times \frac{-e^{-a\tau} + 1}{\tau} - \frac{-e^{-2a\tau} + 1}{\tau} - 2a \right) \\
&\to -\frac{\sigma^2}{2a^3} (-2a) \\
&= \frac{\sigma^2}{a^2}
\end{aligned}$$

as $\tau \to \infty$.

The function B is strictly concave, because its derivative

$$B'(\tau) = e^{-a\tau}$$

is a strictly decreasing function of τ. It follows that the function $B(\tau)/\tau$, which is the slope of the chord between $(0, B(0))$ and $(\tau, B(\tau))$, is a strictly decreasing function of τ.

Similarly, the function v is strictly convex, because its derivative

$$v'(\tau) = B(\tau)^2 \sigma^2$$

is a strictly increasing function of τ. It follows that the function $v(\tau)/\tau$, which is the slope of the chord between $(0, v(0))$ and $(\tau, v(\tau))$, is a strictly increasing function of τ.

Exercise 7.3 The derivative of the bond yield with respect to $\bar{r}$ is

$$\frac{\partial R(r,\tau)}{\partial \bar{r}} = 1 - \frac{B(\tau)}{\tau}$$

The function $\tau - B(\tau)$ has value zero at zero, and its derivative is

$$1 - B'(\tau) = 1 - e^{-a\tau} > 0$$

This implies that $\tau - B(\tau) > 0$ and

$$\frac{\partial R(r,\tau)}{\partial \bar{r}} = 1 - \frac{B(\tau)}{\tau} > 0$$

when $\tau > 0$.

We know from Proposition 7.4 that $B(\tau)/\tau$ is a decreasing function of τ. In fact, the derivative is negative for $\tau > 0$:

$$\frac{\partial}{\partial \tau} \frac{B(\tau)}{\tau} = \frac{ae^{-a\tau}a\tau - (1-e^{-a\tau})a}{a^2\tau^2} = \frac{(a\tau+1)e^{-a\tau} - 1}{a\tau^2} < 0$$

for $\tau > 0$. To verify that the last expression is indeed negative when $\tau > 0$, notice that it has the same sign as its numerator. The numerator is zero at $\tau = 0$ and negative when $\tau > 0$. To see the latter, calculate the derivative of the numerator:

$$\frac{\partial}{\partial \tau}[(a\tau+1)e^{-a\tau} - 1] = ae^{-a\tau} - (a\tau+1)ae^{-a\tau} = -a\tau e^{-a\tau} < 0$$

Hence,

$$\frac{\partial^2 R(r,\tau)}{\partial \tau \partial \bar{r}} = -\frac{\partial}{\partial \tau}\left(\frac{B(\tau)}{\tau}\right) > 0$$

when $\tau > 0$.

It follows from Proposition 7.4 that

$$\frac{\partial R(r,\tau)}{\partial \bar{r}} = 1 - \frac{B(\tau)}{\tau} \to 1 \quad \text{as} \quad \tau \to \infty$$

and

$$\frac{\partial R(r,\tau)}{\partial \bar{r}} = 1 - \frac{B(\tau)}{\tau} \to 0 \quad \text{as} \quad \tau \to 0$$

The derivative of the bond yield with respect to r is

$$\frac{\partial R(r,\tau)}{\partial r} = \frac{B(\tau)}{\tau} > 0$$

which directly implies that

$$\frac{\partial R(r,\tau)}{\partial r} \to 0 \quad \text{as} \quad \tau \to \infty$$

$$\frac{\partial R(r,\tau)}{\partial r} \to 1 \quad \text{as} \quad \tau \to 0$$

$$\frac{\partial R(r,\tau)}{\partial \bar{r}} + \frac{\partial R(r,\tau)}{\partial r} = 1$$

$$\frac{\partial^2 R(r,\tau)}{\partial \tau \partial \bar{r}} + \frac{\partial^2 R(r,\tau)}{\partial \tau \partial r} = 0$$

and

$$\frac{\partial^2 R(r,\tau)}{\partial \tau \partial r} = -\frac{\partial^2 R(r,\tau)}{\partial \tau \partial \bar{r}} < 0$$

Exercise 7.4 We find the maximum point of the forward rate curve by calculating the derivative of $f(r,\tau)$ with respect to τ:

$$f_\tau(r,\tau) = \alpha - \sigma^2 \tau$$

It is zero if and only if

$$\tau = \tau^* = \frac{\alpha}{\sigma^2}$$

and it is positive at lower values of τ and negative at higher values of τ. Hence, $f(r,\tau)$ is a strictly increasing function of τ for $0 \le \tau \le \tau^*$, it reaches a maximum at $\tau = \tau^*$, and it is a strictly decreasing function of τ for $\tau^* \le \tau$.

The maximum value of f is

$$f(r,\tau^*) = r + \alpha\tau^* - \frac{1}{2}\sigma^2\tau^{*2}$$

$$= \alpha\frac{\alpha}{\sigma^2} - \frac{1}{2}\sigma^2\frac{\alpha^2}{\sigma^4}$$

$$= \frac{\alpha^2}{2\sigma^2}$$

We find the maximum point of the yield curve by calculating the derivative of $R(r,\tau)$ with respect to τ:

$$R_\tau(r,\tau) = \frac{1}{2}\alpha - \frac{\sigma^2}{3}\tau$$

It is zero if and only if

$$\tau = \tau^{**} = \frac{3\alpha}{2\sigma^2} = \frac{3}{2}\tau^*$$

and it is positive at lower values of τ and negative at higher values of τ. Hence, $R(r,\tau)$ is a strictly increasing function of τ for $0 \le \tau \le \tau^{**}$, it reaches a maximum at $\tau = \tau^{**}$, and it is a strictly decreasing function of τ for $\tau^{**} \le \tau$.

The maximum value of R is

$$R(r,\tau^{**}) = \frac{1}{2}\alpha\tau^{**} - \frac{\sigma^2}{6}\tau^{**2} + r$$

$$= \frac{1}{2}\alpha\frac{3\alpha}{2\sigma^2} - \frac{\sigma^2}{6}\frac{9\alpha^2}{4\sigma^4} + r$$

$$= \frac{3\alpha^2}{4\sigma^2} - \frac{3\alpha^2}{8\sigma^2} + r$$

$$= \frac{3\alpha^2}{8\sigma^2} + r$$

Exercise 7.5 *Proof of Proposition 7.5.* Recall that for $0 \le s \le u$, we can express $r(u)$ in terms of $r(s)$:

$$r(u) = e^{-K(u)+K(s)}r(s) + e^{-K(u)}\int_s^u e^K \alpha\, dx + e^{-K(u)}\int_s^u e^K \sigma\, d\hat{W}$$

We shall calculate $I(s;t)$ by integrating each term separately. The integral of the first term is $B(s;t)r(s)$. There is little to be said about the second term. As for the third term,

$$\int_s^t e^{-K(u)}\int_s^u e^K \sigma\, d\hat{W}\, du = \int_s^t \int_s^u e^{-K(u)}\sigma(x)e^{K(x)}\, d\hat{W}(x)\, du$$

$$= \int_s^t \int_x^t e^{-K(u)}\sigma(x)e^{K(x)}\, du\, d\hat{W}(x)$$

$$= \int_s^t \sigma(x)\int_x^t e^{-K(u)+K(x)}\, du\, d\hat{W}(x)$$

$$= \int_s^t \sigma(x)B(x;t)\, d\hat{W}(x)$$

where we have interchanged the order of integration in accordance with Proposition 2.17. So,

$$I(s;t) = B(s;t)r(s) + \int_s^t e^{-K(u)}\int_s^u e^K \alpha\, dx\, du + \int_s^t \sigma(x)B(x;t)\, d\hat{W}(x)$$

Exercise 7.6 *Proof of Proposition 7.6.* The formula for m could be proved by using the conditional Fubini theorem (Theorem B.28), but that would require verification of the condition that

$$E\int_0^t |r(u)|\, du < \infty$$

A more direct proof goes as follows. Recall that the conditional mean of $r(u)$ is

$$E(r(u) \mid \mathcal{F}_s) = e^{-K(u)+K(s)}r(s) + e^{-K(u)}\int_s^u e^K \alpha\, dx$$

Hence,

$$E(I(s;t) \mid \mathcal{F}_s) = B(s;t)r(s) + \int_s^t e^{-K(u)}\int_s^u e^K \alpha\, dx\, du$$

$$= \int_s^t e^{-K(u)+K(s)} r(s)\, du + \int_s^t e^{-K(u)} \int_s^u e^K \alpha\, dx\, du$$

$$= \int_s^t E(r(u) \mid \mathcal{F}_s)\, du$$

As to the variance,

$$v(s;t) = \int_s^t \sigma(x)^2 B(s;t)^2\, dx = \int_s^t \sigma(x)^2 e^{2K(x)} \left(\int_x^t e^{-K}\, du \right)^2 dx$$

Define a function $g(x;t)$ by

$$g(x;t) = \left(\int_x^t e^{-K}\, du \right)^2$$

It is continuously differentiable with respect to t, with

$$g_t'(x;t) = 2e^{-K(t)} \int_x^t e^{-K}\, du$$

Hence,

$$g(x;t) = 2 \int_x^t e^{-K(y)} \int_x^y e^{-K(u)}\, du\, dy$$

Now,

$$v(s;t) = \int_s^t \sigma(x)^2 e^{2K(x)} \left(\int_x^t e^{-K}\, du \right)^2 dx$$

$$= \int_s^t \sigma(x)^2 e^{2K(x)} g(x;t)\, dx$$

$$= \int_s^t \sigma(x)^2 e^{2K(x)} 2 \int_x^t e^{-K(y)} \int_x^y e^{-K(u)}\, du\, dy\, dx$$

$$= 2 \int_s^t \int_x^t \int_x^y \sigma(x)^2 e^{2K(x)-K(y)-K(u)}\, du\, dy\, dx$$

$$= 2 \int_s^t \int_s^y \int_x^y \sigma(x)^2 e^{2K(x)-K(y)-K(u)}\, du\, dx\, dy$$

$$= 2 \int_s^t \int_s^y \int_s^u \sigma(x)^2 e^{2K(x)-K(y)-K(u)}\, dx\, du\, dy$$

When $0 \le s \le u \le y$, the conditional covariance of $r(u)$ and $r(y)$ is

$$\mathrm{cov}(r(u), r(y) \mid \mathcal{F}_s) = e^{-K(u)-K(y)} \int_s^u e^{2K} \sigma^2\, dx$$

Hence,

$$v(s;t) = 2 \int_s^t \int_s^y \int_s^u \sigma(x)^2 e^{2K(x)-K(y)-K(u)}\, dx\, du\, dy$$

$$= 2 \int_s^t \int_s^y e^{-K(u)-K(y)} \int_s^u e^{2K} \sigma^2 \, dx \, du \, dy$$

$$= 2 \int_s^t \int_s^y \mathrm{cov}(r(u), r(y) \mid \mathcal{F}_s) \, du \, dy$$

$$= \int_s^t \int_s^t \mathrm{cov}(r(u), r(y) \mid \mathcal{F}_s) \, du \, dy$$

Exercise 7.7 *Proof of Proposition 7.7.* The result can be verified ex post by the following calculations:

$$\int_0^y B_t(s;t) \sigma(s) \, d\hat{W}(s) = \int_0^y e^{-K(t)+K(s)} \sigma(s) \, d\hat{W}(s)$$

$$= e^{-K(t)} \int_0^y e^K \sigma \, d\hat{W}$$

$$= e^{-K(t)} \left[e^{K(y)} r(y) - r(0) - \int_0^y e^K \alpha \, ds \right]$$

and

$$f(r(y), y; t) - f(r(0), 0; t) = e^{-K(t)} \int_y^t e^K \alpha \, dx - \frac{1}{2} v_t(y;t) + e^{-K(t)+K(y)} r(y)$$

$$- e^{-K(t)} \int_0^t e^K \alpha \, dx + \frac{1}{2} v_t(0;t) - e^{-K(t)} r(0)$$

$$= -e^{-K(t)} \int_0^y e^K \alpha \, dx - \frac{1}{2} [v_t(y;t) - v_t(0;t)]$$

$$+ e^{-K(t)} \left[e^{K(y)} r(y) - r(0) \right]$$

$$= -\frac{1}{2} [v_t(y;t) - v_t(0;t)]$$

$$+ e^{-K(t)} \left[e^{K(y)} r(y) - r_0 - \int_0^y e^K \alpha \, ds \right]$$

$$= \int_0^y \left[-\frac{1}{2} v_{st}(s;t) \right] ds + \int_0^y B_t(s;t) \sigma(s) \, d\hat{W}(s)$$

Exercise 7.8 *Proof of Proposition 7.8.* By differentiating the function $B(s;t)$ with respect to t, we find,

$$B_t(s;t) = e^{-K(t)+K(s)}$$

and

$$B_{tt}(s;t) = -a(t) e^{-K(t)+K(s)}$$

Hence,

$$a(t) = -\frac{B_{tt}(s;t)}{B_t(s;t)}$$

By differentiating the function $A(s;t)$ with respect to t, we find,

$$A_t(s;t) = e^{-K(t)} \int_s^t e^K \alpha \, dx - \frac{1}{2} v_t(s;t)$$

$$= e^{-K(t)} \int_s^t e^K \alpha \, dx - \int_s^t \int_s^u \sigma(x)^2 e^{2K(x)-K(t)-K(u)} \, dx \, du$$

or

$$e^{K(t)} A_t(s;t) = \int_s^t e^K \alpha \, dx - \int_s^t \int_s^u \sigma(x)^2 e^{2K(x)-K(u)} \, dx \, du$$

Differentiating again gives

$$e^{K(t)} \alpha(t) - \int_s^t \sigma(x)^2 e^{2K(x)-K(t)} \, dx = e^{K(t)} a(t) A_t(s;t) + e^{K(t)} A_{tt}(s;t)$$

$$= e^{K(t)}(a(t) A_t(s;t) + A_{tt}(s;t))$$

or

$$\alpha(t) = a(t) A_t(s;t) + A_{tt}(s;t) + e^{-2K(t)} \int_s^t \sigma^2 e^{2K} \, dx$$

Exercise 7.9 From

$$\frac{dP(r(s),s;t)}{P(r(s),s;t)} = r(s) \, ds - B(s;t) \sigma \, dW(s)$$

it follows that

$$d \ln P(r(s),s;t) = \left[r(s) - \frac{1}{2} B(s;t)^2 \sigma^2 \right] ds - B(s;t) \sigma \, dW(s)$$

Hence, the differential of the process $R(r(s),s;t)$ is

$$dR(r(s),s;t)$$

$$= -\frac{1}{t-s} d \ln P(r(s),s;t) - \frac{1}{(t-s)^2} \ln P(r(s),s;t) \, ds$$

$$= -\frac{1}{t-s} \left[r(s) - \frac{1}{2} B(s;t)^2 \sigma^2 \right] ds + \frac{1}{t-s} B(s;t) \sigma \, dW(s)$$

$$- \frac{1}{(t-s)^2} [-A(s;t) - B(s;t) r(s)] \, ds$$

$$= \left[\frac{A(s;t) + B(s;t) r(s)}{(t-s)^2} + \frac{\frac{1}{2} B(s;t)^2 \sigma(s)^2 - r(s)}{(t-s)} \right] ds$$

$$+ \frac{B(s;t) \sigma(s)}{t-s} dW(s)$$

$$= \frac{R(r(s),s;t) + \frac{1}{2} B(s;t)^2 \sigma(s)^2 - r(s)}{t-s} \, ds + \frac{B(s;t) \sigma(s)}{t-s} dW(s)$$

SUGGESTED SOLUTIONS TO EXERCISES

E.1 Solutions for Appendix A

Exercise A.1 *Proof of Proposition A.2.*

1: Since $\Omega \in \mathcal{F}$, it follows that $\emptyset = \Omega^c \in \mathcal{F}$.

2: Since $A_n \in \mathcal{F}$ for all n, $A_n^c \in \mathcal{F}$ for all n, and so $\bigcup_{n=1}^{\infty} A_n^c \in \mathcal{F}$. Consequently,

$$\bigcap_{n=1}^{\infty} A_n = \left[\bigcup_{n=1}^{\infty} A_n^c \right]^c \in \mathcal{F}$$

3: $A \setminus B = A \bigcap B^c \in \mathcal{F}$ by 2.

Exercise A.2 1: Since Ω^c is empty, it is countable, and so $\Omega \in \mathcal{A}$.

2: Suppose (A_n) is a sequence of sets in $\mathcal{A}$. To show that their union is in $\mathcal{A}$, distinguish two situations. First, if all of the sets A_n are countable, then the union is countable, and so it is in $\mathcal{A}$. Secondly, if one of the sets A_n has countable complement A_n^c, then the complement of the union is countable, because it is contained in A_n^c. Hence, the union is in $\mathcal{A}$.

3: If $A \in \mathcal{A}$, then either A or A^c is countable, so either A^c or $(A^c)^c$ is countable, and so $A^c \in \mathcal{A}$.

Exercise A.3 A sum of no numbers is understood to be zero, so $\nu(\emptyset) = 0$. If (A_n) is a sequence of disjoint sets, then

$$\nu \left(\bigcup_n A_n \right) = \sum_{i \in \bigcup_n A_n} p_i = \sum_n \sum_{i \in A_n} p_i = \sum_n \nu(A_n)$$

This shows that ν is a measure, and it is a probability measure because

$$\nu(\mathbb{N}) = \sum_{i \in \mathbb{N}} p_i = 1$$

Exercise A.4 *Proof of statements 3 and 4 of Proposition A.7.*

3: Define $B_n = A_1 \setminus A_n$ for all n. Then B_n is an increasing sequence. Set

$$A = \bigcap_{n=1}^{\infty} A_n$$

Then

$$\bigcup_{n=1}^{\infty} B_n = A_1 \setminus A$$

Use the result from 2:

$$\mu(A_n) = \mu(A_1) - \mu(B_n) \to \mu(A_1) - \mu(A_1 \setminus A) = \mu(A)$$

We have used the assumption that $\mu(A_1) < \infty$ to ensure that the expression $\mu(A_1) - \mu(A_1 \setminus A)$ makes sense.

4: Define the sequence (B_n) as in the proof of 2 of the proposition. Note that $\mu(B_n) \le \mu(A_n)$ for all n. Then

$$\mu\left(\bigcup_{n=1}^{\infty} A_n\right) = \mu\left(\bigcup_{n=1}^{\infty} B_n\right) = \sum_{n=1}^{\infty} \mu(B_n) \le \sum_{n=1}^{\infty} \mu(A_n)$$

Exercise A.5 *Proof of Proposition A.11.* Set

$$\mathcal{H} = \{A \triangle N : A \in \mathcal{G} \text{ and } N \in \mathcal{N}\}$$

It has to be shown that $\mathcal{H} = \tilde{\sigma}(\mathcal{G})$. Clearly

$$\mathcal{G} \cup \mathcal{N} \subset \mathcal{H} \subset \tilde{\sigma}(\mathcal{G})$$

We shall show that $\mathcal{H}$ is a sigma-algebra. Since it contains $\mathcal{G}$, it contains $\tilde{\sigma}(\mathcal{G})$, and hence it equals $\tilde{\sigma}(\mathcal{G})$. Now the other equalities in the proposition follow from the general properties of the symmetric difference operator.

Why is $\mathcal{H}$ a sigma-algebra? First, it is clear that $\Omega \in \mathcal{H}$. Secondly, if $D \in \mathcal{H}$, then there exist $A \in \mathcal{G}$ and $N \in \mathcal{N}$ such that $D = A \triangle N$. But then

$$D^c = (A \triangle N)^c = A^c \triangle N \in \mathcal{H}$$

Thirdly, if D_n is a sequence of sets in $\mathcal{H}$, then there exist sets A_n in $\mathcal{G}$ and N_n in $\mathcal{N}$ such that $D_n = A_n \triangle N_n$. Set

$$A = \bigcup_{n=1}^{\infty} A_n$$

$$D = \bigcup_{n=1}^{\infty} D_n$$

and

$$N = A \triangle D$$

Then

$$N = A \triangle D = \left(\bigcup_{n=1}^{\infty} A_n\right) \triangle \left(\bigcup_{n=1}^{\infty} D_n\right) \subset \bigcup_{n=1}^{\infty} (A_n \triangle D_n) = \bigcup_{n=1}^{\infty} N_n \in \mathcal{N}$$

Hence, $N \in \mathcal{N}$ and $D \in \mathcal{H}$.

Exercise A.6 *Proof of Proposition A.12.* The set $\hat{\mathcal{F}}$ is a sigma-algebra. First, it is clear that $\emptyset \in \hat{\mathcal{F}}$. Secondly, suppose $D \in \hat{\mathcal{F}}$. There exist $A \in \mathcal{F}$ and $N \in \mathcal{N}$ and B such that $B \subset N$ and $D = A \triangle B$. But then

$$D^c = (A \triangle B)^c = A^c \triangle B \in \hat{\mathcal{F}}$$

Thirdly, $\hat{\mathcal{F}}$ is stable under countable unions. To see this, let D_n be a sequence of sets in $\hat{\mathcal{F}}$. There exist sequences of sets $A_n \in \mathcal{F}$ and $N_n \in \mathcal{N}$ such that $D_n \triangle A_n \subset N_n$ for every n. Set

$$A = \bigcup_n A_n$$

and

$$D = \bigcup_n D_n$$

Then

$$A \triangle D = \left(\bigcup_{n=1}^{\infty} A_n \right) \triangle \left(\bigcup_{n=1}^{\infty} D_n \right) \subset \bigcup_{n=1}^{\infty} (A_n \triangle D_n) \subset \bigcup_{n=1}^{\infty} N_n \in \mathcal{N}$$

Since $A \in \mathcal{F}$ it follows that $D \in \hat{\mathcal{F}}$. This completes the proof that $\hat{\mathcal{F}}$ is a sigma-algebra.

Since for any $A \in \mathcal{F}$, $A = A \triangle \emptyset$, it is clear that $\mathcal{F} \subset \hat{\mathcal{F}}$.

Next, $\hat{\mu}$ is well defined. Let $D \in \hat{\mathcal{F}}$, and suppose there exist $A, \tilde{A} \in \mathcal{F}$ and $N, \tilde{N} \in \mathcal{N}$ such that $D \triangle A \subset N$ and $D \triangle \tilde{A} \subset \tilde{N}$. Then

$$A \setminus N \subset D \subset \tilde{A} \cup \tilde{N}$$

and so

$$\mu(A) = \mu(A \setminus N) \leq \mu(\tilde{A} \cup \tilde{N}) = \mu(\tilde{A})$$

Similarly, $\mu(\tilde{A}) \leq \mu(A)$, and so $\mu(A) = \mu(\tilde{A})$. Hence, $\hat{\mu}(D)$ is well defined.

Furthermore, if $A \in \mathcal{F}$, then obviously $\hat{\mu}(A) = \mu(A)$.

Next, it will be shown that $\hat{\mu}$ is a measure. First, it is clear that the values of $\hat{\mu}$ are non-negative. Secondly, it has to be shown that $\hat{\mu}$ is countably additive. Let D_n be a sequence of disjoint sets in $\tilde{\mathcal{F}}$. There exist sequences of sets $A_n \in \mathcal{F}$ and $N_n \in \mathcal{N}$ such that $D_n \triangle A_n \subset N_n$ for all n. Set

$$A = \bigcup_n A_n$$

$$D = \bigcup_n D_n$$

and

$$N = \bigcup_n N_n$$

As before,

$$A \triangle D \subset \bigcup_{n=1}^{\infty} N_n = N \in \mathcal{N}$$

Since $A \in \mathcal{F}$, it follows that $\hat{\mu}(D) = \hat{\mu}(A)$. Since

$$A \setminus N \subset \bigcup_n (A_n \setminus N_n) \subset A$$

we know that

$$\hat{\mu}\left(\bigcup_n (A_n \setminus N_n)\right) = \hat{\mu}(A)$$

Observe that

$$\hat{\mu}(D_n) = \hat{\mu}(A_n) = \hat{\mu}(A_n \setminus N_n)$$

Furthermore, since $A_n \setminus N_n \subset D_n$, the sets $A_n \setminus N_n$ are disjoint, so that

$$\hat{\mu}\left(\bigcup_n (A_n \setminus N_n)\right) = \sum_n \hat{\mu}(A_n \setminus N_n)$$

Combining these observations, we find

$$\hat{\mu}(D) = \hat{\mu}(A)$$
$$= \hat{\mu}\left(\bigcup_n (A_n \setminus N_n)\right)$$
$$= \sum_n \hat{\mu}(A_n \setminus N_n)$$
$$= \sum_n \hat{\mu}(D_n)$$

This shows that $\hat{\mu}$ is countably additive.

Finally, to see that $(\hat{\Omega}, \hat{\mathcal{F}}, \hat{\mu})$ is complete, let C be a null set in $\hat{\mathcal{F}}$, and let $B \subset C$. There exist null sets A and N in $\mathcal{F}$ such that $C \triangle A \subset N$. But then $B \triangle A \subset A \cup N$. Since $A \cup N$ is a null set in $\mathcal{F}$, it follows that $B \in \hat{\mathcal{F}}$.

Exercise A.7 *Proof of Proposition A.16.*

1: The Borel sigma-algebra $\mathcal{B}(\mathbb{R})$ is generated by those bounded intervals that contain their right end-point but not their left end-point. The real line can be covered by a sequence of such intervals. It follows from Proposition A.4 that the product sigma-algebra

$$\mathcal{B}(\mathbb{R}) \otimes \cdots \otimes \mathcal{B}(\mathbb{R})$$

is generated by the set of products of such intervals. Those products are exactly the rectangles in $\mathbb{R}^k$, and by definition, they generate the Borel sigma-algebra $\mathcal{B}(\mathbb{R}^k)$. Hence the result,

$$\mathcal{B}\left(I\!\!R^{k}\right) = \mathcal{B}(I\!\!R) \otimes \cdots \otimes \mathcal{B}(I\!\!R)$$

2: For a fixed $x \in I\!\!R$, set

$$\mathcal{F} = \left\{ A \in \mathcal{B}\left(I\!\!R^{k}\right) : A + x \in \mathcal{B}\left(I\!\!R^{k}\right) \right\}$$

It is easy to check that $\mathcal{F}$ is a sigma-algebra and that it contains all rectangles. But then $\mathcal{F}$ contains all of $\mathcal{B}(I\!\!R^{k})$.

3: In dimension one, any singleton set is the intersection of two intervals, and hence it belongs to $\mathcal{B}(I\!\!R)$. Any singleton set in higher dimensions is a product of one-dimensional singletons, and hence, by (1), it is in $\mathcal{B}(I\!\!R^{k})$. Any countable set is a countable union of singleton sets, and hence it is in $\mathcal{B}(I\!\!R^{k})$.

Exercise A.8 *Proof of Proposition A.8.*

1 and 2: Define a measure $\bar{\lambda}$ on $(I\!\!R^{k}, \mathcal{B}(I\!\!R^{k}))$ by

$$\bar{\lambda}(A) = \lambda(A + x)$$

for $A \in \mathcal{B}(I\!\!R^{k})$. It is easily verified that $\bar{\lambda}$ is indeed a measure. It is also easily seen that the three measures λ^{k}, $\bar{\lambda}$, and $\lambda \otimes \cdots \otimes \lambda$ assign the same measure to rectangles $(a, b]$. But then they must be identical, because of the uniqueness statement in Theorem A.17.

3: First, let $x \in I\!\!R^{k}$. It follows from Proposition A.16 that $\{x\} \in \mathcal{B}(I\!\!R^{k})$. If $k = 1$, then

$$\lambda(\{x\}) = \lambda\left(\bigcap_{n=1}^{\infty} (x - 1/n, x] \right) = \lim_{n \to \infty} \lambda((x - 1/n, x]) = \lim_{n \to \infty} 1/n = 0$$

If $k > 1$, then it follows from 1 that

$$\lambda^{k}(\{x\}) = \lambda(\{x_{1}\}) \times \cdots \times \lambda(\{x_{k}\}) = 0$$

Finally, if $A \subset I\!\!R^{k}$ is countable, then it is the union of a countable number of singletons, each of which has measure zero, and so A has measure zero.

Exercise A.9 Let $C \in \hat{\mathcal{B}}(I\!\!R^{k})$ and $x \in I\!\!R^{k}$. We need to show that

$$\hat{\lambda}(C + x) = \hat{\lambda}(C)$$

Let $\mathcal{N}$ be the set of null sets in $\mathcal{B}(I\!\!R^{k})$:

$$\mathcal{N} = \{A \in \mathcal{B}(I\!\!R^{k}) : \lambda^{k}(A) = 0\}$$

There exist $A \in \mathcal{B}(I\!\!R^{k})$ and $N \in \mathcal{N}$ and $B \subset N$ such that $C = A \triangle B$. Because λ^{k} is translation invariant, $\lambda^{k}(N + x) = 0$, so $N + x \in \mathcal{N}$. Now $B + x \subset N + x$ and

$$C + x = (A + x) \triangle (B + x)$$

Hence,

$$\hat{\lambda}(C + x) = \lambda(A + x) = \lambda(A) = \hat{\lambda}(C)$$

Exercise A.10 *Proof of Proposition A.25.*

1: Since every $f \in H$ is measurable with respect to $\sigma(H)$, and since $\mathcal{A}' \subset \mathcal{F}'$, it is clear that $\mathcal{A} \subset \sigma(H)$, and so $\sigma(\mathcal{A}) \subset \sigma(H)$. Set

$$\mathcal{G}' = \{ B' \in \mathcal{F}' : f^{-1}(B') \in \sigma(\mathcal{A}) \text{ for all } f \in H \}$$

It is easily verified that $\mathcal{G}'$ is a sigma-algebra. Since it contains $\mathcal{A}'$, it also contains $\sigma(\mathcal{A}') = \mathcal{F}'$, so $\mathcal{G}' = \mathcal{F}'$. This implies that every $f \in H$ is measurable with respect to $\sigma(\mathcal{A})$. But $\sigma(H)$ is the smallest sigma-algebra with that property, so $\sigma(\mathcal{A}) = \sigma(H)$.

2: All the mappings $f \in H$ are measurable if and only if $\sigma(H) \subset \mathcal{F}$. But since $\sigma(H) = \sigma(\mathcal{A})$, this is true if and only if $\mathcal{A} \subset \mathcal{F}$.

Exercise A.11 *Proof of Proposition A.29.*

1: The inverse image of $A_i \in \mathcal{F}^i$ is

$$\Omega^1 \times \cdots \times \Omega^{i-1} \times A_i \times \Omega^{i+1} \times \cdots \times \Omega^n$$

which is measurable.

2: The inverse image of a product set

$$A_1 \times \cdots \times A_n \in \mathcal{F}^1 \square \cdots \square \mathcal{F}^n$$

is $A_i \in \mathcal{F}^i$.

3: If $A^2 \in \mathcal{F}^2$ then

$$\left(f^1\right)^{-1}\left(A^2\right) \in \mathcal{F}^1$$

and so

$$\left(f^1 \circ f\right)^{-1}\left(A^2\right) = f^{-1}\left(\left(f^1\right)^{-1}\left(A^2\right)\right) \in \mathcal{F}$$

4: If f is measurable, then it follows from 2 and 3 that all the f_i are measurable. Conversely, if all the f_i are measurable, then

$$f^{-1}\left(A_1 \times \cdots \times A_n\right) = f_1^{-1}\left(A_1\right) \times \cdots \times f_n^{-1}\left(A_n\right)$$

is measurable for every product set

$$A_1 \times \cdots \times A_n \in \mathcal{F}^1 \square \cdots \square \mathcal{F}^n$$

It follows from Corollary A.26 that f is measurable.

5: By Proposition A.16, the open sets in $I\!R^k$ generate the Borel sigma-algebra on $I\!R^k$, and the open sets in $I\!R$ generate the Borel sigma-algebra on $I\!R$. Since f is continuous, if $G \subset I\!R$ is open, then $f^{-1}(G)$ is open and, hence, measurable. It follows from Corollary A.26 that f is measurable.

Exercise A.12 *Proof of Proposition A.30.* By Proposition A.15 and Corollary A.26, it suffices to show that $f^{-1}((-\infty, d])$ belongs to $\mathcal{B}(C)$ for all $d \in I\!R$. There is nothing to prove if $f^{-1}((-\infty, d])$ is empty. Otherwise, set

$$x = \sup\{ c \in C : f(c) \le d \}$$

Then $f^{-1}((-\infty, d])$ equals $C \cap (-\infty, x]$ or $C \cap (-\infty, x)$, and in either case it is measurable, since the intervals $(-\infty, x]$ and $(-\infty, x)$ belong to $\mathcal{B}(I\!R)$.

Exercise A.13 *Proof of Proposition A.35.*

1: Since $f = g$ almost everywhere, there exists a null set $N \in \mathcal{F}$ such that the restriction of f to $\Omega \setminus N$ equals the restriction of g. Since the restriction of g is measurable with respect to the sigma-algebra inherited from $\mathcal{G}$, so is the restriction of f, and so f is almost everywhere measurable with respect to $\mathcal{G}$.

2: Since f is measurable almost everywhere with respect to $\mathcal{G}$, there exists a null set $N \in \mathcal{F}$ such that f is measurable on $\Omega \setminus N$ with respect to the sigma-algebra inherited from $\mathcal{G}$. Choose an arbitrary element $\omega' \in \Omega'$ and define g by

$$g(\omega) = \begin{cases} f(\omega) & \text{if } \omega \in \Omega \setminus N \\ \omega' & \text{if } \omega \in N \end{cases}$$

Then $f = g$ almost everywhere, and g is measurable with respect to $\mathcal{G}$ because it is measurable on both N and $\Omega \setminus N$.

3: It is clear that if f is measurable with respect to $\mathcal{F}$, then it is also almost everywhere measurable with respect to $\mathcal{F}$. Conversely, if f is almost everywhere measurable with respect to $\mathcal{F}$, then there exists a null set $N \in \mathcal{F}$ such that f is measurable on $\Omega \setminus N$. It is also measurable on N, because completeness implies that all subsets of N are measurable. Hence, f is measurable.

Exercise A.14 If the family $\{X_i : i \in I\}$ is independent and $i, j \in I$, $i \neq j$, then the random variables X_i and X_j are independent.

Conversely, suppose X_i and X_j are independent whenever $i, j \in I$, $i \neq j$. This implies that they have zero covariance. Let $J \subset I$ be finite. The random variables X_i, $i \in J$, are jointly normally distributed and have zero covariance. But that implies that they are independent. Hence the family $\{X_i : i \in J\}$ is independent, and so the family $\{X_i : i \in I\}$ is independent.

E.2   Solutions for Appendix B

Exercise B.1 *Proof of Proposition B.1.*

1: Every simple function h with $0 \leq h \leq f$ almost everywhere also satisfies $0 \leq h \leq g$ almost everywhere, so the supremum defining the integral of g is taken over a set which is at least as large as the set over which the supremum defining the integral of f is taken.

2: $\int f \, d\mu = 0$ if and only if every simple function h with $0 \leq h \leq f$ almost everywhere is zero almost everywhere. This is certainly true if f is zero almost everywhere. Conversely, suppose $f > 0$ with positive probability. Set

$$A(n) = \left\{ \omega \in \Omega : f(\omega) \geq \frac{1}{n} \right\}$$

for positive integers n. Then

$$\mu(A(n)) \to P\left(\bigcap_m A(m) \right) = \mu(\{\omega \in \Omega : f(\omega) > 0\}) > 0$$

Hence, there exists n such that $\mu(A(n)) > 0$. Now the function

$$h = \frac{1}{n} 1_{A(n)}$$

is simple, it is not zero almost everywhere, and it satisfies $0 \le h \le f$ almost everywhere.

3: If f takes the value $+\infty$ on a set A of positive measure, then for every integer n, the function $n1_A$ is a simple function with $0 \le n1_A \le f$ almost everywhere. Hence,

$$\int f \, d\mu \ge \int n1_A \, d\mu = n\mu(A)$$

for all n, which implies that $\int f \, d\mu = +\infty$.

Exercise B.2 *Proof of Proposition B.3.*

1: Suppose $f \le g$ almost everywhere. Then $f^+ \le g^+$ and $f^- \ge g^-$ almost everywhere. By Proposition B.1,

$$\int f^+ d\mu \le \int g^+ d\mu$$

and

$$\int f^- d\mu \ge \int g^- d\mu$$

Either the integrals of f^+ and g^+ are both finite, or the integrals of f^- and g^- are both finite. So

$$\int f \, d\mu = \int f^+ d\mu - \int f^- d\mu \le \int g^+ d\mu - \int g^- d\mu = \int g \, d\mu$$

Equality holds if and only if

$$\int (g - f) \, d\mu = 0$$

By Proposition B.1, since $g - f$ is non-negative, this is equivalent to $g - f = 0$ and almost everywhere.

2: Since $(f + g)^+ \le f^+ + g^+$ and $(f + g)^- \le f^- + g^-$, $f + g$ is integrable above if f and g are integrable above, and $f + g$ is integrable below if f and g are integrable below.

In either case,

$$(f + g)^+ + f^- + g^- = (f + g)^- + f^+ + g^+$$

Hence,

$$\int (f + g)^+ d\mu + \int f^- d\mu + \int g^- d\mu = \int (f + g)^- d\mu + \int f^+ d\mu + \int g^+ d\mu$$

which implies

$$\int (f + g) \, d\mu = \int (f + g)^+ d\mu - \int (f + g)^- d\mu$$

$$= \int f^+ d\mu - \int f^- d\mu + \int g^+ d\mu - \int g^- d\mu$$

$$= \int f \, d\mu + \int g \, d\mu$$

3: Note that $(-f)^+ = f^-$ and $(-f)^- = f^+$. Hence it is clear that $-f$ is integrable above (below) if and only if f is integrable below (above). In either case,

$$\int (-f) \, d\mu = \int (-f)^+ \, d\mu - \int (-f)^- \, d\mu = \int f^- \, d\mu - \int f^+ \, d\mu = - \int f \, d\mu$$

4: Use the linearity result from Proposition B.2.

Since $(af)^+ = af^+$ and $(af)^- = af^-$, it is clear that af is integrable above (below) if and only if f is integrable above (below). In either case,

$$\int af \, d\mu = \int (af)^+ d\mu - \int (af)^- d\mu$$

$$= \int af^+ d\mu - \int af^- d\mu$$

$$= a \int f^+ d\mu - a \int f^- d\mu$$

$$= a \left(\int f^+ d\mu - \int f^- d\mu \right)$$

$$= a \int f \, d\mu$$

Exercise B.3 *Proof of Proposition B.6.* First, suppose X and Y are simple random variables. Then

$$XY = \sum_{x \in X(\Omega), y \in Y(\Omega)} xy 1_{X^{-1}(\{x\})} 1_{Y^{-1}(\{y\})}$$

Since X and Y are independent, the events $X^{-1}(\{x\})$ and $Y^{-1}(\{y\})$ are independent for all $x \in X(\Omega)$ and $y \in Y(\Omega)$. Hence,

$$E(XY) = \sum_{x \in X(\Omega), y \in Y(\Omega)} xy P\left(X^{-1}(\{x\}) \cap Y^{-1}(\{y\})\right)$$

$$= \sum_{x \in X(\Omega), y \in Y(\Omega)} xy P(X^{-1}(\{x\})) P(Y^{-1}(\{y\}))$$

$$= \left[\sum_{x \in X(\Omega)} x P(X^{-1}(\{x\})) \right] \left[\sum_{y \in Y(\Omega)} y P(Y^{-1}(\{y\})) \right]$$

$$= (EX)(EY)$$

If X and Y are non-negative (but not necessarily simple), define sequences (X_n) and (Y_n) of simple random variables by $X_n = \psi_n(X)$ and $Y_n = \psi_n(Y)$, where

(ψ_n) is the sequence of functions defined in the text. Then X_n and Y_n are independent, $0 \leq X_n \leq X_{n+1}$ and $0 \leq Y_n \leq Y_{n+1}$ for all n, and $X_n \to X$ and $Y_n \to Y$. Hence, $X_n Y_n \leq X_{n+1} Y_{n+1}$ for all n, and $X_n Y_n \to XY$. By the monotone convergence theorem, $EX_n \to EX$, and $EY_n \to EY$, and, because X_n and Y_n are independent,

$$E(X_n)E(Y_n) = E(X_n Y_n) \to E(XY)$$

Since $E(X_n)E(Y_n) \to (EX)(EY)$, it follows that $E(XY) = (EX)(EY)$.

If X and Y are integrable (but not necessarily non-negative), then

$$E|XY| = E(|X||Y|) = (E|X|)(E|Y|) < \infty$$

because $|X|$ and $|Y|$ are independent. Hence, XY is integrable. Furthermore,

$$
\begin{aligned}
E(XY) &= E[(X^+ - X^-)(Y^+ - Y^-)] \\
&= E(X^+ Y^+) - E(X^+ Y^-) - E(X^- Y^+) + E(X^- Y^-) \\
&= EX^+ EY^+ - EX^+ EY^- - EX^- EY^+ + EX^- EY^- \\
&= (EX^+ - EX^-)(EY^+ - EY^-) \\
&= (EX)(EY)
\end{aligned}
$$

Exercise B.4 Since $|f_n^+| \leq g$, g^+ is integrable, and $f_n^+ \to f^+$, it follows from the dominated convergence theorem that f_n^+ and f^+ are integrable (f_n and f are integrable above) and that

$$\int f_n^+ \, d\mu \to \int f^+ \, d\mu$$

Observe that

$$0 \leq f_n^- \to f^-$$

If f^- has finite integral, then it follows from the dominated convergence theorem that

$$\int f_n^- \, d\mu \to \int f^- \, d\mu$$

If f^- has infinite integral, then it follows from Fatou's lemma that

$$+\infty = \int f^- \, d\mu \leq \liminf_n \int f_n^- \, d\mu$$

and, hence, as when f^- has finite integral,

$$\int f_n^- \, d\mu \to \int f^- \, d\mu$$

Combining the results, it follows that

$$\int f_n \, d\mu \to \int f \, d\mu$$

Exercise B.5   Set $A = \{(\omega, t) : 0 \le t \le f(\omega)\}$. By Tonelli's theorem,

$$
\begin{aligned}
(\mu \otimes \lambda)(A) &= \int 1_A \, d(\mu \otimes \lambda) \\
&= \iint 1_A(\omega, t) \, d\lambda(t) \, d\mu(\omega) \\
&= \iint 1_{[0, f(\omega)]}(t) \, d\lambda(t) \, d\mu(\omega) \\
&= \int \lambda([0, f(\omega)]) \, d\mu(\omega) \\
&= \int f \, d\mu
\end{aligned}
$$

Exercise B.6   1: Let $\mathcal{H}$ denote the set of all countable unions of sets in $\mathcal{B}$ and all complements of such countable unions. To show that $\sigma(\mathcal{B}) = \mathcal{H}$, it suffices to show that $\mathcal{H}$ is a sigma-algebra.

It is clear that if $A \in \mathcal{H}$, then $A^c \in \mathcal{H}$. The empty set is the union of an empty set of sets in $\mathcal{B}$, and hence it is in $\mathcal{H}$. Hence, Ω also is in $\mathcal{H}$.

Suppose A_n is a sequence of sets in $\mathcal{H}$. To show that their union is in $\mathcal{A}$, distinguish two situations. First, if all of the sets A_n are countable unions of sets in $\mathcal{B}$, then the union is a countable union of sets in $\mathcal{B}$, and so it is in $\mathcal{H}$. Secondly, suppose one of the sets A_n has a complement A_n^c which is a countable union of sets in $\mathcal{B}$. The complement of $\cup_n A_n$ is a union of sets in $\mathcal{B}$. It is a union of countably many sets, because it is contained in A_n^c. Hence, the union $\cup_n A_n$ is in $\mathcal{A}$.

2: Since

$$
\{\omega \in \Omega : X(\omega) \le 0\} = \bigcup_{x \le 0} B(x)
$$

this set is a union of sets in $\mathcal{B}$. Since X is normally distributed,

$$
P\{\omega \in \Omega : X(\omega) \le 0\} > 0
$$

and

$$
P\{\omega \in \Omega : X(\omega) > 0\} > 0
$$

while $P(B(x)) = 0$ for all $x \in \mathbb{R}$. Hence, neither $\{\omega \in \Omega : X(\omega) \le 0\}$ nor $\{\omega \in \Omega : X(\omega) > 0\}$ is a countable union of sets from $\mathcal{B}$, and so $\{\omega \in \Omega : X(\omega) \le 0\}$ is not in $\sigma(\mathcal{B})$.

Exercise B.7   The constant EX is measurable with respect to $\mathcal{G}$, and if $B \in \mathcal{G}$, then by Proposition B.6,

$$
E[1_B EX] = E[1_B]EX = E[1_B X]
$$

Exercise B.8 If $0 \le a < \|X\|_\infty$, set

$$A(a) = \{\omega \in \Omega : X(\omega) \ge a\}$$

Then $P(A(a)) > 0$, and using the Liapounov inequality,

$$\|X\|_\infty \ge \|X\|_p \ge \|a 1_{A(a)}\|_p = P(A(a))^{1/p} a \to a$$

as $p \to \infty$.

Exercise B.9 It follows from

$$|X_n - X| \le |X_n| + |X| \le 2Y$$

that

$$|X_n - X|^p \le (2Y)^p$$

almost everywhere, for all n. Since $(2Y)^p$ is integrable and $|X_n - X|^p \to 0$ almost everywhere, it follows from the dominated convergence theorem that

$$\int |X_n - X|^p \, d\mu \to \int 0 \, d\mu = 0$$

Hence, $\|X_n - X\|_p \to 0$.

Exercise B.10 Suppose $X_n \to X$ in $L^\infty(\mu)$. Given $\epsilon > 0$, set

$$B(n, \epsilon) = \{\omega \in \Omega : |X_n(\omega) - X(\omega)| > \epsilon\}$$

There exists a positive integer $N(\epsilon)$ such that $\mu(B(n,\epsilon)) = 0$ for $n \ge N(\epsilon)$. Set

$$B(\epsilon) = \bigcup_{n \ge N(\epsilon)} B(n, \epsilon)$$

Then $\mu(B(\epsilon)) = 0$, and $|X_n(\omega) - X(\omega)| \le \epsilon$ for all $\omega \in \Omega \setminus B(\epsilon)$ and all $n \ge N(\epsilon)$. Set

$$B = \bigcup_{m=1}^{\infty} B(1/m)$$

Then $\mu(B) = 0$, and $X_n(\omega) \to X(\omega)$ for every $\omega \in \Omega \setminus B$.

Exercise B.11 *Proof of Proposition B.33.* Suppose $X_n \to X$ in $L^p(P)$. Let $\epsilon > 0$. If $p = \infty$, then

$$P(\{\omega \in \Omega : |X_n(\omega) - X(\omega)| \ge \epsilon\}) = 0$$

when n is so large that $\|X_n - X\|_\infty < \epsilon$. If $p < \infty$, then

$$\epsilon^p P(\{\omega \in \Omega : |X_n(\omega) - X(\omega)| \ge \epsilon\}) \le \int |X_n - X|^p \, dP$$

$$= ||X_n - X||_p^p$$
$$\to 0$$

as $n \to \infty$. Hence,

$$P(\{\omega \in \Omega : |X_n(\omega) - X(\omega)| \geq \epsilon\}) \to 0$$

as $n \to \infty$.

REFERENCES

[1] L. Arnold. *Stochastic Differential Equations: Theory and Applications*. Wiley, New York, 1974.

[2] K. J. Arrow. Aspects of a theory of risk bearing. Yrjö Jahnson Lectures, Helsinki, 1965. Reprinted in [3, 1971].

[3] K. J. Arrow. *Essays in the Theory of Risk Bearing*. Markham, Chicago, 1971.

[4] L. Bachelier. *Théorie de la spéculation*, volume 3 of *Annales de l'Ecole Normale Supérieure*. Gauthier-Villars, Paris, 1900. English translation in [22].

[5] C. A. Ball and W. N. Torous. Bond price dynamics and options. *Journal of Financial and Quantitative Analysis*, 18:517–531, 1983.

[6] M. Baxter. General interest-rate models and the universality of HJM. In M. A. H. Dempster and S. R. Pliska, editors, *Mathematics of Derivative Securities*. Cambridge University Press, 1997.

[7] A. Bensoussan. On the theory of option pricing. *Acta Applicandae Mathematicae*, 2:139–158, 1984.

[8] P. Billingsley. *Probability and Measure*. Wiley, New York, second edition, 1986.

[9] P. Billingsley. *Probability and Measure*. Wiley, New York, third edition, 1995.

[10] F. Black and M. Scholes. The pricing of options and corporate liabilities. *Journal of Political Economy*, 81:637–654, 1973.

[11] R. H. Cameron and W. T. Martin. Transformation of Wiener integrals under a general class of linear transformations. *Transactions of the American Mathematical Society*, 58:184–219, 1945.

[12] R. H. Cameron and W. T. Martin. Transformation of Wiener integrals by non-linear transformations. *Transactions of the American Mathematical Society*, 66:253–283, 1949.

[13] J. Y. Campbell, A. W. Lo, and A. C. MacKinlay. *The Econometrics of Financial Markets*. Princeton University Press, 1997.

[14] A. Carverhill. A note on the models of Hull and White for pricing options on the term structure. *Journal of Fixed Income*, September:89–96, 1995.

[15] K. C. Chan, G. A. Karolyi, F. A. Longstaff, and A. Sanders. An empirical comparison of alternative models of the short-term interest rate. *Journal of Finance*, 47:1209–1227, 1992.

[16] S. T. Cheng. On the feasibility of arbitrage-based option pricing when stochastic bond price processes are involved. *Journal of Economic Theory*, 53:185–198, 1991.

[17] K. L. Chung and R. J. Williams. *Introduction to Stochastic Integration*. Birkhäuser, Boston, first edition, 1983.

[18] K. L. Chung and R. J. Williams. *Introduction to Stochastic Integration*. Birkhäuser, Boston, second edition, 1990.

[19] R. V. Churchill. *Fourier Series and Boundary Value Problems*. McGraw-Hill, New York, second edition, 1963.

[20] R. V. Churchill and J. W. Brown. *Fourier Series and Boundary Value Problems*. McGraw-Hill, New York, fourth edition, 1987.

[21] G. M. Constantinides. A theory of the nominal term structure of interest rates. *Review of Financial Studies*, 5:531–552, 1992.

[22] P. H. Cootner, editor. *The Random Character of Stock Market Prices*. MIT Press, Cambridge, Massachusetts, 1964.

[23] J. C. Cox and C. Huang. Optimal consumption and portfolio policies when asset prices follow a diffusion process. *Journal of Economic Theory*, 49:33–83, 1989.

[24] J. C. Cox and S. Ross. The valuation of options for alternative stochastic processes. *Journal of Financial Economics*, 3:145–166, 1976.

[25] I. de Pinto. *Traité de la Circulation et du Crédit*. Marc Michel Rey, Amsterdam, 1771.

[26] G. Debreu. *Theory of Value*. Yale University Press, 1959.

[27] E. DiBenedetto. *Partial Differential Equations*. Birkhäuser, Boston, 1995.

[28] M. U. Dothan. *Prices in Financial Markets*. Oxford University Press, 1990.

[29] D. Duffie. Stochastic equilibria: Existence, spanning number, and the 'no expected financial gain from trade' hypothesis. *Econometrica*, 54:1161–1183, 1986.

[30] D. Duffie. *Dynamic Asset Pricing Theory*. Princeton University Press, first edition, 1992.

[31] D. Duffie. *Dynamic Asset Pricing Theory*. Princeton University Press, second edition, 1996.

[32] D. Duffie and C. Huang. Implementing Arrow-Debreu equilibria by continuous trading of few long-lived securities. *Econometrica*, 53:1337–1356, 1985.

[33] D. Duffie and W. Zame. The consumption-based capital asset pricing model. *Econometrica*, 57:1279–1297, 1989.

[34] P. H. Dybvig and C. Huang. Nonnegative wealth, absence of arbitrage, and feasible consumption plans. *Review of Financial Studies*, 1:377–401, 1988.

[35] E. Dynkin and A. Yushkevich. *Controlled Markov Processes*. Springer-Verlag, New York, 1979.

[36] S. N. Ethier and T. G. Kurtz. *Markov Processes: Characterization and Convergence*. Wiley, New York, 1986.

[37] R. P. Feynman. Space-time approach to nonrelativistic quantum mechanics. *Review of Modern Physics*, 20:367–387, 1948.

[38] A. Friedman. *Stochastic Differential Equations and Applications*, volume 1. Academic Press, New York, 1975.

[39] I. I. Gihman and A. V. Skorohod. *Stochastic Differential Equations*. Springer-Verlag, Berlin, 1972.

[40] I. V. Girsanov. On transforming a certain class of stochastic processes by absolutely continuous substitution of measures. *Theory of Probability and Applications*, 5:285–301, 1960.

[41] L. Hansen and R. Jagannathan. Restrictions on intertemporal marginal rates of substitution implied by asset returns. *Journal of Political Economy*, 99:225–262, 1991.

[42] J. M. Harrison. *Brownian Motion and Stochastic Flow Systems*. Wiley, New York, 1985.

[43] J. M. Harrison and D. Kreps. Martingales and arbitrage in multiperiod securities markets. *Journal of Economic Theory*, 20:381–408, 1979.

[44] J. M. Harrison and S. Pliska. Martingales and stochastic integrals in the theory of continuous trading. *Stochastic Processes and Their Applications*, 11:215–260, 1981.

[45] J. M. Harrison and S. Pliska. A stochastic calculus model of continuous trading: Complete markets. *Stochastic Processes and Their Applications*, 15:313–316, 1983.

[46] H. He and N. D. Pearson. Consumption and portfolio policies with incomplete markets and short-sale constraints: The infinite dimensional case. *Journal of Economic Theory*, 54:259–304, 1991.

[47] D. Heath, R. A. Jarrow, and A. Morton. Bond pricing and the term structure of interest rates: A new methodology for contingent claims valuation. Unpublished, 1989.

[48] D. Heath, R. A. Jarrow, and A. Morton. Bond pricing and the term structure of interest rates: A new methodology for contingent claims valuation. *Econometrica*, 60:77–105, 1992.

[49] T. Ho and S. Lee. Term structure movements and pricing interest rate contingent claims. *Journal of Finance*, 41:1011–1029, 1986.

[50] C. Huang. Information structure and equilibrium asset prices. *Journal of Economic Theory*, 35:33–71, 1985.

[51] C. Huang. Information structures and viable price systems. *Journal of Mathematical Economics*, 14:215–240, 1985.

[52] C. Huang. An intertemporal general equilibrium asset pricing model: The case of diffusion information. *Econometrica*, 55:117–142, 1987.

[53] J. C. Hull and A. White. Pricing interest-rate derivative securities. *Review of Financial Studies*, 3:573–592, 1990.

[54] J. C. Hull and A. White. 'A note on the models of Hull and White for pricing options on the term structure': Response. *Journal of Fixed Income*, September:97–102, 1995.

[55] K. Itô. Stochastic integrals. *Proceedings of the Imperial Academy of Tokyo*, 20:519–524, 1944.

[56] K. Itô. On a formula concerning stochastic differentials. *Nagoya Mathematical Journal*, 3:55–65, 1951.

[57] F. Jamshidian. An exact bond option pricing formula. *Journal of Finance*, 64:205–209, 1989.

[58] F. Jamshidian. The preference-free determination of bond and option prices from the spot interest rate. *Advances in Futures and Options Research*, 4:51–67, 1990.

[59] F. Jamshidian. Bond and option valuation in the Gaussian interest rate model. *Research in Finance*, 9:131–170, 1991.

[60] R. A. Jarrow and D. Madan. A characterization of complete securities markets on a Brownian filtration. *Mathematical Finance*, 1:31–44, 1991.

[61] M. Kac. On distributions of certain Wiener functionals. *Transactions of the American Mathematical Society*, 65:1–13, 1949.

[62] I. Karatzas. *Lectures on the Mathematics of Finance*, volume 8 of *CRM Monograph Series*. American Mathematical Society, 1997.

[63] I. Karatzas, J. Lehoczky, and S. E. Shreve. Optimal portfolio and consumption decisions for a 'small' investor on a finite horizon. *SIAM Journal of Control and Optimization*, 25:1557–1586, 1987.

[64] I. Karatzas and S. E. Shreve. *Brownian Motion and Stochastic Calculus*. Springer-Verlag, New York, 1988.

[65] R. S. Liptser and A. N. Shiryayev. *Statistics of Random Processes I: General Theory*. Springer-Verlag, New York, 1977.

[66] H. P. McKean. *Stochastic Integrals*. Academic Press, New York, 1969.

[67] R. C. Merton. Lifetime portfolio selection under uncertainty: The continuous time case. *Review of Economics and Statistics*, 51:247–257, 1969. Republished with revisions as Chapter 4 in [72].

[68] R. C. Merton. Optimum consumption and portfolio rules in a continuous time model. *Journal of Economic Theory*, 3:373–413, 1971. Republished with revisions as Chapter 5 in [72].

[69] R. C. Merton. An intertemporal capital asset pricing model. *Econometrica*, 41:867–888, 1973. Republished with revisions as Chapter 15 in [72].

[70] R. C. Merton. Theory of rational option pricing. *Bell Journal of Economics and Management Science*, 4:141–183, 1973. Republished with revisions as Chapter 8 in [72].

[71] R. C. Merton. On the pricing of contingent claims and the Modigliani-Miller theorem. *Journal of Financial Economics*, 5:241–250, 1977. Republished with revisions as Chapter 13 in [72].

[72] R. C. Merton. *Continuous-Time Finance*. Basil Blackwell, Oxford, 1990.

[73] S. M. Müller. On complete securities markets and the martingale property of securities prices. *Economics Letters*, 31:37–41, 1989.

[74] L. T. Nielsen. Understanding $N(d_1)$ and $N(d_2)$: Risk-adjusted probabilities in the Black-Scholes model. *Finance*, 14:95–106, 1993.

[75] R. E. Paley, N. Wiener, and A. Zygmund. Note on random functions. *Mathematische Zeitschrift*, 37:647–668, 1933.

[76] S. Pliska. A stochastic calculus model of continuous trading: Optimal portfolios. *Mathematics of Operations Research*, 11:371–382, 1986.

[77] J. W. Pratt. Risk aversion in the small and in the large. *Econometrica*, 32:122–136, 1964.

[78] L. C. G. Rogers. Which model for the term-structure of interest rates should one use? In M. H. A. Davis, D. Duffie, W. H. Fleming, and S. E. Shreve, editors, *Mathematical Finance*, pages 93–115. Springer-Verlag, New York,

1995.

[79] L. C. G. Rogers and D. Williams. *Diffusions, Markov Processes and Martingales: Itô Calculus*, volume 2. Wiley, Chichester, 1987.

[80] H. L. Royden. *Real Analysis*. Macmillan, New York, second edition, 1968.

[81] W. Rudin. *Principles of Mathematical Analysis*. McGraw-Hill, New York, third edition, 1976.

[82] P. A. Samuelson. Rational theory of warrant pricing. *Industrial Management Review*, 6:13–32, 1965.

[83] W. A. Strauss. *Partial Differential Equations: An Introduction*. Wiley, New York, 1992.

[84] M. E. Taylor. *Partial Differential Equations I: Basic Theory*. Springer-Verlag, New York, 1996.

[85] A. N. Tychonoff. Uniqueness theorems for the heat equation. *Matematica Sbornik*, 42:199–216, 1935.

[86] G. E. Uhlenbeck and L. S. Ornstein. On the theory of Brownian motion 1. *Physical Review*, 36:823–841, 1930.

[87] O. Vasicek. An equilibrium characterization of the term structure. *Journal of Financial Economics*, 5:177–178, 1977.

[88] D. V. Widder. Positive temperatures on a semi-infinite rod. *Transactions of the American Mathematical Society*, 55:85–95, 1944.

INDEX